182937

970.004 Haley, James L.
HAL
    Apaches, a history
    and culture
    portrait

DATE			

APACHES:
A History and Culture Portrait

Also by James L. Haley:

THE BUFFALO WAR:
THE HISTORY OF THE
RED RIVER INDIAN UPRISING OF 1874

APACHES:
A History and Culture Portrait

JAMES L. HALEY

Doubleday & Company, Inc., Garden City, New York
1981

182937

ISBN: 0-385-12147-4
Library of Congress Catalog Card Number 76-42331

To my mother, who bore me twice

Contents

BOOK THREE

Preface

So much has been written about Apache Indians during the past century that new material about them must bear some considerable burden of justification. The histories of the different tribes, and particularly their military defeat at the hand of the United States, have been hashed and served over and over. However, much less has been written of the astonishingly rich and varied Apache culture, and virtually all that has been done is readily accessible only to academic and professional ethnologists.[1] And least of all has been written to relate the tragic Apache history to those of its roots that lie deep in the tribes' own cultural complexes. It is the principal thesis of this book—its justification, if you will—that it is not possible to understand meaningfully the Apaches' history, except to view it through the glass of their complicated Life-way, the demands that it made of their actions and daily conduct, and the way it shaped their perception of outsiders.

In writing Apache history it is insufficient, though it seems inevitably done this way, simply to describe a battle with its dust and blood and blazing guns. It makes exciting reading, of course, but it does not guarantee any deeper perception of why it happened or what the Indians were even doing there. As a factual example, it is common enough to find references to a skirmish that took place in late April of 1880, during the flight (or kidnapping) of the Mimbres chief Loco and his following from San Carlos. Descriptions of the firefight assume a richer meaning once it is learned that the warriors had turned and fought to gain time for others in their band to complete an important religious ritual—a Puberty Ceremony—for a girl who had come of age. A simliar example is seen in the Apache warrior whom the white soldiers nicknamed Peaches, who was indispensable as a scout to General Crook during the 1883 invasion of Mexico. It is widely published that Peaches was a deserter from the band of the minor chief Chatto. It is less widely circulated that Peaches did not quit the war trail until he witnessed the death of his "partner"; and less known still that the other men of Chatto's band, far from labeling him coward or traitor, understood the trauma that losing one's war partner could cause, and even gave him enough food to last until he returned to the agency.

Aside from such specific instances, a general knowledge of Apache culture is also essential to a sensitive understanding of their history. It is one thing to read of General Carleton's order forbidding Mescaleros to leave Bosque Redondo to gather their principal food plant, the agave called mescal. But when one has in the back of his mind how and the scale on which mescal was gathered, and its sociological as well as nutritional aspects, then Carleton's order takes on a significantly different complexion. By the same token, although I have not made it an explicit concern of the historical narrative, it is hoped that after an adequate exposure to Apache culture, when one reads of the death of an Apache Indian—or ten, or eighty—that it will be regarded in a more human context than simply one more historical statistic.

Any book that attempts to depict the cultural and historical progress of the "Apache Indians"—*all* of them—necessarily pleads guilty to at least some degree of artifice, for during most of the period under examination the different tribes were only marginally aware of the welfare (or even, in some cases, the existence) of the others. To do less, however, would fail to place the history in any meaningful cultural perspective, and would also subvert the attempt to place their cultural development in some historical perspective.

Significant traps lie in the two extremes that must be avoided in trying to distill the broad unifying elements of Apachean culture to give the beginning student an appreciation of them. Too extensive a treatment of tribal variations, however interesting to a specialist, would lose the audience to whom this book is directed. But too much simplifying for the sake of general understanding would also defeat the purpose, by mashing the wonderfully discreet tribal flavors into a tasteless and not even very representative gruel. It is a tricky recipe to follow, and one which I doubt will ever be perfected.

Generally, a usage in this text states a rule to which there may be numerous exceptions on an individual or group basis. One band may relate a traditional myth differently than another, but where it seems to be the case that the exceptions prove the rule, only the major version is used. Where it is written that Apaches used either sotol wood or juniper bark for a given purpose, it should be assumed that sotol was used where it was more conveniently obtained, and juniper bark where it was more prevalent. Otherwise, so much time could be spent delineating ethnobotanical variations that the broad scheme of Apache use of naturally occurring plants would be lost. Similarly, a detailed coverage of Goodwin's classifica-

tion of the Western Apache clan system, masterful though that is, would
be meaningless to the non-specialist. While it is essential for the reader to
know that intricate relationships existed among the sixty clans, it is not
strictly necessary for him to know that the ndi-nde-zn clan of the White
Mountain group could not marry into the duc-do-e or be-iltsohn clans of
the Cibicues, or the tcilda-ditl-uge clan of the San Carlos.

The best to which a single-volume culture portrait can aspire is to be
cubist, in the sense that it must try to see the subject from different directions at once, giving the viewer as much an overall impression as a detailed
reproduction. Although broad cultural divergences that evolved among the
Apache tribes are covered sufficiently, I have endeavored to keep the lines
straight and general enough to make the material digestible to a first-time
reader in Apache culture.

There are at least a couple of things that this book is not. It does not,
first of all, claim to be a history from the Apache viewpoint. Only Apaches
can do that. During the early years of "revisionist" academic scholarship,
the rather pretentious notion that a white would tell an "Indian's version"
of American history gained some currency when it was necessary to reverse
a long trend of historical sentiment that implied, as a practical matter,
that the Indians got what was coming to them. The latter view is now,
one hopes, dead beyond raising, but hopefully the former is now discarded
too, in favor of a view that Indians can speak well enough for themselves.

Nor does the present volume aim to be a ferreting out of new detail to
shed yet more light on an already exhaustively researched subject area. A
quick glance at the bibliographies of Dan L. Thrapp and other military
scholars makes it pretty convincing that additional inquiry there, while
perhaps yielding some few fruits, would prove less than continually re-
warding.

Rather, this volume is intended as a different perspective of known facts
—a blending, I hope, of two fields of scholarship, Apache history and
Apache ethnology, that have heretofore been related but, puzzlingly, segregated. I do not know why this should have been so; the theme has been
touched on by many different writers but never really carried home. As
early at 1886 J. P. Dunn tried to give some cultural background, but at
that time very little of the Apache Life-way was even known to whites.
Lockwood's *Apache Indians* of 1938, a standard reference work, purviews
Apache culture in its early pages, but few ties are made to the historical
material that follows. Indeed, it seems not to have been until 1976, in
Angie Debo's admirable biography of Gerónimo, that the sizable body of
published ethnological data was seriously examined for its historical import. And since then a few books, such as Donald Worcester's *The
Apaches*, have also seemed more interdisciplinary in their approach. My
own reading of the cultural treatises, myth cycles, and early-day interviews
yielded historical perspectives that were sometimes startling—for instance,

the fact that lame old Nana, who electrified the Southwest with a raid that was unparalleled for speed and stamina, was in fact a *di-yin* (shaman) through the power of the Geese, and was credited by his own people with having a supernatural source of those qualities. Why this avenue of investigation has not been more closely pursued before now is a mystery to me.

These have been the principal guidelines followed in putting this book together, and had they been the only ones the job would have been greatly (and joyfully) simplified. But, if history has a single lesson to teach, I think it is that there are no easy answers to difficult questions. And among all the chapters of history that there are to read, the only consistency is that not one of them is all black or all white; real history is a study in grays. Only rarely does one encounter a real hero or a real villain; mostly history is populated by just plain people, like you, or me. The misfortune is that it seems not to be in our nature to accept this view of the past as fact. We build up our heroes and craft out villains, and space them through the history pages much like—and sometimes with a motive similar to—a decorator furnishing a difficult room: we use them, somewhat mechanically, to give definition to an empty and awkward space. If we can't comprehend the real story, we'll simplify it to something easier and live with the image, and try not to mind the reality.

Hence it ought to be axiomatic, but does not seem to be, that a historical narrative reveals as much about the point of view and limitations of the narrator, as it does give insight into the subject. This must especially be borne in mind when the subject is one about which opinions are as passionately divergent as with the history of the American Indian.

The writing of Indian history also suffers from the related complication of having become increasingly politicized in our own time. It has evolved from (for lack of better terminology) an Old School into a New School. It is but a slight exaggeration to assert that for generations of literary commentators, the Indians seem to have had it coming to them. They were seen as primitive obstacles to the progress of civilization, violent and unordered, inevitably to be swept from before its approach. There were exceptions to this sentiment, of course, such as the classic *A Century of Dishonor*, but by and large, it is only since the publication not that long ago of a few important watershed books like *Cheyenne Autumn* and *Bury My Heart at Wounded Knee* that scholarly opinion has swung the other way. Historical thought, like history itself, has swings of its pendulum, and indeed this one has swung so fast that the meaning of much of the scholarly vacillation has to be questioned. Savaging the morality of American expansion seems to have become all the rage. I do not think it too cynical an observation to make that where in a communist autocracy history is rewritten to suit the ruler in power, in America history sometimes seems to be re-evaluated to suit the social trends in fashion. Instead of writing by regulation of censors, much recent writing in American Indian history seems regulated by undertowing chants of "Four legs good, two legs better," and if the current writer in American history does not jump on the Poor Little Indians bandwagon he risks, if not his reputation, certainly the favor of the times. This very emphatically does not assert that there is ever a final, definitive "history" of any topic to which nothing can be added. Every new generation of scholars must add its insights and raise its questions. But, in the Old School, white people on the frontier were the heroes and Indians were the villains; in the New School, Indians are the heroes and whites the villains. A historian of any detachment at all has to question whether we have truly rethought the subject or simply switched wardrobes on the characters.

When my first book, The Buffalo War, came out a few years ago I found myself fitted with the lapel label (or perhaps beanie cap) of a revisionist historian. This must have been because virtually all the previous written history of the 1874 South Plains War had come from the Old School—Colonel Wilbur Nye in particular, fine writer that he was—that just did not give a balanced picture of the horrendous problems that the South Plains Indians had to face. Among historians whose minds are comfortably settled about American history, there were inevitably some of the Old School who thought I was trying to be liberal and trendy, and some of the New School who felt I was toeing the Old line. What I found most gratifying were those who accepted the book for what I intended, as I have already termed it, a study in grays. On balance, though, thanks certainly to the magnitude of the leftward leap—for so it was perceived—of The Buffalo War from previous writing, I started the book on Apaches being identified as one of the New School.

Yet there are things about the New School of Indian history that bother me, which for all my desire to be accepted by the academic community, will not go away.

First, its underlying notion that the "white men" took the land away from "the Indians" strikes me as somewhat simpleminded, for the reason that it creates an image of pre-Columbian North Amercia as an idyll of primitive city-states populated by buckskinned yeomen who knew and respected the lie of boundaries. Across North America, or most of it anyway, nothing could have been further from the truth; a tribe of Indians held their territory as long as they could keep other Indians from taking it, and no longer. The Eastern Apaches—Lipans, Mescaleros, and Jicarillas—wound up in New Mexico because they were driven from the South Plains by the Comanches. The Comanches had to do it because they were driven down from the North Plains by the Sioux. If any analogy can apply, it would likely be to billiard balls banking around a table. One provocative conclusion suggested by this is that, today, when a certain tribe of Indians files a lawsuit claiming a given parcel of land as their own by right of heritage, the chances are that it was not theirs, particularly, by heritage at all, but by right of conquest. Or, rather, it was theirs by racial heritage, but by tribal conquest. If that which is legitimately won by conquest can be, legitimately, lost by conquest, then what was the unique factor of the white conquest that causes the vilification by the modern historical community, when Indians conquering Indians is to be accepted as part of the natural order?

A few possibilities suggest themselves. Could it hinge on the sheer magnitude of the conquest, that one tribe fought merely one other tribe, where the whites carried all before them? That does not seem to get at the heart of the contemporary anti-white sentiment, and besides, there are precedents in pre-white exposure times. The Sioux began their expansion westward from the Algonquian woods sometime after 1600, and eventually reached the Rocky Mountains after having knocked off tribe after tribe.

Could it hinge on some feeling that for tribe to fight tribe is more acceptable than for race to fight race? That seems possible, but I am not going to be the one to make that argument. My own impression of American expansion is that it was aimed toward the land itself more than distaste for who was on it. Americans may have killed Indians to get their land, but we also killed Mexicans to get the Southwest and probably would have fought the English to get Oregon. Up until the close of our territorial expansion we never seemed to play much in the way of favorites as to whom we were willing to kill for more territory. Yet there was undeniably some factor of race involved that needs further examination. Most white people on the frontier believed that they were racially superior to the Indians. And almost any tribe of Indians that one can name viewed themselves as created first and the favorite of the Creator, superior to other people whether white, Mexican or other Indians. Apaches were certainly no exception. There seems to be an underlying acceptance within modern liberal academia—the New School—that when Indians assume this stance, it is some kind of noble primitivism, and when whites assume this stance, it is called racism. What this leads to is a kind of retrospective application of a double standard of conduct that may just be the missing crux that sets the white conquest apart from intertribal wars.

The suggested conclusion is that white civilization, having pretended to enlightenment, should have been enlightened enough to see conquest as immoral; for Indian to fight Indian was all right because they didn't know any better. Why should this be so? Putting aside the obvious qualm that this conclusion expresses liberal arrogance at its most tasteless, its usefulness is still limited because it leads to a logical irony that approaches non sequitur. It says that a culture may permissibly grow and expand and progress (and by historical reality, consume other cultures' lands and lives and selected traits) without obligation, until it attains a state in which it realizes that it has committed tortious horrors and has to give back as much of what it has taken as its conscience—or the litigating conquered —demand. By this scale, the only reward for self-awareness is guilt, or at least the self-imposed obligation to stagnate.

We seem to have little difficulty in affixing the decorum of conduct when two technologically advanced cultures expand to a meeting point. They might war over the boundary for a bit, but eventually they settle down and set about trading goods and ideas and influences as freely, or as little, as they wish. If one impinges on the rights of the other, it is usually easy enough to identify the aggressor. The real pangs of conscience come when the advanced civilization confronts a primitive one whose livelihood is marked by hunting, gathering, raiding, and perhaps some agriculture and craftsmanship. At such a meeting, two urges typically assert themselves within the advanced society. The first is to claim dominion over the primitive culture's incompletely or inefficiently used resources. The other is to bestow (or, in contemporary sentiment, inflict) its own culture on the other, to alleviate the readily perceived ignorance and needless suffering. The reality on the American frontier was, of course, that the Anglo-American culture responded most strongly to the first drive, but it is undeniable that there was also a strong influence to "improve" the Indian circumstances, and that is not to be arrogantly dismissed—as it is these days—by an assertion that the Indians needed no "improvement." A nineteenth-century observer of Apachería, and there were a few, beheld a culture in which the elderly were abandoned to death by starvation, and in which twins were regarded as a result of natural imbalance, and one was killed at birth. Tuberculosis was believed to be caused by worms, and owls were dreaded as incarnate Evil. That which they desired, and could not craft for themselves, the Apaches obtained by pillage, and even in the best of times there were risks associated with living at the outer pale of white civilization. Both the Apache and the Anglo-American world-views were inflexibly ethnocentric, and it solves no problems today to bless the first as picturesque and damn the second as craven. To those who meant the Apaches well, the ignorance and suffering and violence of their life-style were plain to see; if it was wrong to exercise coercion to assimilate them into a more advanced state, would it not have been more wrong to have left them entirely alone?

On the other hand, who are we now to judge? What standing does white society have to say that it was wrong for Indians to abandon their elderly to death by the elements, when we abandon our own elderly to rest homes whose regulation is so slipshod that some are nothing but death houses? How can we moralize that it was depraved for Apache *bi-zhahn* (widows and divorced women) to give themselves to returning raiders in return for a share of the spoils, when in some circumstances we have legalized prostitution? How can we say it was wrong for Apaches to kill certain classes of infants at birth, when we can seriously debate the propriety of killing babies still in the womb? These are hard questions, and will never be satisfactorily settled by relying upon a catalogue of heroes and villains.

It is altogether too easy to assert that the white conquest of North America was a just and moral thing, and that modern Indians are owed nothing more than an equal footing with everybody else, when the conscience is stricken that, clearly, they are owed much more than this. But— and this is a very unpopular thing to say these days—it is also too easy to make the accusation that the white conquest of North America was entirely wrong. Today's Indians sue in courts of law to recover damages for their losses: but, if war was illegitimate, then Indians who subsisted by raiding and pillage were as guilty as the white people who vanquished them. And if war was legitimate, what standing do losers have to claim foul? Yet what kind of people would not fight in defense of their homes? What seems to be called into question is nothing less than the legitimacy of the ponderous rise and fall of civilizations themselves, occurring over a stretch of centuries. Did cavemen have a right to be cavemen, or should France sue Italy for inflicting her with the Roman heritage of paved streets and running water? Have we elevated troglodytehood to a defensible right at the law? Or perhaps, and this is profoundly to be hoped, we are just now arriving at a new level of consciousness by which primitive peoples can be elevated in health and science, without being forced in exchange to give up their culture and property. The remaining question, as far as the American Indians are concerned, is the extent to which it should be retroactive, and the proper measure of reparation. Should a tribe of a few dozen or hundred survivors be awarded the entirety of their aboriginal territory, amounting perhaps to millions of acres worth billions of dollars, or enough to practice their culture in security and comfort? How can the loss of a way of life even be measured in dollars? It cannot, of course, any more than one can fix a value on the gains of medicine and education. (Sadly, there is a legitimate query to be made into exactly how much benefit of Anglo culture has, in fact, been made available to Indians.)

All of this exposition is by way of saying that I have been convinced, in writing about Apache history, not to take sides. Where I have perceived treachery by white men, I have called it so, and equally so with treachery by the Apaches. I have tried, wherever I have been conscious of it, to weed out the temptation so common today to imply that a tactic or strategy was proper within the arsenal of the Indians, but immoral when used by anybody else. To take sides in writing history is to seek those ephemeral easy answers. Much more important, to write history without taking sides is the only way I can express my personal opinion that surely, by today's stage in our development, the time has come to stop debating whose fault our history is, and begin trying to understand what it has meant, and proceed from here.

There is one level, however, at which I have been willing to make judgments, that of the personal performance of individuals. In the last fifteen or twenty years, history books have made much of what we call the "forces of history" to explain the nature of wars and the rise and fall of peoples. To an important extent, certainly, individuals' choices of action are dictated by circumstances over which they have no control. Unfortunately, however, the notion of the forces of history has almost replaced Jesus Christ in forgiving the sins of the world. The longer I study Indian history, the more I am struck by the repetition of violence that was started, not by the march of civilization or fiat of government or ignorant rapacity by supposed savages, but rather by common criminality on the part of just plain folks. Personal avarice has little to do with the forces of history, and the acts of profiteers from Castaño de Sosa in 1590 to Bob Tribolett in 1886 were the acts of individuals out to make a buck. Likewise, the fomenting of trouble by power-lusting chieftains like Chunz, Pion-se-nay or—I am sorry to say it—Gerónimo, spoke much more forcefully of their individual ambitions than of the drifting of their people on the ebb and flow of historical tides. The forces of history provided the circumstances, to be sure, but violence seldom started until somebody sought to manipulate those forces to his own advantage, whether among the whites, for monetary gain, or among the Apaches, for sociopolitical advancement.

The forces of history can thrust strangers into the same arena and make them interact, but it is the men themselves who must bear responsibility for their conduct. It is unacceptable for people to kill and pillage one another, and then on looking back point to the forces of history and say, "They made me do it." Surely judgment cannot be so easily escaped.

Perhaps the greatest comfort is to be taken from the performances of the good men who appear in the history of Apachería—men who sought peace and understanding as vigorously as they fought when they had to, like Crook, or Victorio; men who defied majorities of their own race to do what was right, like Calhoun, or Colyer, or Loco; men whose great friendships searched out their own tenuous paths to peace in the midst of pandemonium, friendships like those of Jeffords with Cochise, or Eskiminzin with Whitman and then Clum. There is enough good in the history of Apachería to persuade me that if people like these had held sway over the chancrous influence of the Ourys and Carletons and Wilburs, the Gerónimos and Juhs and Skinyas, that the history would have been different.

Unlike many of my colleagues, I cannot believe that, in the Apache instance at least, war and suffering were inevitable. Only ambition and greed made them so. I suppose one might argue that ambition and greed are themselves forces of history, but that seems merely semantical, and certainly shows a low expectation of human nature.

If war had really been inevitable, there would be little reason to feel guilty about it; not so if war was avoidable but indulged in anyway. This leads me to believe that contemporary Anglo-American scholarship feels guilty about Apache history—indeed, Indian history generally—not because the wars were inevitable, but because so many crimes and injustices were worked upon the Indians. Today's question of Indian reparations then becomes one, not of Anglo social guilt or governmental guilt, but of affixing social and governmental obligation based upon the past crimes of individuals.

It remains only to be said that change, as opposed to war, probably is inevitable, and I have a hard time working up much guilt over the fact that Indian cultures have had to adapt and evolve. One may arguably state change as a function of time: for instance, if one wishes to preserve a forest, one preserves it certainly from fire, only to lose the forest anyway to overgrowth and disease, because fire is part of a forest's natural dynamics. People today who wish to "preserve" Indian cultures should keep in mind that nothing that is alive can be permanently preserved without first killing it. The only way to "preserve" any Indian culture in that sense is to put it in a helium case as one would a document, or a mummy. Our misunderstanding of this owes to the fact, I think, that much of today's Anglo sympathy for the plight of the Indian has degenerated to the subjective and insipid; many of us have abandoned Indians in favor of what I could only call Indian Chic. Of course, enough material has been produced recently positing the degree to which this view by the New School is a product of our own postwar guilt and self-hatred, that the point need not be too finely made here. Anyone's view of the past is affected by his perception of himself and his society, but to force the subject of one's history to wallow in a pit of contemporary social demonology, and then present the surprised and blinking tarbaby as a historical reexamination, strikes me as scholarship that will not bear the test of time. How can we hold, for instance (as I was taught in a couple of courses, by the way), that the Apache acquisition of Pueblan Indian religion was a stage of natural development, but that their acquisition of Christianity is a sign of cultural dissembling? Cultural evolution is a continuing thing, and to say that this influence furthers it while another pollutes it, is a subjective imposition from the outside, and I must confess to a certain amount of residual colic from New School professors who have tended—in my experience, anyway—to use their historical specialties as proving grounds for their own bitterness, atheism, and disappointment with life. Either an Indian denies his heritage every time he takes a pill or drives to church or files a lawsuit, or else these acquisitions from another culture do not reach the heart of "Indianness" at all, and, of course, they do not. The only way to preserve Indian culture as a living and developing thing is to preserve it within its environment—to enlarge the reservations, give the tribes internal autonomy, and leave them alone. Inevitably this crosses the grain of both the diehards of the Old School who would dilute the Indian identity into the tangle of Anglo culture, and the guilty liberals of the New School who would somehow feel better about themselves if they could see millionaires in beads and feathers (and also, curiously, the political Indians who would wring the guilty liberals for every dollar they can get).

Austin, Texas
November 1979

Preface:
NOTES

1. "Since 1930 much information has been gathered by anthropologists, linguists, and historians, but it is hard for ordinary people to get at, and ignorance of Indian ways and beliefs is as universal as it was one hundred years ago." Sonnichsen, *The Mescalero Apaches*, p. 29.

Acknowledgments

Source materials on Apache Indians are found today as readily as they are largely because so many others have already sniffed them out and listed them. A contemporary book about Apaches is remiss if it does not at least momentarily bend the knee before the brilliant scholarship that has gone before, including but not limited to the ethnological inquiries of Grenville Goodwin and Morris Opler, and the historical research of the great Bancroft and the Bandeliers, and more recently, the military analyses of Dan L. Thrapp and the preservation of Apache traditional history by recorders such as A. Kinney Griffith, Wilbur Nye, and Eve Ball. Without their earlier work, there would be precious little to write about now.

The greatest of my personal debts for additional research in this book are owed James C. Martin and Mary Van Zandt of the Special Collections of the University of Texas at Arlington; Tommie Whitely of the Southwest Collection, Texas Tech University; and Lori Davisson of the Arizona Historical Society. Thanks are also due for helps and favors from my friends Bob and Shirley Stigler of Lubbock, Texas; and my much admired mentor (though he may yet disown me), Dr. Elliott West, Assistant Professor of History at the University of Texas at Arlington.

When it was time for Yusn Life-giver to let people onto the world, he called the children of White-painted Woman before him. "The people will need weapons to hunt with and live," he said.

He laid before them a gun, and a bow and arrows. Killer of Enemies was older and he got first choice. He took the gun. Child of the Water had to take the bow and arrows.

Killer of Enemies became the father of the white-eyes, and Child of the Water became the father of the Indians. That's how they got to be different, they say.

BOOK ONE

The Earth Is New

In the beginning Yusn, the Life-giver, created the universe. Nobody knows just how he did it, but he did it and that is all.[1]

When it came time to form the earth, Yusn told four power-spirits to do it for him. They were Black Water, Black Metal, Black Wind and Black Thunder. Together they fashioned the earth, but when they were finished they saw it was no good. It was cold and dead. To make it live, Black Water gave it blood by causing the rivers to flow. Black Metal gave it a skeleton of hills and mountains. This way it was strong. Black Wind breathed life into the earth by causing the wind to blow. The earth was there in the universe, but it was cold, so Black Thunder clothed the earth in trees and grass. This way it was made warm.[2]

In the beginning there was no darkness and Sun shone all the time. Night was kept prisoner in a sack, and Yusn gave the sack to Badger to guard.

One day Coyote saw Badger carrying that sack and thought he had things to eat in there. Coyote started walking with Badger and said, "Old man, you look pretty tired. Why don't you let me carry that sack for a while?"

Now, Badger knew Coyote was a tricky fellow and said, "No, you just think there's something to eat in there, but you're wrong. There's nothing to eat in there at all. I was given this sack to protect and not let anybody look inside."

"No, old man, I just want to help you. I know there is no food in there. I've been watching you and you haven't been in there once to get any. Look how tired you are." Coyote didn't mean that at all. He just said it.

"Well, all right," said Badger. "I guess I am pretty tired," and he gave the sack to Coyote and they walked along. Pretty soon Badger had to defecate. "I'm going over there a minute," he said.

No sooner was Badger in the bushes than Coyote said, "Now I'm going

to get something to eat." He opened the sack right there and Night escaped. It was dark all over, very dark so that you could hardly see anything.

The creatures that were pleased with having night were the four-legged
animals; most in favor of it were predators and those of evil power, like
Bear and Snake, and also Owl-man Giant and other monsters that don't
exist anymore. The birds and flying insects did not want night at all. They
wanted daylight all the time, so they got together and made a plan.

The birds called in all the animals and said, "We don't like you. You're
trashy. You want night and we want day. Let's have a moccasin game and
see who wins. If we win, it will be daylight forever and we can kill you all.
If we lose, you can have dark and kill us. We bet our lives."

The animals said, "All right."

They set up a moccasin game. This was the first one, and we play ours
now because they did it that way. Each side buried four moccasins in the
ground. They made score-keeping staves out of yucca leaves. Today we
play with sixty-eight of them, but back then they used more, I think. One
side hides a little bone in a moccasin and wins a point if the other side
can't guess where it is. If they do guess it, they get the bone and hide it.
At first all the staves are taken by both sides from a big pile in the middle,
and when those are gone they take from each other until one side is
beaten and has none left. We can only play the moccasin game in winter,
at night, because they did it. That's the only time we can talk about it,
too.

They started playing and it was about even. At midnight things were so
close that both sides started to cheat. Gopher was with the animals. He
burrowed down under the moccasins and watched. When the animals had
the bone, he moved it every time the birds guessed correctly. The birds
hid some of their staves up Turkey's leg so the animals would think they
were closer to winning than they were. Before this turkeys had no tendons
in their legs, but now they do because of this.

Just when it looked like the animals and monsters were going to win,
the birds took the extra staves out of Turkey's leg. Roadrunner had been
sleeping, and he was the best player of all. The other birds woke him up
and got him to play for them, while they themselves started singing songs
that had power in them, to ruin the animals' luck. When they sang,
Gopher went blind and couldn't help the animals anymore. This is why
gophers have little eyes now, they say.

Pretty soon it got so close that Coyote got up and left the animals. He
stood in the middle by the fire and said, "I am going to help whoever
wins." That was just like him!

When the animals' position became nearly hopeless, Owl-man Giant
got up and said, "I'm going to get away now. I can't run fast because my
penis is so big." He left as fast as he could but his penis kept getting in

the way, so he had to start carrying it. Pretty soon the sun came up and he knew the birds had won the game. He ran some more, but soon he was so tired he had to rest. He lay down under some cholla cactus and put his penis up in the branches for shade.

Pretty soon he heard the birds coming for him. He tried to run away but his penis got caught in the cholla thorns. They were sticking him. "Ow, my penis!" he said.

The birds came up and right there they killed Owl-man Giant. Then they went after the others. Before they could kill all the night creatures some of them, like Owl and Snake, escaped, and still live today. The animals they killed do not live on the earth anymore. But some of them got away.

Therefore, Night still exists for a time, and it is full of danger for the day birds and good animals.[3]

Sun is as huge as a mountain. Moon is as big and bright as Sun, but Night interferes with it. Once in a while Sun or Moon will go into the sky and the world is very dark.

During the summer the days are long because Sun's moccasin strings are made rotten by all the rain, and he is slowed as he stoops to mend them. During the winter he gets new strings of yucca fiber, and he runs faster, so the days are shorter. That's how they say it is.

The Earth Is New:
NOTES

1. The Genesis myths of the Apaches, which portrays beings in a human form, is purely indigenous, not composite like that of the Navajo. Curtis, *North American Indians*, Vol. I, p. 4. However, the mythology of the Western Apaches speaks of a place in the valley of the Little Colorado River that they once shared with the Pueblans and Navajos alike, which is one of the few time-shrouded links between the Apaches and the Navajos. Goodwin, *Social Organization of the Western Apaches*, pp. 66–71.

Variations of the genesis account and the succeeding mythology are numerous and sometimes contradictory, but the purview is cohesive enough that we can extract a simplified picture. Among the three bands of Chiricahuas there was close alignment in the details of the various myth cycles, except for the generally greater sophistication among the Tci-he-nde Mimbres, which is consonant with their more advanced state on other cultural fronts. Their trickster myths tend to substitute Jackrabbit for other creatures as a foil to Coyote, and their mythology generally evidences their earlier and more frequent contact with Europeans. The split in 1913 of the Chiricahuas between Fort Sill, Oklahoma, and Mescalero, New Mexico, had not by the Second World War

caused any noticeable divergence or specialization in the telling of the myth cycles. Opler, "Myths and Tales of the Chiricahua Apache Indians," p. viii.

2. Basso, "In Pursuit of the Apaches," p. 39.

3. The myth of the first moccasin game is perhaps the single most wide-
spread of the Apache folk tales, and variations of it are legion. See Opler,
"Myths and Tales of the Chiricahua Apache Indians," pp. 23–27; Hoijer,
Chiricahua and Mescalero Apache Texts, pp. 14–16; Goddard, "Myths and
Tales from the San Carlos Apache," pp. 43–44; Goodwin, "Myths and Tales
of the White Mountain Apache," pp. 148–50; Bourke, "Notes on Apache Mythology," p. 211; Goddard, "Jicarilla Apache Texts," p. 207; Mooney, "The
Jicarilla Genesis," p. 198; Opler, "Myths and Tales of the Jicarilla Apache Indians," pp. 231–34; Opler, "Myths and Legends of the Lipan Apache Indians," pp. 87–96.

SOUTHERN ATHAPASCAN INDIANS
(all groups shown in gray)

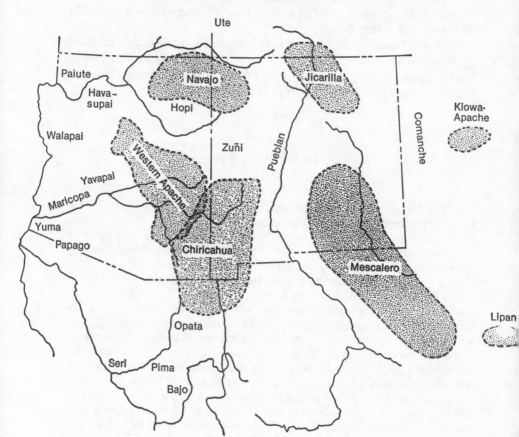

DIVISION OF WESTERN APACHE GROUPS
(after Goodwin)

ARIZONA

NEW MEXICO

Little Colorado River

Prescott

N. Tonto

MOGOLLON RIM

S. Tonto
(1 band +
6 semi-bands)

Cibicue
(3 bands)

Verde River

Salt River

Fort Apache

White Mountains
(2 bands)

Globe

San Carlos

Gila River

Gila River

Gileños
(San Carlos)
(4 bands)

Tucson

Tombstone

Tin-ne-áh:
The People

It must owe in large part to the violence that so long flamed on the surface of Apache-American relations, that Apache culture remains one of the least understood of all the American Indians.[1] Scholars generally feel that the body of popular literature on Apaches is a confused tangle of mysteries and half-baked hip shots. One authority wrote that "In terms of precise ethnological knowledge, the Apache are, with the possible exception of the Ojibwa, the least-known surviving North American group of any like . . . importance."[2] While this may no longer be true among professional ethnologists, it certainly does still hold as far as knowledge among the general public is concerned. From the time the Americans first reached them, the Apaches have been secretive about their customs and ceremonies. One of the best of the earlier Apache historians wrote that those Indians' fearsome reputation was enhanced by "the fact that the Apaches are among the least known of the Indian tribes. . . . they maintain a jealous reserve as to their habits, particularly those of a religious character."[3]

The confusion has in large part hung on to the present day. One of the great modern students of the Southwest wrote of the Western Apaches that they "are one of the most written-about peoples of the Southwest and yet they remain, in my opinion, the most poorly understood by white men. Apaches complain constantly that all the history which is in print misrepresents them, yet so far no Apache autobiographer or even rough chronicler has emerged . . . For the most part, nontechnical writings on Apaches tell more about the colorful personalities of American military men and Indian agents than they do about the Apaches."[4] Although the confusion today is slowly lessening, much ground has still to be covered before the white population as a whole can understand these richly enigmatic Indians.

The mysteries of the Apache origins commence at once, with the uncertainty that surrounds the source of their name. The term "Apache" is most widely believed to stem from *ápachu*, the Zuñi word for enemy, which that tribe applied to another Athapascan people, the Navajo.[5] There are other possible origins, however. It could come from *apátieh*, as a mistaken use by whites of the Yavapai self-designation.[6] One of the Mexican tribes that the Apaches frequently preyed upon had a word, *ápache*, or "raccoon," which is an accurate description of the traditional eye-masking war paint of the Tci-he-nde Chiricahuas. Again, it could come from the name that the Yuma Indians gave the Apache-associated Yavapai: *e-patch*, meaning "men that fight."[7] The derivation might even have been Spanish, from *apachurrar*, meaning "to crush."[8] The Apaches, predictably, called themselves simply "The People": *Tin-ne-áh*.[9]

At the opening of historical times, the Apaches had, to an uncertain degree, settled into two broadly divided groups, a Western, and an Eastern, or Plains. The latter were Apaches whose life-style had been more influenced by the proximity of the Indians of the southern Great Plains: the Jicarilla Apaches, who inhabited the mountains and grasslands of the country that became the eastern part of the New Mexico-Colorado border, and the Lipan Apaches, ranging from eastern New Mexico and trans-Pecos Texas, southeast as far as San Antonio. The Western division contained three tribes, the Mescaleros, the Chiricahuas, and those termed simply Western Apaches. The Mescaleros, whose ways were touched to a lesser degree by Plains cultures, lived about the upper Rio Grande in the heart of New Mexico, southwest of the Jicarillas and west of the Lipans, and ranging south at various times deep into Old Mexico. The Plains influence was virtually absent among the three groups of Chiricahuas; they lived just west of the Mescaleros, from west-central New Mexico south into the Sierra Madre of Chihuahua and Sonora. Further west even from them were the five major groups of Western Apaches, whose territory is generally described as eastern Arizona south of the Mogollon Rim: just to the west of the Chiricahuas were the White Mountain Apaches, whose territory was the largest of all the Western Apaches, stretching from the Pinaleno Mountains in the south to beyond the White Mountains in the north. This group was divided into two bands, the Eastern, which was one of the largest and most powerful of all the Apache bands with a population of about fifteen hundred, and the Western, the band that was most often called by the popular name Coyoteros, although the taxonomy is very confused.[10] To the southwest of the White Mountain Apaches were the four bands of San Carlos or Gileño Apaches, ranging from the Santa Catalina Mountains northeast of Tucson to the country around Miami and Globe. North of the Gileños and northwest of the White Mountains were the three bands of the Cibicue Apache group, and northwest from them were the Southern and Northern Tonto groups, whose range extended as far northwest as Flagstaff.

(A few writers—not many—also include in general Apache treatments two other tribes of Indians, the Navajos and the Gattackas, or Kiowa-Apaches. Most writers exclude them, and this seems the more sensible approach.)[11]

That the tremendous chunk of geography described was the Apache homeland, *Apachería*, is a fact much more settled than the question of how they got there. Linguistically, they were of the ancient Athapascan stock, and there is a general agreement that the beginning point of their migration lay in the Pacific Northwest, in the wooded valleys of the Mackenzie and Yukon rivers. From here, however, the unanswerable questions deepen the Apache mystery: why did they leave, and when, and by what route did they arrive in the mountain-wrinkled deserts of the Southwest? The most accepted theory is that they abandoned the Northwest and pushed south over the Rockies sometime after A.D. 1000, and burst through the Uto-Aztecan tribes to ravage the Pueblans. Repercussions were still noticeable in the mid-1500s, at the coming of the Spanish.[12] Not all scholars agree with that explanation, and at least a few offer the alternative theory that after the Apacheans left the Northwest, they migrated first to the western portions of the Great Plains, and then turned southwest only when forced by pressure from other tribes.[13]

What seems to have been overlooked in the debate is the possibility that the plains-migration theory may be true for some Apache tribes, but not for others. It is known for certain that at least one Athapascan group wound up in the South via the plains, the Gattackas or Kiowa-Apaches.[14] Further, there is evidence of an early divergence in the migratory histories of the western and eastern divisions, seen in the fact that, during reservation days, the Western Apaches had no knowledge (or at least no memory) of the more easterly tribes such as Mescaleros and Jicarillas, until late in the nineteenth century.[15] One also notes the lack of plains elements in the cosmogeny and mythology of the western tribes, which should not have been the case if they had spent much time on the prairies. The lost truth, of course, could lie anywhere within—or even without—this spectrum.

Another debate goes on as well, arguing when the Apaches first arrived in the Southwest. Some believe that the Western Apaches reached the Mogollon Rim, the precipice that overlooked their promised land, by 1400.[16] Others think that the lack of early (sixteenth-century) Spanish documentation implies their absence, and insist that there is "no evidence" that Apaches inhabited Arizona before 1550.[17] Most believe they arrived before the Navajos, some after; and some, that the Navajos did not even evolve until after they became separated from the Apache mainstream.[18] Nobody knows. About all that is asserted with confidence is that after the Apaches did stake a claim to the Southwest the five tribes became increasingly insular. With the aid of geographical barriers they developed independent variations of their common cultural heritage; by historic times they had become self-sufficient enough that, although they remained passingly cordial with others of their kind whose territory bordered on theirs, their relationships became more distant. With the exceptions perhaps of an occasional marriage or joint raid,[19] common ties dwindled until the people perceived themselves first as members of their tribe, and only secondarily as part of a larger entity.

In population the Apaches were probably never overbearing in their numbers. However, their ferocity and reputation cast a shadow far beyond their size, and the early white transients and settlers who lived in that shadow frequently overguessed their strength by large if understandable exaggerations. The usually unflappable John Cremony, who lived among the Chiricahuas in the mid-nineteenth century, believed there was an all-told sum of 25,000 Apaches.[20] The easily flapped George Catlin thought there were 30,000.[21] In point of fact, vast Apachería probably never contained more than 10,000 of the Tin-ne-áh, and the true figure lies more likely between 6,000 and 8,000.[22]

Although the Apaches did not make it a social point to marry outside their own tribe, the men readily took captive women to wife, and captive children of both sexes were often adopted into the community and married. Surprisingly, the practice seems to have had little impact in diluting the Apaches' ethnic purity as a definable people. Aleš Hrdlička, a turn-of-the-century researcher who took it upon himself to go after the Apaches with a measuring tape, was impressed with their racial homogeneity. He found the average Apache noticeably on the small side—the men about five feet six inches tall and the women five feet—but the adults were hardy and athletically formed.[28] The men were characterized by square shoulders and deep runners' chests, with evenly proportioned limbs that were lithe and very strong without being muscle-bound. The women were noted for the fine regularity of their features, and clear, dark eyes and complexion. For a woman to have—as many did—demurely small hands and feet was considered an asset of great beauty by her people.

Of course, the pursuit of physical generalities does not accomplish much more now than it did in Hrdlička's time, for at least two reasons. First, contemporary society tends to regard any mention of racial "characteristics" as not only irrelevant, but motivationally suspect; and, second, it tends to obscure the fact that among the Apaches, as among all peoples, a group of individuals may exhibit the gamut of physical extremes. Some were very thin and some were corpulent. Some were outsized and some were very short. Some were possessed of great physical beauty, and some were terribly homely. Nevertheless, the Apaches themselves were proudly conscious of their racial uniqueness, and early informants often paired mental and moral qualities with an observation that So-and-So was a "good-looking young fellow."

Tin-ne-áh: The People:
NOTES

1. Frederick W. Jackson, in the introduction to Gerónimo, *Geronimo's Story of His Life*, p. 19.
2. Kroeber, "Cultural and Natural Areas of Native North America," pp. 37–38.
3. Dunn, *Massacres of the Mountains*, p. 310.
4. Spicer, *Cycles of Conquest*, pp. 593–94. In the years since this was written, Apaches have come more and more to have their own say about their history to a readership wider than their small monographical audience. One notes, for instance, the popular interest in such books as Betzinez, *I Fought with Geronimo*; Barrett's edition of Gerónimo, *Geronimo's Story of His Life*; Niño Cochise, *The First Hundred Years of Niño Cochise*; and the superb *Western Apache Raiding and Warfare*, as told to Grenville Goodwin by such lucidly informative survivors of pre-reservation Apachería as Anna Price, Palmer Valor, and John Rope. Of comparable quality but on a less celebrated scale one can turn to such accounts as Eve Ball's conversations with Asa Daklugie and James Kaywaykla. Such recountings are very useful, but unfortunately are often limited to personal reminiscences. The cultural aspects of the recounted history are generally implicit and their impact is hence lost on the less expert audience.
5. Hodge, "Handbook of Indians North of Mexico," p. 63.
6. Curtis, *North American Indians*, Vol. I, p. 5.
7. Hodge, "Early Western History," p. 442.
8. Davis, *Truth About Geronimo*, p. 1.
9. There are of course many spellings and variants of this word: *Tinneh, Diné, Indé*, etc. *Tin-ne-áh* is probably close to generically correct. Ogle, *Federal Control of the Western Apaches*, p. 5, n. 13.
10. One of the best summations of the confused situation is from Frederick Webb Hodge: "No group of tribes has caused greater confusion to writers, from the fact that the popular names of the tribes are derived from some local or temporary habitat, owing to their shifting propensities, or were given by the Spanish on account of some tribal characteristic; hence some of the common names of apparently different Apache tribes or bands are synonymous, or practically so; again, as employed by some writers, a name may include much more or much less than when employed by others." "Handbook of Indians North of Mexico," pp. 63–64.
11. The Navajos of northeastern Arizona were, to be sure, linguistically Athapascan, of the same ancient stock as the Apaches, but the two were seldom on friendly terms with one another, and the Apaches themselves have never considered the Navajos to be more than distant relations. Even during times of peace, the Apaches traded with the Navajos; Apaches never traded among themselves, but only with those whom they considered outsiders. Goodwin, *Social Organization of the Western Apache*, pp. 83–84.

The Kiowa-Apaches can only marginally be considered Apaches in a meaningful definition of the term. Their earliest cultural affiliations were with the Kiowa Indians in the Belle Fourche country of Wyoming. From that time on through the reservation period they never associated with any but the Kiowas, and their migration to the South Plains duplicated the Kiowas', who tolerated them as impoverished camp followers. *See* Mooney, "Kiowa Indians," p. 245. Hence they are given in this book a status similar to that of the Navajos, that of a non-Apachean, yet still southern Athapascan tribe.

12. Fehrenbach, *Comanches*, p. 25; Mails, *People Called Apache*, p. 13, citing the *Dictionary* of the White Mountain Apache Culture Center.

13. Terrell, *Apache Chronicle*, p. 20.

14. See note 11, supra.

15. Goodwin, *Social Organization of the Western Apache*, pp. 85–86.

16. Ibid., pp. 63–68.

17. Hodge, "Handbook of Indians North of Mexico," p. 63.

18. Kroeber, "Cultural and Natural Areas of Native North America," p. 35. He considered that "three or four hundred years ago the Navajo constituted a small and culturally scarcely indistinguishable fraction of the Apache," and noted that their great proliferation and prospering coincided with their closer assimilation of Pueblan Indian cultural traits (although he stopped short of speculating a cause-effect relation).

19. Mails, *People Called Apache*, p. 13.

20. Cremony, *Life Among the Apaches*, p. 142.

21. Catlin, *Last Ramble Among the Indians*, p. 180.

22. Bartlett, *Personal Narrative*, Vol. II, p. 385; Thrapp, *Conquest of Apacheria*, p. viii.

23. Turner, in his introduction to Gerónimo, *Geronimo's Story of His Life*, p. 24.

The Slaying of the Monsters

With Yusn in the beginning was White-painted Woman. She had no mother or father. She was created by the power of Yusn. He sent her down to the world to live. Her home was a cave.

Some say there were no other people in those days, but I don't know about it. They say that's what the monsters lived on, so there must have been some. There weren't many, though, and they had a real hard time.

There were four monsters. They killed people and ate them. They were Owl-man Giant, Buffalo Monster, the Eagle Monster family, and Antelope Monster.

I don't know if they mean the same Owl Giant that the birds killed after the Moccasin Game. The stories are mixed up. I think maybe it was, because this one started off with a big penis, like the other one.

They say, once Owl-man Giant caught a woman and put her in his basket. Instead of taking her home to eat, he took her up on a high bluff and let her out. He said, "I want to have intercourse with you."

The woman said, "All right."

He said, "Get over there and bend over."

Owl-man Giant stood behind her a little way off. When his penis got hard it went out and knocked the woman off the bluff. Owl-man Giant got real mad and said, "This is no good at all!"

He got out his knife and cut most of it off and it fell over the cliff. He left himself just a few inches. This is why men now have little penises, they say. You can still see the place today; there is a long rock at the bottom that was his penis. This is why they must mean the same Owl Giant as in the Moccasin Game.

Owl-man Giant was really awful but a couple of times people got away. They say once two women went out to pick berries and they saw Owl-man Giant coming. They saw they couldn't get away, so they took their clothes off and played dead. Owl-man Giant wouldn't eat someone already dead. He had to kill them himself.

He came around and saw them lying there. He squeezed their breasts and played with their vaginas but they didn't move. After a while he got bored and left, then they ran away.

Another time they say a woman and a boy were picking berries when Owl-man Giant came around. He caught them and put them in his basket. He was carrying them home to eat. When he passed under a big tree they jumped out on a limb. After a while Owl-man Giant got tired and sat down to rest. He looked in the basket. The woman and boy had defecated before they jumped out. He saw the excrement in there and got mad. He looked back and saw them running away. He chased them and was gaining on them. The woman and boy were running as hard as they could and crying, but he was too fast for them.

Brown Horned Toad saw them running and said, "Wait! Hold up there. What's this about?"

They told him Owl-man Giant was about to catch them and eat them.

Horned Toad said, "Pick me up. That big fellow is afraid of me."

They stopped running and picked Brown Horned Toad up. In just a second Owl-man Giant got there and started to club them. They held Brown Horned Toad up and it was just like he said. Owl-man Giant screamed and cried and ran away. He was afraid of that Horned Toad!

With White-painted Woman in those days was a boy named Killer of Enemies. He was either her brother or her son. The stories say different. Owl-man Giant really tormented that boy but never tried to kill him; I don't know why. He was just mean to him. He would watch Killer of Enemies go hunting and take the meat away from him and mess up whatever he was doing. Killer of Enemies never resisted; he just cried and let it go. He wasn't good for much, I guess.

Life then was really hard, and one day White-painted Woman was praying about it. Something told her, "When it rains, you have to go lie down under that place over there, where the rain makes a little waterfall. Spread your legs and let the water run in." She did that. When the water ran into her vagina, lightning hit her there four times and she was pregnant.

The spirit told her, "You must call the baby Child of the Water," and she did.

When the baby was born the spirit came back and told her, "If Owl-man Giant finds this baby he will kill him and eat him. He will look all over every day. You have to hide him under the fire. He won't look there. If you can keep this baby till he is old enough to shoot a bow, he will kill all the monsters. When he wants a bow, you make him one. Don't worry over how little he is."

White-painted Woman spent a lot of time crying and praying how to keep Child of the Water alive. She kept him in a hole under the fireplace outside the cave. Every day she took him out to nurse him and clean him up and play with him.

One day something told her, "Owl-man Giant must be coming!" She just had time to get Child of the Water under the fire before he came into the camp.

He said, "I heard a baby crying. You give him to me so I can eat him!"

White-painted Woman looked very sad. "There is no baby here," she said. "It was I who made the noise. I am very lonely for a little baby so I cried like one."

Owl-man Giant said, "Let me hear you do it."

White-painted Woman tried real hard, and she cried just like a little baby cries! Owl-man Giant wasn't satisfied, but he left anyway. After that he came around more often.

Another time, she took Child of the Water from under the fire and was cleaning him up when she said, "Owl-man Giant is coming!" She got Child of the Water under the fire, but Owl-man Giant ran into the camp before she could hide the dirty cloth.

He said, "Ho! I thought you had a baby. That is a baby cloth, and that's his feces. You give him to me right now or I'll find him."

White-painted Woman started to cry. She said, "No, I made that myself to look like a baby's feces."

Owl-man Giant said, "I think you're lying to me. Show me how you did it."

White-painted Woman went over to a sotol plant that had bees in the stalk. Lots of them do. She mixed some of the honey and plant juice and spread it next to Child of the Water's feces. That Owl-man Giant couldn't tell the difference. She said, "I am so lonely for a little baby that I was pretending like I had one." That Giant had to mutter something and leave.

Every time he came around looking, White-painted Woman thought up something to fool him.

After a few years, Child of the Water was still a little boy. He got too big to keep under the fire, so White-painted Woman kept him in the back of the cave. One day a big thunderstorm came up, with lightning and thunder. He looked outside and said, "I want to go kill Owl-man Giant and the other monsters now."

White-painted Woman took him away from the entrance and said, "No. It is too dangerous out there now. Wait longer, till you are bigger." But he went back.

This happened four times. On the fourth time, Child of the Water pointed outside and said, "That is my father speaking out there."

When he said that, White-painted Woman took him outside. She told Lightning, "Your son knows you."

Lightning said, "How do I know this is my son?"

She answered, "Test him."

Lightning had him stand over to the east, and black lightning struck him. He stood to the south and blue lightning struck him. Yellow lightning struck him on the west, and white lightning on the north. Child of the Water was not hurt or frightened at all.

After he had tested him, Lightning said, "My son." Then he told White-painted Woman, "Let him do what he wants."

Soon after, White-painted Woman made him four arrows of grama grass. That's why they use grama grass in ceremonies now, they say, because that's what they were made of. She also made him a bow, but I don't know what kind of wood she used.

Child of the Water said, "I am going hunting."

Up to now, Killer of Enemies had killed many deer, but Owl-man Giant always took the meat away from him. This time Killer of Enemies wanted to go hunting with Child of the Water. Child of the Water didn't want him to, but he went along, anyway.

Killer of Enemies killed a deer, and they started to cook some meat. Soon they heard Owl-man Giant coming. Killer of Enemies became afraid and started to cry.

Owl-man Giant walked into the clearing. He said, "Ho! You have killed a deer for me. I'm going to eat it!" He took the meat from the fire and put it over where he was standing.

Child of the Water went and took it back. He said, "You're not going to eat our meat anymore."

Owl-man Giant said, "I ought to kill you right here." He took the meat back and said, "I'm going to eat your meat and turn it into feces."

Child of the Water took it back again. He said, "You have eaten our meat for the last time."

The meat changed hands like this four times.

Killer of Enemies was sitting there, crying.

"Who do you think you are?" said Owl-man Giant. "What can you fight with? Let me see your arrows."

Child of the Water held out his four little grama grass arrows. Owl-man Giant laughed and took the arrows from him. He looked them over and wiped his anus with them. Then he threw them as far away as he could.

Child of the Water had to go find them and clean them off. When he got back he said, "Let me see your arrows."

Owl-man Giant pointed to a stack of four big sharp pine logs. "Those are my arrows," he said. Child of the Water walked over and looked at them. They were so big he couldn't lift them, so to get even he raised his breechcloth and scratched his backside on them.

He said, "I am Child of the Water. I am going to kill all you monsters, starting with you. We're going to fight each other right now. We can each shoot four times."

Owl-man Giant was still laughing. He said, "All right, but you have to let me shoot first."

Child of the Water said, "All right."

Killer of Enemies was sitting there crying, scared.

Child of the Water stood on the east side, facing west. There was thunder and lightning in the distance. Where he stopped there was a blue rock at his feet. It said, "Pick me up. Your father sent me." He picked it up and held it.

"Get ready now," said Owl-man Giant.

Child of the Water saw the first big log arrow coming. He waved the rock and said, "Let it pass over my head. Shu!" The log went over his head and shattered on the ground.

When he saw the second log arrow coming he held out the blue rock and said, "Let it strike in front of me. Shu!" The arrow shattered on the ground in front of him.

When the third arrow came he said, "Let it miss on this side. Shu!" and it was so. When the fourth arrow came he said, "Let it miss on the other side. Shu!" and it happened.

Then Child of the Water got his bow and little grama grass arrows and said, "Now you hold still."

Owl-man Giant said, "I am not afraid." He was wearing four coats of solid white flint.

Child of the Water shot his first arrow. Owl-man Giant picked up a rock and said, "Let it pass over my head." The arrow hit him right over where his heart was. It blasted one of the flint coats and knocked him over a little hill.

Child of the Water shot the second arrow. Owl-man Giant held out another rock and said, "Let it hit in front of me." This arrow struck him over the heart. It broke the second flint coat and knocked him over another little hill. The same thing happened on the third arrow.

When Child of the Water shot the fourth arrow, Owl-man Giant had only one flint coat left. You could see his heart beating under it. He held out the rock and said, "Let it pass on the side." But it shattered the last coat and went into his heart. He was knocked over a fourth hill and lay there, dead. You can still see the place today. There are four little hills and piles of flint. We get power from that place! My father-in-law has been there.

Killer of Enemies stopped crying and was happy. He started to sing:

> *We have killed the Giant.*
> *It will be good now.*
> *Owl-man Giant, dead he lies there,*
> *For we have killed him.*

He put some of the meat back on the fire and sat there eating, happy.

Child of the Water cut off Owl-man Giant's head. It seemed too heavy to lift, but he feinted three times and picked it up on the fourth. He put it on Killer of Enemies' back and they went home. They took some of the meat, too.

White-painted Woman had been crying for the two boys. She was afraid Owl-man Giant would kill them. When she saw what they brought back she danced and sang, and gave the women's shrill of applause, the same sound as women make today at Puberty Ceremonies. It is a loud, high cry, while they do their tongues this way. It is a way of celebrating. This was the first time it was done on earth.

Child of the Water said, "I am going to kill the Buffalo Monster now."

Buffalo Monster lived in the middle of a big prairie, where he kept watch for people or smoke from their campfires. Whenever he saw something, he would run over and kill the people. Child of the Water got to the edge of the prairie, and started thinking about how to kill the Buffalo Monster.

Pretty soon Gopher came along. He said, "What are you thinking so hard about?"

Child of the Water said, "I have to kill that Buffalo out there, but I don't know how to get close enough."

Gopher said, "It's easy. I will help you. Whenever he runs out after someone, you run toward where he is resting until he starts to come back. Then you lie flat in some low place. When you get close, lie still and wait for me."

Child of the Water did just as he said. After four times he was very close to the Buffalo Monster. Gopher came up out of the ground. "Now I'm going to show you where his heart is. When you shoot him, it has to be right in his heart or he can't be killed. I'm going to dig four tunnels. The first will go right to under his heart. The other three will be under this one. After you shoot him he will dig after you with his horns, but you just keep going from one tunnel to the next."

Gopher went over to Buffalo Monster and said, "My children are cold and I have nothing for the nest. Let me have some of your long hair to warm it up."

Buffalo Monster said, "All right, take what you need."

Gopher chewed off the hair right over Buffalo Monster's heart. You could see it beating! Then he went down into a hole. A little later he came back up, right next to Child of the Water. He said, "The tunnels are ready."

Child of the Water went into the tunnel, until he could look up and see Buffalo Monster's heart beating. He drew his bow and shot right through it.

Buffalo Monster bellowed and started digging into the ground with his horns after Child of the Water. He ran down the tunnel and jumped into the second. Buffalo Monster followed him, and Child of the Water ran down this tunnel and jumped into the third. Still it followed him, but it was slowing down. Child of the Water jumped into the fourth tunnel; when he got to the end he turned around. Buffalo Monster was still after him, but going slow. Just before it reached him it fell down, dead.

When he had killed it, Child of the Water cut off its head and took it home to show White-painted Woman. It was big and heavy, but because he picked it up on the fourth time after three feints it was made light enough. When White-painted Woman saw it she danced and sang, and gave the women's shrill of applause like they do now at the Puberty Ceremony. That was the second time it was done on earth.

Child of the Water said, "Now I am going to kill the Eagle Monsters," and he made himself a war club. He went back out to Buffalo Monster's body and cut its guts out. These he filled with its blood and wrapped around himself, and went out on a prairie.

The father Eagle Monster saw him. He swooped down and picked him up and took him high. Soon he dropped him down onto some rocks. The intestines broke and blood was all over, but Child of the Water was not hurt at all because he was inside. The father Eagle Monster thought he was dead and took him up to his nest on a high cliff.

He put Child of the Water before his children and said, "This is for you to eat."

When the baby Eagle Monsters started to peck at him, Child of the Water rose up a little and said, "Ssss."

The baby Eagle Monsters were scared of that. They told their father, "We can't eat this! It is hissing at us!"

The father Eagle Monster got a little angry. He said, "Wounds make a noise like that. Go on and eat it. I'm going out again."

When he was gone pretty far, Child of the Water got up. "When will he come back?" he asked.

The little Eagle Monsters said, "When male rain comes."

"When will your mother come back?"

They said, "When female rain comes."

"All right," said Child of the Water. He got his war club and waited behind the branch where they landed. Pretty soon it started to rain real hard, with lightning and thunder, and the father Eagle Monster flew into sight. Child of the Water got ready. Just as he landed, Child of the Water bashed him with his club and knocked him off the cliff. He was dead.

Soon the rain slackened until there was just a little drizzle, and the mother Eagle Monster flew in. Just as she landed, he hit her in the same way and killed her.

Child of the Water got back in the nest. "Which one of you can fly the best?" he asked.

They all said, "The little one there."

So he killed the others and threw them out. He got on the little Eagle Monster's back and said, "Take me down."

When they were back on the ground, Child of the Water hit him in the head with his club, too, and killed him. As he stood over the body he thought, "There ought to be good birds in the world."

He plucked a feather from it and held it over his head. "Let this be a good eagle," he said. He let it go, and before it fell to the ground it turned into an eagle, the kind we have now, and flew away.

Child of the Water pulled another feather and did the same. "Let this be a nighthawk," he said, and it was so. He did this until he had created all the kinds of birds we have today. Then he took the body home to show his mother; White-painted Woman danced and sang when she saw it. She gave the shrill of applause, and this was the third time it was done on earth. They say this is how birds were made, but I don't know. It was the birds who won daylight at the Moccasin Game, so maybe that story shouldn't come first. It always does though. Sometimes they get mixed up.

Only one remained, Antelope Monster. He was the worst, I guess, because he could kill with his eyes, just by looking at you! He had a big black spot between his eyes from the blood of men and women he killed this way; antelopes still have this spot today because he did, they say.

Antelope Monster lived in the middle of a big prairie and kept watch for people to go and kill. Child of the Water crept close to the edge of the prairie and watched this monster, trying to figure out how to kill him. But for once he got scared and started to cry. Lizard came along and saw him. "What is it?" he asked.

Child of the Water said, "I have to kill that big Antelope out there, but I don't know how to do it. He kills with his eyes!"

Lizard said, "Don't cry. I know what to do. Take four of those yucca drills that you make fires with and make arrows out of them. Shoot them just as far as you can away from him. Where they hit there will be smoke. When he sees smoke, he thinks there are some people there and charges over fast to kill them. When he goes off, you move closer. I'll help you. When he comes back, I'll cover you with my body. He can't see me because my body is the color of the ground."

Child of the Water made the arrows like Lizard said and came back to the edge of the prairie. He drew the bow as tight as he could and shot the first fire-drill arrow to the east. It went a long way, and where it hit there was a big column of black smoke. Antelope Monster saw it and charged over there as fast as he could. Child of the Water ran toward the middle of the prairie until Antelope Monster started to return, then he fell down flat and Lizard jumped on his back and covered him. He shot his second arrow to the south and it made blue smoke. Antelope Monster ran off again and Child of the Water got closer. He shot his third arrow to the west and it made yellow smoke, and he got closer. The fourth arrow he shot to the north and it made white smoke. Antelope Monster charged out again, and when he came back he fell down dead of exhaustion. Child of the Water didn't have to shoot him at all!

He took its head back to White-painted Woman, and she danced and sang more than ever, and gave a loud shrill of applause. This was the fourth time it was done on earth.

All the people-killing monsters were dead, and the world was safe for people to increase. That's when there started to be more of them around, I guess. I don't think they were yet just like us, but pretty close, maybe.[1]

The Slaying of the Monsters:
NOTES

1. The supernatural characters, White-painted Woman, Killer of Enemies, and Child of the Water (the kind of beings that ethnologists refer to as culture heroes), and the Slaying of the Monsters are the central elements of the mythology of all the Apache tribes, though there is wide variety and contradiction among them. I have chosen to follow most closely the Chiricahua version for its directness and simplicity that does not sacrifice the prominence of the four-part color-directional symbolism. Opler, "Myths and Tales of the Chiricahua Apache Indians," pp. 2–14; Hoijer, Chiricahua and Mescalero Apache Texts, pp. 5–13. The Mescalero telling of the Monster cycle is quite similar generally to the Chiricahua. Ibid., pp. 183–88.

In the other tribal versions things become more tangled. The Western Apaches, Jicarillas, and Lipans reverse the roles of Killer of Enemies and Child of the Water; in fact, an optional translation of "Killer of Enemies" is "Monster Slayer," which I have avoided because of the confusion that would result from calling him Monster Slayer when it was not he, but Child of the Water, who killed them. One obvious solution would have been simply to use the Western Apache names. However, the Western Apache version of the Monster cycle is much more complex than the Chiricahua and fraught with interrelated elements. Goodwin, "Myths and Tales of the White Mountain Apache," pp. 3–4, 10–26; Goddard, "Myths and Tales from the White Mountain Apache," pp. 93, 115–20; Bourke, "Notes on Apache Mythology," p. 210; Goddard, "Myths and Tales from the San Carlos Apache," pp. 8, 13–19, 30–35, 40–41. To combine the best elements of Chiricahua and Western versions into the most textually workable would result in the kind of artificial blend which, as the preface explains, I have tried to avoid. (Probably the surest way to escape confusion is to accept the text and avoid chapter end notes.)

The Jicarilla cycle is the most simplified, blending, for example, the killings of Buffalo Monster and Antelope Monster in the same story. These versions are amply recorded in Goddard, "Jicarilla Apache Texts," pp. 197–99; Opler,

"Myths and Tales of the Jicarilla Apache Indians," pp. 48–49, 58–65, 75–76; Curtis, *North American Indian*, Vol. I, pp. 62, 65–68; Russell, "Myths of the Jicarilla Apache," pp. 255–58; and Mooney, "Jicarilla Genesis," pp. 200–8. The Lipan cycle is contained in Opler, "Myths and Legends of the Lipan Apache Indians," pp. 13–23, 28.

Readers who wish a more detailed breakdown of the different elements will find a marvelous topical index in French, "Comparative Notes on Chiricahua Apache Mythology," pp. 103–11, which also records these same elements as found in the similar cycle of the Navajo Indians.

Some scholars have taken interest in the fact that the chief characters of Apache mythology form a loose sort of Trinity: Yusn the Life-giver, White-painted Woman, and the principal culture hero, Child of the Water. This has prompted speculation that the mythology as it developed may have been influenced by early contact with Spanish missionaries. The age and source of these mythological figures (Yusn et al., not the missionaries) unfortunately cannot be pinned down, although the great Opler believed that the name Yusn was a corruption of the Spanish Dios. *Apache Odyssey*, p. 142; "Myths and Tales of the Chiricahua Apache Indians," p. 3, n. 1. Virtually all the tribal cycles of both the creation and the culture heroes contain some stories or variants that stem very directly from Christian influence—an aboriginal flood, Child of the Water returning from the dead as savior, etc. I have omitted these as extraneous to the accepted cycle, though their existence must be acknowledged. It will be noted, however, that I have omitted them *not* because I consider them inauthentic or un-Apache—that argument is handled in the preface—but for the same considerations of space and unity that ruled out use of the Jicarilla or Western versions.

Spanish Antecedents

Beginning early in the sixteenth century, the Spanish conquistadores in Mexico began sending exploratory feelers into the country to the north. At the rate of one every several years, a column of bearded, halberd-bearing Spaniards trekked like an armored caterpillar into the pebble deserts of what we now call the American Southwest, until the country became more familiar sometime after 1600. To the various bands of Indians, who were probably Apaches, they independently applied a bewildering series of names, based on geographic locales, peculiar traits or foodstuffs, or the names of apparently powerful chiefs. It undoubtedly happened that several bands were sometimes lumped under one name, and one band sometimes called by several names (and indeed the make-up of the bands themselves changed), until the true identity of the people referred to has been lost in the antiquity of the usage: Carlanas, Mansos, Palomas, Farallones, Natagés, Vaqueros, Querechos, and any number of other names that are as easily forgotten in their contemporary meaninglessness.

It is possible that Cabeza de Vaca encountered Apaches in 1528; Fray Marcos de Niza likewise, in 1539. Francisco de Coronado probably met some Eastern Apaches in 1540,[1] although the Indians referred to as Querechos by his scribe, Pedro Castañeda de Nájera, could possibly have been other Indians. The name was a Pueblan word that meant "buffalo eater," and at this time the Eastern Apaches—Lipans, Mescaleros, and Jicarillas, all three—ranged farther out onto the buffalo plains than they did in later years, after the range was claimed by the Comanches. On these first meetings Castañeda characterized the Querechos as "a kind people and not cruel."[2]

One of the first violent affrays between the Spanish and Indians who were probably Apaches—they were called Indios Vaqueros in this instance—took place in 1590. The importance of the fight goes far beyond the happenstance of the early date, however, for it prophesied not just the occurrence of Apache hostility but an aspect of its nature that has gone largely unacknowledged by history: it was brought about not by governmental policy or military bloodlust or innate savagery on the part of the Indians. It was precipitated by a maverick adventurer, unsanctioned by his government, out to seek his fortune. In short, a little man's great ambitions for himself. The legendary exploits of Cortez and Pizarro haunted and chafed the lean young gentlemen in New Spain, who wanted to achieve equal celebrity and wealth for themselves. This one in particular, Gaspar Castaño de Sosa, was fed up with the ennui of being the acting lieutenant governor of Nuevo León. He left the haven of civilization on July 27, 1590, for a footloose look-see with a force of 170 colonists and militia to the region of the Pueblos, with the gleam in the back of his mind of that eternal Spanish will-o'-the-wisp, gold. One night a band of Vaqueros rushed his camp and stole some stock, and one of Castaño's friendly Indians was killed in the fracas. A party of men went out after the Vaqueros, overtook them, and killed a few. Four were captured; three were kept to interpret, and the other hanged.

The incident was not the only one that left the Apaches with a bad taste of the Spanish, for Castaño was not the only adventurer afoot in their country.[3] The others slipped out secretly, in part probably because of the fate of Castaño himself. He had claimed the land in the king's name, but without the king's permission, for which he was arrested and exiled to China.[4] The opportunity to colonize for the king was very much an honor (and chance to reap a fortune) that was the crown's prerogative to bestow, and hence a way for the king to pay a debt or compel a service or loan. Spain's overseas ambitions were dealt a setback in 1588, when the English navy of Queen Elizabeth obliterated the "Invincible" Armada, and not until ten years later was a royal colonizer selected to organize the interior frontier of New Spain.

The lucky man was Don Juan de Oñate, a powerful man from a powerful family, a grandson-in-law to Cortez, and more important, a man with the family fortune to do the job without burdening the royal treasury any further.[5] In early summer of 1598, at the head of a massive (for that time) expeditionary force,[6] he planted sword and cross by the Rio Grande near the site of later El Paso and claimed the country for the Spanish king and Catholic Church. When he entered the Rio Grande Valley in late June the Indians of the pueblos were so demoralized by the size of his army that they promised their allegiance, and even evacuated the pueblo that Oñate named San Juan when he told them to, to provide housing for his train. The yoke so gently accepted was not so easily shaken off, however. A revolt late in the year at the sky-pueblo of Acoma cost a thousand Indians dead, and two more rebellions in early 1599 cost another thousand. After this the Pueblans bowed their heads and did as they were told, which included the construction of a provincial capital city, Santa Fe, by 1610.

Oñate was soon enough aware that the countryside about the subjugated pueblos was roamed by a wild and powerful tribe of Indians, and it was he who first gave them the name Apaches. Some contact with the wild Indians was established and priests were sent out into the mission districts that Oñate organized—such as Padre Francisco de Zamora to the Apaches who were eventually grouped under the name of Jicarillas—but overall, the violence that attended the civilizing process (an irony if ever there was one) was such that little conversion was effected. The Apaches did not really despise the Spanish from the beginning, however. They raided frequently for supplies, but the genuine hatred was awarded gradually, as it was earned.

Indeed, the history of the early Spanish performance in the Southwest first raises the question that recurs with ever greater importance in Apachería, and is still important in our own era of Indian claims and lawsuits for astronomical damages in land and money: When do the crimes of individuals become the guilt of government? When enough crimes are committed? When the crime is done by one whose name is followed by the title and rubric of authority, even when he acts on his own (as Castaño did)? Or does guilt merely require that authority see a crime coming at private hands and fail to prevent it? In a time and place as disorganized and primitive as New Spain, where the government was inextricably bound up in the personality (and flaws) of the one or few who administered it, the question is more easily answered than on the later American frontier. If the occasional incursion of a glory seeker like Castaño had been the worst that Apachería had to endure, it would have been bad enough. Almost from the beginning, however, during Oñate's own regime, the government splattered itself so heavily with graft, corruption, influence peddling, and slave trading as to stand convicted under any test of guilt that one can choose.

Large tracts of the new province were awarded to important men as *encomiendas*, feudal fiefdoms to which the Indians were bound, and from their labor the lord payed a tax-tribute to the governor. Trading in Indian slaves was illegal, but there was ore to be dug in the mines, and soon, looms to be worked in the mills. Genteel families—the *encomenderos*—needed quiet servants to pad about the haciendas. The northern frontier was far from the viceroy, and the viceroy was even farther from the king; with the Pueblan Indians already subjugated, excursions against the Apache menace came frequently to be nothing less than slaving expeditions. And the Apaches, predictably, began to retaliate by taking Spanish and Pueblan women and children captive. Much of the Spanish slaving was done in the name of the Church: one might not hunt slaves, but nothing prevented him from trying to save the soul of a captured Indian by subjecting him to the Christianizing influences of instruction—and labor. It was an obscene blasphemy, practiced probably more by the civil officials than by the clergy, although the priests were by no means guilt-less.

What this introduces is the notion of dividing the authority to deal with Indians—either subjugated or still wild—between the army and the Church, which is another theme that recurs many times in the history of Apachería. To Catholic Spanish conquest, the conversion of heathens was a very major consideration, probably equal in importance to the territorial acquisition itself. Unfortunately, as one might expect from an endeavor that required men dedicated to arms to co-operate with men dedicated to God, it didn't work, and Church and military frequently worked at cross-purposes from one another. Most of the men regarded the Indian as soulless, a species of animal barely above an ape. To kill an Indian was no greater loss than to kill a horse or cow; less of a loss, actually, for there were more Indians than head of stock. The priests, for all their misuse of Indian labor and their perverted convert-or-die theology, did truly deplore the loss of unransomed souls. Each faction also sought the authority for its own sake, the governors trying to preserve the order of the crown, which not just incidentally preserved their own wealth and status, and the leading clergy entertaining some vision of a wilderness theocracy. Each faction held real power—both could order arrests—and the feuding became so bitter that the common soldier sometimes didn't know whom to obey; the governor could execute him, and the Church could damn his soul, and then execute him as well. None of this was lost on the Indians, either Pueblans or Apaches, and they came to view the cross of Christ with increasing circumspection and distaste.

In 1630, after nine years' experience on the frontier, one of the most conscientious of the missionaries, Fray Alonso de Benavides, wrote an eloquent *Memorial* to King Philip IV. In it he bore witness to the brutality and depravity of slaving expeditions that the governor sent against Indians who in some cases were not even hostile. He related one instance of an Apache chief who, through the friar's persistent instruction and the chief's equally persistent application of mind, had almost been won over to the Church, only to perish at the eleventh hour, with the loss of his unredeemed soul, in a raid by enemy Indians that was sponsored by the provincial governor. The chief died, not fighting, but holding forth his rosary, begging for his life in the name of the Virgin Mary. On returning to Santa Fe the raiders were greeted with such scorn and hostility that the sorely embarrassed governor tried to pin responsibility on the leader of the expedition. Benavides reported, however, that the Indians "already know who is at fault, and that God ought to be adored above all things."[7]

Blame was seldom so easily affixed, and it is not difficult to understand why, by the middle of the seventeenth century, the Mescalero, Jicarilla, and Lipan Apaches had begun taking more serious revenge on the Spaniards and the weaker Pueblan tribes who now clung to them for pro-

tection. Some scholars believe, and it is probably true, that until this time
the Apaches had forborne excessive violence against the Spanish and their
wards because the newcomers had not yet wrought sufficient pollution of
the native culture for the Apaches to perceive them as a malevolent
influence.[8] But a more practical factor of moment was the promise of commerce with the Pueblans and their protectors. A couple of trading posts
were established on the northeastern frontier of the Spanish holdings, to
which the Lipans, Jicarillas and Mescaleros brought in buffalo hides and
other native produce to exchange for grain, trade goods and trinkets. The
peace was not uninterrupted by sporadic violence, by any means, but the
mutual benefits of the trading relationship outweighed, for the time being,
a desire to inflict mortal damage on the adversary.

After about 1650, however, Indian raids increased among the villages of
the eastern fringe of Spanish settlement, a tenuous line of squalid hamlets
strung north to south along the Rio Grande in central New Mexico. The
southernmost of the pueblos, and one of the Apache trading posts, was
Jumanos, located probably on or near the site of Gran Quivira ruin; by
chance it was also the closest one to the home range of the largest of the
Mescalero bands, in the Sierra Blanca east of the White Sands. Jumanos
pueblo therefore suffered probably a disproportionate share of the Mescalero raids, but the increase in Apache hostility became noticeable across all
the northeastern frontier. Throughout that decade they preyed upon the
roads and villages, and also, significantly, received into their ranks the
disaffected Pueblans who cared to join them. The Apaches knew well
enough that the tales of hunting and freedom that circulated back to the
settlements caused increasing unrest among the Pueblans still under the
yoke, and they took advantage of the opportunity.

Meanwhile, the conflict between the Church and the military reached a
boiling point in New Mexico under the governorship of Don Bernardo
Lopez de Mendizábal, who came to power in 1659. As his battle with the
frontier priesthood over control of the Indians grew, it underwent that almost inevitable metamorphosis from general disagreement over policy to
bitter, slanderous personal attacks. In the process the Indians, including
the increasingly troublesome Apaches, were all but lost sight of. They
found themselves less a primitive race to be controlled and elevated, and
more a means to other men's ends. It was a role they would play many
times over the next two hundred years. As the Franciscans accused the
governor of subversion and irreligion, and Mendizábal responded with
charges that the missionaries corrupted themselves with Indian women
and made slaves of the natives to further personal goals, the Apaches
watched, sometimes quietly and sometimes from beneath the war turbans,
but always with perception, and they gained a perhaps keener insight into
Western civilization than those caught up in its struggles. (It was the
priests who won this particular battle, as Governor Mendizábal was

arrested in 1662 by officers of the Inquisition, after he had sent a small squadron of soldiers under his chief lieutenant to mock and whip some fifty lashes apiece some religious attendants on their way to celebrate the feast of San Buenaventura, the patron saint of Jumanos. Neither the governor nor his aide ever reappeared.)

Once the Eastern Apaches had set themselves to the expulsion of the Spanish from their country, they received an unexpected assist from the capricious nature of the Southwest, in the form of the dual scourges of famine and pestilence to weaken the Europeans and the Pueblans who served them. From the late 1650s, crops failed year after year; the entire decade of the 1660s was one of desperate, terrible privation. No grain whatever was harvested in 1667, 1668 or 1669, until Spaniard and Pueblan alike were reduced to parching and eating rawhide utensils, "and the greatest misfortune is that they can no longer find a bit of leather to eat, for their herds are dying."[9] Roadsides and ravines were littered with the dead, and one of the Franciscans reported that four hundred fifty had starved to death at Jumanos alone, which was a terrible proportion of the population. Times were not good for the Apaches either, but as they roamed free, living on buffalo and mescal, they watched, and waited, and raided, ferociously: "They hurl themselves at danger like a people who know no God, nor that there is any hell."[10]

On the heels of the famine came a ravaging tide of what was probably smallpox. In 1672 the eastern tribes of the Apaches sensed the time had come, and they struck the villages and pueblos with an intense rapacity that carried everything before them. Even proud Jumanos, with its almost finished cathedral, was finally evacuated of its five hundred surviving families and abandoned, to be lost to history forever.

Throughout the period of hardship, certain of the Pueblo Indians continued to grumble against the Spaniards, and the Apaches, quick to sense the wedge that could be driven between master and subject, used what influence they had to back the malcontents and press for a broadly based rebellion against the Europeans. Under the leadership of a Pueblo shaman named Popé,[11] that was precisely the result achieved. On the tenth day of August 1680, the northeastern frontier of New Spain exploded like a penetrated magazine. Within a short space of time, one third of the European population of the Rio Grande region lay dead. The rest, with the loyal Christian Indians who survived the carnage, fled in undignified disarray, not stopping until they had reached El Paso del Norte or some equally remote bastion of safety. The Rio Grande valley north of there was left completely in the possession of the victorious Indians. To follow up the triumph, the Mescaleros and other eastern bands followed the Spanish south, killing Europeans wherever they could be cornered.

Throughout the 1680s and 1690s the Plains Apache extended their domain south and west; El Paso itself and the outlying settlements became

regular victims of the turbaned Mescalero warriors, whose raids extended
sometimes down as far as Chihuahua. The few successes that the Spanish
had with their punitive expeditions failed to deal a mortal blow to the
Apaches; rather they served to educate and give them experience in the
European war method. After a daring raid on El Paso in 1682, for instance, the punitive Spanish column managed to capture twenty-two of
the culprits and kill a few others,[12] but similar expeditions in later years
generally gained them nothing. Diego de Vargas and a Spanish army retook the pueblos in 1692, and by 1695 attempts were again made to settle
the upper portion of the Rio Grande, but the new colonists found themselves largely at the Apaches' mercy. The Camino Real, the "Royal Road"
that linked the New Mexico pueblos with the larger southern settlements
became such a target of Mescalero violence that a hundred-mile stretch of
it north of El Paso was called by a new name: Jornada del Muerto: the
passage of death.

The closing years of the seventeenth century were the high water mark
of Plains Apache power. The Mescaleros roamed virtually unchallenged
from Chihuahua north to the Rio Grande pueblos, and the Lipans east of
them, out onto the South Plains at least as far as present Kansas. After
1700, however, they were opposed by a new force that was more powerful
than any they had known: the Comanche Indians, a Uto-Aztecan tribe
from the northern Great Plains who had been forced to migrate south by
a mushrooming westward expansion of the Sioux. With unnerving horsemanship and a ferocity more than equal to the Apaches' own, the
Comanches in their buffalo-horned war bonnets opened a struggle for control of the game-rich country of the South Plains, and slowly but surely
began to wrest the land from the Apaches. Apparently, the back of
Apache resistance was broken somewhere east of the Pecos River in the
early 1720s, when a force of Lipans and their allies were put to rout in an
epic battle that was said to have lasted more than a week.[13]

As early as 1717 it was clear that the Comanches were also giving the
Jicarilla Apaches a bad beating, and reducing that tribe's territory with almost every new raid. The Jicarillas were in a particularly bad way—much
worse than the Mescaleros—for they were losing their domain not only to
the Comanches, but also to the Utes on their north and the Apache-
related but unfriendly Navajos on their west. The Jicarillas had nowhere
to turn for aid but the Spanish, who had by now mostly recovered from
the Popé disaster and were repopulating the Rio Grande valley in increasing numbers. Thus, while other Apaches met the Spanish resurgence with
stiff resistance, the Jicarillas were reduced to ingratiating themselves to
them to have any chance at survival. A new governor in New Mexico, Antonio de Valverde y Cosia, showed himself warm to the Jicarilla subjection
when he enlisted two hundred of them into a large army to fight the
Comanches, but the enemy, who raided at will, proved too elusive to

corner in a disadvantageous battle. Jicarilla dependence on the Spanish increased further when, in 1724, the Comanches mounted a devastating raid against them, decimating their ranks of warriors and carrying off as many as half their women and children into captivity.[14] The Spaniards seized the opportunity to plant missionaries among some Jicarilla groups, and the Indians in their desperation tried to please the Franciscan padres by making crosses. Valverde was skeptical of so much eagerness, and when an order arrived from the viceroy that a presidio was to be built some 130 leagues out from Santa Fe, a council of war decided that this was too risky to be practical.[15] Over the next fifty years, however, as the Spanish repopulation of the Rio Grande gained in security, more Jicarillas served under Spanish arms, and for protection the tribe came to dwell almost exclusively in the immediate vicinity of the pueblos.

During the height of the Comanche rapacity, probably a majority of the Mescaleros stayed in their mountain retreats, in hiding, but many others of them migrated south, re-establishing their bands in the Davis and Chisos mountains of trans-Pecos Texas, the Sierra del Carmen; indeed, some mountain lairs were established as far away as Coahuila. From there they undertook raids as far distant as Saltillo, some seven hundred miles from their Rio Grande home. Much of the new country was extremely difficult, and virtually all of it was less productive in game and food plants than their upper Rio Grande, and during the 1730s and 1740s the exiled Mescaleros raided with desperation among the Spanish settlements for goods and provisions. The Europeans, for their part, kept after them with punitive expeditions and slaving raids. Their fortunes varied from humiliating defeats at Apache hands to the capture, in 1737, of a leading Mescalero chief named Cabellos Colorados (Red Hair). The chief's Apache name and the reason behind the Spanish appellation remained mysteries unsolved, for he was taken in bondage to Mexico City, where he disappeared. The state of Chihuahua undertook the formality of a declaration of war against the Apaches in 1748, but it was little more than an acknowledgment of pre-existing fact, and through the decade of the 1750s the turn of battle seemed to edge against the Spanish.

In the northeastern quadrant of New Spain, the region that became known as Tejas and later anglicized to Texas, Spanish relations with the Apache Indians divide rather easily into three periods. There was open hostility from the first contact in 1689 to 1749; a friendship and ostensible alliance from 1749 to 1770; and a return to warfare from 1770 to the end of the royal Spanish government.

In the first instance the Europeans behaved shortsightedly. The original mission in this part of the country, to the Tejas Indians of the low, humid pine forests near French Louisiana, sought to aid that tribe and their allies the Tonkawas and Comanches, and array them against the Apaches.[16] It

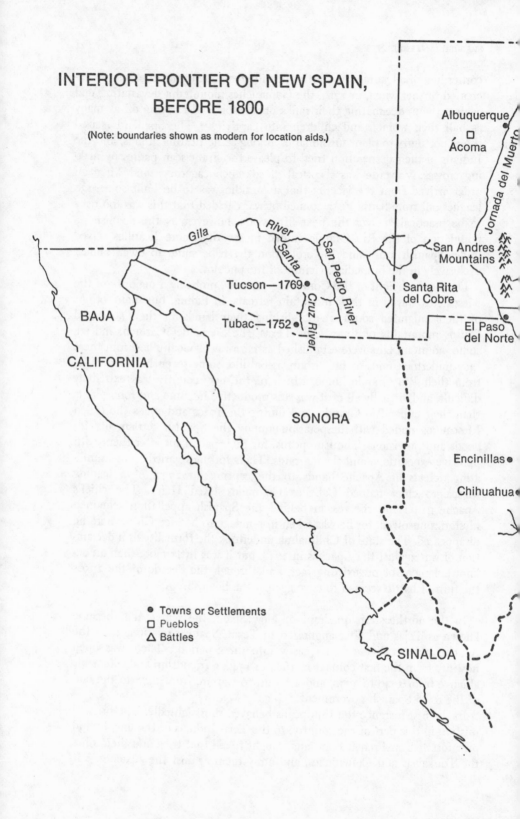

INTERIOR FRONTIER OF NEW SPAIN, BEFORE 1800

(Note: boundaries shown as modern for location aids.)

Gila River

Santa Cruz River

San Pedro River

Jornada del Muerto

Albuquerque

Ácoma

San Andres Mountains

Tucson—1769

Santa Rita del Cobre

Tubac—1752

El Paso del Norte

BAJA

CALIFORNIA

SONORA

Encinillas

Chihuahua

● Towns or Settlements
□ Pueblos
△ Battles

SINALOA

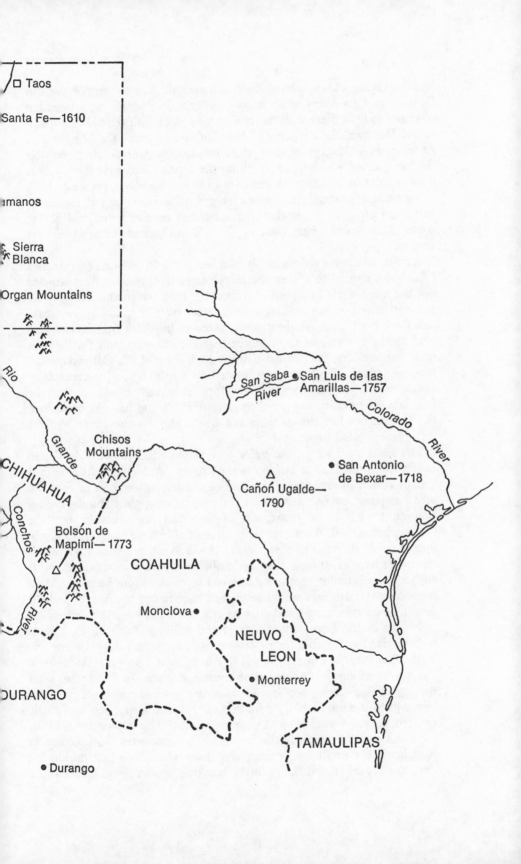

□ Taos

Santa Fe—1610

umanos

Sierra
Blanca

Organ Mountains

Rio

Grande

Conchos

CHIHUAHUA

Chisos
Mountains

San Saba
River

San Luis de las
Amarillas—1757

Colorado
River

San Antonio
de Bexar—1718

△
Cañon Ugalde—
1790

Bolsón de
Mapimí— 1773

△

COAHUILA

River

Monclova ●

NEUVO
LEON

● Monterrey

DURANGO

● Durango

TAMAULIPAS

was the Lipans who inhabited the brush and hill country east of the Rio Grande, and for many years it was the friendly Indians who were encouraged to fight them, so little combat took place with the Spanish themselves. However, the founding of San Antonio in 1718—the Mission San Antonio de Valero, guarded by the Presidio San Antonio de Bexar—on the San Jacinto, which was well within the Lipan range, gave the Apaches a focal point on which to concentrate their revenge. Over the next thirty years, raids and atrocities were exchanged with rather postal regularity, and more often than not the Lipans finished on the losing end of the count. They were far from done in, though, and had one or two tricks yet to play.

A group of Lipans rode brazenly into San Antonio de Bexar in 1749 and broached a request to talk to the missionaries. The commandant scowled but the friars excitedly agreed to a meeting, from which the soldier garrison was barred, as the Indians wished. After years of spurning the Christian God, the Lipans asked for peace, asked to buy back Apache prisoners held by the priests, and finally asked that a mission be built for them in their own country, the San Saba River, a tributary of the Colorado, more than a hundred miles to the northwest. This was far beyond the protective ability of the garrison, and what the Lipans did not reveal was that the San Saba River valley was not their country at all, and had not been since the Comanches had driven them out of it. The Apaches were laying a vastly complicated trap.

The effort by the energetic *padre presidente* of San Antonio de Valero to establish some kind of mission to the Lipans dated at least from 1743.[17] The inert bureaucracy showed itself unresponsive, as usual, so in 1745 the priest proposed not one new mission but four, strung out along the Indian frontier, to effect the conversion of not only the Apaches but the Comanches as well. After four years more of silence the angry padre submitted a wild proposal to abandon San Antonio altogether and relocate it on the Pedernales, though this was probably intended as much to see if anybody was listening as it was a serious suggestion. From his viewpoint a mission on the San Saba would be the first ever among the Apache Indians deep in their own range, and that chance must not be lost to either his own fears or the hearty skepticism of the military. And the Franciscan wish to give the Apaches their own mission was given additional impetus by the fact that the Lipans who did stay more or less near San Antonio de Bexar were eating the fathers out of house and home. In seven years after the 1749 peacemaking, the San Antonio Apaches had consumed good behavior gifts of more than 2,700 bushels of corn and beans, 200 beef cattle and horses, and a huge amount of trade goods.[18] The request for a Lipan mission circulated through the imprecise and confused bureaucracy of New Spain for a still longer time, and there is evidence that during the wait, the Lipans seeded their plot by breaking up the Spanish-Comanche friendship. They seem to have raided small Comanche villages, notice-ably dropping Spanish articles for the survivors to find, and then raided outlying Spanish settlements, leaving behind hardware captured from the Comanches.

Not until 1757 was the decision finally made to establish the Lipan mis-sion and presidio, to be called San Luis de las Amarillas. Aside from the religious motive, approval was finally given, in part, because the Spanish believed they were getting the better of the deal from at least three an-gles.[19] To give the Lipans their own mission more than a hundred miles away would get them out of San Antonio, where they were not only a burden on the granary but even during their periods of uncertain quiet they were a source of consternation to the populace. Also, the very existence of the new mission and presidio would show the flag and distend Spain's line of civilization farther into the wilderness than it had ever been (thus serving some notice to the French that they were not alone in that part of the continent). And there was lastly that lure to which the Spanish had always proved so peculiarly susceptible: tales of silver mines in the San Saba region.

Selected to be *padre presidente* of the new Mission San Luis de las Amarillas was Alonso Giraldo de Terreras. He was no stranger to Apaches, as three years earlier he had presided over a short-lived Mission San Juan Bautista, built for the Lipan Apaches just south of the Rio Grande. After less than a year the Indians had burned the mission and vanished, and Terreras blamed the failure in substantial part on the mission's distance from the Indians' home territory northwest of San Antonio. These Indians appear to have been closely related to the San Antonio Lipans, but were probably not the exact same people, as was once believed.[20] The San Luis mission opened with five priests under Terreras, guarded by a presidio gar-rison under Colonel Don Diego Ortiz de Parilla. A few Lipans wandered in from time to time, mostly to make excuses for the absence of the rest. In early March of 1758, all the Lipans who had been about the mission crept away, traceless. Shortly thereafter, on March 15, the garrison watched as *Indios*—they did not know what kind—whipped their horse herd away from its pasture. Parilla sent a message to Terreras asking him to gather his priests and sacred articles and repair to the presidio, but he refused. The next morning, Mass was disrupted by a din of unearthly, gobbling whoops from outside the mission. Outside, Terreras gasped as he beheld his death: some two thousand Comanche and Wichita Indians, mounted, circling the mission, whooping and demonstrating their ferocity. One of the priests, named Molina, Colonel Parilla, and a few of the garri-son soldiers survived the butchery. Everyone else was killed. The govern-ment was outraged at the Comanches, and in August of 1759, Parilla headed north again with a punitive expedition of not less than six hun-dred, including—the Spanish weren't wise to them yet—well over a hundred Lipans, who disappeared when the fighting started. The army met with disaster near the Red River, at the hands of a combined horde of French-directed plains and woods Indians, and Parilla was sent off to stand trial for incompetence.

The question of how much of the Lipan scheming on the San Saba was maliciously forethought, and how much of it was skillful playing by ear of a complicated fact situation, is probably unanswerable. In either case, the Apaches had continued for a period of years making precisely the right moves. They played cannily on the ignorant piety of the Spanish padres, they perceived and capitalized on the Spanish misconception of intertribal relations and territorial limits, and they very likely disguised their raids to turn the Spanish and Comanches against one another. Overall, it was a masterwork of barbaric shrewdness that would have done credit to the intellectual capacity of any supposedly primitive people. At least, that has been the judgment of history, and it is intrinsically accurate, but in the history books the telling of it seems tinged with an element also of approbation. Whether that approval would have been extended had the roles been reversed—that is, had it been the Spanish who led on the Apaches (as they did, plenty of times)—is doubtful.

Spanish exploration of the northwestern interior was later in coming and more sporadic. Antonio de Espejo may have reached the region of central Arizona, and perhaps encountered some Western Apaches, in 1582. For a long time thereafter the region remained largely unknown, too far west of the Rio Grande to be influenced by its missions, and too far east of California to be influenced by the missions of the coastal Camino Real. For the few soldiers and padres who ventured into the area, Apache hostility began sometime in the early 1670s.[21]

Beginning in 1687 and laboring for nearly a quarter of a century after, the remarkable Padre Eusebio Francisco Kino[22] worked to bring order to the district, and in the face of attacks by hostile Apaches (who sacked the mission at Cocosperra in 1698)[23] the valleys of the Santa Cruz and San Pedro began slowly to be settled and productive. In the mid-eighteenth century two settlements were founded on, and possibly helped define, the western fringe of Apachería: Tubac in 1752, and further north, Tucson in 1769.[24] Beyond their protection, though, Apaches became more earnest in their depredations, and the hopefully productive river valleys began to wither on the vine of settlement. Fray Francisco Garces, whose Mission San Xavier del Bac was located in the region to serve the Pima and Papago Indians, traveled extensively in 1775–76, but gave the Apache country a wide berth. He proposed a plan to control the growing menace by ringing their territory with presidios, the same strategy that was employed some hundred years later.[25]

By 1766, however, Apache victories both here and farther east in New

Mexico, and in Texas, made it clear even to the confused and cumbersome bureaucracy of New Spain that something new and vastly different would have to be done or the entire interior would be wasted by Indians. But the method by which they decided on a policy pointed up the single greatest weakness of the colonial government: from the time they decided to do something drastic, it took nine years to do it. A thorough review of the situation required the years 1766 to 1768, another year for a recommendation to be given to the military council and be forwarded to Spain, and three years for an official policy to come back in 1772. More years were spent in planning and marshaling forces, until by 1775 a vast army of more than two thousand had been assembled to strike into the Mescalero country of the northeastern frontier.

In the meantime, the Apaches continued to have things very much their own way. One Mescalero band in particular had almost made a game of coming in to El Paso from their nearby lair in the Organ Mountains, concluding a peace only to violate it to their hearts' content while sweeping back to their hideout. Only once, apparently, in July of 1766, did the garrison genuinely best them, when Don Pedro José de la Fuente followed them home and punished them. Elsewhere, another significant win over the Mescaleros was claimed in the Bolsón de Mapimí of southeastern Chihuahua, which resulted in the Indians being driven northward from that portion of the country. Most other expeditions were defeated by a combination of the Mescaleros' skill and the extreme terrain of the mountains.

In the opening years of the 1770s a group of Apaches—possibly the same ones beaten by Fuente—satisfied the commandant of the garrison at El Paso that their desire for peace was genuine. The captain, Don Pedro del Barrio, admitted them to the settlement and treated with them, evidently with some success. When word of this reached his superiors, Barrio was relieved of command and replaced with Don Antonio Darioca, who was instructed to seize the Indians the next time they showed themselves. That the Apaches knew of the change in management was doubtful, since Darioca managed to take a few women prisoners. He shipped them off to labor in the textile works at Ensenillas, which was a favored end point for Indian women taken in slaving raids.[26] The once peaceably inclined Mescaleros staged a revenge raid in 1774 against the pueblo at El Paso, ravaging Darioca's own horse herd while killing ten men. Barrio's removal was not to be the last time a subordinate officer was punished and scourged for attempting to arrange a peace when the popular sentiment wanted a war, but the parallel seems almost to have been lost on historians concerned with the post-Civil War American Southwest.

The campaign of 1775, which aimed to ensnare the Apaches within three converging troop columns, ended to the Spaniards' satisfaction, as they claimed in fifteen battles to have killed 138 of the Indians, taken 104

prisoners, and captured nearly two thousand head of stock. Few details of
the engagements survive, although the Europeans hit on and refined at
last a successful technique of stalking and killing Apaches. One must "proceed silently at night," wrote Felipe de Neve, "without fires; to hide during the day and to send out spies to hunt trails; to investigate every noise
and finally to surprise the foe." He presaged George Crook by ninety-six
years.[27]

Another campaign the next year was intended to finish what the first
had started; it did, and it brought disaster to the Mescaleros. The Spanish
had struck an alliance with the new masters of the South Plains, the
Comanches. The European soldiers pressed along a broad front, driving a
large number of Mescaleros before them, into the waiting arms of the
Comanches near the Colorado River of Texas. The Comanches proved
themselves to be of greater cruelty in war than the Spaniards, and it was
said that three hundred Mescalero families were cut down.[28] From such a
massacre the Mescaleros could not possibly recover in either numbers or
power, and in December of 1777 they sent in a peace feeler to the presidio
at El Paso. They were wasting their time, for peace negotiations on the
heels of a tremendous victory were seldom a hallmark of Spanish diplomacy. Moreover, larger changes than ever before were being worked upon
the frontier government, and policy was in flux.

The bureaucracy's nine-year pregnancy on changing the frontier administration was about to bear further fruit. In 1776 the Indian-plagued northern frontier from Texas on the east to the Gulf of California was completely excised from the Viceroyalty of New Spain and re-established as a
separate government, the Interior Provinces, to streamline its management. To head it was named one of the best men available, Teodoro de
Croix, a capable military leader and planner, and a resourceful civilian administrator. Among his envisioned reforms were increasing the efficacy
of protecting a garrison's horse herd by reducing it to a small number of
the finest animals, instituting a willingness to pair diplomacy with force in
dealing with the Apaches, but when diplomacy failed, increasing the ability to hit the Indians hard with military might by rearranging outposts
among the most strategic locations. He also intended to tax wealthy merchants and landowners to defray the cost of their better defense. In
1777–78 he convened three large conferences, one at San Antonio de
Bexar, one at Monclova in Coahuila, and one in his headquarters in
Chihuahua City. Of each group he asked sixteen questions about what to
do with the Indians. The answers were virtually unanimous, and the
resulting policy, for practical purposes, intended the doom of the Apaches.
The Comanches were to be humored at all costs, even in their attacks on
Apache rancherias. The diplomacy amounted to an attitude that Apaches
who kept the peace with the Spanish would not be attacked, but neither

would they be actively protected, and Apaches who turned on the Spanish would suffer a war of extermination.[29]

During his tenure De Croix played skillfully upon a rift that had been growing between the Lipans and the Mescaleros, driving in a wedge just big enough to engender violence between the two that forced the Lipans to sue for peace with the Spanish. The Mescalero bands that had migrated into Chihuahua also asked for a settlement; De Croix housed them in the deserted San Francisco pueblo with the understanding that they were to become agricultural, but the scheme failed before long. Unfortunately for the government of the Interior Provinces, good men were at a premium in the Spanish new world, and De Croix was transferred to take over as viceroy of Peru. He was replaced by Jacobo Ugarte. After the failure of the San Francisco agricultural experiment, little diplomacy was used on the Mescaleros, and one of the more successful military commanders against them was Juan de Ugalde, the governor of Coahuila. In the five years 1779 to 1783 he undertook four separate expeditions against them, each one meeting an appreciable amount of success. Whenever he turned his back, though, the Apaches swept in behind him. The governor of the province of Texas, Domingo Cabello, reported in 1780 that "there is no instant day or night when reports of barbarities and disorders do not arrive from the ranches. . . . unprotected as we are, this can only result in the complete destruction and loss of this province." After his Mescalero campaigns, Ugalde retired to Mexico City for a much needed rest, but again, as soon as he was gone, the angry Apaches, under one Mescalero chief in particular named Zapato Tuerto, inflamed the frontier behind him. They raided deep into old Mexico and completely sacked two settlements, Gruñidora and Sabana Grande.[30]

Within this same time frame, to the west of the action in Texas, Don Juan Bautista de Anza was sent into New Mexico to make a peace and alliance with the Comanches against the Apaches, but to do that he first had to gain the Comanches' respect. He headed one campaign against them in the fall of 1779, but no more money was available for him until 1783. When he was re-equipped he fought numerous successful actions against them that resulted in a treaty in 1785, and Comanches began to accompany him on sorties against the Apaches. Of Apache activity farther west, "all records of the time contain a general complaint of never-ending depredations; but of campaigns, disasters, and other events from year to year, practically nothing is known."[31]

The Spanish handling of the Apache question took on yet another new complexion with the installation of Bernardo de Gálvez as governor of the Interior Provinces in 1786. In a famous directive to General Ugarte called "Instructions for Governing the Interior Provinces," he advanced a new theory, clever from the Spanish point of view but diabolical in the eyes of many historians, that the Apaches might be more easily conquered by peace than by unremitting war. But what a peace: the plan provided for the issuance, after the cessation of hostilities, of firearms to the Apaches, but firearms of sufficient antiquity and poor repair that they would need constant tinkering by trained gunsmiths, which would render them useless in the event the Indians returned to war. The Apaches were also to be issued as much liquor as they could hold, for they had acquired the same fondness for the Spaniards' aguardiente that was the curse of other Indian tribes. Apaches kept in a bleary stupor would, it was hoped, be more easily broken to Spanish rule than when sober and sharp-witted, and with luck they would become so addicted to distilled spirits as to depend on the Spanish for their supply, thus rendering war additionally unpleasant if not unthinkable.

Old-guard line commanders thought the Gálvez "Instructions" were insanely unworkable, but pacification by dissipation was not the only strategy of the Gálvez regime. Spanish ties with the Comanches were strengthened to maintain pressure on the Eastern Apaches, beginning in 1787. Some scholars believe that the Comanche alliance was a mistake, and that this portion of the Gálvez policy should rather have been to aid the Apaches against the Comanches.[32] This is probably true, for the alliance as it was made depended to a large extent upon consistent conduct from the Comanches, which was not forthcoming. The Comanche range extended too far beyond the limit of Spanish territory to guarantee effective control of them, and the Spanish thus found themselves with two enemies instead of one.

However, Gálvez's sagacity paid off for the most part, although here and there serious flare-ups did occur. Lipan raiding in the eastern part of the frontier occasioned the return to battle of Juan de Ugalde, who assembled a formidable army in 1790 that included both Wichita and Comanche Indians. The force trapped and massacred several hundred Lipans in a canyon west of San Antonio de Bexar; the location later became known as the Cañon Ugalde, later anglicized to Uvalde, now the seat of Uvalde County, Texas.

The Gálvez system of buying off the Apaches and keeping them drunk drained between $18,000 and $30,000 per annum from the colonial treasury, and whether because it was working or because both the Apaches and the Spaniards were exhausted after three generations of war, the eighteenth century closed across Apachería in a lull of relative peace. The Western Apaches, who remained largely uncowed by military efforts, were partly subdued by the issuance of rations and supplies, and other Apaches in that area had their hands full with a war against the Navajos. The result for the Spanish was considerable economic prosperity all across the northern frontier. El Paso del Norte and other main population centers bloomed, new settlements were established, and the livestock and other industries reached impressive proportions, Franciscan missionaries, either combating the influence of the Gálvez policy or succeeding because of it, began to make some progress with religious instruction of the Apaches. The peace lasted about a quarter of a century, the longest such period ever recorded.[33]

Spanish Antecedents:
NOTES

1. The most readable treatment of these and other expeditions, indeed of the whole Spanish era, lies in the humbling scholarship of the great Hubert Howe Bancroft. See his *History of Arizona and New Mexico 1530–1888*, pp. 1–145.

2. Winship, *Journey of Francisco Vazquez de Coronado*, p. 60.

3. Bancroft, *History of Arizona and New Mexico 1530–1888*, pp. 92–100.

4. Josephy, *Patriot Chiefs*, p. 80.

5. An order from the king to the viceroy in 1583 instructed him to license only those expeditions that were not to be at crown expense. Bancroft, *History of Arizona and New Mexico 1530–1888*, p. 93.

6. Ibid., p. 124. The expedition counted 400 men (130 with dependents), 83 wagons and 7,000 cattle.

7. Benavides, *Memorial*, ed. Hodge and Lummis, trans. Ayer, p. 57.

8. See Adams, *Geronimo*, p. 22.

9. Bandelier and Bandelier, *Historical Documents*, Vol. III, p. 272.

10. Ibid.

11. A succinct re-creation of the Popé rebellion can be found in Josephy, *Patriot Chiefs*, pp. 65ff.

12. Hughes, *Beginnings of Spanish Settlement in the El Paso District*, p. 335.

13. Thomas, *Forgotten Frontiers*, p. 60; Bolton, *Athanase de Mezieres*, Vol. I, p. 25.

14. Thomas, *Forgotten Frontiers*, p. 58.

15. Bancroft, *History of Arizona and New Mexico 1530–1888*, pp. 236–37.

16. Dunn, "Apache Mission on the San Saba River," pp. 379–80.

17. Ibid., pp. 381–82. A more detailed account of these earlier attempts is Dunn, "Missionary Activities Among the Eastern Apaches Previous to the Founding of the San Saba Mission," pp. 188–93.

18. According to a detailed résumé drawn up by the Franciscans of their expenses, the Lipans had gone through 2,670 bushels of maize, 60 bushels of beans, 133 beef cattle, 76 horses (also used for food), 91 strings of pepper, 7½ cargas 16 tercio of salt, 22½ cargas of sugar cane, 13 cargas 5 tercio of tobacco, 4,555 varas of assorted cloth, 239 hats, 642 blankets, 458 knives, 196 bridles, 17 pots and kettles and 132 pesos worth of trinkets. "Memoria de lo que se gasto en la pacificación de los Apaches," quoted in Dunn, "Apache Mission on the San Saba River," p. 380.

19. This is mentioned in Fehrenbach, *Comanches,* p. 200, and there is further consideration of it in the Dunn articles.

20. Dunn, "Missionary Activities," p. 197.

21. Bancroft, *History of Arizona and New Mexico 1530–1888,* p. 170, gives the date 1672; others differ somewhat.

22. Two good accounts of Padre Kino's work are Bolton, *Rim of Christendom,* and Wyllys, *Pioneer Padre.*

23. Bancroft, *History of Arizona and New Mexico 1530–1888,* p. 354.

24. Thrapp, *Conquest of Apacheria,* p. 6.

25. Curtis, *North American Indians,* Vol. I, pp. 4–5.

26. Thomas, "Antonio de Bonilla and Spanish Plans for the Defense of New Mexico, 1772–78," pp. 198–99.

27. Thomas, *Forgotten Frontiers,* pp. 63–64.

28. Thomas, *Teodoro de Croix,* p. 17.

29. Nelson, "Juan de Ugalde," p. 459. Gunnerson, *Jicarilla Apaches,* p. 256, considered this somewhat of an oversimplification, which it is.

30. See Thomas, *Forgotten Frontiers,* pp. 5–9; Nelson, "Campaigning in the Big Bend of the Rio Grande in 1787," pp. 200–27.

31. Bancroft, *History of Arizona and New Mexico 1530–1888,* p. 378.

32. Nelson, "Juan de Ugalde and the Picax-Ande Ins-Tinsle," pp. 438ff.

33. Bancroft, *History of Arizona and New Mexico 1530–1888,* pp. 378–79.

The People Are Set Out

When Yusn had set people out onto the world, he decided there had to be two kinds. He called the children of White-painted Woman before him and said, "Here are two weapons. Choose which you want to live by."

He had laid before them a gun, and a bow and arrows. Killer of Enemies was older and he got first choice. He took the gun. Child of the Water was left with the bow and arrows.

Killer of Enemies became the leader of the white-eyes, and Child of the Water became the leader of the Indians. That's how they got to be different, they say. I have heard that Killer of Enemies nearly took the bow and arrows, but thought better of it. Then we would have been the whites, I guess.[1]

Back in the early times no one down here on the world had fire. It was not allowed. The only beings on earth who had permission for fire were a camp of Firefly People high up on a bluff. The people down below were cold and had a hard time, and had to eat raw meat. They didn't know how to get up that bluff to get fire from the Flies.

One time Coyote was going around the base of that bluff and saw some of the Fly Little Boys playing the arrow game. He started to play with them and pretty soon he won all their arrows from them. He said, "Listen. I have won all the arrows but you gave me a hard time for them, so I'm going to give you some back. In a while I'm going up the bluff there and tell your fathers how good you are. I will give the arrows to the boy that tells me about the trail."

The oldest Fly Little Boy said, "Our fathers have told us never to talk about that."

"I already know about it," said Coyote. "I just want to see if you do. I think you fell down here and can't get back. If you don't know the path I'll take you up. I just want to help you out." He didn't mean that at all. He was just trying to find out about the trail.

"We can't talk about that," said the oldest.

Coyote said, "Well, I guess you don't want any of these arrows, then."

The youngest Fly Little Boy didn't have much experience. Finally he said, "I know how to do it! You go to that big piñon pine over there and tell it to bend over. It does that three times, and on the fourth time you catch hold and it carries you over."

Coyote said, "That's just right." He gave that boy some arrows, just a few, not nearly as many as he let on.

Coyote went over to that big piñon and told it to bend over. Sure enough, it bent down three times, a little lower each time. On the fourth time Coyote grabbed hold of one of the branches and it carried him up over the top of the bluff.

He went into the camp of the Flies and said, "Listen here, you people! We down there have killed all your enemies. We want you to have a big dance and celebrate what we have done for you."

Those Flies were listening to him and said, "All right."

Coyote said, "Go ahead. Have a good time. I'll be back in just a minute."

Those Flies got a dance going and Coyote went off. He found a juniper tree and tied little strips of bark under his tail. Then he went back to the dance. "I am going to celebrate with you now," he said. In the middle of the dancers was a big fire. Coyote danced over to the fire and waved his tail in it.

One of the Flies saw him and said, "Hey, old man, you're going to catch your tail on fire!"

Coyote said, "No, I won't. This is just how I celebrate." He did that several more times.

One of the Flies saw him look back to see if his tail was burning and said, "I think he is trying to steal our fire."

Coyote said, "Don't talk silly. I'm showing that I'm so happy I don't even feel the fire. See?"

Finally he left his tail in the fire long enough and it started to burn. Then all at once Coyote got out of that camp and ran away. The Flies all said, "There he goes! Get him! He got our fire from us!"

That Coyote ran hard, and his tail was burning so hard he set fire to everything along the way. A bunch of the Flies were chasing him and a bunch were trying to put out the fires. Finally a couple of them flew away to find Wasp. They told him, "Make it rain, old man! Coyote has got our fire and is setting the world on fire. Hurry up!"

Wasp got up and made it rain. (They say, this is why today when we see lots of wasps, we think it will rain.) The rain started putting out all the fires, even the one on Coyote's tail.

Coyote saw it start to rain and he ran to where some bees had a hive in a sotol stalk. When he got there he had just a little fire left, under his tail, where it was scorched yellow. Coyotes still have this place, they say.

He got the bees to hide the fire in the stalk, and this is how we got fire. We still make our fire drills from sotol stalks, because the fire is in it.

Coyote got it for us, even though he nearly burned the world up doing it. He was a rough fellow, but he tried to help us out.[2]

When Yusn made Killer of Enemies chief of the white people, Child of the Water and White-painted Woman told him, "You can't stay with us anymore. You better go live with those people."

Killer of Enemies didn't want to do it. He was crying. Child of the Water didn't let Killer of Enemies take anything with him from their camp, except his gun. Killer of Enemies kept a turkey as a pet. He took that, too, and went to live with the white people.

There weren't many white people in those days. They were poor and having a hard time. They didn't have much to eat. Killer of Enemies saw this and got discouraged. He sat down by his turkey and started crying again. He said, "How am I going to take care of these people? They don't have anything!"

Then that turkey spoke up. He said, "Don't worry about it. They're going to have lots to eat." Right there that turkey swelled up, you know how turkeys do. When he shook his feathers, corn fell out all over. The white people gathered it up and this turkey showed them how to cook it. Then he shook himself again, and more corn fell out. Turkey showed them how to plant it and take care of it. This is how the white people came to have corn. Sometime later the Indians got corn, too, but I don't know how. The stories are not clear. They get mixed up.

Killer of Enemies started crying again. "All the deer are in that other country," he said. "How will these people get meat to eat?"

Turkey said, "Stop crying. Stand up and be a man. You are a child of White-painted Woman and have lots of power. Use it. You have to be clever to lead these people."

Human beings did not have cattle in those days. Only the Crow People had permission for cattle. During the day they let them out to graze on the earth, but took them into the ground at night. Nobody knew how to get them.

Killer of Enemies turned himself into a little puppy. He found some Crow Little Boys and wagged his tail and started to play with them. They liked him a lot. The Crow Little Boys took him home and asked to keep him, but the Crow Men were suspicious. They said, "Where did he come from?"

Killer of Enemies kept playing like a dog, but always he was looking around trying to find out about their cattle. Near the camp of the Crow People was a certain stump, and finally Killer of Enemies saw what happened. Every day at sundown, the Crow Men drove their cattle toward this stump. One of them kicked it four times, and the ground opened and the cattle went in. He watched this several nights and it was just the same. No guards were posted.

Late one night when the Crow People were asleep, Killer of Enemies turned himself back into his human form. He went to this stump and kicked it four times. The ground opened and the cattle started coming out. The noise of driving these cattle away woke up the Crow Men. They said, "Get him! He's taking out our cattle! There he goes!"

They all ran after him but it was too late. Killer of Enemies took these cattle to his people and said, "Now you have meat. You will live on these from now on."

Before Yusn separated the peoples, Killer of Enemies had done the hunting for White-painted Woman and Child of the Water. When he left, the Apaches had a hard time getting meat because Child of the Water had little experience. Yusn told the Thunder People to go down out of the sky and hunt for them, and this is how the Indians ate.

After a time Yusn told White-painted Woman and Child of the Water, "I want you to come up and live with me in the sky now."

They got ready to go. First they taught the Apaches how to behave. They should be good, and brave and generous. They should always share with each other and be grateful for what they have. They should give things to poor people who are having a hard time.

Right before they went to heaven, White-painted Woman called the Apaches to her. She told them, "I am going to leave you some of my power to help you out. When each one of your girls has her first period, you are going to dress her up pretty and have a big ceremony for her. It will last four days. During this time she will have my power to bless you and make things go well for you. A girl should keep herself pure for this time and not let any men have her."

When White-painted Woman had said this, she and Child of the Water went up into heaven. This happened near the Hot Springs in New Mexico, where four prairies come together.

The Apaches started off well, but soon they began to go bad. They started getting drunk and laying around. The Thunder People were still doing their hunting for them. The Apaches said, "You are not bringing us enough meat. You should be doing better so we can get fat."

The leader of the Thunder People said, "From now on you will hunt for yourselves. See if you get fat now." Then he led his men back into the sky. They were angry. Sometimes they shot their lightning arrows down at people to scare them. Even today, now and then some person who is not grateful for what he has will get shot with lightning and killed. This is why that happens, they say.

Chihuahuan Desert and Mountains. Although Apaches were well adapted to survival in the desert, they were primarily a mountain people. The Chisos Mountains of far western Texas, shown here, are patched with open meadows and stands of oak and ponderosa pine that provided the game and resources to shelter a band of Mescaleros. *Photo by the author.*

El Exmo. Sr. D. Bernardo de Galvez, Conde de Galvez Caballero pensionado de la R.ª y distinguida Orden Española de Carlos III. Comendador de Bolaños en la de Calatrava, Teniente Gral. de los R.ª Exercitos Inspector Gral. de todas las tropas de América Cap.ⁿ Gral. de la Provincia de la Luisiana y dos Floridas Virrey Gob.ªy Capi.ª tan Gral. del Reino de Nueva España, Presidente de su R.ª Audiencia, Superintend.ʲᵉ Gral. de R.ª Hac.ᵈᵃ y Ramo de Tabaco Juez conservador de este, Presid.ᵗᵉ de su Junta y Subdelegado de Correos en el mismo Reino & Hijo é inmediato succesor del Exmo. Sr D. Matías de Galvez, de edad de 38 años

Lit. de la V.ᵈᵃ de Murguia é hijos

Bernardo de Gálvez was installed as governor of the Interior Provinces in 1786, and proposed to control the Apaches by keeping them drunk and dependent upon the Spanish for material goods. *Courtesy the Texas State Library, 1/174-12.*

A small rancheria. *Courtesy the National Archives.*

Dorothy Naiche, the chief's daughter, in her Puberty Dress. *Courtesy the Smithsonian Institution, National Anthropological Archives.*

Western Apache warrior. Note turkey-feather war cap with studs, and war club secured to the right hand by wrist loop. *Courtesy the Arizona Historical Society.*

Apache babies in cradleboards. Amulets protected infants from wicked powers. *National Archives.*

Apache Ganh impersonators, or Mountain Spirit dancers. The photographer and date are not recorded, but the dancers are either Mescalero or Chiricahua, identified by the spindly shape of the headdresses; Western Apache headdresses usually spread in the shape of an open fan. It was probably taken fairly late—perhaps the 1890s or early 1900s—for the kilts are wool instead of buckskin. The posing youngster is in the part of the clown, a role permitted one his age, unlike that of a dancer. *Smithsonian Institution.*

"An Apache Princess: Granddaughter of Cochise," as labeled by the photographer, Ben Wittick. *National Archives.*

Apache women gathering wood; note use of the tumpline across the foreheads. *Arizona Historical Society.*

Apache woman tanning hides. *Arizona Historical Society.*

This clever-looking woman is Huera, the wife of Mangus; she believed in the old Apache way and was renowned for the quality of her tizwin. The army's insistence on reservation sobriety quite possibly threatened to lessen her social position. That would have been sufficient motivation for her to encourage resistance and even a breakout, as Gerónimo claimed she did. *Arizona Historical Society.*

The penalty for infidelity: facial mutilation. This is Nal-tzuk-ich ("Cut Nose"), who was an informant for General Crook during the campaign of 1883. *Courtesy the Museum of New Mexico, photo by Ben Wittick.*

When the Thunder People left them, the Apaches went very hungry for a time. They just got real bad. They were lying around drunk and having sex everywhere. They were fighting and stealing. Finally they started getting sick and lots of them died. Then they were sorry.

Yusn took pity on them. He told the Ganh spirits to come out from under the mountains and teach them ceremonies to get well. The Ganhs were wearing beautiful clothes and had wands and headdresses that were full of power.

The Apaches listened to everything the Ganhs taught them. When the Ganhs were ready to go back into the mountain, they got together and the leader said, "Listen. These people are doing all right now, but when we're gone they will do like before. We have to leave drawings of ourselves on the cliff face. When they get tired of being wicked they will remember us and do like we taught them."

The other Ganhs said, "That's right." Each one drew his picture on the cliff face, and then the Ganh spirits went back into the mountain.

It happened just like the Ganh leader said. The Apaches went back to doing no good, until they agreed they had to change. The only way to get along was to do right.

They studied those pictures on the cliff. Some men dressed up and did ceremonies like the Ganhs did. They found out that when they did this way, they had power just like the Ganhs.

All that is just about how it is now, with the white people over here, and the Indians over there.

The People Are Set Out:
NOTES

1. Several different accounts can be found of this first dividing of white men from Indians. Some identify the choosers as Killer of Enemies and Child of the Water. Hoijer, *Chiricahua and Mescalero Texts*, pp. 13–14. Others just say two men. Opler, "Myths and Tales of the Chiricahua Apache Indians," p. 2. See also Bourke, "Notes on Apache Mythology," pp. 210–12; Goddard, "Myths and Tales from the White Mountain Apache," p. 118; Goodwin, "Myths and Tales of the White Mountain Apache," pp. 8–9, 19–20. Another myth describes the choice not between weapons, but between subsistence food types. Opler, "Myths and Tales of the Chiricahua Apache," p. 14.

2. The theft of fire from the Fireflies by Coyote is, like the tale of the Moccasin Game, basic to the scheme of the Apache genesis. Published accounts include Goddard, "Myths and Tales from the San Carlos Apache," pp. 41–43; Goodwin, "Myths and Tales of the White Mountain Apache," pp. 147–48;

Hoijer, *Chiricahua and Mescalero Apache Texts*, pp. 17–18; Opler, "Myths and Tales of the Chiricahua Apache Indians," pp. 51–53; Russell, "Myths of the Jicarilla Apache," pp. 261–62; Opler, "Myths and Tales of the Jicarilla Apache Indians," pp. 269–72; Goddard, "Jicarilla Apache Texts," pp. 208–09; Opler, "Myths and Legends of the Lipan Apache Indians," pp. 109–11. Like the Moccasin Game, this myth was also known to the Navajo Indians. See also Daklugie, "Coyote and the Flies."

The Spanish Become Mexicans

In 1800, some old Spanish copper diggings that dated from sometime before 1680 were rediscovered at Santa Rita del Cobre, in the Continental Divide country of present southwestern New Mexico. This was in the very heart of the territory roamed by the Tci-he-nde Mimbres, the Red Paint People who were the easternmost of the Chiricahuas. A Chihuahua businessman, Don Francisco Manuel Elguea, purchased the interest in 1804, and negotiated an agreement with the most influential Tci-he-nde chief, an affable and intelligent man called Juan José Compe, to mine the metal under strict conditions imposed by the Apaches.[1]

In the east, the Mescaleros were at peace, some of them even continuing their tutelage at the Catholic missions, others having found employment as herders on the sprawling stock ranches. But, although they were at peace, the Apaches were not reduced in the manner that Bernardo de Gálvez had envisioned. When Zebulon Pike passed through San Elizario in 1807, he noted that the Apaches "appeared to be perfectly independent in their manners and were the only savages I saw in the Spanish dominions whose spirit was not humbled."[2]

Through the same period, the history of the Jicarilla Apaches had been as vacillating as it was busy. In 1803 they plundered Pecos pueblo, which led to punitive forays by the New Mexicans, but their hostility lessened somewhat when Governor Chacón concluded a treaty with them the next year. The Apaches agreed to serve as scouts on an exploratory journey to the Missouri River country. In August of 1804 a force of Jicarillas and Ute Indians, with whom they had fashioned a very strong alliance, accompanied Chacón on an expedition against the Navajos. But in spite of the improving relations, Spanish misapprehension of Apache ways led to more trouble. Not all the Jicarillas had joined in the peace with Chacón, and those who held aloof continued to raid sporadically. When Chacón's threats against them went unheeded he made a treaty with the Navajos, and that so angered the lately friendly Jicarillas that they too joined in some raids, and in answer Chacón went even to the Comanches for aid against the Jicarillas. The deterioration was dramatic and, seemingly, unthought. No policy was involved, only a series of instinctive reactions, from both sides. In 1810 the Jicarillas finally suffered two military disasters that resulted in a general peacemaking followed by several years of quiet. In the first one, the Jicarillas and their affiliated Utes ventured onto the prairies to hunt buffalo. There they ran afoul of the new masters of the plains, the Comanches, and were badly beaten. In the second, the Jicarillas and Utes volunteered to aid the Mescaleros, who were under a combined attack by Spanish, Comanches, and Kiowas. After a second whipping the Jicarillas decided to abandon the warpath and made a peace with the Comanches.[3]

Once they quit making trouble, however, they were paid no attention by anyone and their trade declined until they were left in poverty. If they had no enemies, they also had no friends, and increasing numbers of them turned for comfort to Gálvez's aguardiente. The alcohol problem was complicated by a new influence: in the opening years of the nineteenth century, American fur trappers began to penetrate the southwestern mountains in their search for pelts. In New Mexico they often employed Jicarillas as guides, a job at which the Apaches, of course, excelled. The mountain men frequently paid the Indians in whiskey, which they found superior even to the aguardiente, and from that time forward the cheap stuff complicated every problem of their existence.

The peace that Bernardo de Gálvez managed to establish in the 1790s ended with the triumph of the Mexican Revolution in 1824. With the new government preoccupied with establishing itself with some chance at survival, the royal Spanish agreements with the Apaches were ignored and old understandings allowed to fall into disrepair. Soon the disgruntled Apaches began breaking out in increasing numbers, and once they were back at war, the Mexicans discovered that Gálvez's principal object, the breakdown of Apache might, had not been obtained. Not only were the Apaches not broken-down drunks, they were more than a match for about any force the Mexican Government could muster out against them.

In Mescalero country the stretch of road northward from El Paso once again lived up to its name, Jornada del Muerto. The new enclaves of settlement begun hopefully during the final years of the royal administration were abandoned to the Apaches as raids increased. Within a few years all travel outside the major towns was hazardous and the outlying areas were virtually denuded of once plentiful livestock.

After ten years of independence the Mexican position against the Apaches had become emphatically desperate. In 1835 Don Ignacio Zuñiga, who was the long-time commander of the presidios of northern Sonora, asserted that since 1820 the Apaches had killed at least five thousand settlers, which convinced another four thousand to flee, forced the abandonment of over one hundred settlements, and caused the virtual depopulation of the interior frontier. No one remained outside the major centers, except "the demoralized garrisons of worthless soldiers."[4] In the northern part of Sonora the troop garrisons managed to hold the towns of Tubac and, farther north, Tucson, but elsewhere the country was left to the Apaches.

The state of Sonora resorted to paying a bounty on Apache scalps in 1835. Beginning in 1837 Chihuahua state also offered bounty, 100 pesos per warrior, 50 pesos per woman, and 25 pesos per child,[5] nothing more or less than genocide. Historical commentary on this fact is so unanimous and vituperative in its damnation of it (and rightly so), that one is embarrassed to try to slip in a gentle word for the Mexicans, and doubly so when so much of Mexican conduct toward Indians was undeniably deserving of scorn. Yet it seems to have been too easily forgotten that the predicament on the northern frontier was extreme, and that desperate governments, like desperate people, are capable of resorting to desperate acts. One of the more unsavory aspects of these particular bounties was that scalps brought in were only rarely, if ever, provable as Apache. Many of them were doubtless taken from passive Indians, gutter drunks or back-street prostitutes; few questions were asked. And one scholar has noted that aside from the immorality and inefficiency of the practice, it was foolishly undertaken because the goal was unattainable.[6] In their mountain and desert haunts the Apaches were virtually inexterminable, and the attempt at genocide only increased their hatred of the Mexicans while affording the Mexicans in turn no possibility of success.

One factor that is easy to forget in studying Apache history is that the "American" period—that time when the Apache bands began to be occupied as much with Anglo-Americans from the north and east as with the Mexicans—did not begin until very late. It was not until after 1850 that the Anglo population formed any significant portion of the whole in New Mexico. A certain few of them, however, were already quite familiar with the territory. Zebulon Pike had passed through before 1810, and since that time there had been a thin but colorful parade of American explorers, trappers, and adventurers. Once they began to notice them, the Apaches called the Americans by a generic term, *pindah-lickoyee*: White-eyed Enemies (or Outsiders).

The inauguration of the Santa Fe Trail in 1822 quickened the commerce between the United States and Mexico, and awakened capitalistic senses to the commercial potential of the region. Sylvester Pattie and his son James, for instance, became involved in the Santa Rita mines. Many others who followed the frontier for its promise were, inevitably, less successful, and it was principally the latter who took notice when the states of Chihuahua and Sonora opened the bounty season on Apache scalps.

Up to this time the Apaches had paid the pindahs little mind, except when they came laden with goods to exchange for the Indians' protection. One American who gained the trust of the Apaches was James Johnson, who successfully cultivated a warm friendship with the great Tci-he-nde chief Juan José.

When the Mexican states began offering bounty on Apache scalps, Johnson modified the nature of his commerce somewhat. On his last trading expedition to the Juan José Mimbres, Johnson threw a large feast for the Indians, and when he judged that they had had enough to drink, he invited them to help themselves to a large mound of trade goods he had piled up for them. The celebrating Indians took advantage of the offer, unaware that Johnson had concealed behind the stack of gifts a cannon charged with grapeshot and iron scrap. At Johnson's signal the gun was fired, with terrible effect, as Johnson himself pointed his pistol at the stunned chief and shot him dead. Johnson collected fat bounties for the effort, but the Indian war he started blazed unchecked for years.

Here and there the Mexican garrisons of the presidios were able to score an upset over the raging Apaches, as happened about 1840 at the Hueco Mountains, about thirty miles east of El Paso. There a local band was practically annihilated by the death of over a hundred. But for the most part the regular troops were ineffectual. The Santa Rita mines, of course, were abandoned in 1838 to the fire storm of Apache fury over the cannon surprise. The Tci-he-ndes had chosen a new chief to take the place of Juan José. His name was Mangas Coloradas (Red Sleeves), powerful, ferocious, cunning, probably the greatest chief the Mimbres ever had. Curiously, the Apaches laid Johnson's treachery at the Mexican doorstep and not the American; Mangas maintained indifferent relations with the pindahs, but to the Mexicans he was an absolute terror. The major town of Fronteras in Sonora had fallen by 1848, and that seems to have been the low point in Mexican fortunes.

The Spanish Become Mexicans:
NOTES

1. The details of the rediscovery of the Santa Rita mines are quite tangled. However, a pretty good summary is found in Bancroft, *History of Arizona and New Mexico, 1530–1888*, p. 303.

2. Quoted in Terrell, *Apache Chronicle*, p. 150.

3. Mails, *The People Called Apache*, p. 351.

4. Farish, *History of Arizona*, pp. 78–79; Ogle, *Federal Control of the Western Apaches, 1848–1886*, p. 29.

5. Adams, *Geronimo*, p. 53.

6. Thrapp, *Conquest of Apacheria*, p. 9.

Coyote's Journey[1]

Coyote went out on a journey.

Pretty soon he saw a couple more coyotes sitting around a rock. It was a big, round rock, bigger than they were. They were sitting there, talking about it.

"Tell me about this rock," said Coyote.

"You just leave it alone," they said. "We know about you. You're a pretty rough fellow, so you'd better have respect for this rock. It is a living rock. It can go fast over the ground, so you just be careful."

Coyote said, "That's silly talk. You two fools don't know anything at all! No rock can do that."

"Well then, do what you like," they said.

Coyote jumped on that rock and defecated all over. He came down and said, "See? You think a rock can move!" He was laughing at them.

He started to go away, but that rock left its place and rolled after him. Coyote was surprised a little and said, "Well, I guess I am faster than you are." He started to trot, but that rock kept up with him. Coyote told the rock, "Well, now you'll see how fast I really am." He ran as hard as he could, but that rock stayed right behind. It was rolling just like it was in a landslide!

Pretty soon Coyote got scared and ran into a little hole. That rock went right to the hole and stopped it up.

Coyote tried to talk his way out of it, but that rock didn't move. Finally Coyote said, "I am sorry for what I did. Let me out and I'll clean it off." The rock moved to one side a little and Coyote got out and washed off the feces.

When he was done, that rock rolled back to where it was, and Coyote went off.[2]

Coyote went on his journey again.

Pretty soon he came to a fat little tip beetle standing way up on end.

Coyote said, "I am he who eats only fat. Hurry up and finish what you are doing and I will eat you."

Tip Beetle said, "You be quiet and go away. They are talking under the ground, so don't bother me."

Coyote said, "Tell me what they say. Hurry up, or I'll eat you anyway!"

Tip Beetle said, "They say a rough fellow did something to Walking Rock a little bit ago. He is to be killed. They are coming up to kill him."

Coyote said, "You wait here. I'll be right back. I left something over there." He didn't mean that at all. He left that part of the country and never went back.[3]

Coyote went on his journey again.

Pretty soon he came to a river. Turkey was sitting in a tree by this river. Coyote came around and saw Turkey's reflection in the water. He said, "I am he who eats only fat. Come up here and let me eat you."

Turkey's reflection didn't move. Coyote said, "Well, I'm going to get something to eat," and he jumped in the river to catch Turkey. He came out when he couldn't find him down there, but in a little bit he saw him again. He jumped in again and couldn't find him, so he got out. "Now, where did that Turkey go?" he said. This happened many times.

Finally Coyote got so tired he lay down on his back under the tree. When he looked up he saw Turkey on a branch.

"Poor Coyote," said Turkey. He leaned out and defecated, and it fell right on that Coyote.

Coyote surely got mad. He said, "That's just how it is! Well, I'm going to get him right now." He got an ax and chopped that tree down. As it fell, Turkey flew to the next tree. Coyote chopped it down, too, but Turkey flew to the next tree. This happened many times. Finally Coyote got mad and went away.[4]

A little later Coyote saw Turkey walking in the woods. He said, "Right here I'm going to get even with him." He hid in the bushes and waited. When Turkey came by, Coyote jumped out and caught him. "All right now, listen," he said. "I am busy, so you go to my camp. Tell my wife to kill you and cook you for dinner. I'll be home about dark."

"All right," said Turkey. "You caught me, now I have to do what you say."

So Turkey went to Coyote's wife, and told her, "Listen. Your husband can't find any meat today. He told me to tell you to boil all the sinews and bowstrings in the house for dinner. You have to have intercourse with me while they are cooking. He will be home at dark."

Coyote's wife said, "All right."

About dark Coyote came home. "That Turkey is going to taste good," he said. When he sat down to eat, his wife gave him the boiled up sinews and bowstrings.

"What is this?" said Coyote. He was very angry and said, "Didn't that Turkey give you my message?"

His wife said, "Yes," and she told him what Turkey had said.

"Coyote got no sense!" He called himself by his name when he got mad sometimes. "Going through this country and got no sense! Let me see what he did! Spread your legs!"

She did that.

Coyote put his hands over his mouth. "Knife and awl!" he said. He used language like that. "I haven't done that much to you in all the time we have been married!"

I think she smiled a little and went inside. Then Coyote left again, hungry.[5]

He went on his journey again.

Pretty soon he came to a big dead tree. Partway up the trunk, just out of his reach, he saw a fat brown lizard. Coyote said, "I am he who eats only fat. Come down here and let me eat you."

Lizard said, "Old man, you leave me alone. I am saving the world."

Coyote said, "Don't talk silly. What do you mean?"

"I am holding up this big dead tree," said Lizard. "The sky is resting on top of it. If I let go the sky will fall."

Coyote got scared. "Let me help you," he said. He ran to that tree and pushed against it.

"Good!" said Lizard. "You wait here while I go get my children to help us." He got down and ran off as fast as he could. You know how a lizard runs, like this.

Coyote stood there a long time, pushing against that tree just as hard as he could. Finally he got so tired he couldn't help it anymore. He looked around till he saw a little hole, then all at once he ran away from that tree and jumped into the hole and took cover. He lay there a long time, frightened.

After a time he saw the sky wasn't going to fall at all. When he saw how Lizard tricked him, he said something nasty and went away.[6]

Coyote went on his journey again.

Pretty soon he came to a fat little mouse. Coyote said, "I am he who eats only fat. Right here I'm going to eat you!"

Mouse was already caught and didn't know what to do. Back in these times, whatever you said would happen, came true. This is still true a little; that's why we don't swear much. Anyway, this Mouse said, "Don't you eat me, old man. If you do you'll have to break wind and fart."

Coyote said, "I don't care. I fart all the time anyway. Come here! Hurry up!" He took that Mouse and was going to eat him.

Mouse said, "Old man, you just better wait. I'm telling you, whoever eats me will have terrible farts. It will make you sick and push you around and you will be ashamed with a crowd of people around."

Coyote said, "I don't care. I am never around crowds." Right there he ate that Mouse. He swallowed him whole.

He went on his journey again, and pretty soon he came to a big camp of other coyotes. That night there was a dance and they told Coyote, "You look like you're all right. Come to this dance."

That night at the dance he saw a real pretty Coyote Young Woman and wanted to dance with her. He really wanted her to like him! He went over to talk to her, but just when he started to say something he had to break wind. He tried to hold it but he couldn't. His face got a little funny and he farted real loud and it pushed him over a little. He started to make an excuse but before he could talk it happened again. Everybody started laughing at him and he was very ashamed. (This is why people today are ashamed to fart in a crowd, they say, because of this.)

Coyote ran over to a little sapling and caught hold of it, but that didn't help him. He was farting and bumping up and down. He got real sick.

He tried to defecate but he couldn't. He put a finger up his rectum but that didn't help. He couldn't vomit, either. Finally he put that same finger down his throat. There was a little excrement on it and that made him throw up. The Mouse came up and ran off.

These people were still laughing at him. One said, "You ate a whirl-wind!"

Coyote said, "It's your father who ate a whirlwind!" He was very angry and left those people laughing there. He was still farting a little but got better. He never went back to that place.[7]

Coyote went on his journey again. "I am hungry for a rabbit," he said.

Jackrabbit saw him coming and heard this, and there was no place to hide. This was in pretty open country, I guess. Over there a Jackrabbit Old Man died. This Jackrabbit skinned him. He filled the skin full of rocks and set it by the trail.

Coyote came around and saw that Rock Rabbit. He said, "I am he who eats only fat. Right here I'm going to eat you!"

He jumped on that Rock Rabbit and took a big bite. "My teeth!" he said. "Ah, my teeth!" It surely did hurt him. When he saw what it was he said something nasty and went on.

In a little while he saw Jackrabbit sitting by the trail. There was no place to hide, and he was sitting there, still. He didn't move at all. Coyote came up and sat down and looked at him. He didn't say anything. After a time he went on.

After he went a little way he looked back, and that Jackrabbit was still there. Twice more he did that. The fourth time he looked back, Jackrabbit was running away fast.

Coyote said, "Coyote, stupid son of a Coyote! Never will get any sense. Going to starve because he got no sense!"[8]

Finally Coyote sat down and thought about it. He said to himself, "Old man, you been silly about all this. You have to change it all." He was going to be smart about getting something to eat.

He went along and found a coat, a blue coat that had been lost by a soldier. He took this coat and pretty soon he came to a camp of Prairie Dog people. He called them all around and said, "Listen, you people. All day I have been fighting the soldiers. I killed them all and took this coat from one of them. All your enemies are dead, and I want you to have a victory dance about it."

These Prairie Dogs said, "All right," and started celebrating.

Coyote said, "That's right. Have a big time. I am tired and going to rest. I'll be back to dance in a little while." These Prairie Dogs went on dancing, and Coyote went off and filled in every one of their holes. Then he found a mulberry tree and made a war club.

He went back to the fire and started dancing. He said, "Now I am going to show you how I killed the soldiers." He took that war club and started hitting the ground with it. Then all at once he started clubbing those Prairie Dogs. They tried to get into their holes but they were stopped up. He killed every one of them this way.

When he was through he looked around and said, "Well, old man, you did pretty good." He took all the Prairie Dogs and put them in two places in the fire, the fat ones over here and the poor ones over there. Then he covered them over in the fire and said, "Now I am going to sleep while they cook."

While he was sleeping, Mountain Lion came around there and saw it all. He said, "Well, this old fool isn't good for much." He took every one of those Prairie Dogs except a couple of the skinniest and started to go away. Then he stopped and said, "I think I'll just fix him a little." He went back and squeezed Coyote's face skinny and pulled his nose out long. Then he left.

When Coyote woke up he said, "They're going to taste good." Then he said, "Wait a minute! What's wrong with my face?"

He felt of his face and said, "That old Mountain Lion did this! That's just how it is! When I have eaten I'm going to go fix him." He got into the fire and saw all those Prairie Dogs were gone. "Knife and awl!" he said. He was very angry. Finally he found those two little skinny ones and ate them, anyway. Then he went looking for Mountain Lion.

After a while he found him. There were Prairie Dog bones all around and he was asleep. Coyote said, "Right here you are going to get it!" He went up to Mountain Lion and pushed his face in flat and pulled his whiskers out. Then he left.

When Mountain Lion woke up he said, "What's wrong with my face? It wasn't like this before."

This is how Coyote and Mountain Lion got to look like they do now, they say. Before this they looked more like people, I guess.[9]

I am talking about fruit.[10]

Coyote's Journey:
NOTES

1. Of the sixty or seventy Coyote stories and surviving fragments, I have edited for presentation here some that comprise the greater part of the sub-cycle Coyote's Journey, or Coyote, He Trots Along, concerning his comical and ill-executed foraging expedition. For a more extended discussion of Coyote and his place in the mythology, see pp. 128, 158, infra.

2. Published renditions of Coyote and Walking Rock, whose elements of course vary in certain particulars, include all three of Opler's treatises: "Myths and Tales of the Chiricahua Apache Indians," pp. 35–36; "Myths and Tales of the Jicarilla Apache Indians," pp. 335–36; and "Myths and Legends of the Lipan Apache Indians," pp. 117, 121–22. Also, Hoijer, *Chiricahua and Mescalero Apache Texts*, pp. 20–21; and Goddard, "Jicarilla Apache Texts," p. 234.

3. Published renditions of Coyote stories with the elements of Coyote and Tip Beetle again include all three Opler works: "Myths and Tales of the Chiricahua Apache Indians," p. 36; "Myths and Tales of the Jicarilla Apache Indians," pp. 301–2; "Myths and Legends of the Lipan Apache Indians," pp. 148–49. See also Hoijer, *Chiricahua and Mescalero Apache Texts*, p. 21.

4. The tale of Coyote trying to catch Turkey's reflection was very prevalent among the Jicarillas. Russell, "Myths of the Jicarilla Apache," p. 264; Goddard, "Jicarilla Apache Texts," pp. 233, 235; Opler, "Myths and Tales of the Jicarilla Apache Indians," pp. 274, 292, 332. See also Opler, "Myths and Tales of the Chiricahua Apache Indians," p. 41; Goodwin, "Myths and Tales of the White Mountain Apache," p. 188; Opler, "Myths and Legends of the Lipan Apache Indians," pp. 145, 152–53.

5. The Chiricahua cycle does not connect this second incident with Turkey as immediately following the first. Opler, "Myths and Tales of the Chiricahua Apache Indians," p. 69. One Western Apache version follows that tribe's penchant for sometimes substituting Big Owl in the role of Coyote (the same Big Owl that is the Western Apache equivalent of the Chiricahua Owl-man Giant); it does, however, combine the two elements in the same story. Goodwin, "Myths and Tales of the White Mountain Apache," pp. 186–88. On balance the two incidents seem closely enough tied together to have them so here without doing violence to the rest of the sub-cycle as here presented, which is closer to the Chiricahua. See also Goddard, "Jicarilla Apache Texts," p. 233; Opler, "Myths and Tales of the Jicarilla Apache Indians," p. 291; and Opler, "Myths and Legends of the Lipan Apache Indians," pp. 144–45.

6. The Chiricahua renditions of Coyote and Lizard can be found in Opler, "Myths and Tales of the Chiricahua Apache Indians," pp. 36–37; and Hoijer, *Chiricahua and Mescalero Apache Texts*, pp. 21–22. This tale is also well known among the Western Apaches, although the White Mountains reverse the roles and have Coyote playing the trick on Gray Fox, who is his frequent nemesis in the cycle of that tribe. Goodwin, "Myths and Tales of the White Mountain Apache," pp. 193, 199; see also Goddard, "Myths and Tales from the San Carlos Apache," pp. 74–75. Compare Opler, "Myths and Tales of the Jicarilla Apache Indians," p. 279; Opler, "Myths and Legends of the Lipan Apache Indians," pp. 149–50.

7. Outside of the Opler collections, the elements of this story seem to be limited to the White Mountain Apaches, in an episode concerning Coyote and Bear. Goodwin, "Myths and Tales of the White Mountain Apache," p. 172. See Opler, "Myths and Tales of the Chiricahua Apache Indians," pp. 65, 71; "Myths and Legends of the Lipan Apache Indians," pp. 116–19; "Myths and Tales of the Jicarilla Apache Indians," pp. 279–80, 303–4.

8. The tale of Coyote and Rock Rabbit is recorded in the Opler treatises: "Myths and Tales of the Jicarilla Apache Indians," pp. 299–300; "Myths and Legends of the Lipan Apache Indians," p. 147; "Myths and Tales of the Chiricahua Apache Indians," p. 34. The latter rendition divides the piece into two separate stories; a second Chiricahua version is Hoijer, *Chiricahua and Mescalero Apache Texts*, pp. 19–20. Although this is the only one of the presented sequence to employ Rabbit as a foil to Coyote, it was a peculiar trait of the Tci-he-nde Mimbres (Eastern) Chiricahua mythology to substitute Rabbit for the many other antagonists in the Coyote cycle. See also Goodwin, "Myths and Tales of the White Mountain Apache," p. 170. A story similar to Coyote and Rock Rabbit was popular among the Navajo Indians.

9. I have taken the liberty of editing this story down from what is really a more extensive narrative. In the Chiricahua cycle it is carried over as many as three separate tales. Opler, "Myths and Tales of the Chiricahua Apache Indians," pp. 37–40; Hoijer, *Chiricahua and Mescalero Apache Texts*, pp. 22–24. However, the elements are so sequential that the editing seems indicated. For the Jicarilla rendition, see Russell, "Myths of the Jicarilla Apache," p. 264; Opler, "Myths and Tales of the Jicarilla Apache Indians," pp. 272–74; Goddard, "Jicarilla Apache Texts," p. 230. See also Goodwin, "Myths and Tales of the White Mountain Apache," pp. 166ff.; Opler, "Myths and Legends of the Lipan Apache Indians," pp. 151–56.

10. A Coyote story, or a series of them, if several are told, was traditionally ended by an offhanded assertion that one has been talking about some good and beneficent thing. It was intended as an appeasement to Coyote, who was thought to be unappreciative of his role as the butt of so many amusing stories.

BOOK TWO

They Have Power

Each thing in the world—the animals, the plants, the sky and stars and lightning—has a power behind it that makes it do what it does. What you can see is only a little of the whole thing. The power is in the spirit part. Some people can learn to reach the spirit part of something, and they become its shaman.

There is power in everything!

The sources of the Apache religious complex are unknown. Certainly their religion was the product of generations of evolving beliefs and ceremonies, but the source of the germ inspiration still puzzles scholars. Some of its important facets—the significance of pollen, the color-directional symbolism, and the power of the Ganh impersonators—probably originated with the Pueblan tribes.[1] Its primary concern was with the power that saturated the universe, how it affected man, and how man might acquire some control over it and turn it to his own use. Virtually all things in the universe, animate and inanimate, tangible and heavenly, real and mythological, were believed to have some power, or some spiritual counterpart or supernatural duality, that could influence the course of earthly happenings. Man, by approaching the earthly or comprehensible form of a thing, could attain for himself a tiny portion of the power that belonged to its supernatural governor. When this happened he became its *di-yin*, or its shaman, or medicine man.

There was no restriction on one's age or sex to be given a power. Sometimes women were approached, and even children, though this was rare indeed. One could acquire power in either of two ways. In some cases, the power broached itself to the individual, either spontaneously through a vision or sudden frightful happening, or when induced by prayer and self-deprivation. People who got their power in this way were accorded particular respect. In such a case of revelatory power acquisition it virtually always happened that the power made the first approach; only rarely was an active seeker judged acceptable. (The "power quest" was an integral part of the religion of the Plains Indians, of course, and predictably the Eastern Apaches who felt their influence set greater stock in it than the Westerns and Chiricahuas.) When the power sought out its own shaman, it typically could indulge in some flattery to persuade him to undertake the ceremony, advising that he had been under observation for a long time and was judged to be the one most worthy of bestowing it upon. Or, in the first contact, the power might lay down the general terms of the ceremony and ask the person if he were interested, and if he were, a later meeting at a given time and place was arranged. One approached by a power was not bound to accept the ceremonial knowledge; to be a di-yin through a particular power might entail the abandonment of a favorite food or activity. The acquisition of a power was a serious and reverent thing and not to be undertaken lightly. Of course, a contacted person might simply not be interested, although he would certainly give some consideration to his personal safety before he rebuffed a cosmic force.

Much more usually, knowledge of how to approach a power could be taught, for a price, by a di-yin who already held it. Ceremonial power, like physical prowess, waned with the passing of years. To be effective a ceremony had to be performed exactly, and this involved the memorization of a precise series of sometimes several dozen acts, songs, chants, and prayers. As a man grew old his voice weakened, his gestures became less forceful, and he might even get his lines mixed up and harm his patient. Hence, when a di-yin became too old to minister decisively, he might if he wished confide his ritual to a younger man. However, the individual capabilities of each man came into play. As one Chiricahua explained, "Wind said to Lightning, 'See that mountain over there. If I want, I can split it in two pieces.' Lightning answered, 'I also.' They both had power to do the same thing, but the power of the wind is not the power of the lightning."[2] Some men had a greater receptivity to supernatural power than others, and moreover the new holder of the ceremonial knowledge had to be acceptable to the power itself before he could perform effectively.

From first to last the relationship between a di-yin and his power was a personal one, although not always smooth and sometimes even strained. That the di-yin could perform the power's ceremony did not imply the power's approval of every use; it retained the great mass of its force, and in a given instance could use it to defeat the di-yin if it wished. Once a man acquired a power's ceremony he was its keeper, and bore the responsibility of seeing that no other used it fraudulently or tried to imitate him. Just as being given a ceremony increased one's personal income by the tributes he demanded, just so was the di-yin beholden to his power, who could demand of him payments up to and including human sacrifice. This last usually took the form of a power telling a di-yin what men would be killed in battle, with the command that they not be forewarned. For a di-yin to obey such an order was not witchcraft, but sometimes the shaman would refuse his master, abandon the ceremony, and defy the power to do its worst to him personally, before he would act as accomplice to the sacrifice of friends or relatives.

Once a di-yin gained knowledge of a ceremony he did not necessarily begin to "practice" immediately. The power might instruct him to keep it secret until it was actually needed, or for some arbitrary length of time. The personal flamboyance of the individual was also a factor in determining how widely he sought to disseminate the news that he had gained a power. Once he did begin his ministry, though, he had no way of knowing to what extent the power had been granted, except to experiment and feel his way. The height of power was believed to come at the prime of life, peaking in the early to middle thirties and waning progressively thereafter. But in no way was the gift an irrevocable one. If the holder abused it or failed to show continual respect and reverent gratitude, it could be withdrawn in an instant, leaving the person not only without power, but defenseless against a supernatural force that could punish him.

When a di-yin was approached by another Apache with a request for a curing ceremony, he was not bound to accept it, and there were several reasons why he might turn it down. Although most sickness caused by the powers had easily recognized symptoms, a person could misjudge the nature of his illness, and the di-yin would know that his power could not help him. The patient might be too near death for him to risk his reputation trying to save him. Or, especially in the case of very severe or prolonged illness, it might be suspected that the patient was being witched, in which case the di-yin who treated him would be matching his power against the sorcerer's, and if he were not the stronger of the two, the di-yin might save the patient's life only to transfer the evil and die himself. Sometimes personal animosity toward the sick person or his family might incline a di-yin to refuse a request, but the patient could usually overcome this and compel his assistance by invoking the use of the di-yin's given name.

If, in spite of everything that could be done to save the life, a patient died, no fault or shame accrued to the shaman who had presided. It was simply assumed that the powers against which he had been fighting (or witch, if that were the case) were too strong for him. Too many failures, of course, would tip people off that he had lost his efficacy, but usually the di-yin would reach the same conclusion along with them, and would stop practicing before he could be considered a charlatan.

There is a great temptation today to wonder what, aside from their prayers and chants, the di-yins did to cure the sick and augur happenings. Apaches who were from time to time treated by shamans, and who recalled the ceremonies to white researchers, were uniformly emphatic in their affirmation of their accuracy. It is easy—probably too easy—to conclude that Apaches who were not themselves shamans were taken in by hoaxers and sleight of hand artists. But whether they were or not, the debate itself is, essentially, pointless. The existence of the powers and power attainment were as real to the Apaches as hospitals and drugs are today, and whatever amount of their illnesses and cures may have been psychologically induced or suggested (and this undoubtedly played some part), the ceremonial power of the di-yins was, to the Apaches, reality.

An Apache shaman was not a "general practitioner." One who acquired the ceremony of a particular force specialized in the services associated with it, whether healing a particular sickness, bringing rain, or whatever. Some few individuals who were both worthy and receptive to the powers might acquire two or even several ceremonies. When a di-yin acted, it was usually in the role of healer, but in addition those associated with certain powers also gained a reputation for skills or crafts associated with them. For instance, a di-yin through Bear could not only cure bear sickness, but might also gain fame for physical strength or wrestling. A di-yin through Bat might be a famous horseman; those who knew Goose might be riders or runners of strength and stamina.

Some di-yins who gained ceremonial knowledge of warfare also gained political influence through this medium. Power for war came most often through Wind, Lightning, or some celestial body such as North Star. A di-yin for war was taken on a raid whenever possible; he could consult his power on whether to make a certain attack, and where the safest camping places were. There were different means of divining the location of an enemy; a Chiricahua who had power through Morning Star would trace a cross of pollen on his left hand and hold it aloft toward his governor, waiting for a lightning bolt to point out the enemy's whereabouts. Another would stay in communion with his power, praying and chanting and holding his arms in the air, waiting to be turned to face the proper direction. Di-yins for war were also responsible to make protective amulets for the warriors' gear, and fashion the sacred war objects that an adolescent apprentice carried during his novitiate.

One of the most famous of the latter-day di-yins for war, a member of the Bedonkohe group of the Nde-nda-i Chiricahuas, was once credited with stopping the sun. According to one of his followers, "We were going to a certain place, and Geronimo didn't want it to become light before we reached it. He saw the enemy in a level place, and he didn't want them to spy on us . . . So Geronimo sang, and the night remained for two or three hours longer. I saw this myself."[3] Gerónimo was said to have accomplished this through his command of "Enemies-against Power." This power—*indah keh-ho-ndi*—was the most powerful possession of a di-yin for war, and it was this that he called upon in making or blessing shields and *izze-kloth* war charms.

There was a second class of person who held power. Probably as an avenue to make misfortune more bearable, all the Apache tribes shared a concept of witches, evil sorcerers who turned their power against an individual or the community. A witch was a person who had acquired a power but kept it secret, or a known di-yin who cast spells secretly in addition to performing his public function. It was part of the duality of the universe that a person could be approached by a power for the attainment of evil ends, as well as beneficent ones. That was one way to become a witch; the other was to acquire a good power and twist it to wicked ends. One could never really tell who was a witch; those who were under suspicion were whispered about and watched by the community, but there were few ways to be sure. One of their identifying traits was the practice of incest, and to be caught in a sexual act with a relative was tantamount to an admission of guilt.

Witchcraft was of two kinds. One, called "love magic," had to do with influencing the sexual desires of others. Its use was not thought too dire an offense unless made too strong. Some Chiricahuas were known to employ a variation of a deer-bringing ceremony to return home husbands of wives who were lonely or abandoned. Young men of the Jicarillas could, in the flame of passion, play a particular kind of flute within the hearing of the intended mate, which was thought to be irresistible. These practices served basically worthy ends. The second kind, however, malicious sorcery, was held to be of awesome wickedness. No more terrible charge could be leveled against someone than the accusation of sorcery.[4] The punishment for it, even when seen only in its partner crime, incest, was almost inevitably capital. The mode of execution was frequently by burning alive. The witch, whether a man or woman, was hung by the wrists from an overhanging tree branch, the feet barely touching a pile of firewood. (One distinguishing feature of the Mescalero religious complex was a fear of witches that was exaggerated even for Apaches. Some experts believe this might have been a result of their nearer exposure to the witch-ridden Indians of the Rio Grande pueblos.[5] During periods of particular unrest or suffering, witch-hunts were not uncommon and di-yins were heavily employed to protect the innocent from their awful power.)

They Have Power:
NOTES

1. Opler, *Apache Odyssey*, p. 27.
2. Opler, *An Apache Life-way*, p. 210.
3. Ibid., p. 216.
4. Basso, *The Cibicue Apache*, p. 73.
5. Opler, *Apache Odyssey*, p. 27.

Power Is in It

By far the most potent of the beneficent powers was attainable through *ha-dintin*, the pollen of cattails, corn, or other plants; tule cattails were thought best. The good that came through pollen was non-specific, imparting an aura of peace and favor wherever it was used: in blessing new-born infants or attendants of a Puberty Ceremony, healing the sick, or generally spreading good. Strangely, this cornerstone of all curings and ceremonies was itself gathered without special ritual; the pollen-heavy tops of the cattails were cut off when they were ready, in the autumn, and the heads shaken over a piece of undyed buckskin.

Additional power for good was associated with the four cardinal directions—east was the holiest, then west, north, and south—and also from the colors sacred to each direction, black (or less commonly, green) for the east, yellow for the west, white for the north, and blue for the south. The power of the directions was also non-specific, and there is no better example of the degree to which religious observance suffused the Apache Life-way. Not being set aside for a period of concentrated worship and then forgotten, the holy good of the directions was drawn upon in virtually every activity of each waking hour: that which was begun, was best begun to the east. That which had to be repeated, was best repeated four times, once for each direction, and perhaps one additional time in homage to the zenith. The number four and the multiples of four came to have significance in themselves. The adolescent war novice's cap was adorned with four feathers; he carried four arrows in his quiver, and his apprenticeship lasted through four expeditions. The girls' Puberty Ceremony lasted four days, and concluded with a run to the east. Deer to be butchered were turned to the east, and a game of hoop-and-pole began from the east. There was no phase of Apache life set apart from the consciousness that it must be done in a holy manner, and the result was perhaps the most complex religious system of all the Indians in North America.

There were a host of minor sources of good power. Ashes were carried in tiny bags to frighten ghosts at night. Katydids were associated with a bountiful corn crop; they were never harmed and were occasionally prayed to. Crows were usually associated with wicked powers, but their appearance before a hunt brought luck.

One of the most frightful—although not necessarily evil—powers manifested itself on earth as lightning, and a large part of the rituals of power attainment were concerned with it. Among the most potent medicine amulets were those fashioned from the wood of a lightning-blasted tree. Lightning was considered to be the arrows of the Thunder People, and the thunder their shouting. To be hit by lightning was to be struck down by them, usually but not invariably for evil, and near misses were considered dire warning and occasioned terrible dread. The sudden terror caused by a close lightning bolt, especially if it were so close that the burning could be smelled, signaled the onset of lightning sickness. Its symptoms included fever and vomiting, clammy extremities, and a generally queasy and insecure feeling; once it was identified, a di-yin with lightning power was sent for to cure it.

Lightning was avoided. During electrical storms red items were hidden, pinto ponies were not ridden, captive fawns were turned loose, and no food was eaten for the duration. People who were so flagrant as to eat during a thunderstorm, even if they were not struck, were sure to lose their teeth. During electrical displays people would imitate the call of the nighthawk, which they believed was able to dodge the fiery arrows of the Thunder People.

One of the more potent of the baneful powers was represented by Bear. This animal was avoided studiously, as were its trails, lairs, droppings, and anything connected with it. When a spiritualistic human manifestation was perceived in them, bears were considered to be the reincarnated ghosts of people who had been criminals in their earthly lives, who were made to live as bears in punishment. Thus a bear might be killed as an act of mercy, but killed at the greatest possible distance, and the remains were not disturbed.[1]

Physical contact with a bear was not necessary to contract bear sickness. To catch a breath of the musty, sickening odor of the animal was almost as potent a cause, as was the fright caused by a bear's sudden appearance by a trail. Bear sickness was evidenced by a general malaise or tiredness, the prevalence of bears in one's dreams or a constant troubling memory of the incident of exposure. In serious cases there might be a limb deformity or withering, or one might exhibit symptoms of madness, hydrophobia, or grand mal epilepsy. When an inadvertent contact with bear odor or droppings or a den was made, an Apache might go to considerable lengths to fool the power into thinking it had not been contacted. When a bear trail happened to be crossed, it was customary to say, "It was a year ago," to keep the spirit away. It was practically impossible to recite the Creation myth or much of the Coyote cycle without referring to Bear, and some caution was used in the mention; he disliked being called by his actual name, but took it better when referred to as Ugly Buttocks or Wide Foot. At the conclusion of a Bear story the teller would assert something like, "Now we have been talking about pollen and fruit and other good things," to fool Bear into thinking that he had not been discussed.

The same ruse was also used at the conclusion of stories dealing with any of the canine animals, including the Coyote cycle. Of the dog family, foxes were considered to be the least harmful. A fox had little power of its own, but an appearance at night near a rancheria was believed to foretell a death. During reservation days, dogs were often kept as semi-feral pets, but were still considered an overall negative influence. They were not allowed near infants or toddlers, and they were kept away from men during hoop-and-pole play, as the men wanted no interfering harm during the heavy betting. Dead dogs were touched only unwillingly, for the bodies could cause sickness. "When you have a disease from a dog," said a Chiricahua, "the saliva comes down as it does with a mad dog. You get a little crazy and go 'Aaaa!' "[2]

A molested coyote had the ability to bring misfortune or accident, but these were less dreaded than coyote sickness itself, which was characterized by blindness or facial disfiguration, crossed eyes, or perhaps disabling cramps of hands or legs. Di-yins who held coyote power were accorded particular respect; knowledge of a coyote ceremony was believed to hold good for disorders associated with other canines.

Of all the baneful powers, Snake was the only one addressed by polite kinship forms. When encountered, a snake was spoken to with deference and asked to keep its harmful influence away. "My grandfather, I'm a poor man and have a hard time," one might say. "Go away and don't bother me." In religious belief, little distinction was made between poisonous and non-poisonous snakes; some could of course cause a greater sickness by the strength of their venom, but the power association was what was most feared. Skin disorders such as sores and peeling were associated, understandably, with snake sickness.

Care was taken to keep infants away from snakes, but if a snake were found in a rancheria the Apaches could not kill it. During the reservation days, however, a white man could be called upon to kill and remove it. It was of course taboo to eat snakes, or lizards, or any animal that did eat them, like roadrunners and turkeys. Most Apaches rarely even talked about snakes except in expletive, but to wish verbally snakebite or snake sickness on another was thought impious and likely to backfire. When Snake was mentioned in the mythology, the Chiricahuas resorted to the same trick used to fool Bear into not noticing; Snake was more commonly referred to as Yellow Flowers.

Many animals had lesser taboos connected with them. Because of the peculiar association between bats and horses, a person once bitten by a bat risked death if he ever rode a horse again. Horses themselves, or mules, were thought harmful only if they were molested or abused. Thus, while they were frequently killed for food or ridden into the ground during a war, a man did not deliberately mistreat an animal; if he did he risked horse sickness and a di-yin with horse power would have to be consulted. Turtles and gophers could cause sickness and were not touched except by those who had their power. One stung by a vinegarroon was believed to get sick from the line of dots that went out from the wound, but would not die unless the dots completely encircled his body. Similarly, a person stung by a centipede was thought to have one day of life left for each of the legs on its body. A special respect was accorded spiders, and they were not harmed because of a fascinating bit of imagery: the strands of a web were associated with sunbeams, and it was believed that if one destroyed a spider, the sun would weave a web inside the offender and kill him. There was also a belief that if a spider was killed its relatives would go looking for the guilty person and take revenge. When a spider did happen to be killed it was customary to tell the departing spirit, "It was not I," and then name an enemy as the guilty one.

Some birds were considered harmful to some extent. Crows were considered to be the most evil bird of their size. Some Apache mythology associates them with the first bringing of death onto the world; among those who did not make that connection, the presence of a crow was still considered a bad omen, and most Apaches were afraid to imitate their call. The aversion to raptors—hawks and eagles—was due mainly to their partial diet of snakes. Eagle feathers were of important use both functionally and ceremonially, and eagles were frequently killed, or raised and plucked. In handling them either dead or alive, however, care was taken not to touch the talons or beak, as those were the parts that touched snakes.

Interestingly, on war raids deep into Mexico some Apaches had encountered parrots, and were demoralized to hear a bird imitate human speech. The only way a bird could talk, it was said, would be to have a witch inside.

Infinitely more dreaded than the power surrounding the foregoing was the wickedness associated with Búú: the Owl. Bear and Snake were reasons to exercise caution, but owls were the earthly presence of the Evil Dead, and the Apaches were terrified of them. A renowned war leader could be set to abject trembling by the hoot and swishing past of an owl at night. Only di-yins who themselves held owl power or the equivalent ghost power were not afraid of them. Apaches who lived good lives and died went to the underworld; wicked people went into owls. The only way to drive an owl away from camp was to throw flaming torches at it. The dread of owls was branded so early and strongly into the consciousnesses of children that, if they lost virtually every other trait of the Life-way, they still feared owls. Owl sickness, like the other power sicknesses, could be caused not only by physical contact, but merely by the fright caused by an owl's sudden and unexpected appearance. The sickness entered the body just at the time the scare occurred; it took a di-yin with owl power to cure it, and such shamans were accorded great respect.

The hoot of an owl could symbolize different things. It could be a sign that the hearer or one near him was going to die; it might be a ghost trying to contact the upper world, through the call. Early informants readily admitted that they were as frightened by the hooting as they were of the bird itself. Confided one, "Some say they hear it say, 'I am going to drink your blood.' "[3]

Even more feared than owls were the beings that possessed them, the ghosts, for, while one always knew that an owl was the presence of a ghost, a ghost did not necessarily need to take that form to get near a person and harm him. Ghosts could manifest themselves in a number of ways. They could make noises that approached speech, or they could appear as shapeless, glowing amorphae that came and went. Perhaps the most dreaded kind of appearance was in dreams. "I get like that," said one Apache. "The door opens and they get closer and closer. I want to get up and fight, but I can't move. I can just say, 'Ah!' "[4] This was ghost sickness, and had to be tended by a di-yin who knew ghost power to exorcise the faintness and disorientation. The most dangerous dream was that in which food was offered by one's dead relatives; if it was accepted it was a sure sign of impending death, and belief in this omen was so strong that it probably scared some of its victims to death by suggestion.

The most common way to contract ghost sickness was through burial of the dead. One's spirit did not pass down to the underworld at the instant of death but stayed around the place for a while. Relatives who had to touch the body to bury it were liable to get ghost sickness and there were cleansing ceremonies to keep it away.

Even outside of handling the dead, daily caution was needed by everyone, for ghosts were not difficult to conjure, and in fact could be summoned quite by accident. One never knew where a ghost could appear; a spirit retained forever the ability to come from underground and visit the scene of its death, thus any place that was ever a death-site kept the potential for a visitation. Sometimes the bonds of affection with earthly people were not severed properly, and the ghost would respond to the mention of its name. Hence it was a very bad thing to speak the name of a deceased, and to do so in the presence of his relatives was an insult. Spirits also responded to whistling; as a rule, whistling was not allowed after dark, and for a careless whistle to be answered by a sudden sigh in the wind was demoralizing.

When it was necessary to travel at night, Chiricahuas dusted some ashes on their faces, and carried little bags of ashes. When unaccountable frightening noises happened nearby, a pinch of ash was thrown in that direction to keep the danger at bay. Persons slept with ashes under their pillows for the same reason.

Although powers usually revealed themselves only to their chosen di-yins, the forces of the cosmos were not limited to influence only through them.

People can do many things to change the weather. If everything is dry and you want it to rain, kill a lizard or snake and turn him belly up. Or wait for a still night, one when there is no wind at all, and light a big fire, so the smoke will go up high without blowing around. Twirling a bull-roarer helps, and there are some songs about the Ganhs. When you see a ring around the moon you know it will rain soon.

If it has been raining too much and you want it to stop, the best thing is to draw a circle with charcoal around your backside, then show your anus to the clouds. That should stop it right there. Also, catch some lice and bind them with sinew to a rock.

A common individual could also receive warning of events about to take place. One of the most important signals, especially to the Chiricahuas, was the muscular tic or tremor. Each person had to learn by experience the meaning of his own tremor-signs, by correlating their occurrence with subsequent events. A particular kind of tic to one person could have a different meaning to another, but generally, a tic beneath the eye was a bad sign, as was a fibrillation or tremor of the outer thigh muscle. A tremor of the inner thigh or arm muscles foretold good.

Scarcely less important were dreams. Here again, an individual had to interpret the meaning of his own dreams by remembering them and closely observing events that followed, but there were generalities. To dream of the sacred ha-dintin pollen, fruit, or festivity was good. Dreams foretelling misfortunes or personal disaster were those concerning floods, losing teeth, or being chased or trampled by animals. Dreaming of fire was also ominous, but its effect was negated by getting out of bed immediately after the dream and lighting a fire. But the most dreaded dreams of all were, predictably, dreams of the dead, and particularly of recently deceased relatives. As mentioned before, if in one of these dreams the person accepted food offered by the dead one, he knew his own death was very near. Remarkably, however, to dream of one's own death or the death of a

family member were good signs, because they were taken to mean the opposite. Hence to dream of one's own good health was unlucky, but to
dream of personal sickness or accident meant the opposite would occur.

There was one other important aspect of the Apache religious complex.
All the elements through which power could be obtained were lesser entities of the universal scheme. There was no such thing as acquiring power
through Yusn Life-giver, or through White-painted Woman, Killer of
Enemies, or Child of the Water; these holiest of spirits comprised a
pantheon above earthly intervention. They were acknowledged and revered for the examples they had set the Apaches to live by, but were not
to be bothered with day-to-day problems. In the early troubled times of
the mythology, when Apaches had been not long out on the ground, it
was Yusn who sent the Mountain Spirits—or Ganhs—to help them out,
and it was the Ganhs who remained their link to the high cosmos.

One version of the Mountain Spirit myth told that when Yusn brought
the Apaches out upon the earth to live, he did so only after instructing
them how to walk in the holy Life-way. They should be kind to each
other, generous to the poor, and respectful in hunting and warfare. The
Apaches made a good beginning but soon were consumed in pettiness and
mean living. Yusn was displeased, but took pity and sent to them representatives of the supernatural beings, the Ganhs, to instruct them anew in
the proper way to live. The Ganhs, beautifully dressed in their buckskin
kilts and elaborate hooded headdresses, demonstrated the good Life-way
and gave the Apaches powerful ceremonies to end diseases and invoke
blessings. Soon, however, the Ganhs became disgusted with the recalci-
trant Indians and returned to their homes in the sacred mountains. Before
leaving, they etched carvings of themselves in a cliff face for the Apaches
to ponder when they became sick of their wickedness. This the Indians
finally did, and they determined to recapture and hold on to the proper
Life-way by imitating the dress and dances of the Mountain Spirits in
times of need or great joy.

From that early mythological time up to the era when the Ganh dance
was transformed from religious rite to tourist attraction, a certain few men
who were taught the intricate ceremonies acquired the right to don the
kilts and headdresses and dance, whether for the health of the very sick, or
to secure blessings for a girl who was passing into womanhood.

In the Ganh dance there was no belief in actual transubstantiation.
That is, a man impersonating a Mountain Spirit was not believed to become a Ganh himself. When performing, however, he was touched with
their power, and very strictly was not to be called upon or recognized verbally by anyone in the assemblage.

If a person was very seriously ill, the di-yin who was treating him could
call upon the Ganh impersonators to help him in a curing ceremony, and

the result could be a night-long frenzy to drive away the sickness that was so frenetic that one early ethnological observer called it the "Devil Dance." Typically, songs and chants began in the early evening; after nightfall they became louder and more intense as the torches of the Clown—a caricature of the Ganhs who helped break the tension with his buffoonery—and four or perhaps more Ganhs approached the camp. After numerous feinting approaches, the Clown was the first to enter the area, several times dashing through twirling a bull-roarer, each time having to be coaxed back by louder and louder singing. When the Ganhs finally entered they would be carrying a large wand or perhaps a trident in each hand. The point of the ceremony was for the Mountain Spirit impersonators to lay their wands on the sick person, transferring the sickness from the patient onto the wands, where it could then be blown and shook back into the air. Throughout the treatment, in which the Ganhs might enter and depart as many as a dozen times, the participants could perform a kind of Wheel Dance that could go on continuously until morning. There were endless variations on this very basic outline of a Ganh curing ceremony, depending upon what the di-yin in charge called for.[5]

Another form of curing rite, this one most prominent among the Western Apaches, was the Medicine Disk Ceremony. Although Apaches were not as widely known for their sand paintings as the Navajos, medicine disks were circular sand paintings sixteen feet across or even larger. Elaborately designed and executed, they had to be created, used, and obliterated in one day. The primary design was usually of concentric rings, embellished with various signs, symbols, and representations of Ganhs. The ceremony was done with the assistance of a Ganh impersonator, and the patient might walk the circles, from the outer to the inmost, there to sit down during the rituals.

Power Is in It:
NOTES

1. Davis, The Truth About Geronimo, pp. 110–11.
2. Opler, An Apache Life-way, p. 226.
3. Ibid., p. 230.
4. Ibid., p. 233.
5. Reagan, "Notes on the Indians of the Fort Apache Region," p. 330.

Herbalism

When Yusn set up the world, he gave all the plants a purpose. You can do something with everything. Nothing is wasted!

The Apaches did not believe that all illness was attributable to transgressions against the powers. A second class of sickness was comprised of the natural maladies that could be tended by the patient himself or his family, or if they became more serious could be handled by a trained herbalist or di-yin for healing.

The simplest of personal discomforts could be attributed to a number of sources, and were usually pooh-poohed with humorous wives-tales. Sneezing, for instance, was a sign that someone was thinking of the sneezer. Warts were caused by rescinding gifts, and a ringing in the ears was a sign that one was the subject of another's conversation.

Those sicknesses that did need attention were treated with a wide variety of home-prepared remedies. The Apache use of plants and herbs was widespread and astonishingly thorough, and there exist some startling examples of the precocity of their pharmacology. Dee-o-det, who continued as the leading shaman of Cochise's Tsoka-ne-nde Chiricahuas until the turn of the twentieth century, prepared a tonic from a weed known to the Apaches as *zagosti*. He fed the brew to the elderly in winter to keep their blood thin. An extract of this plant was later incorporated into the drug coumadin, a blood thinner commonly given to cardiac patients.[1]

According to Apache informants the best herb for colds and throat trouble was osha root (*Ligusticum porteri*), which was either chewed on or mixed with tobacco and smoked. A stuffy nose was treated by rubbing it with a mixture of ground osha root and water; the same was done to the forehead for a headache. In extreme cases the osha root was boiled and drunk. Another remedy for head colds was to crush and sniff strongly pungent wildflowers and weeds, although caution was given not to abuse the medicine and inhale it like a snuff. Sage, mixed with tobacco and smoked, was good for congestion.

Ear trouble was treated with drops prepared from salt and screw bean (*Strombocarpa pubescens*). Hair disorders like dandruff were treated with rubbings of certain tree saps and a couple of other herbs. Eye disorders—trachoma became a serious problem during the general breakdown of the Apaches' health late in the reservation period—were treated with a wash made from shavings of oak roots.

The standard remedies for diarrhea and constipation were, for the first, a solution of Apache plume (*Fallugia paradoxa*), and for the second, cudweed flowers (*Gnaphalium decurrens*). The flowers were picked during the fall bloom, then boiled and dried; they would keep indefinitely, and when a laxative was needed they were brewed like a tea.

When stomach, intestinal, or rectal discomforts became prolonged, a di-yin for healing who was proficient in the use of the enema tube might be summoned. Chiricahua shamans were noted for this especially. After the tube was inserted, herbal decoctions were forced by breath into the patient's body, after which poultices were applied and kept on with a mixture of ocher and grease. Hemorrhoids were believed amenable to this type of treatment. Blood in the stool could be treated this way, or else by drinking a solution of ground cinquefoil root.

To the Chiricahuas, disorders of a sexual nature were among those that required the services of a di-yin, either as herbalist or in conjunction with a herbalist. For excessive menstrual flow or cessation of periods without pregnancy, the shaman would administer a power-associated tea prepared from shavings of lightning-blasted wood, marked with ha-dintin pollen before being drunk. Intricate and lengthy prayers were spoken at this curing. Venereal diseases were also so serious as to need a di-yin who knew a ceremony to cure them.

Once the Western Apaches were exposed to venereal diseases, they were not as alarmed by them as the Chiricahua, and treated them with a mineral mud from Carrizo Creek (the medicinal value of the mud was believed, on later examination, to lie in its sodium sulfate and sodium magnesium chloride content). Failing that, compresses were made with extracts of *Populus tremuloides* (quaking aspen) bark; in women the infected vagina was packed with it, and among men the affected area was plastered with it. A large volume of bark and herb teas was also used in treatment.[2]

During the later reservation days, tuberculosis took such a fearful toll that di-yins who knew herbs and a ceremony to cure it were very important people. Apaches believed that tuberculosis was caused by worms, thus the curing concoctions consisted mainly of powerful purgatives administered during the course of lengthy prayers and chants. The Chiricahuas developed a cure from *Perezia wrightii* root, called "narrow medicine."

The powdered root was put in water and heated, not over a fire, but by placing four ritual heated stones in it. As the mixture foamed it was dusted with pollen and offered to the cardinal directions before being given to the patient to drink; the patient also was crossed with pollen and prayed over; then he was placed in the sun's heat until he vomited up or defecated the worms. "It works either way," said the informants who swore by the remedy. "Lots of people get well from taking it."[3] A shaman who knew the narrow medicine ceremony could charge a huge fee to perform it, as much as a horse. The overdoses that resulted from the medicine being administered by quacks—or from self-treatment by those who simply could not afford to hire a di-yin—were believed to lead to suicide.

Not all home remedies were herbal; some were what anthropologists call "sympathetic." For instance, mumps were treated with poultices prepared from grease and ashes of burned plant bulbs, the significance of the medicine stemming from the physical similarity to the swollen glands.

Another type of non-herbal remedy was the combating of pain with other pain. Sometimes joint aches were treated by lighting small chips of charcoal over the place and letting them burn to ashes. No ceremony or di-yin was needed for this, but there were some rules, such as not watching the flame as it burned. Pain from a rotting tooth was sometimes treated by placing the tip of a hot awl into the cavity. Some use of heat was more gentle: rheumatic joints were eased with a smear of warmed grease and ocher, or perhaps a heated stone or shell. Frostbite was treated with a mixture of grease and piñon gum.

Apaches were surprisingly advanced in the physical repair of injuries. They seem to have been rather more adept at setting broken limbs than the Indians of the plains, where a relatively simple fracture could result in a lifetime deformity. Splints were usually fashioned from cedar bark, as among the Western Apaches, or sotol slats among the Chiricahuas. They also knew the use of more complicated devices, such as buckskin trusses to apply pressure to hernias.

One of their more curious medical treatments was bleeding; a headache, fatigue, or rheumatism might be alleviated by opening a vein with a thorn. One wonders, however, whether this might have been copied from early Spanish physicians.

The occurrence that most seriously frightened Apaches was rampant spread of communicable diseases, especially the later ones—such as smallpox—brought by the Europeans. Epidemics were retarded among their population by the use of trail signs. One death emblem in particular, a dead owl or an owl effigy, with the head turned toward the infected area, was placed in an approaching path to warn travelers away. The same effect was accomplished by hacking all the limbs but one from a trailside tree; to draw attention to this sign, a twist of grass might be tied around the trunk. Sickness was kept outside one's home during an epidemic by burning piñon and juniper boughs inside the wickiup. The poor ventilation of the dwelling created a thick concentration of smoke, and the head of the household kept the members of his family there until they couldn't stand it any longer. To the Chiricahuas, both earthquakes and sudden thunderstorms were signs of approaching epidemics, and ceremonies could be undertaken to ward them off.

Herbalism:
NOTES

1. Cochise, *The First Hundred Years of Niño Cochise*, p. 110.
2. Reagan, "Notes on the Indians of the Fort Apache Region," p. 314.
3. Opler, *An Apache Life-way*, p. 223.

In This Way We Live

Apache camps or villages have traditionally been termed rancherias. They were established and grew matrilocally, which is an ethnological way of saying that newly married couples went to live near the wife's family. Typically, a rancheria was limited to members of an extended family (or among the Western Apaches, other clan relatives), but the practice of several extended families living in a general proximate area frequently resulted in larger, but more scattered, encampments. Use of the term rancheria is almost universally applied among Western Apaches and Chiricahuas. Possibly because the more eastern tribes lived under more Plains Indian influence, historians have been more content there with the terms camp and village.

Among the more westerly Apache groups, and variably less so toward the eastern, shelter for each family was provided by the wickiup, a small semispherical or dome-shaped brush hut of a size and luxury that varied with the abundance of local building materials. (The Apaches of the Gila River, for instance, had notably smaller and poorer wickiups; those of the White Mountain group near Fort Apache were considered the sturdiest and most spacious.) The construction frame was a circle of poles or saplings bent over and tied together at the center. The spaces between the poles were thatched with whatever natural cover was available—yucca leaves or scrub in the desert, grass in the transition zone, and reeds in a river bottom. A smoke hole was left open at the top but it was not always effective. Canvas was stretched across the exterior to minimize drafts, and a skin or blanket flap served as a low door. Constructing the wickiup was women's work, and it usually took perhaps four hours.

The less settled bands like the Nde-nda-i Chiricahuas frequently used semipermanent shelters inferior to the real wickiup, but they were quickly constructed and it was no great loss when they had to be abandoned. They were built of brush and sticks laid on a conical framework of poles similar in shape to the Plains Indian tipi.

Most Mescaleros and Jicarillas preferred to live in hide-covered tipis of the Plains Indian model, although these dwellings were neither as large nor as well constructed as those of the Plains Indians. The Eastern Apaches retained the matrilocal arrangement of the villages, and did not adopt the complicated tipi-circles of the Plains Indians. And, after the Apache fashion, tipi entrances faced the east. Some Mescaleros did prefer the wickiup, and both kinds of dwelling could be seen in a Mescalero village. The Plains tipi was scarcely known among the Western Apaches and Chiricahuas, except a few of the Tci-he-nde Mimbres, the nearest neighbors of the Mescaleros, who did choose to live in them.

Often seen next to the wickiup—or tipi, for that matter—was a large brush arbor, or ramada, that became known as the "squaw cooler." It provided light shelter for outdoor work or eating.

There was little regulation in camp life. In times of war or other insecurity a few lookouts were posted over a rancheria at night. Usually there was no ceremony or special method in selecting a sentry, just whoever wanted to. In times of known danger, however, the chief might select the best men to stand guard.

If rain during the night extinguished all the embers of the previous day's fire, another might be readily started with the fire drill. This consisted simply of a flat stick of sotol, or less frequently yucca, somewhat less than a foot long and about an inch and a half wide. Into a small hole on one flat side, a tapered but blunt-ended drill about a quarter inch in diameter was inserted and twirled with the hands. Grass, bark shreds, and sometimes dry manure was placed around the hole, where the friction heat would ignite it.

Some amount of kindling was always kept in a dry place, and sometimes a slow-burning fuse of juniper bark shreds bound with yucca fiber was lit when rain threatened to dampen kindling. Fire drills were the most troublesome method of starting a fire, however, and were not used if a coal or flint box could be borrowed. Still, a warrior usually carried a fire drill on a raid, in case he became separated from his party and needed a fire.

Camps were moved frequently to find better game or gather a wild food in season, and when it came time to pack up, virtually all the labor fell to the women. They did all the packing, and themselves carried whatever would not fit onto the horses. About the only item not transported was the heavy metate grindstone. The cucumber-shaped mano was taken, but if a metate could not be located near the new campsite, a flat rock with a slight depression was pressed into service. It was believed that if a camp were left exactly as it was when in use, the previous inhabitants would be affected by what happened there during their absence. Thus, when the place was deserted, it was "mothballed" by smoothing over the fire pit and placing the brush bed frames in a central pile. Nevertheless, when a bear or other animal of wicked power rummaged through a vacant camp and left droppings, some adverse effect was sure to manifest itself on the people.

If a stream was in flood and had to be crossed, fair-sized rafts could be fashioned of logs and crosspieces; the whole construction might be twelve feet long and a yard or more wide. Small bullboats were made by stretching rawhide over a simple cross-frame. They were not sculled but pulled across the stream by swimmers.

Equipping and handling the horses was the man's job, although women could usually manage to rope and saddle one. The Mescaleros devised a flat-cantled variation of the Plains saddle, but for most of the Apaches, until Mexican or American saddles became plentiful through trade and raiding, saddled horsemen were the exception rather than the rule. Most horses were ridden bareback or astraddle a hide or blanket cover.

The Western Apache riding saddle was constructed of a cottonwood frame, taken from properly shaped tree forks that could be whittled to the right form, and saddle skirts were added by lashing two flat boards onto the frame. Over this a wet rawhide was fitted and sewn into place. It contracted as it dried, and became secure. Pack saddles were much less elaborate, being simply padded aparejos of the Mexican type. Completing the equipage were oak stirrups, a braided rawhide quirt, a rope bit and bridle, and yucca fiber hobbles. Sometimes, too, "horse moccasins" were carried to pad the animal's hooves if he went lame.

Rope was usually made by braiding together strands of yucca fibers. This was suitable for use as bridles, as was rope of braided horsehair. The strongest ropes were of braided strips of rawhide, although single-strand rawhide rope was much more common.

Although Apaches were among the first North American Indians to acquire horses from the Spanish, they never put them to such extensive use as the Plains tribes, and in reservation and pre-reservation times they never learned the art of breeding horses. They did, however, develop sophisticated ways to care for them. Perhaps the most common of the many techniques to break a wild horse to the saddle was to tether a freshly caught animal for several days, denying him food and water. When he became used to human presence, the owner would lead him through the deep sand of a stream bank to drink his fill. With the horse mired in the sand and weighted by a distended belly one could saddle and mount the animal with a minimum of difficulty.

When horses were needed to cross a desert, and there were no water holes nearby, enough trouble was taken to feed them cactus pulp, but to the Apaches horses remained a convenience, not the necessity they became to Plains Indians. Long after Apaches acquired a formidable degree of horsemanship, when hard pressed in battle they would loose their stock and fight on foot among mountain rocks, which was a mode of combat much better suited to the environment. Much greater emphasis was placed on a man's endurance afoot than on horseback. It seems likely that over a long period of time this proved of benefit to the Apaches. One scholar has considered that a large part of the Plains Indians' vulnerability to white conquest was their almost umbilical dependence on white men's guns and white men's horses. These foreign influences so mutated the Plains culture that by the time it peaked in the 1800s, their dependence on the articles of white culture crippled their ability to wage effective war. The Apaches never made so great a concession. When Plains warriors were unhorsed they were left virtually helpless; when Apaches were dismounted they were more effective than ever. They could traverse rougher ground and hide themselves more easily. It seems possible that Apache resistance was as lengthy and successful as it was in part because of their relative cultural purity and less impaired harmony with their very particular and demanding environment.

We Hunt Them

The procurement of meat was the man's duty always, except when the women were invited to participate in a rabbit surround. To the Chiricahuas, hunting, unless another animal was mentioned specifically, meant deer hunting. This was by far the most important meat source; they were hunted all year round, though they were known to be fattest and the skins were in top condition in the late fall.

Not surprisingly, a great many beliefs and behavioral customs attended such an important responsibility. The presence of crows near the rancheria, a bird not usually appreciated, was thought favorable because of their part in the Coyote myth about the release of animals across the earth. From the day before stalking a deer, a man ate no strong-smelling foods that the prey might detect; his own body odor he masked with a smear of animal fat or bone marrow. Great care was taken not to make statements of confidence beforehand; such brass would be sure to spoil the luck. For the same reason, burden baskets to carry the meat home were not taken out. The powers were believed to take more pity on a hungry hunter, thus meals were not eaten right before a hunt.

Although several men might leave camp together for the hunting ground, once they arrived they separated and worked either alone or sometimes in pairs. To get close enough to shoot an arrow a hunter often employed a deer mask, fashioned from the stuffed head of a deer, that was fitted onto the shoulders. A skillful stalker approaching from downwind might get within a very few feet without causing alarm. Some does could be called by blowing across a leaf held horizontally between the lips; the resulting noise was thought to resemble the bleat of a fawn.

Once a deer was taken, the process of skinning and butchering it was a blend of practicality and ceremony. Child of the Water had laid down the rules when he had hunted on the earth, and to violate them could result in harm or spoil the luck of the next hunt.

Long time ago they say.

This young man lived with his grandmother. One day they needed meat, and she sent him out to kill a deer. She told him how to kill and butcher it. "Be careful," she said. "Do not butcher it under a white pine tree."

The young man wondered why she said that. He went out and killed a deer. "I'm going to find out what she meant," he said.

He carried the deer to a white pine and started to cut it up. Pretty soon he heard someone coming through the brush. It was a woman. "My husband," she said. "Husband, come here and let's do something in the bushes."

This young man was ashamed. He had never been married. He ran for his camp, and the woman chased him. When he got back he told his grandmother about it. "I told you not to do that," she said. She dug a hole under the fire and hid him there.

Right then the woman ran into the camp. "Where did my husband go?" she said.

"There is no man here," said the grandmother. "Do you see one?"

The woman squatted down and urinated. "Water, find my husband," she said, and it ran down into the fire. "You hid him under there." She ripped up the fire and pulled the young man out of the hole. "Come on, husband, do it with me right here." She got on her back and lifted her legs.

He looked between her legs and saw her vagina had teeth all in it, chewing all around. It was Vulva Woman! "Woman, the only way I will have you is in a wickiup. You build a wickiup and we'll do something together."

Vulva Woman was building the wickiup, and this man went out and got four sticks of hard wood. When he came back, she was in there in the wickiup, on the bed. "Come on and let's do something," she said. She had her legs in the air and she was wiggling around.

"All right," he said. He put in the first three sticks of wood into her vagina, but she chewed them all up. The fourth one finally broke off her teeth, and after that he had to live with her.

There are rules about cutting up a deer. You have to do it a certain way, or something like this will happen. That's why they tell this story.

When a man skinned a deer properly, he laid its head to the east, and thereafter did not walk around the front of it, nor did he step over or straddle it. The tendons to the lower legs were severed to keep the legs limp. "They look too much like a dead person does if they are stiff,"[1] said the Chiricahuas.

If a man were afoot, he carried as much as he could back to his rancheria, and strung the rest in a tree until he could return. The hooves and head were always taken home to ensure continued luck. A successful deer hunt was considered a gift of nature, not the result of individual prowess, and selfless generosity was expected of the hunter in sharing the meat. This pressure was so strong that often, by the time he gave portions to the elderly, the widows, and virtually anyone who asked it of him, the hunter might get home with only a tiny portion of the carcass. "I used to sneak in at night," confessed one. "That's what some do."[2] If a man killed a deer but had not yet butchered it, and was found by a second, unsuccessful hunter, the second one could in fact claim as much of the kill as he wished. However, the possibility that on any given day the situation might be reversed prevented abuses of this particular rule. More difficult to resolve was the case of two men hunting as a team. The rule was that the one who actually shot the deer got the meat, his partner, the hide. One of the best enjoyed Chiricahua stories was of two such hunters:

My grandfather told me this story.

Two partners went out hunting; both were good hunters and could shoot straight. Soon they found a big deer, right near them. It was so near that neither could miss him.

"You shoot him cross-cousin," said one.

"No, I have meat cousin. You shoot him," said the other.

"I need a buckskin. I say you shoot him."

"You're making me mad, cousin. You shoot him, right now."

The deer heard them fighting and ran away. The partners didn't get anything, and went away mad at each other. For a long time they didn't speak to each other at all.

When freshly prepared, meat was usually either broiled or fried, but sometimes it was boiled into a stew and dumplings were made to go with it. Frequently meat was preserved for long periods by jerking it into thin sheets and drying it.

During consumption of the deer carcass the respectful restrictions continued, because unappreciative use could spoil the luck in the next hunt. Bones were not cast aside but neatly piled, to avoid the impression of throwing the deer away. Similarly, hot meat was not blown upon to cool it; just as in curing ceremonies, where blowing on the patient blew the "sick" away, so here blowing on the meat would blow the deer away. If, in spite of observing all the customs, a man had poor luck in hunting, he could go to a di-yin who knew a ceremony for help.

Another important source of meat was the pronghorn antelope. Head masks were employed in stalking the animals; this required more skill than with deer, however, because pronghorn were found on the open plains, and were much fleeter when danger was detected than were the deer of the forest edge. When large numbers of men on horses were available, pronghorn were taken in mounted surrounds in which a whole herd might be decimated.[3] Ceremonies similar to the deer rites were also used in hunting pronghorn, although the antelope were neither as numerous nor as important.

In hunting both deer and pronghorn, when a perfect skin was desired—that is, one unblemished by a bullet hole or arrow puncture—the animals were run down by horse relays, roped, and strangled, or else slashed where skinning incisions would be made anyway. Such perfect hides were sometimes needed for religious ceremonies, although running the animals in this manner was thought to spoil the meat by increasing the amount of blood in the muscles at the time of death.

Other large animals of Apachería—elk, mountain sheep, and mountain goats—were also hunted for both meat and hides, but they were not commonly found. Head masks were not used in hunting the elk because they were slower and thought to be more stupid than deer and pronghorn.

Buffalo were not found in the Western Apache range, nor in that of the Nde-nda-i or Tsoka-ne-nde Chiricahuas. They did appear rarely in the territory of the Tci-he-nde Mimbres, and when they did they were hunted and utilized. Eastern Apaches had a greater exposure to them. The Mescaleros hunted buffalo occasionally, and the more northeasterly and Plains-like Jicarillas a great deal, often in company with the Utes.

Of all the large game, unborn young were eaten and considered a delicacy. However, viscera were apparently not so much prized by Western Apaches as by some other Indians; of the animals they used for food, stomachs might be opened, washed, and broiled. At one time they ate beef intestines raw, but later broiled them. Chiricahuas, too, were not fond of the stomachs, although they did prepare a dish by filling a deer's stomach with blood, wild onions, and chilis, and cooked it until thick. Head meat was sometimes eaten but was not thought desirable.

Apaches, and especially Chiricahuas, did not hesitate to supplement their meat diet with wood rats. When a burrow was discovered, the escape exit was searched out; such a disturbance was made at one end that the rat fled from the other, where it was shot or clubbed. No distinction was recognized between rats and opossums, except that the latter tasted better.

The hunting of rabbits constituted part of the stalking training of boys too young to take larger animals. During hard times the men also hunted them, sometimes by shooting, sometimes by forcing them out of their burrows. Occasionally, and partly perhaps as a social lark, the men took the women on a rabbit surround or clubbing. A distinction was made between jackrabbits and cottontails, in favor of the latter. It was said that the Tci-he-nde Mimbres had little prejudice against jackrabbits, but the other two Chiricahua groups would not eat them. Youngsters also hunted squirrels, and they were eaten readily, but it would have been demeaning for a man to take them.

There was prejudice against eating prairie dogs, although it was done from time to time. Some of the Apaches believed that they ate snakes, which is probably attributable to their having observed snakes descending into prairie dog holes in search of prey. The Chiricahuas had a way of cooking such small mammals, of roasting them whole until half-done, then skinning and gutting them before the cooking was finished.

Most Apaches would not hunt the peccary, or javelina, classifying it with the white man's hogs as a snake-eater and therefore nasty. Peccary hunts were not unknown, however, among the Nde-nda-i Chiricahuas. Cattle from Mexico, and later from American ranchers, were slaughtered and eaten during raids, but were seldom kept for any length of time. About the only effort made at herding was to loose them in a canyon to turn feral, then hunt them like any other game as they multiplied. Horses and mules, after they were introduced, were killed and eaten, but only when other sources failed.

Mountain lions were considered edible but not too desirable. They were, however, killed at every opportunity because their hides made the best available arrow quivers. Badgers, otters and beavers were also killed for the pelts; badger skin was a favorite material for making acorn or piñon nut sacks.

Among the Apache tribes the desirability of wildfowl as a food source varied widely from one local group to another; some would not eat them, others felt no objection. Doves seem to have had the widest acceptance, but few would eat turkeys, which were, because of their consumption of insects, revolting. The few birds that were eaten were usually cooked by boiling.

Birds were very much hunted for their feathers, however, particularly eagles. Chiricahuas constructed a conical brush blind out in the open, where it would afford a convenient roost. Birds that took to it were shot from within. Eagles were either shot, or trapped by placing snares around carrion. If, as occasionally happened, an eagle gorged itself on carrion until it had difficulty flying, it was chased down and clubbed. Sometimes young eagles were taken from the nest and kept until mature, at which time they were plucked. While captured eagles were released after the plucking, a unique superstition, doubtless of mythological significance, governed the killing of clubbed adults. "The eagle is not left alive intentionally, but if you hit it and think it is dead and then after it is plucked it gets up again, you leave it alone."[4]

To the Western Apaches the eating of any fish was forbidden; they were unclean, categorized in the same family as snakes, lizards, and amphibians. The Chiricahua also, before the reservation period, did not eat fish, but the restriction was less severe. All fish were called by a generic term; there were no separate words to distinguish different kinds. Fish were also related to epidemics, although they were not sources of power.

Long time ago they say.
Many of our people got very sick. They were burning up fever and real hot. The di-yins took them down to the river for a curing sweatbath. Everybody who was sick went.
When they came out of the sweathouse they all jumped into the cold water. They were supposed to do this, just like we do it now. They swam across the river and came out on the other side. There they all died. Everybody that was sick died.
Those who were not sick were very mad at the di-yins. They thought they were witches and murdered the sick people. The people were going to kill all the di-yins right there. All at once the dead people turned spotted, just like the fish in the river. Then the people knew it was the wicked spirits of the fish that did it. Not one of us has eaten fish since that day. We think they are the spirits of bad women. We don't eat them at all.[5]

We Hunt Them:
NOTES

1. Opler, An Apache Life-way, p. 320.
2. Ibid., p. 323.
3. Cremony, Life Among the Apaches, pp. 203–5.
4. Ibid., p. 329.
5. See Reagan, "Notes on the Indians of the Fort Apache Region," p. 295.

Food All Around

To the different Apache tribes there were, in addition to the four seasons of the year, six time divisions having to do with the gathering of wild foods: Little Eagles (early spring), Many Leaves (late spring and early summer), Large Leaves (midsummer), Thick with Fruit (harvest time, late summer to early fall), Earth Reddish Brown (late fall), and Ghost Face (winter).[1] In fact, years were counted in terms of harvest, each harvest meaning not one time of reaping but the entire yearly cycle.

One of the first foods to be available for gathering in the time of Little Eagles was the narrow-leaved yucca, the central stem of which was harvested before the blossoms appeared. The slender stalks were often eaten soon after gathering, roasted on a bed of live coals and with the burned outer skin peeled away. Thicker stalks were usually cooked in underground baking pits, which were holes lined with stones, the cooking food covered with damp grass and earth. A medium-sized pit—about four feet long and a yard deep, would bake a load of yucca stalks in rather less than a day. After baking they could be dried and stored for up to a year, then soaked to soften them again before eating, or else pounded into a mixture with available fruits, like that of the broad-leaved yucca. The stalks of the narrow-leaved yucca were not considered the best eating, but they were plentiful and they kept well, which made them of importance during the barren seasons. After their flowers appeared during Many Leaves the stalks were not fit for consumption, but the flower clusters were harvested and boiled in soups, either alone or with meat, or else they were boiled and then dried and stored. When the flower buds of another species of yucca became available they were opened, dried, and strung like peppers on thin sticks. These were used as sweeteners in beverages.

Also available during the season of Little Eagles were the tule rushes, which contained two edible portions, the new shoots and the long white root bulbs.

Late spring was an especially busy time for nearly all the Apache tribes, because their single most important food plant, an agave or century plant known as mescal (*Agave utahensis*), was ready then. Before they bloomed the stalks could be cut and prepared like narrow-leaved yucca, but much more important was the basal cluster of leaves that contained the heart. The women usually gathered and cooked mescal in communal bakes, perhaps a half dozen women leaving for the dry hills to stay as long as several days. It took that many women a couple of days to gather a ton of the cabbage-sized heads, each woman trimming the sharp points of the leaves until the head resembled a giant artichoke, marking it with a sign to identify it as her own. Typical advice for gathering mescal was remembered by John Rope, a well-known Western Apache informant, that "if you get a mescal head ready to cut off, don't stand on the lower side of it; always work on the upper side. If you stand below it while you cut, it will roll on you, and its sharp points will stick into you. If you cut it off and are about to chop away the leaves from the head, don't open your eyes wide. Close them halfway so the juice won't get in them and blind you."[2]

To cook the mescal hearts a huge baking pit was dug, a yard or more deep and ten to fifteen feet across, located as centrally as possible in the harvest area. This was filled with firewood and atop that were flat rocks. The wood was ignited with ceremony and praying and left to burn down, after which a foot-thick layer of wet grass was thrown over as quickly as possible. Then the mescal, another layer of wet grass, and a layer of dirt a foot or so thick. Atop the mound another fire was lit and kept burning until the food was cooked, which could be one or more days, depending on their size and quantity.

Baked mescal would spoil quickly if not preserved, and if the women gathered and cooked the food away from their rancheria the heads would often be loaded in burden baskets and carried back to dry in the sun. After drying, the baked mescal could be stored for some time, was nutritious, and tasted somewhat like squash. Most of the hearts, however, were pounded into thin sheets and preserved with a glaze prepared from the juice extracted during the pounding. Three mescal heads could be pounded into a sheet about four feet long and a foot and a half across; in this candied form the food would keep almost indefinitely, and sometimes a sheet was folded to form a kind of pouch in which to store the dried, roasted mescal hearts already mentioned. Many mescal expeditions were made during this season, before the plants bloomed and ruined them for food.

Many Leaves was also the time when the first of a number of wild onions were ready. These were usually boiled in soups with other vegetables and meat, but were also eaten raw. The locust trees were beginning to bloom, and their flowers were boiled, either to be used at the time in soups, or to be then dried and stored. Later in the year the bean pods of the same locust trees were collected just before they were ripe. The pods were dried and ground into a sugary substance that was either eaten raw or boiled. During early summer the women could also scrape the powdery inner surface of western yellow pine bark for a sugary sweet, but this much trouble was usually gone to only when other sources were in short supply. The first of the sumac berries to ripen also appeared during Many Leaves, when the red berries of *Rhus microparpa* were gathered, washed, and dried. Often these were ground and mixed with mescal for variety.

The long fruiting season of the one-seeded juniper began with mid-summer, the time of Large Leaves. The berries were good tasting and had a mild laxative effect. When very ripe they were eaten raw, or mashed to remove the seeds, or squeezed for the juice; berries not quite ripe were boiled to soften them. The first of the wild seeds and grains were ready for harvest in midsummer, threshed by brushing them around by hand in a sack, winnowed by scattering them from the sack onto a waiting hide. Seeds were either boiled into a gruel or ground to flour and used in making breads.

The transition from middle summer to late summer brought with it a profusion of wild berries. Strawberries were almost invariably eaten fresh. Raspberries were either eaten fresh or crushed and dried, and molded into cakes. The earliest of the wild grapes were ready at this time, and some of them were dried and stored as raisins. Chokecherries and mulberries, which became available soon after, were treated in much the same manner as raspberries. At about this time wood sorrel, a wild green, became available in the mountains, sometimes eaten raw and sometimes with other related plants, and also certain wild potatoes that were usually eaten raw. These spoiled after about two weeks.

One of the first of the early fall foods was the tornillo, or screw bean; these could be eaten raw or ground into a sweet flour. For the more southwesterly Apaches the fruit of the giant saguaro cactus was ready for harvesting around the first of September. It, too, was caked and preserved. A desert yucca known as the Spanish bayonet also provided food in the form of its beanlike seedpods; the seeds were not consumed, just the pods, which were boiled or roasted. In the higher elevations the broad-leaved yucca was ready to be harvested in the fall. Most of the fruits, called datiles, were gathered before being entirely ripe, and roasted over coals. Then the skin was peeled off as the fruit was split and the seeds removed. The datiles were pounded and glazed in their own juice, and dried in the sun for about two days; these would keep very well and were often relied on in the winter. They could also be preserved by picking when very ripe, and split and dried without roasting. Currants, hawthorn fruits and alligator juniper berries were gathered in the mountains at this time, but they were not usually common. A greater reliance was placed on sweet red algerita berries, which were cooked into a jellylike substance. Mesquite beans were also sought in the fall; they were boiled into a gruel or ground into a flour for making a kind of pancake. Walnuts were greatly prized during the fall; they were either picked green, split, and dried, or else picked ripe off the ground and eaten fresh.

Probably the second most important source of gathered plant food was, for most of the Apache groups, the nut of the piñon pine. To gather the pinecones sometimes whole bands would work together, even the men. The nuts were removed by drying or roasting the cones; the nuts could be eaten as they were or mixed with a variety of other foods. Most often they were parched on trays set among coals, and then ground into flour. Then they could be baked into a kind of thick bread or boiled into a soup. Tremendous quantities of piñon nuts were gathered in season and stored for long periods. Of less importance were the nuts of the western yellow pine; they were considered edible, but they were smaller and more trouble to gather. Live oak and Gambel oak acorns were gathered in their season, to be eaten raw, or lightly roasted and dried. The latter preparation could be worked into jerked meat with some fat to make a kind of nutritious pemmican that kept well and was suitable for eating anytime with no further preparation. Another type of acorn, called *chechil*, was eaten raw but also had a wider variety of uses. The ground kernels could be mixed with flour, one part to five, and used in bread.

Sunflower, pigweed, spurge, dropseed grass, and tumbleweeds were all gathered for their seeds in the fall, and food seasonings were acquired from locust pods, anglepod seeds, and lamb's-quarter.

In addition to the succulents like mescal and yucca, different cactuses provided a variety of food products, and women sometimes undertook long journeys to obtain particularly desirable ones in season. The sweet red fruits of the large pitahaya cactus were ready in late summer, ready to pick as soon as the pods opened. Although these were often dried and caked they remained sticky and very sweet. Nipple cactus fruits matured about the same time. Prickly pear fruit was rubbed clean of its spines with sand or leather and eaten raw, or it too could be dried and glazed for later use. All the sweeter cactus fruits could, alternatively, be prepared into a buttery spread.

Honey, of course, was a great treat at any time of year. During their foraging the women always kept an eye out for hives found in the stalks of sotol, narrow-leafed yucca, and mescal. The ground hives of another kind of bee were opened after the insects were killed one by one as they left the exit. The Chiricahuas had a small ritual before opening a ground hive, indulging in a bit of hopeful speculation by drawing a large circle on the ground, praying for the hive to be that big. Tree hives were rendered safer by pacifying the bees with heavy smoke, and cliff hives were broken by stones from a sling and recovered as the bees abandoned a fallen chunk. Often young boys who found a hive would make a war game of recovering the honeycomb, making battle against the angry insects and showing their bravery by withstanding the stings. Frequently this turned into quite an exhibition that the adults would watch obligingly.

In the days before extensive European contact, wild tobacco was obtained from the leaves of a small desert annual, which were picked and dried in the sun. The resulting smoke was pleasing and mild, but the plant was so scarce that the tobacco was usually mixed with dried sage and sumac to stretch its use. Both it and Europeans' tobacco were extremely valuable in the older times, although less so as the latter became more plentiful during the reservation days. Mostly the tobacco was consumed by wrapping cigarettes of green oak leaves, but a few individuals did make short, cylindrical pipes by brushing wet clay over a wooden mold. Although smoking was an acceptable activity, boys were discouraged from it until they underwent their war novitiate, and only immodest women indulged in it before middle age, especially in public. A Chiricahua made certain not to be carrying anything bloodstained when he smoked, on pain of ill luck.

It is almost certain that all the Apache tribes practiced some agriculture before the appearance of the pindahs. The extent to which it was practiced by one particular tribe or other is, however, uncertain. This is for different reasons. First, for any rule that can be deduced about one group or band, local exceptions exist. Second, during the years when the federal government sought to coerce all the Apaches into plowing, an Indian's assertion of his knowledge of farming tended to vary with what he hoped to accomplish with the answer. An Apache who stood to gain some rations by it would claim more familiarity with and amenability to agriculture than would one who was in a foul mood or seeking to avoid work or residential commitment. Third, latter-day informants gave hopelessly irreconcilable accounts to ethnologists.

The Jicarillas were probably least inclined to farming, owing as much to their latitude and altitude as to their Plains Indian-like life-style. The Mescaleros cultivated crops when they had to, but their experience of the terrible example of the Spanish reduction of the Pueblan Indians kept them alert to the advantages of the more mobile existence of hunting and gathering.

Of the three groups of Chiricahuas, the Tci-he-nde Mimbres possessed the most advanced agricultural system. The first crop they knew was corn, later supplemented by pumpkins, squash, melons, onions, and chili. In the vicinity of their beloved sanctum of Ojo Caliente they worked an irrigation system, utilizing mud plugs to stop the flow in the ditches as needed. Apparently, the Mimbres even developed a farm "system," in which a few men refrained from hunting to specialize in raising vegetables. Hunters brought them meat, and the farmers allowed anyone to take what he

Apache men playing Hoop-and-Pole. *Smithsonian Institution, National Anthropological Archives.*

Na-de-ga-ah, an Apache outlaw who terrorized the Fort Apache region until hunted down by his own people. *National Archives.*

A di-yin for war: Gerónimo of the Nde-nda-i Chiricahuas. This is a late photograph that probably dates from the Fort Sill years; the di-yin's cap appears to be the same in which he posed many times during that period. The buckskin shirt appears to be Mescalero in design and may date from his marriage to Katie. *Courtesy the Eugene C. Barker Texas History Center, University of Texas.*

James S. Calhoun, first governor of New Mexico Territory and, concurrently, Superintendent of Indian Affairs. He was so broken down by New Mexico service that when he finally left for the States he took his coffin with him in the wagon, and had to use it. *Museum of New Mexico.*

This fanciful illustration is from the memoirs of General John R. Bartlett, showing hostile Apaches attacking his train. *Courtesy the Texas State Library, 1/174-31.*

Edwin Vose Sumner, Lieutenant Colonel of the 1st Dragoons. *National Archives.*

General James H. Carleton, striking a characteristic pose: energetic and well-meaning, but inflexible, defiant, and frequently wrong. *Museum of New Mexico, Copy of U.S. Army Signal Corps Photo.*

San Juan, a Mescalero Apache chief of the reservation period, in typical Mescalero dress. *National Archives.*

This view of the newly occupied Fort Sumner bears out John Cremony's contemporary description of the Bosque Redondo ("Round Grove"), that it consisted of "a few scattered trees, by no means thick, even in the densest portion." *Museum of New Mexico, Copy of U.S. Army Signal Corps Photo.*

needed from the field. There was no buying and selling or trading, however; the prohibition against actual commerce among the Tin-ne-áh stayed in force, and all was done on the basis of gift giving. It was said that the Mimbres fields were up to thirty acres in extent, with each man tending his own plot. If this account of specialization was accurate (and it seems from Mimbres agent's reports that it was), it represented an important advancement over the other Apache bands, where labor having to do with crops was for women, children, and the elderly, with the men helping perhaps only with the most difficult plowing.

The lesser dependence of the Nde-nda-i on agriculture than the Tci-he-nde Mimbres was made inevitable by the poorer soil of their range, their more open exposure to raids by Mexicans and enemy Indians, their more predatory habits, and their need to move frequently in search of water and wild foods. In fact, it is possible that the Nde-nda-i did not cultivate at all until perhaps shortly before the earliest American arrivals in the 1820s. When a garden plot was started, though, the crops were not segregated but all grown together. In his old age Gerónimo recalled that "We planted the corn in straight rows, the beans among the corn, and the melons and pumpkins in irregular order over the field. We cultivated these . . . as there was need."[3] These unfenced patches were much smaller than those of the Tci-he-nde, usually about two acres in size, and frequently held and tended in common by more than one family. Plowing and sowing was the women's work, but care of the crops was usually left to children or the very elderly.

The agriculture of the Tsoka-ne-nde Chiricahuas was, predictably, advanced somewhere between the Tci-he-nde and Nde-nda-i. They knew agriculture and practiced it occasionally, but they did not care for it and were not dependent upon it.

Apache agriculture reached its highest development among the Western tribe, where it assumed not only economic but sociological importance as the determinative factor of clanship. When Apaches first entered central Arizona, where arable land was at a premium, the best sections were apparently soon settled and farmed on a semipermanent basis by groups of people who claimed them as their own. Not all the families in these groups were related to one another by blood, thus a second framework of kinship was developed—the clans—defined according to where one's people had their farms in season. Eventually the clans came to have much wider influence in Western Apache sociology than simply determining where one had a right to grow food (indeed their most important practical aspect was to prevent local intermarriage), but the origins of the vastly complex clan systems lay in their early-acquired sophisticated idea of agriculture and communal ownership of farmland.

The Western Apaches were also unique in their highly ritualized mythology that made it a point to explain the origin of different food crops and thus place agriculture within the native scheme of things, as opposed to the simpler Chiricahua view, for instance, that hunting and gathering were essentially Indian activities, and farming was acquired from the pindahs.

This man's mother arranged for him to marry Vulva Woman. Maybe she didn't know who it was. I don't know. This man and Vulva Woman went off to live together. She lived a long way from the man's relatives. When he started to have intercourse with her he saw she had teeth down there and knew who it was, so he jumped up and ran. Vulva Woman chased him a long way, and not many men got away from her. When the man had opened a little distance between them he ran into a clearing by a stream. There was an ugly old woman tending a squash patch. It was Frog. "Get away from my squash!" said Frog Old Woman. "You just got married and you might wither it up if you get in it."

"Help me, grandmother!" he said. "Vulva Woman is after me. Hide me in the squash."

"All right," said Frog Old Woman, so she hid him in the squash.

Just after that Vulva Woman ran into the clearing and saw Frog Old Woman sitting there. "Where did that man go?" she said.

"What man?" said Frog Old Woman.

"His tracks go right there into that squash. I'm going to get him!"

Frog Old Woman got up and pushed her. "Get away from my squash! You might be menstruating or pregnant and you'll wither it up if you get in it."

Vulva Woman kept prowling around the edge of the squash patch, looking for that man. "You won't find anybody," said Frog Old Woman, "I'm going to stay right here and make sure you don't get into my squash." Vulva Woman stayed around a long time, but finally went off along the creek, looking for her husband. When she was gone, Frog Old Woman said, "She is pretty far away now. Come out of there."

When he came out Frog Old Woman said, "Over there is a hole in the rocks where Rock Squirrel Old Man lives. You can hide there awhile and he will take you home. But first I am going to give you some squash seeds. You come from a good place and they will grow there. Plant them to a hand's depth, and don't plant them near where a gopher lives. When they come up, don't let new married men get near them, and don't let pregnant or menstruating women get near them. That will wither them up."

So the man took the seeds and went into Rock Squirrel Old Man's hole. Rock Squirrel Old Man covered up the hole so Vulva Woman could not find him, and he said, "Tomorrow I am going to take you home, grandson." The man was a long way from home, but Rock Squirrel Old

Man had a power, and when they set off they got there almost at once.
So the man planted the seeds and that is how we have squash.[4]

The most important and widespread crop was corn, although sometimes
in the mythology it is linked more closely to the pindahs. Several different
ways were devised to prepare it. New ears were roasted or boiled and eaten
whole, including the cob; young ears were also steam baked underground
in a process similar to cooking mescal. When taken out of the pit they
were dried, shelled, and could be stored for long periods. In the Chiricahua rancherias, several women would operate as a team to roast and shell
the corn, some to rip off the husks, some to tend the cobs as they parched
on the fire, and some to cut off the kernels and spread them in the sun,
where they stayed for a week or more. Finally the kernels were stored in
parfleches to be used when needed. Much of the fall harvest was ground
on the metate into corn meal, which was used to prepare a variety of corn
cakes, soups, mushes, and, most important, tortillas. The Chiricahuas also
learned to make a kind of tamale by wrapping cornmeal in the husks.

Virtually all Apaches who farmed utilized pumpkins, which were picked
when half ripe and boiled. Seeds were eaten along with the meat, without
salt.

Food gathered or grown in times of plenty was often cached and walled
in cliffside caves. These could be either personal storehouses or constructed with varying degrees of communality; sometimes a whole extended family kept one. Spare goods and camp equipment were banked
there, too, as insurance against losing all one's personal belongings in a
raid by an enemy. Such a cache usually had a rock-lined floor laid over
with oak branches. On these were carefully stacked parfleches of mescal
and yucca fruit cakes, with the layers of food separated by thin layers of
grass. The technique of walling the cache up was similar to that of burial
crypts: the stacked rocks were plastered over with mud so as to be indistinguishable from the surrounding cliff face.

To have spent so much time in the deserts and semi-arid country, the
Apaches produced a surprising variety of drinks and beverages. Even in
the worst drought, basic moisture needs could be met by chewing the
moist inner tissue of different cactus species. Barrel cactus was favored for
this; the melonlike interior was chewed after the top was lopped off. After
runoff had carried away most of the water from a rain, basal leaves of the
agaves retained a fairly large amount that was sipped through reed straws,
when no other water was available. Apaches did not dig for water in dry
stream beds of the tree-lined watercourses, knowing the water was too
deep to reach. Rather, they would seek out a dry waterfall in the mountains, where they could obtain a little water in the rocky basin at the bottom.

A very nutritious milklike juice was prepared by crushing, boiling, and straining whole walnuts, including husks and shells, sometimes mixing in mesquite beans as well. Not all the husk could be strained out of the thick liquid, however, and as it was swilled in the mouth the inedible fragments were spat out. As one informant said, "It's just the opposite from chewing tobacco."[5]

The *chechil* acorns were toasted brown, ground, and brewed into a kind of coffee, as was bark of the Gambel oak. The most popular teas were made from cota and lip fern.

The white men's whiskey and Mexican distillates were not the first intoxicants to which the Western Apaches and Chiricahuas had been exposed. They had two powerful indigenous brews of their own, called *tula-pah* and *tizwin*. Although some early writers treat them as virtually the same beverage they were markedly distinct, each prepared by a laborious and time-consuming process.

Tula-pah was a potent corn beer. The first step in its preparation was to make the kernels sprout, which was done in summer by a brief and shallow planting, and in winter by moistening them and storing them in the warmth under sleeping blankets. When the shoots were visible the kernels were dried and pulverized; it was at this stage that any added ingredients, like small amounts of locoweed or rootbark of the lignum vitae, were mixed in. From here the mixture was boiled in water for some hours, after which the liquid, or "white water," was drained off, and the grain mixture reground. The whole was then recombined and boiled a second time before cooling. Fermentation required twelve to twenty-four hours, but the stuff had then to be quickly consumed as it spoiled after another twelve to twenty-four hours. In addition to the pleasurable side effects, Apache advocates of tula-pah stoutly protested its nutritional and medicinal value. "It's corn," said one, "and it feeds your body."[6] It also had diuretic properties and was a powerful laxative.

It seems generally believed that the technique of making tizwin originated with the Chiricahuas, who passed it on to the groups of the Western tribe. It was prepared from mescal plants and involved a simpler recipe than tula-pah. The mescal hearts were cooked until they assumed a thick, gluey state. They were then squeezed to extract the liquid, which was set aside to ferment.

Both tula-pah and tizwin had a legendary taste that, according to the whites who sampled them, only an Apache could appreciate. Because both brews spoiled so quickly, large quantities of them had to be hurriedly used. Thus bringing in a batch of stuff was usually the occasion of a large social gathering. All too often, these were drunks that were as wild as they were unpredictable; one might take a violent turn, and the next might degenerate into a sexual orgy that Apaches in their right minds would find unconscionable and disgusting.

Food All Around:
NOTES

1. Opler, *An Apache Life-way*, pp. 354–55.
2. Goodwin, *Social Organization of the Western Apache*, p. 166.
3. Gerónimo, *Geronimo's Story of His Life*, p. 71.
4. This account of the acquisition of squash by the Apaches is drawn from the version of the White Mountain group, which is much more interrelated with other elements. See Goodwin, "Myths and Tales of the White Mountain Apache," pp. 71–76.
5. Opler, *An Apache Life-way*, p. 362.
6. Ibid., p. 370. See also Reagan, "Notes on the Indians of the Fort Apache Region," pp. 28ff.

A Good Woman Is Busy

In addition to gathering, cooking, and preserving foods, the Apache women bore a heavy responsibility with camp chores.

Gathering wood was women's work. They were not strong enough to haul heavy logs, but made bundles of sticks and brush about a yard long and a foot and a half across. The wood bundles were tied with a special rope, a single strand of rawhide about fifteen feet long, tanned just enough to make it pliable so it could be tied. The wood bundle was secured by wrapping one end of the rope around either end of the sticks, with the remainder left slack in the middle. The woman then ran this tumpline across her shoulders or forehead to carry the wood back to the rancheria.

A woman was expected to hollow and dry gourds, the best of which were obtained in Old Mexico, for use as water containers. She also crafted spoons and dippers from them, as well as from tree knots or burls, and leaves of the broad-leafed yucca.

The preservation of animal skins was strictly the work of the women, although they did sometimes require a man's aid in pulling and stretching a particularly large or tough hide. To prepare the skin a woman scraped the remaining flesh from the inside, with a sharpened bone or stone in the days before trade knives were available. She then soaked the skin for two or three days to loosen the fur, then draped it over a "tanning pole," which was a short log leaned diagonally against a tree trunk. After scraping the hair off with a sharpened horse rib she pegged the skin out to dry in the sun, which took another couple of days.

Deer hides were usually tanned, and to prepare the buckskin for clothing or carrying bags, the woman first prepared a tanning paste by steaming together fat and deer brains, working it to the desired consistency with her fingers. She immersed the rawhide in the paste or else worked it in by hand until it softened. After it was pliable she hung it in the sun for a short while, then wrung it out and began the laborious process of working it by pulling and stretching. "She works it all over and on both sides as it dries," said one Apache. "If she starts early in the morning, she gets through about noon with this stretching. Once in a while she stops and lets it dry some more. By the time she is finished, it has turned into buckskin."[1] Summer was the best time to tan hides, as the work could be spread out over a longer period. In winter the process had to be completed in one operation or the work was uneven and unattractive.

Buckskin turned stiff again if it was allowed to become wet, and if this happened a woman had to rework it as needed by going over it with a stone. Once dampened, however, buckskin could not be restored to its original quality.

Variations of this method of preparing hide were followed when different products were wanted. Moccasin soles had to be thick and tough, and the rawhide used for them was not stretched beforehand. When making blankets the fur was left on the hide; the woman did not soak it but pounded it soft after fleshing, then rubbed the tanning paste into the inner surface before stretching and pulling it.

To fashion saddlebags the hide also was not soaked at any time. When removed from the carcass it was placed inside up to dry in the sun. When it dried the woman turned it over and shaved the fur away, then turned it back over to flesh it. She worked the tanning paste in to soften it, then cut out and sewed the saddlebags. The hide was not yet entirely dry, and she placed a quantity of dirt in each bag so they would keep their shape until they were dry. The same sewing method was used as in making clothes, first puncturing thread holes through the skin with an awl, then sewing the pieces together with deer or other sinew.

The parfleche storage bag was more trouble to make; cowhide was used for these and it was more difficult to work. Virtually all Apache parfleches were of cowhide, which points to their relatively recent adoption. They were probably first acquired from the Mexicans, but the Jicarillas, Mescaleros, and Lipans probably acquired them somewhat simultaneously from the Plains Indians, who used a quantity of parfleches made from buffalo hide. The rawhide that went into parfleche making was fleshed from the inside, but frequently some of the fur was left on after trimming. The woman pounded it heavily to the desired thinness, and pounded it still more along the lines where the folds would be. From this the pattern was cut out, and the pack folded and tied with rawhide rope. Of the more western Apache groups the finest parfleches came from the rancherias of the Tci-he-nde Mimbres, who embellished them with decorations that others did not bother with.

The women were responsible for making all the smaller bags and containers used around the rancheria. Small water containers were pounded from rawhide, as were shallow saucerlike trays that served much the same function as the woven tray baskets. Badger skins were favored to make pouches for storing acorns and piñon nuts, and buckskin for bags used to store the sacred ha-dintin, and for awl cases. The last named skin utensils were often created with as much thought to their art as their utility. Awl cases were frequently heavily fringed, beaded, and decorated, to be hung in the wickiup and displayed when not in use.

Because camp was moved so often, a woman's housewares in the earlier days were fairly limited, to the *tus* water jug, knives and baskets, perhaps a cooking pot or two, and her grindstones, the metate and mano. After the advent of Spanish and then American trade, though, she might have a large coal oil tin for boiling, a metal skillet to replace the simple flat frying stone, and a few other manufactured utensils. She also usually kept a particular pounding stone that was suited to her hand, for working hides.

None of the Apache tribes wove cloth.[2] The Navajos, with whom the Apaches were seldom on friendly terms, are believed to have learned it from the Pueblans after the Popé rebellion of 1680, but the skill did not pass on to the Apaches. The Mexican tribes on which the Apaches preyed also wove little. Apache clothing therefore was prepared from animal hides, their first exposure to woven textiles coming from the white-eyes. Once cloth was seen, though, it was generally desired and traded for, which increased to some extent their later dependence on white-manufactured goods. Most hide garments were of course buckskin, stitched together with threads of sinew, although Mescaleros also shredded mescal fiber for that purpose, sewing it through thread holes punched in the skins with an awl.

Outer garments were frequently decorated with different colors, and various dyes were employed. Algerita roots were soaked and boiled to obtain yellow, mountain mahogany bark and roots were boiled for red, and walnut juice for a dark brown. Contact stains, obtained by rubbing colored clays into the hide, wore off and had to be reprocessed periodically.

The aboriginal dress of the Apaches was simple and adequate. The basic garment for the men was a substantial—indeed almost voluminous compared to those found on the Plains Indians—breechcloth, that wrapped around the waist and fell as far as the knees in front and was perhaps ankle length behind. In warm weather the men went bare chested, but for winter they had long-sleeved buckskin shirts, fringed on the shoulders and lower sleeves, with round neck holes. The standard garment for the women was a simple two-piece outfit of a mid-length buckskin skirt and a top that extended to perhaps past the hips. Apache women took to colorful trade cloths with a passion during the reservation days and became quite famous for their truly voluminous, multitiered ankle-length dresses of the brightest possible colors.

Apache moccasins were functional footgear of rawhide soles and buckskin uppers. Their principal distinguishing features were their length, sometimes reaching the thighs, and a peculiar round tab that extended vertically from the extremity of the toes. Taste in moccasins varied among the Chiricahuas and Western Apaches. The Tci-he-nde Mimbres men often preferred low-cut types, but among others it was a matter of pride and influence to have the uppers reach the knees or thighs. One factor in distinguishing a Chiricahua moccasin was a strip of red paint along the seam that joined the sole to the upper. In virtually all cases, the flat, turned-up toe-piece was purely decorative and might be painted in a variety of ways. (C. F. Lummis, however, believed that the toe-piece served as protection against cactus thorns.)[3]

When worn functionally, the uppers were rolled down to a practical length, and small objects or a knife kept in the folds. When the tough rawhide soles finally wore through, the moccasins were not necessarily thrown away. After removing the old soles the uppers could be restored. The lower part of the uppers, where the sole had been attached, was buried in the ground after a rain and sprinkled occasionally to keep it damp. After about a half day they could be removed and reworked to fit the new sole. If the moccasins were of the high, thigh-length boot kind, the scuffed and ragged area around the sole might simply be cut away and the uppers pulled down, softened and reworked to fit a new sole. In this way one pair of moccasins would last a very long time, growing progressively shorter until worn down to ankle length. Notwithstanding this practicality, Apache women, whether out of modesty or vanity, were said to be more careful than men to wear only high moccasins.

Eastern Apache men usually wore ankle moccasins of the Plains Indian kind. Sometimes a moccasin could be identified as Mescalero by the presence atop the foot of a beaded stripe, narrowing to a point at the toe.

Apache women gave considerable attention to their hair, shampooing it with lather from an aloe called soapweed, brushing it with tips of grass bristles, and spreading it on outstretched arms to dry. For virgins or unmarried women among the Western Apaches, the hair was vertically bundled at the nape of the neck and wrapped in the *nah-leen*, or hair bow. This was a piece of leather shaped like a bow or hourglass, worn vertically with the upper and lower loops decoratively studded with beads or brass knobs. The strands that fastened the nah-leen to the hair were usually of brightly colored cloth and hung well down the back. When a woman married she destroyed the hair bow and let her hair cascade down her back and shoulders, shaped off squarely at the bottom. Failure to destroy the hair bow at marriage was a serious insult to her husband, signifying as it did that she might take lovers.

Among the Chiricahuas the nah-leen was fashion, without significance to a woman's status or sexual availability. A particularly rich or important Chiricahua woman might have her hair groomed by her female slave-captives, and the hair bow was generally worn until the woman was sufficiently advanced in years to give little further thought to her hair.

Apache women became quite adept at devising jewelry from new elements as they became available. Necklaces had seemingly always been crafted from endemic substances like mountain laurel seeds, or dried roots punched out to make beads. Once trade beads were acquired many women habitually wore heavy layers of necklaces. When commerce items began to include the small circular trade mirrors, they were often ringed or fringed with beadwork and worn as sun-reflecting pendants. Chiricahua women also tattooed in moderation, with small circles or line patterns on cheeks and forehead. Western Apache women were fond of red face paint, but they used it—and tattoos—sparingly.

Apache men also wore a considerable amount of jewelry, some of it decorative and some of it with power significance. Facial painting and tattooing was usually decorative and non-ceremonial, and largely a matter of personal taste. A man who had lightning power, however, might, for instance, tattoo himself with the appropriate symbols. Facial tattoos were usually dark blue, small, and geometrical. Use of the tattoo among either sex was never terribly widespread; the technique was probably not endemically Apache, but acquired from the Yavapai during contact with them. The men plucked their facial hair as soon as it appeared; whiskers were considered unmanly. Outright vanity among the men was not uncommon; some dandies even wore perfume bags of mint to attract attention from the ladies.

The clothing, hair dress, jewelry, and other accouterments of the eastern tribes of Apaches were greatly influenced by Plains Indian fashions, and sometimes bore not that much similarity to those of, say, the Western Apaches.

The Apaches were not accomplished potters. They were familiar enough with the technique to fashion some cups, jars, and some very large cookpots and kettles, but they were crudely done and decorated simply when at all.[4] Pots were always made by the women, and some believed that men were not allowed in the vicinity during the process. The usual method was to grind clay to a very fine power and then mix it with water to the proper consistency. The woman worked the clay into a coil, smoothing it as it was built up with her hands or a paddle. She applied the juice of nipple cactus or prickly pear as a glaze and let it dry in the sun. On a hot day it would be ready to fire in about three hours, depending on the size of the vessel. The woman then placed the pottery in hot ashes or coals, turning it frequently to bake evenly; she knew the pot was done when it made the proper sound when she struck it with a stick. Most of the pots were used for boiling, but drums were also made by tightly stretching buckskin over the tops and tieing them fast.

Some women, particularly the bi-zhahn, divorcees and widows, supported themselves by making pots for the rest of their group, giving them away in expectation of gifts of meat and other goods. Notwithstanding such specialized effort, pottery always retained its utilitarian nature, and Apache pots were not decorated to any great degree; they were usually brittle and did not last any great length of time.

Of all the Apache camp crafts, basketry probably attained the highest degree of sophistication and beauty, although sight was never lost of the need for utility. Exactly when Apaches began making baskets is unclear, although there is reason to believe that they learned the art from captives taken from other tribes. Some experts have noticed that the development of Apache basketry parallels that of the neighboring Yavapai Indians, and they may have learned the art simultaneously if not together.

The best time to gather basketry materials was in the winter, because less time was consumed in drying the fibers than when they were taken in another season. Different colors of fibers were obtainable, green from the fresh outer leaves of the yucca, white from the inner leaves near the stem. Yellow could be produced by igniting grass placed among the green yucca leaves before gathering. Some red could be found in the root tendrils of the narrow-leafed yucca. Black fibers, which were used ceremonially at the Puberty Ceremonies, were obtained from the outer coating of unicorn plant, or devil's-claw, seedpods.

Because of the dearth of pottery, water was usually stored and transported in the *tus*, an open wicker jug caulked inside and usually out with piñon pine gum. It was woven by twining, often sumac and less frequently mulberry. The Gileños Apaches who settled at San Carlos acquired a preference for using willow twigs, and the White Mountains sometimes used the very young shoots of squawberry bush. Different materials were not generally mixed; the one plant selected was used to make the entire jug, with the warp formed of whole twigs, the weft of split ones. They were not dried or prepared beforehand, but were applied fresh from the plant, bark and all, so the tus could be made at any time of year. A weft shoot was usually divided into thirds, the woman biting into the large end of the twig and guiding the split down to the smaller end with her fingers. In cross section the split shoots resembled pie slices, and these were scraped with a knife before being worked into the jug.

There were two approximate sizes of the tus, the smaller used for water, the larger for holding tizwin beer. The necks could be either very narrow or relatively large, with a wooden handle attached to either one or both sides.

The piñon pitch was gathered shortly before, either broken off the trunk of the tree when found hardened, or pried loose if it was still sticky. (If the latter kind of pitch was gathered, the collecting basket was lined with grass to keep it from sticking.) Back in the rancheria the pitch was softened by heating it in a pot. While there were no restrictions on who could be around while the woman was weaving the tus, the Chiricahuas believed that a woman had to be alone before she could begin applying the gum caulking. She poured the hot, gelatinous pitch from the pot into the inside of the tus, where she worked it evenly by rolling around a heated stone. The outside, too, was usually caulked, but this step might be omitted. The gum was spread around the exterior by a buckskin covered paddle or a piece of cowhide with the hair left on. A better-made tus had cedar fibers or some similar filling rubbed into the chinks of the weaving before the gum was applied. Because of the trouble involved in heating the piñon gum, and because the feeling among some groups that only women should be present was an opportunity for a social get-together, a number of jugs were usually caulked at the same time.

The tus was regarded as a strictly utilitarian vessel, and little effort was spent to make it attractive. Usually the jugs had a rough and careless weave that gave them a rather lopsided appearance and an uneven lip. They were seldom decorated, but sometimes a woman would cake the outside fibers in ocher before caulking, and the color would be discernible through the gum. Sometimes also a woman would smooth the outside pitch with her hands before it had entirely cooled.

The cooling process was not lengthy and a tus could be used the same day it was caulked. A leaking one was easily repaired by reheating and smearing the gum. When water was stored in the tus it was common to cover the opening with oak leaves to keep it cool and enhance the flavor. Drinking water was not stored in the tus for long periods as the water would begin to taste of the gum. Most Apaches did not carry a tus as a canteen during light travel, but there was a special kind which had a double neck that gave it an hourglass shape. It could be wedged under the belt or strung from the saddle, and it was taken on longer journeys.

The deeply capacious *tuts-ah*, or burden basket, was also constructed by twining, with withes usually of mulberry or sumac, or again, willow at San Carlos. These were used for hauling firewood or baked mescal heads to the rancheria, or for gathering wild plant foods. To manage the heavy loads the burden baskets were better made than the tus jugs. The combination of strength and flexibility was obtained by using a large number of warp twigs, with a few—usually four—equally spaced ones thicker than the others to form a supportive framework. Additional strength was found in the protective bottom plates or coverings of buckskin or rawhide. The principal means of transporting burden baskets during the food gathering was by a forehead strap anchored to two of the thicker warp fibers.

Although principally thought of as a camp utensil, the tuts-ah was more commonly decorated than the water jugs. The most often used design was a series of colored lines woven in such a way as to create bands of black, red or yellow checkerboards. If these and the more elaborate designs ever possessed religious or mythological significance, the meanings were discarded during reservation days, and the designs were used simply for artistic enhancement. Western Apache burden baskets often had in addition buckskin fringes on the bottom and spaced along the rim. Among the more functional-minded Chiricahua, decoration was generally limited to a few colored lines and perhaps some tin cones to dangle from them.

The most widely used basket around the wickiup was the *tsah*, or shallow tray basket. It was indispensable in carrying seeds or other loose food items; it was placed among hot ashes for parching; and it was used in winnowing seeds from chaff after threshing. In some places the favored materials for making a tsah were a foundation warp of sumac with a sewing material of yucca, although the highest degree of artistry was reached in tray baskets made of willow, cottonwood, and devil's-claw. The tsah was woven with a different technique—coiling—than the twined tus and burden basket, and those made during the reservation period are considered the finest Apache contribution to Indian basketry.[5] Some Apache women, especially around San Carlos, became experts at the blending of different colored patterns and created designs of tremendous beauty and originality.

The willow twigs used for warp material could be gathered in any season. The bark was peeled away immediately and the twigs could be stored. In fashioning the warp, three twigs were used, two very slender and one a little more stout. The curvature of the basket sides was determined by the placement of the thicker stem in relation to the other two. In coiling, as one warp stem was covered by the weft another was inserted, and weak spots were avoided by staggering the lengths of warp. The cottonwood sewing material was best gathered and split during the hot months, when the bark was easily removed, though it could be boiled loose when gathered at other times. The cottonwood also could be stored. The jet black seedpods of the devil's-claw (a burr, *Martynia parviflora*) were gathered when they matured and fell from the plants during the autumn. Mostly the devil's-claw was found in flats near stream beds or in other areas of richer, moister soil, as the plant was less hardy than other desert burrs. The wickedly spectacular seedpods, about two inches long and an inch in diameter, each terminated at its outer end in two pincerlike, curved, fish-hooked tendrils about eight inches long. The extremely sharp hooks were the means of the plant's spreading its seeds, the tendrils sticking fast to animals' legs or people's clothing. It was the black outer fiber of the horns that was used in the coiled baskets, the covering being peeled away in thin strips after soaking, peeling from the hook back toward the pod. The fibers curled somewhat while drying, and in this state they were stored until the woman was ready to scrape and trim them for working into the basket. The latter step was an important one, for greater care was taken to make the tsah a utensil of beauty than with other baskets, and the fibers had to be even and regular to avoid a patchy appearance. Though devil's-claw was used principally for its decorative effect, it was also about the most durable and resilient of desert weaving fibers.

The most frequently used motifs in decorating baskets almost surely once had power significance, but this became so blurred in the later reservation days that the meanings of some have been lost. The cross, which was often utilized, probably invoked the beneficence of the cardinal directions. Stylized men and dogs were frequently incorporated, the dog probably hearkening back to Coyote, but the reason for desiring his usually baleful influence is a mystery. The use of geometric abstracts like triangles and linked diamonds originated in some cases among other tribes. The diamond motifs, which represented quartz crystal charms to the Yavapais, were evidently appropriated by the Apaches to symbolize mountains and clouds. One of the oldest and most striking Apache designs is a peculiar geometric fret in which a "brickwork" of regularly spaced rectangles is created by a maze of unbroken parallel lines.

Some Apache baskets had in their centers solid black discs of devil's-claw. This was a technique possibly borrowed from the Pima Indians, where such was the traditional practice. It was a sensible design as well, since the bottom of a basket received the most wear and abrasion, and devil's-claw was the toughest of the basket fibers. Another trait seemingly borrowed from the Pimas was the making of large amphora-shaped storage baskets or *ollas*. Also fashioned of the coil weave, the construction of ollas did not begin until late in the reservation period, in response to the commercial trade.

A Good Woman Is Busy:
NOTES

1. Opler, *An Apache Life-way*, p. 377.
2. Tanner, *Southwest Indian Craft Arts*, p. 58.
3. Lummis, *General Crook and the Apache Wars*, p. 41.
4. Tanner, *Southwest Indian Craft Arts*, p. 175.
5. Robinson, *The Basket Weavers of Arizona*, p. 75.

He Makes Weapons

A man's principal chore when around the rancheria was the crafting of his war materials, which included bows and arrows, lances, knives, and war clubs. Apaches never developed the use of the tomahawk,[1] although a few Chiricahuas were known to have fashioned hand axes from blades found at ancient Pueblo dwellings.

ARROWS

Most of a man's time was spent making arrows; each warrior was responsible for securing his own, and when leaving on a raid he usually carried thirty to forty in his quiver and left others in his camp. The Apaches made two kinds of arrows. One, learned from the Navajo, was about two feet in length, made of hardwood, preferably mountain mahogany, Apache plume, or mulberry, and some Chiricahuas became known for arrows of desert broom (*Baccharis sarothroides*). The second kind of arrow was more indigenous and about six inches longer, made of cane or reed fitted with a hardwood foreshaft.

The technique of making arrows was relatively simple. The man selected slender branches of the desired hardwood and cut them to the proper length, then peeled away the bark and scraped them smooth. After drying them about two days, he straightened them as true as possible by working them against a heated rock with a pumice arrow-straightener, or with his teeth, and decorated them with bands of different colored paints to identify them as his own. When reed arrows were made, he selected fresh carrizo that was firm and not too tall and porous. These he straightened between his teeth, and they needed to dry much longer than hardwood, up to two weeks. The hardwood foreshaft was four to six inches long, of which about half was inserted into the reed, and bound with wet sinew and piñon gum. As the sinew dried it bit into the wood and held the foreshaft fast.

In fletching, three equally spaced feathers were used (as such arrows flew truer than those using four)—buzzard, eagle, or hawk feathers from the tail or wing. Turkey feathers were frequently used to fletch practice arrows for youngsters. The feathers were put in place one at a time, with a single strand of wet sinew at the top, and after all were in place the sinew was wrapped securely around the shaft. As the sinew dug into the wood it was sometimes held even more firmly by a small amount of glue or piñon gum. Fletching feathers all faced the same direction, or else the arrow would turn awry in flight, and the arrows were sometimes fluted, either in straight lines aligned with the feathers or in a single spiral to increase the rifling effect. The short hardwood arrows were used principally for long-distance flight, fired holding the bow horizontally, against either large game or an enemy. The carrizo reed arrows were used for lighter shooting, as at birds at short range, shot from a vertically held bow. Some bird arrows were fitted with crosspieces to prevent the missile from passing completely through the target and getting lost.

It is sometimes thought a great curiosity that Apaches did not chip flint arrowheads. Instead, they simply whittled the tips of the arrows to fine points and hardened them in a fire. Flint arrow points were readily utilized when they happened to be found in ancient campsites, and intricately wrought ones were regarded with some awe in the belief that they were left behind by the Thunder People. (Catlin saw some of the latter fitted into arrows and considered the Apaches unexcelled chippers of arrowheads.) Additionally, some stones were found naturally occurring that had a point or edge; or, like slate, could be pounded in the likelihood that one of the resulting pieces would be serviceable.

The use of arrow poisons was not unknown. Some tipped their arrows with snake or spider venom, or smeared them with an extract prepared from a deer's gall bladder that had been rotted by a rattlesnake bite; but most Apaches persisted in shunning anything to do with Snake. The Chiricahuas had one type of poison, the strength of which was shamanistic and unrelated to any inherent potency of the substance. It was prepared from rotting animal blood and prickly pear spines. All in all, the practice of shooting poisoned arrows appears not to have been widespread, and certainly no band ever came to depend heavily upon them. However, Western Apaches had *eh-ehstlus*, a mixture of spit, deer spleen, and nettles, left to rot and then painted onto arrow points. Its makers swore to its physical efficacy, but admitted it was no good if a batch were smelled by a dog. Also, as one of them told Goodwin, "they used to say that if a pregnant woman farted into the poison it would surely be deadly. But . . . it was only a joke."[2]

BOWS

The best bows were considered to be those made of mulberry wood,[3] although locust, oak, and some maples were serviceable. They were single-curved self-bows, three to four feet long. A general rule of thumb was that a bow should not be longer than the length of two arrows; otherwise the arrows would be too short to allow the bow to be drawn fully. Double-curved bows were constructed but only rarely; curiously, they seem to have been known before the single-curved ones were devised, but were discarded as inefficient.

To prepare a bow, the warrior selected a branch, which he stripped of its bark, split, and shaped before allowing it to air dry five to seven days. After it had cured he rubbed it thoroughly with grease as he pulled and flexed it; after this he bent it and tied it securely in the shape he wanted and placed it in hot ashes, watching it carefully to see that it was not singed. The bow kept its shape after this but was cured for about a week and a half more with the binding cord still in place, before being strung for use. The bow was not backed along the inner length, but sometimes, especially after it had become weakened by extensive use, it was reinforced with a circular wrapping of sinew, held in place by smearing the bow beforehand with a layer of hot piñon gum or a glue prepared by boiling animal horns and hooves. A second layer of glue was put outside the sinew wrapping and the bow was left to dry. Sometimes, but not often, horsehair was substituted for the sinew. The forward-facing outer part of the bow was frequently decorated, either with power symbols or with designs by which the maker could be identified.

The best bowstrings were prepared from sinew of a deer's leg or back. The common method was for the maker to soak the sinew in water, peel it into strands, and splice them end to end to form one long string. Bumps were chewed down to an even thickness, and it was then folded over and twisted. Otherwise, he would roll two or three different strings together on his leg. A new bow was not strung at full tension the first time, but was gradually broken in. A warrior usually carried an extra string with him into a fight in case the one in place snapped. In an emergency, mescal fibers would be pressed into service, but very few men preferred them. Less frequently did a warrior also carry a spare stave.

Although visually unimpressive, the Apache self-bows drove their cane or hardwood arrows with surprising force, reasonably effective to a range of 150 yards and quite steadily accurate at 100 yards and less. Arrows striking a tree at short distance frequently drove into the wood until they were not removable—sometimes over halfway; deer shot at short range were usually run through and the arrows recovered beyond.

Each man was also responsible for making a wrist guard to go with the bow. The pattern was cut out of rawhide and pierced with an awl so it could be laced up the back of the hand and wrist; it was the lengthened underside that protected the wrist from the snap of the string. Most guards were plain and utilitarian, but a few were decorated with angled slashes.

The bow cases and quivers that carried the best luck were those of mountain lion skins, often fashioned decoratively with the tails left on to hang down, and sometimes also with red flannel or brass studs. The quivers were carried on an attached sling over the back so that the feathers protruded above the right shoulder. During battle they were shifted to under the left armpit for easier reach. It is believed that it was the Chiricahuas who invented attaching the bow case and quiver together, which the Western Apaches then copied. In making the bow cases and quivers it was the woman who prepared the skin, but the warrior would cut the pattern before letting her sew them. A di-yin was not needed to make or impart power to bows and arrows, but a family's oldest man usually gave advice on the best methods. He made arrows for relatives for nothing, in return for their seeing to his needs. If he were exceptionally skilled he could make bows and arrows for men outside his family and keep an income of presents.

SHIELDS

War shields, called nas-ta-zhih, were not popularly used, which is unsurprising for a people who depended heavily on stealth and ambush. What ones they had were of cowhide, with perhaps buckskin around the sides; they were not large, and were of a lesser quality than the tough buffalo skin shields of the Plains Indians. Shields were traditionally made by di-yins for war, but sometimes a warrior constructed his own, then took it to the di-yin to be hung with amulets and painted with power symbols. Use of a shield implied hand-to-hand combat, and they were carried only by the bravest fighters. Therefore their use was in a way sacred to Enemies-against Power, and a di-yin had to be involved at some point in their making, or there was a risk of angering the cosmos.

For a man to make a war shield he first fleshed green cowhide; if it was to have a convex shape, he dampened and molded it into a shallow depression in the ground, and left it to dry. Ordinarily he hardened the rawhide by pressing it into sand that had been heated with coals. After he cut it to the shape he wanted, he fastened onto the back side either one or two handles. Sometimes the power symbols were painted directly onto the cowhide, and sometimes a buckskin veneer was fitted over it first.

Although very few Western Apaches or Chiricahuas owned shields, the more easterly Apaches were much more comfortable with their use and skilled in their manufacture. Some Mescalero shields, in particular, were of a size and quality almost equal to those of the Plains Indians. Probably because of the power that a di-yin imparted to them, shields were not burned with a warrior's other possessions at the time of his death.

LANCES

Somewhat the same prejudice was felt against lances, which were also of practical use only in close combat. In the early days, lances were little more than slender poles, sharpened at one end, or else bladed with a sharpened tip of mountain mahogany. After a time, however, knives and bayonets began to be attached. These were held in place not by a wrapping of sinew, but rather by a whole section of cow or burro tail slipped over one end and allowed to dry and shrink in place. In the times when the Mexican enemy had muzzle-loading rifles, a warrior would run up and spear him as he was reloading. After the introduction of breech-loading rifles this took considerably more skill. Nevertheless, warriors who wanted to become recognized for bravery had to be proficient in the use of lances. The only technique was to spear at close range; they were not used from horseback or thrown any distance.

Lances were made from a light material, usually sotol stalk or young spruce, averaging seven feet long but sometimes much longer, especially among the eastern groups, whose lances might be in some instances twelve feet long. Western Apache lances were usually plain or simply decorated with blue paint along the upper shaft and red along the lower, with perhaps one or two eagle feathers at the base of the point. Mescalero and Jicarilla lances, even when the same size as the Western, were much more conspicuously decorated and sometimes beaded. They lacked the wrist loop of the Plains Indian lances, but they might, uncharacteristically for Apaches, be tufted with an enemy scalp. Mescalero warriors commonly set tripods of standed lances before their dwellings.

WAR CLUBS

Rather more important to a warrior's possession was his war club, common to all the groups, for which the word was, accurately, "stone carrier," for it was more a primitive kind of mace than an actual club. In its construction, a round, fist-sized rock was placed in a rawhide pouch, connected to the wooden handle by a short length of rawhide that had been worked just enough to make it flexible. In some war clubs this connecting piece was longitudinally slashed and twisted to give it still greater flexibility and prevent the handle from snapping on impact. The handle was frequently covered with buckskin, at the end of which was a loop for the hand and, rarely, a decorative plume of horsehair. The overall length of such a club was one and a half to two feet. They were used, of course, in close combat, or when the owner had crept close enough to a sleeping enemy.

KNIVES

Until the advent of trade knives, those made by the Apaches were little more than crude hiltless, single-edged pointed scrapers of flint or chert. Sometimes rough handles were crafted for them, and they were carried in mostly undecorated buckskin sheaths. Among the Western tribes these were carried simply by thrusting under the belt, without slitting a belt attachment on the back of the sheath; this cut attachment was known to the Mescaleros, though. Jicarillas developed the custom of carrying their knives in sheaths that dangled from loops attached to the belt. By the reservation period, both trade knives and well-crafted sheaths were in much more common usage.

SLINGS

Apache boys who had not yet begun their novitiate in war training spent much time playing with slings. This weapon's place in Apache culture was of questionable origin, but it was not dissimilar to slings found elsewhere in the world. A skilled boy could become astonishingly accurate at a shorter distance, but less so as a target approached the maximum range of 150 yards.

To fashion a sling, a small square of rawhide was worked enough to make it flexible, then perforated with four incisions from one corner to the opposite, which made it flexible enough to fold around a rock, usually one inch by two or a little larger. To each of the other two corners a rawhide string was attached. One string had a loop at the free end, to slip over the middle finger; the other was unlooped, to hold between the first finger and thumb. Apaches twirled a sling about the head once only, because the stone might fly out and either warn the intended prey or possibly hit a bystander. As the sling was brought forward the unlooped string was released and the rock projected.

FIREARMS

Of course, the only firearms Apaches had were those which they stole or traded for; ammunition was always in short supply and they traded for it with Zuñi Indians and contrabandistas. Lack of ammunition was the motive behind many, if not a majority, of the foraging raids made during the reservation period, but ammunition still remained so scarce that they sometimes made bullets out of materials other than lead, including silver and even rocks of the appropriate size.[4]

He Makes Weapons:
NOTES

1. Thrapp, *Conquest of Apacheria*, p. viii.
2. Goodwin, *Western Apache Raiding and Warfare*, p. 233.
3. See Bleeker, *Apache Indians*, pp. 93ff.
4. Farish, *History of Arizona*, Vol. III, p. 222.

They Scout Around

Apaches made an important distinction between raiding and warfare, although both were apparently called by the same term, that meant "to scout."

Raiding was akin to hunting in that it was primarily a means to acquire food and the necessities of life. (However, a man did not usually excel at both. If a warrior gained much wealth by raiding, the powers were believed to feel that he was not much in need of game, and denied him success in hunting.) Raiding was more an economic duty than a military adventure: admiration of skill in raiding stemmed not so much from a man being a good fighter as a good provider, and the few men who would not take part in raids were criticized not for cowardice but for laziness. A raiding party was small—as few perhaps as half a dozen men—and highly mobile. No dance was held beforehand to send them off, and no encounters with an enemy were sought.

Probably most of the Apache raids, of course, were directed south of the American border. Various scholars have perceived how, although they raided frequently and savagely among the villages of northern Mexico, the Apaches were careful not to drive the Mexicans away completely or try to regain the territory. They harvested the peons like a crop or renewable resource, taking what they needed in the way of stock and supplies, but always leaving enough behind for the people to rebuild.

War expeditions, undertaken to avenge one of a raiding party who was killed or for some other perceived injustice, took on quite a different character. War parties were much larger in size than raids, including as many men as wanted to go. It was up to a deceased's relatives to ask their chief to get up a war party, and those who were to participate brought their weapons that they planned to use to a dance just before departing. This was the war dance, or what the Chiricahuas called the "Angry Dance." Typically it would begin with four of the participating warriors approaching the fire from the east and, chanting, they would dance a number of four-square patterns. Women around the perimeter of the fire would whoop encouragement as other warriors joined the dance until it became a general frenzy. The men who were going to fight shot off their guns to show how they would do it to the enemy; occasionally, warriors who had talked big about how much they would do in the next fight, but who were not dancing, were called on by their given names and compelled either to take part or be disgraced. Some men danced a great deal, others only a little; it was a matter of personal inclination. A war dance could go on for more than one night, and sometimes as many as the cardinal four, but in any case the war party left soon after the finish.[1]

Each man took a little food with him, and a drill for making fire, if he owned one, either storing them in his quiver or rolling them into the high uppers of his moccasins. When water was carried it was taken in a length of animal gut tied off for the purpose. War dress for the Western Apaches and Chiricahuas was simple, just their substantial form of breechcloth, moccasins, and a headband. For headgear they did not have the elaborate feather headdresses of the Plains type that many people associate with a stereotypical American Indian. Instead, they wore small hide war caps, looser than what could be called a skull cap, tied with strings under the chin. War caps were frequently decorated with a knot of eagle or turkey feathers on top, and studded with patterns of various sizes of brass hobs or conchos. Some of them were intricately beaded or painted with stars, crosses, crescents, and bands.

When the Jicarillas went to war their dress was much more similar to that of the Plains Indians, although their feather headdresses resembled more headbands circled with erect quills of feathers than the large and more familiar flowing bonnets from the plains. Perhaps the most distinctive war dress of all the Apaches was the Mescaleros'. Although they lived between the Chiricahuas on one side and the Plains influence on the other, for headgear they used neither the war cap nor the feather bonnet. Rather, Mescalero warriors wrapped their heads in lengthy turbans, usually open on top and elaborately decorated with small artifacts and amulets. In the earlier days these were made of skins, but after trade felt became available it was often used, as well as furred skins. The method of wrapping was a matter of individual taste. Some men closed the tops to form caps; when furs were used, some left the tails attached to dangle as ornamentation. Some men did use the more familiar war caps, though they frequently decorated them with such unconventional objects as cow horns, perhaps an adaptation of the Comanches' buffalo horn bonnets. Mescalero war shirts were also quite easily recognized. Usually fashioned of buckskin, they were open down the sides and heavily fringed around the arm seams and down the backs of the sleeves. Their most distinguishing trait was a sizable V-shaped plate or bib down both the front and back, fringed around the outer edge. With the exception of the girls' Puberty Dresses, the Mescalero war shirt was perhaps the most impressive garment possessed by the Apaches, and often they were quite beautiful, rubbed or stained red, brown, or yellow and painted with a variety of symbols.[2]

The man chosen to lead a raid or revenge sortie was selected for that time only; he might be a chief but did not need to be. He had no duties when off the warpath; he was just a fellow with a reputation for leading men. While at war, though, he did not haul wood or water, or cook or butcher meat. He was there to exort the men and give advice, and it was he who divided spoils among them.

In addition to his own gear, each man carried with him a small bag of pollen for its good influence, but the most powerful protection he could take with him was his *izze-kloth,* or medicine cord, a loosely braided string sash of two hide strands twisted about each other, or perhaps four strings braided together, draped across the body from right shoulder to left side. Only a di-yin for war could make them; they possessed immense power, but were to be called upon only in times of present and serious danger.

> *I am calling on sky and earth.*
> *Bats will fly, and turn upside down with me in battle.*
> *Black sky will enfold my body and give me protection,*
> *And earth will do this also.*[3]

Generally it was from the izze-kloth that the bag of pollen was hung. Possession of the medicine cord, which was referred to as Killer of Enemies' bandolier, was believed to sacrifice one's luck at other skills. Thus, if a man were an accomplished fighter, he would not procure one and ruin his hunting and gaming. In addition to the physical amulets he wore, each warrior sought to commune with the Supernaturals to obtain what was known as "Enemies-against Power." These were magic words or phrases given the man by one of the powers, words that, when invoked in the heat of battle or in great personal danger, brought the interest and guidance of the sponsoring power. The concept of Enemies-against Power had strong mythological ties, and it was of premier importance for a warrior to have its confidence when he engaged in a fight. The short incantations were particular and localized in effect; one might turn away an enemy bullet or arrow, another kept one strong in the face of exhaustion, and still another might help the earth in concealing an Apache during hiding.

> *Right here in the middle of this place*
> *I am becoming Mirage.*
> *Let them not see me,*
> *For I am of the sun.*

A man's safety and luck on a raid or at war was also influenced by the conduct of his family during his absence. They were expected to be on their best behavior; some wives kept almost constantly at prayer. The woodpile was kept neatly stacked and the children were not permitted to play on it, for to scatter the wood was to risk the warrior's loss. A similar restriction applied to the disposition of deer carcasses; after eating, the bones were piled respectfully in one place, to keep the raiding party from becoming separated. Each warrior had also to observe his own *gudn-hlsi*, or taboos, such as sexual chastity until return, reference to women as White-painted Woman, and observance of the sacred warpath language.

If a di-yin was with the group, and especially if he was the leader, he might paint the faces of his warriors in the most auspicious manner. The design was a matter of his choice, although some designs became almost traditional: Eastern Chiricahuas often wore a single stripe of red clay across the bridge of the nose; Mescaleros, a large circular daub on either cheek and perhaps a line of smaller daubs across the forehead; Westerns, frecklelike splashes of white.

Although enemy camps were sometimes overrun, it was the Apaches' skill at plotting and executing ambushes that gained their greatest notoriety. These were of three basic types. In the first, the entire party would flee before a pursuing force into an area of heavy brush and poor visibility. Once out of sight they would split and circle, half to the left and half to the right, and pounce upon the enemy from both flanks. In the second, two or three warriors on the fastest horses would show themselves, apparently unsuspecting, to an enemy, who would fire on and pursue them. The decoys, to outward appearance surprised and terrified, would lead the enemy into a prepared crossfire. This was used mainly against American citizens and Mexicans, because the American cavalry caught on to it early. In the third, which was the most frequently used against the army, an enemy force was kept under surveillance until its route could be projected, and an ambuscade was prepared where they were most likely to pass. These last were often so well concealed that not even other Indian scouts could uncover them in time.

Pitched battles were avoided unless the Apaches were sure that they held all the advantages. When out on the trail for a revenge raid, the di-yin, of whom one was almost invariably taken, had a great deal to say about whether a fight was to be provoked at a particular time. If his auguring showed any uncertainty, a more favorable opportunity was awaited. Once a fight was opened and it began to turn against the Apaches and they were forced to break and run, a stranded man might employ the right to call on a comrade by his given name to compel aid. During a rout, recalled one Chiricahua informant, "Maybe P. is the last man and is about to pass me. I call him by his name and say, 'Don't leave me here alone with these people!' Then he would say, 'Well, that's my name,' and he would turn around and begin to fight again."[4] Ordinarily, other people were addressed by relationship terms; use of the proper name was limited to emergencies, and not to render aid when it was invoked shamed the party of whom it was asked, even if performance risked near-certain death.

Mutilating the corpses of killed enemies had at one time been against the custom of the Apaches, and apparently they took to it only in exasperation at Mexican and then Anglo atrocities. After the practice did come into usage, scalps were displayed at the victory dance as deeds were recounted and the bravest men were singled out for honor. There was, however, no concept of *coup*, or the accumulation of war trophies for social distinction. That would have implied indulgence in killing for its own sake, which was not the Apache manner. Even if a great number of the enemy were slain, still only one or a few scalps were brought back, and they were discarded after the celebration. Ever present was the fear of the dead and their return. A few Mescaleros did preserve and flaunt scalps, but not many of them would risk such an offense against the powers, for the Mescalero fear of the dead was accentuated even for Apaches. Among the more westerly tribes, those who had taken or touched a scalp underwent some kind of ghost medicine to keep the victim's spirit away. Some scholars insist rather highly that Apaches never scalped and that accounts of it are the result of "imaginative editing."[5] However, it seems certain that it was practiced to a limited extent. The Western Apache term for it was *bitsa-ha-digihz:* His Head Top Cut Off.

When possible, prisoners were taken in war to obtain information about the enemy's strength and movements. Adult males, however, were almost invariably killed soon after because it was too dangerous to keep them around. Women prisoners were not usually taken in the course of a raid, but when they were, sexual assault against them was rare. A warrior risked losing his luck in fighting if he raped a female captive. However, as one Chiricahua said, "If you can make her love you, all right." Undoubtedly, some women who were too frightened to resist were taken advantage of. The most desirable captives to take were young boys; girls would not bring large tribute when they got married, but boys adopted into the tribe, as they usually were, increased a band's numbers and helped provide food and goods. Sometimes, when a revenge raid netted a male captive, he was brought back to the rancheria alive for the dead man's relatives—usually his female relatives—to torture and kill, and Apache women bereaved by war casualties unquestionably contributed much to the tribe's reputation for the devising of inhuman tortures. They did have to ask the chief's permission to do this, but if he were inclined to allow a merciful death, he could be overruled by a vote of the warriors. If the dead party had been influential or popular, the captive was in for a horrible death.

Such an execution might take place at the victory dance that was held if an expedition returned triumphant from a raid or fight without having lost a man. The first dance at such a celebration might be a round dance of the kind the Chiricahuas called They Come in with the Enemy, but its real center was a face-to-face dance called Enemies, Their Property Dance, for which the women chose partners. If the men had returned with spoils, a warrior who was chosen by a woman to partner her was expected to pay her for the privilege from his share of the goods. (The token payment given the women at the conclusion of social choosing-partner dances was believed to be an outgrowth of this.) The most unique aspect of Enemies, Their Property Dance was that it was about the only time public approval was extended to sexual promiscuity. At this dance, the bi-zhahn, (young widows and divorcees) who had no men to support them, were allowed to strip almost entirely naked and dance lewdly, sometimes even with false genitalia depending from their gee strings. The warrior with whom a bi-zhahn chose to dance had to give her a substantial present, perhaps given her after she had taken him home for a lusty romp on the bed frame. Wives of married warriors did not usually complain about it; men returning from a battle were ready for a good time, and it was the only sexual outlet for the bi-zhahn, from whom this sort of conduct was expected.

At the end of the merrymaking a serious religious dance was sometimes performed. On rare occasions, victory dances were held even if losses had been sustained; mourning was delayed and the names of the dead were not mentioned to dampen the celebrating. The time of the victory dance was considered an auspicious time for marriage, first, because of the festive atmosphere generally, and, second, because the prospective groom was laden with booty to give in tribute to the woman's family. This was particularly true of a young warrior; after he had served as an apprentice for the four raids of his novitiate, his first time out as a full participant he was expected to take a leading part, and often came back with a sizable supply of goods.

They Scout Around:

NOTES

1. According to one of Opler's informants, the warriors who were going out did not themselves shout encouragement to one another. "They just made a noise softly under their breath, like, 'Wah! Wah!' You can't shout in the war dance or in war. The belief is . . . if you shout in battle, many of you will be killed." *An Apache Life-way*, p. 337.

2. See *Material Culture Notes*, p. 128.

3. Goodwin, *Social Organization of the Western Apache*, p. 667.

4. Opler, *An Apache Life-way*, p. 346.

5. Debo, *Geronimo*, p. 5.

Babies

Long time ago they say.

Coyote found two newly born fawns. He saw they were spotted and thought they were very pretty. He found their mother and told her, "I want my children to look like that. How did you do it?"

Doe said, "It is easy. Put your children in a little cleft in the rocks. Cover them with juniper branches and set fire to the wood. When the wood pops and crackles that will give your children spots."

Coyote went home and did that. He put his children in a little cleft and covered them with juniper. He lit the wood and watched but the fire just burned the little coyotes.

Now, don't you try to be like Coyote. In the early times he did bad things and you see what happened. Now you know better.

I am talking about fruit.[1]

Among all of the Apache tribes, children were greatly prized and treasured, both for their own sakes and as economic assets, and the community felt that childless marriages were tragic. Impotence on the part of the husband was, understandably, almost automatically attributed to witchcraft, and he could undergo a curing ceremony to correct it. (It is probably not unreasonable to speculate that, since most cases of male impotence do have a psychological origin, the percentage of cures from such ceremonies was higher than average.) Sometimes, sterility in a woman was attributed to malice on the part of her mother, or the di-yin who had officiated at her Puberty Ceremony. A fertility ceremony for a childless woman included, in addition to chanting and pollen sprinkling, the ritual feeding of eggs and rabbit testicles. Impotence on the part of the husband, frigidity in the wife or sterility on either part, were sometimes regarded—especially among the Chiricahuas—as grounds for divorce. This was less true among the Western Apaches, although these factors were certainly of influence in making a divorce decision. The identity of a sterile party in a marriage was determined easily enough after they divorced, by observing which spouse produced children in the succeeding marriages.

In the few cases where a couple wished to avoid conception, di-yins, frequently women in this case, could administer potions to prevent unwanted pregnancies, prepared either from rock crystal or unripe prickly pear fruits. Food restrictions imposed by such a di-yin had to be kept fastidiously or pregnancy was almost sure to result. Eggs, obviously, were on the forbidden list, and frequently honey.

For the expectant Apache woman, pregnancy was a time of equanimity, of care without dread, work without exertion, and receiving special attention without becoming spoiled. As soon as her condition was apparent she abstained from having sex, a restriction that stayed in effect until the child was weaned. If the father had no other wife, he also was expected to stay continent, and social pressure worked to prevent him from slinking around to find easy women. He was ridiculed if that were discovered.

The mother-to-be did not ride horses, do heavy lifting or anything to jolt or shock the baby. She refrained from eating fatty meat, piñon nuts, or other fattening foods, as it was believed they would make the baby fat and complicate the delivery. Most especially did she not eat intestines, which were, by the obvious physical similarity, believed associated with stillbirths caused by umbilical strangulation. She did not witness ceremonies at which the Ganhs danced, because the sight of them might make the baby dread to come out, and stay inside until the mother was killed. Both parents were particularly careful to avoid arguments with outsiders, for one never knew who was a witch, and to quarrel with a witch could be lethal if the baby were hexed as a result.

The indulgence with which Apache society treated infants and toddlers carried over to expectant mothers, but a woman was ridiculed if she attempted to take advantage of this. Sloth was bad for the baby, and the mother was expected to perform a regular amount of housework. "When you sit on the child after the fifth month it will be harder for you," it was said. "The child gets in the right position for coming out if you move around. The more you are a coward about it, the worse it will be for you."[2]

As the time for birth neared, a baby's activity was thought to be a sign of its sex: an active baby indicated a boy, a quiet one a girl. A few di-yins claimed to be able to influence the sex of an approaching child, but regular defeats at the hands of Nature led to their being taken not too seriously.

Once labor started, all the mother's female relations on her side of the family came, and her husband's female relatives, too, if they happened to live nearby. The husband himself left because his mother-in-law was coming. It was not necessarily taboo for a man to attend a delivery; he could keep his mother-in-law away simply by remaining. But as a matter of delicacy this rarely happened; a man would be embarrassed to witness such a thing among so many women. Personal hygiene was also involved in his leaving, for if he came into contact with the afterbirth he could get joint swelling, the same as if he touched menstrual discharge.

Among all the women who came, there was usually one who was skilled as a midwife, and who had gained the right to perform birth ceremonies. If not, and one was desired—it was not strictly necessary—she could be obtained from outside the family, but a large fee had to be paid her. A midwife with a particularly good record might receive as much as a horse.

Babies were not born from a lying position. The delivering mother knelt on an old blanket or rag of clothing, grasping a post to brace herself. To make the birth fast and easy, she swallowed four small salted pieces of the inner leaves of the narrow-leafed yucca, and her genitals were bathed with a solution of *Erigonum jamesii* root. It was the midwife's duty to massage the mother's abdomen and take the baby as it emerged. When labor was very difficult or prolonged, other specialists or di-yins might be called in to assist. If the infant did not breathe at first, it was not struck but splashed with cold water. For the baby to be strong and healthy but not cry was a good sign.

Almost immediately after the birth, the midwife-di-yin began the birth ceremony, rinsing the infant in lukewarm water. If it had been crying loudly the water might be mixed with an extract of *Parosela formosa* to quiet it. Commonly a newborn was rubbed with a mixture of red ocher and grease, then wrapped in a soft blanket. The specific prayers and incantations depended on the personal method and power of the midwife, but usually the ceremony included the sprinkling of ha-dintin pollen or ashes to the four directions, beginning with the east, and then on the child. While this went on the other women tended the mother, perhaps bathing her genitals again and examining her to see that she had suffered no abnormal damage.

Most Apaches believed that pregnancy was cumulative. One intercourse was not enough to cause it; it had to be developed over a long time. Thus, when a loose woman slept with a number of men and became pregnant, each man was a father of the child in proportion to the number of times he had been with her, and was expected to contribute a like share to the child's support. Such women became the butt of jokes, however, among the fathers. One might say of the child, "He can run fast. His legs must be from me."

Because of the belief in cumulative pregnancy, one occurrence that was always dreaded was the birth of twins. The appearance of two babies could be taken as evidence of the wife's infidelity or excessive lascivious appetite; at the very least it was a sign of serious spiritual disharmony.

When twins were born, it was believed that only one of them would live to adulthood, but the faith was seldom tested, because one of the babies was usually destroyed at birth. If one was a boy and the other a girl, the boy was kept.

Different groups of Apaches handled the matter of the umbilical cord differently. Some cut it with the edge of a yucca blade; others let it dry and fall off. If the baby was a boy, the cord might be buried with ceremony, either among deer tracks, to make him a successful hunter, or among horse tracks, to make him a great raider.[3] Others saw a danger in this, for if the cord were unearthed and eaten by some animal, great harm could come to the baby. More typically, especially among the Chiricahuas, the umbilical cord and its wrapping were placed in the branches of a fruit-bearing tree, in the belief that the infant's life would be renewed each year as the tree produced new life.

The place of birth became holy to that family, and whenever they happened to travel close by they would bring the child to the spot and roll him on the ground to the four directions to renew his spirit.

Nursing of course began as soon as the mother was able; a special soup was prepared for her by boiling bones, that was believed beneficial to abundant milk production. However, if for some reason the mother were unable to nurse the child, the function would be performed by a close female relative.

An infant's first name was usually given at birth, either for a peculiar characteristic or an unusual event attending its appearance; frequently it was suggested by the midwife. This name was not expected to last beyond childhood and was not of great significance. Often it had little descriptive quality of the person later in life; it is frequently cited that one of the fiercest war leaders of the later reservation period, known to the whites and Mexicans as Gerónimo (the Spanish for Jerome), had as a baby name Go-yath-khla, meaning Sleepy, or Yawns. From the baby names, as it was indeed with the adult names, too, it was not possible to know a person's sex just by hearing the name, unless a hint was contained within it, for instance, among the Western Apaches it was becoming for a man's name to bear the virile prefix, heçke, or Angry.

From the time the umbilical cord separated, the infant was tied into his cradleboard, and was seldom removed until old enough to crawl around. The number-directional symbolism suggested the fourth day of life as the most auspicious time for the cradle ceremony.

Cradleboards could only be fashioned by di-yins who had acquired the right to make them, and their construction was a matter of great religious ceremony. In stricter tradition the materials had to be gathered and the construction completed in one day.

A typical cradle ceremony song had elements in common with the cycle of blessing songs usually reserved for the girls' Puberty Ceremony, but with each line referring to a stage of constructing the cradleboard:

Good, like long life it moves back and forth.
By means of White Water in a circle underneath, it is made.
By means of White Water spread on it, it is made.
By means of White Shell curved over it, it is made.
Lightning dances alongside it, they say.
By means of Lightning it is fastened across.
Its strings are made of rainbows, they say.
Black Water Blanket is underneath to rest on;
White Water Blanket is underneath to rest on.
Good, like long life the cradle is made.
Sun his chief rumbles inside, they say.[4]

The three main parts of the cradleboard were the frame, the back slats, and the hood, or shade. The frame was oval in shape, usually made of oak, walnut, or ash. The hood was generally of a lighter material such as Apache plume or mock orange. The Chiricahuas sometimes attached sexual significance to the material used to make the back slats: a girl's cradle used narrow-leafed yucca, a boy's, sotol. The bedding on which the baby was placed might be wild mustard or some spongy sedge; a favorite pillow material was *Solanium trifolium.* The framework and hood were stretched over with buckskin, frequently stained yellow, and each cradle was bottomed with a footboard of oak or ash.

Some were fancier than others, depending on the wealth of the family and the degree of ostentation desired. Poor families usually limited the ceremony to the minimum necessary prayers and rituals. As with other ceremonies, the procedure depended upon the personal medicine of the di-yin officiating, but it usually included brushing the infant with particular designs of ha-dintin or ferrous dust. Cradle and baby were held ritually to the four directions, and there were feints before actually placing the baby on the bed.[5] After the infant was strapped into the cradleboard, the hood was usually decorated with symbols of significance to its sex: crosses and parallel slits for boys, half-moons or full moons for girls. The di-yin often hung protective amulets from the cradleboard, splinters of lightning-blasted wood and bags of ha-dintin, before turning it over to the mother. To these the mother added her own—the stuffed right paw of a badger to keep the infant from becoming frightened,[6] a piece of cholla wood to keep away sickness, and for other purposes, hummingbird claws and snatches of skin from a wildcat. If the cholla wood failed in its charm, to it was added a growth from a parasitized creosote bush.

For the first few weeks of life, the baby was carried horizontally in the cradleboard; he was not carried vertically on his mother's back until the neck muscles were strong enough to hold the head upright. As a packing to absorb the baby's waste, the necessary area was stuffed with soft mosses, or bark of the wild rose ground to powder. To make the skin strong, very young infants were bathed in a solution extracted from *Drymaria fendleri*, and to protect them from skin rashes they were dusted with powdered heart-leafed willow bark.

Among the Chiricahuas, it was necessary to pierce the ears during the first few months, a task usually performed by the maternal grandmother. This was accomplished by applying a heated object to the earlobe, following quickly with a sharp puncture by a bone sliver or thorn. "When the ears are not pierced," it was said, "the child cannot be controlled; he will be wild and go to the bad."[7] Children after the procedure were believed to hear things sooner and grow faster.

The constant confinement in the cradleboard produced a slight flattening of the back of the skull, but not as pronounced as in the cultures where the trait is deliberately enhanced. The bundling also tended to produce a contentment with motionlessness that proved of value later in life to the hunter or raider. Babies were taught very early the value of silence. If an infant sought attention by crying, it was taken from the rancheria, strung from a bush, and ignored until it became quiet. Approval was restored after that. Crying babies could give away the location of a rancheria to a raiding enemy, or foul an attempt to escape. In terrible emergencies it was not unknown, when the survival of the group depended on it, to kill crying babies, or even ones with a reputation for sudden tantrums, when hiding from an enemy.

As a baby's eyes began to work in unison, small baubles were hung from the rim of the hood to engage its attention. The Apaches seem not to have developed any traditional lullabies, but mothers often improvised melodies and lyrics.

After he was old enough to leave the cradleboard, at about six or seven months, a baby crawled freely about the rancheria, with all the adults taking care that he did not get into trouble. He was not allowed to contact harmful scorpions or snakes, or things that had power to harm him, like owl feathers. Other than that, he was mostly free to develop his own powers of exploration and observation. It was considered a bad thing to keep a dog near toddlers, since dogs shared in the power of Coyote. After the cradleboard fell into disuse, it was permissible to keep it and hand it down to the next child, but a new cradle ceremony was held each time it was used.

The spring after leaving the cradleboard was considered the best time for the ritual haircutting. Spring was ideal, for it was the season of renewal and fresh growth. The di-yin selected must himself have had thick hair. Usually the child's face was brushed with ha-dintin pollen, which was not washed or rubbed away but allowed to wear off. With appropriate rites the di-yin cut the child's hair closely, usually leaving one or a few snatches of long strands. (After such a ceremony it was thought excessively funny for the adults to tease the children that they looked like quail.) The shorn hair might then be buried under a fruiting tree, perhaps with a lock of the di-yin's own. It was best for a child to go through four such ceremonies during successive springs, each conducted, if possible, by the same di-yin. After that age, however, the hair was never cut except in extreme mourning, for to do so was bad luck.

Sometime between leaving the cradleboard and the second birthday was time for the elaborate first moccasins ceremony, designed to give the child an auspicious start on the sacred Life-way. It was a time of great rejoicing for the family, and gifts were prepared for everyone who came. Of course, a di-yin who knew a ceremony was employed. After some opening prayers, the di-yin typically would mark with pollen all the family and guests, just before dawn. As the sun broke above the horizon he lifted the baby four times to the east, then as many times to the south, west, and north. The ceremony was patterned on the first one, that White-painted Woman gave Child of the Water. With pollen the di-yin made four footprints on a white buckskin, and then, perhaps in company with the male parent, led the child through his first ceremonial steps. One early account indicated the heavy emphasis on number-directional symbolism: "We led him through these footprints. [The di-yin] said a prayer about Child of the Water and his first step just as the boy took his first step. He said another prayer for the second step and went on until four prayers and four steps were over. Then the boy took four steps by himself. As he did so, they said, 'May he have good fortune.' Now we turned the boy clockwise and brought him back, and he walked the four steps in the same way again. Four times we walked him like this. Then we took him in a clockwise circle four times. After four prayers, [the di-yin] sang four songs. Then we sat down."[8] After another cycle of singing and praying, a child was fitted with his first moccasins with equally measured ceremony. Then the gifts were blessed and given out, and general revelry would continue until dark; at that time the child might be lifted to the moon with prayers that he grow tall. Although, from birth on, the degree to which a child was raised in religious ceremony was the private decision of the family, the conducting of two rituals as holy as the haircutting and first moccasins so early in a child's life left an indelible imprint that adequately prepared the developing personality for the sacred journey along the Life-way.

As the time came for a child to be weaned, frequently after the moccasin and haircut ceremonies, he was gradually introduced to different soft foods. Reluctant children might be forbidden to nurse, but more cleverly the mother would begin daubing her nipples with an unpleasant substance like chili, and tell the child that was what normally happened at this time and it was necessary to take other foods.

Babies:

NOTES

1. Coyote's attempt to spot his children like fawns is a favorite example of him as foolish imitator. According to French, "Comparative Notes," p. 109, the tale appears in the following treatments: White Mountain: Goodwin, "Myths and Tales of the White Mountain Apache," p. 155. Lipan: Opler, "Myths and Legends of the Lipan Apache Indians," p. 141ff. Chiricahua: Opler, "Myths and Tales of the Chiricahua Apache Indians," pp. 70–71. Jicarilla: Russell, "Myths of the Jicarilla Apache," p. 265; Goddard, "Jicarilla Apache Texts," p. 227; Opler, "Myths and Tales of the Jicarilla Apache Indians," pp. 285–86.

2. Opler, *An Apache Life-way*, pp. 5–6.

3. Thrapp, *Victorio*, p. 10.

4. This song is an adaption of a literal translation found in Goodwin, *Social Organization of the Western Apache*, pp. 436–37.

5. For an account of a Mescalero cradle ceremony, see Opler, *Apache Odyssey*, p. 23.

6. Thrapp, *Victorio*, p. 10.

7. Opler, *An Apache Life-way*, p. 13.

8. Ibid., pp. 16–17.

Rites of Passage

The attitude of affection and indulgence that characterized Apache adults' handling of infants and toddlers carried over in some degree to early childhood. The games that children played together were simple and unaffected, at least until they reached an age at which they began to understand the nature of gambling. Boys and girls generally played together until they were perhaps five or six, after which they tended to segregate sexually.

Children were not given any intensive instruction in religion or the powers beyond walking them through necessary rituals like the first footsteps or the haircuts; they were too young to comprehend more than this, and they were left to learn deeper meanings gradually, by assimilation. Whenever it was possible during the nomadic wanderings of a particular group, parents would take a child to the place of his birth and lay him on the ground, rolling him to the four directions in a ceremonial renewal. (Adults, too, might do the same thing in visiting their own birthplaces, which perhaps strengthened their affinity to a given locale and militated against their removal by the government during the reservation days.)[1]

The principal introduction a child received to the elements of the Lifeway was by the telling of fables or morality tales—prominently, of course, the Coyotes stories. Coyote, who did first all the wicked and silly things that men do, illustrated a bad example for the children to contrast with the way they were expected to behave. Non-mythological stories were also used, like that of the man who did not rub grease on his legs after meals. (This was believed to feed the legs just as the food gave nourishment to the body, and was a brief but universal afterdinner activity.) The unlucky person one day found himself in danger, but when the man called upon his legs to run, they told him to run with his belly. The telling of the tribal myths to the children also served to acquaint them with the legendary happenings of their genesis, which was essential to their later understanding of the ceremonies conducted by the di-yins. It was in this fashion

that most children first learned of Yusn, White-painted Woman, Child of
the Water, and Killer of Enemies, and events such as the Slaying of the
Monsters.

Since Apache society was characterized by a high regard for social acceptance and relations, it is not surprising that a great deal of time was
spent training children in manners and etiquette. It was considered very ill
bred for a child to run in and about a camp other than his own. A child
was instructed not to dunk other people's children while swimming; boys
were instructed never to fight with a girl. If one child offered another a
gift, it was to be accepted graciously, at once; it was a serious offense to
hurt another child's feelings—particularly a poor one's—by refusing an
offered present. Children were ordered not to swear, or abuse children
smaller than themselves, not to steal or be unkind to playmates, or to go
into others' camps and eat their food. Table manners were important at
home. Children were trained not to ask for food while it was still cooking,
not to help themselves before others had begun eating, and not to ask for
more than they could eat. When company came, a child was expected to
behave himself maturely, and especially not to walk in front of company
during the act of leaving the wickiup. By far the worst thing a child could
do was make fun of the elderly.

The need for social acceptance was a key factor in the discipline of
misbehavior. Parental disfavor was demonstrated in the same way that social disfavor was shown by the community: by ridicule. A child was given
trust and responsibility that increased with his age; for that to be withdrawn and replaced by sniggering mockery almost always unnerved him
and resulted in a quick improvement in his conduct. Bogeys were also
commonly used to keep a child in line; among the Chiricahua the most
common threat was with the Godeh. The parents did not try to describe
this kind of troll—to threaten to send for him was usually enough for a
small child. When they grew too old to be frightened of the Godeh they
were threatened with the Clown who accompanied the Ganh impersonators when they danced. One of the functions of the Clown was said
to be the punishment of bad children, or else carrying them away in baskets. When children grew dulled by threats that were never consum-
mated, the parents might persuade a big, fat man to paint himself up like
the Clown and ambush the children at play away from the camp. When
he had crept close enough upon the scene he would rush them brandishing
a stick or basket and chase them, whooping and gobbling and throwing
rocks at them, back to their camp. Almost without exception children
demoralized by this treatment behaved perfectly for a considerable time.
If certain children were particularly bad, word would be put out generally
that the next time a Clown appeared in a Gahn ceremony, or at a Puberty
Ceremony, he would single them out and terrorize them, just at the time
they were in awe of the Ganhs and most vulnerable. Fierce-looking old

men for whom the child had expressed fear were also utilized as bogeys; one would sometimes be invited to come over with a big sack and act like he was going to carry the child away. The parents would act as though they approved and would not protect the child, and that, too, usually did the trick.

Corporal punishment was resorted to with the greatest reluctance and as a last resort. Among the Apaches, older youths who caused trouble were not always punished by the father; it might occur that the parent would drag his son to a public place like the hoop-and-pole ground. If another man was there with an incorrigible boy, the two were forced to fight each other until one was entirely whipped. The winner then had to face others until he, too, took a beating. Girls were seldom beaten, although one guilty of sexual promiscuity could be publicly whipped by her father, first for dishonoring the family and second for cheating them out of the marriage tribute that a chaste girl would bring to the family.

Discipline to enforce the frequent imperative for silence was continued strictly. Children who cried were held under a blanket until they stopped, or else had cold water dribbled over their heads. Children who chattered incessantly or otherwise made nuisances of themselves were disciplined in a variety of ways, often to the considerable amusement of the adults. One of the favorite methods was the wild-goose chase. A parent might pick up his tobacco pouch as if to smoke, then express surprise at having left his smoking device at another camp, and send the child to fetch it. The expression "smoking device" was a tip-off to other adults, and when the child went to the other camp and asked for it he was sent on to a third camp and then a fourth, until he might be gone all night. It was then, one supposes, easy enough for the parent to explain to the tired, irritable child that his constant chattering must have caused him to forget where he left it, after all.

At other times children were gotten temporarily out of the grown-ups' hair by means that gave them their first physical training for war or flight. Children were regularly made to bathe in cold mountain streams to strengthen their hearts.[2] Very often it happened that a disruptive boy was instructed to run to the top of a nearby hill and return without stopping; as he got older the hills became higher and more difficult until by the time of his war novitiate he was in superb physical condition.

The war novitiate or apprenticeship of an Apache youth was the step that elevated him from adolescence to full manhood, and also gave the men a way to train him in techniques of warfare and survival in hostile country, while exposing him to only minimal personal hazard. As boys grew older their play centered more and more on imitating adult activities like hunting and raiding. They worked with their practice bows and arrows until they became remarkably accurate in their shooting. At about the age of fifteen a youth felt increasingly outgrown of games and made it known to the men in his family that he wanted to begin his training to be a warrior. Although by this age he had certainly picked up a great deal of lore about warfare and novice conduct, the men would not take him along until they were sure he had learned enough to get by if he were stranded.

There are lots of rules about getting along on a raid or even if you are just scouting about. You have to know them or you can have a hard time all right.

You should always have women prepare you some food in advance— enough for five or maybe seven days.

You should travel only at night across the open places. You can travel during the day in the mountains if you want, but if you cross a desert by day the soldiers or Mexicans would see you and catch you.

If it is a hot day and you want to rest, lie up in brush or grass. Never go to cool shade, no matter what. If there are soldiers around, that is where they will be and you will walk right into them.

For this same reason you must never go to a waterhole during the day. If you are out of water and don't know where to look for some, get to a mountain and look around to see where green things are growing, then lie up somewhere and wait for the night. Don't just go to water in the middle of the day for anything! Wait for dark and scout around to see it is all right.

If you see someone coming, but they are too far away to recognize, find some brush to take cover in, next to a clearing. Make a smoke signal and put it out at once. Go to the cover and see who comes around. Then you can decide what to do.

When the men were satisfied that the youth was ready, they took him to a di-yin for war, who gave him further instruction and also the special equipment of the apprentice's station: the novice cap, drinking tube, and scratching stick. The processing of apprentices was a common activity of a di-yin for war, and if any fee was charged it was inconsequential. The paraphernalia were not particularly charged with power and remained the property of the di-yin, to be returned to him at the conclusion of the noviate for use by the next boy.

The novice cap was similar in appearance to a regular war cap, but it had none of the power that a di-yin could infuse into the latter. Instead, the novice cap was decorated typically with four kinds of feathers: oriole feathers for clearheadedness, eagle down for protection from harm, the leading pinfeathers from either wing of a hummingbird, for speed, and quail feathers to aid in surprising the enemy. For the duration of the raid, the novice could not scratch himself with his hands, but was required to use the scratching stick, or else his skin would become soft. Likewise, he could drink water only through the drinking tube of carrizo reed, or his beard would grow unmanageably.

When he finally left on a raid with the adult warriors—he had to wait for an occasion, as they would not go out just to give him experience—the novice was put under a greater series of restrictions. He could not look back at the rancheria or he would have ill fortune. If he stared up at the sky he would cause it to rain. He could eat only cold food, to make his horse serve him well. While on the raid he must be sexually chaste, and must not eat any head meat or entrails. To the other warriors he must be solemn and respectful; he must do all the camp drudgery—gathering wood and cooking—and he must not sleep until given permission. And very importantly, he must use only the ceremonial warpath language, a system of about eighty mystical euphemisms that were substituted for the common terms for certain objects.[3] The heart, for instance, was referred to as "that by means of which I live"; arrows were "missiles of death," and so on. The warriors for their part observed the restriction of addressing and referring to the novice as Child of the Water, the supernatural being whom the apprentice represented during the training. Although the novice rode at the head of the line of warriors, they were careful to keep him from harm; if a situation developed in which a fight seemed likely, an apprentice was left in safe cover at a distance, but from which perhaps he could see the action and learn from it. To have an apprentice killed on a raid reflected very badly on whoever led it.

A youth's character was believed to reveal itself during the novitiate, and if he showed a tendency to sullenness or indolence, that reputation might hinder him all his life. The consequences of failing the apprenticeship or being dropped for incorrigibility were serious—such a man was not welcome on raiding parties and was doomed to a life of limited income—and failures were few and limited to rare cases of uncontrollable rebellion. A young man rode as an apprentice on four expeditions; after this he was considered a man equal to the others, eligible to marry and establish his own household, and hold and express independent views.

The war novitiate that adolescent boys were required to undergo was no less intricate than Nah-ih-es, the Puberty Ceremony of the girls.[4] Scholars have regarded it as a lovely—and singularly telling—attribute of the Apache Life-way that such a fierce tribe should have as its single most important religious ceremony a four-day rite to usher a girl into womanhood at the time of her first menstrual flow. The anomalies of the Puberty Ceremony only begin there, however. In the Apache religious complex that heavily emphasized the role of di-yins to mediate between the sources of power and the people, this ceremony came directly from the Supernaturals, given to all the people, and was the least shamanistic of all Apache rites. And in a cosmic scheme where the most powerful forces left on earth to cure disease and dissipate evil were the dancers who impersonated the Ganh spirits, it was the only ceremony where the Ganh dancers performed just for the entertainment of the crowd and to spread good luck. From an individual standpoint, it focused community attention upon the intimate physiological mechanism of a girl who was entering a stage of life during which she would be too embarrassed even to eat in front of strangers. (Indeed, some girls found the ordeal so mortifying that they had to be physically coerced by their families to go through with it. Women who had not undergone the Puberty Ceremony were not ostracized or ridiculed, but they were pitied as doomed to sickly health, poor disposition, and early death.) For many girls it would be the most attention they would ever receive, as during those four days the celebrant was considered to have power. As her family began informing the community of the coming event they would, rather than say that their daughter's ceremony was coming, likely use the accepted expression, "She is going to become White-painted Woman." It is doubtful that a real belief in transubstantiation was implied, but during her ceremony a girl was dispenser of the power for good of that supernatural being.

Thus it was very important that a girl come into her Puberty Ceremony chaste. An important part of the ritual was where she blessed each person in the gathering with pollen, and if she assumed the power of White-painted Woman fraudulently she could bring very bad luck to those she affected. A girl who was known to have "gone around" with boys might be denied the ceremony; if she undertook the ceremony and was later learned to have had sexual experience, she might even be banished.

The Nah-ih-es was so elaborate—and costly to the girl's family—that they might begin making preparations as early as a year before they expected her time to come. Extra food was preserved and set aside, and hints could be dropped to relatives who were slow to contribute their share. Gifts from members of the community unrelated to the family also started to arrive; the feasting was open to all, and anyone who wanted to come sent a present. In fact, some people might begin referring to the prepubescent girl by a nickname that meant "She through whom we will have a big time." Most important, the family began acquiring fresh buckskins, either by gift or their own hunting, to begin making the girl's Puberty Dress. If no women in the family had the necessary skill to make this exquisite costume, an unrelated woman was employed, for the workmanship had to be the finest. A Puberty Dress required five buckskins, one for the moccasins, two for the top, sewn flesh side in, and two for the skirt, prepared flesh side out. During the sewing an older woman who knew the proper songs was given substantial presents to sing over it day by day, which sometimes took several weeks. The entire costume was dyed or rubbed yellow, to represent pollen, before being spectacularly finished with fringes, studs, beadwork, tin cone-tinklers, and painted with symbols associated with White-painted Woman: the crescent moon, morning star, rainbow, and sunbeams.

Aside from the celebrant herself, there were three important functionaries necessary to help her through the ceremony, and whose services had to be negotiated and made certain well in advance. The first of these was the girl's attendant, an older, experienced woman who had charge of the girl during the four days of the Nah-ih-es and for four days thereafter. Only certain women could perform this function. They were not strictly considered to be di-yins, but shamanism was involved to a degree; a woman gained knowledge of attendance by learning it from one who already had it, whose personal possession it was. Some attendants could claim supernatural experience with White-painted Woman herself, thus placing the girl's attendant more in the role of priestess than true shaman. When the girl's family reached a decision what attendant was to be approached, they sent the girl over to her with a ritual offering, which the older woman had the choice of accepting or refusing. If she accepted, the two addressed each other from then on as mother and daughter, a special relationship that lasted as long as they lived.

Just as the attendant was in charge of the girl during the Puberty Ceremony, most of the rituals themselves were directed by the singer. His role exhibited less shamanism than that of the attendant; he learned the dozens of songs simply through years and years of paying attention. The most sought after singers were old men who, by community observation, had presided over ceremonies that produced a high percentage of healthy, strong, good-natured, industrious women. If the singer were caught short on paraphernalia the family had to supply them—a deer hoof rattle, basket tray with eagle feathers, plenty of pollen, and a supply of different paints such as white clay and red ocher.

The girl's family had finally to select a di-yin who had power through the Ganhs to choose and prepare dancers for the ceremony. This could be a chancy negotiation for many reasons. One practical aspect was that the di-yin was being asked to miss the party himself; the one who dressed and painted the Ganhs had to stay in a little camp well removed from the festivity. He was being asked for four days of demanding—and dangerous—work. Although the Ganhs at a Puberty Ceremony danced for the entertainment of the gathering, the dancers still represented powerful Supernaturals, and there was some risk involved anywhere in the employment of power; if the di-yin did anything wrong during his work, he risked harm to himself, his dancers, or those at the celebration. The di-yin was also responsible for rounding up four men who were willing to dance, and he might well have trouble getting that many to agree, for the same reasons. Once a Ganh di-yin was engaged, though, he knew he would be well paid for his effort.

The family could not, of course, know exactly when the girl's menarche would begin (as the English language does, the Apache had a special word for the first, as opposed to the regular, menstruation). When the girl told her mother that it had begun, a small ceremony was held immediately afterward for family and good friends, which was a one-day-long abbreviation of the full rite. The real ceremony might then take place as soon as enough people gathered, or it might be postponed awhile—until, say, autumn, to coincide with the harvest, or (as happened more frequently during later reservation days) to allow for a multiple ceremony to be given by different families.

The Puberty Ceremony was held on a large, level open area near the family's encampment. Families who were visiting from some distance away began making temporary camps around the place, except none on the east side, which was left open. The women in the girl's family erected a large, open kind of structure, usually on the south side of the clearing, to begin preparing the store of food they had laid by. There was also built a wickiup in which to house the attendant, unless her own dwelling was close by.

The rite opened with two simultaneous occurrences. Before dawn the celebrant tendered herself to her attendant, and the matron washed the girl's hair in yucca root or soapweed. Just as the sun came up the girl faced the east as the praying attendant marked her with pollen down the part of the hair and across the bridge of the nose. She then dressed her, beginning at the feet, in the Puberty costume. From this instant she was a woman, and for the next four days she was White-painted Woman and had to be addressed so. The attendant soon gave her a ritual feeding, perhaps of cactus fruit crossed with pollen and held out to the directions, placed on the celebrant's tongue after three feints; this gave her good appetite through her life. No men were allowed around the attendant's dwelling during this time; they were occupied anyway, near the center of the clearing, in the other first-dawn rite, erecting the ceremonial structure. Like all aspects of the Puberty Ceremony this varied from tribe to tribe. Among the Mescaleros it was referred to as the Big Tepee, for its conical shape of spruce poles; the Chiricahuas apparently referred to it simply as the Ceremonial Structure. By Mescalero tradition it consisted of four main poles and eight lesser ones, with further cut saplings demarcating the runway to the east. The Chiricahua structure consisted of four poles and a simple clear area to the east, unbounded. In most cases the poles, shorn of branches except those at the top, created a home for White-painted Woman that was between twenty-five and thirty-five feet tall. It is impossible for a brief description to convey the meticulous character of everything connected with the Nah-ih-es; just in the raising of the Big Tepee, everything was aligned with the directions, done in multiples of four, prayed and sung over incessantly and according to exacting ritual, and sprinkled with pollen. At the top of the Big Tepee fluttered a bunch of grama grass and two eagle feathers, to guarantee the safety of the structure.

Inside the attendant's wickiup, the matron affixed two more eagle feathers to the back of the celebrant's head, to guarantee good weather, and began instructing White-painted Woman in the restrictions she must observe during the ceremony and four days thereafter. Much like the novice in war, the female puberty celebrant could scratch herself only with a stick, on pain of leaving scars, and drink only through a reed tube, or else risk rainstorms. White-painted Woman was further admonished to be cheerful and gracious, but not to laugh or make fun of people as she might normally do. Breaking this rule would result in premature wrinkling. She must not under any circumstance wash off the pollen with which she was to be coated again and again over the next four days; it must be allowed to wear off naturally. She was reminded of the household tasks that would be her life's work, and told to reflect solemnly on what it meant to be a good woman. The gathered crowd would be watching her behavior closely, for as with the war novice, an adolescent's lifelong character traits were believed to establish themselves during the rites of passage. When the celebrant and attendant were ready, they left the wickiup and approached the center area where the singer was directing the erection of the Big Tepee.

The singer by now was involved in the cycle of what were called Dwelling Songs: one set for raising the poles and slipping them into the holes that had been dug to support them, a second set for leaning the poles together and tying them fast.

> The home of the long-life dwelling ceremony
> Is the home of White-painted Woman.
> Of long life the home of White-painted Woman is made,
> For Killer of Enemies has made it so,
> Killer of Enemies has made it so.[5]

At each mention of the Supernaturals or some object sacred to them—turquoise or the sun—the attendant would cry the same shrill, ululant sound of applause with which White-painted Woman greeted the deaths of the Monsters in the Genesis. In fact, an alternate way of referring to the attendant was the expression She Who Makes the Cry.

When the framework had been made secure, the women who had been preparing food at the south edge of the grounds came in a procession and set heaping baskets of food in a line from the east of the ceremonial dwelling. The singer blessed the trays with pollen and a boisterous meal was enjoyed before the house of White-painted Woman was finished by covering its floor with spruce branches and fastening walls of horizontally tied oak branches, with the door left open to the east. When the hearth was dug it was time for the most important series of rituals of Nah-ih-es: blessing the people, the molding, and the run. The attendant laid a buckskin in the southeast of the Big Tepee, and as the celebrant knelt the older woman marked her again with pollen—across the bridge of the nose and down the part of the hair—and was marked in return. As a tray basket laden with little sacks of pollen was set before the girl a long line of people queued to the south. When each person entered the house he offered pollen to the directions and marked the face of White-painted Woman with it, in the same pattern already established. The girl in turn blessed him with pollen and prayed for his good luck and long life. These exchanges with the people were strongly believed to be curative; young women brought their babies to be blessed, and when an older lame person entered the Big Tepee the girl might briefly massage an aching joint.

When the blessings were over, the attendant stretched the girl face-down on the buckskin and gave her a lengthy massage, praying that she would be molded into a good life, that she would be industrious and have a good disposition, and live a long and happy life.

That done, the attendant took pollen from nut- or fruit-bearing trees and traced four footprints toward the east on the buckskin, and led the celebrant ceremonially through them. Then the tray basket of pollen and the ritual paraphernalia were taken to the east of the Big Tepee a distance of perhaps fifty to seventy yards. When the crowd had gathered, the attendant pushed White-painted Woman out the entrance to run, clockwise, around the basket and back. As the girl jogged off, the attendant again gave the shrill of applause, with the other women joining in, and any men who wanted further good luck could trot after the celebrant. This was repeated four times, with the basket being moved closer to the ceremonial structure each time. When she returned from the last run White-painted Woman shook the buckskin to the directions to banish sickness from her people; her family then scattered a basketful of presents onto the skin and enjoyed the scramble as everyone tried to claim one. At this stage the celebrant retired to rest and hear more instruction, as the public gathering turned into a general party. The women gossiped and played the stave game, old people reminisced, the men played hoop-and-pole, everywhere there was racing and gambling.

For a long time before evening, at his small camp removed from the noise of the Puberty Ceremony, the di-yin through Ganhs had been preparing and painting the four dancers and, perhaps, a Clown, if someone wished to dance that role. Getting the Mountain Spirit dancers and their equipment ready was important and tiring work for the di-yin; one of the Ganh-making songs collected by Morris Opler illustrated the dominating and powerful imagery of the ceremony:

> In the middle of the Holy Mountain,
> In the middle of its body, stands a hut,

> *Brush-built, for the Black Mountain Spirit.*
> *White lightning flashes in these moccasins;*
> *White lightning streaks in angular path;*
> *I am the lightning flashing and streaking!*
> *This headdress lives; the noise of its pendants*
> *Sounds and is heard!*
> *My song shall encircle these dancers!*[6]

Well after night had fallen and the dancing fire had been lit to the north of the Big Tepee, the arrival of the Ganh dancers was heralded by the clattering of their headdresses. As they performed the spectacular cycle of traditional dances to entertain the crowd, the singer was within the ceremonial structure leading the girl and a few other women in a quiet, mystical long life dance. When they were done and the Ganhs were through with their performance, the remainder of the night was allotted to social dancing to amusing and risqué songs.

The second and third days and nights of the feast were less ceremonial than the first; the emphasis was simply on having a good time. The celebrant remained under her restrictions, but not until the fourth night was there a new cycle of concluding ceremonies. The conclusion came with the final performance by the Ganhs, at which they had the good-natured right to roust everybody into the dancing circle, aid the girls in choosing partners, and even danced themselves in the social round. The end of Nah-ih-es was usually signaled when White-painted Woman led a saddle horse to her singer in payment for his services and retired for her four days of recovery with the attendant.

The sociological aspects of both the male and female rites of passage were many, but certainly the most important was the provision of a spiritual portal through which an adolescent could enter the adult world. The ceremonies communicated full-fledged acceptance of them in the adult circle, while at the same time giving solemn notice of what kind of conduct was expected of a grown member of the community.

Rites of Passage:
NOTES

1. Gerónimo, *Geronimo's Story of His Life*, pp. 25–26.
2. Thrapp, *Victorio*, p. 10.
3. See generally Opler and Hoijer, "The Raid and Warpath Language of the Chiricahua Apache."
4. A great deal of material has been published about the Puberty Ceremony, in addition to treatment in the standard works. See generally Nicholas,

"Mescalero Puberty Ceremony"; Whitaker, "Nah Ih Es: An Apache Puberty Ceremony"; and Arnold, "The Ceremony of the Big Wickiup."

5. Opler, *An Apache Life-way*, p. 96. Opler noted very perceptively that, this being a Chiricahua Dwelling Song, the reference to Killer of Enemies hearkened back to a time before that tribe replaced him as the culture hero with Child of the Water.

6. Ibid., p. 108.

Courtship and Marriage

Long time ago they say.

Coyote found a beautiful woman and wanted to make love to her. He was a scoundrel and did that with anybody at all. He took her for a walk in the woods. Just when they were ready for intercourse Coyote saw her vagina was full of teeth and got scared. It was Vulva Woman! Instead of entering her himself he put in a stick of wood, but she chewed it all up. So he put in a rock and broke all her teeth, and then she was smooth just like women are now.

The woman said, "You have made me valuable. I am worth horses and different things now." Today men still give horses and things for women when they get married.

Coyote was a rascal and did many bad things in the old time, but he tried to help us. Many things he got for us we could not do without now.

I am talking about fruit.[1]

From the age at which boys and girls ceased playing together, and especially from the early teens, they began to exhibit an embarrassed self-consciousness in front of the other sex that increased with age and began to diminish slowly only with marriage, and in most cases continued for some time after marriage. A few young people, of course, passed through adolescence with poise and self-assurance, but as a rule boys in their late teens and girls in their middle teens would do anything to avoid calling attention to themselves. A boy would ask an older relative to go into a group of people to do errands he would normally do himself, if he saw girls that he knew. A girl would assume the habit of not eating where young men could see her. If she encountered a boy on a path she would look the other way, and if spoken to, make no answer. If a boy were asked—even by his family —to perform some task, he might refuse to move, or else leave, if it would make others notice him. To outsiders this awkwardness gave the appearance of a surly and unco-operative attitude.

Entrance to the Cochise stronghold. *National Archives.*

General Oliver O. Howard. *National Archives.*

Heske-hlda-sila, called Diablo, chief of the White Mountain Apaches.
National Archives.

Camp Grant in 1871, at the time of the massacre.

Royal Emerson Whitman, 3rd Cavalry. *Arizona Historical Society.*

Eskiminzin, a chief of the Arivaipa Apaches, with two of his children. *National Archives.*

The Camp Grant Massacre trial, Pima County Courthouse, Tucson, December 1871.
Arizona Historical Society.

George Crook, Lieutenant Colonel of the 23rd Infantry. *National Archives.*

But the growing feelings surfaced eventually, of course. As a rule, a first overture of personal interest was the province of the girl. A bolder one might come upon a boy and express admiration for a possession of his and ask him to make her one. Commonly, more tact and more company were involved; a girl might hint to a boy that she and her friends had so much work to do in the field that it would be nice for some boys to help them out. Or she could say that she and her friends would like to go out and cut mescal, but they had no boys to cut and haul firewood for them. Having more people in the company and ready work at hand made lulls in the conversation less painful, but personal embarrassment still played in the logistics of an encounter. Most young people working together were too bashful to leave for a drink of water, and one who failed to start work fully refreshed was in for a miserable day, for a sudden disappearance into a clump of bushes was unthinkable. (There was even a case of one mortified boy banishing himself from his companions for two months after a spectacular, though accidental, flatulation.) Perhaps the best opportunity a girl had of showing a boy she liked him was to choose him—perhaps more than once—as her partner at a social dance. A girl who had been well coached by her female relatives would look away shyly while touching him on the shoulder, and the chosen boy might be so embarrassed that he dragged his feet or missed steps through the whole thing. (If that happened, a wise girl dragged her feet, too.) But it was a beginning. A girl's elders were not bashful at helping her out; sometimes an aunt or other authoritative figure would accompany her to a dance to point out boys of good character and family, and among the Western Apaches, of eligible clan.

From such a subtle start, pursuit was mostly the place of the boy, for girls were always lectured against chasing. A courting youth might begin mooning about paths that the girl was known to frequent. If she seemed pleased, he could really sound out her interest by killing small game and leaving meat outside her wickiup. If she cooked something up and brought it over to his camp, he was in business.

A welcome respite from the discomfort of dealing with the opposite sex was afforded by the peculiar relationship that existed between a person and his or her cross-cousin. This was a child of either sex of one's father's sister (paternal aunt), or mother's brother (maternal uncle), as opposed to parallel cousins, the offspring of paternal uncles and maternal aunts. A chosen cross-cousin could by mutual agreement become the target and source of an endless exchange of puns, pranks, practical jokes, and other fun. Cross-cousins were a resource often used to good advantage to arrange meetings away from camp in which, at first, the suitor and his cousin would sit and talk, in proximity to the girl and her cousin. The two couples might even talk briefly back and forth. After a few such rendezvous, the cousins would playfully decide to take a walk together and the couple would be left alone. This was a critical time, and all too often the more fearful party called the cousins back before they wandered beyond hailing.

Eventually the couple would have to begin meeting on their own, and there began a tragicomic quadrille of arranging to meet, meeting, and usually being too embarrassed to exchange more than superficial small talk. By this time the whole community knew that they were going together, as confirmed by the fact that at the social dances the young man might put his arms around her, draping her as he did so with his blanket, as they danced together. This was also the stage at which premarital liberties were most likely to occur, in spite of repeated stern warnings against them to the girl by her family. Most couples were far too bashful, but premarital intercourse did sometimes occur, although it was a very serious offense against the girl's family, and a quick forced marriage usually resulted if they found out. In fact, many Apaches considered premarital violation to be a more serious crime than the theft of another man's wife, for to ruin a maiden robbed her family of the bride presents they could exact for marrying off a virgin. A used girl—one who, as the Apaches said, already had a brand on her—commanded much smaller tribute.

A typical couple, once they made their wish to marry known, took no part in the negotiations and left it entirely to their families. If an agreement between them was reached, the boy's family sent over the bride presents, perhaps three horses, one of them with saddle, bridle, gun, blanket, and buckskins. Soon after, the girl would arrive in the young man's family camp, or be escorted there by an older female relative, or perhaps one of the boy's female relatives would be sent to fetch her. Exact form was not important; they managed.

After the strain and embarrassment of a courtship, it is not surprising that once a couple were considered married (they did not address each other by given names, but used the reciprocal term that meant "you with whom I go about"), it frequently took a while to become accustomed to one another. There seems to have been little developed notion of anything like a honeymoon, but a couple did what they were comfortable doing. A man who knew that he and his bride were well at ease with each other might have prepared a temporary camp in a secluded place where they were sure of being alone; they might stay there for from one to three weeks before settling among his wife's people. Another couple might be so terrified at the prospect of sleeping together that they prevailed upon sympathetic cross-cousins to stay with them at first. Night would find them four in the bed, the bride and groom on the outside, petrified and motionless; the groom's male cross-cousin slept next to him, the bride's female cross-cousin between him and the bride. Tact and good judgment of the moment dictated when the cross-cousins would leave the newlyweds alone to face each other.

The couple eventually established a permanent residence at or near the wife's family cluster, and the son-in-law became a producing member of that economic unit. Ties with the man's family remained cordial; some time after the marriage, perhaps a couple of months, the wife's female relatives carried over to them a large feast of prepared food. Smaller exchanges of gifts continued for as long as a year, but the young man was still a part of his wife's family. The most remarkable new relationship that he began was the undertaking of mother-in-law avoidance. An Apache woman had no restrictions against contact with her husband's mother, but a man was forbidden to look on, speak to, or have any contact with his wife's mother. One early informant told an ethnologist that "the mother of the wife is the cause of all domestic trouble and is a woman to be shunned. The Apache believe that if a man looks at his mother-in-law he will become blind."[2] This almost certainly overstates the case, however, for most avoidance relationships were carried on in respect and deference.

Although the majority of Apache men never kept more than one wife at a time, it was permissible for him to take others. About the only restriction was that he not take a second wife unless he had the means to support her, which frequently meant that a new wife was not taken until several years after the first. A man with more than one wife could house them in the same wickiup or allow them to establish separate households. Four wives was about the limit for a Chiricahua man, but among the more stable and agricultural Western Apaches, a man might be able to support more as he got older and wealthier. A man with many wives was considered fair game for good-natured joking, but not ridicule. In the case of one elderly White Mountain man, his friends sparred with him whenever he appeared dressed up, saying that he must be after another woman. To these he retorted with a twinkle, "The time was when I visited all six wickiups every night, but now I only visit four. I am getting old."[3]

If a man did desire a second wife, the rule followed was that of sororal polygyny, the practice of choosing the new wife from among the first wife's sisters or female cousins. (If an unmarried girl did not like her brother-in-law whom she might have to marry, she could discourage him by requesting, at the time of the first marriage, an avoidance relationship similar to that he owed her mother, or by requesting that he speak to her only in special polite speech forms, which he was then virtually bound to do.) If a wife's family had no more available women to marry off, a husband was still expected to seek their permission before marrying outside the family. The earlier enthnologists sometimes attributed the Apache man's adherence to sororal polygyny to his baser instincts, but the fact was that the obligations a man assumed to his wife's family were so involved that his life was much simplified by owing all his duties to the same group. The family ties of a man with three or four unrelated wives were soon in chaos. If the new wife was in fact chosen from among the existing in-laws, the husband was required to give no further bride presents to her parents. There was no custom of "ranking" wives into a pecking order, but terms of address within a polygynous marriage were exact. Children of the first wife addressed the second wife, if she were their mother's sister, as aunt. Wives from outside the mother's own family were addressed as stepmother.

Marital infidelity was discouraged, but its existence was recognized in a practical way; the first adulterer, of course, was Coyote, and men were believed doomed to repeat the sins and follies that were first his. A number—indeed, a disproportionate number—of stories in the Coyote cycle concern his ceaseless efforts to have sex.

Coyote was going around.

He came to this camp of other Coyotes. He saw one Coyote Woman working outside a wickiup. He said, "Where is your husband?"

This Coyote Woman said, "He is out hunting."

Coyote was hanging around there, talking. Finally they went into the wickiup together. Pretty soon the husband came home with some meat. He heard them in there in the wickiup. Coyote was saying, "Is this good?"

She said, "Yes, this is good."

Coyote said, "Is that good?"

She said, "Oh, that is good."

Coyote Woman's husband got mad and threw the meat over by the fire. "Let's see what is so good!" he said. He took out his gun and ran in there and caught them. He said, "All right. You two sit over there." He was ordering them around. He had them covered with his gun. "Old man, I'm going to let you see what is good. She is going to put four little rocks in the fire and let them get hot. She is going to dip them in tallow and you are going to eat them. If you live through that, you can have everything. I will leave and never come back." He told her, "Go on, heat those rocks. Hurry up!"

When the first one was ready, he made Coyote swallow it. He said, "Is it good?"

Coyote said, "It is very good." He said to himself, "I am not afraid. I am a di-yin. I have lots of power!"

When the second one was ready, Coyote Woman's husband made him eat it. He said, "Is this one good?"

Coyote said, "This one is good, too." Then he told himself, "I am a di-yin."

When the third one was ready, Coyote Woman's husband said, "Is that good?"

Coyote said, "That is good." To himself he said, "Well, I used to be a di-yin." His face was getting a little funny.

When the fourth one was ready, the husband said, "Is it good?"

Coyote looked at him and fell over dead. This Coyote told his wife, "Take him out away. He's trash. Throw him over the cliff."

She did as she was told. When she came back she looked as if she had been crying. He got mad and said, "Were you crying for him?"

She said, "No, I ran into a branch."

He got out his knife. "You come over here. Hurry up! I'm going to cut your nose off! That will fix you!"

Coyote Woman ran over to her mother's, where he couldn't follow. She hid out there a long time.

I am talking about fruit.[4]

It was true that an Apache husband tended to be quite jealous, and severe with his wife when he believed her guilty of wrongdoing. He might beat her, for instance, if she failed to destroy her maiden hair bow, or if he caught her participating in a social dance. The worst punishment she faced was the husband's right to slit off her nose if she committed adultery. The white-eyes were horrified to discover the practice, but Apaches held their women's virtue in such esteem that guilty women were thought to have gotten their due. Unfortunately, many husbands tended to be overly jealous, and when this trait was reinforced by the influence of too much tizwin, it resulted in there being a good many more "cut-nose squaws" than actual adulteresses. When the military authorities banned the practice during the reservation days, a great deal of trouble ensued over what the Apaches—the men and the elderly, anyway—considered an unreasonable infringement of a just procedure. (Often, too, there was pressure exerted by a husband's family to be severe with his wife, as a matter of preserving the family honor.)

Wronged women had fewer alternatives. Some Apaches believed that the blue-green algae of the genus *Nostoc*, when given in potion, reduced a spouse's proclivity to philander. Very rarely, a rightfully jealous wife would kill her husband, usually as he slept, without community or affinal punishment, but no one would ever marry her subsequently. The only sensible recourse was divorce.

An Apache divorce involved no more procedure than the ceasing of cohabitation. There did not have to be agreement between husband and wife in the matter; the decision of one was enough. Although the wife could have some difficulty if the husband attempted to hold her by force, an escape was usually easy to engineer because her family lived in the immediate vicinity and she undoubtedly would have told them of marital trouble beforehand and sought counseling from them. A wife's family, however, usually advised against separation when possible, because the son-in-law was a provider within their economic unit. The community was much slower to recognize a divorce when children were involved, and occasionally the leaders and headmen would exert their influence to effect a reconciliation. If the couple were adamant, babies invariably stayed with their mother, as did small children, usually. The father, particularly if he was of an influential family, or if he accused the wife of injurious conduct, could claim older children, especially sons. Both events served to increase further the economic burden on the woman's family, although at the time of divorce the woman did keep all her personal property. This included the wickiup she had made and her household utensils—in short, virtually everything except her husband's war gear and other personal belongings. Once a man was divorced he owed his wife's family no more duty or responsibility, although he did continue the avoidance and respect relationships where they were present.

Long time ago they say.

This Coyote was having a hard time with his wife. They were fighting all the time. Her family were all against him. She got them on her side.

One day Coyote had enough. "I'm going to live somewhere else," he said. But he decided to get even first. He told his wife, "I am hungry for a rabbit. I am going hunting."

His wife said, "You are a grown man. You shouldn't hunt rabbits. That is for women and children. Maybe I'll tell my family about it so they can laugh at you."

But he left anyway. He was only gone a little bit when she heard him call her. She went outside. He was just out of sight in the brush. He said, "Why, here is a rabbit in this hollow log, right here. I can't reach him. Go get your mother! She has little bony arms and she can reach in and catch him. Hurry up! This is woman's work, anyway. I'll go over here where I can't see her."

His wife said, "All right."

Coyote's mother-in-law came over, and Coyote covered his head and went into some bushes. She bent down and started reaching into that hollow log. She got about halfway in, and all at once Coyote ran over and pushed her and she got stuck. Right there he lifted up her dress and had intercourse with her.

She was calling out, but she was inside the log and no one could hear. When Coyote was through he went home. He told his wife, "That rabbit got away."

Later, Coyote's wife heard what had happened and questioned him about it.

Coyote told her, "You talk like a witch! I never looked at your mother! I never saw her!"

Coyote's wife said, "Somebody did something to her while she was in that log."

Coyote said, "You people are witches! I'm leaving here." He packed up and left, and never went back, but he was satisfied.
I am talking about fruit.[5]

The lack of formality attached to divorce did not lessen its seriousness. Moral standards remained high, and the social pressure against divorce was sufficient to guarantee that it was not undertaken flippantly. Women, especially, who had a record of marital trouble were not well thought of by the community. Because of the close supervision of maidens, it was usually the divorcees who provided the sexual initiation of adolescent boys. The word for divorcee, bi-zhahn, had itself an unsavory connotation (its fuller expression meant "already-used woman"), and not many prominent men were willing to risk marriage to a woman who had been married before. However, the institution of marriage was so important to the Apaches for its spiritual and practical aspects that if a bi-zhahn wished to remarry, she could almost always come up with some man desperate for a wife to keep house. Indeed, it was said that a few young men, who had never been married before, preferred to wed bi-zhahn for their greater experience at camp labor—not to mention lovemaking—and the lads wished to spare themselves that lengthy period of gnawing embarrassment and ambiguity and self-consciousness that was part of a conventional courtship, by settling down as quickly and matter-of-factly as possible.

Although the most common cause of divorce was probably infidelity, other offenses qualified. Excessive gambling or brutality on the part of the husband could result in divorce, as could laziness, sexual incapacity, or unwillingness to perform necessary chores, by either party.

In cases where a marriage ended not in divorce but in the death of one of the partners, the customs of levirate and sororate were invoked, by which the surviving member was "bound" to the family of the deceased until a suitable remarriage with one of the deceased's kin could be arranged. In the case of a widower, he would go into deepest mourning, perhaps not even going out to hunt, while his in-laws supplied him with the necessities of living. In time, his dead wife's eldest unmarried sister would come to him, and he would have no choice but to marry her. If she did not like him, but a younger sister or female cousin did, then that woman would come to him with the sister's authority, and he would have to marry her. If none of the eligible women in the family declared for him, his economic responsibility to them ended after a period of time, perhaps a year, after which he was considered single and free to marry whom he chose. To remarry sooner than this, or to remarry before being formally freed, was a deep insult to the dead wife's memory and her family would be sure to cause trouble. The only cases where the sororate did not apply were the few men who kept more than one wife. If the general practice of sororal polygyny (sister marriage) had been followed, the husband remained in the family in any case. However, in the event that a man had a surviving wife not related to the dead wife's family, the husband's responsibility was to the surviving wife. If over a period of time a man was widowed by the deaths of unrelated wives, neither family had a claim on him.

The same kinds of rules applied to a widow's obligation to her husband's brothers and male cousins. The widowed woman continued to live with her own family, but the selection of a new mate was the right of the husband's family, unless there was an indication that no other men in the family wanted to marry her.

The advantages of levirate/sororate adherence were that it provided for continuity of not just the immediate family, but the extended family as well, and minimized the effect on the children of their temporary orphanage.

Unlike some Indian tribes, the Apaches never found a niche in their society for sexual deviation. Because incest and perversion were attributed to witches, male homosexuals, when found out, were accused of witchcraft and usually killed. However, if a man merely showed effeminate tendencies—staying with women, playing too much at the stave game, taking no part in raids or the hoop-and-pole game—he was just laughed at. He was not considered dangerous or a witch unless he actually made a sexual advance on another man; thus a considerable distinction was recognized between homosexual tendencies and overt acts. Homosexuality was also forbidden to women, but very late in the reservation period women who lived together were not unduly hounded if they had no families to shame. Otherwise, for a woman to show interest in masculine activities such as riding and shooting was considered a desirable trait, if not carried to excess. Because of the narrow margin of existence, for a woman to be able to ride well, shoot straight, and run with stamina gave her a better chance of survival than one completely dependent on her husband or relatives. In very rare cases a woman, usually one who knew a power, took full part in masculine activities and even raided and fought with as much courage and cunning as the men; an unmarried sister of the chief Victorio, named Lozen, comes to mind. However, such behavior was accepted as spiritually motivated, and not a matter of sexuality.

Male informants to early twentieth-century ethnologists were unanimous in their conviction that Apache men never masturbated; the thought was horrifying. However, some of the Apache informants had heard that a few single women abused themselves with dildos made from the spongy inner tissue of cactus. Women could seldom be coaxed into discussing such things.

This couple were living together. They had no children, and didn't seem to be very happy, but nobody said anything. The other people around noticed this woman was gone a lot from her camp when her husband was out hunting.

A couple of times he came back earlier than usual and noticed his wife was not around. He asked around and the other people said, "She goes up in the brush over there. We don't know what she does."

One day he followed her. He saw her go into the brush, and she went to this place and squatted down. She was moaning and going up and down a little. Finally she got up and shook her dress down. Then she left.

He went over to where she had been. She had a little cactus with the skin and thorns cut off. It was like a penis coming out of the ground, that was how she had cut it. "Why, she's no good," he said.

This man took out his knife and almost cut it off at the ground. He just left it standing by a little. Then he went home. He didn't say anything to his wife.

The next day she went to the brush and that cactus broke off in there. When she got home she told her husband she was sick but wouldn't talk about it.

This woman couldn't urinate and began to bloat up. Finally she had to tell him about it.

He sent for an old di-yin to help her. He put a little hook up in her and pulled it out. When he did, her urine went all over and she was very sick, but got better. Her husband said, "I ought to kill you, but I have pity for you. I don't want to see you again. We're not married anymore. You better go live someplace else."

He could have killed her if he wanted. That's how we used to do.[6]

In general, the personal shyness of the Life-way left the Apaches sexually diffident and unsophisticated. It was not unknown for even a married man to admit he did not know the names of all a woman's parts; those who did know them, and talked about them, were considered boors unfit for polite company.

Courtship and Marriage:
NOTES

1. This version of the smoothing of Vulva Woman is the Chiricahua. See Opler, "Myths and Legends of the Chiricahua Apache Indians," p. 70. The Western Apache telling of it is, predictably, more detailed, more intricately tied into a larger cycle, and more fraught with religiously symbolic overtones.

2. Reagan, "Notes on Indians of the Fort Apache Region," p. 301.

3. Goodwin, *Social Organization of the Western Apache*, p. 352.

4. Elements of this myth are common to all five Apache tribes. See God-

dard, "Myths and Tales from the San Carlos Apache," p. 68; Goddard, "Myths and Tales from the White Mountain Apache," p. 132; Opler, "Myths and Tales of the Chiricahua Apache Indians," pp. 63–64; Goddard, "Jicarilla Apache Texts," p. 224; Opler, "Myths and Tales of the Jicarilla Apache Indians," p. 288; Opler, "Myths and Legends of the Lipan Apache Indians," pp. 126, 130. The element was also present in the Navajo mythology.

5. I have taken the liberty of elaborating on some elements of this tale to make them explicit to a primarily white readership, where they would not need be pointed out to Apaches. See Opler, "Myths and Tales of the Chiricahua Apache Indians," pp. 40–41; and Opler, "Myths and Tales of the Jicarilla Apache Indians," pp. 313–14.

6. Sexual stimulation by means of cactus was an element more common to Navajo mythology than Apache. Cf. Opler, "Myths and Tales of the Chiricahua Apache Indians," p. 89; and Opler, "Myths and Tales of the Jicarilla Apache Indians," pp. 369–70.

The Social Order

Social relations between Apache tribes and among the divisions of each tribe were, curiously, shaped almost as much by aloofness and hauteur as by any feeling of confederation. While there was a recognition that all people among the Tin-ne-áh were more alike than outsiders, ethnocentric snobbishness had important local applications in deciding to whom duties were owed or how much respect need be shown. Among the Western Apaches the Tonto group were probably the most insular, but the bands of the Cibicue group felt isolated as well. "The people living here on the Cibicue, and [the other Cibicue bands] are all like one people," said one. "It is just as if we were Americans and the rest of these Apaches around us were foreigners."[1] Although outwardly identical even to knowledgeable whites, Western Apaches could tell at a glance what group one belonged to by the slightest variations in clothing or mannerism, and each group considered itself a bit pre-eminent among the others. The White Mountain Apaches, for instance, considered themselves superior to the Tontos, as expressed in one of their myths, that "Long, long ago our people were one of many living on this earth. [Yusn] gave us our language and culture before all the other people. That is why we have everything there is . . . To the Tontos he did not give all—only about half what we received from him. That is the reason their voices are small and that they eat all kinds of things—hawks, coyotes, lizards—that we cannot eat because we would get sick."[2] (The Tontos were also looked down upon by the Chiricahuas, whose name for them was bìnì-é-diné: People Without Minds, which could likely be the source of their Spanish name, Tonto, or fools.)

The lack of close-knit feeling among the different groups of Western Apaches was, however, probably more than made up for by the complicated relationships that existed between each individual and other members of his clan. The clans were briefly introduced in the section on agriculture, for their having originated at the settlement of the early farming plots. They came to be thought of as a second kind of family apart from blood kin, complete with family ties and duties to help in revenge raids, etc. Eventually there came to be sixty of the clans, each taking its name from either a physical feature at or near the aboriginal farming plot or a unique trait of the clan. One of the most important clans, for instance, that of the chief Diablo, was named for Odart Mountain near the head of Bonita Creek, nadotsusn: Slender Peak Standing Up People.

Since clans were considered a second kind of family, marriage within the same clan was forbidden as incestuous. Each clan was considered to be closely related to a few others, and intermarriage was likewise impossible, although the rule was not strictly kept as more distant relationships became indistinct. Western Apache clanship was traced matrilineally; therefore a man always remained a member of his mother's clan, while his children were members of his wife's clan. Since residence was matrilocal and there was frequent intermarriage between different groups, clans in time came to crosscut group boundaries as readily as they crosscut blood ties. Thus each individual person was centered precisely in a bewildering constellation of group, family, and clan ties and duties. Relation by clanship was so complicated that a girl in search of a husband had to rely on elderly relatives for determination of who was eligible. (For instance, a girl of the ndi-nde-zn [Tall People] clan living among the White Mountains group could not marry into the duc-do-e [Flies in Their Soup People] clan or be-iltsohn [Made Yellow People] of the Cibicues, nor the tcilda-ditl-uge [Bushes Sloping up Growing Thickly People] of the San Carlos.) Apaches who had reached the age at which they could sit for hours and reminisce to each other about their relatives took great delight in discovering suddenly that they were some way related to someone they had known all their lives. For present purposes, it can be generalized that a person owed the same duties to his clan relatives as he did to his blood relatives, only to a somewhat lesser degree.[3]

Aside from clanship there were other, lesser, ways of exhibiting the closeness of a relationship between two bands, or within a community. The Apaches made an important distinction between gift giving and actual commerce or bartering. Trade as such was carried on only with people unlike themselves, not of the Tin-ne-áh. In fact, the presence or absence of commerce between two groups was sometimes used by early ethnologists to help determine the degree of kinship felt; with people considered to be like themselves the Apaches exchanged gifts. Within a given community, those relationships that were regarded as special—for instance, that between a woman and the older one who had attended her at her Puberty Ceremony—were marked by an increased exchange of presents. The gift ethic had a much wider application than this, however, and even unrelated members of a community exchanged presents. This had its practical side, as commerce within a group would have required some specialization of labor, which was known in only a very few situations, and then only where someone had acquired a particular skill. Of course, gifts were given in the surety that others would be received. For generosity to be repaid in kind was the social norm, and the importance of personal ownership was de-emphasized to the extent that a free flow of wealth was virtually assured. Selfish people were ridiculed. One's social prestige hinged largely upon his generosity, and he knew his friends would aid him when he needed something. In this attitude, to be ashamed to accept a gift was taken as an indication of worthlessness, and an indication that the generosity would not be repaid. On any acceptance it was implicit that the beneficiary was under obligation to the giver until the gift was repaid, though immediacy was not important. To give without asking a return was considered comely, but generous people seldom suffered.

In fact, a reputation for generosity was a cardinal element of being considered for a position of leadership. Although every man was born with an identifiable social situation, if he exhibited bravery, skill, good judgment, fairness, and generosity, he could rise to become a leader; even some Mexican captives adopted into a tribe attained a measure of influence. If a man came from an important family he was expected to maintain their standards, but even a lowborn man was required to conduct himself with socially acceptable restraint and wisdom if he wanted to be a leader. Acquisition of wealth (by industry, not by greed) was helpful in rising to leadership, particularly to a man who started off poor, as was a good marriage to an influential family. It follows, then, that there was never any one pre-eminent chief over all of a tribe of Apaches. Each extended family was steered by its patriarch, who was followed with the consensus of the family; government of a local group was by a council of the heads of extended families, of whom one was generally acknowledged the most capable leader. He was then considered a *nantan*: chief, as it were, of the local group. The wisest and most successful leaders of the local groups could, in turn, rise to influence a still wider circle of people. At times, dominating and charismatic personalities could command the unanimity of almost an entire band; Mangas Coloradas of the Tci-he-nde Mimbres (the Eastern Chiricahuas) was such a one. Usually, however, there were at least a few leaders to choose from of approximately equal stature; among the Mimbres after the death of Mangas, most people followed the lead of Victorio, but some followed Nana and some Loco.

At council meetings of the local groups the acknowledged leader more or less presided. Of slightly less importance were men who were distinguished for wealth, bravery, and wisdom, and also important di-yins. It was the leader's responsibility to decide a question, but he always gave careful weight to the opinions expressed by others, not only for their intrinsic merit, but because he knew his position depended on their confidence in him. Only seldom would a leader decide an issue against the advice of a majority of his headmen. (Women were usually permitted to attend councils, but were silent unless they had something they considered of great importance to say.) The rule of leadership by ability was strongly enforced. Chieftainship was hereditary only insofar as the son fulfilled the promise of his birth; if he proved not to be the ablest leader, others supplanted him. This was very possibly the fate of Mangus, the son of Mangas Coloradas, who was never able to keep more than a small following. And, just as one's personal power and ability to lead in battle waned with age, so did the chiefs begin to lose their influence with advancing years and infirmity. Usually this happened gradually and willingly, often with the old man himself suggesting a replacement. He might then retire to enjoy a position of respect as family head and concern himself with lesser affairs of the camp.

For anyone aspiring to leadership it was imperative that he be able to speak gracefully and effectively, not only in council but in casual conversation as well.

Greetings were preferably quiet and dignified; rowdiness at seeing someone after a long absence was considered boorish. However, loneliness for absent friends and relatives was keenly felt, and there were special ceremonies to relieve it, such as ritually placing a basket four times over the head. Relatives or close friends reunited after a lengthy or harrowing separation might hold each other quietly for several seconds before any talking began.[4]

Considerable restraint governed the use of personal names in conversation or reference. Children were taught early on never to address a person by his given name except in the most earnest gravity, personal grief, solemnity, or mortal danger. A request accompanied by use of the proper name could not be refused unless it asked the physically impossible, and even in that case it was likely to be the person unable to comply who was ashamed more than the petitioner. A di-yin who would otherwise refuse to treat a patient could be compelled to by calling him by his name. In battle a warrior who was in danger of being left to the enemy could get help by calling on a companion by name. It followed, then, that to invoke a person's name flippantly or in derision was a serious insult and likely to result in a fight.

In everyday speech a person was called by his relationship to the speaker, or some other identifying term. The given name was also avoided in third-person reference, and often great trouble was taken to arrive at some characterization. Nicknames were used, frequently of a humorous or teasing nature, but never where the nicknamed persons could hear them. For casual meetings on a path or about camp there were no general expressions of greeting equivalent to, say, the English "Good morning," and it was up to the individual to open conversation with a witty remark or question. Small talk and gossip were discouraged, but as in any society, trade in them was active.

Use of the term *Ašoog'd* (thank you) was restricted to situations where the benefit conferred was extraordinary and beyond what one could have expected. A small gift might be acknowledged in a small way ("Yes, we can use some meat," for instance), and it was acceptable to receive it without any remark at all. *Ašoog'd* was a serious professing of gratitude and beholdenness to the giver, and was never used as perfunctory politeness. This was another of the many facets of the Life-way that left whites with the impression that Apaches were sullen and resentful, when in most cases nothing was further from the truth.

Hand and arm gestures were important in speaking, especially in a group. To indicate a particular person or object, a speaker might incline his head; pointing with the hand was impolite and denoted exceptional emphasis or disapproval. However, to gesture with two fingers at a person when he wasn't looking indicated to the company that the speaker either had been playing or was about to play a joke on him. A wink accomplished much the same purpose. Outrageous requests could be made of a person by first sticking out one's tongue at the intended butt of the joke, when he could not see it, to tip off the others that a joke was being initiated. It was not unheard of for a serious request to be masked in this manner to avoid the embarrassment of being refused. To speak or listen with the hands placed on the hips indicated that the conversation was being taken in jest. This was most frequently done by the speaker in mock scolding, but when he found himself confronted with a like gesture it meant he was carrying the joke too far. The akimbo stance was also used to deflate the arguments of one giving unwanted advice, and to mime the conduct of conceited people. Amazement or dumbfounding was denoted by the common gesture of clapping the hand over the mouth.

An Apache who wanted respect was careful not to indulge in vices or crude behavior, but the community tolerated moderate personal flaws like disagreeability. Greed, of course, was not respected, but perhaps the worst trait one could exhibit was indolence. Within a household a woman's jobs were so specifically hers that if she were slow to make utensils or gather wood, the husband would not complain as long as she managed adequately. Somewhat more pressure was on the men, as they were expected to provide meat and booty to the extended family as well. In either case, chronic and telling dereliction could bring about pressure from either side of the family for a divorce. In the cases of people or family units who were lazy and contributed less than their share of a group's income, they were usually supported in part by gifts from the extended family. Such charity, however, was accompanied by advice, exhortation, or scolding, and the social pressure for all to contribute to the extent of their ability was great enough that better behavior generally resulted. Incorrigible spongers were, curiously, not driven from the group, but neither were they respected. Others ridiculed them mercilessly with comments or even nicknames like Feces Jutting Out,[5] implying that one was too lazy even to wipe himself.

The Social Order:
NOTES

1. Goodwin, *Social Organization of the Western Apache*, p. 8.
2. Ibid.
3. Grenville Goodwin probably did more than any other white man to explain the mysteries of Apache kinship. See ibid., Appendices E, F, and G, pp. 588–629.
4. Bleeker, *Apache Indians*, p. 82.
5. Opler, *An Apache Life-way*, p. 465.

They Have a Big Time

By late in the reservation period, social dances were held without needing any particular excuse. Among the Western Apaches there were two kinds. One was similar to the Puberty Dance, except there was no particular celebrant. The more common was a Wheel Dance where the single women could choose their partners. A sizable fire was lit in the middle of the dancing area, and on the west of it were the drummers, singers, and the men who wanted to dance. Around the edge of the area sat those who were not dancing and their families. The single women formed into pairs and made the spoked wheel around the fire; once the dance started, each pair would stride into the selection of men and a woman would tap on the shoulder the one she wanted to dance with. Though it was considered an invitation, compliance on the part of the men was mandatory, and they could be physically compelled to dance with their sponsors. Once chosen, the dancers returned to the wheel and faced each other, about a yard apart, and danced a simple time-step of a few paces forward and a few backward, so that the wheel revolved slowly. The affairs were effective social mixers lasting through the night, and a great time was had by all, except perhaps by the men who were chosen by women they didn't care for.[1]

Cooking up a batch of tizwin or tula-pah was almost a sure signal for a social gathering. The brew was prepared in substantial quantities and spoiled rapidly, so if friends were not invited over it would go to waste anyway. Known boors and troublemakers were seldom invited to parties, as a host desired to keep things as quiet as the expected revelry would allow. It was rude to attend a drinking party uninvited, although there were usually a few gate crashers, who were not turned away. A boy might begin going to tizwin parties when he was fourteen, a girl somewhat older, depending on her reputation and her parents' strictness. At the drinking fests the beer was served by the woman who had prepared it, using a single cup-dipper that was passed around the circle. The cook herself usually drank the relished "squeezings" as a reward for her trouble. Tizwin parties became something of a neutral ground in which everyday social restrictions were relaxed, and almost anybody could take license for conduct that would otherwise earn them community censure. Thus women, for instance, might take the men's place in singing and drumming, and sometimes a party ended in disorder or even a sexual orgy.

A round of telling the traditional myths and stories also provided an opportunity to get together, particularly during the long nights of winter. Indeed, the favorite myths, the Coyote cycle and those involving Snake and Bear, could only be told during this season, when the latter two entities were hibernating.

An old man, or sometimes an old woman, who was skilled in storytelling was always in demand, adding to the legends his own personal sagacity and humor, or making sly comments about those of the present company who found themselves in problems similar to those being recounted. Sometimes storytelling sessions occurred spontaneously, but more typically they were announced in advance so a crowd could gather. Just as often, a talented storyteller would be sought out with a request to tell the legends, but in any case it was assumed that the speaker would give the listeners a meal for having honored him with a chance to display his art. If, as it frequently happened, the stories continued all night, the presents were more substantial to make up for the speaker's having "robbed" his visitors of their rest. Diversion during the performance was offered by the opportunity to thump or tickle those who had dropped off to sleep. The Coyote cycle especially had the reputation for inducing drowsiness, and if one simply could not stay awake he was allowed to slumber. Some of the Coyote stories were thoroughly randy, and a thoughtful storyteller would warn his audience that he was ready to tell some "very funny stories" to give those who were in a respect relationship with each other (sweethearts, for instance) a chance to leave to avoid the embarrassment. If a raconteur were giving an especially good rendition the audience would interrupt him with verbal applause of "Ao, ao!" or other encouragement.

Most Apaches were so bashful about the performance of normal body functions that if one had to leave in the midst of a storytelling or other social gathering, some excuse was generally made to ask pardon. It was embarrassing just to walk out, because everyone would know the purpose of the errand. A common excuse for a man was to tend his horses, or for a woman, to check on the children. (No excuse was needed when two close friends were alone together without their families; one would simply say he was leaving for a minute.)

Usually there was smoking at social gatherings, especially after tobacco became more plentiful during reservation days, although boys and women were discouraged just as at other times.

Virtually all the sporting and gaming events were accompanied by wagering that in any culture but the Indian would be considered desperate. It seems understandable, therefore, that people who came to depend heavily on their gambling winnings frequently knew a power and a ceremony to help them, and these aids were a jealously guarded secret. In fact, early anthropologists working among the Apaches wrote that an Indian could eventually be coaxed into discussing any topic save two: witches, and his gambling ceremony. It was very important for a youngster to learn early the nuances and strategies of the various games, because at any given time his immediate personal wealth could depend heavily on his skill. And as befits a quick and intelligent people, even the younger children played their games with shrewdness and aplomb.

One of the favorite boys' games, for instance, was the arrow contest, using the toy weapons their fathers had made for them. One boy would shoot an arrow into a target area such as an earthen embankment, then the second would shoot, trying to touch or cross the arrow of the first. If he missed there was no consequence; if he succeeded he won the first boy's arrow. Players of this game quickly learned to shoot their worst arrows as targets to be possibly lost, and to attempt to win arrows with their best and truest-flying ones, when there was no chance of losing them.

A large portion of the adults' spare time was taken up in sports and gaming, divided between sports of physical prowess and games of chance.

The men played their own versions of the arrow contests of the boys, and also the marble games and the Heads and Tails game. Wrestling was very popular among the men, with local champions gaining some measure of renown and even contesting with the champions of other bands or groups. In one much enjoyed sport a man famed for his strength had a rawhide rope tied around his waist, with three pullers at the other end. A fourth man was called upon to sit on the wrestler and try to hold him down. Wagers were laid on whether the strong person would be able to throw his opponent, rise, and outpull the three smaller men straining to stop him. One-on-one wrestling matches began with the contestants grasping each other about the waist, after which any trick or hold could be used to throw the opponent from his feet. There were no time counts or pinning rules; once a man lost his balance and any part of him other than his feet touched the ground, he was done.

Racing, both afoot and on horseback, was popular with everybody. In the short footraces, stepped off as perhaps two hundred paces, women could compete against the men, and sometimes they won. The contestants began not from a crouch but from a braced stand, and time was kept by old men at the finish who counted. Much longer cross-country races were also held, but were less frequent. Straightaway horse races were held on the same track as the footraces. A cross-country bareback horse race was about a day's ride, but in this the women did not compete with the men, although they did race among themselves.

The Chiricahuas were noted for a wildly brutal team sport called shinny that combined the tougher elements of soccer and hockey. The object of the game was to put a wood or buckskin ball about the size of a tennis ball between the opposing team's goalposts. The goal was usually two properly spaced trees, and the playing field was up to half a mile long, of any width. As many as two dozen people of both sexes could play, evenly divided into teams. Each player carried a stick about a yard long with a crook at the end, to strike the ball, and sometimes a straight one to protect himself from the whacks of his opponents. The ball could be hit with the stick or also kicked to advance it, but not touched with the hand. There were no fouls, penalties, or time periods. Each goal counted as one point and the play proceeded continuously until one side gave up. The issue of what team defended which goal was decided by the equivalent of a coin toss, using a flat stone wet on one side and dry on the other. Play was begun with a face-off in the center of the field, with each of two representatives trying to bat the ball to his own players.[2]

A much less rowdy sport was similar to the white man's horseshoe throwing contests. A small hole was dug at either end of a playing field about thirty paces long. Each contestant had two stones, slightly smaller than the holes. The object was to stand at one end of the field and cast one's rocks into the hole at the other end. To do so successfully with both stones netted the player ten points; with one stone, four points. If both players put one stone in the hole, they canceled each other, without score. If one player put both his stones in the hole and his opponent only one, he got four points. If both players threw perfectly in one turn, the last to throw netted the four points. Otherwise, the rock coming nearest the hole earned one point for its owner; if both his stones were closer he got two points.

By far the most important sport played by Apache men was hoop-and-pole. Not only were women forbidden to play this sport, it was also taboo for them even to approach the grounds. The hoop-and-pole field was something of a men-only club or retreat, and if a thoughtless woman should pass nearby, the men would stop their play and hold their poles high in the air to warn her away.

In this game a small hoop somewhat more than a foot in diameter was rolled down a sort of alley, and just as it was about to fall, each of the two contestants slid his long, tapering pole after it in such a fashion as to cause the hoop to fall on the butt end of the piece. Both the hoop and the poles were notched with point markers, and a player accrued points based upon how many pole notches were within the hoop and how many knots on the hoop's crosspiece were over the pole. The playing field was about thirty feet long, aligned east to west, with a rock at either end to mark the boundary, and a third stone to mark the center. The area was carpeted with a smooth layer of grass or pine needles so the hoop would roll evenly. Play began from the center stone, first to the east, then the west; the hoop was rolled underhanded toward the end of the field, where there was a ridge of grass. Once the hoop bounced over this and began to wobble it was time to release the poles. Scoring varied by individual agreement, but the crosspiece of the hoop had either thirty or fifty marking knots across the distance, and there was also a fixed number of scoring notches along the rim of the hoop and on the pole butts.

It was very important for a youngster to learn skill at hoop-and-pole because huge sums were nearly always wagered on the games. Only men who knew a hoop-and-pole ceremony could make the equipment, some indication of the seriousness with which the men took this sport. Each player closely guarded his luck during a game. While play was in progress it was forbidden to walk around the field from the east. Dogs, because of their association with Coyote, were not allowed in the vicinity, and a contestant might drop out of play if another man stepped on his shadow.

The women's counterpart of the hoop-and-pole was their lively stave game, which can be loosely described as combining the merits of backgammon and to a lesser extent monopoly. The object was to advance one's counter along a circle of stones, with the number of spaces being moved in each turn decided by the throw of marked staves. To make the playing area, forty small place-marking stones were set in groups of ten in a circle on the ground, with the four gaps, called the rivers, aligned with the cardinal directions. The heavy flat rock against which the three staves were cast was in the center of the circle. The staves were six to eight inches long, fashioned out of round sticks that had been split longitudinally so that one side was flat and the other round. The flat side was usually painted or striped red or black, the round side, yellow or white. Although the scoring varied by agreement in each game, in most cases a stave throw in which all landed flat side down netted a move of ten spaces; all flat side up, five spaces; two flat sides up, three; one flat side up, one or two. If moving a counter ended in one of the gaps, or rivers, the player had to go back to the beginning. When only two women or two teams were in the contest, the counters were moved in opposite directions; if several were competing individually all the counters moved in the same direction. If one's turn landed her on a stone already occupied, the space was claimed by the newcomer and the previous holder was sent back to the start. When this happened in team play, two partners could occupy the same space. A woman or team who got to move ten stones on one throw automatically got a second turn. Numerous variants of this basic game existed;

sometimes, although not frequently, the men joined the women in a mixed competition of the stave game, but it was a decidedly feminine sport and men who played it too often were criticized.

Long time ago they say.

Coyote was watching some Prairie Dog Young Women playing at staves. They were very pretty and he wanted one of them. That's the way he was. Some men are still that way, just because he was.

He got his friend Gopher and said, "See that Prairie Dog Young Woman sitting over there, the prettiest one? I want her real bad, but she wouldn't care for me at all. I want you to tunnel over there where she is sitting. Come up and make a little hole right under her."

"All right," said Gopher, and he did it.

Coyote went into the tunnel and looked up that little hole. He saw her sitting there and got excited. When his penis got hard he pushed it through the hole to make love to her.

This Prairie Dog Young Woman was sitting there playing at staves, when she felt something bumping against her underneath. She looked down and saw what it was going up and down.

Prairie Dog Young Woman got the big flat rock from the middle of the stave circle and dropped it on Coyote's penis. "Do it with this rock," she said, and they all ran away.

I am talking about fruit.[3]

Another of the important recreational sports, and one which, curiously, was nearly always played just for fun and exempted from betting, was called slap-the-ball, and it was especially popular among the Chiricahuas. Although from a simple description it appears to be a derivative of the pindahs' baseball, it was apparently known and played long before baseball was invented. The playing field was in the shape of a diamond perhaps sixty paces square. At the base of the diamond a large circle was drawn on the ground, big enough to contain all the members of one team. The other three bases were just large enough to hold three or four players. Slap-the-ball was informal enough that the size of the field and the competing teams could be varied by agreement, but it required at least four on a team to make a good, lively contest. The object of the game was for as many runners as possible from the slapping team to make a complete circuit of the bases before one of their number could be hit with the ball by an opponent.

The contest began with a combination of the wet-or-dry rock toss and face-off. The opposing teams lined up facing each other, and the ball, just large enough to fit comfortably in the palm of the hand and fashioned of soft buckskin stuffed with grass, was rolled between them. As this was done the stone was tossed in the air and one man called it wet or dry. If he guessed correctly, all his team dashed for the big circle, hoping to get there before one of the opposition could pick up the ball, throw it, and hit one of them with it. If they all succeeded in getting into the circle, they were ready to play. If one of them were hit, the other team tried to get into the circle before one of the first team could get to the ball and hit back. The scramble went on until one team was safely in the circle.

The leader of the team not in the circle, which was to play defense, spaced his men around the field. One of them, the pitcher, stood before the big circle and tossed the ball into the opposing players. If one of the batting team were hit while out of the circle it counted as an out, but usually the ball was tossed underhanded into the circle, where one of the men batted it with his open hand. It was against the rules to catch the ball and throw it, but some men became so skilled at this form of cheating they were difficult to call. A struck ball had to go forward into the defending players to count as a hit. The best description of play was from a Chiricahua informant: "I am the first man to hit it, say. I try to place the ball so that I can get to the first circle before getting hit. If I get hit by a man on the other side who picks it up and throws it at me before I get to the first circle, as soon as I'm hit I run for the ball. My team, as soon as they see me get hit, run out and try to help me. The other team, as soon as I am hit, run for the big circle. If I or one of my men gets the ball and hits one of them before he gets in the circle, my side is still in and can keep on batting.

"If I hit it up high in the air and a fellow on the other team gets under it before it hits the ground, he can hit it away, and all on his side run for the big circle. . . .

"But, if I hit it and make the first little circle, my second man is up. The pitcher watches me and tries to hit me when I am out of the circle. If my man hits it and someone on the other side standing near the circle where I am gets it, I do not have to run. More than one can get in one circle. . . ."[4] If the first circle got filled up with none left to slap the ball, the pitcher would stand in his place and toss the ball up in the air until one of the slappers took a chance and ran to the second circle. Each man to make a complete circuit scored a point for his side. Play of slap-the-ball might continue for hours, until it was called off by mutual consent and exhaustion.

One of the most important of the sedentary games was played only in winter and only at night. This was the moccasin game, the only one of the games to possess mythological significance; this was the contest that was arranged between the birds and animals near the beginning of time, to settle whether the world would be clothed in darkness. The object of the game was, first, to guess within which "moccasin" the opposing team had hidden a small bone, and second, having won the bone, to hide the bone in one's own set of containers and garner points as the opposition wrongly guessed which it was in. To begin a contest a fire was lit in the middle of a level area, and the teams took their positions on opposing sides. The bone that was to be hidden was a small, rounded one, as from the ball of an animal's socket joint. It was not hidden in actual moccasins, but rather in small hide bags or in grass-covered holes in the ground. The privilege of being the first team to hide the bone was decided by the wet-or-dry rock toss. The first team to hide the bone concealed their moccasins behind a blanket, until they called "ready" and let it down. A representative from the other team held a striking stick, about two feet long and carved with the images of the birds who were victorious in the First Game. After making up his mind, he whacked the bag he believed contained the bone, as the hiding team sang boisterous songs about the First Game to confuse him. If he guessed the right bag, the bone was won and went over to the striker's team to hide. If, however, he guessed wrong, points were awarded the hiding team from a store of yucca-leaf counters. There were sixty-eight such counters, worth one hundred four points. Sixty-four of the counters were plain and valued at one point each; four were fringed and worth ten points apiece. If the striker missed the proper bag by one on either side, the hiders were awarded four points or counters; if he missed by two or more, the hiders got ten points. The hiding team kept possession of the bone as long as the striking team failed to guess its location. When it was finally lost, the roles were reversed and the new hiding team had a chance to win counters. All the counters awarded came from a central bundle, until this was exhausted, and then the team making faulty strikes had to pay the hiders from their own winnings. The game continued until one team had won all the counters.

Throughout the game the myth-songs were sung to confuse the opposition and bring luck upon oneself. When one team seemed on the brink of disaster they sang a song that the birds had used in the First Game, when they were about to lose, and it had saved them. Once a song had proven lucky it was continued until it lost its efficacy. The moccasin game was attended, of course, by heavy betting, with smaller side bets attending each separate move. There were endless variations of the moccasin game. In one a striker who missed the mark was allowed to try again, without relocating the bone, on something of a "double or nothing" basis; in another the hiders were permitted to conceal the bone not in the moccasins at all but on the person of one of their number, but with a penalty to be paid when they were found out.

After considerable white exposure, Apaches developed a deck of playing cards that were faced with, instead of numbers, a series of designs, symbols, and stick figures. Apaches with the time to spare became engrossed in complex games, the vagaries of which few whites were able ever to penetrate.

They Have a Big Time:
NOTES

1. Reagan, "Notes on Indians of the Fort Apache Region," p. 315.
2. Opler, *An Apache Life-way*, pp. 445–46.
3. Elements of this story are found in Opler, "Myths and Tales of the Chiricahua Apache Indians," pp. 53–54, and also his "Myths and Legends of the Lipan Apache Indians," pp. 186–89.
4. Opler, *An Apache Life-way*, pp. 446–48.

Crime and Punishment

It has seemed to be the case that in more primitive and non-technological societies, where social acceptance plays a large role in governing one's conduct, crime is less a problem than in urban, developed and acquisitive ones. So it was with the Apaches.

Whatever conflicts between individuals arose, cursing and verbal abuse were relatively rare. In mythological times, it was believed, whatever one person wished for another, would come true, whether good or evil, and belief in the power of verbalism persisted. There were, of course, general expletives and imprecations, one of the more severe of which was the exclamation "Knife and awl!" Although no exact meaning of the phrase is known, it had the force of a vulgarity and a wife might be scandalized to hear her husband utter it.

To tell a person he was no man or not any good was a serious pronouncement, and even more so was to tell one to his face that he was "trashy." To use anything stronger than these might result in the death of one of the disputants. To tell someone to go to the underworld, or to wish verbally his death, implied a witch-power to bring about the result, and was not done. An exclamation concerning one's body waste was also very bad, but by far the worst thing a man could be called was the product of witches. Part of the nature of witches was incestuous perversion, and to call a man the son of witches would certainly, among the Chiricahuas, result in the abused party hissing the ultimate acceptance of a challenge: "*Ahagahe!*" After that was said, one of the two would shortly be dead or severely beaten.

A woman had resort to a particular insult when she was exasperated beyond reconciliation. Toward the scorned party she would extend her right fist, with the thumb between the first and second fingers. Suddenly she would fling the fingers open, exclaiming, "Smell this!" The action had a sexual connotation of the worst and most demoralizing kind.

In a society as materially simple as the Apache was, where many chattels either changed hands frequently by gift or wager, or were easily manufactured for oneself, theft was seldom a problem. It was also true that the lack of mass production resulted in most goods being easily identified as to ownership, so stolen property could not be openly used, anyway. In cases where theft was found out, no more serious action was taken than forcing the burglar to return the goods to the owner. He was also talked about and ridiculed, and was open to suspicion of being a witch. It was not unknown, however, especially among the Western Apaches, for a man who stole and butchered another's stock, to be killed by the owner when guilt was proved.

Animals were also sometimes subject to punishment. According to one anthropologist, stock animals that trampled a field were marked as rogues by cutting off their ears.[1]

Punishment of a murderer was the responsibility of the victim's family; there was no socially imposed punishment. Typically this meant insistence on the death of the murderer, although the option rested with the family to settle for less—either corporal punishment, or a payment of valuable goods. After a murder the killer's family had three choices. First, if he had been a chronic troublemaker, they could either hand him over or kill him themselves. If either of these were done, the victim's family had no further claim against them. Second, they could allow or help him to escape until a money payment could be arranged. The victim's family was not bound to accept such a payment, and if they refused it, the murderer's family faced the threat of a revenge murder by the victim's relatives. Third, they could side with their man and defy the victim's family, in which case an extended blood feud might result. Such feuds were rare, however, because the groups' leaders would step in and exercise their considerable influence to prevent further bloodshed.

If a property settlement were first refused, there remained one plea for clemency that was hard to ignore, that in which the murderer's mother or another female relative stood before the victim's family, calling them by their names and begging for mercy while stripping herself naked and groveling.

Habitual criminality was often dealt with by banishment; and once the culprit had been told that he "had better go live someplace else," word spread effectively enough that he usually could not take up residence in any nearby camp. Such a man became a loner in the wilderness, existing as a predatory highwayman against his own race until, if he became troublesome enough, he was hunted down and killed by an execution squad sent to dispatch him. A few such men gained considerable local notoriety as a constant threat to travelers through their haunts, and were held up as a kind of bogey to little children. One such outlaw, named Na-de-gah-ah, terrorized the countryside around Fort Apache for years until he was caught and killed by his own people. His career began in 1881, when he murdered another Apache for his horse, which was particularly fine. Na-de-gah-ah's relatives, no doubt fearing a revenge killing, chased him off and sent for the Apache army scouts, who captured him. He escaped prison in the spring of 1882, killing a scout who was his kinsman and taking his gun and ammunition. He hid out in the mountains around Fort Apache for three years, supporting himself on plunder taken from whites and Apaches alike. In 1885, Indians living in his territory held a dance in the hope that he would come down to attend; he did, and was taken prisoner by scouts concealed in surrounding brush. He escaped again soon after, again killing his guard. A short time later, however, he showed up at a round of storytelling; a middle-aged woman recognized him and held him down until her husband could get his gun and shoot him.

Virtually all the Apaches agreed that the killing of Na-de-gah-ah was a service well performed, but the fear of a revenge killing from his relatives was, in spite of his worthless character, great enough that the couple responsible moved from the vicinity.[2]

This kind of criminal came to have a curiously important impact on Apache–white relations during the reservation days, for they frequently committed depredations against whites just as they did among their own kind, and those crimes were frequently blamed by the whites on Indian hostility in general. Furthermore, it was not unknown, just as was true among whites, for exiled Apache criminals to find each other in the wilds and live together in camps that were very literally dens of thieves. Sometimes large war parties had to be organized to wipe them out. It was also true during the reservation period that the question of social obedience in the rancheria sometimes paralleled the question of war or peace with the whites, as roughneck elements would sometimes leave the camp of their own choice and set up freebooting "robbers' roosts" of their own until they caused a war or were exterminated, or both. The cases of Chunz and others in 1873 and Na-tio-tish in 1881 come first to mind.

Crime and Punishment:
NOTES

1. Reagan, "Notes on the Indians of the Fort Apache Region," p. 301.
2. Betzinez, I Fought with Geronimo, pp. 126–29. See also Davis, The Truth About Geronimo, pp. 192–93.

Death, Burial, and Eternity

In the beginning everybody was to live forever and it was all right. There was no death. Maybe they never thought of it, but one day they had to make a decision about it.

Coyote did not want death in the world. He said, "I'm going to throw a stick in the river. If it sinks, people will begin to die. If it floats, it will be all right." He threw in the stick and it floated.

Then Raven said, "No, I have the say here." I don't know where he got that authority; I guess he just had it. He said, "I'm going to throw a rock in the river. If it floats, there will be no death, but if it sinks, people will begin to die." He threw in the rock and it sank right there.

That is how death got started. Now, when ravens come around we don't like it at all.[1]

As an Apache became older, he took progressively less part in camp life and duties, and the status of the elderly in society declined accordingly. It was part of the religious complex that one's personal power lessened with age. In a way, one's life-span was regarded as cyclical, and when an elderly person's mental faculties began to weaken it was said that he was returning to his childhood. Important di-yins and chiefs kept influence and were listened to with respect as long as they displayed strong minds, but aside from that, one's last years were regarded as a time of harmless folly and senility to be endured until death brought release. Not even the mighty White Mountain chief, Diablo, was spared this fate. If an elderly person lived with his family, he used the poorest clothing and bedding and ate the worst food, and his needs were tended to last. Of course, the family saw to his comfort and cared for him, but within the priorities demanded by their thin existence. This treatment of the old did not lessen family bonds or affection. It was simply accepted that younger people did harder work, and required most of the nourishment and care. The survival of the band depended on those of working age and it was only sensible that their needs receive first attention. The elderly were given light tasks to perform, and they did them ungrudgingly and the best they could within their limitations. It proved that they were still useful to the community. If an old person lived alone, he was left mostly on his own, but if, for instance, he was too ill to cook, he was fed communally.

When an elderly Apache finally became too infirm to get about on his own, he might eventually be "thrown away," or left to die. This was a practice that horrified white people, but in reality it was the most practical response to the Apache's harsh living conditions. A group's survival might depend at any moment on being able to flee a sudden attack, or spend days on the move trying to elude an enemy. The risk of collective annihilation was just too great a price to pay for carrying the elderly. Even in peacetime, extensive migrations had to be undertaken to gather seasonal foods, and camps had to be moved frequently to prevent one spot from becoming too polluted to live in. In both cases, the transportation of helpless old people was burdensome in the extreme. When an old person was "thrown away," the family usually gave him some provisions, lying that they would soon return; the old one was then left to wait for death.

Generally the elderly did not resent this practice. They knew the rules of their existence even better than the young, and they had themselves left elderly people to die. There was, to be sure, pathos in facing death in such a way, but most accepted that their life had come to its end with a grace and nobility consistent with the Life-way.

Generally, little mourning was shown for those who had lived full and lengthy lives. Except for great chiefs, where a public funeral and display of grief at the passing of a good and generous man were warranted, a very old person who died might acceptably, if he came from a poor family or had few relatives, be left in his wickiup, laid along the north wall with his head to the east, after which the dwelling was pushed in. The family then moved away from the vicinity, for the Western Apaches shared the Chiricahua view that a spirit could linger in the proximity of its demise until Owl bore it to one of the four homes for the dead.

On the other hand, enormous grief was felt at the deaths of infants or children. One of the early anthropologists to study the Western Apaches observed the funeral of a baby in particularly tragic circumstances. At the time he wrote, in 1908, authorities still referred to Apache households by the numbers on their metal census tags; it was a degrading practice and was eventually discontinued, but the account has been left intact as a brand on its time: ". . . there was a tula-pah drunk on the ridge on which D25 lived. The fourteen-day-old baby of D25 was given some of the drink by its mother and died from the effects the next day. When the writer came . . . he found D25 lying face down in the dirt in his yard. A few minutes later he saw Mrs. D25 and noticed that she was crying. He at once went to the house. The little one was still alive. A medicine man was singing over it. At 2 P.M. all hope for its recovery was abandoned and the preparation for the death feast was begun, tula-pah, etc., at several of the camps of the ridge. About sunset the baby died. As it was dying nothing out of the ordinary was done, except that ashes were sprinkled on it. For hour after hour before it died all mourned and wailed, the father, twenty-four years of age, out-wailing his wife and mother. At the death of the child, all present, both men and women, joined in the death wail, the man's mother wailing in the house, his mother-in-law outside, as she was not allowed to enter the house while her son-in-law was there . . . The next morning D25, aided by his wife, dressed their baby for the funeral. D25 then left his house so that his mother-in-law might enter and view the corpse. At about 10 A.M. . . . the corpse was taken to the hills and buried."[2]

If an infant had already been fitted into its permanent cradleboard, the most common method of burial was for him to remain in it. The parents would carry the bundle far away from the camp and hang it in a tree or bush, next to a tus jug of water to refresh the baby on its journey to the hereafter. The particular example of D25 was also evidence of the foolishness that could go on at a tula-pah or tizwin bout; the mother was doubtless quite drunk when she fed the brew to the baby, and she was probably roundly criticized for her stupidity. The serving of tula-pah after the death, however, was common, as it helped start the spirit auspiciously on its journey. In this regard it had much the same intent as the drinking at curing ceremonies, which was that all events, even the most somber, happened well if they occurred in an atmosphere of warmth and cordiality. Also demonstrated was the practice of wallowing, as the infant's father sprawled himself in the dirt. This form of distress was never widely discussed but appears to have been evenly spread among both Western Apaches and Chiricahuas.

If a child were stillborn, or died after having outgrown its cradleboard, the body was hastily buried in the normal fashion. The cradleboard, however, was mutilated with knife slashes to prevent its reuse, and strung in a tree to the east of the rancheria. To touch it or bother it ever again were under strict taboo.

Death itself was not a widely discussed subject. The Apache fear of death and the spirits of the dead discouraged talking about it in loose abstractions. When talking of the deceased, the term for "dead" was not generally used; more common was the reference "He Who Is Gone." Death was no thing to commemorate, and there were no death songs. Since Apache economy revolved about hunting, and some pets were kept in the rancherias, a child's first exposure to death was in most cases not traumatic. Adults did not explain the deaths of people to children in terms of ghosts until they were old enough to understand their awful significance, although—owing largely to the incessant warring against Mexicans—deaths and grieving were plainly and commonly seen. Indeed, Kaywaykla asserted to Eve Ball that he was seven years old before he knew that people could die of natural causes.[3]

Children were, however, instructed at a necessary time in funerary etiquette, for instance, that if one witnessed a funeral procession one must either cry and wail out of respect for the bereaved family, or else look away; it was rude just to stare. One of Morris Opler's informants recalled that when he was very small he asked his grandmother "where they were taking a dead man who was being carried away. She told me not to look . . . Then she told me that they were putting the man away; that he couldn't walk, or dance, or eat, or sing by himself anymore; that they were putting him under the ground.

"'But if they are putting him under the ground, how will he keep the dirt out of his eyes,' I asked. She explained to me that he was all fixed up so that no dirt would get in his eyes. It was the first time I had ever thought about death. I began to ask more questions of my grandmother, but she told me that he couldn't come back anymore and to stop talking about it.

"A few days later we children played funeral. We killed grasshoppers and buried them.

"I wasn't afraid until I was about seven years old. Then I learned about ghosts, and from that time on I was pretty much afraid."[4]

Once a person died it was the responsibility of his immediate family to bury the corpse. Sometimes a particularly close friend was asked to help, but it was a difficult thing to request. All family members recognized their duty to help if they were needed, although some might try to find a tactful way to avoid it if possible. Sometimes a kinsman of the deceased would travel to nearby camps and inform them of the death, and friends might gather to keep a kind of wake outside the wickiup where the preparations were being made. Here, too, tula-pah might be served to those who came in an attempt to start the spirit on an auspicious journey; if the death were of a notable person and many came, a meal could be prepared for them while they discussed the deceased's good qualities, and leading men might make consoling speeches.

Inside the wickiup, the body was washed and the hair combed out, by brothers and spouse if the deceased was a man, or by close female relatives if a woman. This varied, of course, according to who was available; about the only restriction was that a man's body could not be tended by his mother-in-law. They dressed the deceased in his best clothes and painted his face. If the death had occurred in the early morning, the funeral might be held the same day, but if not then, certainly on the day after. The man's body was wrapped in a good blanket and mounted on his horse—or his favorite horse if he had owned several—and his good possessions were loaded on. A small niche or cave in a canyon wall was the preferred grave, but a shallow depression at the base of a hill was acceptable; sometimes a grave was dug even on open ground, when that was necessary. Talk about death and funerals to early ethnologists was rare enough that accounts of customs varied widely, probably reflecting that talk between different tribes and groups about it was so rare that different practices developed at different places. A Chiricahua asserted that the body was interred with the feet to the east and head to the west; a Western Apache gave an opposite account. Both agreed that bodies were buried stretched to full length and never doubled up. In some places, bodies were removed from wickiups by cutting a hole on the east side; some simply carried them through the door. As a funeral progressed through a rancheria, those acquainted with the deceased or his family joined in the crying and wailing to show their respect; strangers turned and looked away. The place of interment was usually kept a secret by those comprising the party. Cliff graves were walled over with such skill as to prevent their accidental discovery, and hole graves were covered and weighted securely enough to prevent unearthing by scavengers. Over a period of time a dead person's kin visited the grave a few times—the good four was a common number—to see that it was undisturbed. Some groups completed a funeral by sprinkling an unbroken circle of ashes around the grave to keep the ghost from wanting to roam. Apaches who acquired the custom of firing rifle shots at funerals may have picked it up during the reservation days, from white military funerals. Some Apaches adopted the practice of returning from a burial separately, and none by the trail on which they had gone out, being careful not to look back. This was thought to prevent the ghost from wanting to follow.

The goods that were transported to the gravesite were buried with the body, and the deceased's horse was shot at or near the grave; sometimes the horse, too, was buried with the body. Back at the rancheria, the deceased's wickiup and his remaining possessions were burned, and the site abandoned. The Apaches sought to make the separation between the two worlds total, first, because the deceased's other belongings might be of use to him in the afterlife, second, because their continued presence on earth would remind the family of the death and prolong their grief, and third, because the ghost might return to punish anyone who used his goods. There was also some feeling that to continue to use a dead person's belongings implied an expectation of inheritance, or a purposeful waiting or longing for another's death, which was a horrible thought. Children whom the deceased had named might have their names changed to lessen the memory.

Among the Western Apaches, a portion of the farming plot of the deceased's clan was left fallow for up to three years, for the use of the dead.

However, one exception to the rule of destroying the deceased's personal property was food. Not only was it too precious to be wasted, but it was to a degree thought of as communal property. Just as in life a healthy man and industrious woman provided for an extended family of dependents, when one of the providers died the extra food was used, and hidden caches were dealt with similarly. When a single woman died leaving an amount of stored food, it was divided among her relatives. (Also, a warrior's shield, if he owned one, was not destroyed but passed on to a younger relative, because the shield when consecrated by a di-yin was thought to acquire a power and existence of its own.)

To show their respect to the family, non-relatives in the same camp refrained from wearing bright clothes where the bereaved could see them, and the deceased's name was not spoken again. If he had a common name, extensive euphemisms were employed for a time to keep from saying it. After a passage of years, however, it was not only permissible but quite an honor to approach a family with a request to give the deceased's name to a child or newborn. Such a request was accompanied by a substantial gift, such as a saddled horse laden with a gun and blankets.[5]

The curing ceremonies undertaken by those who had prepared the body for burial to ward off ghost sickness varied widely in their intricacy and duration. The fear of ghosts reached an extreme among the Mescaleros, but among the Western Apaches eventually evolved into little more than a ritual washing of hands.

Apache thinking about the hereafter was never unified or consistent. This is clear from the many different characterizations in the mythology, and from the irreconcilable versions offered by different informants to different researchers. The Chiricahua view of the afterlife tended to be that it existed just below the surface of the ground—hence the ease with which ghosts could return. The entrance to the underworld was through a great inverted cone of loose sand, a view perhaps acquired by observation of ant lion pits; at the bottom of the great cone was a windowlike opening to the nether region. A person who was dying was considered to be slipping down the side; one who recovered from a deep coma had successfully scrambled out of the pit. Some, a very few, sank so far down that they could look into the underworld, and upon their recovery tell about it. Said one who had looked in and returned, "The same ways we have here are carried on down there too. . . . The people remain the same age as they were when they died. There is no sickness, death, pain, or sorrow there. Those who were good and those who were bad are down there together . . . It is just as though everything is transferred to a different country."[6]

Other Apaches' concepts of the hereafter differed somewhat from the Chiricahua. The Western Apaches, for instance, believed that there existed at the infinity of the four cardinal directions four separate homes for the dead, and a deceased had his choice of which to live in. These were the homes of the four demigods who helped shape the world, and who dwelt there to hold it up.

All Apaches apparently shared the belief that life was more meaningful in the hereafter, and that the ceremonies that occurred on earth occurred also on the other side. A person spent his time at what he was best at on earth, and the old life of hunting, gathering, and raiding was followed in joy—a conviction no doubt cemented by the increasing horror of reservation life, and the other aspects of Anglo-American domination that began at about the midpoint of the nineteenth century.

Death, Burial, and Eternity:
NOTES

1. These are the roles usually assigned to Coyote and Raven in the Lipan and Jicarilla versions. In the Chiricahua (Opler, "Myths and Tales of the Chiricahua Apache Indians," p. 28) and White Mountain (Goodwin, "Myths and Tales of the White Mountain Apache," pp. 177–78) tellings, the roles are reversed. In the latter, Coyote cast into the river not a stick but a hairbrush and mano tied together.

Other versions listed in French, "Comparative Notes," p. 105, include: from the Lipans, Opler, "Myths and Legends of the Lipan Apache Indians," pp. 38–39. From the Jicarillas, Goddard, "Jicarilla Apache Texts," p. 194; Opler, "Myths and Tales of the Jicarilla Apache Indians," pp. 44–47, 268; and Russell, "Myths of the Jicarilla Apache," p. 258. From the White Mountains, Goddard, "Myths and Tales from the White Mountain Apache," p. 138.

2. Reagan, "Notes on the Indians of the Fort Apache Region," p. 318.

3. Kaywaykla, *In the Days of Victorio*, p. xiii.

4. Opler, *An Apache Life-way*, p. 26.

5. Goodwin, *Social Organization of the Western Apache*, p. 530.

6. Opler, *An Apache Life-way*, p. 478.

BOOK THREE

Pindah-Lickoyee

Of all the sisters born into the American union, New Mexico arrived after perhaps the most strenuous labor. During the Mexican War, effective control of the area lay with the Missouri Volunteers. Before passing on to California, General Kearny did foster a semblance of civil control, but its life ended with its governor's, William Bent, in the Taos rebellion of 1847. When peace arrived the next year and New Mexico became the 9th Military Department, governance passed from the Volunteers to regular troops under Colonel John M. Washington. Formation of a territorial government was snagged for three years by the impassioned debate in the federal Congress on the allowance of slavery in the new territory. Not until the Compromise of 1850 answered the question in the negative was a civil executive finally established.

The new possession was physically massive, including all of present-day New Mexico and Arizona (except the later Gadsden Purchase), as well as a strip along the southern borders of Colorado and Utah. Its population was about 100,000. Of the roughly 40,000 Indians, some tribes were friendly or debilitated enough to cause little concern. The principal threats to life and property were from the 2,000 Utes, 10,000 to 12,000 Navajos, and 6,000 to 8,000 Apaches. The non-Indian population of approximately 60,000 was primarily Mexican, almost entirely concentrated along and thinned out away from the Rio Grande valley.

Soldiers were few and supplies were short, but one resource that the American Government never found in short supply was promises. When General Kearny's Army of the West first invaded New Mexico in the late summer of 1846, the first settlement they occupied was Las Vegas, a frowsy adobe village at the southeastern foot of the Jicarilla-dominated Sangre de Cristo Mountains. From a plaza rooftop the commanding general addressed his new subjects, saying that the Mexican Government had never protected them from Indians. "The Apaches and Navajos come down from the mountains and carry off your sheep, and even your women,

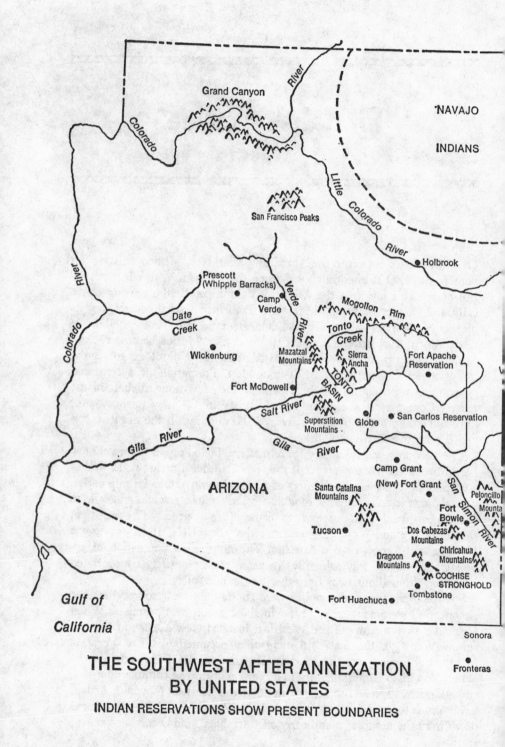

THE SOUTHWEST AFTER ANNEXATION
BY UNITED STATES

INDIAN RESERVATIONS SHOW PRESENT BOUNDARIES

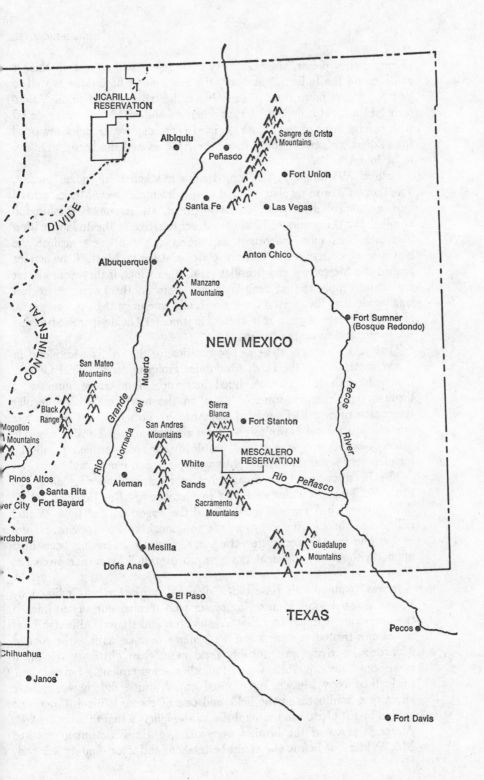

whenever they please," he said. "My government will correct all this. It will keep off the Indians."[1] Actually the army might have done as well to look to its own protection. In early November 1847, the Missouri Volunteers had not yet occupied El Paso when a band of Mescaleros made off with several head of their stock. A hard chase of seventy miles rewarded the soldiers with twenty dead oxen; the Apaches and the horses were not to be found.[2]

Colonel Washington's year-long tenure was active in Indian pursuit. The thousand or so regulars allotted to the defense of New Mexico arrived only a handful at a time, so to augment his resources Washington enrolled five companies of local volunteers to strike at the Indians within his reach. His most important expedition was northwest against the Navajos, which resulted in a minor parley and treaty. Most of the actions against the Mescaleros and Jicarillas (and other tribes, if they were hit, for few white people at that time knew one from another) were on such a small scale that they served more effectually to enrage than to cow them, and Apache depredations east of the Continental Divide increased during the spring and summer of 1849.

That year also brought new opportunities for the wilder Mescaleros in Texas, most notably the Davis Mountains group under the chief Gómez. The gold rush to California lured increasing numbers of immigrants through their country, some of them on the newly established regular stagecoach runs to El Paso from San Antonio. Fort Bliss was put on the line at the Paso del Norte to give some protection, but horrible roadside carnage—burned-out wagons and hastily dug graves—testified to all the travelers that protection by the army was spotty and inadequate.[3]

The Jicarillas and Utes became bolder in the plundering along the Santa Fe Trail. At Point of Rocks in October of 1849 Jicarillas led by third-ranking chief Lobo Blanco pillaged the wagon train of J. M. White, killing him and carrying away his wife and daughter. The Indians, according to one investigator, were acting out of anger at having been fired upon, "without any sufficient cause or provocation," by soldiers from Las Vegas.[4]

It was at about this time that Colonel Washington was relieved by Brevet Colonel John Munroe, an officer who seemed unready to quench the many small ground fires that Washington had started. Although he is sometimes treated as a man bereft of energy or imagination, the root of Munroe's inactivity was probably little more than obstinacy. He liked good books, smooth whiskey, and the other accouterments of civilization; he loathed New Mexico and wanted out. Munroe did, however, have effective subordinates in the field, and one of them, William Grier, was guided by Kit Carson to overhaul the White killers a month after the fact. Although seven of the hostiles were killed, a Jicarilla woman executed Mrs. White just before she could be retaken, and upon finding her body the soldiers made some little ceremony of vowing vengeance. The daughter was never recovered, although Congress passed a special appropriation of $1,500 for her ransom.[5] Grier's force made camp that night in the deserted rancheria. After dark some of the men heard a noise in the surrounding willow brush; they armed themselves and made a search, and soon found an abandoned Indian baby, strapped in its cradleboard. It was Dr. James A. Bennett who discovered the infant, and he recorded the subsequent event in his memoir: "An old gruff soldier stepped up and said, 'Let me see that brat.' I handed it to him. He picked up a heavy stone, tied it to the board, dashed baby and all into the water, and in a moment no trace of it was left. The soldier's only comment was, 'You're a little feller now but will make big Injun bye and bye. I only wish I had more to treat the same way.'"[6]

In May of 1850, more Jicarillas and Utes struck the Santa Fe Trail, waylaying an eastbound mail train. It's eleven men were all killed. The troops who inspected the site were under Lieutenant Ambrose Burnside, whose graphic report was widely published, scandalizing polite people and finally drawing enough attention to the New Mexico problem that serious changes came under consideration.

Once in possession of New Mexico, the American army found itself less than entirely sure of exactly what it possessed, and some of its sorties went out not so much to fight anybody as just to get the lay of the land. One expedition left San Antonio, Texas, early in 1849 to survey a new road through the six hundred wilderness miles to El Paso. After covering two thirds of the route they reached the Davis Mountains and ran afoul of a large group of Mescalero Apaches. These southerly Mescaleros—and some Lipans probably rode with them, too—had the just reputation of being more warlike and truculent than those in the homeland of New Mexico's Sierra Blanca. These particular two hundred warriors rode under the chiefs Chinonero, Cigarrito, and most prominent (and dangerous), Gómez. The intransigence of both parties nearly erupted into a fight before a talk could be staged. The Corps of Engineers lieutenant in charge bought the forbearance of Chinonero and Cigarrito with presents, and the latter helped them escape Gómez's planned attack. The soldiers got away in a nightlong, harrowing, storm-blown flight toward Limpia Canyon.[7]

Another party left Doña Ana in early June 1850, to explore the Organ Mountains and Tularosa Basin, and they wound up in the middle of the Sierra Blanca, the very heart of Mescalero isolationism. At the midpoint of the nineteenth century these Apaches lived under the headship principally of the chiefs Barranquito, Josecito, and Santana. Of the three, Barranquito was by far the least sympathetic to the white people and the quickest to fight, Josecito remains little known but probably counseled a middle course, and Santana later proved himself loyal in friendship to the

Americans. When the pindah soldiers encamped on his doorstep, though, Santana sent word that he would smash them if they came any closer. The lieutenant in charge reported that he "was informed that there were about two thousand warriors waiting for me; and my command not being sufficient to engage so large a band of Indians, I thought it more prudent to retire. . . ."[8]

> Long time ago they say.
> Coyote was going along and saw a Jackrabbit. "Well, I'm going to get something to eat," he said, and took in chasing that rabbit.
> Finally Jackrabbit saw a little stump and ran into it. It wasn't much at all. Coyote was right behind him. When he got to the stump he stuck in his hand to catch him.
> All at once Jackrabbit grabbed hold of Coyote's hand. He called out, "Grandmother, get me that knife! Hurry up! I'm going to cut off his hand!"
> That Coyote started howling and begging for his hand. Finally Jackrabbit said, "All right. Go away and don't bother me." Coyote left there and never went back.
> I am talking about fruit.[9]

Santana probably would have done well to muster one tenth of the two thousands of warriors that the lieutenant feared; it was an outrageous bluff, but it worked.

However, the increasing numbers of white men in their territory led various Eastern Apache bands to seek some peaceful rapprochement. At midyear of 1850, the chiefs of the Sierra Blanca Mescaleros sent word in to the military that they were willing to give up all their captives and stolen property in exchange for a treaty. In a remarkable attempt at comprehensiveness, the chiefs took the initiative of calling councils with Jicarillas and Comanches to prevent the peace being wrecked by unincluded holdouts.[10] This Mescalero-Jicarilla effort gained no quick response, but the bands involved continued mostly to forgo raids among the pindahs to see what developed. That fall, a group of the wilder Texas Mescaleros contacted the garrison at San Elizario, near El Paso, to investigate the chances for peace. They were well treated and promised to come back, but never did. This was probably not because the Indians were undependable, but rather that they were led by two lesser chiefs, Simón Porode and Simón Manuel, who if they had been criticized by the more powerful Gómez, probably could not have stood up to him.[11]

The latter contact also illustrated a shortcoming on the American side, when the army major in charge at San Elizario (the locally celebrated Jefferson Van Horne) noticed that he was authorized only to fight Indians, not treat with them, and requested instructions whether it was permissible—as he hoped it was—to encourage them with food and presents. In response to the increasing contacts, some semblance of organization began to form during 1850 to deal with the New Mexico Apaches. The mines at Santa Rita were opened again with the establishment of Fort Webster nearby; but war was not to be the principal instrument of diplomacy, first, because these early relations with the Apaches were still good enough that they could be encouraged by peaceful means to take up farming, and secondly because there were fewer than 13,000 men in the entire army, and fewer than 1,400 in New Mexico to fight them. Even to Americans, peace is attractive when there is no army to do the fighting.

More importantly, one James S. Calhoun was appointed to the combined office of governor of the territory and superintendent of Indian Affairs for New Mexico. He was old and sickly, but a very bright man and a capable administrator. One of his first efforts was to relieve the misery of the Jicarillas. To evidence the genuineness of their desire for peace the first chief, Francisco Chacón, turned in a herd of sheep that had been stolen by Navajos, in March of 1851. Calhoun managed to sign a treaty the next month with Chacón's Jicarillas, and also with two Mescalero chiefs, Lobo and the more well-known Josecito.[12] The superintendent sent word that he would come out soon to the Jicarillas, and left Santa Fe in May to ease their wretched starvation. His first contact, however, demonstrated the power of the forces that opposed him.

He reached the Pecos in the co-operative company of Colonel Munroe on May 16 and distributed some of the grain to the Jicarillas at Anton Chico. A band of the Comanches who occasionally crossed over from the Texas Panhandle also came in to parley, but comancheros who made their business running guns and liquor to the Indians (and who stood to lose that business if the Indians settled down) convinced them that they were going to be murdered, and they fled. Messengers found the Comanches and persuaded them to return, and at the conclusion of a satisfactory conference the chief promised to return with his band to make a treaty. As they neared Anton Chico the same thing happened again—this time they stampeded in such a panic that they left their camp goods behind—and Calhoun gave up in disgust, after sending out more emissaries to return their possessions.

Of this exercise in frustration Calhoun related an entire account to the Indian Commissioner, articulately denouncing the comancheros, whose interest lay with continued Indian unrest, concluding that "*power* is wanted in this Territory to catch the infamous. . . . Are these things never to be remedied? Give me the authority and *means* and I will remedy it."[13] He admitted, however, that he did not understand the nature of the Indians' faith in the comancheros. He never had, actually. Six months before, he asked, "Why is it that these traders have no fears . . . when these same Indians show . . . a determined hostility to all who remain quietly at home?"[14] The reason was, of course, that the comancheros were a steady source of supplies (especially arms and ammunition), and the liquor that the Apaches—the Jicarillas most miserably—had grown so fond of. The bizarre relationship of Mexicans trading with Indians who preyed on other Mexicans had become so solidified during the preceding two centuries that it could not change just because a pindah suddenly lived in the governor's palace.

Yet, with the Mescalero and Jicarilla treaties under his belt, Calhoun received the visit of a "Gila" (probably a Chiricahua) chief and heard another earnest profession of peaceful intentions.[15] He still felt he had reason to believe that Apache affairs in his administration would get off on a hopeful foot. To follow up this friendly meeting, Calhoun began to make preparations to visit the Chiricahuas at Santa Rita to make a treaty. His good design fell apart, however, when he applied to the army for an escort and was told, in effect, to go to hell.

The principal reason for this was that in July of 1851 the military hierarchy had undergone a change of tremendous import to the Indians of the territory. Command of the Department passed from Munroe to Edwin Vose Sumner, lieutenant colonel of the 1st Dragoons, a burly, disagreeable, and contentious man who loved a good fight almost as much as he hated the Indian Bureau. With his thundering voice, piercing eyes, and shock of white hair and beard, he terrorized bureaucrats and his troops alike. But he was neither a bad man nor a bad soldier; at most times he possessed a clear mind, a firm grasp of his responsibilities, and, usually, at least one serviceable plan to bootleg Indian control from the Bureau. He was a man who proved himself capable of the pettiest insults and meanness to civil authorities, but in genuine crises his strong common sense usually held sway over his personal inclinations.

Sumner arrived with instructions to completely reorder the military structure of his Department, as a result of a still broader change in Washington of frontier defense philosophy. Until this time, the troops had been stationed in the towns themselves, riding out after Indians when needed but mostly, it was charged, succumbing to the laziness and vice of city living. To gain more effective Indian control, lessen the cost to the government of civilian contractors, and improve the morale of the soldiers, emphasis was now to be placed on the construction and maintenance of posts and forts at militarily strategic passes and junctions, far removed from the towns. The posts were to be constructed by the troops themselves of local materials, and they were to grow and produce as much of their own food and supplies as practicable. In addition to this, Sumner was to crush Indian resistance.

With fewer than 1,400 men in the whole Department, that was a huge task to wrestle. Sumner went at it with his customary energy and decision, and within a month of his assuming command he had removed the big garrison from Santa Fe and re-formed the headquarters as Fort Union, at an important junction on the Santa Fe Trail, some one hundred miles east of the city, and himself set out west at the head of a small army to battle the Navajos. In their country he left behind a five-company garrison at the post he named Fort Defiance. In a few weeks he returned and established more forts, manning them with garrisons evacuated from El Paso, Doña Ana and Socorro. To watch over the Chiricahuas at Santa Rita del Cobre he established Fort Webster; to ride shotgun on the Jornada del Muerto he placed Fort Conrad on the northern end and Fort Fillmore where the California Trail crossed the Rio Grande, near Mesilla. The next year he placed a small military camp in the heart of Jicarilla territory and still another further north to intimidate the Utes. The scheme was much more sensible than keeping the soldiers in the towns, and although the location of posts was constantly adjusted and fine-tuned, the system itself endured until the close of the frontier.

However, Sumner came to New Mexico with a powerful inconsistency in his orders. He was to pursue an aggressive policy toward the Indians, yet he was to co-operate with Governor-and-Superintendent Calhoun. The first instruction was much clearer to his understanding than the second, which grated on his nature and his philosophy. Thus, when Calhoun applied for an escort to the Chiricahuas at Santa Rita, he met a cold rebuff, and the chance for an early treaty with the tremendously powerful following of Mangas Coloradas was lost. Calhoun complained of the lack of co-operation from the military—a plaintive refrain echoed many times over the next thirty-five years—but the trip never took place.[16]

Pindah-Lickoyee:
NOTES

1. U. S. Senate, Exec. Doc. No. 7, 30th Cong., 1st sess., Vol. 3, p. 27 (1848), quoted in Utley, *Frontiersmen in Blue*, p. 42.

2. Bieber, *Marching with the Army of the West*, p. 343.

3. See Rippy, "The Indians of the Southwest," pp. 363ff.

4. *Condition of the Indian Tribes*, p. 328.

5. Details of the White massacre may be found in Sabin, *Kit Carson Days*, Vol. II, pp. 618ff.; also Bennett, *Forts and Forays*, pp. 25ff.

6. Bennett, *Forts and Forays*, p. 25.

7. Secretary of War, *Annual Report* for 1849, pp. 284–85. See also Bieber, *Exploring Southwestern Trails*, pp. 271–81.

8. Secretary of War, *Annual Report* for 1850, p. 73.

9. The elements of this method of escape from the trickster are found in Opler, "Myths and Tales of the Chiricahua Apache Indians," p. 40; Hoijer,

Chiricahua and Mescalero Apache Texts, p. 20; and Opler, "Myths and Tales of the Jicarilla Apache Indians," p. 299.

10. Sonnichsen, *Mescalero Apaches,* pp. 61–62. Of all the agreements that the Apaches had made with Spanish authorities, many were ruined when their terms were violated by Indians who had not been party to them. For Santana and Barranquito to recognize this factor and move to correct it (if indeed that was their aim) showed perception keener than that of many who sat on the other side of the bargaining.

11. This is speculation on my part, but too much white-written history of Indian–American relations fails to consider the difficulties that peace-minded Indians faced within their own camps. Of course, Simón Porode and Simón Manuel could have been taking a ride at the soldiers' expense, but I doubt it since they brought their families into San Elizario with them. The transactions are recorded in Secretary of War, *Annual Report* for 1850, pp. 112–13.

12. Calhoun, *Official Correspondence,* pp. 314–16.

13. Ibid., Calhoun to Lea, June 30, 1851.

14. Calhoun to Lea, Oct. 15, 1849, quoted in Keleher, *Turmoil in New Mexico,* p. 55.

15. Calhoun, *Official Correspondence,* p. 290.

16. Ibid., pp. 394, 415.

New Fort Grant was established after the Camp Grant Indians were removed to San Carlos and the older post's location proved unhealthy. *National Archives.*

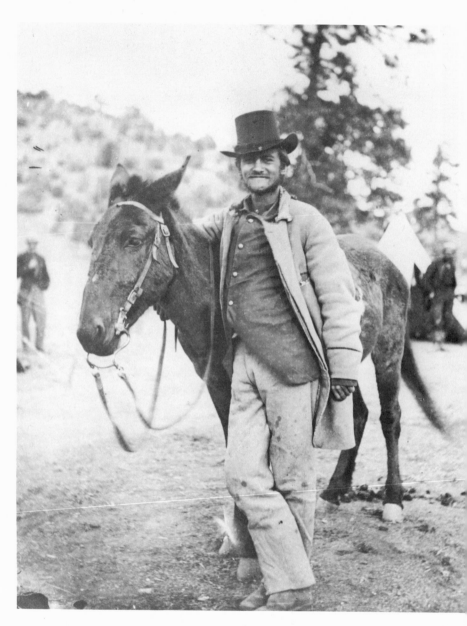

Frederick W. Loring, a promising young writer from Massachusetts, shown here with his mule, "Evil Merodach." Photo taken two days before his killing by Indians from the Date Creek Reservation. *National Archives.*

John Philip Clum. *Arizona Historical Society.*

At San Carlos in 1875, Agent Clum strikes a characteristic pose, flanked by the powerful Diablo (l.) of the Eastern White Mountain Apaches and Eskiminzin (r.) of the Arivaipas. *Naitonal Archives.*

The San Carlos Apache Police, c. 1876. Matching pantaloons were a gift from Arizona citizens. Agent Clum is at fore of column, lower center. Bearded man in white shirt (1.) is Clum's interpreter, Marijildo Grijalba. *National Archives.*

Partial view of Camp Apache, in the mid-1870s. *National Archives.*

Naiche, the second son of Cochise; on the death of his elder brother he became hereditary chief of the Tsoka-ne-nde Chiricahuas. *National Archives.*

Mangus, son of Mangas Coloradas, was the last Apache leader to surrender. *National Archives.*

Mangas and the Boundary Commission

In the early 1850s Apache raids into Old Mexico, carried out largely by the two western tribes—Chiricahuas of the Continental Divide country, and Western Apaches proper of eastern Arizona below the Mogollon Rim—increased to such an extent that one estimate suggested that four hundred Mexicans were killed in the two years 1851 to 1853.[1]

There were three major bands of Chiricahuas[2] that bridged the gap between the Mescaleros on the east and the Western Apaches, to both of whom the Chiricahuas were well known and with whom they freely associated.

Almost immediately east of the White Mountain group of Westerns were the Tci-he-nde, or Red Paint People; their name derived from their traditional war paint, a single, broad stripe of red clay across the face.[3] These most northeasterly Chiricahuas centered about west-central and southwestern New Mexico state (as it was eventually defined), and clustered most densely around the area of Santa Rita del Cobre and the hot mineral springs nearby on the west side of the Rio Grande. In historic times, whites have called them most frequently the Warm Springs or Ojo Caliente, the Mimbres or Mimbreños (Spanish for "willows"), or Coppermines Apaches. Their most famous latter-day chiefs included Mangas Coloradas, Victorio, Nana, and Loco, and in this book the designation Mimbres is limited to this band.

Just to the southwest of them were the Tsoka-ne-nde; the name is untranslatable, but they are thought of as the middle, and most insular, Chiricahuas, who inhabited primarily the Dragoon, Chiricahua, and Dos Cabezas mountain ranges and the connecting deserts. Under the leadership for many years of their most famous chief, Cochise, who was probably only just coming to prominence in 1851, they have never been widely called anything but Chiricahuas.

To the south and southwest of them, living almost entirely in the Sierra Madre of Old Mexico, were the Nde-nda-i, the so-called Enemy People.

Their territory was not as rich in game and plant food as that of the other Chiricahuas, and this thinner existence altered their life-style. They were less attached to one particular home range and roamed more widely than other Chiricahuas, their functioning social units were smaller—the local family group, called the gó-táh—and they were more dependent upon raiding to acquire basic necessities of life. Because of this, the more sedentary Western Apaches considered the Southern Chiricahuas to be little more than predatory drifters. One informant was almost certainly talking about the Nde-nda-i when she said that they "were mean people . . . I don't know where they lived; they were like Coyotes and lived any place."[4] Their two most famous latter-day chiefs belonged to different gó-táhs: Juh (pronounced Hwū) was a Nednhi (a variant form of Nde-nda-i), and Gerónimo was a Bedonkohe.

To the pindahs who encroached inexorably into their territory they were all simply Chiricahuas, and it seemed only a matter of time before Americans would become victims of an attack by those Apaches. One of the first raids recorded was committed, probably by Gileños or Mimbres, on February 2, 1850. They struck eastward at the Rio Grande village of Doña Ana, killing one man and wounding three. A small military unit gave chase, and as the town lay unprotected in their absence, more Apaches entered the settlement and stole stock freely. A special investigator was dispatched to discover what had happened. When Indians were found who could talk about the incident, they explained the conduct by saying their wild game food was gone, and the pindahs forbade them to depredate among the Mexicans. "We must steal from somebody," they said, "and if you will not permit us to rob the Mexicans, we must steal from you, or fight you."[5]

At first, the question of whose citizens they were robbing, which depended upon the demarcation of a boundary line between the United States and Mexico, was an issue of indifference to the Apaches. Mexicans were Mexicans to them. (That attitude changed, of course, once they learned how convenient it was to escape one country's army by crossing into the other's territory.) The question of the boundary was, however, important to the two nations involved, and in the summer of 1851 two official surveying expeditions, one Mexican under General García Conde and one American under General John R. Bartlett, embarked to stake off the line.[6] When Superintendent Calhoun heard of the expedition, he recommended that an Indian agent be detailed to facilitate the commission's inevitable contact with Indians, particularly the Eastern Chiricahuas that he knew as "Gilas," but again his purpose was frustrated. To army men like Sumner, to have an Indian Office in Santa Fe was insulting enough, but to have a Bureau agent along on a military expedition was something they didn't have to, and would not, stand for.

The commission established their base near the old mines at Santa Rita del Cobre, and Bartlett himself traveled extensively throughout the region, everywhere being told of the ferocity of the Apaches. To his own observations things did not seem so bad, except in Sonora, where he was sobered by the sight of "depopulated towns and villages; deserted haciendas and ranches, elegant and spacious churches falling to decay; neglected orchards, teeming with fruit, and broad fields, once cultivated."[7] At the Sonoran capital of Ures Bartlett fell ill, and while he was recuperating a number of Apaches rode brassily through the town and liberated Apache captives from the prison.

At the time the Boundary Commission entered the southwestern part of New Mexico for the survey, the single greatest leader the Apaches had was a physical giant as well as a domineering personality: Mangas Coloradas (Red Sleeves), of the Tci-he-nde Mimbres. He was a truly striking figure with a hulking body and disproportionately large head. Born sometime in the early 1790s, Mangas was fast becoming an old man, but still he possessed cunning as impenetrable as the thick mat of hair that hung down to his waist. His lips were thin and tightly drawn, his nose aquiline, his eyes bulging. He had succeeded to the chieftainship of the Mimbres on the death of Juan José in James Johnson's cannon surprise. Within the caution that must always be used in calling an Apache leader a chief, Mangas Coloradas' following was large and exceptionally cohesive, and he commanded great respect among the Tsoka-ne-nde and Nde-nda-i bands in addition to his own.

The commission had been at their task for some six weeks before Mangas Coloradas paid his first visit, accompanied by his closest captains, Ponce, Delgadito, and Coleto Amarillo. In his reports Bartlett characterized Mangas as a man of "great influence among the several Apache tribes. . . . a man of strong common sense, and discriminate judgment; he has none of the savageness . . . that we anticipated from the many vague rumors afloat." As a white soldier's first glimpse of the great Mangas this is a particularly illuminating characterization, for it shows from whence and how far he was eventually driven to hold the Southwest in ice-veined terror. Bartlett also expressed high regard for the chiefs Ponce and Delgadito, whom he termed "reasonable and practicable" men of "more than ordinary character, intellect and influence." The general also thought the strength of the Mimbres' immediate friendship to the Americans especially remarkable because, he continued, "they have all been viewed by the inhabitants of this country as cruel, bloodthirsty, implacable enemies, and too often assuming them to be so, they have been treated . . . worse than brutes. No attempts have been made to conciliate them, but on the contrary, many flagrant acts of injustice have been committed against them and much done to exasperate them and increase their hostility." He went on to recommend the establishment of an agency for Mangas' tribe, but General Sumner was not listening.

The Apaches, for their part, were equally impressed with Bartlett and his men. There was in Mangas' entourage from time to time a minor war leader of the Nde-nda-i, in the prime of life, once named Go-yath-khla, later much more famous under the name Gerónimo. Many years later he recalled that "These were the first white men I ever saw. . . . We could not understand them very well, for we had no interpreter, but we made a treaty with them by shaking hands and promising to be brothers. Then we made our camp near their camp, and they came to trade with us . . . Every day they measured land with curious instruments and put down marks which we could not understand. We gave them buckskin, blankets, and ponies in exchange for shirts and provisions. We also brought them game, for which they gave us some money. We did not know the value of this money, but we kept it and later learned from the Navajo Indians that it was very valuable."[8] (Actually, while these may have been the first white men that Gerónimo had ever seen, Mangas himself was known to have had a talk with General Kearny's party during the late war.)

Meals and sojourns were exchanged freely, but the promisingly warm relationship was wrecked by two unfortunate incidents which, while Bartlett handled them as well as anyone could have, still exhibited such insensitivity to the Apache Life-way that Mangas' protection was lost.

After some months the Mimbres became secure around the Americans to the degree that on one visit to Santa Rita they brought with them, purely incidentally, two small Mexican boys captured on raids into Sonora. The Apaches saw nothing untoward with the fact; they brought their own children into town just as readily, but once near enough to Santa Rita to dare it, the boys decided to attempt an escape. The Mimbres camps were only a very few miles from town, and on an occasion when the prisoners found themselves left nearly alone in camp (captives were rarely held under close guard), they slipped away and ran for the American surveyors' camp.

The tent nearest the Apache village, and fortunately away from the path the Indians used in going to Santa Rita, was that of John C. Cremony, a soldier, interpreter, scout, and all-around colorful frontiersman. His camp was about six hundred yards from the tent city of the other whites, and isolated from them by a low hill. He had started housekeeping here because he thought the setting idyllic, and had even dammed a small brook to create a bathing pool.

By the time the Apaches spied the fleeing children and chased them to Cremony's camp it was too late to reclaim them. As they approached, Cremony and another man, a Mexican, emerged with the two boys from his tent, the Mexican with a ready carbine, Cremony with not less than four pistols, two holstered and one in each hand. When the angry Mimbres surrounded them and signed for them to relinquish the prisoners, Cremony cocked his revolvers and told the Mexican to cock his carbine. They stood back to back with the boys between them, circling warily while making their way along the path to the commissioner's tent. After about two hundred yards the group rounded the hill and became visible to the other Americans in the camp, a number of whom went out and escorted the besieged group into the camp.

The Mimbres were furious, and as soon as news of the incident reached Mangas Coloradas and Delgadito they went in to Santa Rita to demand the boys' return from Commissioner Bartlett. They received a shock when Bartlett explained to them that article of the Guadalupe Hidalgo treaty by which the United States was obligated to return to Mexico all Mexican captives recovered from the Indians. It was the first the Apaches had heard of it.

"You came to our country," Mangas countered stiffly as Cremony translated. "Your lives, your property, your animals were safe; you came and went in peace. Your strayed animals were brought home to you again. Our wives, our children and our women came here and visited your houses. We were friends! We were brothers! Believing this we came among you and brought our captives, relying on it that we were brothers and you would feel as we feel. We concealed nothing. We came not here secretly or in the night. We came in open day and before your faces, and we showed our captives to you."

Bartlett repeated the American position as clearly as he could, but another of the Mimbres chiefs, either Delgadito or Ponce, who was also present, protested, "Yes, but you took our captives from us without beforehand cautioning us. We were ignorant of this promise to restore captives. They were made prisoners in lawful warfare. They belong to us. They are our property. Our people have also been made captive by the Mexicans. If we had known of this thing, we should not have come here. We should not have placed that confidence in you."

Yet again Bartlett repeated the limits of his authority, but the Tci-hende chiefs insisted that "the owner of these captives is a poor man. He cannot lose his captives, who were obtained at the risk of his life and purchased by the blood of his relatives. He justly demands his captives. We are his friends, and we wish to see this demand complied with. It is just, and as justice we demand it."

The argument dragged on tensely for days, when Bartlett finally agreed with Mangas' and Delgadito's initial suggestion that he buy the boys. To have purchased them himself would have been illegal, but he had two Mexicans on his payroll, and he arranged to finance the deal so that one of the Mexicans could buy their freedom. But then the Apache headmen came into Santa Rita once more and announced that the bargain was off. "The owner does not wish to sell," they said. "He wants his captives." Mangas had undoubtedly brought pressure to bear on the boys' owner to sell, but the situation illustrates that even a leader of Mangas' stature faced considerable limitations in imposing his will on his people, and it was the chief's obligation to stand up to the pindahs for the man's decision.

"I have already told my brother that this cannot be," answered Bartlett. "I speak not with two tongues. Make up your minds."[9] At last the Mimbres spokesmen relented, but said the owner would demand twenty horses at the very least for the two boys. Then Bartlett, whose only fault until then had been perhaps some lack of imagination, did the unforgivable: he looked at the Indians and laughed.

"The brave who owns these captives does not wish to sell," they insisted. "He has had one of those boys six years. He grew up under him. His heartstrings are bound around him. He is as a son to his old age. He speaks our language, and he cannot sell him. Money cannot buy affection. His heart cannot be sold. He taught him to string and shoot the bow, and to wield the lance. He loves the boy and cannot sell him."

It has been suggested[10] that at least some of the last argument was aimed at Bartlett's pity to get better terms for the boys' owner. This was probably true, but to some extent it was probably also a sincere claim. Furthermore, there was more to that reference about a son to his old age than Bartlett conceded. In the Apache experience food was seldom superabundant, and elderly people—especially old men—while treated with respect, were not pampered. For such an old man, particularly if he were poor or from a small family (for instance, if he were widowed after a long marriage, he would have only modest claims for help from either his own or his wife's family), to lose two potential suppliers of food after spending his last good years training them in Apache survival and hunting, would have been a calamity that no price—even the twenty horses at which Bartlett laughed—could have fully recompensed. And, although there seems to be no evidence that it surfaced, yet another argument lay implicit in the desire to keep the boys. If the Apaches had already begun training the youths for the warpath, which apparently they had, they must have thought it unwise to relinquish them, and their knowledge, back to the hated Mexicans.

Bartlett finally settled the affair by leading the Mimbres to the commissary, where he displayed about $250 in various trade goods and offered them in payment. The Apaches accepted them and left.

After a time there appeared to be hope that the quarrels over the two Mexican boys had left no permanent scars in the American's relations with the Apaches. Social and trading visits were resumed, and Bartlett presented Mangas with an elegant suit of clothes which, to the delight of the commission, were promptly altered to meet the practical necessities of the environment. (He removed the seat of the breeches, for one thing.) "During this time," wrote Bartlett, "the members of the Commission went about freely in small parties or alone, for twenty or thirty miles around our camp, and were on no occasion molested. They also visited the

Apache camps, where they were well received. Our wagons with stores went unprotected to and from the Surveyors, and their attendants, who were scattered for fifty miles along the line, where the escort could afford them little protection." The Americans' stock was also entrusted almost entirely to the Apaches' mercy. Although Mangas' camp was only about four miles from Santa Rita, the best pasturage was at Delgadito's camp, eight miles away.

Then, suddenly, news raced through the camps that one of the commission's Mexican hands, named Jesús López, had shot one of the Apache men. The Mimbres leaders made no attempt to disguise their outrage and went to see Bartlett, whom they discovered already had the man in custody, and he interrogated López in the Indians' presence. Only one other man had witnessed the shooting, and from these two the story emerged that one of the Apaches had tried to buy a whip from López. When López refused, the Apache grabbed at it but López shoved him back and picked up a rock. Then, it became clear, López chunked the stone aside, picked up a rifle, and, after keeping the Indian covered for several seconds, shot him point-blank in the chest. The commissioner's behavior at the questioning convinced the Mimbres that the incident was an isolated one, not involving the Americans as a whole, and that widespread violence was not called for. However, the Tci-he-nde were beginning to perceive the foreign presence in the country as deleterious, and the budding friendship cooled alarmingly. If the warrior lived, they said, they would be content that López's wages be given to the man's family. But if he died, the Mexican would have to be turned over to them to be executed.

At the commission's hospital the desperately wounded Indian received the best possible attention; his friends visited him to make certain the Americans were doing all they could. But after a strong fight for his life that dragged on for a month, he died. To show his respect Bartlett ordered a coffin, but the Mimbres scornfully took his body away for burial by their customs.[11] And when they were through, the angry, resolute Indians returned to Santa Rita for Jesús López. Bartlett met them, and knew that for once he was facing real trouble. "The great chief of the American people," he began patiently, "lives far, very far, towards the rising sun. From him I receive my orders, and those orders I must obey. I cannot interfere in punishing any man, whether an Indian, a Mexican, or an American. There is another great chief who lives in Santa Fe. He is the governor of all New Mexico. This great chief administers the laws of the Americans. He holds court wherein all persons charged with crimes are judged. He alone can inflict punishment when a man has been found guilty. To this great chief, this governor, I will send the murderer of our Apache brother. He will try him, and, if found guilty, will have him punished according to the American laws. Such is all I can do. . . . It is all I have a right to do."

The Chiricahuas were not at all satisfied, and it was soon after this that the commission's stock began to disappear, and other signs of hostility increased. In spite of both Bartlett's earnestness and Mangas' genuine feeling of betrayal, there were evidently other factors involved that neither side articulated.

In the first place, an agent from Governor Calhoun would have been very useful to have around; Sumner kept trouble brewing with his imperious decisiveness, and Bartlett went so strictly by the book that he couldn't deal effectively with problems when they arose. The army seemed unable to find a middle latitude of conduct. Secondly, the whole content of the Guadalupe Hidalgo treaty should have been explained to the Apaches, insofar as it affected them, at the beginning, all at once. That knowledge of the treaty was parceled out to them bit by bit as they violated its mysterious terms must have created some feeling that the pindahs were making up the rules as they went along.[12] Another source of confusion to the Apaches, as Delgadito complained, was that while they were to be divested of their captives, no serious effort was made to recover those Apaches held as slaves in Mexican households. The enforcement was so prejudiced that shortly after Bartlett left the country, one army observer could write that "it is very doubtful whether a settlement can be found in the valley of the Rio Grande not possessed of Indian slaves. These poor creatures are bought and sold like horses or mules, and it seems rather too much to expect that the Indians shall deliver up the Mexican prisoners in their possession to the authorities which countenance openly the sale and slavery of numbers of their tribe. . . . [P]rotection from plunder, which we are expending so much money to extend to the [Mexicans], could with equal justice be extended to the Indian."[13] Apart from this, it generally went without notice that Mexican prisoners among the Apaches had a far better lot than Apache slaves among the Mexicans. Mexican girls among the Indians eventually might marry into the tribe, and could become highly respected. The boys became warriors—as those recovered by Bartlett were being trained to be—and even rose to influence as war chiefs.[14] But whatever positions they came to hold, the key factor was that they were assimilated into the society almost as equals, and indeed became important sources of fresh blood in small bands. Male Indian children among the Mexicans were doomed to servitude of the meanest and most bestial order; the girls almost invariably became prostitutes, as far from the will of White-painted Woman as one could go. Sonora and Chihuahua maintained their scalp bounty on Apaches, and open season continued. It was a situation that no people could accept and hope to survive. Thus they severed the ties.

Fortunately for Bartlett, his work in Mimbres country was almost completed, and by the time the commission left the members were for practical purposes dismounted, having lost about three hundred head of stock. Indeed, it was said, although probably rashly, that only the constant troop commotion around Fort Webster stood between Mangas and a massacre of the whole commission.

Mangas and the Boundary Commission:
NOTES

1. Lockwood, *Apache Indians*, pp. 39–40.
2. Different authors recognize different numbers; I am following the one who seems most sensible, Opler, in "An Outline of Chiricahua Apache Social Organization," pp. 178–80. Even this simplified categorization must admit to some degree of artificial imposition. To the Chiricahuas themselves, before and even after the white concentration policy demolished the geographic significance of their band divisions, a person's localized affiliation was of more immediate importance than his band. White people, for instance, regarded Gerónimo as a Chiricahua; Apaches regarded him as a Bedonkohe. Eve Ball, letter to Sylvia Dunn, Mar. 25, 1957, Southwest Collection, Texas Tech. University.
3. Kaywaykla, *In the Days of Victorio*, p. xiv.
4. Goodwin, *Social Organization of the Western Apache*, p. 84.
5. Bowman to Assistant Quartermaster, Apr. 21, 1850, quoted in U. S. Senate, Exec. Doc. No. 1, 31st Cong., 2nd sess., Vol. I, pp. 295ff. (1850).
6. For a general history of the work of the Boundary Commission, see Faulk, *Too Far North, Too Far South*.
7. Bartlett to Stuart, Feb. 19, 1852, in Bartlett, *Personal Narrative*, pp. 226–39. Most of the extensive quotations that follow, particularly of conversations with Apache headmen, are doubly preserved, once in Bartlett's memoirs, with a closely similar version in Cremony, *Life Among the Apaches*, both quoted in many secondary treatments. Differences between the two primary accounts exist but are insignificant.
8. Gerónimo, *Geronimo's Story of His Life*, p. 129.
9. The time-honored imagery of "white man speak with forked tongue" is a good place to warn the reader of what is called in journalism "noise." Undeniably, Indians (including Apaches) frequently spoke in an imagic fashion, but I can't help but wonder how much of their phraseology, especially after many of them learned enough English to communicate, was in a way a "playback" of what early interpreters rendered from their native expressions into such stylistic gewgaws as "forked tongue," "heap big," and the insertion of "um" after a verb: "kill 'um," "take 'um," etc. It reminds me of a scene I saw in a movie once, where one character asked another, "Why you talk this way?" The other answered, "I don't know; I thought you wanted me to."
10. Adams, *Geronimo*, p. 60.
11. To Apaches the idea of taking a dead body off in a box was incomprehensibly horrible. Kaywaykla, *In the Days of Victorio*, p. 20.

12. A still finer twist in treaty making was employed later on. In an 1852 treaty with the Utes and Navajos, the provision against raiding in Mexico was added after the Indians had signed it. Greiner to Lea, June 30, 1852.

13. Pope, *Report of Exploration*, p. 19.

14. Opler, *An Apache Life-way*, p. 468.

Mangas Triumphant

At the end of summer, 1851, the plight of the white prospectors in the copper mines region worsened when Fort Webster was deactivated so the troops could follow and protect Bartlett. The mines were left unguarded, and it was rumored—with some evidence—that Mangas Coloradas was fashioning an alliance with the Navajos.[1] Moreover, many of the Apaches in Old Mexico, aware of the new boundary, moved north beyond the reach of the Mexican soldiers, which weighted New Mexico Territory with more even than the usual number of Apaches. In spite of the tension, Mangas was at this point probably not beyond reason in his distaste for the pindahs. He considered the whites skulky and inferior and he did not like them, and Bartlett had (although rudely) increased his sophistication in dealing with them, but Mangas was an intelligent and practical man who knew when to bend with the wind. His willingness still to bargain may be seen, first perhaps in the failure of a Navajo alliance to materialize, but secondly and more importantly in his manner of seeking redress for the wrongs that were still done his people.

The miners at Santa Rita continually provoked him, and from time to time in fact killed Apaches with virtual impunity. During the autumn, Department Commander Sumner reported, "a Mexican at the little town of San Antonio, assailed and killed two Apaches and dangerously wounded a third, while they were gambling together.

"The Indians came in the next day and demanded that the man should be confined for trial—this was done, and the Indians left satisfied, but as soon as they were gone, the murderer was permitted to go at large again, and when the Indians heard of it, they became furious."[2] The fact that Mangas' Indians required not the man himself (as they had Jesús López), but merely that he be held and tried, must speak significantly of their acquiescence to play by the white man's rules.

Nevertheless, some writers have suggested that Calhoun's plan to send an agent among the Mangas Mimbres would have accomplished little good, for the reason that the Apaches believed they had driven Bartlett away, and were in no mood to give concessions that they didn't have to.[3] This is probably more true than not, but with the additional reason that it would likely have proven impossible to find anyone to treat the Indians any more perceptively than Bartlett had. Nevertheless, it was not yet true that the only way to bring Mangas to terms was to crush him militarily.

All that soon changed, however, for there remained the scraggly string of prospectors working the Santa Rita mines. A new strike had been made at nearby Pinos Altos, and the increasing population was a bothersome new thorn in Mangas' side, that he began to scheme to get rid of.

Long time ago they say.

Coyote saw some prospectors, white men, coming along toward him. They had fine horses and pack mules with lots of goods, and Coyote decided he would get them. He knew about white men. He went beside the road and defecated, then he took off his hat and held it over the feces. Pretty soon the prospectors got there.

"What have you got under there?" they asked.

"I have my wonderful bird under here," said Coyote. "He is black and yellow and red, and he knows everything in the world. Anything I want to know, I just ask him. He is worth a lot!"

Those white men whispered among themselves and then asked, "Can he tell you how to get money?"

"Yes, he tells me that all the time."

Those prospectors started getting excited. "Let us see him."

"No, he only talks to his owner."

"Sell him to us, then."

"No, he's worth too much."

"Look. We'll give you everything we have. Horses, mules, goods—you can have it all."

Coyote held back a minute and then said, "Well, all right. But listen. I have owned this bird a long time and he likes me. You'd better let me get pretty far away before you reach under and get him, or he'll fly after me."

"All right," they said.

"You see those four ridges over there? When you see me get over the last one, then you can reach under and grab him."

"All right," they said.

So Coyote took their horses and pack mules, and just as he left he said, "When you reach under, grab him hard. If he gets away you'll never see him again." Then he went off toward the four ridges.

When the prospectors saw him go over the fourth one, they got ready. All at once they reached under the hat. They grabbed real hard in that stuff and it came out between their fingers.

Oh, were those white men surely angry! They said they were going to

*get that Coyote and they went away after him, but his head start was too
much. Soon the prospectors got hungry. They had already killed the game
in the country and their food was packed on the mules. So they went
around hungry for a time, and then they starved to death.*

I am talking about fruit.[4]

During the fall, Mangas Coloradas rode into Pinos Altos and tried to
persuade the miners to leave for Sonora, where, he said, the riches were
such that Pinos Altos was worthless by comparison. He knew where gold
was and he would take them there, and besides it would be warmer there
during the coming winter. Seeing in this a trick to lure them out and kill
them, the prospectors tied Mangas to a post and whipped him until he
could barely stand. Then they let him go, and the single most powerful
leader of the Chiricahua Apaches stumbled away amid a cacophony of
hoots, jeers, and taunted threats. It would have been far, far better for the
miners, and hundreds of others, if they had finished him there.

When he regained his health Mangas Coloradas set off on a rampage
that by the end of February 1852 had demoralized every effort to contain
him. On the twenty-ninth (it was a leap year), Calhoun reported to
Washington that since his last writing, "the Indians have become bolder
and bolder, and . . . we receive daily information of new outrages and
murders committed by them. Such is the daring of the Apache Indians
that they openly attack our troops and force them to retreat, or become
victims. . . . an Escort no longer affords any protection."[5] Raiding
Apaches pounced on the mail carriage from the village where the two
Apache gamblers had been murdered; its men were slain and burned with
the wagon. More Apaches attacked the mail wagon from San Elizario,
killing one and wounding two of its ten-man escort from Fort Conrad; a
messenger sent to bring help also fell. A federal wagon train from Fort
Webster to the copper mines was picked off and plundered; only the
teamsters managed to escape. A group of soldiers pursued Apaches just
after a murder near El Paso. During the chase, "two sergeants and a Corporal were in advance of the company when Indians sprung from an ambush, butchered them before the eyes of the men, and forced the Company to retreat."[6] The list went on and on and on.

Nor was Mangas' anger confined to the immediate vicinity of Santa
Rita. In defiance of the hated treaty restrictions, the traditional raids into
Sonora and Chihuahua continued. In the western portion of New Mexico
Territory, which later became Arizona, only two settlements remained,
Tubac and Tucson, whose combined population shriveled to just over one
thousand souls.

During the time of strife Calhoun's hand was stronger against Sumner's
military regime than it otherwise would have been, thanks to the second
office he held, governor of New Mexico Territory. And it was by virtue of

this position that the Department commander agreed, during the terribly menacing spring of 1852, to furnish one hundred stand of firearms to Calhoun to equip a militia. Sumner quickly changed his mind in favor of leading a major campaign himself, but Calhoun urgently protested that there were so few troops in the territory that if an expedition were outfitted the settlements would be left defenseless. There was a general consensus that Calhoun was right, and the militia got their guns.

Fortunately, only the Chiricahuas were at war. Apaches east of the Rio Grande were credited with having behaved themselves since the May 1851 treaty. They were, however, beginning to feel neglected, and Calhoun wrote that they "are being tampered with, and are growing restless."[7] He intended to meet with them on March 15 to settle them down again.

Near the end of April a migrating band of almost a hundred Jicarillas passed through on their way to the Pecos, causing John Greiner, their agent and Calhoun's aide, concern at their continued debilitation. "The facility with which they could get liquor at the groceries, and their fondness for it occasioned much trouble," he wrote.

"These Indians are very poor, very hard to govern, and from their continually roaming through the settlements, there is danger to be apprehended from collisions between them and the citizens."

Still, he remained hopeful. "The talk held with them at Pecos, and the presents there distributed, has produced the most beneficial results.—They intend to settle down and manufacture Tenajos[8] and baskets to trade with and a number of them are beginning to plant. Chacone their head Chief has strongly recommended them to cultivate the land, and this year has set them the example himself."[9]

In an effort to salvage a peace out of the Mangas holocaust, Governor Calhoun appointed Charles Overman of Socorro special Indian Agent for the purpose, but the groundwork for Overman's success was already being formed as the Mimbres raids fell off dramatically during the spring. During the preceding fall and winter Mangas had vented his wrath with virtually unimpeded murder and pillage, including at times the diabolically imaginative torture of captives. (It is doubtful whether Mangas should be saddled with personal blame for incidents of torture, as the mode of death of a prisoner probably remained the prerogative of the family of a warrior lately killed by whites. Still, the horror of it did at least as much to panic the civilian population as the actual extent of the depredations.) Mangas was probably tired of fighting and saw the peace as a chance to rest up. Contacts were established, and arrangements made to hold a peace conference.

Since early January Calhoun had been continually ill, stricken with attacks of jaundice and catarrh that left him bedridden for weeks at a time. Once he began to suspect that he would not recover, he began to lay plans to return to Washington, and turned the bulk of his Indian Office work over to the ablest of his agents, Greiner. By the middle of April Calhoun grew daily weaker, and desiring to return to the States to die, he arranged a smooth transition of his powers before he left. He issued a proclamation jointly with Colonel Sumner[10] that if he died before a replacement arrived, Sumner would discharge his executive duties and Greiner would continue to act as superintendent of Indian Affairs. Calhoun departed in late May, taking his coffin with him, accompanied by his secretary, son-in-law, and (dutiful to the end) five Pueblo Indians on a mission to Washington. He died near Kansas, Missouri, at the end of the month.

Before word of his death reached back to New Mexico, Calhoun's labor bore fruit. On June 28 a large number of Chiricahuas, Mangas Coloradas among them, came in to make a treaty, which was done after four days of talks. It was recorded that during the conference, Greiner asked Mangas why he insisted on maintaining a war with Mexico. The chief answered, "I will tell you. Some time ago my people were invited to a feast; aguardiente was there; my people drank and became intoxicated, and were lying asleep, when a party of Mexicans came in and beat out their brains with clubs." Mangas went on to recall for him James Johnson's murder of Juan José, "At another time a trader was sent among us from Chihuahua. While innocently engaged in trading . . . a cannon concealed behind the goods was fired upon my people, and quite a number were killed. . . . How can we make peace with such people?"[11]

Just over a week later a second treaty was concluded with the Mescaleros. A group of thirty had come into Santa Fe at about the same time as the Chiricahuas, and they were joined by a few Jicarilla observers. Greiner spent just over thirty-five dollars on gifts and a celebration, and the Mescaleros signed the treaty in fairly good humor after balking at the requirement that they no longer raid in Mexico. Eventually they worked up sufficient enthusiasm for the new peace that, after they left Santa Fe, they sent word back in to Greiner to try to meet them at Bosque Redondo— the "Round Grove" at a bend in the Pecos River about a week's journey east of the city—for a big council they were arranging with Comanches.[12]

In between the making of the Mimbres and the Mescalero treaties, serious trouble arose between Greiner and Colonel Sumner, who suddenly announced that he was taking over from Greiner as acting superintendent, although Greiner could accompany him to a third treaty meeting, another one with "Gila" Apaches, if he wished.[13] It was a blatant repudiation of the clearly drawn agreement with Calhoun; Greiner was shocked and angry, but unlike later agents who could have taken his example, he refused to endanger the promised peace by engaging in a jurisdictional shoot-out with the military. After lodging a strong protest and spelling out his position to both Sumner and Indian Commissioner Lea,[14] he submitted to army authority and went along in the inferior position Sumner gave him. The Apaches were very nervous and refused to come in to Santa Fe, so the conference was held at Ácoma pueblo. Greiner knew that it was he the Indians trusted and not the army, and that if he sat home in a huff the negotiations might come to nothing, or worse than nothing. While asserting that "The kindest feelings exist I believe between Col. Sumner and myself—and I am inclined to believe he acted from a conviction of duty," Greiner went on in saying of the appropriation to be made for the Apaches, that "you may be sure it will be better expended by the Indian Department than by the War Department in powder and bullets."[15]

In addition to the new trouble with Colonel Sumner, Greiner was also becoming acquainted with the bureaucratic inertia of the Indian Office, noting in his first report since Calhoun departed, "I shall send to the Department my accounts monthly, and draw for the amount expended . . . Not a line has been received from the Department for two months."[16]

Despite these troubles, Greiner could report with genuine accuracy as well as optimism that as of the end of June 1852, "*Not a single depredation has been committed by any of the Indians in New Mexico for three months. The oldest inhabitant* cannot recollect the time when this could have been said with truth before."[17] And, at the end of July, "another month has rolled around with scarcely a complaint lodged against them. People in small parties—even single persons travel through their Country without being molested, and I think they can be kept so if the people of New Mexico will only let them alone."[18]

Mangas Triumphant:
NOTES

1. The Navajo chief Manuelito either was or became Mangas Coloradas' son-in-law. If Mangas had wanted a full war then, he could have commanded as many as four hundred Navajos in addition to his own Mimbres. Cremony, *Life Among the Apaches*, p. 84. However, when total war did come a few months later, the Navajos appear not to have been a part of it. The great Tsoka-ne-nde Chiricahua leader Cochise, who was probably just coming into his prime, was known to be a son-in-law of Mangas. Thrapp, *Conquest of Apacheria*, p. 14, speculated that if Mangas' using his daughters to form marriage alliances was a deliberate attempt at inter-band unity, he must have been the first Indian since Tecumseh to attempt it. I wonder, too, in the opposite direction, to what extent leaders of smaller bands sought to affiliate themselves with the great Mangas.

2. Sumner to Jones, Feb. 3, 1852. The pertinent letters are reproduced in Calhoun, *Official Correspondence*.

3. Ogle, *Federal Control of the Western Apaches*, p. 33.

4. Two views of this rather incisive treatment of white prospectors' dual penchant for avarice and gullibility are Opler, "Myths and Tales of the

Chiricahua Apache Indians," p. 51; and Goodwin, "Myths and Tales of the White Mountain Apache," pp. 196–97.

5. Calhoun to Webster, Feb. 29, 1852.

6. Calhoun to Lea, Feb. 29, 1852.

7. Ibid.

8. These are a kind of water jar.

9. Greiner to Lea, April 30, 1852.

10. Calhoun and Sumner, Proclamation of April 21, 1852.

11. Farish, *History of Arizona*, Vol. II, pp. 151–52.

12. The inclusion of Comanches in this case and a couple preceding, raises the interest to know which Comanches these were. This probably cannot be known for certain, but I suspect they were of the Kot-so-te-ka band, either then or shortly after under the chieftainship of the remarkable Mow-way, who was known to have raided as far west as Santa Fe, and who at one time or another cultivated some kind of relationship with the Mescalero Apaches. See Wilbur S. Nye, *Plains Indian Raiders*, p. 298.

13. Sumner to Greiner, July 3, 1852.

14. Greiner to Sumner, July 4, 1852.

15. Greiner to Lea, July 31, 1852. A treaty did eventually result; see Kappler, *Indian Affairs: Laws and Treaties*, Vol. II, pp. 598–600. Greiner probably knew that he was giving Sumner more than due credit in alleging their friendly relations; the following winter Sumner received a reprimand for the flagrant usurpation. Conrad to Sumner, Dec. 23, 1852.

16. Greiner to Lea, June 30, 1852.

17. Ibid.

18. Greiner to Lea, July 31, 1852.

General Garland's War

In April of 1853 a new governor arrived in the territory, William Carr Lane. At Santa Fe he endured a flurry of petty humiliations from Colonel Sumner, who removed his headquarters to Albuquerque rather than suffer through a welcoming ceremony, and took the flag with him and refused to return it.

For three months, though, Lane managed to call Sumner's bluffs better than Calhoun had, until in July a new Secretary of War, Jefferson Davis, finally began to perceive Bull Sumner as a liability in Indian control and relieved him. In New Mexico Sumner had made many more enemies than friends, and he was glad to go. It is a little too easy for a history establishment now sensitive to Indian injustice to write off Sumner as an obstructionist and blackguard. The differences between him and the civil authorities were primarily philosophical, and only mirrored in small the tremendous battle that raged nationwide between the War and Interior departments over Indian control. Still, measured against the chances for co-operation or even peace with the Apaches that were lost as a result of his tempestuous quarreling, Sumner probably did more than his share to keep the Apaches in turmoil. He was replaced by John Garland, a brevetted brigadier general who was quiet, efficient, popular, and willing to co-operate with civilian authorities when he believed good Indian management would result.

At the end of May 1853, Josecito and a small cluster of Sierra Blanca Mescaleros rode into Santa Fe to keep in touch. They said they were having good luck with their crops, and they still hoped for a fort to be established in their range to protect them.[1]

Lane concluded other agreements with the Mangas Chiricahuas, by which the Indians were to receive heavy rations for one year, including breeding stock and instruction in farming, and lesser rations for three years thereafter. Without waiting for the Senate to ratify his treaties, he assembled a large portion of the Mimbres at the site of Fort Webster and spent a goodly sum of money on their behalf. However, Lane was replaced in August of 1853 by a new chief executive, David Meriwether, who arrived to discover that Lane had spent virtually all his money and the Senate had repudiated his treaties. The Mimbres found themselves left to face the coming winter without the promised aid from the pindahs, and in a rage they resumed raiding.

Their resentment increased further when Fort Webster was put back on the line by stationing a new garrison there to protect the exploding population of whites: settlers, surveyors, and prospectors, in addition to transients en route to the gold diggings in California. In fact, the providing of a southern rail route to California was the principal motivation for the Gadsden Purchase, which rendered the work of the Boundary Commission dead letter. (One provision of the Gadsden agreement canceled the clause of the Guadalupe Hidalgo Treaty that required the United States to prevent her Indians from raiding in Mexico. Although this may be seen as simply a *de facto* recognition that it was an impossible goal from the start, it has also been noted that whatever gain there was in the lessened responsibility was offset by moving the boundary further south and including more bands of Apaches in American territory.)[2] At any rate, during the winter of 1853–54 the angry Mimbres lightened the civilian frontier of an estimated $100,000 worth of goods, and took several lives during the raids.

One facet of Lane's administration had been the removal of all Indians from east of the Rio Grande to agencies west of that river, a plan spurred in part by new trouble among the Jicarillas. In 1852 a number of them allied with Utes and, novelty though it was, some Navajos, for a raid against Arapahoes and Kiowas, but instead they turned and committed depredations on white settlers. When Lane called them in to agencies at Albiquiu and Taos, they relied on him and came in, but they were given spoiled rations and the crops they planted failed.[3] When repudiation from the Indian Commissioner forced Lane to recant and cut their supplies, their resentment was almost as extreme as their circumstances.

Governor Meriwether had a sterner jaw for Indian administration than Lane, and did not, evidently, perceive the hostility as the result of broken promises. To his mind, of the feed-them-or-fight-them alternatives, feeding them hadn't worked, so he would fight them.[4] Once again Ute-Jicarilla raiding parties began to lurk about the Santa Fe Trail, seeking plunder enough to keep their families alive. A party of about thirty under their third chief, Lobo Blanco (of the White massacre), absconded with cattle owned by the man who held the beef contract at Fort Union. Thirty dragoons of the 2nd Regiment clattered out after them and engaged Lobo Blanco's warriors on March 4, 1854, south and east of the post about fifty miles, near the Canadian River. The dragoons came off the better; the lieutenant in charge shot Lobo Blanco repeatedly, but the chief did not die until he was finished by a boulder dropped on his head.[5]

Near the end of the month, more Jicarillas were seen on the Taos–Santa Fe road, mounted, probably, on horses stolen by Gómez Mescaleros in west Texas and sent north to trade.[6] The commander of the military post near Taos sent out a sixty-man company of 1st Dragoons to see what they were up to. The Indians were a very large raiding party under the first chief, the erstwhile farmer Chacón, out to avenge Lobo Blanco and, probably, secure some provisions for his own following. He had with him something on the order of, it was estimated, 200 to 250 warriors. In the Embudo Mountains at Cieneguilla, some twenty-five miles south-southeast of Taos, Chacón prepared an ambush for the pindah soldiers and waited. The dragoons obligingly entered the trap, which Chacón triggered at the perfect instant. In a three-hour holocaust every man in the company, save two, was hit. Thirty-six made it back to Taos; twenty-two were killed and abandoned. The officer in charge, Lieutenant John W. Davidson, lived to fight another day.

The Battle of Cieneguilla marked the high point of Jicarilla resistance, as from that hour the army marked them for doom. General Garland was aghast when he learned by special courier of the disaster; he sent orders to the commander at Fort Union, Philip St. George Cooke, to "humble them to the dust."[7] When the directive reached Union, Cooke was already after them with every man he could muster: two hundred regulars, a company of artillerymen, who had found their cannon swabs and ramrods snatched away and replaced with muskets, and thirty-two Mexicans and Pueblo Indians picked up in Taos as scouts, under guide-turned-agent Kit Carson.

By now it was April, but the spring countryside was still covered with a thick, smothering crust of snow, and more fell every day as Cooke headed his angry army west into the wilds. Chacón's sign was quickly discovered and Cooke pursued it, across the Rio Grande and still further in forced marches that gained on the Ute-Jicarilla party, Chacón was likely surprised at the unusually vigorous chase and possibly overconfident after the easy rout at Cieneguilla. With about 150 warriors he crossed the Rio Caliente and spaced them around a rocky cliff to treat Cooke as he had Davidson. The Pueblo scouts defused the ambush before it could spring, however, and Cooke attacked with vigor and precision. He divided his command, part to flank Chacón from a nearby ridge, part to attack him frontally, part to cut him off from his horses, and part to flush him from the boulders where he was waiting. The Jicarillas were completely undone, and escaped in disarray as soon as they saw how Cooke held the advantage. Although Chacón lost only five dead and six wounded, virtually all the horses and camp stores were lost to Cooke, who kept what he needed and destroyed the rest. It was believed that some members of the hostile families, to the number of seventeen, became separated from their men and fled into the snow to die of cold and hunger. Although it can be wondered whether Chacón would have turned and fought if he had been unencumbered by his women and children, the nearby presence of his dependents probably had little effect on the outcome.[8]

For the next two months Garland kept columns of troops crosshatching the Jicarilla country, mostly without serious effect but enough to keep Chacón wary and apprehensive. On June 4, however, an Indian-hating Yankee named James H. Carleton, a brevetted major in the 1st Dragoons, was guided by Kit Carson to a Jicarilla village of twenty-two lodges in the Raton Mountains near the Colorado border northeast of Taos. Although a few of the Indians were killed before the rest escaped, the incident was more notable as a presage of Carleton's later career in New Mexico, and his association with Kit Carson.

The next month the Jicarillas sent a peace feeler in to Santa Fe, which was hostilely rebuffed. Still, Chacón had seen the hopelessness of the situation, and he began to move his people near the agency at Albiquiu, hoping to obtain mercy. There were, inevitably, bad incidents from time to time, and the more warlike Jicarillas went north to continue raiding with the Utes, but for this majority of the tribe that followed Chacón, their fighting days were over forever.

During the Jicarilla fighting, the Gómez Mescaleros in the Davis Mountains of Texas had a field day jumping on travelers and wagon trains at Eagle Springs.[9] It was the (mostly) peacefully struggling Sierra Blancas, however, who were blamed, and it was against them that General Garland sent a 180-man punitive column. The nonplussed Sierra Blancas managed to scramble out of the way and there was no fighting. In October of 1854, seven of the southern Mescaleros (one of them a chief) were killed when troops chased them from one of their Eagle Springs ambushes. Many of these bands apparently now retired across the Rio Grande, beyond the reach of the soldiers but still conveniently able to hit into west Texas. Troop concentrations began to build in New Mexico, as on New Year's Day of 1855 ten Apaches—either Texas Mescaleros or hungry disaffected Sierra Blancas—discovered. They made the mistake of stealing stock close in to Santa Fe, and soldiers chased them down and killed them to a man.

General Garland was convinced that the trouble emanated from the Sierra Blancas, and laid plans for a major expedition against them. To fight them in the winter, he reasoned, would be difficult on the dragoons, but even worse on the Apaches. The principal area of contention was two hundred miles east of the Rio Grande, in the cattle ranges about the Pecos River. The strategy was to converge troops on the area from different directions; the strongest column of about eighty dragoons left the newly established Fort Thorn a couple of days after Christmas, under the command of Captain (later Confederate General) Richard S. Ewell. The long march to Anton Chico on the Pecos was across ice-sheeted terrain, treeless and exposed to numbing blasts of wind. When they reached Anton Chico they were advised that the cattle-stealing Mescaleros had retired to the south and the columns would have to follow. The combined force of fifty infantry and over a hundred dragoons plowed south down the Pecos to the Peñasco, then a long march west up that stream to the eastern slope of the Sacramento Range. This led them to the most sheltered area in the region, which was also a main winter camp of the Sierra Blanca Mescaleros. The first time soldiers sortied through their country the Apaches simply tried to stay out of the way, but as the lookouts kept Ewell's column under scrutiny, the leaders got ready to fight. The pindahs were headed right for them, it was winter, and there was nothing in the frigid wilderness on which to support themselves if they fled, so there was little else to do.

During the night of January 17, warriors tried unsuccessfully to burn the command out of their camp, and all the next day maintained a moving siege as the troops crept up the Peñasco. Whenever the Mescaleros got too close, Ewell ordered a charge to disperse them, but his animals were too broken down by the 450-mile trek to catch the well-mounted Indians.[10] Reporting that fifteen of the warriors had been shot from their horses, Ewell sensed that he must be nearing an important prize, judging from the vigor of the defense, and indeed soon was able to estimate that there were perhaps three hundred lodges within a few miles. The next afternoon he entered a quiet, snow-dusted canyon that contained two abandoned rancherias, one in the main part and a second, smaller one in a side canyon. Ewell decided to spend the night in this place and detailed one of his junior officers, a respected and popular captain named Henry W. Stanton, to investigate the second rancheria. Shortly thereafter Ewell suddenly heard a staccato eruption of gunfire and sent a relief party afoot to see what had happened. The village's inhabitants had retreated to just beyond its perimeter, when Stanton saw them and charged after them. The Apaches got away after killing one of Stanton's men. After chasing them a good distance up the valley, the captain galloped too far ahead of his men and got cut off; in a short time he managed to rally his men and, not seeing where the Indians had gone, turned back. About three quarters of a mile from the rancheria he was ambushed and another of his men killed, a private who was dismounted and lanced after he killed one of the warriors. Stanton himself stayed in the rear to cover his group's retreat, until he was killed by a single shot in the head. After this the Mescaleros disappeared and left no track for the scouts to follow, although Ewell saw smoke signals to the south and guessed that was the direction they took. Ewell hurriedly buried his dead and struck out after them, in two days reaching the heights of the Guadalupe Mountains. By now he was losing about ten

horses per day to cold and exhaustion, and he soon returned to the
Peñasco, where he found the bodies of his three dead men disinterred and
half eaten by scavengers, their burial blankets gone. The report carried the
implication that it was the Mescaleros who had looted the corpses, which
would have been an exceptionally desperate thing for a Mescalero, with
his fear of the dead, to do. Back on the Peñasco, the Sierra Blancas tried
once more to burn Ewell out of his camp, but were thwarted. With his expedition almost totally broken down, Ewell headed up the Bonito, then
north to the Manzano Mountains. He crossed the range at Point of the
Mountains and returned to his post.

About fifteen of the Mescaleros dogged him all the way back to Fort
Thorn, where on February 23 they raided a grazing station some distance
out. All four of the herd guard were badly wounded but managed to fight
the Indians off. The Mescaleros took out south again, determinedly followed by units from Fort Thorn and then Fort Bliss at El Paso, but they
got away.

Although only one Apache had been killed, Ewell's campaign was a bad
beating for the Sierra Blancas, because the pindahs had taken a war into
their deepest sanctuary, driving them from their camps in the horrible
weather of the Ghost Face season, when little food could be gathered.
They knew that a new agent, Dr. Michael Steck, had been appointed to
their affairs, and they went to him and begged for peace. The army was
reluctant and a little disgruntled, as General Garland had readied a
strike force double the size of Ewell's, but Steck managed to stay their
hand long enough for the bested Indians to march down to Fort Thorn
to plead their case. There Governor Meriwether's hawkish attitude changed
abruptly when he saw their condition. "I found these Indians . . . the
most destitute imaginable," he wrote. "I relieved their immediate wants
and directed Agent Steck to issue them a limited amount of provisions,
from time to time, as they might apply for relief and their necessities
seemed to require it."[11] The Sierra Blancas signed the treaty that was
given them, by which they agreed to live under the guns of a fort at the
confluence of the Bonito and Ruidoso, and were allotted a reservation.[12]
It is somewhat painful to speculate whether there need have been a
fight at all, if the Sierra Blancas had been rationed and encouraged when
they asked for such a fort the year before. And the fort, not to write too
florid a finish to the campaign, was named for the fallen Captain Henry
Stanton. The twenty-seven-mile-wide swath from the Pecos to the mountains has, with considerable boundary adjustment, remained the Sierra
Blanca reservation to this day. The treaty was never ratified by the federal
government, but Agent Steck, a conscientious and forthright man, settled
down to the agency at Doña Ana to make do the best he could.

Even as Captain Ewell was preparing to march against the Mescaleros,
the time bomb of Jicarilla hunger and misery and alcoholism that Cal-

houn and Greiner had both warned about finally exploded. The element that had refused to surrender with Chacón was a sizable one, and on Christmas Day 1854, over one hundred Utes and Jicarillas ravaged a settlement on the Arkansas River. Fifteen white men died; women and children were taken prisoner and the livestock stampeded. In January of 1855 a punitive expedition of regulars went out against them. The troops managed to surprise a large force of the hostiles as they were engaged in a frenzied war dance. In a blinding fusillade some forty of the Indians were killed, and six children taken prisoner. Only after a second fight, however, in which the hostiles lost thirteen more dead and all their supplies were lost, did they sue for peace. In meeting with the agent they said they went to war only because of the desperation of their circumstances.

Soon after this, Jicarilla resistance gave its last hurrah. More raids were committed, and in a final battle they killed some two dozen soldiers. The governor declared war on them, but by 1856 relative peace had returned to northern New Mexico. Kit Carson became agent to the Jicarillas and Utes, and he worked out an arrangement with land baron L. B. Maxwell to hire the Indians as hunters, herders, and artisans. And many of them abandoned themselves more resignedly than ever to the whiskey bottle.

To the Mescaleros, Dr. Steck showed himself to be a fair but very tough administrator. The initial provision made to the Sierra Blancas was insufficient for their needs, and with the wild game nearly all gone, they took to stealing and butchering white-owned stock—a horse, a cow, a mule, any animal they could lay their hands on. Steck refused to allow the excuse and informed them that they would not be rationed again until the stock was replaced. The hopeless Indians had little choice but to migrate back to the Sierra Blanca and try once more to live off the land. They managed, barely, for some months before coming back down to Fort Stanton to beg for food, and they were allowed to butcher a decrepit old mule that had fallen down dead in its corral.[13] Steck again refused to feed them until they replaced the animals they had stolen. Although on the surface this seems to have been an almost bizarrely unreasonable position, Steck's motives were certainly good ones. He knew that the Mescaleros could never live in peace until they swore off thievery; the white civilians wouldn't let them alone as long as they were losing animals, and the Apaches had to be made to realize this. And, a couple of months after the confrontation, the Sierra Blancas turned in forty horses which, ironically, they probably had had to steal to replace what they had eaten. With his conditions met, Steck gave them a liberal ration of five beef cattle and thirty fanegas of corn, which was to become their monthly ration (one fanega is a bit more than one and a half bushels). It was a peace that held for a long time.

During the summer of 1854, Congress finally got around to appropriating a workable sum—$30,000—for the Mimbres Chiricahuas. Governor Meriwether did not use any of it, however, until the summer of 1855, after they had been sufficiently impressed by Garland's whipping of the Mescaleros and Jicarillas. The dual incentive of, on one hand, liberal subsistence, and on the other hand, seeing their neighboring cousins thrashed and savaged, rendered the Mimbres eminently amenable to a new treaty, and Dr. Steck's duties were expanded to include instructing them in farming and civilized behavior.

General Garland's War:
NOTES

1. Abel, "Indian Affairs in New Mexico under the Administration of William Carr Lane," p. 343.
2. Ogle, *Federal Control of the Western Apaches*, p. 37.
3. Mails, *People Called Apache*, p. 352. By this time Kit Carson had risen dramatically in influence with the Jicarillas, gaining their confidence and even settling disputes between quarreling factions.
4. Hoopes, *Indian Affairs and their Administration*, p. 172.
5. Bell to Cooke, Mar. 7, 1854; Garland to Thomas, Mar. 29, 1854.
6. Commissioner of Indian Affairs, *Annual Report* for 1854, p. 378.
7. Garland to Cooke, April 7, 1854, tense changed.
8. Details of this campaign can be found in Rodenburgh, *From Everglade to Canon with the Second Dragoons*, pp. 178ff.; Sabin, *Kit Carson Days*, Vol. II, pp. 660ff.
9. Sonnichsen, *Mescalero Apaches*, pp. 69–71.
10. Secretary of War, *Annual Report* for 1855, pp. 56ff., quoted in Sonnichsen, *Mescalero Apaches*, pp. 74–75. Sonnichsen took a view here, as elsewhere in his fine book, sympathetic to the Sierra Blancas, but did not speculate on how or where they got such fresh horses.
11. Commissioner of Indian Affairs, *Annual Report* for 1855, p. 186.
12. Kappler, *Indian Affairs: Laws and Treaties*, Vol. I, pp. 870ff.
13. Sonnichsen, *Mescalero Apaches*, p. 82.

Dr. Steck

Strong, high-minded, independent, stern, and caring, Michael Steck became a credit to the principle of civilian Indian administration. Originally, he had pulled up his Pennsylvania-German roots and come to New Mexico to get his sickly wife into a warmer climate. From his first post as Mescalero agent, his ability and energy—and his rare popularity with the Indians—led to a quick rise in office, until President Buchanan appointed him superintendent for New Mexico.

Steck was already well known among the Tci-he-nde Mimbres, and when he visited them he was received with impressive warmth. They professed their interest in farming, and when the time came to do the actual work, they set to with a will that few would have predicted. The successful crops they raised in 1855 encouraged them to the extent that the more extensive 1856 planting met their needs for all that year and well into 1857.[1] It was apparent that Steck had stumbled onto a successful formula of Apache control: treat them with scrupulous fairness, give them meaningful work to occupy their active and resourceful nature, and reward them generously and tangibly for doing right. It was a deceptively simple idea that was hit on only infrequently during the American period of Apache reduction.

To the Mescaleros he sent a half dozen men to teach them farming, starting with seventy acres of vegetables and grain in the spring of 1856, and a larger project two years later near the place where Alamogordo was later established. Barranquito was dead,[2] and his place of influence was taken by his son Cadette, who spoke as strongly for peace and co-operation as his more turbulent father had desired to fight. Although this period gave the weary Sierra Blancas a much needed breather, these were still far from good times and the Mescaleros were besieged by troubles from without and within.

From outside they were beset by citizen "ranger" forces, which were vigilante posses of Indian-hating ranchers and businessmen disgusted with the army for stopping their war short of exterminating the Mescaleros. In a pattern that became surprisingly fixed over the years, the rangers would spend some little time gathering their courage in a saloon and then, taking a few bottles with them, stage a sneak attack on some unsuspecting village of treaty Indians and kill those slowest to run away—which usually meant the women and children. In February of 1858 just such a force, the "Mesilla Guard," as they called themselves, put on this sort of raid near the Doña Ana agency. They killed about eight before the survivors managed to reach the town and obtain protection. The disgusting incident almost ignited an Indian war when word of it reached the still powerful Gómez, who reached Doña Ana shortly after with about a hundred very angry warriors. Dr. Steck managed to talk him out of fighting, however, by promising that the army would deal with the problem. General Garland was, in fact, furious and threatened to withdraw the garrison if the civilians were so ready to "defend" themselves. Such drunken cowards, he wrote, "have no claim to the protection of the military, and will receive none."[3] He probably meant it, and with Gómez at their doorstep the militia bowed their heads and asked the army to stay.

In April, though, the vigilantes pillaged another Sierra Blanca rancheria, close by Fort Thorn, and killed several more. The commanding officer at the post couldn't believe his eyes, reporting that the Indians of that village "have been at peace and on friendly terms with all in the vicinity; have been daily in and about the garrison, quiet and well behaved."[4] He arrested nearly forty of the freewheeling vigilantes and confined them at the post, an unprecedented action that raised a storm of protest. But, though the clamor reached clear to Washington, none of the perpetrators were punished beyond that inconvenience.

From within, the Sierra Blanca villages were tormented by the ubiquitous comancheros and their whiskey. The Mescaleros had become almost as pathetic in their desire for the stuff as the Jicarillas, and so extended their protection to the bootleggers. The problem remained for decades, but Steck's more immediately serious trouble was that the constant drunkenness precipitated such quarreling that after a time perhaps a half dozen of the Mescaleros had been killed in disputes. In the Apache Life-way this opened the possibility of legitimate retaliation and perhaps then blood feuds, but fortunately the worst trouble subsided and Steck took care to keep the agricultural plots of unfriendly groups separated.[5]

Still, the situation was well enough in hand that when the intractable Gómez saw the Sierra Blancas dependably rationed every month, he started hanging around, too—but Steck would have none of it. He did not need to know the ceremonies of the war novitiate, and the anticipation with which an Apache youth awaited it, to sense how quickly Gómez could lure the young men out for plunder. Steck's stance was perfectly acceptable to Cadette and the other peace chiefs. They were trying so hard to behave themselves that even the army had to acknowledge it. Military and agency records for 1857 show that Gómez returned to his old ways, but this time the commander at Fort Stanton made sure that General Garland knew that the Sierra Blancas were innocent. "After the closest inquiry and strictest investigations," he reported, "I am convinced that the Indians in this neighborhood are in no way connected with them."[6] A few months after this, Cadette brought in stock that his men had captured from renegades, who had taken it in raids. The officer who receipted for the animals praised that "These people have all along shown the most friendly disposition, and are doing all they can to prevent the other Mescaleros from depredating."[7]

By and large, Steck's program worked well enough that when the next Apache turmoil arose, it came not from his Mescaleros or Mimbres, but from bands in the Mogollon Mountains farther west who were not included in his responsibility and who had not yet felt the press of American troops.

The Western Apaches were the last tribe to be able to follow the old life unhindered. Although they sometimes traveled for commerce to the Hopi and Zuni Indians—indeed the volume of trade was said to be appreciable—the Westerns were more concerned with war and raiding. In northern Mexico were the Opata Indians, against whom they fought frequently. They were on bad terms with the Yuman Indians of western Arizona (it was not yet Arizona, of course), raiding often among the Walapais and Havasupais, and sometimes suffering raids in return. (By curious contrast, most of the Western groups enjoyed cordial relations with the Yuman Yavapais, particularly so among the San Carlos and Tonto Apaches. San Carlos women were sometimes taken as wives by the Walkamepa Yavapai, and Tonto women by the Wickedjasapa Yavapai.)[8] Pimas, Papagos, and Maricopas were considered bitter enemies. Probably because they were furthest removed from the border of other Indians' ranges, the White Mountain Apaches seldom raided against the western Arizona Indians, but spent more time than the other groups raiding the peons of Old Mexico, and that was the root of the present trouble. Finding their war trails south made hazardous by the presence of troops in the new Gadsden area, some of the Western Apaches, most likely the White Mountains, turned their raids eastward toward the Rio Grande.

After one of the Rio Grande raids an army unit pursued the Apaches deep into the part of the territory that later became separated as Arizona. The soldiers retook several stolen animals after a chase of three hundred miles, but inflicted little damage on the raiders to recompense so much effort.[9] It was an endless business. Fort Buchanan was put on the line in the middle of the Gadsden Purchase, but during 1857 the Western Apaches became more adept at eluding patrols and again stepped up their raids into Old Mexico, and once they were there they wreaked havoc practically unchecked. It cannot be ascertained which groups of the Westerns were the most active in the Mexican plunder, but the question is not terribly important since they all seem to have been going at it whenever they wanted. After the close of the frontier, Western Apache informants seemed to regard the Mexican raids of the late fifties as the height of the good old days, and were seldom hesitant to talk about them.

Only after Apaches murdered the Navajo agent was a major expedition mounted against them, a small army of 400 under the command of Colonel Dixon S. Miles. Two important fights took place in late June of 1857, both of them defeats for the Apaches. In unexplored territory near the headwaters of the Gila River, Miles killed forty-two and captured thirty-six of a large band he had trapped about thirty-five miles from Mount Graham, and then destroyed their crops. A second force of soldiers to the north trapped the important chief Cuchillo Negro, killing him and six others while taking several families captive, in the Cañón de los Muertos Carneros. The bested Indians sued for a peace conference with Steck and the military commander of the Department.[10] The Apaches admitted they had been raiding, but the government for the time being did not undertake their closer supervision, and held the reaction to a stern warning that more raiding would be followed by more war. To Steck, though, the chief result of the campaign was the loss of the peaceful Tci-he-nde Mimbres, who had been farming for two and a half years. Shaken by the explosion of war all around them, Mangas Coloradas and his captains scattered their families into the safety of the mountains, and waited.

In the wake of the largely victorious fighting, different plans were submitted to the Washington authorities to change the broad complexion of frontier defense and Apache management. Some proposals had a view toward pacification of the Indians, others aimed for extermination, but in the nation's capital both sides of the bureaucratic feud—War and Interior —entered curiously lethargic doldrums. Congress authorized no adjustment of either the number or configuration of army posts or Indian agencies, and in fact the War Department found itself having to reduce the number of soldiers defending the southern frontier of the New Mexico Territory.

Meanwhile, the Mangas Mimbres returned to their cornfields and, for the most part, behaved themselves under Dr. Steck's watchful guidance. Steck noted that their numbers were beginning to be seriously reduced by exposure to white men's diseases, and he reported that they endured with surprising patience the crimes and indignities committed by whites in the locality. Transients were, again for the most part, allowed to travel through their territory in safety, and Steck turned his attention farther west, to the White Mountain band of the Western Apaches. These Indians had been heartily participating in the raids into the Gadsden

Purchase, and by visiting them in friendship Steck managed to win some amount of control over them.

In Washington, the increase of raids into the Gadsden area prompted the dispatch of a special agent to report and make recommendations. This resulted in the putting forward of a broad scheme that would have placed the area in virtually complete military governance, but most of the citizens opposed it. This civilian rejection of too high a military profile even in the face of the Indian menace seems telling of something—perhaps the knowledge that too many troops keeping an eye on real trouble would make it difficult to fake depredation claims. At any rate, civil authorities held a peace talk with several Chiricahuas near Apache Pass in December of 1858. Steck of course was present, and to him the Indians vowed not to molest the Overland stagecoaches, although Steck would have felt better about it if they had agreed to remove farther north. In February of 1859 Steck journeyed to the Cañón del Oro to meet with about 300 Pinalenos, who claimed to represent many times that number, and they also pledged to behave themselves.

During the summer of 1859 the army undertook an extensive reconnaissance of Apachería to get a comprehensive grasp of the situation.[11] The military found the farming Tci-he-nde under Mangas Coloradas still at peace with Americans but raiding in Mexico, although at Steck's suggestion a post was established again to protect the Santa Rita mines. To the west and south the Tsoka-ne-nde and Nde-nda-i Chiricahuas were still refraining from molesting the stage route, and what little stock they had stolen they claimed they mistook for Mexican-owned animals. The Western Apaches had quite plainly continued to rake in plunder from Sonora, and to help control them, a post—Fort Breckenridge, later called Camp Grant—was established on the San Pedro River at the mouth of Arivaipa Creek, but not before some of the Westerns had raided the Patagonia Mines and killed a leading civilian.

Steck was troubled by the increasing infirmity that plagued the farming Mimbres, whose fields now stretched three miles along the Santa Lucia River. Although he believed they might become self-sufficient, the number of their men had decreased from about 400 to perhaps 150, and diseases and alcoholism continued to take their toll. Steck wished them to be given a reservation as far from white people as possible, but failing that, they should at least be removed north of the Gila. His energetic efforts at pacification were bringing him into increasing conflict with the military, which believed that many of the bands he was cajoling into peace could not be controlled until they had been given a good beating. Steck was not anti-army; in fact, he advised the construction of a large post north of the Gila to control the concentration of Apaches he would try to collect there. The difference was one of method of control: Steck wanted forts dotting crucial points of Apachería to keep the warlike cowed (which was in fact in agreement with Bull Sumner's original deployment plan), but the Department commander, T. T. Fauntleroy, preferred to muster punitive expeditions as needed. One such force did push deep into the territory of the Pinalenos, but the officer in charge of the 200-man expedition saw the reason of Steck's side, after most of his horses were stolen or dead of exhaustion. Such ineffectual sallies, Steck reasoned, served more to upset and anger the Apaches than control them. To offset this influence, Steck met constantly with Indians—800 in the Burro Mountains in late October, 400 Tsoka-ne-nde Chiricahuas soon after on the San Simon, and finally a huge conclave of 2,500 Westerns near where the town of Safford was later established. Everywhere he advised them to leave whites alone and move north of the Gila.

In 1860 the federal government finally established a Gila Reservation, a plot of ground fifteen miles square, astride the river. It was much too small to subsist them, and except for Steck's, no serious effort was made to collect them there, and the Indians who did come in deserted the place when the Civil War started. In fact, for several months from late 1859 into 1860, little effort was made above the level of the individual agencies at planning what to do with the Apaches. Dr. Steck was as busy as ever, but in the higher circles of government almost all attention was focused on the threat of war between the states. Most of the Apaches were pretty well left to themselves, and in late 1860 friction increased once more between the New Mexican miners and the Tci-he-nde Mimbres of Mangas Coloradas.

The mines at Pinos Altos were beginning to play out, and the miners not only felt the monetary pinch but, easily distracted from hard work when it did not pay richly in gold, they had more time to get into mischief and steal stock from the Apaches. The Mimbres, of course, retaliated. The miners would organize and go Indian hunting, and the disease-ridden Mimbres were in a poor position to resist. "This I have been anticipating for some time," reported Steck, "as there are now and have been for some months, three or four hundred people at the Pino Alto Mines, a majority of whom were not taking out gold enough to support them."[12]

One such series of incidents led to an altercation between a posse of miners under a colorful pioneer named Tevis, and a group of Mimbres led by an important chief named Elias. A few words were exchanged before the pindahs opened up on the Mimbres and the chief was killed. Tevis, an acquaintance of Elias for some time, wrote that the chief had "sat on his horse . . . not over two hundred yards away, and cussed us in English— and in good English, too. I asked if any of the rangers could lift him out of his saddle, and one by the name of Davis . . . raised his gun, and before the smoke cleared away, Elias lay stretched on the ground."[13]

After later trying to calm the enraged Chiricahuas, their acting agent, Pinckney R. Tully, gave a different version, writing that "Elias, one of the

Apache captains, and I believe the best Indian in the tribe, done [sic] all
he could to get to the Americans, to tell them who he was and ask them
what they were killing his people for, but he could do nothing. He still
kept going to the miners and they firing at him, until he was finally shot
dead."[14]

> Long time ago they say.
> The Foolish People had a camp over there. Soldiers were camped
> nearby and these Foolish People thought they were friends.
> One day the soldiers came and started shooting them down. Instead of
> running or fighting, they started to discuss it. They asked, "What are they
> shooting at us for?"
> After they were mostly dead, one of those remaining said, "We better
> get away from here!" They ran off, but by then the soldiers had killed
> most of them.
> They were fools, that's why they got killed.[15]

An army officer was sent out to investigate the affair, and in his report
to Dr. Steck he accused that the prospectors "have no proof that this party
[of Indians] has anything to do with" the thefts that brought the incident to pass. Steck in turn conceded that local bands may have been
guilty, but that "where one [animal] has been stolen by Indians, four have
been stolen by white thieves." Steck wrote that he did not know what the
Chiricahuas would do, but now that the miners had organized, the
Apaches were not strong enough to fight them, and "The only result I
dread is that they will remove to the Republic of Mexico . . . and from
there maraud upon the property of our people."[16]

The new Indian superintendent in New Mexico, Colonel James L.
Collins, had been rather quiet on Apache policy, but in the fall of 1860 he
suddenly broached a radical new plan to control them by moving them
into pueblos like those of the Rio Grande valley. This scheme would almost certainly have been doomed to failure, given the vastly different Life-
way of the Apaches from the Pueblans, but he never had a chance to try
it. In the tradition of the miners who had bullwhipped Mangas Coloradas,
stupidity was ready to strike again on the frontier.

Dr. Steck:
NOTES

1. Ogle, *Federal Control of the Western Apaches*, p. 37.
2. Sonnichsen, *Mescalero Apaches*, p. 83.
3. Secretary of War, *Annual Report* for 1858, p. 293.

4. Ibid., p. 289.

5. Commissioner of Indian Affairs, *Annual Report* for 1858, p. 195. See also Reeve, "Federal Indian Policy in New Mexico," pp. 14ff.

6. Commissioner of Indian Affairs, *Annual Report* for 1857, p. 576.

7. Ibid., p. 576.

8. Gifford, "Southeastern Yavapai," p. 197.

9. Ogle, *Federal Control of the Western Apaches*, p. 38.

10. Documentation for this brief campaign is found in U. S. Senate, Exec. Doc. No. 2, 35th Cong., 1st sess., Vol. II, pp. 135ff. (1857).

11. U. S. Senate, Exec. Doc. No. 2, 36th Cong., 1st sess., Vol. II, pp. 306ff.

12. Steck to Collins, Dec. 14, 1860, quoted in Thrapp, *Victorio*, p. 68.

13. Tevis, *Arizona in the '50's*, pp. 200ff., quoted in Ibid., p. 69.

14. Ibid., p. 71.

15. Stories of the Foolish People comprise a minor cycle among the Jicarilla, Lipan, Mescalero, and Chiricahua Apaches. In discussing the Chiricahua version similar to this (Opler, "Myths and Tales of the Chiricahua Apache Indians," p. 85, n. 1), Opler speculated that some of the Foolish People myths served to teach lessons in their telling. This particular story so closely parallels the fate of the chief Elias that one wonders whether perhaps some of the Foolish People stories were formulated after particularly terrible events in Apache history, to guard against their reoccurrence.

See also Hoijer, *Chiricahua and Mescalero Apache Texts*, p. 37; Opler, "Myths and Legends of the Lipan Apache Indians," pp. 206ff.; and Opler, "Myths and Tales of the Jicarilla Apache Indians," p. 364.

16. Quoted in Thrapp, *Victorio*, pp. 68–69.

Apache Pass

By the opening of the 1860s the leading chief of the Tsoka-ne-nde Chiricahuas was an athletic man in the prime of life named Cochise. Between thirty-five and forty years old, he was described as about five feet nine inches tall and perhaps 160 pounds in weight. His face was shaped by a high forehead and large, straight nose, and his body bore numerous spattered pocks of buckshot. He was a son-in-law of Mangas Coloradas, and he led a following as devoted to him as the Tci-he-nde were to Mangas. He sheltered them mainly in and about two impregnable natural fortresses, one in the Chiricahua Mountains and the other in the Dragoon Mountains, to the southwest of the Tci-he-nde in what is now southeastern Arizona. Cochise was a fearsome warrior, a shrewd tactician, and a good provider—which meant a skilled raider—and his singular popularity with his people indicated that he was a strong and compassionate leader to his dependents. Though the Mexicans were terrified of him, he seems to have been well thought of by white men who knew him. When Cochise promised Dr. Steck that he would forbear molesting the stagecoaches on the southern route, he went his word even one better, and took a contract to deliver wood to the Butterfield station located in his range, in Apache Pass near the Puerto del Dado spring.

There had been some touchy moments, of course. In early March of 1859 some Apaches, perhaps or perhaps not of Cochise's tribe, apparently seized the stage station and held the three employees hostage. Serious trouble was averted, however, when as the Indians were standing guard outside in a driving rain, a single mounted man approached the station. The leader of the Apaches went out to meet him and lowered, "*Tu capitan?*"

The man replied in the negative and held out a crucifix.

"*Tu padre?*" asked the chief.

"*Si,*" he said. "*Yo padre.*" It was Joseph Priest Machebeuf, an aide to the bishop in Santa Fe.

The chief extended his hand, exclaiming, "*Bueno! Como le va?*"[1] It is sometimes forgotten in southwestern history that Apaches often respected the safety of pindahs with spiritual connections, much as they accorded deference to their own shamans.

These Apaches inquired of any troop movements that Machebeuf knew about, and on hearing that a squadron was only a short distance behind him, departed with a cordial "*Adios, padre.*"

The station attendants swore that they had been saved from certain death, but the truth of it was happily untested, and in sum their relationship with the Cochise Chiricahuas was a good one.

There entered the story at this juncture one of those characters that historians wish they did not have to spend much detail on. John Ward was lately of San Francisco, California, where he had served on the celebrated Vigilance Committee, from which he was a "castoff."[2] (One might query, if he was a failure as a vigilante, just what he *was* good for.) He arrived in Tubac in 1857, and homesteaded a ranch located some twelve miles west of Fort Buchanan. There he lived with a woman not his wife, one Jesúsa Martínez. They had one child themselves and she had had two previously; the eldest, named Felix, was about twelve years old. Early in 1861, Apaches of unknown origin raided the Ward ranch, ran off stock, and escaped with the boy Felix in tow. Ward rode to Fort Buchanan for assistance; a scouting party went out and reported that the culprits had split into three groups, and their trail could not be followed. (The raiders were probably White Mountains or Pinalenos; Felix Martínez, or Felix Ward, grew up near Fort Apache, in the camp of the father of a famous Apache informant, John Rope.[3] As an adult he took the name Mickey Free and gained much celebrity as a scout for the army.) John Ward wanted action, though, and to get it he informed the garrison that the raid had been committed by the local Chiricahuas.

At the end of January a company-sized patrol of about fifty men was sent to Apache Pass, under the command of Second Lieutenant George N. Bascom, 16th Infantry. Bascom, a twenty-five-year-old West Pointer from Kentucky who had been in Arizona only a few months, was accompanied by the rancher Ward and an interpreter named Antonio.

Bascom had no difficulty contacting Cochise. On February 4 the chief with several of his men came into Bascom's camp for a parley. While Cochise was denying that he had anything to do with Felix Ward, Bascom's tent was being surrounded by soldiers, whereupon the lieutenant informed the Indians that they were under arrest until the boy should be brought in. With startling quickness, Cochise flashed out a knife, ripped through the rear wall of the tent, and bolted past the cordon of infantry. The soldiers were so surprised that they let him pass. They recovered their senses and opened fire before he was out of range, but all of the fifty or so rounds failed to hit him.

Curiously, in neither of Bascom's reports of the Apache Pass affair—a summary dated February 14 and a more detailed account on February 25—did he mention a word about this incident, which the Apaches memorialized as the "Cut Through the Tent." Rather, Bascom laconically noted that, "feeling confident that they had the boy I captured six Indians and told the Chief Ca-Ches that I would hold them as hostages until he brought in the boy; he denied having taken the boy, or having been engaged in depredations in the vicinity of the Fort, but said it was done by the Coyoteros and that they then had the boy at the Black Mountain, and if I would wait ten days at the Station he would bring him in; to this I consented."[4] The implication of his reports is that Cochise was allowed to leave freely, and that his reappearance after only two days instead of ten and the subsequent events were the result of Apache treachery. The weight of history has judged otherwise.

The next day[5] Cochise and some of his men visited the Butterfield station, accompanied, as Bascom reported, "with Francisco a Coyotero Chief with about five hundred warriors, and I raised a white flag." The lieutenant went out to parley, but "suspected from their actions that all was not right" and retreated. Cochise then called the stationmaster, a stage driver named Wallace, and a hosteler away from the building for a conference. Bascom ordered them back into the station because, he told them, he had no hostages to exchange for them if they were captured. Bascom evidently felt that the six Apaches he did hold were reserved for Felix Ward, and not to be wasted before the boy materialized. The three men paid Bascom no attention, however; they knew Cochise well enough and went on out, but as they neared him Cochise made his move to capture them, thinking to exchange them for the Apaches held by Bascom. Wallace was nabbed, but the other two broke and ran back to the building. The Indians opened fire and killed the stationmaster, but failed to hit the hosteler. Soldiers inside the station panicked, however, on hearing the gunfire, and believing the fleeing innkeeper to be an attacking hostile, shot him, too.

Toward evening Cochise's Apaches overhauled and captured a small wagon train two miles west of the stage station, and took more hostages. Skirmishes flared up between the Apaches and Bascom's infantry on the fifth, and on the seventh or eighth. The only white casualties were two sergeants reported slightly wounded. However, Bascom got word through to the fort that he needed a doctor and reinforcements,[6] indicating that he was either harder pressed than he let on, or wanted more men to make a clean sweep of the area.

On the sixth, Cochise let himself be seen by the soldiers, reportedly with the stage driver Wallace as hostage and interpreter, saying he would trade the white man and sixteen government mules for Bascom's Apache prisoners. The lieutenant refused to deal unless Felix Ward was handed over. In the evening, Bascom received a note from Wallace, that Cochise had other prisoners, and would trade. It is conceivable that the stalemate dragged on as long as it did because Cochise had sent out messengers to try to recover Felix Ward, or perhaps he was just stalling until he could figure out how to recover his men; but, after the unimportant skirmish on the seventh or eighth, there was no activity from the Indians for some days.

On February 10, the post surgeon from Fort Buchanan, Bernard J. D. Irwin, reached Bascom with his escort; in his entourage were three Coyotero Apaches captured during the journey. Later, reinforcements of seventy men from Fort Breckenridge under First Lieutenant Isaiah N. Moore also rode into the camp.

Nothing more was seen or heard of Cochise. Lieutenant Moore scouted the vicinity with his troops, "travers[ing] 'the mountains three days to assure myself," he reported, "visiting their camps, which I found to have been hastily abandoned, but did not see one fresh track in the whole march."[7] It seems possible that some Apaches—perhaps the captives—sent them on wild-goose chases after nonexistent hostiles. "While they searched," said Gerónimo later, "we watched them from our hiding places and laughed at their failures."[8]

Perhaps Cochise thought the massing of troops in Apache Pass signaled a major campaign against him,[9] or perhaps he finally abandoned hope of getting his captive men back and decided to leave them for dead. For all he knew, they were dead already. All that is certain is that on February 17 or 18 the soldiers found Cochise's white prisoners, executed, shockingly mutilated. Cochise of course got the blame for this, and undoubtedly he approved of the killings, but the torture slayings were probably, again, the responsibility of the female relatives of those men abandoned to Bascom. However, some of the captured Indians were said to be near relatives of Cochise, and if that were the case some of his own women would likely have participated in the atrocity.

Bascom's scouts having discovered no fresh Indian sign, the command went into camp for a final night at the station and started back to Fort Buchanan the next morning. "When near the scene of the massacre," wrote Bascom in his report, "I took the six warriors I had prisoners to the grave of [the] murdered men, explained through the interpreter what had taken place, and my intentions."[10] Bascom then had the six Apaches tied hand and foot, and hanged them from nearby trees. Actually, Bascom's written account claims for himself a little more brass than he had really shown immediately before the executions. At first he resisted the idea of hanging the prisoners, but Irwin testily insisted that the three Coyoteros were his own responsibility and he meant to hang them, whatever Bascom did; Irwin also ranked Bascom and said he would assume responsibility if

Bascom would support him. Only then did the reluctant young lieutenant relent and carry out the act.

Irwin's later attempt at vindication, that his insistence on hanging the six Indians was "demanded and justified by the persistent acts of treachery and the atrocious cruelties perpetrated by the most cowardly and intractable tribe of savages infesting the country,"[11] seemed to reveal rather more about himself than about Cochise. Bascom need not have worried about the killings; he was given an applauding citation for his conduct and promoted three months later.

It is difficult to comprehend the full consequence of the failure of Bascom, thanks to John Ward, to concede Cochise's innocence of the kidnapping. The chief had always been regarded as a fair, honorable, and intellectually capable man, and now by no doing of his own he was branded otherwise. If indeed it had been his relatives that were hanged it certainly fanned the flame of his temper, but it was his overall perception of a broader treachery that finally set his feet on the warpath. And now his depredations were more furious than anyone could have imagined. By one scholarly estimate, for two months after the Bascom affair the avenging Indians killed an average of twenty white people every week.[12] Another opinion was that the ten long years of his hostility cost approximately five thousand lives[13] in raids and battles, a retribution so terrible that his earlier reputation was all but forgotten.

After devastating the Apache Pass vicinity, the Apaches struck twice in quick succession on the Tucson–Tubac road. In the first instance they raided a fortified way station at Canoa, some miles from Tucson, wrecking the place and killing two men camped there. The Indians were still in the immediate area when two more men came riding into Canoa, driving some stock. One was a Mexican, the other was middle-aged pioneer William Rood, whose ranch was about four miles away. They had come through Canoa about an hour previous, on the trail of some strayed horses, and had talked to the two men whose corpses they now discovered. Quickly the Apaches jumped them also, wounding Rood through the left arm with an arrow, and took out chasing them; many of the Apaches were unmounted and ran along behind. After Rood's horse began to tire and slow and he saw he would be caught, he turned from the road and galloped across the desert to find some cover. The Apaches followed him instead of the Mexican, forcing Rood to hide in a small mudhole thicket. In a remarkable display of the courage and nerve that is born of desperation, he killed, he said, nine of the Indians and had one bullet left before they gave up and rode away.[14]

The Tucson–Tubac road, in fact, became impassable, and before long Apache pressure forced the total abandonment of the ancient Spanish settlement of Tubac, the one-time headquarters of Juan Bautista de Anza.[15]

Tucson itself, though not abandoned, dwindled in population until only two hundred remained to tough it out.[16]

Another casualty of Cochise's rage was a party of half a dozen tough and well-armed pioneers under Free Thompson. They were west-bound through Doubtful Pass when they were pounced upon by, it was believed, Cochise and Mangas Coloradas both. It took the Apaches three days and cost them more than forty dead to kill them all. Cochise later said that "they were the bravest men he ever knew or heard of, that if all his band were equal in bravery he would undertake to whip the whole United States."[17]

In late March of 1861, the superintendent of the stagecoach line informed his Tucson agent (who happened to be William S. Oury; remember him for later), that the southern route of the Butterfield Stages was being abandoned for a more northerly one. The move was slated for April 1, but on one of the last scheduled runs, Cochise Chiricahuas ambushed the coach as it passed Stein's Peak. The driver and conductor were killed in the first volley, then the Apaches followed the unguided mules for a mile and a half before the coach was wrecked. The three passengers were captured and tortured to death.[18]

Cochise and about a hundred warriors attacked the herd guard at Fort Buchanan itself; some troops who went out in pursuit were almost totally annihilated. The situation was so grave that the Indian Commissioner sent a special agent to send back a first-hand report and make recommendations. This emissary quickly concluded that there was no help for things until the Indians should be soundly beaten, and he suggested—without much imagination—that a new fort be raised in the Chiricahua country to control them.

By now, however, the Civil War was on in the East, and not many people in Washington cared what happened in New Mexico.

Apache Pass:
NOTES

1. Horgan, *Lamy of Santa Fe*, p. 269.
2. Farish, *History of Arizona*, Vol. II, p. 30.
3. Goodwin, *Western Apache Raiding and Warfare*, p. 309, n. 56.
4. Bascom to Morrison, Feb. 25, 1861, quoted in Sacks, "New Evidence on the Bascom Affair," p. 266.
5. As it frequently happened on the frontier, the exact chronology of events was lost when men at the scene were unsure of the exact date or later remembered it faultily. The Bascom incident has always been exceptionally tangled in this regard. See Utley, "The Bascom Affair," and Sacks, "New Evidence on the Bascom Affair."

6. According to Thrapp, *Conquest of Apacheria*, p. 17, medical assistance from the posts was not sent out to field commands for another twenty years.

7. Moore to Meury, Feb. 25, 1861, quoted in Sacks, "New Evidence on the Bascom Affair," p. 265.

8. Gerónimo, *Geronimo's Story of His Life*, p. 132.

9. This was the opinion of Thrapp, *Conquest of Apacheria*, p. 18.

10. Bascom to Morrison, Feb. 25, 1861, quoted in Sacks, "New Evidence on the Bascom Affair," p. 267.

11. Irwin, "Apache Pass," p. 374.

12. Ogle, *Federal Control of the Western Apaches*, p. 45, n. 87.

13. Farish, *History of Arizona*, Vol. II, p. 32.

14. A brief description of the Rood affair is found in Thrapp, *Conquest of Apacheria*, pp. 3-4. Additional material is found in Weight and Weight, *William B. Rood*; Pumpelly, *Across America*, pp. 45-47. In 1870 Rood drowned amid evidence of foul play while prospecting north of Yuma.

15. Torrans, "Tubac's Rightful Place in the Sun," p. 368.

16. Dunn, *Massacres of the Mountains*, p. 331.

17. Farish, *History of Arizona*, Vol. II, pp. 59-60; Comfort, *Apache*, pp. 253-55.

18. See Oury's account in Tucson *Star* of July 20, 1879. Apparently, moves had been under way even before the Apache troubles to shift the route northward, the maneuvers stemming from Republican congressmen who had always favored the northern route. Of the forty stations that once watched over the Butterfield Route, the one in Apache Pass is one of the few of which any trace remains. See Mulligan, "Butterfield Trail," p. 367.

The Civil War's
Southwestern Sideshow

For the white citizens in the western half of New Mexico that was becoming known as Arizona, the start of the War Between the States on April 12, 1861, could not possibly have come at a worse time. With Cochise at the towering height of his fury, orders went out to the military installations on the western line to pull back as far east as the Rio Grande. Fort McLane was deserted on July 3 and the garrison retreated to Fort Fillmore. Fort Breckenridge was abandoned and destroyed on July 10 as its soldiers fell back to Fort Buchanan. Dr. Steck fled his post three days later and left for Santa Fe, the last agent the Mimbres would have for a long time, and on the twenty-first the Apaches saw the hated Fort Buchanan itself evacuated and fired as those pindahs, too, marched east. Cochise and his watchers, perched high in their mountain overlooks, saw it all, and with the citizens all but helpless before him, it was a bloody time in the Southwest.

The Confederate troops had already occupied the posts in trans-Pecos Texas during June, including Fort Davis and Fort Bliss, after which they turned into New Mexico.[1] Lieutenant Colonel John R. Baylor of the Mounted Rifles occupied Fort Fillmore on July 26, and in the Organ Mountains he captured without resistance seven Union companies under Major Isaac Lynde. A federal force was whipped at Val Verde, where, parenthetically, Cochise's nemesis George Bascom, since promoted again to captain, was killed. The Southerners' advance finally stalled at Glorieta. Baylor proclaimed himself governor of the "Territory of Arizona," created by himself, and retained that civil office after he was succeeded in military command by Brigadier General Henry Sibley. With his title and office confirmed by the Confederate Congress, Baylor set up his capital at Mesilla and settled down to deal with the Apaches. The question of how to do it was not a hard one for someone who hated Indians as much as he did.

Skirmishes with the local Mescaleros began almost immediately, leaving several dead on both sides.[2] Farmers who had tilled under the protection of federal posts had stampeded out of the region, leaving the ripening crops for the Mescaleros, many of whom returned, momentarily unchecked, to the old life of raiding and plundering. A party of Sierra Blancas got the short end of a fire fight on July 25, and after that they continued to pillage but stayed fairly close to their home range.[3]

The power of the Davis Mountain Mescaleros of Gómez and his rowdies, however, was something to be dealt with more seriously, and before sending men to battle against the wily Indians, a peace treaty was tried first. The effort centered on a chief called Nicolás, an active raider who had been thoroughly contemptuous of white men and their peace speeches. He accepted an invitation to enter Fort Davis and negotiate. He flourishingly agreed to befriend the new authorities, and even clambered into a stagecoach for the long ride to El Paso to seal the pledge with Confederate peace commissioners. At a glittering (at least under the rather frowsy circumstances) fête given in his honor, Nicolás rendered a very pretty speech: "I am glad I have come. My heart is full of love for my pindah brothers. They have not spoken with forked tongues. We have made a treaty of peace and friendship. When I lie down at night the treaty will be in my heart, and when I arise in the morning it will still be there. And I will be glad I am at peace with my pindah brothers. Enju!"[4] After toasts and cheers he got back on the stage for Fort Davis, in the company of that post's new commander. Twenty miles out from the fort, Nicolás swiped the colonel's side arm from its holster and flew out the door, disappearing before the coach could stop. The whole thing had been a lark, and the next day he and his warriors surprised the Fort Davis stock herd, killed two of the guard, and pounded away with abundant horses and cattle. It was enough to give sincere Indians a bad name.

Nicolás and his raiders had not gone far when they were overtaken by a small detachment—one officer, Lieutenant Reuben E. Mays, and thirteen men. Too easily they retook a hundred head of horses and continued trailing, encouraged, until they came upon a narrow canyon that had ambush written all over it. Lieutenant Mays and his scout read the signs correctly but were cajoled by the men—green Texas Volunteers—into proceeding. Nicolás and the hundred warriors who followed him were waiting, and only the Mexican guide escaped the firestorm. A rescue party failed to locate any of the corpses.[5]

To subjugate these and other Apaches, Governor Baylor organized two volunteer forces, thirty-five "Arizona Rangers" and thirty "Arizona Guards," although exactly what kind of show he expected a few dozen citizen volunteers to make against the vast Apache menace is questionable. Undaunted, Baylor sent his volunteers to re-open the Mesilla–Tucson road on March 20, 1862, and his orders to the Guards commander caused quite a stir when they reached the East: "I learn . . . that the Indians have been in to your post for the purpose of making a treaty. The Congress of the Confederate States has passed a law declaring extermination of all hostile Indians. You will therefore use all means to persuade the Apaches or any tribe to come in for the purpose of making peace, and when you get them together kill all the grown Indians and take the children prisoners and sell them to defray the expense of killing. . . . Leave nothing undone . . . and allow no Indian to escape."[6]

The brutality of this directive caused the Confederate President, Jefferson Davis (the same man who as the American Secretary of War had removed Bull Sumner ten years before) to dismiss Baylor from his office. However, the change mattered little, for the Confederate jig in the Southwest was about up. Despite its victories here and elsewhere early in the war, the Confederacy was never in a position to hold New Mexico in the face of any serious federal push to retake it, because their lines of supply southeast to San Antonio were horrendously overextended through barren country that was watched over by Gómez, Nicolás, and other chiefs equally crafty and truculent. When the Union offensive came in summer of 1862, the rebels vacated their posts even quicker than the loyalists had the year before. They fell back to the El Paso area, and then even Fort Davis was evacuated, and almost instantaneously looted and sacked by celebrating Mescaleros. Most of the credit for the reoccupation of New Mexico fell to volunteer forces from Colorado, but of greater importance to the Apaches was the California Column, 1,800 volunteers marching eastward under the command of Brigadier General James H. Carleton, the same blustery, self-righteous Yankee dragoon officer who had fought Jicarillas for John Garland in 1854.

Carleton's army lumbered quietly through Arizona until they reached Apache Pass, the scene of the Bascom debacle, which they found blocked by a still rampaging Cochise and, now, Mangas Coloradas. In retrospect, it is starkly amazing that Mangas kept the peace as long as he did. For seven years he had tried to tend his farms, during which time he had been threatened and abused by Indian-hating settlers, buffeted by troop movements, and kept insecure by the government's desire for him to move here or there or somewhere else. He had watched his warriors, perhaps once four hundred strong, sicken and die in their fields until fewer than half that number remained. Dr. Steck was a good man; they all knew that— even the wildest of the Nde-nda-i war captains, known as Gerónimo, admitted Steck was a good man,[7] but where was he now? Elias had been a good man, too, and he was dead. Cochise, Mangas' son-in-law, was a good man, and he saw his relatives hanged from trees by a pindah nantan. And now, every ounce of Mangas Coloradas was at war, at Cochise's side.

It was June 25, 1862, when the foremost detachment of the California Column, 140 of the 1st California Cavalry under Lieutenant Colonel Edward E. Eyre, reached the Puerto del Dado spring and discovered a num-

ber of Chiricahuas under a white flag. Eyre expressed his peaceful intentions as three of his men who became separated from the rest were cut
down in their tracks. That night the Indians attacked and managed to
wound Eyre's surgeon. It was rare indeed for Apaches to engage in hostilities at night, for killing after dark was somehow associated with Owl and
undead spirits. Why Cochise would undertake such a venture in the absence of extreme emergency is a first-class mystery.

On July 14, a second contingent of about 120 infantry entered Apache
Pass. They had marched forty miles that day in the oven of a desert summer, and had had no water. Mangas and Cochise commanded the
approaches to the spring and watched from ambush. When the fore of the
column was only a half mile from the water, and thinking of little else,
the rear had passed into the vise and the Apaches opened fire, killing one
pindah and wounding another in the first fusillade. Soon, however, the Indians learned an important lesson about fighting white soldiers: part of
the force was made up of a small artillery detachment. Two light how-
itzers were wheeled up, and when the barrels could finally be elevated
enough, they began methodically booming in response to the cracking
puffs of rifle smoke on the mountainsides. There was a great deal of noise
and blasted rubble, and although the Apaches were suitably impressed and
somewhat frightened, they dug in for several hours more. They managed
to kill another pindah and wound a fourth before retreating from their positions. A few of the Apaches were probably killed by the bursting shells,
but white claims of the casualties inflicted by the artillery—up to five
dozen dead—were badly exaggerated. The commanding officer sent a half
dozen men off to warn his supply train, several miles to his rear. No
sooner were they away than they were beset by Apaches, who managed to
slow them down by shooting most of their horses. The detail might have
been wiped out but for a lucky shot from one John Teal:

"The old chief . . . had got to a bunch of Gaita grass & was lying on his
belly on the opposite side with his rifle resting on the bunch pointed strait
[sic] at me, which caused me to drop from the horse on[to] the ground
& the indian shot the horse instead of me. The horse left & I laid
low. . . . We kept firing till it was dark when a lucky shot from me sent
the chief off in the arms of his indians."[8] The wounded leader was almost
certainly Mangas Coloradas. The engagement was broken off and Mangas
was transported to Janos, where a doctor managed to save his life.

With the strategic importance of Apache Pass so dramatically illustrated, Carleton established a major post at the site, named Fort Bowie in
honor of a colonel in the California Volunteers. And, while the fights with
Cochise and Mangas in the pass had little effect in slowing the Chiricahua
onslaught, Fort Bowie remained an intrusive threat that the Apaches had
to keep an eye on, and the fort was not taken off the line until 1894.

General Carleton finally took command of the Department of New

Mexico on September 18, 1862, delegating active command of the western half—the District of Arizona—to a newly billeted brigadier, Joseph Rodman West. Like Bull Sumner, "General Jimmy" Carleton was not a wicked man; he was a seriously flawed man whose miscasting generated wicked results. His was an exaggerated personality. His good qualities, his energy and efficiency and desire to do right and do it well, were considerable, as were his shortcomings: tyranny, inflexibility, and self-righteous conceit. A man with his tendency to autocratic dictation should never have been placed in a position to use it so freely. New Mexico in her ravished disorganization needed a strong governor; she got an emperor. Martial law was extended for years after the need had passed, and travel between towns was strictly regulated by military passport. To politicians and his superiors he was an able and witheringly effective correspondent, and he seemed to his enemies untouchable.

Carleton left the subjugation of the Mimbres and Chiricahuas to General West, while he turned his own attention—through the impressed service of an unwilling Kit Carson—to the Mescaleros.

Barely a week after assuming command (lethargy was not among his many faults), Carleton ordered that Fort Stanton be reoccupied, and directed Carson out with five companies of volunteers, with the instruction, "All Indian men of that tribe are to be killed whenever and wherever you can find them. The women and children will not be harmed, but you will take them prisoners, and feed them at Fort Stanton until you receive other instruction about them. If the Indians send in a flag and desire to treat for peace, say to the bearer that when the people of New Mexico were attacked by the Texans, the Mescaleros broke their treaty of peace, and murdered innocent people, and ran off their stock; that now our hands are untied, and you have been sent to punish them for their treachery and their crimes; that you have no power to make peace; that you are there to kill them wherever you can find them; that if they beg for peace, their chiefs and twenty of their principal men must come to Santa Fe to have a talk there."[9]

From the Apaches' perspective, they might as well have had Baylor back. The height of the Confederate advance into New Mexico had never given them control of the whole Territory, and in the portion not surrendered by Union forces, some face of civil responsibility for Indians had been maintained. Dr. Steck had been previously relieved of the superintendency to concentrate his talents on the Mimbres agency, where he remained until compelled to leave. The new superintendent appointed a leading citizen, Lorenzo Labadie, agent to the Mescaleros. He was a man of courage and strength who also felt the Apaches' suffering. In many ways he was the equal of the good Dr. Steck, combining sensitivity to the Indian plight with a stern grasp of frontier reality. The same day that Carleton ordered Fort Stanton reoccupied, Labadie reported that the

Mescalero chiefs had been signaling their desire for peace for some two months, and in that time had exercised closer control over the disaffected rowdies who committed the raids. Still, none had come in to his agency, and the depredations had been serious, and he supportively agreed to the idea of Carleton's campaign to herd them back in. He certainly would not, however, have condoned the exterminationist tone of the General's orders to Carson.

Indeed, Carson himself scarcely knew what to do with them. He was a soldier, not an executioner. Most of what the Mescaleros stole, they ate; their subsistence raids had made them neither fat nor powerful. They had lost the campaign before it started, and they knew it and Carson knew it. But the columns took the field.

One came back empty-handed, but another happened across the small following of the elderly chief Manuelito. The leader was taking his people to Santa Fe to plead for an end to the violence. After sighting one another the Indians and militia neared each other warily. Manuelito raised his hand in the peace sign and walked toward the pindahs; at an order from Captain James Graydon, gun barrels were suddenly leveled and a volley was fired. Manuelito was killed, also five other men including his second chief, José Largo, and a woman. As the Mescaleros fled, the hoorawing volunteers rode down and killed five more and wounded several before they could get away. The militia rounded up the captured stock and returned to Fort Stanton; somewhere during the flush of victory, some of the stock was disposed of, at an appropriate fee. The charitable assumption is that this was to help defray expenses, as the saying went.

Kit Carson was mortified, and even Carleton was sufficiently moved to instruct Carson that if he were satisfied that the fight "was not fair and open,"[10] he should attempt to return the stock to the survivors of Manuelito's band. One hopes that made them feel better, but the war was not canceled. Indeed, it intensified, as the Sierra Blanca and Guadalupe Mountains regions were scoured by one sortie after another. The climactic action occurred in early November, initiated not by Carson's New Mexico militia but by Carleton's own Californians. Captain William McCleave managed to sneak undetected upon the main camp of Sierra Blancas, located in one of their favorite strongholds, Dog Canyon in the Sacramento Mountains, above the White Sands. He routed them, with the Mescaleros fighting a delaying action with what little ammunition they had. Once they had extricated themselves, they fled the Sacramentos and did not stop till they reached Carson at Fort Stanton.

Obeying his instructions, Carson sent a delegation escorted by Agent Labadie and a guard of soldiers to Santa Fe. There Cadette surrendered to Carleton with what dignity was left him: "You are stronger than we. We have fought you so long as we had rifles and powder; but your weapons are

better than ours. Give us weapons and turn us loose, and we will fight you
again; but we are worn out; we have no more heart; we have no provisions,
no means to live; your troops are everywhere; our springs and waterholes
are either occupied or overlooked by your young men. You have driven us
from our last and best stronghold, and we have no more heart. Do with us
as may seem good to you, but do not forget that we are men and
braves."[11]

Carleton, it turned out, had just the thing for them. His energetic nature had already seen to the end of the war, and he had laid out a new reservation just for them, at another frequently used Mescalero campground,
the Bosque Redondo on the Pecos River. Carleton told Cadette that they
could negotiate a peace when he had gathered his people, all of them, at
the Bosque.

While Carleton was mopping up the Mescalero trouble, his number
two, General West, had gone into action against the Mimbres and
Chiricahuas, obeying Carleton's order to "immediately organize a suitable
expedition to chastise what is known as Mangus Colorado's [sic] Band of
Gila Apaches . . . the punishment of that band of murderers and others
must be thorough and sharp."[12]

The stars were beginning to juxtapose themselves ominously for the
aging Mangas after his months of incessant warfare at the side of Cochise.
By now he was probably at least seventy, and he had been chief of the
Tci-he-nde since the murder of Juan José. He must still have had firm control of his mental powers, though, or he would have fallen from influence,
and he must still have been strong, because he continued to lead raids,
and Apaches would not follow a decrepit man into battle. He might have
lived several more years. Mangas and his people were camped in the vicinity of Pinos Altos. Though the place held ugly memories for him, the
miners who had beaten him were long since dead or driven away. Now a
new group of white-eyes was entering the territory. About forty rough and
woolly pioneer prospectors under the general leadership of Joseph Reddeford Walker were riding west, returning to Arizona after a remarkable
circuit that had taken them gold hunting to California, east through the
Grand Canyon country to Colorado, and down the continental spine that
divided the New Mexico Territory. As they entered the Tci-he-nde
Mimbres country, they had skirmished with the Apaches a few times. According to one member of the Walker party, Daniel E. Conner, the prospectors decided that if they could kidnap Mangas and hold him until they
vacated the country, "we would be able to proceed with far less
difficulty."[13] The member of the group selected to lead the attempt was a
colorful Southerner named Jack Swilling.

The Walker party's brainstorm coincided with a decision in the military that peace would never come to the Southwest while Mangas lived. So, when Swilling set about the kidnap he obtained assistance from a military detachment under Captain Edmond D. Shirland, 1st California Cavalry. There was nothing obtuse or baroque about the plan: they sent word out that the army wanted to have a peace talk, Mangas came in, and they took him. When he appeared he was seen to be wearing plain blue overalls, cut off at the knees, a checkered shirt, and a sombrero, much too small to settle on his gigantic head, tied with a string under his chin. Conner noted his high, aquiline nose, "his one delicate feature," his sharply receding chin and forehead, bulging eyes, and thick, straight, waist-length hair. The chief was spirited away to a reoccupied Fort McLane; soon thereafter, General West also arrived and held a private interrogation of Mangas before turning him over to a guard detail. Then, allegedly, West instructed one of the guards almost coyly to make very particularly certain that Mangas did not under any circumstance escape, and asked if his instruction were understood. It was.

Daniel Conner was standing guard duty that night, and in his memoir he recounted that "About 9 o'clock I noticed the soldiers were doing something to Mangas, but quit when I returned to the fire and stopped to get warm.

"Watching them from my beat . . . I discovered that they were heating their bayonets and burning Mangas's feet and legs. This they continued to do [until] Mangas rose up on his left elbow, angrily protesting that he was no child to be played with. Thereupon the two soldiers, without removing their bayonets from their Minié muskets each fired quickly into the chief, following with two shots each from their navy six-shooters. Mangas fell back . . . and never moved.

"An officer came, glanced at the dead body and returned to his blanket. . . . In twenty minutes all was still again. The next morning I took some trinkets from the body. . . . A little soldier giving his name as John T. Wright, came to the dead body and scalped it."[14]

A little later Mangas' corpse was dumped in a shallow grave, but before long an army surgeon with an interest in such things had it unearthed and decapitated. He boiled out the head and sent the skull to noted phrenologist O. S. Fowler, who measured it and declared it larger than Daniel Webster's. It is hard not to recall here John Russell Bartlett's summation of Mangas' qualities upon their meeting in 1851. Probably no Indian in the Southwest tried so hard to keep peace with the white men, and was so hated for his trouble. Of all the Apaches who fell by white hands, Mangas Coloradas was the greatest tragedy. When charges of brutality were finally brought against General West over Mangas' killing, he defended that he had detailed seven men "including a non-commissioned officer, over Mangas to be sure he could not escape . . . and [he] was killed at midnight while he was rushing his guard to escape." He lied. West also as-

Lieutenant
Charles B. Gatewood.
National Archives.

A group portrait of Gatewood's Apache scouts, taken at the conclusion of the Victorio campaign. Man at top is Sam Bowman, Chief of Scouts; Lieutenant Gatewood immediately below him. *National Archives*.

Beduiat (Victorio), great leader of the Tci-he-nde Mimbres after the murder of Mangas Coloradas. For many years this was believed to be the only photograph ever taken of him; legend had it that his hair became tousled when he lost his headband in a struggle to make him pose for the camera. *National Archives*.

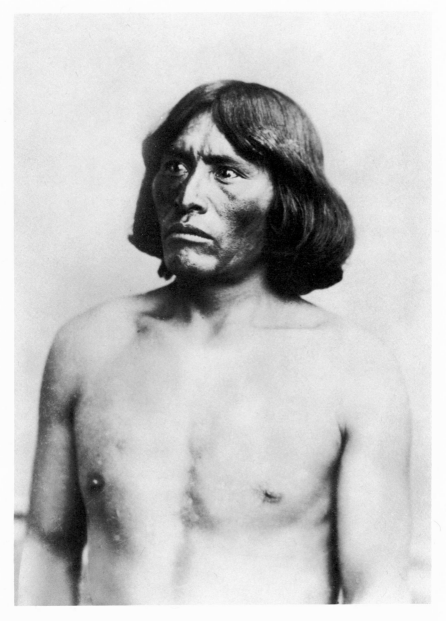

Beduiat (Victorio). In this recently discovered picture, Victorio's thick, short-cropped hair appears to have a natural wave and is exceptionally well groomed. *Arizona Historical Society.*

Fort Davis, West Texas, as it appeared in the 1880s, about the time Grierson outmaneuvered Victorio. *Texas State Library, 1/141-1.*

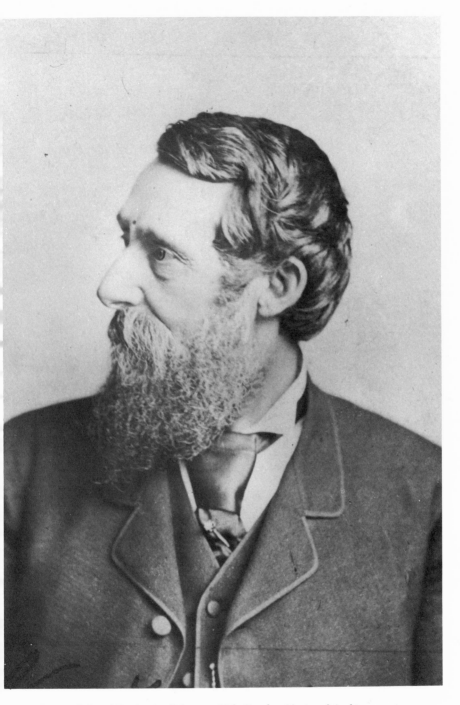

Colonel Benjamin Grierson, 10th Cavalry. *National Archives.*

Nana, leading chief of the Tci-he-nde Mimbres after the killing of Victorio in October 1880. At the age of about seventy-three he led a thousand-mile blitz across New Mexico that was one of the most spectacular of all Apache raids. *National Archives.*

Apache scout Dead Shot, convicted and hanged for sparking the mutiny at Cibicue. *National Archives.*

Western Apache scout, believed to be Dandy Jim, also hanged for his part in the Cibicue mutiny. Note extraordinary quality of the war cap. *Arizona Historical Society.*

serted that Mangas had been captured "red-handed in a fight with the soldiers."[15] That was also a lie.

Without Mangas in bondage to ensure their safety, the Walker party slipped through Doubtful Pass in the dead of night, when the Apaches were least likely to attack.

The Civil War's Southwestern Sideshow:
NOTES

1. For a more detailed history of this incursion, see Kerby, *The Confederate Invasion of New Mexico and Arizona, 1861–62.*

2. *The War of the Rebellion*, First Serial, Vol. IV, pp. 19ff.

3. Twitchell, *Leading Facts of New Mexico History*, Vol. I, p. 321.

4. Sonnichsen, *Mescalero Apaches*, p. 93, citing Raht, *Romance of Davis Mountains*, p. 148.

5. *The War of the Rebellion*, First Serial, Vol. IV, p. 26; see also Utley, "Fort Davis Guidebook."

6. Baylor, *John Robert Baylor*, p. 13.

7. Gerónimo, *Geronimo's Story of His Life*, p. 131.

8. Teal, "Soldier in the California Column," p. 41.

9. Sabin, *Kit Carson Days*, Vol. II, pp. 702–3.

10. Ibid., p. 705.

11. Cremony, *Life Among the Apaches*, p. 201.

12. Myers, "Military Establishments in Southwestern New Mexico," p. 21.

13. Conner, *Joseph Reddeford Walker*, p. 34.

14. Ibid.

15. McClintock, *Arizona*, Vol. I, p. 177.

Bosque Redondo

General Carleton was probably the only man in New Mexico who wanted a reservation at Bosque Redondo. The Indians didn't want it, and the stockmen on the Pecos who would lose cattle to the Indians certainly didn't want it, but Carleton's was the only vote that counted, and he sent an army detail to lay it out and establish a new post—Fort Sumner—to be ready to keep the new inmates in line. With that group was John Cremony. He had come east again as a California Volunteer, and he was among the first to remark what a misnomer Bosque Redondo was. The "Round Grove" was little more than a scrawny picket of cottonwood trees that followed a gradual bend in the Pecos River, "a few scattered trees," he wrote, "by no means thick, even in the densest portion."[1]

When the post was manned, one of the garrison registered a more subjective opinion about "this terrible place . . . The Rio Pecos is a little stream winding through an immense plain, and the water is terrible, and it is all that can be had within 50 miles, it is full of *alkili* [sic], and operates on a person like castor oil—the water, heat it a little, and the more you wash yourself with common soap the dirtier you will get."[2]

The reservation was not large in extent, some forty square miles, and while the Apaches had often used the thin stands of cottonwood as a campground, they doubtless never considered the place as a permanent abode. They were a mountain people, and there were no mountains on the Pecos. But it was the only refuge from a war of extermination, and by March of 1863, some four hundred had reported in, and soon a crop was planted. Some, however, refused and slipped away, and there was sporadic violence all summer. There had been considerable intermarriage with the Tci-he-nde Mimbres, and perhaps a hundred Mescaleros went west to join them; Mangas was dead, but great war leaders remained in Delgadito, Nana, and an increasingly influential warrior and chief named Beduiat, known to his Mexican prey as Victorio. Others certainly went to Texas and Chihuahua to join the Mescaleros and Lipans there. And some others defied Carleton to do his worst by raiding in his back yard. A lone soldier was waylaid between Fort Stanton and Santa Fe and burned alive; this was the way Mescaleros executed witches, but whether done for hatred or exorcism, the horror was the same. An officer's wife and her maid were ambushed while bathing in a hot spring. And, of course, cattle disappeared from the ranches. Most of the Mescaleros, however, followed Cadette to the Bosque.

Once he got his Indians fenced at the Bosque, Carleton decided that they needed education, and to this end he wrote the famous bishop of Santa Fe, Jean Baptiste Lamy, that he respectfully begged "that you will name some clergyman of energy, and all those qualities of patience, good temper, assiduity and interest in the subject so necessary in one who is wanted to teach the Indian children now at Fort Sumner, not only the rudiments of an education, but the principles and truths of Christianity."[3]

Carleton even fetched the bishop for an inspection tour of the reservation. Lamy listened in his insightful way to Carleton's characteristically trumped-up summation of the readiness of the Bosque Indians for a Christian school, and he dispatched a priest to start the work. Lamy recognized, however, the potentially explosive strife at the place, and wrote his Society that, "the Government seems determined to make them live in these reservations and nowhere else."[4] The bishop held some hope for the Bosque school but hope fizzled, as did the school, when his requests for government money and supplies went unheeded. Carleton's own postal bombardment of Washington had finally netted a school building and some supplies from the army, but the enterprise never really prospered.

It was probably just as well, for the Mescaleros found little at Bosque Redondo to fan a desire to be educated in the pindah schools, anyway. During repartee with John Cremony on the subject, the ordinarily agreeable chief Cadette silenced him with what Cremony backhandedly conceded was an irrefutable argument: "You say that because you learned from books, you can build all those big houses and talk with each other at any distance, and do many wonderful things. Now, let me tell you what we think. You begin when you are little to work hard, and work until you are men in order to begin fresh work. You say that you work hard in order to learn to work well. After you get to be men, then you say, the labor of life commences; then you build the houses, and ships, and towns and everything. Then, after you have got them all, you die and leave them behind. Now, we call that slavery. You are slaves from the time you begin to talk until you die; but we are free as air. We never work, but the Mexicans and others work for us. Our wants are few and easily supplied. The river, the wood and plain yield all that we require, and we will not be slaves; nor will we send our children to your schools, where they only learn to become like yourselves."[5]

Most of the Mescaleros had their hands full just trying to survive. The crowded conditions and their inability to move created sanitation problems. The army issued them tainted rations, diarrhea from the river water was inescapable, and they were susceptible to the meningitis that broke out. The hospital at Sumner, complained the chief medical officer, "is a regular tumble-down concern; even rain comes through the roof—in fact I may say the place is only fit to keep pigs in."⁶

The situation held some promise of improving, after the weather cooled and the Mescaleros harvested a modest crop. They found they had a champion in their agent, Lorenzo Labadie, and what was more, Michael Steck was back as superintendent of Indian Affairs for New Mexico, his Mimbres agency having been shut down by the increasing hostility. Cadette was satisfied with their leadership. The work was backbreaking—tending the farms and digging irrigation ditches—but the Indians liked Steck and Labadie, and were willing to try.

But then the Navajos came. After settling the Mescaleros to his satisfaction, Carleton sent Kit Carson at the head of another army northwest into the Navajo country. There had been altogether too much raiding from that quarter to suit the general; the Navajos were a more settled tribe than the Apaches and less skilled in warfare, and their dusty flocks of sheep and bright green peach orchards made easier targets. Carson waged a campaign of destruction that presaged Sherman's in Georgia, and soon the four to five hundred Mescaleros found their guaranteed exclusive reservation overrun by some eight *thousand* Navajo captives. The Apaches were hopping mad; Steck and Labadie knew that the two tribes loathed each other, and protested to Carleton, but he was inflexible. He had settled upon the plot of ground at Bosque Redondo as a great, centralized concentration for all the reduced Indians in New Mexico.

From the beginning the Navajos used their vastly superior numbers in every way they could to bully the Mescaleros out of whatever they wanted: the best campsites, the best farmland, even the ripened crops. Fights erupted constantly, as Agent Labadie reported, "the Apaches in defence of their fields and gardens, and the Navajoes in endeavoring to destroy them. The commander of the post made use of every means to prevent these abuses, but without effect. They fought; Navajoes were confined in the guard house; shots were sometimes fired at them by the guard, but all could not prevent them from stealing from the Apaches; in fact, their fields were, in some cases, completely destroyed. . . ."⁷

About the only thing that the Apaches had going for them was that they were, by far, the better warriors; they were unable, being outnumbered twenty to one on the little reservation, to battle openly, but they got their chances. Carson had not by any means corralled all the Navajos into the Bosque, and those still out frequently passed nearby with stolen plunder. The army was not so busy civilizing and pacifying the Mescaleros that they missed the advantage of letting them vent their spleen on punitive expeditions against the Navajos. The first one in November of 1863 was a miscarriage, but in December more Navajos struck nearby, and thirty Mescaleros went after them, led by Agent Labadie and the school-teacher sent by Bishop Lamy, Father Fialon. When troops from Fort Sumner finally caught up with them they found the remains of a holocaust of a fight, and twelve dead Navajos; one of the Mescaleros was killed. Even Carleton had to grump that they did pretty well, although he hinted that things might have gone even better if his Volunteers had got there first instead.[8]

Just after New Year's Day, 1864, a large group of Navajo raiders got to within a mile of Fort Sumner and rounded up horses belonging to the army, in addition to about sixty owned by the Apaches. Sixteen soldiers, with Labadie and sixty Mescaleros, gave chase, and after a few miles the Navajos drew into a small valley to ambush them. The fight lasted from before noon until dark, when the Navajo survivors slipped away, less most of the stolen horses. Some fifty-two of the Navajos were reported to have been killed.[9]

The administrative affairs at the Bosque, meanwhile, were as turbulent as ever, and Carleton's own correspondence about his project entered a weird fantasy of contradictions. One letter praised the Mescaleros and the next damned them. One report called them "the happiest people I have ever seen,"[10] and the next would call them "that noted band of murderers."[11] He was up to his elbows in the minutiae of the place, at one point deprecatingly excusing himself because "my anxiety is so great to make this powerful nation, which has surrendered to us, as happy and well-cared for as possible." He interfered with the local authority over the trivia of boards and nails and the hours of labor, only because he believed that "you will enter into the spirit which animates me for their good."[12] But, when Steck tried to reason with him that canning eight thousand Navajos into the same camp with five hundred Apaches was a disaster waiting to happen, and that the Navajos should be allowed to return home, Carleton could explode that "this [is] positively forbidden by myself . . . the Navajos shall never leave the Bosque if I can prevent it."[13] When the Mescaleros were hungry, Carleton sent a memorandum suggesting that they be allowed to glean fields for additional seed grain. But the Mescaleros wanted to leave long enough to hunt, and gather and roast some mescal. Steck gave his permission, and even Captain Cremony agreed this would be beneficial; he could have a hunting party out and back in two days (they returned with several dozen antelope). Carleton was furious, ordering the commander at Fort Stanton that "No Mescaleros have a right, even with a pass, to come back from Fort Sumner into their country to make *mescal*. . . . You will kill every Mescalero *man* that can be found without a passport."[14] Carleton's despotism might have been tolerable if he had been as enlightened as he thought he was, but it would have been easy for one unacquainted with him to believe that he had lost his mind.

The hunting excursion that Captain Cremony escorted provided about the only diversion that the Apaches had during these long months, and it left Cremony suitably impressed with the efficacy of mounted-surround hunting. Once they were well away from the hubbub of the Bosque, the party rode to the top of a high, broad-vistaed hill, from where they could decide what section of the country to hunt in. While pausing to deliberate, Cremony enjoyed a smoke and also distributed a number of the cigaritos among the Apaches. The Indians must have been impressed by this generosity, as at this date tobacco was probably difficult for them to get at any cost. When a likely place for a hunt was selected the warriors formed two lines, the front one about six hundred yards ahead of the rear, with the men in each line spreading out until the lines were some two miles across. The formation moved out, and once a herd of antelope was seen about a half mile distant, the two flanks of the first line galloped out ahead and encircled them, followed shortly by the second line. No man in the hunting lines was ever more than fifty yards from the next, and that distance narrowed as the noose constricted. Nearly ninety antelope were taken, with only a negligible number succeeding in escaping.[15]

Carleton angrily "refused to have any such act repeated."[16] The Mescaleros would live or die at the Bosque, and Carleton sent orders to Fort Sumner that if Dr. Steck showed himself and tried to interfere, he was to be escorted from the place by a military guard.[17] Steck was livid and wrote scorching letters to Washington; in response he was reminded that a war was in progress, and if he could not get on with Carleton perhaps he should resign.

To Cadette's Indians, life or death became a close question. The 1864 crop failed; supplies from the war-ravaged East dwindled to nothing; and Carleton ordered one reduction upon another in their rations. In an effort to separate the Mescaleros and Navajos, Labadie finally gave in to Navajo pressure and assigned developed Apache farms to Navajos, and gave the Mescaleros new ground to break.[18] The 1865 crop was a disaster; late frost, spring hail, and summer drought and disease and insects riddled it. Carleton began accusing Labadie of graft and corruption and ran him off the reservation, even though the officer accused of being his accomplice was acquitted in a court-martial.[19] Labadie remained in the vicinity and re-established the agency off the reservation limits, but Cadette had had enough. He was heard to say with a glower that his people had been promised a reservation of their own, and meant to have it, but he said nothing detailed. On the morning of November 4, the Apache village was found to contain nine sick or crippled Apaches. Everyone else had left, and soon the invalids were fetched away as well. Their trails went east and south and west and north, dividing and subdividing until even the idea of pursuit was abandoned. They had dissolved into their country like salt into water; they could have done so at any time before, but had chosen to give the pindah government every possible chance. They remained in hiding for seven years.

After the Mescalero exodus the reservation at Bosque Redondo declined. Carleton was relieved in the fall of 1866. A year and a half later, General Sherman arrived to inspect the Navajo remnants, shook his head, and let them go home.

Bosque Redondo:
NOTES

1. Cremony, *Life Among the Apaches*, p. 200.
2. Horgan, *Lamy of Santa Fe*, p. 316, quoting Pettis to wife, Feb. 26, 1864.
3. Carleton to Lamy, June 12, 1863. This and the following letters cited are reproduced in *Condition of the Indian Tribes*, the Congressional Joint Special Committee report published in 1867, pp. 109ff. Several are quoted in Sonnichsen, *Mescalero Apaches*.
4. Horgan, *Lamy of Santa Fe*, p. 316.
5. Cremony, "The Apache Race," p. 207.
6. Commissioner of Indian Affairs, *Annual Report* for 1866, p. 150.
7. Labadie to Steck, Oct. 22, 1864.
8. Carleton to Thomas, Dec. 23, 1863.
9. Commissioner of Indian Affairs, *Annual Report* for 1864, p. 202.
10. Carleton to Usher, Aug. 27, 1864.
11. Carleton to Thomas, Nov. 15, 1863.
12. Carleton to Crocker, Oct. 31, 1864.
13. Carleton to Thomas, Mar. 19, 1864.
14. Carleton to Smith, May 1, 1863.
15. Cremony, *Life Among the Apaches*, pp. 203–5.
16. Sonnichsen, *Mescalero Apaches*, p. 106.
17. Carleton to Smith, May 1, 1863.
18. Dunn, *Massacres of the Mountains*, p. 340.
19. Carleton to Assistant Adjutant General, Mar. 22, 1865.

Like Lizards We Run

After helping out with the capture and killing of Mangas Coloradas, Joseph Reddeford Walker and his party continued westward, and discovered gold in central Arizona in May of 1863. The resulting rush led to the founding of Prescott, which usurped a sizable chunk of land that had belonged to the Tonto Apaches.[1] Until this time, that sector of the territory had been relatively quiet, but the sudden presence of a boomtown with its attendant wildmen eliminated any possibility of coming to terms peacefully with the Indians. To the government the mining enterprise was more important than negotiations with natives, and Fort Whipple was soon established (one of the few stockaded forts in the West) to protect the town.

As so sickeningly many times before on the southwestern frontier, the hostility between the white-eyes and, this time, the Tontos, began out of ignorance and preconceived notions, and was started by the settlers. The first recorded incident of violence[2] occurred at "Walker's Diggings" near Prescott, when two Apache boys came into the ramshackle town, probably to trade, but were shot down by the miners. It was probably in revenge for these murders that a party of about fifteen Apaches attacked prospector George Goodhue on the road to Prescott and killed a couple of his party. In leaving the scene of that attack these Indians, in turn, were ambushed by another miner, an escaped convict from Australia called Sugarfoot Jack, who killed either two or three of them. And so the cycle had begun afresh. Usually the Indians had surprise and the terrain going for them, but the pindah gold diggers were one up in their superior weapons and the moral depth to which they would stoop. Here as elsewhere, one of the favorite recreations of the miners, combining sport with self-preservation and a chance to prospect new ground, was the staging of Indian hunts, and no man in early Prescott was more successful at organizing them than a thirty-two-year-old Alabaman named King S. Woolsey.[3]

Woolsey ran a ranch east of Prescott, farther from the protection of the town than most of the others, so he lost more stock than most to the Apaches. In one particular raid, one of his neighbors lost several head of cattle and determined to form a punitive raid, and Woolsey volunteered to head it. After several days' scouting to the lower Verde, the group ran out of food, so a miner named Peeples and a small group visited a Pima Indian village and shortly returned with the rations, as well as reinforcements that included some Pima and Maricopa Indians. On January 24, 1864, the party that then totaled about forty men descended into a wash somewhere south of the Salt River. The weather promised a beautiful day but the ground in the wash was very rough, forcing the group to travel in single file. As they skirted a bare slope they looked up and suddenly beheld about 250 Apaches staring at them in total silence. The Indians, who could have been either Tontos or Pinals, had also been in the act of rounding the mountain shoulder, and the confrontation was swift and dramatic. They must have seen that they outnumbered the pindahs five or six to one, but they did not attack. As the Woolsey group dismounted and prepared to defend themselves, one of them noted dryly that they seemed to have found more stock than they probably wanted. Instead of fighting, peaceful halloings were exchanged, and several of the Apache leaders came down the slope, and were seated on a blanket to attempt a parley. When it became apparent that none of the Indians spoke any English, the whites, as they smiled and nodded and pointed, began jocularly picking out and discussing their targets. The shooting started at the touch of a hat brim.[4] The most important Apache casualty is believed to have been a leader named Par-ra-muc-ca.

Another of King Woolsey's brainchildren, the famous "pinole treaty," has become a cherished piece of Arizona folklore, but its documentation is rather sketchy and some scholars doubt whether it actually occurred. Woolsey was said to have arranged a peace talk with the Indians, and as a good will gesture gave them a large ration of cornmeal (pinole) that he had laced with strychnine. Twenty-five Apaches were supposed to have died from it.[5]

Whatever the moral shortcomings were of the citizenry that was building the area, they soon numbered enough to gain a political voice, and Arizona became a Territory of the United States in 1863. Organization did not render the frontier less savage, however; in fact, a tax base was virtually nonexistent, and the territorial legislature met its expenditures by owning a mine named—with what one could now see as devastating symbolism—the Vulture. Nor were King Woolsey's expeditions the only ones out, and through 1864 Apache-hunting excursions became quite the thing to do.

The violence in the Prescott region was to some degree offset by more hopeful developments a little farther east, and 1864 was notable as the year in which the large and powerful White Mountain Apache tribe began their curiously peaceable relationship with the American army.

The recognized chief of the Eastern band of the White Mountains was also the single most influential leader among all the Western Apaches. His name was Heske-hldasila, translated variously as Angry, Right Side Up or Angry, Constantly,[6] called by the whites Diablo. He commanded a following that was probably unprecedented among the Western tribe. "Father had keener wits than anyone else," according to his daughter, Her Eyes Gray, later known to the pindahs as Anna Price, one of Grenville Goodwin's most knowledgeable and reliable informants. "He would let a man speak to the people. If the man talked poorly the first time, Father would think it over . . . Then if he spoke poorly and said something a second time, Father would send him off with his family. He would never come back.

"If a man was told to do something by my father, he had to do it. If he refused, Father could run him out of the local group. I saw this happen three times . . . My father had the right to drive off a subchief or family head of any clan but his own."[7] In each of the three instances referred to, the persons banished were orphaned blood relatives that Diablo himself had adopted, and each case resulted in the outcast's death.

Impetus for contact with the White Mountains came from General Carleton. While pouring most of his energy into the attempt to breathe life into his grotesque creation at Bosque Redondo, he also declared the doom and extermination of Chiricahuas and Western Apaches who opposed him. At one point he penned a suggestion of mutual co-operation to the governor of Sonora, Don Ignacio Pesqueira, that read almost like a dinner invitation: "If your excellency will put a few hundred men into the field on the first day of next June, and keep them in hot pursuit of the Apaches of Sonora, say for sixty or ninety days, we will either exterminate the Indians or so diminish their numbers that they will cease their murdering and robbing propensities and live at peace."[8]

Carleton also assured the citizens in Arizona of his commitment to unrelenting war on the Indians who terrorized their towns and ranches. Although for one reason and another the great campaign never materialized, he did send a force to establish a post on the upper Gila. The command fought several actions in reaching the area, and once Camp Goodwin was a reality, messages went out to the White Mountain bands. Instead of resisting, Diablo accepted the army presence and agreed to live peacefully. Given the turmoil over the increasing white presence, especially among the Tontos, who now raided to the very outskirts of Prescott, this seems remarkable. However, it serves to illustrate the independence that the bands of the Western tribe maintained from one another, in spite of their friendship. Moreover, the White Mountains were the most isolated of the Western Apaches, and had experienced little army contact.

From that standpoint their acceptance of the fort and troops was consistent with the hospitality that Mangas had shown the Boundary Commission in 1851. Diablo was not carried away with affection for the pindahs, but he recognized at once the futility of trying to fight them. He saw their material superiority and was once heard—and it was a rare thing for an Apache—to complain of Child of the Water's having taken the bow instead of the gun: "All about us enemies [Europeans] have good food. Sun did this. He made things the way they are . . . He feeds us just like the birds; we eat the seeds out of every bush. I wonder how Sun feels about us when we eat. Like lizards, we run about this country."[9]

Through the rest of Arizona, depredation and horror prevailed, but Diablo pledged his people to peace from the beginning.

It was a curious tack for Carleton to take, but in April of 1865 he sent his inspector-general, Nelson Davis, to arrange a peace conference with Tci-he-nde and Chiricahuas at Pinos Altos.[10] The Apaches, represented among others by Acosta, Nana, and Beduiat (Victorio), indicated a willingness for peace, if they could remain in their homeland. Carleton's terms were equally simple: Bosque Redondo or death. Three of the lesser Mimbres chiefs, the brothers Salvador, Pasquin, and Cassari, had little incentive to give in. Their father, Mangas Coloradas, had gone among the whites to speak of peace. By now they knew what had happened to him: "They cut off his head and boiled it in a big black pot."[11] An impasse was reached, and Davis concluded his peace mission with the exclamation, "Death to the Apaches, and peace and prosperity to this land is my motto!"[12]

The good Dr. Steck had not given up trying, fuming to the Indian Commissioner, "There are no Indians in this Department more faithful than the Mimbres band of Apaches, when at peace. . . . they were driven by the treachery of our own people into their present hostile condition."[13] It still got him nowhere.

For the previous fifteen years, the history of Apachería had been guided by the personalities of a few strong men. For the next five years, however, Indian affairs in the Southwest sank into stifling doldrums of confusion created by the army and Indian Bureau alike. Massive army reorganization in 1866 left Arizona ruled not from Santa Fe, but from California. Generals grumbled and snapped at each other over the best way to kill Apaches,[14] and "posts were established, abandoned, moved, and renamed with bewildering rapidity as the Indian threat shifted or disease appeared or water gave out or supply problems grew critical."[15] Dr. Steck finally quit the Indian service in disgust, and as the Interior Department dawdled and stalled over policy, agencies were set up and shut down as Apaches appeared from time to time to ask poignantly what had happened to the man they considered to be the only honest, straight-talking representative ever sent to them. With so little interest from Washington officialdom, the civilian "ranger" forces took to the saddle again. The posses would be authorized and outfitted, only to be triumphantly disbanded after some sordid little massacre of a sleeping rancheria of women and children, as the warriors took unending revenge upon the roads and ranches. The confusion was so general that the Indian Commissioner had to concede that "Apache relations were governed by the course of events rather than by the adoption of a policy." One of the closest scholars of that period emerged from a textual recitation of the minor disasters and insults with the rather weary comment that 1871 opened "with the usual picture of distress and woe."[16]

Buried within the matrix of turmoil, however, one hopeful new sign in Apache management glimmered for a moment before being snuffed out. In December of 1866, Colonel Charles S. Lovell ordered his subordinate, Colonel Guido Ilges, commanding Camp Grant, to respond favorably to local Pinalenos who had been asking for peace terms. Ilges treated with them and reached an amicable agreement to keep them fed and supplied until they could settle down. With greater speed than he ever showed in prosecuting a campaign, Department Commander General Irvin McDowell replied, scandalized, that the agreement was "irregular, injudicious and embarrassing."[17] The Division commander over McDowell, H. W. "Old Brains" Halleck, agreed, and ordered the colonels' rebuke. The Indian Commissioner and Secretary of Interior condemned the agreement, not because it promised peace, but probably because they were not the ones who made it, and if allowed to stand, it would put peaceful Indians under army control and bruise the prestige of the Interior Department. As it had been before and would be again, God help the men who tried to become friends when others higher up and far away had told them to kill each other.

The Arizona legislature condemned the very idea of peace with the Apaches as "a monstrous and most expensive farce,"[18] and within a few years memorialized the federal Congress that "our people have made their home here, and have no other, but unless protection is given to them, the constant decimation . . . will soon sweep from the country all traces of civilization, except for deserted fields and broken walls."[19]

McDowell's successor as commander of the California Department, Edward O. C. Ord, had little difficulty in seeing through that game, though: "Almost the only paying business the white inhabitants have in [Arizona] is supplying the troops. . . . If the paymaster and quartermaster of the army were to stop payment in Arizona, a great majortiy of the white settlers would be compelled [to leave]. Hostilities are therefore kept up with a view to protecting the inhabitants most of whom are supported by the hostilities."[20] (General Sherman had reached the same conclusion and grumped about the propriety of starting a second war with Mexico to make them take Arizona back.) The situation was an obscene merry-go-round by no means uncommon on other Indian frontiers, but accentuated in Arizona by its isolation from any other areas of white commerce. The unsavory businessmen and government contractors whose interest lay in keeping the wars hot became known collectively as the "Tucson Ring" or "Indian Ring." Since the talks they had with one another and the decisions they reached were always informal and unrecorded, and since they saw the necessity of covering their tracks from the eyes of the army or government reformers, the very existence of the Ring cannot be proved. Their activity, however, was undeniable, and their influence became perhaps the most vicious specter in the history of the Southwest.

Beginning in 1869 President Grant's famous "Peace Policy" started making itself felt—howbeit gently—in Arizona, which gave some direction if little force to Indian management there. A Board of Indian Commissioners was established to advise the President on Indian affairs, and a voice of influence was given to religious organizations. Their policy was grounded on the notion that it must be nobler (and the army had to agree it was cheaper) to feed and civilize the Indians rather than fight them. An attempt was finally made to define a workable boundary between civil and military authority, and it was agreed that the Indian Office would have responsibility for all Indians on the reservations, and the army would be called on to deal with hostiles who were off the reservations. While this looked on paper to be just the thing, it left the Arizona Apaches in a limbo, for although they had been through many agents and agencies, they did not own an acre of ground that the federal government conceded to be their own. To iron things out, the secretary of the Board of Indian Commissioners, Vincent Colyer, was sent West. At Fort Defiance in Navajo country he held a conference with a number of Apache headmen, and reported that they were ready to be subsisted.

Colyer's success with them had been prepared by the patient labor of an army lieutenant, Charles Drew, an acting agent to the Tci-he-nde and Chiricahuas at an agency located at Ojo Caliente (Warm Springs), in the heart of Tci-he-nde country. The Mimbres were overjoyed by the location of Drew's mission, and by 1870 some 500 of them under Victorio, Nana, and a third and very important leader named Loco, had come in. Drew also tried to bring in the elusive Cochise, who had been inquiring about peace terms, but did not succeed until the 1870–71 winter. When Cochise came in, the population of Apaches affiliated with the Ojo Caliente agency rose to probably well over 1,200.[21] Soon, however, pressure from local white settlers caused the Ojo Caliente agency to be removed sixty miles to the northwest to Tularosa, a place that the Mimbres and Chiricahuas both hated. A few years before, one of the unsuccessful peace missions to Cochise had attempted to convince him to move to Tularosa, and he had refused. "That is a long ways off," he said. "The flies on those mountains eat out the eyes of horses. The bad spirits live there."[22] Rather

than migrate to the evil, haunted place, Cochise picked up and removed
to his own country in the Chiricahua and Dragoon mountains of southeastern Arizona; the Mimbres under Loco and Victorio mostly drifted
eastward to visit the Mescaleros, who were finally about to be returned to
their old reservation at Fort Stanton in their own country.

Vincent Colyer's mission still could not call the Apache mood hostile,
and recommended the liberal expenditure of funds to work the peace policy on them. None were available from the Interior Department, so President Grant authorized the army to establish what were called, without
adornment, "feeding stations" in the western part of Apachería.

Like Lizards We Run:
NOTES

1. Mails, *People Called Apache*, p. 29.

2. This is according to Thrapp, *Conquest of Apacheria*, p. 26, citing news
clippings in the Los Angeles Public Library. Conner, *Joseph Reddeford
Walker*, pp. 148ff., contains his memoir of the incidents. See also Farish, *History of Arizona*, Vol. III, p. 32.

3. King Woolsey was probably the most prominent pioneer character in the
early history of the Prescott region. More details of his life and Indian-hunting
hobby are contained in Woody, "Woolsey Expeditions of 1864."

4. The Par-ra-muc-ca incident is treated in Ogle, *Federal Control of the
Western Apaches*, p. 48; Dunn, *Massacres of the Mountains*, p. 337; Conner,
Joseph Reddeford Walker, pp. 171ff.; and others, including Thrapp, McClintock, Browne, and Woody. These opening pages of Arizona history illustrate
perfectly, and it is the only time it need be mentioned, that finding source
material on what happened in Arizona is never as difficult as making sense
out of it.

5. Woody, "Woolsey Expeditions of 1864," p. 159; Ogle, *Federal Control
of the Western Apaches*, p. 48, n. 109; McClintock, *Arizona*, Vol. I, p. 186.

6. Goodwin, *Western Apache Raiding and Warfare*, p. 34.

7. Goodwin, *Social Organization of the Western Apache*, p. 679.

8. Carleton to Pesqueira, Apr. 20, 1864.

9. Goodwin, *Social Organization of the Western Apache*, p. 678.

10. There was no shortage of motives for Carleton to explore the chances
for a settlement—on his terms, of course—with the Tci-he-nde. The terms of
enlistments of his California Volunteers were coming due; with the Civil War
ended the government was slashing the size of the regular military; and at a
time when Carleton could have really used them, the civilian ranger militias
showed little zeal once there was a possibility of serious combat. Ogle, *Federal
Control of the Western Apaches*, pp. 49–52.

11. Kaywaykla, *In the Days of Victorio*, p. 48.

12. Davis to Cutler, May 3, 1865.

13. Steck to Dole, Mar. 20, 1865.

14. As one sad example of the bickering among the billets, in spring of 1867, the California Department's commanding general, Irvin McDowell, ordered General John Irvin Gregg, of the District of Prescott and Upper Colorado, to maintain his aggressiveness. Gregg responded with general orders declaring all Indians in his sizable district—which included Apaches in the east to some California tribes in the west—to be hostile if off the reservation, even if they had safe-conduct passes from their agents. "He certainly simplified the question of what Indians were to be fought," wrote McDowell, but aside from usurping Indian Bureau powers, Gregg was expanding his military activity beyond the point of moral justification, to say nothing of tactical and financial feasibility. Utley, *Frontier Regulars*, p. 192.

Miffed at the criticism, Gregg issued new orders once he learned that McDowell had countermanded his first ones, but not what McDowell anticipated. The new directive authorized troop movements only against large war parties who attacked whole settlements or seized roads. "Attacks upon trains and travellers and the stealing of stock, by individuals or small parties of Indians, cannot be considered hostile acts, but as offenses against the common law; the same as if committed by white citizens." General Orders No. 12, June 11, 1867, quoted in Thrapp, *Conquest of Apacheria*, p. 54.

And so on it went, until citizen abuse of the army reached an unprecedented level.

15. Utley, *Frontier Regulars*, p. 177.

16. Ogle, *Federal Control of the Western Apaches*, p. 79.

17. Ibid., p. 64. "Old Brains" Halleck's view of Apaches was as forthright as they came: "It is useless to negotiate with these Apache Indians. They will observe no treaties, agreements, or truces. With them there is no alternative but active and vigorous war, till they are completely destroyed, or forced to surrender as prisoners of war." Dunn, *Massacres of the Mountains*, p. 339.

18. Ogle, *Federal Control of the Western Apaches*, p. 64, n. 25.

19. *Memorial and Affidavits Showing Outrages Perpetrated by Apache Indians in the Territory of Arizona for the years 1869–1870*, p. 6.

20. Secretary of War, *Annual Report* for 1869, p. 124.

21. Hodge, "Handbook of Indians North of Mexico," p. 64.

22. Vanderwerth, *Indian Oratory*, p. 126.

Always Live in a Rough Place[1]

Originally established in 1859 as Fort Arivaipa, later renamed Fort Breckenridge and then Fort Stanford, Camp Grant occupied a crucial position of Arizona geography, the outlet of Arivaipa Creek into the San Pedro River, about sixty miles northeast of Tucson. To the south swept the San Pedro Valley; depopulated and left to the conquering Apaches since 1762,[2] it gave them an unobstructed plain to the plunder fields of Sonora. West of the post was the Camp Grant wash and the Tucson Road. Ten miles to the north was the Kearny Trail to California. To the east Camp Grant commanded, via Arivaipa Canyon, the approaches to the Sulphur Springs Valley and the upper Gila basin. One possible route for a transcontinental railroad passed right by the fort. Near the head of Arivaipa Creek, some miles up from the San Pedro, were springs that provided the only permanent water supply for miles. From the springs downstream to where, in the driest periods, the remnants of the creek sank into the sand, the constant moisture created a miniature but sharply defined ecosystem not more than a hundred yards across. It was along and about this threadlike oasis that one band of the Gileño Apaches, the Arivaipas, had established their semipermanent farming plots.

By the closing month of 1870, responsibility for Arizona's safety had fallen to Brigadier General George Stoneman, who chose, much to the disgust of the citizens, to undertake its defense from his headquarters in California. The 3rd Cavalry was rotated into Arizona service in November, and among the officers who arrived in Tucson that month was First Lieutenant (and brevetted Colonel) Royal Emerson Whitman, to assume command at Grant. He was a native of Maine, and a man of good education. During the Civil War his pronounced qualities of Yankee stubbornness and sound intellectual capacity elevated him through the ranks from sergeant to a respected officer. When he got his first look at Camp Grant he must have thought it was the end of the earth; little more than a rectangle of squalid adobe buildings around a dust bowl of a parade ground. For something over two months his command proceeded with no major occurrences.

In February of 1871, five old Indian women came into the post under a white flag, telling Whitman they were in search of a boy whom they believed the soldiers had taken prisoner some months before. The women were Arivaipa Apaches, from the band of a younger chief named Eskiminzin. They were very ragged and frightened-looking, and it seems likely that it was the old women who came in because their band was apprehensive about the army's intentions toward them; if Indians were to be killed, then they could easier afford the loss of five old women than five warriors. Whitman treated the women kindly, however, feeding them and co-operating in every way, and they stayed two days. When they left, they asked if they might return with more of their people, to which Whitman agreed.

Eight days after their initial visit the old women returned, this time with a few other Indians. They brought some goods to sell so they could buy manta canvas to make new clothes, to replace their present rags. The appalling condition of their clothes might be taken as evidence, first, of the deteriorating game conditions that accompanied white settlement, and, second, that they had probably not been raiding, at least extensively, or they would have had some newer garments or material (although, of course, it was the elderly who wore the poorest clothes). Once again Whitman handled them with courtesy, and when the Apaches told him that many of their band wanted to come in, he encouraged them to have their chiefs come in for a talk. He promised he would protect them, and even if the conference went badly they would be allowed to leave unharmed.

In a few days more the Apaches returned again, with their chief Eskiminzin, a Pinal chief known to the whites as Capitán Chiquito, and a third chief, named Santo. With them they had about twenty-five Indians, the largest number yet to come in, and probably significantly, enough to make a fight of it if the pindahs proved treacherous.

Whitman found Eskiminzin a friendly, barrel-chested family man, remarkably short even for an Apache, with a stocky, well-fleshed face of even proportions and only moderately high cheekbones. His name, prefixed by the common masculine nominative "Angry," meant Men Stand in Line for Him: Häčkí-bánzín. Himself a Pinal, he had married into the Arivaipas. Eskiminzin told the lieutenant that his people were weary of being in constant danger from the troops, and they wanted to settle down in their ancestral territory along Arivaipa Creek. They wanted to make peace and plant crops, and they asked Whitman to give them tools and issue them rations until a harvest was ready. Over the years this was a common enough recitation to be made by a bargaining Apache, but in this instance it was almost surely made in good faith. In fact, Arivaipa Creek contained three of the aboriginal farm plots that gave rise to the Western Apache clan system.

Whitman explained to Eskiminzin that he had no authority to make a treaty with his people, a correct assertion, seen in the four-year-old example of Colonel Ilges.[3] Instead, Whitman suggested that if they wanted to enroll and settle down they go to the White Mountains, where there were already peaceful Apaches and supervision. However, he ran afoul here of the Apaches' tribal social schisms. Eskiminzin refused to move, telling Whitman, "That is not our country. Neither are they our people. We are at peace, but have never mixed with them." This was true. The Arivaipas, as well as the other Gila bands, had contacted the White Mountains only infrequently. Most of what intratribal society they had was with Southern Tontos and Cibicues, not White Mountains,[4] although it was true that Eskiminzin himself was by marriage related to Diablo.

"Our fathers," the chief went on, "and their fathers before them, have lived in these mountains and have raised corn in this valley. We are taught to make mescal our principal article of food, and in summer and winter here we have a never-failing supply. At the White Mountains there is none, and without it now we get sick. Some of our people have been at Goodwin and for a short time at the White Mountains, but they were not contented, and they all say, 'Let us go to the Arivaipa and make a final peace and never break it.'"

Since Whitman was without power to negotiate a treaty, the talks might have ended there, but the Yankee lieutenant decided to creep out on a limb. If he could pacify these bands, others might come in, and if things went as well as they promised, the whole Indian question in his area might be brought to a peaceful resolution. So he told them they could come in and he would issue them rations, a pound of beef and a pound of corn or flour per day per adult, and he would let them gather mescal as they needed it. And, he said, he would write his commander and see if their plan was satisfactory.

Eskiminzin and the others left to gather in their bands, and Whitman on February 24 wrote Department Commander Stoneman at Drum Barracks, California, recounting what had taken place, and asking his endorsement and instructions for the future. Four days later he wrote a second, more complete report, sent it by special messenger to accompany the first, and settled back anxiously to wait.

Around the first of March Eskiminzin returned with his entire band of about 150 Arivaipas; by the fifth, other groups had doubled that number. Soon the figure leveled off at about 500 Indians, which was a sizable portion of the Gileño group of the Western Apache tribe. Whitman could see the Indians were desperately poor, and needed money to buy supplies and cloth that in former days they could have obtained easily enough by raiding. Therefore, he made an arrangement with Eskiminzin's Arivaipas to gather hay for the fort, at the rate of one penny a pound. In two months, they and the other bands who came in, brought in 150 tons, worth $3,000, which made them, in Apache terms, wealthy. Before long not only the women and children but the warriors as well—and this was an important breakthrough—submitted to labor. To encourage them Whitman canceled his agreements with "other Indians" who[5] had been doing the job, and he made arrangements also for local ranchers to take on Apaches as hired hands.

The lieutenant was firm with his Indians but took care not to be harsh or unfair. At first, he took a census and fed them every other day, but as matters smoothed this was relaxed to every third and then every fifth day. As the season lengthened, lower Arivaipa Creek turned foul and dried up, and Whitman gave his permission to the Apaches to relocate five miles upstream, where the springs kept the water pure and flowing. The Apaches got on well with neighboring ranchers, and became contented to such an extent that some of the men began selling their weapons. By the end of March Whitman still had no reply from General Stoneman, but his unofficial "reservation" was flourishing. He kept the Apaches under the closest possible scrutiny, though, keeping his guard up against any treachery, "Knowing as I did," he said later, "that in case of any loss to the Government . . . I should be the sufferer."[6]

But observe as he might, he could discover no wrongdoing, and the scheme continued to go well. "I made it a point to tell them all they wished to know. They were readily obedient and remarkably quick of comprehension. They were happy and contented and took every opportunity to show it. They had sent out runners to two other bands which were connected with them by intermarriages, and had received promises from them that they would come in." Nor was this unjustified optimism on the part of the one man. Other soldiers in the post, civilian employees of the army (including veteran Indian haters), and even the citizen ranchers who were persuaded to hire Apaches—all were in agreement that something profoundly remarkable and significant was happening. To the Apaches Whitman came to occupy the position almost of a patron saint. He personally attended all the hay weighing, and even asked whether they thought they were being fairly treated in their trading and purchases from white people. Only once, apparently, did Whitman overstep the bounds of their trust, when he asked if they might supply scouts to fight other, hostile Apaches. Eskiminzin admonished him: "We are at peace. We are not at war with those Indians." Besides, he added, his people might one day be forced out of Camp Grant, and how would the other Apaches receive them if they had scouted for the army? Eskiminzin did hint, however, that his people might help Whitman fight his enemies, if he would help them fight the Mexicans. Whitman dropped the subject.

Long time ago they say.
This Cow was standing at a river getting ready to cross. A Coyote came up and looked at the river. He said to the Cow, "I want to get across, but the water is too high. I am afraid."
The Cow said, "I'll let you hold onto my horns when I go over there."
"No, I might wash off and drown," said Coyote. He was really acting scared.
"Well, I'll let you grab hold of my tail."
"No, I would still be afraid."
"Well, I don't know what I can do for you."
"Let me get inside your rectum," said Coyote.
That Cow was embarrassed and didn't want to do it. But she really wanted to help that Coyote and said, "All right. Get in."
Coyote crawled up inside her rectum and the Cow swam the river. Just as she got out on the other side, that Coyote bit her in there and killed her, then he came out and had a big meal.
Coyote was a rascal and shouldn't have done that, but that Cow was a fool. She didn't know the difference between helping somebody and letting him take advantage.
I am talking about fruit.[7]

Around the first of April a new commander, Captain Frank Standwood, arrived to take over the reins at Grant. Whitman briefed him on what he had been doing, and Standwood approved the arrangement and instructed him to carry on.[8]

In the middle of April, Whitman finally received a communication from General Stoneman's headquarters, but on tearing open the envelope he found only his original letters, with an adjutant's note that they had been improperly filed. In his rush to get off both letters, Whitman had neglected to write on the outside fold of each a brief résumé of its contents. Although the incident is often cited as bureaucratic bungling at its worst, it has been theorized that Stoneman did read the letters, "but used the briefing as an excuse to return [them] without action. Stoneman knew of the situation at Camp Grant. . . . [His] motives can be explained, perhaps, by the fact that he was harried by the citizens about his 'feeding stations,' and did not wish formally to assume responsibility for establishing yet another one."[9] What this implies is that Stoneman was willing to bask in the sunshine of a successful venture, but would let Whitman bear the consequences of a failure, which was politic if somewhat underhanded. However, it may also just be possible that Stoneman was mindful of the abortive 1866 treaty with the Pinals and Arivaipas, and, approving Whitman's action, sought to prevent its similar destruction by a higher authority by keeping it as quiet as possible.[10]

On April 24, Captain Standwood left on an extensive scout through southern Arizona, leaving Whitman in command with a garrison of only one company—about fifty men.[11]

Six days later, at half-past seven in the morning of April 30, a messenger from Camp Lowell just outside Tucson, interrupted Whitman's breakfast with news that a large force of armed citizens from that town were on the loose and were believed headed for the Camp Grant Apaches with the intention of massacring the rancheria. Word would have reached Whitman sooner, but the leaders of the Tucson mob, the influential Oury family on the white part and Elias family on the Mexican, had cannily staked out sentries and sealed the road until their success was assured. Reacting swiftly to the news, Whitman sent out two interpreters to warn the Indians and direct them to come into the post without delay. But they were too late.

When the order to attack had been given, the 148 Tucson civilians—six whites, forty-eight Mexicans, and ninety-four Papago Indians—moved in on the unsuspecting Gileños with ruthless resolution. Eskiminzin, awakened by the shrieks and gunshots, warned his family while snatching up his youngest daughter and fleeing into the darkness. He eluded detection and got away. "Men, women and dogs were clubbed," wrote one of the white attackers, William H. Bailey. "I never saw so many dogs in such a small place . . . Some Apaches that escaped the clubs of the Papagoes tried to climb the side of the gulch. They were shot down by the Mexicans and Americans on the side of the gulch." In thirty minutes it was over; the Tucson raiders rendezvoused on the San Pedro River above the fort. By eight o'clock they were eating breakfast, "in the full satisfaction," wrote leader Oury, "of a work well done."[12]

"My messengers returned in about an hour," wrote Whitman, "with intelligence that they could find no living Indians. The camp was burning and the ground was strewed with their dead and mutilated women and children."[13] On their return, Whitman offered a $100 reward to whoever would go into the mountains and explain to the survivors that the soldiers had no part in the horrible deed. There were no takers. He also sent the post surgeon, Dr. Conant B. Briesly, with a wagon and about twenty men to bring back wounded.

"On my arrival," reported Briesly, "I found that I should have but little use for wagon or medicine; the work had been too thoroughly done. The camp had been fired, and the dead bodies of some twenty-one women and children were lying scattered over the ground; those who had been wounded in the first instance had their brains beaten out with stones.[14] Two of the best-looking squaws were lying in such a position, and from the appearance of the genital organs and of their wounds, there can be no doubt that they were first ravished and then shot dead. Nearly all of the dead were mutilated. One infant of some ten months was shot twice, and one leg hacked nearly off. While going over the ground, we came upon a squaw who was unhurt, but were unable to get her to come in and talk. . . ."

With no one willing to go into the mountains to contact the survivors, Whitman went out with a burial party the next morning, hoping that by burying the dead with a great demonstration of respect, the others would see him and come down. The gravedigging took the greater part of the day, and toward evening his effort began to be rewarded. "They began to come in from all directions," he wrote, "singly and in small parties, so changed in forty-eight hours as to be hardly recognizable, during which time they had neither eaten nor slept." As the searches continued more bodies were found until there was a total of 125, more or less, one fourth of the entire camp. Only eight of the dead were men; those who were not away hunting had tried to take cover to fight, but to no avail.

"Many of the men, whose families had all been killed, when I spoke to them and expressed sympathy for them, were obliged to turn away, unable to speak, and too proud to show their grief. The women whose children had been killed or stolen were convulsed with grief, and looked to me appealingly, as though I were their last hope on earth." Many prostrated by sorrow began to cry what Whitman believed were their death wails, which struck him as "too wild and terrible to be described."

"I did what I could," he continued. "I fed them and talked to them, and listened patiently to their accounts. I sent horses into the mountains to bring in two badly wounded women, one shot through the left lung, and one with an arm shattered." The latter proved to be the wife of Capitán Chiquito;[15] she recovered, as did the other.

Amazingly, the surviving Pinals and Arivaipas continued to express their confidence in Royal Whitman and their affection for him. When Eskiminzin was able to compose himself to speak, he told Whitman that "my women and children have been killed before my face and I have been unable to defend them. Most Indian in my place would take a knife and cut his throat, but I *will live* to show these people that all they have done, and all they can do, shall not make me break faith with you as long as you will stand by us and defend us, in a language we know nothing of, to the great governor we never have nor never will see." It was a stunning testimonial to the justice and humanity, and above all the effectiveness, of the policy of kindness that Whitman had begun by exceeding his authority, alone and at enormous risk to his career, and had maintained in the face of the most provocative and slanderous criticism from Tucson.

Aside from the dead, something else preyed on the minds of the Apaches. Twenty-nine of their children were missing, taken prisoner by the Tucson marauders. "Get them back for us," they pleaded to Whitman. "Our little boys will grow up slaves, and our girls, as soon as they are large enough, will be diseased prostitutes, to get money for whoever owns them. Our women work hard and are good women, and they and our children have no diseases. Our dead you cannot bring to life, but those that are living we gave to you, and we look to you, who can write and talk and have soldiers, to get them back." The emphasis on feminine purity was of course part of the Life-way, but it was especially marked among Eskiminzin's Arivaipas. Camp Grant's interpreter and mail carrier, William Kness, who had acquired little affection for Apaches in his twenty-six years on the frontier, deposed, "I never met with as great regard for virtue and chastity as I have found among these Apache women."

Of twenty-nine Arivaipa and Pinal children who were taken captive at the massacre, only two escaped. Five were later recovered from Arizona citizens. The rest, twenty-two, were taken to Sonora and sold.

Some years before, probably when Eskiminzin had only just become a chief, the venerated Diablo of the Eastern White Mountains had expressed distrust of the Indians who lived in the desert country, not just Pimas and Papagos but Yavapais and Southern Tontos as well. "They are all against you," he advised Eskiminzin. "Whenever the women go after saguaro fruit, you stay on top of a hill to watch out for them. That's the way you will keep your wife a long time. Don't sleep late in the morning with your children. Wake up early and talk to them. Go about the camp early in the morning. The Pima might have surrounded you in the night, and thus you will save your children . . . Don't live with your people on a trail. Always live in a rough place on the side of a hill."[16]

Eskiminzin had become trusting, and lax on almost every point; in the massacre he lost both his wives and five of his children. It was said that the sentries posted to guard the camp were engaged in a card game at the time they were silently clubbed.

Always Live in a Rough Place:
NOTES

1. A fine introduction in general reading to the Camp Grant affair is Schellie, *Vast Domain of Blood*. Despite its unfortunate title and fictionalized format, it is a work of good scholarship, readable and engrossing. An excellent piece of source material, and the source of most of the extensive quotations in this chapter, is the documentation of Vincent Colyer's investigation, found in Commissioner of Indian Affairs, *Annual Report* for 1871.

2. Hastings, "Tragedy of Camp Grant," p. 146. (The location of Camp Grant was moved in 1873, and the post renamed Fort Grant. Crook, *General George Crook: His Autobiography*, p. 165, n. 6. Both the location and the personnel of Arizona garrisons changed so frequently that I have not burdened the

text with extensive explanations of their lineages, in order not to wander too far from an Apache orientation. Readers interested in this facet of Arizona history should see the fine summary of Brandes, "Guide to History of the U. S. Military Installations in Arizona.") Bishop Lamy pondered Spanish ruins during a pastoral visit in 1878. Horgan, *Lamy of Santa Fe*, p. 336.

3. See Brandes, "Guide," p. 50.

4. Goodwin, *Social Organization of the Western Apache*, pp. 58–59.

5. Thrapp mentioned this in *Conquest of Apacheria*, p. 83, but did not name the tribe of "other Indians." If they were Papagos, who lived not too far away, it might help explain their motive for participating in the subsequent massacre.

6. San Francisco *Alta*, Feb. 3, 1872. This is another important piece of source material.

7. The tale of the foolish cow is one of the most widespread of the Coyote stories. French lists seven different versions, from every corner of Apacheria. See Goodwin, "Myths and Tales of the White Mountain Apache," pp. 118–19; Russell, "Myths of the Jicarilla Apaches," p. 263; and Opler, "Myths and Tales of the Chiricahua Apache Indians," p. 66, as representative.

8. It is here that the unanswered questions about the Camp Grant massacre begin to multiply: Did the approval come from Stoneman or was it Standwood's own? If it was from Stoneman, did Standwood tell Whitman so? Did Whitman ask Standwood if he had heard anything of his letters? Had he?

9. Hastings, "Tragedy of Camp Grant," p. 150 n.

10. Officially or unofficially, Stoneman almost inescapably must have known and approved of Whitman's actions, for he circumstantially confirmed them on April 1, when he ordered Standwood to continue the feeding. Further complicating the question—and it seems to be one of the red herrings that Arizona citizens were so clever at reeling up from the deep—one of the white participants in the massacre, Walter DeLong, later claimed that Standwood came to Camp Grant with orders to treat the Apaches as prisoners of war. This was true even according to Whitman, but the red herring lies in the subtlety of DeLong's implication that POWs should not have been subsisted; that is a false impression, for Indian POWs were commonly fed by the army during their dependency. See DeLong's account in the Lamprey manuscript, New York Public Library.

11. One wishes there were some clues, other than circumstance, that Oury and the other leaders struck when they did to take advantage of Standwood's absence with most of the manpower, but that is a spoor of evidence which, if true, they managed to erase.

12. This and previous excerpt are from Hastings, "Tragedy of Camp Grant," p. 153. Interesting background on the Elias family can be obtained from Officer, "Elias Family," pp. 378–80.

13. This and following passages are from Commissioner of Indian Affairs, *Annual Report* for 1871, pp. 488ff.

14. Braining and facial disfigurement were peculiar traits of Papago and Pima warfare. Spicer, "European Expansion and the Enclavement of Southwestern Indians," p. 144, began to make the point that the rather lumpy classification of Pimas and Papagos as "peaceful" is a misnomer arising from

the considerable passage of time since their subjection. On the frontier, Indians who fought against the white men were labeled "warlike," etc., and those
who fought with them were "peaceful," irrespective of the fact that both
groups fought. The appellations had little to do with absolute characteristics. I
have seen not much in Papago behavior at this time to commend them to the
general platitude of being "peaceful."

15. Thrapp, *Conquest of Apacheria*, p. 91.
16. Goodwin, *Social Organization of the Western Apache*, p. 688.

The Peacemakers

If, as some believe, General Stoneman's cat-and-mouse game over authorizing a feeding station at Grant was aimed at self-preservation, it availed him nothing; President Grant relieved him from responsibility for the Arizona Department effective May 2. It was the result largely of the furor that grew out of the massacre, aided by pressure from Arizona's Governor A. P. K. Safford. Stoneman's replacement took command on June 4: George Crook, lieutenant colonel of the 23rd Infantry and brevetted major general. Crook entered Arizona reluctantly, amid controversy and a hiss of disapproval from the rest of the officer corps. The argument stemmed from the fact that Crook had been given a command in his brevetted rank, which was a virtually unprecedented breach of the seniority system. As a junior lieutenant colonel he had in effect been promoted over the claims of forty line colonels to a position theretofore reserved for brigadier generals. The irregular appointment had been opposed by the Secretary of War and General of the Army Sherman. However, Crook was enjoying some amount of celebrity for his creditable victories over the Paiute Indians, and President Grant bowed to Governor Safford's argument that to appoint a proven Indian fighter was the only way to handle the Apache problem.

George Crook himself found the situation an embarrassment and tried to dodge the command rather than become outcast from other officers. It was an attitude consistent with his courtly demeanor and high principles. He habitually shunned the egotistical ostentation that kept other officers in the public—and presidential—eye; in fact he seldom even wore his uniform. He rarely drank or used profane speech; he was concerned for the welfare of the men and officers who served under him. With Crook duty came first, and he could stay in the saddle as long as any man. Probably his greatest single drawback was a combination of inflexibility with some amount of mental dullness. Except where his keen sense of military advantage rescued him, he tended not to recognize his mistakes, and once he had assumed a course of action based upon faulty information or wrong impression, he might continue that course heedless of mounting evidence against him. Academically he was undistinguished, the lowest-ranking graduate of West Point ever to attain a major general's billet. His spelling changed from moment to moment, but once he turned his mental faculties upon an enemy he studied them until he gained an uncanny ability to think as they did and anticipate their movements. His reputation in Indian fighting was one of tenacity aimed at effective precision and swift conclusion. But he did not, he most emphatically did not, favor extermination of the Indians. In peace he was known to govern Indians firmly, consistently, and with scrupulous fairness.

In addition to the controversy attending his appointment, General Crook brought with him to Arizona some extraordinary and revolutionary theories of Indian fighting. The first was the substitution of pack mules and hired civilian packers for the conventional army wagon trains to transport supplies in the field. Wagons served well enough in plains campaigns, but to fight Apaches it was necessary to follow them into their most remote mountain haunts, and before the close of the Apache wars Crook's long pack trains became a hallmark of desert warfare.[1]

Second, and by far the more controversial, was his belief that Apaches were so singularly well adapted to their harsh environment that they could never be conquered by white troops alone. The soldiers were unused to the desert and had nothing like the physical conditioning or stamina of the Apaches. The Indians could exist for indefinite periods of time hiding in small groups in the mountains, concealing their trails so effectively that no white tracker could follow, and dismounted their warriors could jog incredible distances across the bleakest desert. Left to their own devices in fighting Apaches the soldiers were, wrote Crook, "helpless."[2] Their only hope lay in cracking Indian solidarity, winning sympathizers inside the rancherias, turning the Apaches upon themselves. They must enlist whole companies of friendly Apache scouts and skirmishers with war skills equal to the hostiles' own, expecting this to be as damaging to hostile morale as to their military advantage. Crook's was a sound theory, but it was not without its opponents in an army that was tacitly, but pervasively, ethnocentric. It was a strategy not entirely without precedent, however; Bautista de Anza had utilized it nearly a century earlier, and General Ord had espoused the idea only two years before.

Later on in June Crook traveled to Tucson in the company of his aide, Captain Azor N. Nickerson, and his favorite scout, Archie MacIntosh, and paid a courtesy call on Governor Safford, who took the opportunity to inform Crook of the frontier civilian view of the Camp Grant raid. He gave the general such an earful that ever afterward Crook refused to condemn the Tucson businessmen for their effort, and although he had not yet met Lieutenant Whitman, Crook acquired a hatred for him that never diminished. Because of this erroneous antipathy Crook misinterpreted nearly all subsequent events concerning Whitman, and the lieutenant had then to pay for those risks he took on behalf of Eskiminzin's people, becoming the most visible victim of Crook's one great personal flaw.

Crook also began forming a bad opinion of Eskiminzin, but with rather more justification. A few weeks after the massacre, the Arivaipas returned to Camp Grant to settle, but were attacked—perhaps inadvertently—by a column from Camp Apache. That was enough, and he told Whitman he was leaving. The chief then stopped by to see a white farmer who had befriended him, named Charles McKinney. After a friendly meal and smoke, Eskiminzin pulled out his pistol and shot him dead. It was a demonstration to his people, he said, that they could never have friends among the pindahs. (And, probably not just coincidentally, it was a way to reassert his own leadership after he had brought his people so much misery by trusting the whites. Indeed, one might wonder whether, but for the presence of the garrison at Grant, Eskiminzin might have carried out his object lesson on Whitman, and whether that might have been his original purpose of going into Grant to see him.) With his band left destitute by the massacre and the torching of his rancheria, Eskiminzin soon after raided an army wagon train between Tucson and Fort Bowie. He lost thirteen of his men dead, however, on discovering that the wagons were guarded by riflemen concealed inside; he then disappeared into the mountains, uncontacted for several months. Thus, when Crook came onto the scene every report he had of Eskiminzin was bad—except, of course, Whitman's—and the commanding general marked him for neutralization at the first opportunity.

One of Crook's first substantive actions was to interview every officer in his command, draining each one of his store of information on Arizona geography, Apache character, "and every other item of interest that a commander could possibly want to have determined."[3] From among his junior officers he selected a curious pair for his aides-de-camp, one a hard-living, brawling Scot, Lieutenant William J. Ross; the other, Lieutenant John Gregory Bourke, an intelligent, witty, and sophisticated Philadelphian who later studied Apache ethnology with skill and perception. Bourke had just passed his twenty-fifth birthday on June 23, but he had been in the army ten years, having attended West Point after fighting in the Civil War.

Five weeks after his arrival Crook was ready for his first extensive scout of his domain. He departed Camp Lowell, just outside Tucson, on July 11 with five companies of 3rd Cavalry (B, D, F, H, and L), heading southeast to the strategic Camp Bowie in the heart of Cochise's territory. The force of two hundred arrived at Bowie on the fourteenth for a stay of three days. The general suspected, probably correctly, that Cochise kept Camp Bowie under observation, and so had his men sneak away after nightfall on the seventeenth for an offensive swing through Chiricahua country. They camped that night just to the southwest of the Dos Cabezas Mountains, and the next day noticed several signs of Indian presence. At one point Crook saw dust rising a good distance down the Sulphur Springs Valley. Guessing the Indians were riding for a low range of spring-watered hills between the Pinaleno and Dos Cabezas ranges, he dispatched Captain Alexander Moore with a force to seize the spring and ambush the Indians as they approached. Instead of taking the spring, however, Moore led his command straight out onto a table-flat plain where the Indians easily saw him and fled. Moore said he had sought to cut off the Indians' trail, but Crook, incensed at having lost "one of the prettiest chances of giving the enemy a severe blow,"[4] believed Moore had deliberately warned them away to prevent having to fight them. The Indians were thought to be a raiding party on their way home from Mexico.

Writing that "I saw it was useless running down the horses and men trying to catch them," Crook turned instead toward Camp Grant, and after that undertook a very roundabout scout of the eastern portion of the territory: out of Arivaipa Canyon to the Gila, down the Gila to San Carlos, and then north to Camp Apache, where he arrived on August 12.

In the vicinity of Camp Apache Crook found a number of rancherias of peaceful Apaches, mostly White Mountains and Coyoteros, but among them also the village of the Pinal Capitán Chiquito. After the bloodbath at Grant, Chiquito overcame his aversion to mixing with White Mountains and fled to Camp Apache to settle. After many long talks Crook convinced the Indians that he sought their best interest, and he used the opportunity to begin enlisting several warriors as scouts to help fight hostiles. The White Mountains, too, began to be receptive to the army, and several of them joined.

While Crook was in these negotiations, a party of six men—three Mexicans and three Apaches—rode into the camp and produced a letter from the agent at Cañada Alamosa, O. F. Piper. Their mission, the paper said, was to seek out Cochise and persuade him to surrender. Crook wrote that "two of this party were recognized by several as being Cochise's worst men." One of the messengers was Loco, an influential chief in his own right, but of the Tci-he-nde Mimbres, not the same branch of the Chiricahuas as Cochise. When Crook continued that "I felt very suspicious that they were there in the capacity of spies," he probably ran off the track. The general, perhaps unaware that Cochise and his people had spent the previous winter with Agent Piper,[5] forbade the six to proceed further. But as they did bear a safe-conduct pass, he regretfully let go the chance to arrest and shackle the Chiricahuas, and with some huffy remarks about the Indian Bureau sent them back where they came from.[6]

Shortly before leaving the Camp Apache area Crook divided his command, keeping two companies, B and L, for himself, assigning the other three to Captain Guy V. Henry, who was to take them and the newly enlisted Indian scouts on an extensive shakedown march westward down the Salt River toward Camp McDowell, giving battle to any hostiles found. Mindful that he wanted Apache scouts in service for a long period, Crook instructed that for a time care must be taken that none of the trailers be exposed to danger.[7] They were to be used to find hostile rancherias, but until they had time to build their morale and self-confidence, no chance should be taken that some might be killed. Also with Captain Henry were a few dozen Mexican scouts whom Crook had taken on at the suggestion of Governor Safford. The governor had highly praised the Mexicans as trailers, claiming that "they knew the country, the habits and mode of Indian warfare, that with ten days' rations on their backs they could march over the roughest country at the rate of thirty to fifty miles a day," and so on. Crook, partly dabbling in pragmatism—and partly in deference to Governor Safford, probably—hired fifty of them for scout duty.

This expedition proved out Crook's theory of having Indian fight Indian, Captain Henry noting that "the Indians were invaluable, and that they enabled him to kill 7 warriors and take 11 women prisoners" in circumstances that would have otherwise yielded nothing.[8] The Mexicans, however, showed themselves much more in their element when massacring sleeping rancherias and selling scalps. Their performance under Captain Henry was so dreadful that Crook shortly dumped them and never again took on Mexican units. It is also possible that at about the same time Crook authorized a brief experiment with Navajo Indian scouts, but they were not used.

As Captain Henry's force headed down the Salt, Crook continued his reconnaissance, leaving the Camp Apache area on August 15, heading northward to the Mogollon Rim. His only guide was his favorite, Archie MacIntosh, who himself knew nothing of the country but had been told that the trail was clear along the Rim. What little trace there was soon played out, however, leaving the column to feel its way almost blindly westward along the thickly forested, chasm-gashed rim of the plateau. One especially hot evening they were forced to make camp where no water could be found, but a timely if too powerful rainstorm supplied them plenty. "The thunder and lightning were terrific," wrote Crook. "Trees were crashed to splinters not far from us. Judging from appearances, this country was subject to such storms very frequently, as in places there were acres where most of the trees had been struck by lightning at some time or other . . . some trees over 150 feet high had been smashed into fine splinters clear to the ground."[9] One wonders at the thoughts of Crook's newly enlisted Apache scouts at such a display of anger by the Thunder People. There is no record of apprehension or desertions, however.

Throughout the march Crook impressed his men with his vigor and fitness. "He was the most untiring and indefatigable man I ever met," admired Bourke. "He was always awake and on his feet the moment the cook of the pack-train was aroused to prepare the morning meal, which was frequently as early as two o'clock, and remained on his feet during the remainder of the day." Crook also absorbed readily the minutiae of the natural history of the region, learning "the name of every plant, animal, and mineral passed near the trail, as well as the uses to which the natives put them. . . . The Indians evinced an awe for him . . . they did not seem to understand how it was that a white man could so quickly absorb all that they had to teach."[10]

The day after the storm they came upon a small spring of crystal water in a sheltered area that was named General Springs in Crook's honor. Soon after leaving there Crook had his first close brush with hostile Indians, not important from any military standpoint but a suitable prelude to his years in Apachería. The general, with his aides Ross and Bourke, Captain Thomas Lee Brent, and packmaster Thomas Moore, was riding well in advance of the two cavalry companies, barely skirting the dizzying dropoff of the Mogollon Rim, when suddenly the unsuspecting officers heard the whisk of several arrows that missed them narrowly and continued on into the forest. As a tribute to the power of the Apache bows, Bourke noted that some of the arrows buried themselves in the soft wood of the pine trees, one of them "as far as the feathers." Crook and the others took cover in the timber as the assailants, about fifteen or twenty Tontos, fired more volleys. Most of the Indians fled down over the rim upon seeing the cavalry nearing at a trot, but two of them lingered a few seconds, partly visible among their sheltering rocks. They branded a deep impression into those whites who had not before seen Apaches stripped to their war regalia. It was "a most repulsive picture," wrote Bourke, "and yet one in which there was not the slightest suggestion of cowardice."

At the last instant before they would be cut off and captured, the remaining two Tontos loosed their arrows, turned, and leaped over the edge of the cliff. From Crook's line of vision he and the others believed for a moment that the two Indians had committed suicide rather than face capture, but when they ran to the precipice they saw instead that "the two savages were rapidly following down the merest thread of a trail outlined in the vertical face of the basalt, and jumping from rock to rock like mountain sheep." Although Crook managed to wound one with a pistol shot, the Tontos continued without slowing. Several other men opened fire on them, but according to Lieutenant Bourke the soldiers were simply too awed and fascinated at the Apaches' nimble flight to shoot accurately.

The next day Crook's force struck the trail that ran from the Little Colorado to Camp Verde, and reached Verde two days after that. Much of the ground they had covered since leaving Camp Apache had never been regularly traveled, at least by white men, and in 1873 Crook had the route mapped as "Crook's Trail," although it was not used for another year.[11] The general's intensive course in Arizona geography and Apache Indians left him with deep impressions. "It is the roughest portion of the continent," he wrote later, "and it *is* impossible for persons not acquainted with it from personal inspection to form any correct idea of its rugged mountains and arid plains. The character of these Indians is such as might be expected under such surroundings. The constant struggle with adverse conditions, with hunger, with exposure to extremes of heat and cold, and to danger of every kind kills in infancy the weak and sickly children; only the strong, perfectly developed child survives. Consequently the adult Apache is an embodiment of physical endurance—lean, well proportioned, medium sized, with sinews like steel, insensible to hunger, fatigue, or physical pains."[12]

After learning of Captain Henry's success with the Apache scouts, Crook determined to proceed with that method to sweep the area of hostiles, and projected five columns based on Henry's model to take the field. While the general had been on the trail, however, the nationwide repercussions of the Camp Grant massacre had finally resulted in action, and emissaries were coming from Washington to treat for peace with the disaffected. "On my arrival at Verde," wrote Crook to the division adjutant, "I saw by newspaper accounts that I had been ordered to suspend all operations until the Peace Commissioners visited these Indians," and he announced he would retire to the stockaded Fort Whipple to see what developed.[13]

The peacemaker from Washington was Vincent Colyer, forty-seven-year-old secretary of the Board of Indian Commissioners. By profession Colyer was an artist, and a very successful one, but much of his time was devoted to humanitarian pursuits (during the Civil War he had organized and commanded a Negro volunteer regiment). In his present capacity he had been among Apaches once before, at Fort Defiance two years previous. Colyer's first stop in the Southwest was at O. F. Piper's agency at Cañada Alamosa to consolidate the reservation there. To his dismay, he found the civilians in southwestern New Mexico still singing the praises of the Camp Grant massacre, exhorting one another to perform a like attempt on the Cañada Alamosa Chiricahuas. The chiefs with whom Colyer sought to negotiate were repeatedly scared away by rumors that they would be killed if they went into the agency, and after some very frustrating weeks Colyer moved on to Arizona. He arrived at Camp Apache on September 2, noting that he was received "very kindly" by the commanding officer, Colonel John Green. Upon learning that a war had been called off pending his performance, Colyer went into talks with the leading chiefs at Apache. He stayed there about a week, declaring the surrounding territory a reservation, and continued on to Camp Grant, where he met Lieutenant Whitman and the post's new commander, Captain William Nelson, on September 13.

In the months since the massacre, the war-weary Gileños had continued to seek refuge in Whitman's care. Eskiminzin was still there and Capitán Chiquito had returned from Camp Apache, but Colyer's mission to them almost collapsed after a remarkable and controversial incident. During the talks it was learned that a force of two hundred armed men from Tucson, under the guise of prospecting, were approaching the rancherias. Colyer instructed that they be kept away, and Nelson, fearing a re-enactment of the April massacre, ordered Whitman and a squad of cavalry out to rout them, which was done. The civilian populace, through the newspapers, shrieked in outrage. The party, it was claimed, numbered about sixty, was engaged in peaceably searching for gold, and had sought permission only to pass nearby, but was instead harassed, terrorized, and forced to flee by Whitman's cavalry. General Crook, held in reins at Whipple, was included in the attacks, and fumed. Since assuming his command, Crook's regard for Whitman had if anything lessened, an attitude that even one of Crook's more admiring biographers concedes was "inexplicable."[14] The conclusion seems inescapable that the small army from Tucson intended either to attack the Grant Apaches again, or else stage a show of force to intimidate and scare Colyer. If indeed they were telling the truth, it is about the only time in Tucson history when such a large portion of the male population took a simultaneous holiday for a lighthearted prospecting excursion.

Colyer extended official recognition to the impromptu reservation at Camp Grant and named Lieutenant Whitman as the agent, he being the only man the Indians trusted. Colyer than moved on to more councils, with the Pimas at Camp McDowell. At Camp Verde he found the Yavapais starving to death; there was little game left to hunt in that area, the reduced Indians had few weapons to hunt with, and when they did go hunting they were in constant danger of attack from the whites. On Colyer's arrival the Yavapai chief had to be fed and given a stimulant before he and the peacemaker could meet. During this time Colyer was approached by the editor of the leading newspaper of Prescott, the *Miner*, who requested Colyer to address a citizen gathering. Colyer refused, noting that throughout his visit the paper had been referring to him in fairly unequivocal terms, calling him in one instance a "treacherous, black-hearted dog."

After completing his mission to the Yavapais Colyer continued on to Whipple, where he met Crook for the first time. The general disapproved of Colyer's enterprise, but the two men had a more or less satisfactory meeting. Crook treated Colyer with respect and deference, and Colyer conceded some points of Crook's Indian philosophy. After meeting Crook, Colyer departed for San Francisco and thence back to Washington. The peacemaker's tour had clarified the reservation issue, but he failed in at least two major objectives. At Cañada Alamosa his messengers had failed to arrange a meeting with Cochise, thanks largely to citizen-inspired rumors that kept the chief in hiding, and at McDowell he was unable to meet with the Tonto chief, Delshay. Several attempts were made to bring him in, but each was aborted or sabotaged. Colyer did investigate Delshay's history quite thoroughly. "He has been at McDowell several times during the past few years," he reported, "and . . . on two occasions he has been dealt with very treacherously."[15]

Despite Crook's show of courtesy to Vincent Colyer, he was badly stung by the peacemaker's endorsement of Royal Whitman and embarrassed by the rough handling of the Tucson mob at Camp Grant. The general was suffering a relentless press attack over the incident, and believed further that Colyer had designed it so, circumventing his authority as Department commander by supporting his enemies and subverting his policies. Made to appear to the civilian population as an impotent nullity, Crook was just too mad not to act. Although Colyer (and for the time being, Whitman, thanks to Colyer's protection) was safe from the general's fury, the orders to disperse the citizen "prospectors" had come from Captain Nelson, who now alone felt the commander's wrath. "You must not forget the duties you owe to the citizens of this government," Crook reprimanded. "Your action in this matter was unwarrantable, as you transcended the limits of your authority, and in future you will be governed by the proper military authorities . . . nor will you unnecessarily provoke the hostilities of the citizens towards the military and the Indians under their protection."[16] It is probably unfair to infer from this that Crook was hoping the Pinals and Arivaipas would suffer another massacre in lieu of a military defeat at his own hands. If the general were convinced that the Tucson party—whether sixty or two hundred—was not of violent or mischievous intent, then Nelson's affront to them could have put the Apaches in danger of a spite raid, thus complicating the army's job of protecting them. Nevertheless, Nelson, who was under orders to co-operate with Colyer to the utmost, seems to have acted correctly and with prudence. From the wording of the rebuke, it seems probable that Crook's anger toward him stemmed mostly from Nelson's having taken instructions from Colyer.

By the conclusion of his mission, Colyer had established interim reservations at Camp Apache, Camp Grant, McDowell, Verde, Date Creek, and Beale Springs. His system of Apache reservations, while frequently adjusted, remained serviceable for a very long time. On the following November 5, however, a terrible incident occurred, proving that any peace with the Indians was only as durable as the dependability of a tribe's worst element. Eight miles west of the small mining settlement of Wickenburg, a stagecoach with eight persons aboard was attacked by Indians believed to be from Date Creek. Six of the whites were killed outright and one was mortally wounded. Among them were three members of the surveying party of Lieutenant George Wheeler, including, perhaps most tragically of all, a gifted young Massachusetts writer named Frederick W. Loring. He had been with the Wheeler expedition in the capacity of correspondent and "general assistant," but his main interest in the Southwest was to broaden his experiences to enrich his writing. In Prescott on November 3, Loring posed for a farewell photograph with his mule, Evil Merodach. His death on the California-bound stage deprived American letters of one of its potentially most facile artists.[17]

When the massacre was first reported there was some belief that it might have been perpetrated by white outlaws or Mexicans, and to be certain of the truth Captain Charles Meinhold was sent from Camp Date Creek to investigate. On November 9 he stated it as his opinion that the culprits had indeed been Indians, and most likely from among the thousand or so contained on the Date Creek Reservation. Although Crook had treated Colyer with studied civility, he was not sorry to see the peace mission fail, if indeed the Wickenburg incident represented a broad failure of policy and was not simply an individual criminal act. The impression lingers that Crook was suspiciously hasty in making that assumption. In fact, Crook expressed delight[18] at Colyer's alleged failure, joined in the humorous comments about "Vincent the Good," and now that the interruption was over, resumed plans for a major expedition. It is easy here to confuse Crook's stern efficiency as a soldier with his motivation. He was no warmonger; he did feel, at least partially correctly, as was shown from time to time on the frontier, that Indians who had never been defeated badly by whites could not be counted on to maintain a negotiated peace when the peace no longer suited the fancy of their rowdier element. The Tonto Apaches were proud, independent, and warlike. Crook believed sincerely that the Colyer mission was a futile exercise and that it was better for the Apaches to suffer a quick, severe beating, to be followed by honest and caring pacification. Crook's delight at Colyer's failure, if such it was, was from this perspective, not that he enjoyed warring on Indians.

Less sensible behavior from Crook was shown in his continuing vendetta against Lieutenant Whitman, and the general was not so busy with his new preparations that he neglected his effort to break him. While Colyer was himself permanently beyond Crook's reach, it was inevitable that Colyer's protection of Whitman would soon cease to be effective. In fact, Colyer was barely out of the territory when Crook preferred criminal charges against Whitman, and on December 4 the lieutenant was court-martialed on two almost comically trumped-up charges containing a total of eight specifications. One charge, that Whitman was guilty of conduct "to the prejudice of good order and military discipline," had but one particular, that he had gambled in a card game on September 1, 1871. Whitman was the disbursing officer of his post, and the charge carried the implication that he had been gambling with army funds. The other charge, of "conduct unbecoming an officer and gentleman," accused Whitman of drunkenness on seven occasions during the preceding thirteen months, beginning in San Francisco in November 1870, "while en route to Arizona," through the end of August 1871, when, it was charged, Whitman "did attempt to seat himself in a woman's lap" at a Tucson picnic. Once before the court Crook's spurious charges, which, historians have noted, "might have been levelled against almost any officer on frontier service,"[19] were quickly thrown out in response to Whitman's pleading in bar of trial that the charges were cumulative and largely fomented by a "citizen Editor of a disloyal paper, abusive of the Army and its officers, and influenced by malice."[20]

The "disloyal paper," the Prescott *Arizona Citizen*, had by this time vilified Whitman beyond credibility. At the time of his arrival in November of 1870, the *Citizen* remarked of him and his companions that they were "fine appearing gentlemen. . . . we believe [they] will prove efficient in their public doings."[21] In the weeks following the massacre and Whitman's outraged condemnation of it, the same journal pictured him as a rolling drunkard, an evil man whose prime motivation for assembling the Indians at Camp Grant was his unnatural sexual attraction to Indian women, "dusky maidens" the paper called them, and fomented a ferocious scandal about him. The soldiers at Grant backed Whitman as best they could. The junior lieutenant, William Robinson, deposed that the *Citizen* had deliberately made it "appear that [he] was a debauched scoundrel and a slave to vice." Robinson expressed ignorance of Whitman's personal life before their association, but said flatly that during the Apaches' presence, "to the best of my knowledge he touched not one drop of liquor," and continued that "the other statement given in the *Citizen* [about Whitman's alleged relations with Indian women] has not the slightest foundation in truth."[22]

When Crook learned that the court had dismissed Whitman's case without action, he was furious. The lieutenant's peculiar pleading resulted in his being found neither innocent nor guilty; Crook complained that this left matters in a worse tangle than ever before by failing either to vindicate Whitman or finally dishonor him. Crook filed a report bitterly condemning the court's decision and began laying plans for another trial. The general's continued vendetta has baffled historians. That Whitman's alleged drunkenness (and he did drink, at least on his own time) was the central issue is hardly credible. Though Crook himself was not a drinker, he managed to wink at the offense enough times when it was committed by his touted Archie MacIntosh. Crook's favorite scout was a rousing boozer, and it was said that while accompanying the general—"en route to Arizona," no less—Crook himself in one instance had to prevent MacIntosh from falling out of the wagon. The best explanation for the trouble

lies in a bad case of first impression outlasting reality, and Crook's suscep-
tibility to stubborn continuance in one frame of mind after he had been
shown to be wrong. Whatever Governor Safford said about Whitman at
that first meeting with Crook, the general believed it too readily and for
too long. Then, too, must be weighed the factor of Crook's own continuing embarrassment over his controversial assignment. To him it seemed
that after having been named Department commander over his own objection, he was stranded in Arizona with Colyer and Whitman and
evidently no person anywhere in authority in the army or the Indian Bureau would sustain his decisions. After he tried once to nail Whitman and
lost, Whitman's very presence was a reproach that had to be done away
with if he was ever to have effective authority in his Department.

In describing Whitman in his autobiography, Crook wrote that the lieutenant had "deserted his colors and gone over to the 'Indian Ring' bag
and baggage."[23] If there was an organized ring it was comprised of the
businessmen who plotted and executed the Camp Grant massacre. Given
the purpose of the ring, Whitman's success at pacifying hundreds of wild
Indians was a direct and serious threat to the war profiteering, and for
Crook to charge Whitman with collaboration was unjust.

Scarcely a week after Whitman wriggled from Crook's clutches, over a
hundred of the Tucson residents and Papago Indians who committed the
Camp Grant massacre were put to trial. When President Grant first heard
of the carnage on Arivaipa Creek he was shocked and angered. Calling the
incident "purely murder," he informed Governor Safford that Arizona
would by presidential order suffer martial law if the perpetrators were not
brought to justice. Grant then ordered District Attorney C. W. C. Rowell
from California to organize the prosecution. The trial opened at the sag-
ging adobe shack that was the Pima County Courthouse in the first week
of December, and for five days there proceeded a farce of the highest degree.

Mexican community leader Juan Elias testified that he was absolutely
certain that an Apache killed in a recent raid on the Papagos at San
Xavier was one he had seen in Camp Grant, identifiable by virtue of a
missing front tooth. For two days this was a mainstay of the defense, until
another defense witness fouled up his story and revealed himself talking to
that particular Indian six months after his supposed death. Elias also
swore that a horse he saw in Camp Grant was one of those stolen from
the San Xavier Papagos, although the *Citizen* had reported at the time of
the raid[24] that of the twenty-three horses stolen, four were killed and the
remaining nineteen safely recovered.

Another expedition member, James Lee, swore that he and some others
had tracked the Indians who raided San Xavier and followed the trail
directly to the Camp Grant village. However, his party had traveled
mostly at night, when tracking was impossible, the trail was three weeks

old, and it followed the main Tucson–Camp Grant trail with all the other traffic. The *Citizen's* own web of sexual intrigue about Lieutenant Whitman came unhinged when the women of Whitman's alleged intentions proved to be the five old women who first came into Grant looking for the captured boy.[25] Later study showed that the source of the fabrication lay in some artful editorial twisting on the part of the newspaper of a pro-Whitman letter previously received.[26] When the jury finally took their instructions and retired, they deliberated for nineteen minutes before finding all the defendants innocent of all the charges.

Throughout December Crook tightened preparations for his war, notifying all the Apaches that they must come in to their agencies and settle down or he would come out to fight them. He established a deadline for them to show themselves for peace at February 16, after which any Indian not at his agency would be considered hostile. About a week before his campaign was to begin, Crook was torpedoed again by higher authority, receiving a message from Division Commander John M. Schofield that the government had decided to try once more to treat with the Indians. The new emissary was Brigadier General Oliver Otis Howard. Although Howard's battle record was in every way commendable—he had lost most of his right arm in the Battle of Seven Pines in 1862—most other officers looked on him with some amusement because of the zeal of his religious faith, which approached fanaticism. It was not unknown for the "Praying General," as they called him, to assemble troops for inspection and harangue them with hymns and sermons. He prayed aloud on his knees in front of people, but President Grant knew that when it really counted, Howard retained a soldier's hard-nosed practicality, and hoped that he would meet with more success than Vincent Colyer had.

Crook was too much an officer and gentleman to criticize Howard's mission openly, but inwardly he was disgusted, and in truth his feeling was not unjustified. Crook had been assigned to Arizona over his own protest to subjugate the Apaches, and was now to be upstaged a second time by a would-be peacemaker. There was reason to his feeling that the interference was undermining his effectiveness; if there was one thing the Apaches responded to, it was truthful speech and consistent action. If Crook were ever to gain the Apaches' respect, it would not be by their seeing him silenced and shackled every time he threatened to move against them. He had just received intelligence from his Indian spies that Date Creek Indians had indeed been responsible for the Wickenburg massacre the previous November. He began planning an expedition to punish them, but with Howard coming he filed it away for another day. (Crook, by the way, had not abated his persecution of Royal Whitman, and pressured General Schofield himself into ordering his rearrest and confinement at Camp Crittenden. This was carried out on March 12, pending yet another court-martial, this time for alleged disobedience.)

Howard learned that the Indians at Camp Grant were greatly agitated, mostly because their beloved nantan Whitman had been taken from them. Howard had Crook overruled, and Whitman was released and reinstated among his Indians while the two generals journeyed from McDowell to Grant to deal with the situation. Evidently it was only now that Crook learned that General Howard and Lieutenant Whitman were very old and dear friends. Though Whitman did not share Howard's religious zeal, they were nearly the same age (Howard was forty-one), were both from Maine, were related by marriage, shared a common humanitarian instinct, particularly regarding the Indian question, and had never let the difference in their ranks complicate an intimate friendship. Crook's bad case of chagrin got even worse when they arrived at Camp Grant and he was forced to observe Howard "parade up and down the garrison, arm in arm with Whitman."[27]

A conference with the Gileños was quickly arranged; Howard and Whitman arrived together, and on alighting from their ambulance (as military coaches were called), they saw Eskiminzin and the other chiefs already seated. As they neared to speaking distance, however, the "Praying General" fell to his knees and begged God to strengthen him in the undertaking. The Apaches were terrified by the weird antic, believing Howard was making evil magic against them, and so hurriedly quit the place, with a few fitful glances over their shoulders. After a few embarrassing minutes Eskiminzin peered around the side of a building and beckoned to Whitman. As he approached him the chief demanded to know who was "that man" and whether Whitman, too, had finally turned against them. Whitman quickly set things straight and the council got under way. The incident was one to raise chuckles then and now, but was also demonstrative of the Apaches' dread of ghosts, witches, and mystical or insane behavior.

Howard managed to recover as many of the Apache children as were still held in Tucson, and shifted their reservation from Camp Grant northward, re-establishing it as the San Carlos Reservation. The Apaches were pleased with both improvements, and Howard confidently effused the question whether they did not think him such a friend that he could come among them even during a war. "You know how wooden an Indian's face can look," said Whitman later in recalling Eskiminzin's reply: "Not unless you want to get killed." To recoup some dignity, Howard asked whether any white man could do that. "Yes," answered Eskiminzin, "so long as [we] remember the Camp Grant massacre, so long *that* man [pointing out Whitman] can come among us, by day or night, in war or peace."[28] Despite the rebuff of Howard's forwardness, when the council broke up Eskiminzin was, as Crook wrote bitterly in his memoirs, "very profuse in his demonstrations of friendship and good will towards General Howard, but he scarcely noticed me, didn't even offer to shake hands with me."[29] (Considering Crook's stand on the massacre and his treatment of Whitman, why he felt Eskiminzin should play up to him is something of a mystery.) Some writers maintain that the Gileños' good impression of Howard lay in his being open about his religion, as indeed they themselves were,[30] but their perception of Howard as a man with a tap into supernatural power probably also helped.

When Crook finally managed to get Howard alone he addressed him abusively, accusing him of taking Whitman's part against Crook to undermine his authority, and of "prostituting" his command by dangling promises of choice assignments in the East before Crook's officers if they would oppose him. Howard was flustered by the sudden attack and tried to explain his long association with Whitman. "He tried to deny and explain, etc.," wrote Crook triumphantly, "but I held up to him the facts," and took some consolation in knowing he had so upset Howard that he "could not go to sleep until he found relief in prayer at three o'clock in the morning."[31] In a less heated meeting Howard managed to calm Crook by agreeing that force must be used to punish the core of Apache resistance, and agreeing in principle to the enlistment of Apache scouts.

During May of 1872, Crook's argument that a lasting peace with Apaches was impossible unless they were first militarily whipped became increasingly supported by facts.[32] Around the middle of the month raiders stole stock from ranchers in the Williamson Valley. A small cavalry unit from Camp Hualpai chased them over a hundred miles before overtaking them and killing four; only one animal was recovered, though.[33] At the same time, Crook was beginning to suffer some embarrassing raids himself. On the nineteenth Indians crept within striking distance of Camp Verde, where they pounced upon and stole the beef contractor's herd. Thirty head were rescued and one raider was killed after a rugged chase.[34] Three days later hostiles pulled Crook's beard again, killing a shepherd and making off with two thousand sheep within a mile and a half of the Department Headquarters at Fort Whipple. Crook himself was absent, but his aide Captain Nickerson and Archie MacIntosh mustered some cavalry and chased them for eighty miles before overtaking them. They got most of the sheep back, but most of the raiders, thought to be either Tonto Apaches or Yavapais, got away.[35] In early June more marauders stole some mules from near Prescott. A small army unit chased and brushed with them as far as Bill Williams Mountain, after which they followed the Indians into a large canyon. The mules were found dead—split open to ventilate before being butchered; the Indians were fought, but inconclusively.[36]

Howard made several adjustments in Vincent Colyer's system of reservations before loading up an Apache delegation and heading back to Washington. Howard's mission had failed in only one important objective, but it was a serious enough failure that on July 3 President Grant ordered him back to Arizona to try once more to reach some kind of agreement with Cochise and the Tsoka-ne-nde Chiricahuas. He had been expecting the instruction, and once back in Arizona set himself up in Camp Apache and sent out messages, but for several weeks he had no luck whatever.

However much Cochise had shown himself desirous of peace at Cañada Alamosa, it was undeniable that southeast Arizona suffered heavily from depredations right up to the time of Howard's second mission. That the middle Chiricahuas acted alone is doubtful; in fact it seems likely that most of the violence was the work of Nde-nda-i bands from farther south. But the violence was there nonetheless. On August 27 a fuzz-faced lieutenant and an experienced corporal en route from Camp Crittenden to Tucson were ambushed in Davidson's Canyon. It was said by others in their party, whom the two had left behind, that the corporal suggested that they not enter the canyon until after dark to protect them from ambush, but his suggestion was ignored by the young officer, who was due in Tucson for court-martial duty. The lieutenant was killed in the attack, the corporal taken alive, bound to a burning tree, and tortured to death.[37] (If the last part of the narrative is true, it indicated the work of Nde-nda-i, perhaps the band under the leadership of Juh, who was notorious for torturing captives.) Seven Mexicans were killed by Indians in the same general vicinity on the same day.

In an attempt to stir up some activity in his search, Howard made a trip to Tularosa in western New Mexico. The Mimbres had been ordered to report to the agency there, and Loco and Victorio had been cowed into coming in, but they loathed the place almost as much as Cochise, who continued to disdain it. Howard persuaded the Mimbres chiefs to remain there for the time being by promising to move them back to Cañada Alamosa in their own country if Cochise could be convinced to remove there as well. This was a chancy condition, for while the Tci-he-nde would be delighted to have a reservation in their own country again, it would be a major move for Cochise and his following, but Howard put his best face on and bulled ahead. He made the acquaintance of Thomas Jeffords, a remarkable forty-year-old scout and pioneer who was said to be the only white man who could take Howard to Cochise. Jeffords and the chief had been acquainted since 1867, and he held the respect and affection of the Tsoka-ne-nde to a degree that was unique on the Arizona frontier. The Apaches knew him warmly as "Taglito." Cochise, whose blood brother he had become in 1870, referred to him as *Chik-a-çay*: my brother. Howard was vastly impressed with Jeffords, but the scout did not reciprocate the regard. At first he considered Howard a sanctimonious windbag, but changed his opinion when Howard showed no reluctance to carry out the mission in Jeffords' company only, without an escort.

The devastation in southeast Arizona had been such that even Jeffords

dared not do it entirely alone; they waited until two young Indians favorably known to Cochise, named Ponce and Chee, could be located. They
agreed to help, if Howard would issue orders protecting their families from
the army while they were gone, and Howard complied.

The party that set out included Howard and his aide Captain Sladen,
Jeffords, the two Indians, two packers, and an interpreter. The journey
south was one of over three hundred miles, and it took them through the
old mining district near and about Santa Rita, where Howard learned they
were in as much danger from white ruffians as they were from Indian attack. Outside Silver City, Howard had to interpose his own stern per-
sonage between his Chiricahua guides and a couple of miners who pulled
their guns on them. As they neared Cochise's stronghold they were visited
with increasing frequency by scouts from the great chief, and to allay any
fears of treachery the two packers and the interpreter were sent back.

Although Cochise's main stronghold was in the Chiricahua Mountains,
his favorite camp lay in the Dragoon Mountains, in a hidden valley some
forty acres in extent that was, for practical purposes, impregnable, ap-
proachable only through a jumbled, boulder-strewn defile six miles long.
They came as near as they dared before making camp, and settled down
to wait. The next morning a man came in identifying himself as Cochise's
brother. Soon after, the chief arrived, too, with his wife and sister, and
second son, a youth named Naiche. Chee and Ponce convinced Cochise
that the one-armed officer was in earnest, and the chief believed it when
Howard agreed to stay while Cochise called in his subchiefs to council.
He would stay, he said, as long as it took. Howard described Cochise as a
man "fully six feet in height, well proportioned, . . . face slightly painted
with vermilion." His collar-length hair was straight and black with a few
strands of silver. "When conversing on all ordinary matters," wrote
Howard, "he was exceedingly pleasant, exhibiting a childlike simplicity;
but in touching upon the wrongs of the Apaches . . . he is altogether
another man."[38]

"You Americans began the fight, and now Americans and Mexicans kill
an Apache on sight," said Cochise. "I have retaliated with all my might. I
have killed ten white men for every Indian slain."[39]

Howard was Cochise's guest for eleven days; after a lengthy conference
among themselves the Chiricahuas agreed to live at peace, on two conditions. First, they must be given a reservation right there, in their own
country. Cochise indicated that he personally would be willing to remove
to Cañada Alamosa, but his captains were not obligated to follow him,
and some had refused. Even a chief of Cochise's influence could not just
order his people about; he faced the same limitations as any headman.
Those who stayed in Arizona would continue to raid and wreck the peace
anyway, and if he could stay there he could control them better. Howard
found this sensible, and agreed. The second condition was that "Taglito"

Jeffords serve them as agent. He was the only man they trusted to deal with them fairly, and they meant to have him. Jeffords tried to escape the duty, but when it was clear that it was not a matter to be negotiated, he reluctantly agreed.

The Cochise treaty was formalized—orally—at Dragoon Springs on October 12, 1872, and Howard departed, thoroughly respected and admired by the Chiricahuas, and as thoroughly despised by most of the miners and ranchers. Gerónimo's following of Bedonkohe Nde-nda-i had been present for the conferences; "He always kept his word with us and treated us as brothers," said Gerónimo, who had had occasion to ride double with the general briefly. "We could have lived forever at peace with him. If there is any pure, honest white man in the United States army, that man is General Howard."[40] When it was time for them to part, Cochise embraced Howard firmly and said, in English, "Good-by." It is a shame that such a good story was marred by one unfortunate repercussion. When Loco and Victorio heard from Ponce and Chee that Cochise had wangled his own reservation in his own country, and that Cañada Alamosa would not be reopened and they were stuck with Tularosa, those chiefs were very bitter and angry. With just a little more perception from Howard toward the Mimbres so much more trouble might have been avoided.

In September, with Howard safely engaged in the search for Cochise, Crook resurrected his plan to punish the Date Creek Yavapais and Tontos. The first column sent out killed seven hostiles and scattered the rest. Later in the same month Crook sent out a force of 5th Cavalry, assisted by scout chief Al Sieber and eighty-six friendly Walapais. In a campaign that destroyed forever the Yavapai resistance to the white takeover, the hostiles were crushed, with about forty of their number killed.

Crook then quickly smashed a clot of hostility among the Walapai Indians of north-central Arizona, and then set about tackling the raiding elements among the Western Apaches, who had been thorns in his side since the Colyer mission, but they proved to be tougher customers. On the morning of September 30 a large raiding party of Apaches—again, tribe unknown but probably Westerns—attacked a ranch within a couple of miles of Camp Crittenden, killing a Mexican and taking three horses. Shortly before noon a cavalry unit of about a dozen galloped onto the scene, but on finding themselves outnumbered by an estimated five or six to one, declined to press the engagement. The Apaches, as was their habit, took cover on a rugged mountain slope, taunting and daring the white-eyes to attack, but instead the lieutenant in command divided his party in two to spread the alarm to nearby ranches. The same Indians ambushed the squad under Sergeant George Stewart about four miles from Crittenden as they were returning to the fort. Four of the six soldiers were killed in a massive volley. The rearmost in the line fled back in the direction they had come; the foremost, the bugler, raced toward the post and narrowly escaped after a desperate chase. The ambush was carried out in the unlikeliest of places, far from cover and on a broad flat. As a tribute to the Indians' skill at hiding themselves in the desert, the lieutenant reported that the fifty or so Apaches had hidden themselves, "in a little ravine, two feet deep and not more than fifteen paces from the road; the place was very open and it would seem almost impossible for them to have been concealed in such a place."[41]

When Howard left the territory in triumph Crook began trying to obtain a "copy" of the treaty, only to discover that apparently it was not committed to paper. He was pretty sure that the southern border of the new Chiricahua reservation was contiguous with the Mexican border, which gave them a safe crossing line at least fifty miles long, whenever they felt like plundering in Mexico. All of Howard's actions were confirmed by an executive order on December 14, leaving Crook to enforce a treaty of whose terms he was unsure, upon Indians who mistrusted him and whom he mistrusted. But for the present he had no choice but to let the Chiricahua question lie.

The Peacemakers:
NOTES

1. See generally Essin, "Mules, Packs, and Packtrains."
2. Crook, "Apache Problem," p. 262.
3. Bourke, On the Border, pp. 108–9.
4. Crook, General George Crook: His Autobiography, p. 164.
5. Utley, Frontier Regulars, p. 201.
6. Agent Piper was not pleased. See Colyer, Peace with the Apaches of New Mexico and Arizona, p. 10.
7. Crook, "Apache Problem," p. 267.
8. Secretary of War, Annual Report for 1871.
9. Crook, General George Crook: His Autobiography, p. 166.
10. This and following quotations are from Bourke, On the Border, pp. 147–50.
11. Thrapp, Conquest of Apacheria, p. 102.
12. Crook, "Apache Problem," p. 261.
13. Crook, General George Crook: His Autobiography, p. 167; Thrapp, Conquest of Apacheria, p. 102.
14. Thrapp, Conquest of Apacheria, p. 104. Crook's nature being as it was, I suspect—although I doubt it can be proven—that either one or two other factors were involved in Crook's determination to break Whitman, aside from his characteristic perseverance in an erroneous policy. First, I can't help but wonder whether Crook, given his evenhanded fairness to other officers on duty in Arizona, perhaps had more evidence against Whitman than he was willing, for whatever reason, to make public. Second, it seems possible that in review-

ing the records of the feeding station at Camp Grant, Crook found certain anomalies and arabesques in the bookkeeping, which he took for corruption, when in fact they had been honestly intended. No man at this time was able to govern Apache Indians strictly by the book and be effective. Sudden exigencies frequently had to be finessed, and even the best agents like Tom Jeffords and John Clum had to juggle accounts to make ends meet (which, by the way, also led to charges of *their* corruption). Unfortunately for Whitman, General Crook lived by the book—usually—and would not have been easily satisfied by an argument of this nature.

15. Colyer, *Peace with the Apaches of New Mexico and Arizona*, pp. 22–27.
16. Crook to Nelson, Sept. 22, 1871. This and ff. cites to army correspondence are reproduced in various secondary sources. See p. 252, n. 4, supra.
17. *Select Picture List*, p. 3.
18. Thrapp, *Conquest of Apacheria*, p. 105.
19. Ibid., p. 108.
20. Ibid.
21. Prescott *Arizona Citizen*, Dec. 3, 1870.
22. Colyer, *Peace with the Apaches of New Mexico and Arizona*, p. 38.
23. Crook, *General George Crook: His Autobiography*, p. 170.
24. Prescott *Arizona Citizen*, April 15, 1871.
25. Thrapp, *Conquest of Apacheria*, p. 93.
26. Hastings, "Tragedy of Camp Grant," p. 156, n. 47.
27. Crook, *General George Crook: His Autobiography*, p. 170.
28. Thrapp, *Conquest of Apacheria*, p. 111.
29. Crook, *General George Crook: His Autobiography*, p. 172.
30. Debo, *Geronimo*, p. 85.
31. Crook, *General George Crook: His Autobiography*, p. 173.
32. This activity is recorded in the National Archives' Army Record Groups 75 and 98, accessibly chronicled by Thrapp in *Conquest of Apacheria*.
33. Mason to Nickerson, May 23, 1872.
34. Wilson to Post Adjutant, Fort Verde, May 24, 1872.
35. Crook to Assistant Adjutant General, Pacific Division, May 28, 1872; Arizona *Miner*, May 25, 1872. See also Nickerson, "An Apache Indian Raid, and a Long-Distance Ride," pp. 693–94.
36. Garvey to Commanding Officer, Fort Whipple, June 13, 1872.
37. Hall to Adjutant General's Office, Aug. 29, 1872.
38. Carpenter, *Sword and Olive Branch*, p. 215.
39. Quoted in Debo, *Geronimo*, p. 87.
40. Gerónimo, *Geronimo's Story of His Life*, p. 140.
41. Hall to Assistant Adjutant General, Department of Arizona, Oct. 1, 1872.

The Tonto War

By late in 1872 Crook had been restrained as long as he could be. Vincent the Good had come and gone, and the peacemaker Howard had done his best (or worst), but still depredations continued. "I think I am fully justified in saying that I have carried out that portion of my instructions which required me to cooperate," wrote Crook of the pacification efforts in September, but "humanity demands that I should now proceed to carry out the remainder of my instructions, which require me to punish the incorrigibly hostile."[1]

After he had been among them for a few months, Crook began to form a more mellow opinion than he first held of his adversaries. "I think the Apache is painted in darker colors than he deserves, and that his villainies arise more from [his] misconception of [the white people] than from his being worse than other Indians." The desert, Crook reasoned, subsisted the Indian only meagerly. To improve himself "he has either to cultivate the soil or steal, and as our vacillating policy satisfies him we are afraid of him, he chooses the latter." Thievery was also better suited to the Apaches' natural temper, he said, yet Crook saw good qualities in them, and believed they wanted only a demonstration of white military strength to soften them for remolding. "I am satisfied," he continued, "that a sharp, active campaign against him would . . . make him one of the best Indians in the country."[2]

However much Crook was at fault in his wrath at Whitman—and he was, grievously so—he had arrived at an understanding of his Apache enemies far more perceptive than that of any other commander who fought them. Whitman had been fortunate to achieve progress with a few bands of Pinals and Arivaipas, accomplished by initiative, good judgment, and perseverance. For the majority of the other Apache tribes, Crook's theory of sharp defeat followed up by intensive and kindly pacification fell far short of the locally espoused extinction ethic, and was the most generous treatment ever offered them. As the date for beginning the operations drew near, no new peacemaker arrived to stay the war again. If one had, it is doubtful whether Crook would have let him proceed. "I had made up my mind," he admitted later, "to disobey any order I might receive looking to an interference . . . feeling sure if I was successful my disobedience of orders would be forgiven. . . . [I]f I was again stopped, I would lose my head anyway."[3]

Crook's strategy for the campaign was planned to be simple and surgically effective, to defeat the hostiles as swiftly and humanely as possible. In the first instance, troop columns would operate with apparent haphazardness, stirring up the country sufficiently for the non-reservation Western Apaches to collect in what had always been their refuge in times of military pressure, the Tonto Basin. Secondly, once the hostiles were herded into the general area, the troop columns would converge inward, encourage surrenders, and annihilate the holdouts.

Later a favorite setting for Zane Grey's and other western romances, the Tonto Basin can be roughly defined as containing the drainage of Tonto Creek, bounded by the Mogollon Rim on the north, the Mazatzal (locally pronounced *mat'-a-zal*) and Superstition mountains on the west and south, and the Sierra Anchas on the southeast. In area the basin covers perhaps fifteen hundred appallingly rugged square miles. Though the broken topography was a distinct benefit to hiding Indians, Crook began his campaign with important advantages, too. He would prosecute the war with fresh troops from the 5th Cavalry and his own 23rd Infantry, recently phased into Arizona duty to relieve the 3rd Cavalry and 21st Infantry. He would open his campaign just at the start of winter, when water would be easier to obtain for his troops, while at the same time the increasing cold would make it ever more difficult for the hostiles to regain food and supplies lost to the army. This strategy was based partly on Crook's correct understanding of the Apaches as a mountain people, knowing that when hard pressed they would fortify—or from his viewpoint, strand—themselves on snowy mountain peaks until they either froze, starved, fought a suicidal action, or surrendered. Crook had prepared carefully for this campaign; he'd had after all little enough else to do during the preceding year. He obtained for his service the most experienced and cunning white guides in the territory: Al Sieber, Archie MacIntosh, of course, Ed Clark, Marijildo Grijalba, and many others whose colorful careers could, and do, fill volumes by themselves. For Indian trackers Crook impressed not only friendly Apaches but also Yavapais, Walapais, and Apache-hating Paiutes, Pimas, and Maricopas. His famous pack trains were outfitted with the best obtainable mules, manned by packers proven capable and not abusive of the animals.

On November 16, 1872, Crook was at last able to commence his operations, intending to concentrate first on taming the extreme northwestern part of Apachería; the first step was to drive the hostiles out of that region down southeast into the basin. That was quickly effected by three expeditions from Camp Hualpai, one to sweep the San Francisco Peaks, one the headwaters of the Verde, and one the Chino Valley. After that they were to unite and clear the vicinity around Camp Verde. Each column consisted of one troop company and a few dozen Indian scouts, and during the two-week marches that took them to Verde they suffered badly from thirst, as it was still too early for the snows. At one point the newly enlisted Indian scouts got thirsty enough at their soldier duty that they nearly deserted, but they were persuaded to stay on. These sweeps were reasonably effective, as many hostile rancherias were burned, a few prisoners taken, and about thirteen Indians killed, eleven of them in a single action by the Chino Valley column, which was led by Paiute trailers.

After sending off the columns from Hualpai, Crook left with his two aides-de-camp, Bourke and Ross, and an escort for Camp Apache, where he enlisted more Apaches as scouts. The Indian Bureau personnel charged Crook with exceeding his authority by taking peaceful Apaches to fight his war, but Crook maintained that the real cause of the accusation was an army census of Camp Apache Indians that suggested the agent had been receiving rations for three hundred nonexistent Apaches.[4] Also while at Camp Apache Crook dispatched a small expedition to McDowell. Feeling their way through the lower portion of the Tonto Basin and striking hostiles where possible, this march took about two weeks and also ended satisfactorily. At one point a detachment of about thirty scouts and regulars endured a grueling thirty-mile night march to attack the rancheria of the Apache chief Delshay, whom Vincent Colyer had been frustrated from meeting. The chief escaped but lost fourteen dead. Shortly after regrouping, the column hit another rancheria, killing eleven and capturing six.[5] The second camp must have had no idea they were being stalked, as the location was revealed to the soldiers by a dog's bark. If the Apaches had known the troops were that close upon them they would have killed their dogs to guarantee silence. When there were no native scouts to sniff them out, quiet and camouflage were two of the Indians' best weapons. On at least one occasion during the Tonto campaign, army regulars marched within a stone's throw of a hostile rancheria and failed to discover it.[6]

Meanwhile, the Hualpai columns had rested in Camp Verde only three days before going back out on December 3, in the company of two other, newly formed units, this time to sweep clean the country west of there. They were out two weeks; they all burned rancherias and drove hostiles before them, but only one force, the most northwesterly, made contact for a fight. The Indians were clearly "not expecting anything from that direction," and were surprised while making camp. Thirteen warriors were killed, three women taken prisoner, and the camp was destroyed. The next day the lieutenant in charge of that column suffered the loss of one Walapai scout in trying to overrun another band of hostiles dug into a

General Orlando B. Willcox. *National Archives.*

Albert Sterling and his Apache scouts. *National Archives.*

Tzo-e, called Peaches, was so grief-stricken by the death of his war partner that he defected in the middle of Chatto's famous raid and returned to the reservation. He willingly guided Crook into the Sierra Madre to bring his people in. *National Archives.*

Chief Loco. After the death of Victorio, cunning but peaceable Loco commanded the largest single following of the remaining Tci-he-nde Mimbres. His left eye was damaged but not blinded in a mauling by a bear. *National Archives.*

Before striking into Mexico, General Crook's invasion force bivouacks near the border. *Arizona Historical Society.*

The new way to chase Indians: a few of Crook's packers and pack mules. *National Archives.*

Apache Indians digging an irrigation canal at San Carlos in the 1880s. *National Archives.*

Apache prisoners of war, 1884. *National Archives.*

Gerónimo, a chief and di-yin for war of the Bedonkohe group of the Nde-nda-i. *National Archives.*

mountainside. All the Verde operations were organized and co-ordinated by Crook's number two, Captain Azor Nickerson, who now sent out yet another column under newly arrived Captain George F. Price with a company of 5th Cavalry and three dozen Yavapai scouts. Price's unit had one brush with hostiles in which nine women and one old man were taken prisoner, but Price quickly scurried back into his base for reinforcements, having found "more country than he could cover and plenty of Indians."[7]

All of Nickerson's columns returned to Verde but left again on December 23 for another two-week stint, now turning eastward to begin combing the Tonto Basin itself.

From Camp Apache Crook continued on to the new Fort Grant, where he arrived on December 7 and promptly organized yet another column, a large one of two cavalry companies and thirty Apache scouts. They were to scour the southern Tonto Basin, with special instructions to strike at Delshay and his equally notorious cohort, another chief named Chunz; eventually they were to report to Camp McDowell. They, too, had good hunting, overrunning a rancheria on December 15, and the next day taking that of Chunz. No hostiles were killed but virtually all the food and camp goods were seized.

Up to this time the Apache scouts had done the bulk of the fighting, and they celebrated on the night of the seventeenth with a war dance. Lieutenant Bourke had gone out with this column, and as the group progressed he kept a close eye on the Indian skirmishers. "The longer we knew the Apache scouts," he wrote, "the better we liked them. They were wilder and more suspicious than the Pimas and Maricopas, but far more reliable, and endowed with a greater amount of courage and daring."[8]

On December 22 these scouts struck again, killing a number of hostiles and taking three prisoners in the south of the Sierra Ancha Mountains. Three days later the Fort Grant expedition rendezvoused with another from McDowell that had come out to assist them. Together they mounted well over two hundred men. The McDowell force and its some one hundred Pima trailers had just routed a hostile rancheria near the Four Peaks region in the extreme southern Mazatzals, just across the Salt River from the columns' meeting point. It was believed that more renegades remained hidden in that area, so at eight o'clock that night the column undertook a silent, perilous night march to the rim of the Salt River gorge. On reaching the precipice after midnight the command rested, while the scouts were sent out to prowl the canyon. When they returned they reported discovering fires on the canyon floor, and accordingly the troops crept into a position to attack and waited the remainder of the frigid night without the benefit of heavy clothing or blankets. When dawn finally broke, the canyon was discovered to be empty, the fires having doubtless been lit as decoys.

Angry and disappointed, the troops were ready to quit the place. First,

though, one of the white guides left with a small group for a rapid exploratory trip to familiarize himself with the country, and discovered almost
immediately that the troops had spent the night less than a quarter mile
from the real rancheria, a small one now abandoned. When they continued their exploring a little more cautiously, some horses and mules were
discovered a little farther on, and just after that, a very large rancheria
perched on an extensively fortified outcropping. In an act of considerable
bravery the guide Joe Felmer and the handful he had with him, charged
the camp and so surprised the Apaches that Felmer took it without loss to
himself while killing a half dozen hostiles. Unaware of the size of the attacking force, the Apaches, a band of Tontos under a chief named Nanni-
chaddi, took refuge in a large overhang eroded back into the cliff wall.
The rest of the command came up in support, but no charge was ordered,
as the Indians were hopelessly trapped. On Nanni-chaddi's front but some
distance away down an arroyo was the Salt River. The depression or cave
in which he had taken refuge was roughly shaped like a shallow U. In the
higher reaches of the rough ground down both sides leading to the river
were the troops. Behind him was a stone wall a thousand feet high. The
soldiers were ordered to take cover and snipe at every warrior who showed
himself, but not to shoot deliberately at any women or children.

When two separate offers of surrender were scorned one of the troop
companies gained the bluff tops and not only began shooting at the cornered Indians but hurling boulders down as well. As the toll of Apache
dead mounted, some tried to escape, either by sneaking away or recklessly
bolting down the arroyo toward the river, but in each case they were
found out and killed. After some hours of siege an intensive volley-fire was
ordered into the hostiles' cave. The next three minutes wrought a horrible
holocaust on the cornered Apaches as every soldier and scout shot down
into the pit as fast as he could handle his rifle. When a charge was finally
ordered and the cave overrun, only twenty women and children, all
wounded, were left alive to surrender. Seventy-six Apaches died, including
every one of the men except one, who hid motionless under a pile of
corpses until the soldiers moved on. Fifty-seven of the bodies were within
the confines of the cave. The soldiers had lost only one man, a Pima
tracker, dead.

Apache social organization was so localized in nature that even this
crushing defeat had little adverse effect on hostile resistance elsewhere,
but the local demoralization was great. The victorious troopers stayed in
McDowell only long enough to be refitted and augmented, and trekked
back out to the Superstitions, bound eventually for Fort Grant. They announced their renewed presence in a brief fire fight on January 15, and on
the eighteenth the surrounding hostiles began showing signs of wanting to
surrender. First a boy came in, then a woman, then an old man walked
into the camp. They were fed and told to go back out and bring in their

band. As the column wound its way toward Fort Grant the Indians surrendered without show, one at a time. Lieutenant Bourke, who had come back out with the expedition, noted that "it seemed as if from behind clusters of sage brush, giant cactus, palo verde or mesquite, along the trail, first one, then another, then a third Apache would silently join the column. . . . When we reported to General Crook again at the post . . . there were one hundred and ten people with us, and the whole business had been done so quietly that not one-half of the command ever knew whether any Apaches had joined us or not."[9] With his Indian scout program proving successful, Crook impressed twenty-six of the newly arrived POWs into his service. The Superstition Mountains were believed clean, but elsewhere the columns stayed out, many of the cavalrymen afoot now because a rampant stock disease had depleted the stables. Throughout the winter Crook's troops waged a ferocious campaign of raids, skirmishes, and fire fights; by Christmas he had nine separate commands operational in the field, many of these splitting frequently into smaller units.

In just over two weeks starting from the first of the year, one detachment of Captain Price's column fought three actions near the Bradshaw Mountains and Agua Fria River, netting eleven warriors dead and nine women and children captured. Shortly after that a unit under Lieutenant Frank Mochler, operating in the heart of the basin, overran a large rancheria on Tonto Creek, killing seventeen against a loss of one. Many other smaller actions also took their toll as the columns crisscrossed the Tonto Basin.

On March 11 a band of Tontos gave Crook the impetus he needed to finish his campaign. A small party of them were laired in a draw not far from Wickenburg, evidently purposing to take another stagecoach. Instead, they fell upon and killed two white passersby, one a remarkable old pioneer named Gus Swain.[10] A third white, an unarmed twenty-one-year-old Scottish immigrant named George Taylor, whose father ran a nearby mine, was taken alive and tortured brutally. Captain Nickerson inspected the site shortly after, writing that the Apaches had shot some one hundred fifty arrows into non-vital portions of young Taylor's body. The ground, he wrote, "was all matted down as he had rolled over and over." Nickerson could not bring himself to relate how poor Taylor was finished off, except to say that it was too "excruciating and beastly" to describe.[11] (The wounds that Nickerson ascribed to having been made by arrows were in fact made by wood splinters. After piercing Taylor with kindling the Indians had set him afire.)

As the final push was begun to cower the remaining hostiles the frequency and effectiveness of the fights increased. Within two weeks of George Taylor's torturous murder, thirty-eight warriors were killed in four separate actions. One unit in particular, under Captain George M. Randall, 23rd Infantry, was instructed to hunt down the Taylor killers. Doggedly Randall and his scouts uncovered their expertly hidden trail, north-east from the headwaters of the New River through the rugged and sometimes lunar Bloody Basin, toward the forking of the Verde River. Just as the trail was beginning to warm, some of Randall's mules strayed, the captain guessing from surrounding plumes of smoke signals that his enemy had captured them. His presence was known, but he managed to keep his location secret. Continuing their slow and silent march, Randall's scouts soon took prisoner a Tonto woman, whom they bullied and threatened into leading them to her rancheria.

The column moved out under cover of darkness, in total silence. All talking was forbidden; their very footsteps were muffled by gunnysacks tied over their boots. After an extensive march the Tonto woman guided them to a hulking parapet of a mountain called Turret Peak, about ten miles west of the Verde opposite the mouth of the East Fork and about twenty miles due south of Camp Verde. Formed by a tortuous intrusion of ancient lava, the mountain was capped by a relatively compact upthrust shaped vaguely like a pillbox, from which the peak took its name.

The woman's rancheria was located on the small level area atop the pillbox, a seemingly invulnerable position accessible only by a jumbled crawl space where a thin section of the summit wall had collapsed. The slightest noise from the soldiers at this stage would have meant disaster, but one by one the troops wriggled silently under the last obstacle, a boulder that had crashed down onto the passageway. Regrouping in one corner of the summit, the soldiers overran the rancheria at first light, killing about twenty-five of the renegade Tontos, again including all the men, it was believed. Some of the women and children got away, but the rest were captured.

The effect of the Turret Peak fight on the remaining hostiles' morale was significant and widespread, as it accomplished what the Salt River Cave fight had failed to do, possibly because there were more survivors left this time to spread the news. If the Turret Peak hideout could be found and smashed, where else could they hide? "So secure did they feel in this almost impregnable position," wrote Crook of the attack, "that they lost all presence of mind, even running past their holes in the rocks. Some of them jumped off the precipice. . . ."[12] Crook was not at the fight, and one hopes he was quoting good authority for the last assertion; Captain Randall's report was subsequently lost from the army files and was never found.[13]

Within days of the Turret Peak fight the beaten Indians began sending peace feelers into the posts. One group cautiously entered Camp Verde and spoke with Crook, and the general called an almost screeching halt to his war. Crook was a skilled Indian fighter, but until he could ascertain the renegades' sincerity he would allow no blood to be needlessly spilled. He ordered signal beacons lit on the hilltops to recall the troop columns, and scouts were sent out to scour the maze of the basin country to locate the other units and stop the violence. The end of the Tonto War shows Crook in his most favorable light. He had shown himself unafraid to fight Apaches in their own country, and as his theory of employing native scouts proved itself, he had whipped them. Between four and five hundred Yavapais and Western Apaches were dead, and the survivors called him the "Gray Fox." But he showed himself unafraid to stop the war, defying the local demand for genocide.

Crook's first dividend from the campaign was the surrender of the chief Cha-lipun at Verde on April 6. Although most of his following seems to have been among Yavapais, Cha-lipun (actually Tčà-libáhń meaning Brown Hat) was himself a Southern Tonto, with most of his Apache following drawn from the Mazatzal band and four of its attached semi-bands.[14] It is likely that his Yavapai following was the result of one or more marriages into that tribe. Cha-lipun, or Charley Pan, as Crook called him, had about three hundred Indians with him, but represented several times that number. His surrender talk with Crook was not only a vindication of Crook's strategy in the Tonto campaign but also justified the general's reliance on Indian scouts. Cha-lipun said to Crook, according to Bourke, that "They had never been afraid of the Americans alone, but now that their own people were fighting against them they did not know what to do; they could not go to sleep at night, because they feared to be surrounded before daybreak; they could not hunt—the noise of their guns would attract the troops; they could not cook mescal or anything else, because the flame and smoke would draw the soldiers; they had retreated to the mountaintops, thinking to hide in the snow until the soldiers went home, but the scouts found them out and the soldiers followed them."[15]

In accepting Cha-lipun's surrender Crook shook his hand, telling him that "if he would promise to live at peace and stop killing people, he would be the best friend he ever had." In establishing the peace Crook showed admirable judgment. On the one hand he told Cha-lipun he was sorry for the war, that his people had brought it on themselves, but now it was over and he would help them live better and protect them from bad whites. On the other hand he issued insightful instructions to his subordinates on governing the former hostiles, advising that the Indians were not to be dealt with severely for committing "what in the civil codes would constitute minor offences, [but] care should be taken that they do not succeed in deceiving their agents and officers in matters of greater import, being careful to treat them as children in *ignorance*, not in *innocence*."[16]

Three days after the Cha-lipun surrender, Crook wrote a formal end to the war, issuing a congratulatory message to his troops,[17] which was soon followed by a citation from Division Commander Schofield.[18]

Not all the columns were brought in, however, because at least one of the principal hostile bands was still out: Delshay continued to roam uncowed. On April 25, though, his rancheria in the northeast part of the basin, near the bend of Canyon Creek, was finally cornered and check-mated. Instead of suffering the fate of those at Salt River Cave and Turret Peak, Delshay surrendered his band, waving a white flag at first firing. The troops were under Captain Randall, who at first rejected the surrender, employing the well-established policy of accepting only after the most belligerent hesitation. No, he said, Delshay had proven himself a bad Indian and must die. At this point, wrote Crook in his abrupt and frequently sarcastic memoirs, "Delshay commenced crying and said he would do anything he would be ordered to do. He wanted to save his people, as they were starving. Every rock had turned into a soldier, and his people were hunted down as they had never been before. . . . He said he had had one hundred and twenty-five warriors last fall, and if anybody had told him he couldn't whip the world, he would have laughed at them, but now he had only twenty left." And, according to Crook, there followed still another admission of the effectiveness of his Indian scout strategy. Delshay "said they used to have no difficulty in eluding the troops, but now the very rocks had gotten soft, they couldn't put their foot anywhere without leaving an impression by which we could follow."[19]

Finally Captain Randall gave in and allowed Delshay to surrender, taking him and his captive band to the White Mountain Reservation. With the last of the renegades finally corralled, the territorial newspapers were almost delirious in their praise of Crook and his troops. A more meaningful recognition of the importance of the first American military victory ever gained over Apaches, was received at Prescott. The first telegraph line to reach that part of the territory had just been installed, and the first message to be received announced that Lieutenant Colonel Crook had been promoted to brigadier general. The promotion jumped Crook again over the forty line colonels who had claims senior to his to the billet, and it was made, again, over the objections of the War Secretary and the General of the Army. Crook was a hero, but it made him a cloakroom full of enemies, among the most powerful and persistent of whom was Nelson A. Miles, colonel of the 5th Infantry. The irregular promotion opened a feud between Crook and Miles that smoldered for thirteen years before exploding.

The Tonto War:
NOTES

1. Crook to Assistant Adjutant General, Pacific Division, Sept. 21, 1872. This and ff. cites to army correspondence are reproduced in various secondary sources. See p. 252, n. 4, supra.

2. Curtis, *North American Indians,* Vol. I, p. 8.

3. Crook, *General George Crook: His Autobiography*, p. 177.

4. Crook to Assistant Adjutant General, Dec. 12, 1872. This and ff. cites to army correspondence are reproduced in various secondary sources. See p. 252, n. 4, supra.

5. Smyth to Crook, Dec. 16, 1872.

6. Farish, *History of Arizona*, Vol. III, p. 325.

7. Nickerson to Assistant Adjutant General, Dec. 26, 1872.

8. Bourke, *On the Border*, p. 203.

9. Ibid., p. 207.

10. For more information on this colorful character see Conner, *Joseph Reddeford Walker and the Arizona Adventure*, pp. 227–28.

11. Thrapp, *Conquest of Apacheria*, p. 134.

12. Crook, *General George Crook: His Autobiography*, p. 178.

13. This according to Thrapp, *Conquest of Apacheria*, p. 136.

14. Goodwin, *Social Organization of the Western Apache*, p. 36.

15. Bourke, *On the Border*, p. 212.

16. General Orders No. 13, Department of Arizona, Apr. 8, 1873.

17. General Orders No. 14, Department of Arizona, Apr. 11, 1873.

18. General Orders No. 8, Pacific Division, Apr. 28, 1873.

19. Crook, *General George Crook: His Autobiography*, p. 180.

The Mysterious Dr. Wilbur

Though Crook had finally given the Western Apaches a sound beating, he faced an equally tough struggle with the Indian Bureau, with whom he still had to share control of the reservations. To represent the army at the Verde Reservation he dispatched Lieutenant Walter Schuyler; for the two big Apache agencies he sent William Brown, leader of the Salt Cave fight, to Fort Apache, and to San Carlos a young Massachusetts Quaker lieutenant named Jacob Almy.

Affairs at San Carlos were deplorable. As the white man's control grew, some Apache customs began to modify to reflect the new force, and around the agencies new expressions said much of the Indians' opinion of the would-be masters and their government. Up to that time it had been customary for an Apache who violated the taboo against killing spiders immediately afterward to protest one's own innocence and name an enemy as the killer. Now new sayings began to emerge in addressing the dead spider: "I did not kill you. The agent killed you," or even, "The President killed you." White people were held up as bogeys to scare little children. "Don't go around white soldiers," one was told, and "don't go around Chinamen. They'll feed you hog meat and turkey meat, and these eat nasty things, anything at all."[1]

George Stevens, who had been the agent, was removed for penning a scandalous letter about General O. O. Howard. Stevens' personal reputation had been one of honesty and integrity, and he was fired and hustled away without having an opportunity to defend himself. The letter, which was later proved to be a forgery, opened the door for an interim agent, Dr. R. A. Wilbur of Tucson. The letter was really written by a noncommissioned officer in the 1st Cavalry, but how Wilbur was awarded the appointment, and whether there was any connection between the two, was never uncovered. Wilbur was a swindler and war profiteer of the most brazen and unapologetic kind, as he himself later admitted with glibness and candor. The agent named to replace George Stevens permanently, a retired army major from Maine named Charles Larrabee, would not take over for months, and until then Dr. Wilbur was to have a free hand at San Carlos.

Wilbur managed to capitalize on inter-band frictions that had broken the Indians settled near San Carlos into two opposing groups: the Pinals and Arivaipas of Eskiminzin and Capitán Chiquito, who would have rather stayed in their home territory; and a group led by three roughneck Tonto chiefs, Ba-coon, Cochinay and Chunz, of whom the last was the worst, a well-known murderer and thoroughly treacherous individual. The two factions' mistrust of each other was sufficient to overcome their aversion to the agent, and Dr. Wilbur's paternalistic reward system encouraged each side to tell him what the other was up to.

When Agent Charles Larrabee finally arrived in early 1874 he found Dr. Wilbur in efficiently manipulative control, and no doubt raking in a fortune in graft. That Wilbur was out to profit as much as possible from his short tenure was apparently clear to everyone but the Indians. He was so little concerned with agency affairs that in one instance, when the interpreter warned him of an impending murder by an Indian of one of the employees, Wilbur responded that the culprit should "wait till I get out of here, and then he can do as he pleases." To keep control as long as he could, Wilbur sought out the beef contractor's local agent and informed him that the new agent, Larrabee, would accept agency beef weighed only after butchering; Wilbur had been accepting it on the hoof, which was an easier weight to falsify, and Larrabee was threatening to cut off a source of graft that evidently had been profitable for both Wilbur and the contractor. What the meticulous Dr. Wilbur had not counted on was that the contractor's agent, Elijah S. Junior, would soon turn witness and testify against him.

Wilbur, according to Junior's later testimony, confided to him that he had told the Indians that Junior was a good man, and they should seek advice from him, not Larrabee, and concluded with the advice that "In case anything happens, Concepción [the interpreter] will notify you in time so you will have a chance to get away."

"I thought at the time," said Junior to the investigating commission, "and I think so still, from Dr. Wilbur's language, manner and actions, that he meant to, or had at the time, used his influence with the Indians by false representations, etc., to have all the white people at . . . San Carlos . . . massacred after his departure therefrom."[2]

When Charles Larrabee learned of the dissatisfactory state of affairs he sent for the Tonto chiefs to come in for an interview. On March 5 the three Tonto cutthroats, Cochinay, Ba-coon, and Chunz, with a fourth Tonto chief, Nezhar-titte, came in for the talk, but when Larrabee and Junior arrived on the scene they found Dr. Wilbur already there, seated among the Indians. As Larrabee strode toward them the interpreter Concepción told him he would not go among them, "not for ten thousand dollars." Larrabee introduced himself to the Tontos, saying that he had been sent by the President to help them all he could, but Nezhar-titte cut him off, saying he had seen him with too many soldiers to believe he intended to help them, with which Chunz agreed.

Dr. Wilbur participated in the meetings, openly influencing the Chunz faction against Agent Larrabee. Elijah Junior's testimony conjured an almost satanic vision: "Dr. Wilbur was sitting by the side of the chief Chunz. When [Nezhar-titte] said to the agent that he had seen him with the soldiers, I saw Dr. Wilbur nod his head several times and laugh, signifying his approbation, and when [Chunz] added that he did not believe the agent was their friend, I distinctly saw Dr. Wilbur nod his head and smile, embracing and hugging at the same time . . . Chunz." Several of the Indians loaded their guns and surrounded Larrabee, at which Junior ran to the agent's quarters for his rifle.

On his return Larrabee ordered him to issue one of his beeves to Bacoon's people to quiet them. Junior did so, and the Indians slaughtered and butchered it with great emotion and ferocity. The crisis passed, but the overall situation did not improve. During the next several weeks Larrabee sought to pacify the Chunz faction with more and more concessions, but Wilbur's continued influence over them was such that they took advantage of Larrabee's effort at fairness. Throughout this time Larrabee virtually ignored the other faction of San Carlos Apaches, that led by Eskiminzin and Capitán Chiquito. Had he taken a more perceptive assessment of his situation he could have used their willingness to co-operate to help control the unruly Tontos. However, relations between the Arivaipas and Tontos had degenerated to an extremely unfriendly level; the effects of crowding different bands of Apaches onto the same small territory were beginning to be felt in force. Eskiminzin's and Capitán Chiquito's people, informed by the Tontos in no uncertain manner that they were no longer welcome, were left virtually to their own devices, and stayed segregated in their own rancheria on the stream about five miles downstream from the Tontos. Larrabee's attempt to deal directly with Wilbur's Tonto thugs left Eskiminzin once again unfairly dealt with.

The first week in May Larrabee finally admitted that he was almost in a state of siege, and requested that troops be sent him to help restore order. On May 8 the commandant of Fort Grant arrived with a cavalry unit and had some serious talks with Larrabee. The agent refused to let the soldiers arrest Chunz outright and remove him, and the troop commander finally assented to aid in the pacification effort, "though I differed with him utterly." After a week of the army presence, the major in charge of the Fort Grant troops assembled and lectured the Indians, telling them Larrabee was replacing Wilbur and must be obeyed. Most of the Apaches appeared satisfied, but the Chunz element remained insolent. Before leaving, the major drew Larrabee aside and said, "The day is coming when you will need me and my soldiers. Send for me. I will come, but I fear I shall only arrive in time to bury your dead body." He then collared General Crook's administrative representative at the agency, Lieutenant Almy, and advised him how best to defend the agency in case of an uprising.

The descent of soldiers upon San Carlos was finally enough to make Eskiminzin and Capitán Chiquito flee into wilderness hiding, though they kept a few informants at San Carlos to report developments, one of the spies being a son of Eskiminzin. It was well that they did so, for about two weeks later the San Carlos bomb finally exploded.

On May 27 somewhat more than a thousand Apaches, four hundred of them armed men, came into the agency grounds for their regularly scheduled issuance of rations. It was the usual social occasion for the Apaches, who bantered, gambled, and played games as Larrabee sifted through the laborious paperwork that attended an issue. But on this occasion Larrabee found his progress dogged by a short, stocky, belligerent Indian from Cochinay's rancheria, an ex-scout named Chan-deisi. He seems to have been a leader in his own right, being identified (the name stemmed from Tčà-ndézń, or Long Hat) as one of the Canyon Creek band of the Cibicue group, himself of the thirteenth clan, drawing most of his following from that as well as the twelfth and twenty-third clans. Over the course of about forty-five minutes Chan-deisi insistently demanded more ration tickets than he was allotted; Larrabee continually refused him, until Chan-deisi suddenly raised his lance as if to kill him. Larrabee's life was saved, curiously enough, by Ba-coon,[3] who had evidently undergone a change of heart and abandoned Dr. Wilbur; Ba-coon shoved Chan-deisi aside, and the latter stormed out of the headquarters building. Outside, it was later learned from Eskiminzin's son, Chunz tried to convince Chan-deisi to kill Larrabee and as many other whites as he could, then hide in the mountains.

Larrabee tried to put the occurrence out of his mind, but a few minutes later scribbled a note to Crook's man, Lieutenant Almy, to bring a guard and arrest the Indian Chan-deisi.

In less than half an hour a detail comprised of interpreter Marijildo Grijalba, a corporal, and five privates arrived, and Larrabee met them at the south side of the compound. He told them to wait for him to locate Chan-deisi, and then started back toward the buildings. The Indians on the agency grounds knew something was amiss and gathered in a noisy group. Before Larrabee returned Lieutenant Almy arrived, and on being told that Chan-deisi was not yet in custody he set off, himself unarmed, toward the mass of Indians to try to quiet them. Before he reached them a shot rang out from their midst, and Grijalba and the others saw Almy start and spin around, clutching his midsection, gasping, "Oh, my God!" Before he could fall he was shot again, through the head, killed instantly.

A wild spree of gunfire erupted at once from the Indians, and the small guard shot back as best they could. One of the soldiers had set his sights on the Indian he saw shoot Almy, but the interpreter Concepción, trying to stop the melee before they were all killed, knocked his rifle away, crying, "Don't shoot!" The attempt was successful, though for his trouble he was accused (but cleared) of complicity, and in the end his removal was recommended. All the Indians present bolted in panic, but before long most of them drifted back to San Carlos and were forgiven. However, the bad element of Cochinay, Chan-deisi, and Chunz, with their following, stayed out and would have to be hunted down and beaten.

When Crook learned of Almy's death he was outraged, ordering troops out to chase the hostiles until they were killed or captured, and replacing Almy with Lieutenant William Rice, who had operated out of Verde during the late Tonto War. Larrabee understandably resigned his agency shortly after, and was replaced in the interim by Major Brown, so San Carlos for the time being at least had a consistent military government with no divided authority.

After the Chunz breakout, however, San Carlos began to be less a problem to Crook than Lieutenant Schuyler's Yavapai-Tonto reservation at Camp Verde. As the summer lengthened the Yavapais, still referred to by the army as Apache-Mojaves, grew increasingly restless, until the most noisome of them began to follow the lead of the Tonto chief Delshay, who was allowed to stay at Verde instead of with the other Tontos at San Carlos. By the middle of September Delshay's faction had become large and obnoxious enough that Schuyler wrote Crook that he thought he should arrest Delshay and remove him. The general concurred that this should be done, but before the deed could be carried out Delshay ambushed the agency intending to kill Schuyler and any others with him. The chief of scouts at Verde, Al Sieber, rounded up his Indian scouts quickly enough to fight them off, and the renegades scattered into the Tonto Basin, which was already roamed by the fugitives from San Carlos. Crook had another war on his hands.

Largely because of the machinations of the evil Dr. Wilbur, Crook had to spend the summer and fall of 1873 laying the groundwork for a second offensive, to chase down and exterminate the poisoned element of Chunz, Cochinay, Delshay, and Chan-deisi, the latter two of whom Crook consistently termed "Del Ché" and "John Daisy." At the same time he replaced Major Brown as San Carlos agent with Major George Randall, of Turret Peak fame. Randall started the chain of events with a remarkable twist when on New Year's Day, 1874, he arrested and confined, of all people, the hapless Eskiminzin. Crook vigorously backed Randall's action, but never clarified the reasons for Eskiminzin's incarceration, except to report that he mistrusted him, and that he saw he was not acting in good faith.[4]

Probably the roots of this lay in Crook's antipathy toward Royal Whitman and Oliver O. Howard.

Eskiminzin managed to escape a couple of days later, and fled for the wilderness again, with his following and numerous others. Most of them soon returned to San Carlos, where because of the unusually heavy winter rains they were allowed to make their camps on higher ground across the river from the agency flat. For some weeks the rains continued unseasonably dense, until the Gila flooded and cut off the rancherias from the agency and Randall's troops. It was at this time that Cochinay and Chunz chose to make their return and regroup their following. For some time tizwin drunks and general mayhem flourished until the inevitable incident occurred. On January 31 Apaches killed two of a party of freighters near San Carlos, and most of the Indians, fearing a reprisal, bolted.

A few dozen of the worst element set off on a string of depredations, including the torture-murder of a family of six near Tempe. Crook had not so many troops as a year before, but still he managed to put four different columns into the field, two into the Tonto Basin from Whipple and Verde, one to the Superstitions from Lowell, and the largest to the Pinal Mountains from Fort Grant. Composed of parts of six cavalry companies, guided by Archie MacIntosh, augmented by a sizable complement of White Mountain trailers and led by Randall himself, the strike force did not move out until a certain target had been located, a large hostile rancheria deep in the Pinals.

Moving by night and hiding by day, Randall neared the village with effective wariness, detouring for miles around a precipitous canyon and making an oblique approach to his objective. The peak on which the rancheria was located was a high one, inaccessible except by way of a few finlike ribs of extruded rubble that spilled down the sides. Just at dawn Randall's men overran the rancheria from three different directions. The surprise was total; twelve of the renegades were killed and twenty-five taken prisoner, but the three principals, Cochinay, Chan-deisi, and Chunz, if they were present, got away.

Later on in the spring, on April 2, a joint action fought on Pinal Creek netted two more important victories over the hostile Tontos. On the first day of the month, Lieutenant Alfred Bache, operating as part of Major (now brevetted Colonel) Randall's Fort Grant force, captured a Tonto woman, who was bullied into leading the troops to her camp. She guided them to within striking distance of one large and one smaller rancheria. Bache generously accorded the honor of attacking the larger camp to a junior lieutenant named Reilly, who had just entered Arizona service and was eager for a fight, while he himself would assault the smaller. Bache gave Reilly Archie MacIntosh and fifteen Indian scouts, with two dozen troops, to get into position and attack the rancheria at dawn. Reilly took the regulars and covered one side of the rancheria, while sending Mac-

Intosh and the scouts far to his left to prevent the Indians' escape. Their maneuvering entailed wading some distance through an icy knee-deep stream, scaling steep slopes to get to the summit, and then crouching, cold, wet, and silent, in cramped positions to await the sunrise.

Bache, meanwhile, was working his way into position around the lesser rancheria, his march covering ground so rugged that his few Indian scouts had to help the floundering regulars over the worst spots. But eventually they, too, crept into hiding just beyond the perimeter of the rancheria, separated by only a few bushes from the smoldering campfires.

As morning broke the simultaneous attacks took the Tontos by complete surprise and caused utter confusion. Reilly's group killed seventeen, Bache's accounted for thirty-one and took fifty prisoners. But again, the ringleaders were absent.

Meanwhile, the column that Crook had sent out from Verde, under Walter Schuyler and guided by Al Sieber, were having a remarkable adventure. In three months on the trail they ranged southeast to the far side of Fort Grant, and by the time they returned they had accounted for twenty-six captives and eighty-three dead renegades. But Dr. Wilbur's Tonto chiefs were among neither tally. They were reported in numerous places, but while their following suffered fearful tolls of dead and captured, the chiefs always managed to escape, a curious string of occurrences to which Crook credited the increasing number of surrenders later into the spring.

But it was impossible for so many units to operate in the field for so long without results. About three miles from Tucson a small detachment of Indian scouts caught and killed Cochinay in the latter part of May. They decapitated the body and carried his head back to San Carlos. During the third week in June a similar fate befell Chan-deisi, whose head showed up in Camp Apache. As the war lengthened, growing numbers of the disaffected gave up the struggle and surrendered. On April 1 a Tonto (or possibly White Mountain) chief named Des-a-lin came in and expressed a desire to co-operate with the whites. Soon after that he made good on his word, bringing in another wanted leader named Pedro. Less fortunate was Eskiminzin, who had been hiding in the countryside since the trouble began eleven months before. Late in April Eskiminzin finally gave himself up at San Carlos, where he was soon arrested, and to make more certain of his stay this time, chained.

In mid-July Des-a-lin finally tracked Chunz to the tilted upthrust of the Santa Catalina Mountains northeast of Tucson. Thirty Indian scouts were dispatched to finish him, and they were joined, predictably, by several volunteers from the town. As the force neared, most of Chunz's band disintegrated, either giving themselves up to the scouts or fleeing wildly while there was still time. Staying with Chunz to the end were six of his worst ringleaders, and they were reported by the deserters to be leaping terror-stricken from rock to rock in a frantic search for a last-minute escape route. Chunz's final position was overrun and he and his half dozen supporters were killed. Their heads were brought into San Carlos on July 25, and were displayed for several days on the parade ground. Only the renegade Delshay was left, but his time was not yet.

The practice of beheading the bodies of wanted Indians seems more brutal and needful of comment now than it did then. The Apache scouts had not lost their traditional aversion to the dead, nor their aversion to mutilation. The heads were ordered taken for purposes of identification (much confusion on the frontier stemmed from mistaken assertions that this or that hostile leader had been killed), for the payment of rewards, and to instill fear into the agency Indians. It was certainly a practice of impeachable morality, but in these instances, at least, it was not done purely for wantonness' sake.

A new agent, John Philip Clum, arrived at San Carlos on August 8, first greeted by the rotting, gore-clotted heads of Chunz and his crew. It was a sight to demoralize any man, but it was an especially stark initiation for a twenty-two-year-old farm boy from New York.

Further south, Tom Jeffords had been experiencing little difficulty keeping the Tsoka-ne-nde Chiricahuas in line, although some trouble was portended by the death, after an illness of several weeks, of Cochise on June 8, 1874.[5] The death of the leader whom they afterward referred to as the Great Chief was a heavy blow to his following, and they took it hard. Agency worker Fred Hughes later wrote that "Quite a number of Indians were camped near the agency, mostly women and children, and they had evidently gathered there to await the news of their chief's death. When it came, the howl that went up from these people was fearful . . . They were scattered around in the nooks and ravines in parties, and as the howling from one rancheria would lag, it would be renewed with vigor in another."[6]

The keening Indians took Cochise's body out into the mountains, and walled it up in one of the crevasses beneath the western foot of Signal Peak. When his grandson Niño Cochise saw the place in 1895 it struck him as "the most peaceful place in the world."[7]

On Cochise's death his elder son, Taza, became hereditary chief. He was a big man—nearly two hundred pounds—bearing some resemblance to his grandfather, Mangas Coloradas. He was broad-faced and quick-thinking, and showed much of his father's bravery and sagacity. Taza was married to Nah-dos-te, a sister of the controversial war di-yin of the Nde-nda-i, Gerónimo; their son Niño was about six months old at the time. Cochise's second son, Naiche, also held some influence but he was too young and inexperienced to hold any real power; and he was by reputation more of a good-time Charlie than a leader.

The Mysterious Doctor Wilbur:
NOTES

1. Opler, *An Apache Life-way*, p. 328.
2. The hearings into Doctor Wilbur's conduct, and Elijah Junior's account, are preserved in microcopies of the National Archives Record Group 75, quoted in pertinent part in Thrapp, *Conquest of Apacheria*, pp. 148ff.
3. This according to Thrapp, *Conquest of Apacheria*, p. 153. The Tonto chief Ba-coon, as Thrapp also noted, was contrarily reported killed in early April of that year, in a squabble with another Indian.
4. Crook, *General George Crook: His Autobiography*, p. 175.
5. Utley, *Frontier Regulars*, p. 367. Also reported as June 7.
6. Quoted in Adams, *Geronimo*, p. 195.
7. Cochise, *The First Hundred Years of Niño Cochise*, p. 134.

Clum and the
Concentration Policy

On reflection, John Clum's appointment as San Carlos agent seems too ludicrous and improbable to have happened. One of the most tumultuous and chronically dangerous Indian agencies in the West was to be administered by a New Yorker aged twenty-two years and nine months. He had been in the West only a short time, collecting weather data with the Meteorological Service of the Signal Corps in New Mexico. His Indian experience was nil and he had scarcely even seen an Apache. One motive that suggests itself for the appointment: the Indian Ring might have been looking for an easily controllable agent, but if that is true, they had it all wrong. Nowhere in the history of the Southwest has there ever been anybody exactly like John Philip Clum.

He had been appointed agent six months before his arrival, on the recommendation of the Dutch Reformed Church, of which he was a member. Under President Grant's "Peace Policy" of giving Indian responsibility to different churches, it was this denomination that received influence in Apache affairs, and whatever trepidation the church leadership may have had over his tender years, young Clum took up the reins with gumption. He was an unusually short man, shorter even than most Apaches, and prematurely bald, except for a fringe of hair over his ears and around the back of his head. His face was tightly drawn but handsome, and soon after his arrival he matured his looks considerably by growing a woolly mustache. He was quick-witted and humorous; on departing Tucson for San Carlos one person tried to warn him away from the reckless venture, Clum responding to the effect that any Indian trying to scalp him would be wasting his time. But it was his other personal qualities that made him so remarkable. Once settled in San Carlos it took very little time for him to demonstrate that he was a prodigiously innovative and competent administrator. He was possessed of seemingly bottomless honesty and conscience, iron nerves in the face of personal danger, and a willingness to observe and understand Apache culture in a way unique to those Indians' experience. When local officials, the Indian Ring, and the army discovered he could not be controlled or bullied, the young man found himself under attacks that never once abated for the duration of his stay. But those who opposed him found his poise and self-assurance absolutely maddening, and were quick to learn that he combined a talent for viperine invective with an almost uncanny political sense of when and where to strike in the bureaucracy to get his way. But most promising of all, John Clum threw himself almost physically into his work, turning to it all his marvelous talent and craftiness, committing himself heart and mind to the betterment of the San Carlos Apaches.

After leaving Tucson en route to his new post, Clum stopped one night at Fort Grant. There he noticed a short, stocky, and very unhappy-looking Indian held in chains. On asking who he was and what he had done, Clum could learn of no particular charge but was told that it was the Arivaipa chief Eskiminzin. He had been transferred to Grant from San Carlos to make doubly sure he did not again escape his confinement. Clum and Eskiminzin had a very long and serious conversation, and Clum promised to see what he could do on Eskiminzin's behalf.

The establishment at San Carlos was enough by itself to be monumentally depressing. "Of all the desolate, isolated, human habitations!" wrote Clum. "Wickiups, covered with brush and grass, old blankets, or deerskins, smoky, smelly. Lean dogs, mangy, inert. A few Apaches strolling around, as wild and vicious as the inmates of an old folks' home." He was shown his adobe residence and noted that the mud-plastered grass roof would do no more than soil the rain as it came through. "Low ceiling," he wrote, "paneless holes in the walls for windows, doors of canvas tacked on frames of poles, with hinges of rope, or strips of leather cut from the leg of some discarded boot. Furnishings in harmony with the architecture, constructed of material salvaged from old packing-boxes. The only substantial feature in this grotesque establishment was the floor . . . good old Mother Earth."[1]

The physical facilities were just an appetizer, however. Once he arrived, young Clum found the military still in full control, and hotly unwilling to let any Indian Bureau agent back into responsibility. Major Randall had been replaced by Major John B. Babcock, on whose memory, like everybody else's, the unsavory Dr. Wilbur and Lieutenant Almy's tragic death were still fresh. For the first time Clum showed what material he was made of, as after three weeks of intensive wrangling that went on at all levels of government, including some fast and intelligent talking of his own, word came down from Washington that Clum was indeed to have full responsibility for San Carlos. A lesser man never would have gotten his foot in the door. The army garrison buckled under to their reduced role, not hopeful of the future, but over a period of several weeks the pugnacious young agent went to work on the seven hundred Apaches who regularly drew their subsistence from San Carlos.

To begin his administration Clum improved the Apaches' personal hygiene, showing them how sickness was made worse by filth, encouraging them to keep their wickiups and squaw coolers free of refuse. He told the Indians he trusted them to manage their own affairs, and he helped them establish an Apache law court with their own judges. He served as chief judge himself.

To bring agency regulations closer to the people, he requested the chiefs to select for him four good Indians to serve as his policemen, and the headmen picked four whose service to Clum was long and fruitful. One was a brother of the reconstructed Des-a-lin, named Tauelclyee. Two others were called Goodah-goodah and Eskinospas. The fourth man had a name that Clum found utterly unpronounceable, so, with a wry whimsy that would prove characteristic he called him after a noticeable personal trait: Sneezer. Most important of all, he put the Apaches to work. Clum could see that when left to themselves they were a vivacious, active people who needed to be kept busy, and the only way to keep them out of trouble while confined to the reservation was to provide them gainful employment. He used a large portion of his budget to initiate an extensive building program, hiring the Indians as construction workers and craftsmen. The scheme provided the Apaches with activity and a consistent reward to which they proved responsive, and it also vastly improved the physical facilities of the agency. It was precisely the system of management that General Crook had insistently pressed for, and its favorable effect was not long in manifesting itself.

By demonstrating his unique caring for them, Clum managed to persuade the San Carlos Apaches to do things they would have done for no other white man. Probably his greatest victory was in disarming them, convincing them that if they turned in their guns they would have no difficulty checking them out to go hunting. Although the Apaches certainly stored some weapons in secret caches, that they turned in any firearms at all was a tremendous step forward. Clum was also quick to perceive the evils of brewing tizwin and tula-pah. He banned their manufacture outright and, for the most part, made the ban stick.

Though the Apaches were unhappy over the loss of their tula-pah, most of them responded to Clum with a shocked, and then affectionate, obedience. He was the first agent they had ever known, in fact the first white man they had known since Royal Whitman, whose treatment of them was based on trust, maturity, deference, and genuine affection. When disputes arose with the army over Indian matters the Apaches saw Clum defend them vigorously and with an ability startling for one his age. Eskiminzin was released and when he returned to San Carlos, the chief used all his considerable influence to gain Clum acceptance among his people, while at the same time the personal relationship between the two men flowered into a tender and remarkable friendship. Clum soon enlarged his San Carlos Apache Police into an elite and intensely loyal strike force of several dozen men, trained by Martin Sweeney, a veteran cavalry sergeant whom Clum hired as his clerk and general assistant. "His military training," wrote Clum, "plus his sympathetic understanding of Apache character, enabled him to teach military tactics to the Indians so that they not only learned how to drill, but enjoyed it, and became excellent soldiers."[2] Over the course of his tenure the crusty sergeant proved an admirable assistant to the brassy youngster. By the end of the summer affairs at San Carlos had attained a smoothness that, while not perfect, no one would have thought possible two months before.

Toward the end of August the long and tragic association of the Tonto chief Delshay with the pindahs finally came to its gruesome end; on the twenty-sixth Clum got a letter off to the Commissioner with the message that Des-a-lin "returned this A.M. having taken the head of 'Del-Chay' and left same with the Commanding Officer at Camp McDowell, A. T." Des-a-lin also brought in tow seventy-six of Delshay's people, and thirty-nine members of his own following who had not been at the reservation since the trouble fomented by Dr. Wilbur.

As one interesting sidelight, General Crook found himself in a bit of a quandary over paying the bounty he had offered for Delshay, as a second group of scouts delivered an ear and a scalp that they claimed was Delshay's at Camp Verde. But, "being satisfied that both parties were earnest in their beliefs," he wrote, "and the bringing in of an extra head was not amiss, I paid both."[3]

It was well that Clum managed to put the San Carlos house in order as quickly as he did, for as the summer ended his real troubles began. The decision had been made, at the Washington level of the administration, that not just the Western Apaches, but all Apaches and "associated tribes" in Arizona and New Mexico were to be concentrated at San Carlos, with the other reservations to be deactivated. Some historians believe the idea was instigated by the nefarious war profiteers, but even if the Indian Ring was not behind the decision, it was still a bureaucratic disaster, and its importance to the rest of late nineteenth-century Apache history can hardly be overstated. The concentration policy, as it came to be called, ignored the Apaches' cultural divisions, and the squeezing of different tribes into the small gravel flat around San Carlos either led directly or contributed indirectly to every subsequent outbreak until the end of the Apache wars.

First implementation of the concentration policy was the removal of some 1,500 Yavapai and Walapai Indians from Camp Verde to San Carlos. For part of 1874 the Verde agent was Dr. Josephus Williams, who when he went mad was replaced by his clerk, Oliver Chapman. General Crook had enjoyed a fairly stable working relationship with Williams, but Chapman, while "probably not as bad as some of the others,"[4] was less satisfactory, and it was just as well that Clum be given their care. What complicated matters was the fact that the Western Apaches already at San Carlos did not want the other tribes there. Most of the Western bands had always been friendly with the Yavapais, but the only two to have intimate contact with them were the Southern Tontos and Gila-San Pedro bands like the Pinals and Arivaipas. The Walapais, however, were traditional enemies of all the bands.

Original authority to carry out the removal was given in a special commission to L. Edwin Dudley, one-time superintendent of Indian Affairs for New Mexico. It was scheduled to take place on February 27, 1875, but Dudley quickly lost control and a fight broke out between the Yavapais and Walapais on one side, and several Tontos on the other. The chief of scouts at Verde, Al Sieber, managed to stop the fight before it got out of hand, and he turned the fifteen hundred Verde Indians over to Clum with few casualties. Clum sensibly had them camp a safe distance from the Apaches and even, using rations as bait, managed to disarm them as he had his other agency Indians.

Clum's working arrangement with the army took a serious turn for the worse when George Crook was replaced as commander of the Arizona Department by General August V. Kautz, who found the upstart agent an affront and set about clipping his feathers. Kautz had no faith in any Indian Bureau personnel and he took on the broad goal of wresting Indian control from them and returning it to the army. His means were direct and very military. No sooner did Clum have the Yavapai-Walapai situation in hand than James E. Roberts, his counterpart at the sister Apache agency, Camp Apache, arrived with the complaint that the military garrison there, under Major Frank D. Ogilby, had virtually ousted him from responsibility and usurped all authority for itself.

The trouble, according to Roberts, began with a disease epidemic that swept through the Cibicue and White Mountain rancherias, resulting in a spree of tizwin drunks to relieve grief and fright. (More probably the tizwin was consumed at curing ceremonies; exorcisms were believed more effective if conducted in a positive atmosphere with social festivity.) But the result was the same, and some of the intoxicated Apaches had gone raiding and whites had been killed. Roberts said he had telegraphed Washington for instructions. Clum's experience with the military thus far was such that, even if he did not think Roberts a capable man, he probably would have backed him.

The Indian Bureau in Washington decided to use the incident to further the concentration policy, and so wired instructions for Clum to proceed to that place and assume control of the White Mountain and Cibicue Apaches there. Accordingly Clum and Roberts left for Camp Apache, but while en route encountered garrison commander Ogilby. The major showed more mettle than Babcock had, refusing to acknowledge the orders and returning to Camp Apache, defying Clum to come take the Indians if he could. But Ogilby did not know what he was up against. The two agents pursued him to Camp Apache and for ten days there continued a battle over authority that, had not the fate of so many Indians been at stake, would have been comedic.

Clum opened the exchanges by ordering the arrest of the army's post physician, whom Major Ogilby had appointed acting agent after Roberts had fled, on the charge of illegally opening Roberts' mail. To facilitate his handling of the Camp Apache Indians Clum ordered a census, but Ogilby got even by ordering a duplicate army counting the same day, and pairing this with a threat to attack those Indians who favored Clum's roll. When Clum insisted that all the agency Apaches were his responsibility Ogilby emptied the guardhouse of its criminals, including two murderers, for Clum to govern as best he could, and then ordered his garrison to deny Clum aid if he applied for military assistance. Inevitably the greatest losers in the squabbles were the Apaches. Except to Clum himself they had been lost sight of, and had become less something to fight than something to fight over. They were no longer regarded so much as a people to administer and care for than as a source to further departmental influence or personal reputation. It was a state of affairs that Clum hated viscerally. Petty harassment was everywhere, as at one juncture an attempt was made to arrest him for riding his horse on the parade ground at excessive speed. But when Clum had had enough he went where only he would have the audacity to go—straight to the top. He clambered aboard a train for Washington and returned triumphant, with ironclad authority to remove all the Indians from Camp Apache to San Carlos.

Not all the Camp Apache bands were willing to make the move, however, even after Clum had Eskiminzin and numerous other San Carlos leaders talk to them. Although the significance was not fully appreciated at the time, virtually all the Apaches who refused to leave were of the Tcatci-dn clan (Red Rock Strata People), whose relationship with Diablo's Nadotsusn had been souring for some years. There had been fighting and loss of life on both sides.[5] But in the end only a few rancherias were left behind, and after the removal was completed Clum's population of Apaches at San Carlos stood at well over four thousand.

Not long after the Camp Apache removal, Clum's inexperience finally got him in serious danger, in an incident that resulted in the death of the Tonto chief turned renegade-killer, Des-a-lin. Clum, in the company of Des-a-lin's brother, the agency policeman Tauelclyee, attempted to tell the chief how to treat his wives. While willing for the good of his people to chase down renegade offenders, Des-a-lin was unready to brook such a shocking and insulting interference into so intimate a matter, and drew a weapon to kill the agent. But before he could do it Tauelclyee raised his rifle and shot him dead. It was a sobering instant for the starchy young Clum, but fortunately the incident did not harm his standing with the rest of his Indians. Tauelclyee's devotion to his new duty moved Clum deeply, and while the policeman mourned for his brother he stayed on the force. "It was my habit," wrote Clum much later, "to caution my Apache Police, when hunting renegades and murderers, to be sure at all times to have their rifles in prime condition and loaded, so that if shooting seemed inevitable they could do it first. I do not think that an officer of the law should . . . wait until the criminal has missed him a couple of times . . . until he joins in the shooting."[6] Here, and later, it was a philosophy that put Clum in good stead.

One of the traits that most endeared Clum to his Apaches was his wry wit and constant banter. Though they had little enough reason to display it, the Indians were possessed of a keen sense of humor, and were delighted when their plucky young agent began tossing about pet nicknames for those with whom he most closely associated.[7] Eskiminzin became Skimmy; of his four policemen, Sneezer already had his name. Goodah-goodah was suddenly Goody-Goody, and Eskinospas was Nosy. The last one, Tauelclyee, haughtily refused any nickname, and Clum respected his feeling. (Clum's interpreter, Marijildo Grijalba, did not come off as well as the others, as the bearded, hairy Mexican found himself answering to Mary.) To Clum's warmth the Apaches responded in kind, shedding much of the cold reserve usually kept in front of pindahs. He later recalled how at one point he noticed that whenever an Apache gave an explanation of something it was almost always hedged with the word "maybe." Once when riding alongside Eskiminzin he asked the reason for this, and the chief responded, "Because we're never sure. Maybe." Clum also discovered that his people were, in their own complex language, irrepressible punsters. The story was once related how, during the reservation days at San Carlos, one of the chief incomes the Apaches had was gathering wood for the agency, the authorization for which was given each Indian in a written order. One man who had gone in to the agency for his ration of coal oil was returning to his rancheria, when he was met by a man going the opposite direction, who asked him, " '*tciz begeda i' tci'?*" or, "Did you get a written order for wood?" The same phrase in a different context also meant "Do they write with wood?" The first man answered, "No, they only write with pencils down there."[8]

As Clum's stay lengthened he learned more and more about the everyday life and customs of his Apaches, and he gained a special fondness for their children. Once, he became inquisitive over a strange noise he heard at the agency, "a succession of mysterious rumblings to the westward, not unlike the reverberations of distant thunder." Mounting his horse to investigate, he rode about three miles distant from the agency compound, where he found the source of the disturbance, a group of Apache children tobogganing down the high gravel shoulder of a mesa. "For a toboggan they had a cowhide," he wrote, "dried hard as a board . . . It would accommodate half-a-dozen Apache kids. The two in front set their feet in buckskin loops attached to the cowhide, to prevent them from slipping off en route. When the kids were safely adjusted, they let go the moorings and plunged down the steep incline at breath-taking speed."[9]

During his stay at San Carlos Clum also became familiar with the sweatbaths, noting that in addition to their medical and ceremonial functions the Western Apaches also used them simply for cleansing. Such bathing was done in private, in a sweathouse just large enough to hold one person and a few stones. In the extreme confinement it frequently happened that the bather would accidentally touch or sit on one of the superheated rocks, and Clum maintained that by eavesdropping on cleansing sweats he considerably expanded his vocabulary of Apache expletives and colorful verbs.[10] Clum also took note of another facet of Apache hygiene, one that perhaps rested him somewhat easier over his premature baldness, and that was the method of ridding oneself of the lice that infested the San Carlos location. He observed the Indians on afternoons when they had free time, spending considerable effort grooming one another in the shade of the squaw coolers to pick out the pests. Periodically one would prepare himself a head plaster of runny mud, which when left to dry suffocated the lice; the pack was then rinsed away in the river. Sometimes, he saw, lousy bedding was cleansed by casting it over an anthill.[11]

In spite of the restrictions and changes that Clum brought upon the Indians, in some respects his administration offered them a partial respite from their continuing cultural denigration. One of the chief obstacles to his progress with them was the adverse effect of the concentration policy itself, and it was not long before it was on the move again. On May 3, 1876, Clum opened telegraphed instructions ordering him to the Chiricahua Reservation on the Mexican border, there to suspend Agent Jeffords, and remove the Chiricahuas to San Carlos, "if practicable." The sweep of those orders must have raised even his eyebrows.

If the Western Apaches had found a quieting influence in Clum, the Cochise Chiricahuas had found the same thing in Thomas Jeffords four years before. Under Cochise's leadership and Jeffords' agency, southeastern Arizona had enjoyed a level of peace not seen since the fight at Apache Pass had inflamed Cochise in 1861. But in the two years since Cochise's death the situation had worsened. Jeffords had come under increasing attack for his virtual dictatorship over the reservation. He was charged with selling ammunition to his Chiricahuas, though the charges ring hollow because the Arizona side of the border had been left mostly alone. Then Jeffords' beef rations to the Indians were ordered cut. One wonders where the attacks and unwise directives were coming from, but the whole business smells of the Indian Ring.

Also, Taza's leadership of the Tsoka-ne-nde had been weakened by factionalizing among his people. Tci-he-nde Mimbres from Ojo Caliente had been using the Chiricahua Reservation as a way station for their raids into Mexico, and some of the worst of Clum's Western Apaches were believed hiding out there. Jeffords managed to avoid serious trouble until he was ordered to cut the beef ration, and had to inform the Indians they would have to hunt more. Most of the Chiricahuas went up into the Dragoons, but while there the divisions within the band were finally rent. A fight broke out, resulting in the death of three Indians. Taza brought his majority following back to the agency, while a smaller splinter group under a lesser chief named Skinya stayed in the mountains, and this group raided increasingly into Old Mexico. The spark needed to blow things sky-high was finally struck around the first of April. A raiding party had just returned from Mexico, led by Skinya's brother, Pion-se-nay, laden with goods and valuables. An employee of the stage station, acting either on his own enterprise or that of the Indian Ring—one can never be sure—offered to sell them white man's whiskey for ten dollars a bottle. Pion-se-nay bought enough to get himself and his men drunk; they attempted to buy more but the vendor refused, probably out of a growing fear of being among intoxicated Apache warriors. The Indians killed him and another employee, took all the whiskey, and as many guns and bullets as they could find, and went back into the mountains for an extended drunk. The next day they stole stock and killed a third white man. Jeffords soon learned of the situation and led a force of troops into the Dragoons. Skinya's camp was found and attacked, but the Indians' position was well chosen, and the soldiers left without overrunning it.

When Clum received his instructions he knew he would have to move with extreme care. For nearly a month he laid plans, applying to the army for military assistance. The army, for once, responded with co-operation, and strategically placed the entire regiment of the 6th Cavalry around the reservation. When he was ready to move, Clum arrived at Sulphur Springs on June 4, with fifty-six of his elite San Carlos Apache Police. Also on June 4 the Skinya faction rode into Taza's rancheria and tried to enlarge their renegade band with warriors from his camp. Taza's men proved loyal, however, and a fierce skirmish broke out that left seven of the renegades dead, including Skinya. Pion-se-nay was gravely wounded but managed to escape with the rest of the survivors. The next day Clum arrived at Taza's camp and convinced him to remove his people to San Carlos. As preparations got under way Pion-se-nay sent word that he wanted to come in to die, and Clum sent Tauelclyee and twenty policemen to fetch him.

Although Taza agreed to the removal, the Chiricahua Reservation had also hosted other bands, who fled rather than go to San Carlos. Of the Nde-nda-i, the Nednhi group under the fat, violent chief named Juh, and the Bedonkohes, under a still minor war leader and di-yin named Gerónimo, sneaked into Old Mexico with about four hundred followers. About two hundred others, probably a mixture of disaffected Tci-he-nde Mimbres and Tsoka-ne-ndes, slipped off northeast in the direction of Ojo Caliente. Thus when Clum set out for San Carlos on June 12 he had in tow only Taza's Tsoka-ne-ndes, numbering 325, about one third the number who had been living under Jeffords' agency.

Clum accounted for the smaller than expected population by writing the Indian Commissioner, in his customary style, that previous estimates had been erroneously high, and that "the imaginary army of four or five hundred formidable warriors had dwindled to the modest number of sixty half-armed and less clothed savages."[12] The fact was, however, that a large number of those "imaginary" Indians had fled to Mexico, with Tom Jeffords' love and complicity. Although General Kautz suspected that Jeffords had previously inflated the counts to hide his own graft, the agent had altered the rolls at the last minute to prevent the flight from being detected and the Indians followed. It was not the freeloading Nde-nda-i that Jeffords was worried about, but the at-home members of Cochise's band. The Tsoka-ne-nde regarded everything about the transaction—Clum, the army, San Carlos, and its Western Apaches—with suspicion. Even Taza, who accompanied Clum on his return, sent his wife Nah-dos-te and infant son to a hideaway in the Sierra Madre, where they remained off and on, remarkably, until after the end of World War I. Throughout that time, few of the Chiricahuas softened either their cynical view of John Clum's bravado or their gratitude to Jeffords. Nah-dos-te and her son, Niño Cochise, their faces charcoaled in mourning, attended Taglito Jeffords' funeral in 1914.

The Nde-nda-i who stayed behind considered the Cochise peace at an end; not only had they lost their reservation and agent, they were keenly aware of why they had lost it, because a profiteering pindah had sold them whiskey and got killed. Southeast Arizona's respite from Indian war was over, as within a few weeks more than a hundred head of stock and some twenty white lives were lost to raiding Apaches. As Clum and his group passed by Tucson he turned Pion-se-nay over to the county sheriff, but the culprit quickly made good an escape and joined the hostiles.

Clum had almost a year to assimilate Taza's Chiricahuas into the scheme of things at San Carlos, and then the concentration policy turned its dubious attention to the Tci-he-nde Mimbres under Victorio at Ojo Caliente. The incentive for this action came when a 6th Cavalry lieutenant saw Gerónimo in that vicinity and reported that the Gerónimo renegades were using Ojo Caliente as their base. At first the removal of the Tci-he-nde Mimbres was not ordered, and Clum was directed on

March 20, 1877, to go to Ojo Caliente with his San Carlos Police, arrest the Chiricahua renegades and return stolen property to its owners. But heavy pressure was being exerted to have the Mimbres removed as well, brought by white settlers in the Ojo Caliente vicinity. There was some justification for this sentiment, as depredations had never entirely ceased.

Clum set out for Ojo Caliente in early April, knowing it would be a long and tiresome journey, with his chief of police Clay Beauford and 102 Apache Police. On April 21 they reached a rendezvous point where they were to have been met by eight companies of 9th Cavalry that had been dispatched to help in the delicate and dangerous operation. But the regulars weren't there and Clum, although he knew from spies that Ojo Caliente contained between 350 and 500 Apaches, perhaps a hundred of them Gerónimo's, brazenly forged ahead. He took with him only twenty-two of his Apache Police, leaving Beauford to follow the next day with the other eighty. But as he reached the agency he displayed admirable cunning as he planned to trap Gerónimo. After nightfall he sent a messenger to Beauford to race his men up from the rear and hide them in the agency commissary before their presence could be discovered.

The next morning Clum sent a runner to instruct Gerónimo to come in with his leaders for a council. Gerónimo was not a chief by heritage, but was a di-yin for war who became so indispensable that he began to garner his own following. As one of the reservation Chiricahuas later explained, "Geronimo got political power from the religious side. He foresaw the results of the fighting, and they used him so much in the campaigns that he came to be depended upon. He went through his ceremony, and he would say, 'You should go here; you should not go there.' That is how he became a leader."[13] He was a mystic with powers of clairvoyance that still defy satisfactory explanation; he had married and raised one family only to lose them in a massacre by Mexicans, and he had little use for them, pindahs, or even non-Apache Indians.

Seventeen of the renegade Nde-nda-i, including Gerónimo, responded to Clum's summons, being met on the agency porch by Clum and six of his police. In his memoirs Clum wrote that he told the outlaws if they listened to him "with good ears" no harm would come to them. Gerónimo, he wrote, shot back "that if I spoke with discretion no serious harm would be done us." Knowing then that their cover had not been blown, Captain Beauford gave a signal, and the doors of the commissary burst open and the bulk of the Apache Police dashed, guns at the ready, to form a picket line across the south end of the parade ground. Six of Gerónimo's men started to flee, but as they turned they saw Beauford coolly sighting them with his rifle, motioning them back. Within seconds all the police were in position and the capture was complete. Beauford, though, was nearly tackled by one of the Nde-nda-i women, who pounced on him with a terrific shriek, wrestling with him until Beauford threw her sprawling in the dirt.

Clum commented, "There are always a few belligerent squaws who insist upon intruding whenever a 'war talk' is in progress." Such behavior was not as a rule encouraged among the Indians, but the woman undoubtedly increased her prestige by attacking Beauford.

When Clum ordered Gerónimo to the guardhouse the leader did not move, but when the confident young man added, "You must go, now," Gerónimo sprang to his feet. "From his demeanor it was evident to all that he was hesitating between two purposes, whether to draw his knife, his only remaining weapon, cut right and left and die fighting—or to surrender. Instantly Sergeant Rip sprang forward and snatched the knife from Geronimo's belt, while the muzzles of a half-dozen needle guns . . . pressed toward him—their locks clicking almost in unison as their hammers were drawn back." Gerónimo glared at them defiantly for a few seconds, then gave himself up, mumbling, "*Enju*," or, "It is well." Although at this point in history Gerónimo was still a comparatively minor figure and the exploits that gained his awesome reputation were still years in the future, Clum for the rest of his long, colorful, and contentious life never tired of speaking and writing about his accomplishment in staging, as he put it, "the first and only *bonafide capture* of GERONIMO THE RENEGADE."[14] Historians usually indulge Clum in his bit of braggadocio, but it should be added that he never emphasized that while Gerónimo had been taken, the equally unsavory Juh was still at large, as was another of the Nde-nda-i recalcitrants, Nolgee. It has become fashionable in the revisionist school of history to write off Clum's feat as treachery, in order to assert that the wild and free Gerónimo was never really "captured." But to some of us a capture is a capture, without finessing definitions, and Gerónimo himself limited his boasting to the truth that he had never been captured in a fight.

In a short time Clum had Gerónimo and some of the others fitted with ankle-irons, and the shackles stayed in place as long as Clum had him. He and the other Indians were bedded down in a corner of the corral which served as a guardhouse, and were closely watched by ten of the Apache Police. When the companies of 9th Cavalry galloped into Ojo Caliente the next day Clum showed unabashed mirth as he displayed his prizes to the quizzical troopers.

Regarding the arrest of those with him, Gerónimo later said, "I do not know why this was done, for these Indians had simply followed me from Apache Pass to Hot Springs [Ojo Caliente]. If it was wrong (and I do not think it was wrong) for us to go to Hot Springs, I alone was to blame."[15] He never understood that he was arrested not for going to Ojo Caliente but for what he did before he got there.

According to one Tci-he-nde account given later, some of Victorio's people asked him to chase Gerónimo away, as he would cause trouble, but the chief refused. "We [Tci-he-nde] were on friendly terms with the towns around us and we were causing no trouble there. But the Tsoka-ne-nde and Nde-nda-i came around. They used to bring in horses stolen from the south, and they got us into trouble.

"Some of our leading men said, 'There are too many Nde-nda-i and Tsoka-ne-nde here. They are bringing in horses. They will get us into trouble.' But our leader, Victorio, wouldn't do anything about it. He said, 'These people are not bothering us.'

"Then a bunch of them came with some horses from the south. There were about seven in the bunch. They had stolen horses from the Pima Indians around Tucson. The Pimas told the missionary there, and he wrote to Washington. Soldiers came and took these men prisoners. They chained them and took them to San Carlos. Then they took all the Tci-he-nde band there."[16]

What the informant was referring to was the fact that the Indian Bureau had changed its mind and decided to remove all the Ojo Caliente Apaches to San Carlos. Clum had sent Beauford home with most of the police force, ordering him to try to apprehend any small bands of renegades they met while en route. Clum kept only twenty-five men for himself to escort the prisoners back, and it was only after Beauford had gone that the local whites pressing for the removal of the Victorio Mimbres carried the day, and Clum received new instructions from Washington. He could not possibly have complied without the co-operation of the Mimbres; to that end he convened a talk with Victorio, and fortunately for Clum the Tci-he-nde consented to the move. Gerónimo witnessed the conference, believing that both he and Victorio were on trial, and that Victorio was found innocent and himself guilty.[17]

On May 1 Clum prepared to start the return journey, having in his charge 110 of Gerónimo's Nde-nda-i and 343 of Victorio's Tci-he-nde. As the mass of people started to move out Clum stopped to speak to an Indian he found sitting on a step, his hair unbound and his head in his hands. At the sound of Clum's voice the Indian groaned and looked up. Clum nearly fainted; the man had smallpox. The last thing he needed or expected was an outbreak of smallpox. After a frantic search he found one of his policemen who had survived the dreaded disease, and he followed the rest of the Indians with the sick wagon, which, in spite of Clum's efforts, became laden with an increasing number of afflicted.

On the third day of the march Clum beheld a phenomenon that temporarily removed some of his plentiful starch. While it was still morning, a young woman who had been walking near the front of the line, split off and went into some high chaparral about a hundred feet from the trail, followed by four other women. Clum heard a man's voice call out a name, and an old woman followed the others into the brush. At this point Clum dispatched Sneezer to see what was wrong. In the time it took him to investigate and ride back the young woman had given birth, Sneezer an-

nouncing proudly to Clum that it was a man-baby. When Clum directed
one of the baggage wagons to lay by and fetch mother and son along that
night Sneezer disapproved of the fuss, advising Clum that many Apache
babies were born on the move; the woman and her baby would catch up
with the rest of them that evening. But somehow Clum just couldn't let
himself do that, and made the orders stick. Chiricahua women were particularly stoic about births. "Today she has a baby," they would say, "tomorrow she is around doing something. Some lie down for an hour
maybe."[18]

By the time they returned to San Carlos on May 20, three more children had been born on the march; some of the Apaches chuckled at the
rash of what they called "bye-'em-bye babies," but Clum reached his
agency with a net loss of four Indians. Although the original sufferer of
smallpox survived, eight of the others who took sick died on the trail.

Anxious to demonstrate to his near five thousand Indians how bad ones
among them would be dealt with, Clum offered Gerónimo to the Pima
County sheriff, but to his disgust no action was taken. This, paired with
the ease with which Pion-se-nay escaped from that officer, raises speculation that the Indian Ring was not anxious to settle the Apache problem,
but that of course is not provable.

At San Carlos young Clum wisely treated Victorio with all the
deference due a chief and warrior of his stature, even naming him to a seat
on the Apache Court. But by now the San Carlos Reservation was simply
too overcrowded for even Clum to keep all the Indians pacified. Intertribal friction reached a critical state, and Victorio's Mimbres were the
most miserable, for as the latest comers they took the brunt of abuse and
probably had the poorest campsites. They missed their New Mexico
homeland terribly, and the constant news received of the raids by Apaches
still roaming as renegades kept them in a state of excitement. But before
Clum could set about resolving these problems, he resigned.

His incessant carping at army policy toward Apaches had made him enemies in the military; his staunch honesty and efficient management made
him enemies in the Indian Ring, and the resultant political pressures
finally turned the Office of Indian Affairs against him. During the summer
of 1877 he found himself spending more time defending himself from his
detractors and scourging his enemies (with characteristic flame) than governing his Indians. To force a showdown he made genuinely unreasonable
demands on the Indian Office, and as soon as he saw he had lost his
influence, he quit. For three years he had fenced like a musketeer, with
one hand overcoming stupendous odds and working a miracle of Indian
management, while with the other hand dazzling, confounding, and until
near the end defeating, the army command of the Arizona Department.
When his resignation became effective on July 1, 1877, he was aged
twenty-five years, eight months. The majority of his Indians were devoted

to him, and the San Carlos Reservation had become almost his empire. But like the empires of history it was held together by the force of one man's personality; in Clum's absence it took only two months for the empire to collapse.

Clum and the Concentration Policy:
NOTES

1. Clum, *Apache Agent*, p. 130.
2. Ibid., p. 140.
3. Crook, *General George Crook: His Autobiography*, pp. 181–82.
4. Thrapp, *Conquest of Apacheria*, p. 162.
5. Goodwin, *Western Apache Raiding and Warfare*, pp. 101–2.
6. Clum, "It Happened in Tombstone," pp. 239–40.
7. Clum, *Apache Agent*, p. 142.
8. Goodwin, *Social Organization of the Western Apache*, p. 559.
9. Clum, *Apache Agent*, p. 145.
10. Ibid., p. 144.
11. Santee, *Apache Land*, p. 10.
12. Clum, "Geronimo," p. 10.
13. Opler, *An Apache Life-way*, p. 200.
14. Clum, "Geronimo," quoted in Thrapp, *Conquest of Apacheria*, p. 174.
15. Gerónimo, *Geronimo's Story of His Life*, p. 144.
16. Opler, *An Apache Life-way*, pp. 462–63.
17. Gerónimo, *Geronimo's Story of His Life*, p. 143.
18. Opler, *An Apache Life-way*, p. 9.

Victorio

During the night of September 1, 1877, the Tsoka-ne-nde renegade, Skinya's brother Pion-se-nay, long since escaped from the Pima County sheriff and recovered from his wounds, furtively rode into the Chiricahua rancherias laden with the wealth taken in more than a year of raiding. He reclaimed his old following and encouraged Victorio and some others to break out of the San Carlos hellhole and return to the old life. The temptation was too strong. Before dawn, 310 Apaches, almost all of the following of Victorio, plus a few Tsoka-ne-nde and Nde-nda-i, bolted toward the east. Also heading the breakout was another celebrated Mimbres chief, Loco. Typical of the inter-band strife that had prevailed, they stole before leaving as much stock as they could find, the property of the White Mountains and Cibicues. The Nde-nda-i war leader and di-yin Gerónimo did not participate in this break. John Clum's replacement, H. L. Hart, had unchained him soon after his arrival, and for the time being Gerónimo stayed on at San Carlos.

It went without saying that any bad faith connected with the breakout was, as far as the citizens were concerned, on the part of Victorio. But, even given the general misery of his unwelcome people at San Carlos, still other factors were involved. Not long after Clum's successor arrived at San Carlos the Indians found their rations mysteriously cut, and times became even harder than before. Then, too, if Clum had used the draw of his tremendous personal magnetism to convince Victorio to come to San Carlos, then the chief might easily have felt betrayed by Clum's sudden resignation only two months after their arrival. But certainly the central issue was that the Mimbres wanted to go home. The attachment of the Tci-he-nde to their Ojo Caliente region was, even for Apaches, remarkable. Time and again they sought it out, in spite of a chain of bitter memories that began as early as Juan José's murder forty years before. White authority at the time decided that the fixation was the result of intractable stubbornness. The twentieth-century deluge of sympathy for Indians ascribes to it a

maudlin sentimentality. Both probably miss the mark, for the area arouad
Hot Springs contained important scenes of the Chiricahua Genesis.

*There is a place near Ojo Caliente where four prairies come together. It
was here that White-painted Woman instructed us in the first Puberty
Ceremony, and then went up to heaven.*
It is a holy place, just full of power![1]

Outraged at the theft of their animals, the White Mountains were
quick to tell Agent Hart of the break, and before the sun was even up a
hastily assembled force of Apache Police and White Mountains volunteers were on the trail after them. Almost immediately the agency Indians
trapped Victorio's people against a steep cliff of Natanes Mountain,
recovered all their stock, and also took that of the renegades. The party
was of insufficient size to overrun Victorio's position, however, and they
returned to San Carlos after securing their horses and mules. Soon after, a
regrouped force took after the renegades again, encountering them not far
from Ash Creek. This time Victorio lost a few of his men killed, and
about thirty of his women and children were taken prisoner. The night
after the fight Victorio slipped his people out of that area and into the
rugged, lava-studded country south of Fort Wingate. To remount his people Victorio stole about a hundred head of horses from area ranchers, but
as he still had hopes of returning to Ojo Caliente, as few whites as possible were killed, perhaps a total of twelve to fifteen.

Nevertheless, his outbreak caused a ferocious uproar among the citizens
of eastern Arizona and western New Mexico, and the military stayed in
close pursuit. After skirmishes that cost the Tci-he-nde more than fifty
dead, nearly two hundred—Victorio not among them—came sullenly into
Fort Wingate and gave up. Some solution had then to be found as to
what to do with them, especially once the original prisoners were joined
by fifty more. Wingate itself was unequipped to handle them, and the
Western Apaches would never have stood for their return to San Carlos.
For the time being they were escorted to their beloved Ojo Caliente,
where Victorio surrendered, as it were, in triumph, in February of 1878.
The general commanding the New Mexico Department, Edward P.
Hatch, told the Mimbres he would use his influence to get Washington to
let them stay, provided they behaved themselves scrupulously.

For almost a year, from fall of 1877 to summer of 1878, they waited
hopefully while the deep and mysterious political currents eddied through
the departments of War and Interior. During that time Victorio's people
labored mightily to stay out of any trouble that could cost them their
home, drawing unaccustomed praise even from local settlers. The Indian
Office seemed satisfied to leave things in this unsettled state, as it resulted
in greater peace than anything else had, but when the army forced a show-

down the decision was made to return the Mimbres to San Carlos. Early in October 1878, two companies of scouts and regulars showed up at Ojo Caliente to take them back.

Victorio, understandably, was enraged. He conceded to the cavalry captain that the army would probably be able to force the women and children into returning to San Carlos, but while the men lived none of them would go back. Then before anyone could stop him, he was gone, fled into the mountains with about eighty, then a hundred, followers, nearly all warriors. The fall of 1878 was unseasonably wet across the Southwest, as a succession of rainstorms rolled over the countryside, making things miserable for everyone. The regulars, frustrated in trying to follow Victorio's washed-out trail, turned their attention to removing the Mimbres women, children, and elderly to the hated San Carlos. About 170 of them were shipped out in December through fiercely inclement weather to Fort Apache. From there they were escorted to San Carlos on mules and afoot, as the road was impassable to wagons. One of the Tci-he-nde girls, badly burned in an accident, stayed at Camp Apache, where she was adopted by the post's fine young physician, Walter Reed.

While the Mimbres families were heavily guarded at San Carlos to prevent Victorio's retaking them, the warriors began the winter of 1878–79 in the southern New Mexico mountains. The harsh weather proved too much for them, however, and in February they descended to Ojo Caliente and again Victorio pled their cause. They would go anywhere, he said, except they would rather die than go to San Carlos. The officer in charge tried to help, and sent a favorable recommendation upward through channels. By April word filtered back that they were to be sent in the other direction, to the Mescalero Reservation at Tularosa; on hearing that, Victorio thought better of his earlier rash promise and fled with his men back into the wilderness.

However, Victorio was simply not satisfied living without the families of his band, as a renegade, and by the end of the spring he was ready to capitulate to the government's demand to go to the Mescalero Reservation. On June 30 he materialized suddenly at Tularosa and announced his good intentions. To his relief the Mescalero agent received them with warmth, promising that if they behaved themselves among the Mescaleros he would try to get their families moved from San Carlos. Victorio stayed on hopefully, but in July there occurred one of those tragic accidents of history that not uncommonly determine the fate of a people. In Silver City, New Mexico, a town built on the Continental Divide in the heart of Tci-he-nde territory, a grand jury of settlers returned criminal indictments against Victorio for horse theft and murder, the news of which the Mimbres greeted with consternation. For a time it looked as if the trouble would pass without incident, but around the first of September a hunting excursion of white men from Silver City passed near Tularosa. Among them were the judge and the district attorney. When Victorio recognized them he automatically assumed he had been tricked, and was now to be tried and hanged. Within the day he had gathered up his warriors and fled, never again to make peace with the pindahs.

It was said that Victorio was in the company of the Mescalero agent when he saw the suspect group of white men, and that he yanked the agent's beard to distract him while he made a getaway. If true, it was remarkable that he didn't kill him, for the blood that flowed in the following months was almost unprecedented. At first Victorio had with him about sixty warriors, but such was his reputation as a leader and fighter that once word of his hostility spread, disaffected Apaches from all tribes flocked to him—Tci-he-ndes, Tsoka-ne-ndes, even a large number of Mescaleros and long-sullen Lipans. It was even suspected, with some cause, that a few Comanches from the Indian Territory, quiescent since their defeat in the Red River War in 1875, rode over to fight under him. It was believed by some that eventually Victorio led a force of 350 fighting men, although that figure seems rather too large.

Two days after the breakout, with his original sixty warriors, Victorio descended upon the horse herd of E Company of the all-Negro 9th Cavalry, near Ojo Caliente. The Apaches escaped with forty-six horses after massacring the eight guards.

Once the alarm over Victorio was spread, troops were put on alert from central Arizona to Fort Davis in West Texas. The heaviest responsibility for capturing him rested with the senior officer in southern New Mexico, Major Albert P. Morrow, and the Department commander, General Hatch, who eventually took to the saddle to co-ordinate the effort. Morrow engaged in a one-on-one chase of the elusive Mimbres chief that is remarkable in Southwest history. One other important army officer came to the fore from the start of the Victorio war. Mustered from Fort Apache with fifteen regulars and twenty Indians of his A Company of Apache scouts, Lieutenant Charles B. Gatewood was ordered to prevent Victorio from seizing his families at San Carlos. Of frail health, with large, liquid eyes and a prominent, highly aquiline nose (his nickname was "Beak"), the twenty-six-year-old Gatewood figured in every subsequent Apache war until he arranged the final Gerónimo surrender in 1886. Gatewood was also one of the not insignificant number of army officers who were openly disgusted by the civilian handling of the Victorio problem. Regarding the conflict between the Mimbres and the white squatters who finally triumphed in their land grab, Gatewood's statement that the terrible war that followed could have been prevented by any man who combined sensitivity to the issues with power to make a decision stick, has not gained a wide following among modern scholarship intent upon showing how irresistible are the forces of history.

Shut off by a cordon of cavalry from running west or south, Victorio was content to lair in the mountains of the Tci-he-nde homelands, his strength growing by the day. Two weeks after the breakout, when they ambushed a party of about four dozen regulars and Navajo scouts, his force had grown to at least 150. In a hot, day-long fight during which the army group was reinforced and their strength doubled, Victorio's men, masterfully concealed on high canyon walls, were not known to have suffered a single casualty. By the time the regulars, Navajos, and reinforcements (some of whom were civilian volunteers) retreated at sundown a total of ten had been killed. Thirty-two head of government stock were killed and twenty-one captured, as were most of the army unit's supplies and baggage.

Once it became apparent that Victorio's immediate goal was not the recapture of his Tci-he-nde families, Lieutenant Gatewood was transferred with his Apache scouts from San Carlos to Major Morrow's command at Fort Bayard, near Silver City. When news reached there of Victorio's first battle win, additional forces, including Gatewood, were put out in pursuit. After a few days' persistent tracking, a trace of the hostiles' passing was discovered. In a drenching rain the pack train was left behind, and by moving swiftly by night the army unit overtook the hostiles on the fourth day. They were deep within the Black Range, described by General Hatch as being so rough that "The well known Modoc lava beds are a lawn compared with them."

The renegades were first contacted by a small number of scouts moving well in advance, who discovered them on the floor of a small canyon, cooking their evening meal. Not suspecting the presence of a larger force, the hostiles caustically invited the scouts down for dinner as the shooting started. The rest of the force quickly rode up from behind, surprising Victorio's men and flushing them up onto the canyon walls, where they took cover for a serious fight. Darkness, however, broke off the engagement soon after it started. Instead of slipping away during the night, Victorio renewed the conflict the next morning, and the fight slowly spread up the canyon floor, the maddening echoes making it impossible to tell who was shooting at whom or from where. It was a situation in which one difficulty of having Apaches fight Apaches became all too apparent. "When the scouts began to appear," wrote Gatewood, "it was impossible for us to tell whether they were hostiles, [until we] heard the fog-horn voice of Sergeant Jack Long bellowing 'Mucho bueno! God d–n, come on!'"

Lieutenant Gatewood was not yet a seasoned Indian fighter, and at one point the fighting became so confused that he took cover on the wrong side of a boulder. "I didn't think there was a sane man in the country," he wrote later, "except the Corporal, who cooly informed me after awhile that I was sitting on the wrong side . . . and pointed out to me the folly of protecting a rock."[2] By the time the hostiles broke off the engagement they were believed to have lost three dead, two men and one woman, which was a lighter toll than Morrow's cavalry suffered. Before Victorio could get away the soldiers tried to recapture some of their stock but were beaten off.

About a month after the breakout Major Morrow succeeded in surprising Victorio's camp and recaptured a good deal of government stock, and several days after that the army learned they were not alone in searching for the Mimbres. Local settlers had formed into posses to hunt Victorio down, one of which, a party of twenty, found him still in the Black Range on October 13. The wily chief easily lured them into the simplest of ambushes and killed six of them before turning his attention to a couple of wagon trains nearby, killing eleven more and taking a woman and child captive. Dead and wounded alike were tossed onto the fired wagons before the renegades pounded off to the southwest, Major Morrow in pursuit with his rapidly tiring 9th Cavalry. After giving his antagonists another beating on October 22, killing by one report nineteen, most of them Indian scouts, Victorio headed his raiders toward Old Mexico.

Still Morrow dogged his footsteps, with some eighty regulars and eighteen Indian scouts under Lieutenant Gatewood, south through the sand and lava deserts into Chihuahua. The cavalry horses broke down in the heat and were destroyed, as water became ever more scarce. Once, wrote Gatewood, "we found a tank of clear and cool water, but . . . a coyote had been killed and disembowelled in it, and it had been otherwise disgustingly poisoned."[3] In two days they covered seventy miles, not an exhausting pace for the Apaches, but it ruined the black soldiers as a fighting unit. On the third day of the march, in the Guzman Mountains near the Corralitos River, Gatewood's scouts found and defused an ambush, slipping behind Victorio's men and opening fire on them with a booming volley. Unwilling to fight at close quarters, the hostiles broke and regrouped on one ridge after another, each higher than the previous one, gradually leading to a sheer rock wall. When Morrow's exhausted troopers reached the base, Victorio's men triggered a landslide, but miraculously no one was injured by it. At this point Morrow tried to outflank his enemy with Gatewood's Apaches, but that maneuver was guessed and broken apart.

Morrow's men had been pressed to their limits; some of them were beginning to show symptoms of thirst madness, and there was nothing to do but lead his mauled command to water. Although Victorio gave ground all during the fight, he had badly bested the dismounted cavalrymen, and the army force crawled back to Fort Bayard, north of the Mogollon Mountains, where they arrived on November 3, 1879. Victorio was for the time being left to the Mexicans, and after the fight on the Corralitos the hostiles repaired to one of their favorite raiding lairs, the Candelaria

Mountains of northern Chihuahua, and the Americans turned their attention back to its usual focus, Arizona.

In the months following the Victorio breakout in September 1877, the Nde-nda-i renegades Juh and Nolgee continued to terrorize most of southeast Arizona and northern Sonora, and indeed were probably guilty of some of the depredations attributed to Victorio. In December of that year they annihilated a wagon train near Stein's Peak on the New Mexico border, killing several men. They took some losses, too, as a homeward-bound scouting expedition surprised their rancheria on December 18, killing fifteen of the renegades and rounding up several head of stock. Gerónimo and other important leaders, including Francisco and Ponce, slipped out of San Carlos on April 4, 1878, so quietly that they were not missed immediately. It was reasoned that they must have linked up with Juh, but their exact location was not learned until July of 1879. It was discovered they were back in business as contrabandistas, selling goods stolen in the United States to merchants in Janos, a continuation of the generations-old love-hate relationship between the Apaches and the Mexicans.

As Victorio rested his men in the Candelarias his force grew in size still further, swelled by an influx of more Mescaleros from the Tularosa Reservation, and from the Mescalero and Lipan bands in the Sierra del Carmen who had always remained away from an agency. Going into the winter of 1879, they flexed their muscles, wiping out two parties of Mexicans out of the little Chihuahua town of Carrizo. Twenty-six Mexicans died in the ghastly massacres. In an angry reaction to the Carrizo killings the most active Mexican officer in the district, General Gerónimo Trevino, launched an expedition against Victorio in late December with four hundred regulars. But almost immediately Victorio eluded him and recrossed into the United States. To meet the renewed threat General Hatch picketed his whole cavalry regiment across southern New Mexico, supported by reserves moved into Fort Bowie in Apache Pass, just across the Arizona border. No sign of Victorio was seen until he materialized in the Black Range, far to Hatch's rear, and the black 9th Cavalry—five companies under Major Morrow—were off on another punishing chase.

Morrow overtook Victorio on January 12, 1880, near the upper reaches of the Puerco River. In a hot fight that lasted all afternoon and evening Morrow lost a sergeant killed and two men hit. Although no hostile bodies were found, Morrow believed several Indians had been wounded. After breaking off his fight Victorio continued moving his band northward; a week later he was overtaken in the San Mateo Mountain; in a second skirmish Morrow lost one of his junior officers killed and two Indian scouts hit. Staging another successful getaway, Victorio turned east and south, across the upper Rio Grande and into the San Andres Mountains, just north of the trans-Pecos extension of west Texas. Still Morrow and his ragged cavalry kept at it, again making contact on February 3, in a canyon near the locally famous watering place known as Aleman's Well. In laying his defensive network Victorio employed a brilliant strategy, stationing his warriors in groups at key places on the canyon walls in such a fashion that as one group was flushed the cavalry would be openly exposed to fire from another. The plan worked faultlessly, and after two days Victorio melted away, again the victor. Almost out of rations and ammunition the exhausted, bewildered, and consistently beaten cavalry turned for home. Only one company was left in the vicinity to keep in touch with the wily Indians, but as soon as they were alone, Victorio turned and smashed them. In an ambush that turned into a total rout the hostiles inflicted heavy losses and captured virtually all the soldiers' food and bedding.

By now it was obvious to General Hatch that besting Victorio would require a better strategy than simply chasing him across deserts. Further, feeling had been mounting in the army that the Tularosa Mescaleros had been continuing to support him with supplies and men; so when Hatch received reliable word that the crafty chief was laired in a large canyon in the eastern San Andres he devised and set in motion a complicated and time-consuming strategy. While reinforcing his own jaded command with four companies from Arizona, two of Indian scouts and two of 6th Cavalry, Hatch planned to take to the saddle himself and meet a second column from Fort Stanton at Hembrillo Canyon on April 7. At the same time, Colonel Benjamin H. Grierson was to ride north out of Texas to Tularosa with five companies of his Negro 10th Cavalry. By delaying Grierson's start Hatch gave himself time to fight Victorio in the San Andres and still close on Tularosa at the same time as the Texas force, to neutralize the reservation Mescaleros by seizing their weapons and stock. And, conveniently, Grierson on his way to Tularosa would pass by the eastern edge of the San Andres, cutting off that direction as a possible hostile escape route.

Unfortunately, not only was Victorio unused to minding army timetables, but almost from the start of the campaign things went wrong. As the Fort Stanton column, under Captain Henry Carroll, approached the San Andres from the north, they stopped and watered heavily from a spring that they discovered, too late, was charged with a near fatal concentration of the mineral gypsum. With his two troops of cavalry rendered nearly useless, in fact almost helpless, Carroll interrupted his march with a frantic search for fresh water. He knew of one spring that he had seen the year before, but on reaching there it was discovered to have gone dry. The only other spring was in Hembrillo, where Carroll led his feeble and vomiting men, arriving in the morning of April 7.

Victorio had learned of the offensive before it ever started, and laid another of his masterful ambushes to fall upon the first soldiers to enter the canyon; and, of course, he held the Hembrillo spring. When the hostiles saw the condition of Carroll's desperately sick and thirsty men they fought like demons to keep the soldiers from reaching the water. One party of regulars did manage to reach it, but then succeeded in filling only a few canteens and lost two of their number killed.

General Hatch, meanwhile, had found his own advance bogged down by a broken pump at Aleman's Well, forcing him to send on ahead 125 troops and scouts under Captain Curwen McClellan, who entered the battlefield on the morning of the eighth to discover that the hostiles had opened the day's fight by pressing their advantage on Carroll's nearly finished troops. In a classic cavalry charge McClellan reached Carroll's command, and together the two forces managed to push the Indians slowly out of the canyon. Victorio quickly saw he had lost the advantage and before he could sustain many casualties led his warriors in melting away to the south.

By midmorning Carroll and McClellan had sent messengers southward to find Hatch and bring him up quickly, but evidently overstated their own situation. The general, under the impression that his carefully mounted expedition was being mauled, scurried his column northward on a trail that skirted the base of the mountains, the same trail that Victorio's people were right then traveling, headed south. The hostiles recognized the situation first and hid themselves trailside until Hatch thundered past. Victorio's leading subchief, an old man named Nana, later said that Victorio "had a bad fifteen minutes" until their way cleared again.

Only one Apache body was found in Hembrillo Canyon, although Captain Carroll, himself and seven others wounded during the ordeal, claimed to have killed three others. When the facts became known concerning Victorio's escape almost beneath Hatch's own horse's hooves, the general had an even greater respect for his adversary, but local settlers and newspapers considered him the fool of the year. But whatever his embarrassment, Hatch marched on to Tularosa to meet Grierson for the disciplining of the reservation Mescaleros. And Victorio had one more trick to play. Popularly supposed to have kept going south all the way to Mexico, Victorio, once the San Andres were clear, backtracked up Hatch's trail to Aleman's Well, breaking open the padlocked troughs to give his people a good watering before sneaking back west to their home territory in the Black Range.

The agent to the Mescaleros at this time was S. A. Russell, whom Grierson characterized as an honest man, but when Grierson arrived on April 12 and explained that his purpose was to disarm and dismount the Mescaleros, Russell protested. Things had been very quiet in that vicinity, and moreover the Mescaleros camped around the agency were there at Russell's express directive, and they had not been bothering anybody.

However, just as that assertion was certainly true of most of the

Mescaleros, it was almost as certainly untrue of a few of them. All during his march north Grierson had seen increasing evidence that Victorio was supported at least in part by Mescaleros, and he would not have recommended action against them had he not been convinced absolutely. He was not an Indian hater, as he had proved time and again during his gentle management of Kiowas and Comanches at Fort Sill in the early seventies. Moreover, after Hatch's fight at Hembrillo Canyon, one of the hostile getaway trails, when finally uncovered, led east toward the Mescalero Reservation. Tularosa, insisted Grierson, had become "a supply camp for Victorio's band." The army would hold sway in this argument, and after Hatch arrived the disarming took place on the sixteenth. They succeeded in assembling about 320 of the reservation Mescaleros, but trouble broke out almost immediately.

Lieutenant Gatewood, with a group of his scouts, saw a party of Mescaleros rounding up stock near the agency. Assuming this was a theft in progress, they attacked, killing two of the Mescaleros. Only later was it learned from an outraged Agent Russell that the Indians had been herding at his instruction. Over this affair there was considerable consternation and unrest among the assembled Indians.

When the seizure of arms finally got under way some shooting broke out, at which most of the Mescaleros who had come in fled up a hillside. Grierson's cavalry charged after them vigorously, and when some of the Apache men tried to fight, a number of them were killed. The controversy over the incident was neither small nor short-lived, but Hatch's plan yielded considerable results, some good, some bad. On one hand, Hatch faced a larger enemy force, as some thirty to fifty of the Tularosa Mescaleros committed themselves openly now to Victorio. But just as significantly, Hatch had finally separated the sheep from the goats; the rest of the Mescaleros returned chastened to their lodges during the night. Grieving for their dead and cowed by the sizable garrison left permanently on station, they were effectively neutralized and denied to Victorio as a sanctuary or source of further supply.

After a few relatively peaceful weeks in the Black Range Victorio made his presence known during the beginning of summer; among the victims of the renewed raids were more than a dozen isolated shepherds. One group of raiders, led by Victorio's reputed son named Washington, swung westward as far as San Carlos, killing three whites in one action and some more in sacking a wagon train. Once again Hatch and Morrow took after them, but their cavalry was simply too broken down to be effective.

Going into the third week in May, Morrow's men exhausted themselves in another hard chase, and the major was approached by one of his scout commanders, H. K. Parker, who requested permission to draw a few days' rations and take his sixty to seventy Indian scouts out for a general reconnaissance. Morrow had nothing to lose and agreed. In four days Parker's trailers found nothing while making their way to Ojo Caliente and General Hatch. Hatch gave them more rations and let them go out again, and on the second day of this excursion Parker's scouts uncovered enough hostile sign to have the command go into hiding until Victorio's rancheria could be located. When it was found, in a canyon at the upper end of the Palomas River, the scouts knew their presence was not suspected, and Parker set about giving the legendary chief a dose of his own. Dividing his command into three units, he stationed them during the night of May 23–24 at strategic places on the canyon walls. One of the groups opened fire into Victorio's rancheria at first light, and the hostiles broke and ran up their principal escape route only to be met by a blasting rifle volley. They then ran down the canyon, straight into the muzzles of the third group. Thinking himself outnumbered and surrounded, Victorio took his people back to their rancheria and began throwing up fortifications and rifle pits.

When Parker saw this he knew he had them cornered, and sent a messenger racing back to Hatch to send more supplies and ammunition. Hatch received the information and dashed off a triumphant news dispatch that Victorio was cornered and done for. But somehow, incredibly, no ammunition ever made its way to Parker. When his scouts were down to five bullets apiece he instructed them not to shoot except in self-defense. Eventually he had to pull back altogether, allowing Victorio to make his getaway. When he exhausted his rations and had to butcher horses for food, Parker finally returned to Ojo Caliente.

No explanation could be given why he was not resupplied, and Parker, to say nothing of the local civilians, was livid; Hatch came in for a storm of abuse from the press that was not entirely unjustified. But even though the hostiles were given no coup de grace on the Palomas, Victorio had still suffered a crippling defeat. Himself wounded in the leg, he had lost perhaps thirty of his people dead, and his following began to break up. Undoubtedly some of them were simply tired of fighting; others may have believed the chief's medicine was broken and a further effort under him was useless. But he still had a potent force of an estimated 150 warriors, whom he led to Mexico to rest and lick their wounds. In their move south they were caught twice more by Major Morrow and his hard-riding cavalry; the hostiles lost about ten more dead, including, it was believed, Victorio's son Washington. Morrow, however, failed to turn or hold them. Back in Mexico the renegades raided through a strip of territory to regain their stronghold, but once there they settled down to a quieter existence, even coming in to trade at a local village from time to time.

Hatch felt certain that Victorio would return as soon as he recovered, and requested that Grierson be sent up from Texas to help out again, but Grierson protested and offered a new strategy. For once the timid, oft-abused Grierson spoke up.

Since the close of the Civil War Ben Grierson had been laboring under severe disadvantages in regard to commands and promotions. The choice jobs and what few promotions there were to be had in the frontier army usually went to boastful, chest-thumping braggarts who clamored and intrigued to get them, and then by spectacular if risky tactics won new honors. Grierson was a gentle man, a music teacher before the Civil War. He was the colonel of one of the army's four Negro regiments and thus the object of some amusement among the rest of the officer corps, many of whom were exponents of a tacit but iron-rooted racism; most of them viewed the black soldiers as tragicomic, shuffling parodies of the ideal white fighting man. Grierson's post, Fort Davis, was one of the most isolated hellholes on the command line, and for all the thirteen years since its recommissioning, it had been the exclusive domain of one or another of the army's only four black regiments, the 9th and 10th Cavalry and 24th and 25th Infantry.[4] Grierson had never attended West Point, and worse, General Sheridan disliked him intensely. Hence, when the bearded music master reared and challenged Hatch's use of him, eyebrows rose across the service.

With the Apaches effectively sandwiched between Hatch's 9th Cavalry on the north and a Mexican expedition of five hundred commanded by Colonel Adolph Valle on the south, Grierson believed Victorio would try to swing wide through West Texas, circling around Hatch's defenses to return to his home territory or possibly the Tularosa Reservation. For Grierson to leave, as Hatch suggested, with a sizable force of his twelve-company command, would have left the Texas frontier undermanned and easy prey to the Apaches. But if he stood pat along the Rio Grande, the Texas frontier would be well defended, and a safe alley to Tularosa would be denied the hostiles. General Ord finally sided with Grierson, and on June 28 Sheridan, too, found himself agreeing.

The strategy with which Grierson responded to the opportunity was a good one, too. Hatch and Morrow had badly worn down their 9th Cavalry with endless goose chases through the desert after the elusive Victorio. Grierson instead planned to station small garrisons at the major water holes along Victorio's projected route, denying their use to the wily Apaches and thereby turning the merciless desert climate against the Indians, whose great strength normally lay in their ability to use it to their advantage.

True to Grierson's prediction, Victorio crossed into West Texas in late July 1880, after a hot brush with the Valle Mexicans. The most important water hole they would have to cross was the Tinaja de las Palmas, in the furnacelike Quitman Canyon, which was held by Grierson himself, with two other officers, twenty-one troopers, and the colonel's teen-age son, Robert.

When Grierson heard of Victorio's approach he fortified his position and sent for help. As Victorio and a large number of followers pounded up the canyon Grierson and his little squadron held them off gallantly until aid arrived. Two columns charged into the fray from both flanks, and the jarred Apaches retired hastily from the field. "Golly," the colonel's son committed incredulously to his diary, "you ought to've seen 'em turn tail & strike for the hills."⁵ The Apaches tried numerous times to pass the water hole, but beaten back on each attempt, Victorio headed west and recrossed into Mexico, leaving behind seven dead. Grierson's strategy was working.

Three days later, on August 2, Victorio made a second attempt, this time managing after two days to evade Grierson's scouts and cavalry, and raced north toward Tularosa along the desolate western escarpment of the Sierra Diablo Mountains. Like a flash Grierson was after him with two companies of the 10th, not actually chasing him, but moving to head him off by seizing the critical Rattlesnake Springs which lay in Victorio's path. In an action reminiscent of his swift movements in the Civil War, Grierson drove his men sixty-five miles in twenty-one hours, an admirable pace even for Apaches, while keeping a protecting mountain range between the Indians and himself. The soldiers encamped at Rattlesnake Springs on the afternoon of August 6 and, reinforced by two more companies of the 10th, they held the water hole in the face of a furious attack by Victorio's thwarted warriors. No Apaches or soldiers lost their lives, but the Apaches were once again denied water and rode away.

Within hours of the skirmish there, the enraged hostiles fell upon a supply train out of Fort Davis that had rounded the end of a mountain range, unaware of the action. Most of the train guard were riding in the wagons and came pouring out to meet the attack, much to Victorio's surprise. The escort kept the Apaches at bay until Grierson charged onto the field and drove them off. Frustrated and probably confused at Grierson's wile and mobility, Victorio led his warriors back to Mexico. Victorio's increasing desperation was suddenly brought to the fore by a remarkable incident. After the second defeat by Grierson, some of the Mescaleros were tired of the escapade and tried to return to their reservation, apparently feeling as much at liberty to dump Victorio and sneak home as to desert Agent Russell and sneak out. This seems well enough within the Apache scheme of individualistic warfare, but in this instance Victorio would have none of it. There was a confrontation, and Victorio killed the Mescalero chief to force the other warriors to stay.

By this time plans for a joint Mexican-American expedition were well under way. Relations between the two countries had been warming since February of 1880, when President Hayes rescinded the June 1, 1877, order that had permitted American troops to enter Mexican territory without Mexican permission, which the Mexicans found hateful and humiliating. The current scheme called for Colonel George P. Buell to cross into

Chihuahua from New Mexico (he left in September), and for Colonel Eugene A. Carr with nearly all the 6th Cavalry to cross from Arizona. Once south of the border they were to link up with a Mexican army of a thousand or more, commanded by the prominent soldier-politician Colonel Joaquín Terrazas, for a sweep through Victorio's Mexican stronghold, the Candelaria Mountains. The grand design fell apart when it was learned that Victorio had moved farther south. Terrazas was aware that two American armies deep in Mexico would cause serious unrest among the people, and he almost certainly was mindful of the political gains he would make by crushing Victorio without American help. Labeling Buell's Apache scouts untrustworthy, he ordered both Buell and Carr out of the country.

After a brief stalk Terrazas trapped the Victorio group in a rugged canyon of the isolated Tres Castillos Mountains. Completing the encirclement of the islandlike upthrust late on October 14, Terrazas attacked at dawn the next day. With no place left to run or hide, seventy-eight Apaches—sixty warriors and eighteen women and children—perished in the holocaust.[6] The fact that Terrazas lost only three dead indicates that Victorio lost his last battle not only by an apparent checkmate; he must have been out of ammunition as well.

According to the traditional version, Victorio himself was shot and killed by an auxiliary scout, a Tarahumara Indian named Mauricio. However, that Victorio's body was positively identified, or that he was even among the dead, was not provable by any Mexican account. Reportedly none of the Mexicans had ever seen him or knew what he looked like, and had he actually escaped, the political fruits of offering any scalp as "Victorio's" might easily have proven irresistible. Victorio's death has been made quite certain by Indian agreement, and also the fact of the survivors of his band turning for leadership to his leading subchief, the cunning, experienced septuagenarian Nana. For killing the Tci-he-nde chief the Tarahumara scout was given a nickel-plated rifle and a bounty of three thousand American dollars by the Chihuahua state government.

Other reported versions of Victorio's end have, predictably, surfaced. One—that he survived and went into hiding the rest of his life—is too contradictory to his personality and the Apache Life-way to be credited. Another had it that his band was massacred, not in battle, but in a village square ambush after they had come in to trade. That was not unknown to happen in Mexico, but the celebration attending such an end to Victorio would not have permitted the fact to be hidden. Terrazas also took seventy prisoners, and it seems unlikely that that many captives would have been taken in a village massacre. Then, too, if any but the Tarahumara named Mauricio had shot Victorio, the size of the reward would almost certainly have lured out other claimants. The Apache tradition, first related by those who discovered the bodies, was that Victorio's people were practically destitute of ammunition, and not until he saw that death or capture was inevitable did the chief commit suicide with his knife.

The small number of Victorio's following to survive Tres Castillos turned for leadership to the dead chief's ablest lieutenant, Nana. He was about seventy-three, tall, crippled with rheumatism and old wounds, but fit, toughly spry, and eccentric—as evinced by the thick gold watch chains that dangled from his ears. Also surviving was Nana's daughter by a Mescalero wife; later known to the whites as Katie, she was married to the rising Nde-nda-i war di-yin Gerónimo. She escaped the massacre with their small boy (later called Robert Gerónimo), who lived to be the last survivor. Between fifteen and thirty others of the band either escaped from the battle or were absent, scouring the countryside for some ammunition.

Once they obtained it, Nana's decimated band took some measure of revenge on the Mexicans. On November 16 they ambushed a party of Terrazas' soldiers, killing nine. As perhaps final evidence that Victorio was killed at Tres Castillos, it was said that among the Mexican dead was a sergeant in possession of Victorio's saddle, and amulets that could only have come from the chief's body. The sergeant's remains were discovered chopped beyond recognition. Soon after, the Apaches attacked Governor Terrazas himself, who was traveling with an escort of ten, of whom nine were killed; that Terrazas escaped was miraculous. After these vengeance killings, Nana's people wandered almost aimlessly west into Sonora, where accidentally they found Gerónimo and linked their weakened band with his. This was possibly the first time Gerónimo saw his son by Katie.

After spending some time with Gerónimo's Nde-nda-i, Nana led in July of 1881 a blitzlike raid across New Mexico that remains his principal claim to celebrity. He took with him fifteen of his own warriors, joined soon by about twenty-five Mescaleros who, themselves rebellious against reservation restrictions, were eager to fight under this incredible old man who had married into their tribe. They moved during broad daylight to the northeast, straight into the Sacramento Mountains. There, in Alamo Canyon on July 17 their path crossed that of two American soldiers, part of a small squad of 9th Cavalry under Lieutenant John F. Guilfoyle. The encounter was as much a surprise to the attackers as to the troops; their quick ambush netted them only three mules and the wounding of the packmaster. When Guilfoyle learned of the incident he took up chase in earnest, beginning remarkable one-on-one pursuit that lasted nearly until Nana left the country again.

Nana sensed the way east blocked by soldiers and turned westerly, through the Canyon del Perro, killing a woman and two Mexicans at the edge of the White Sands. Guilfoyle's men attacked the Indians before they had even left the scene, although no one was killed in the fire fight, and Nana and his men continued to the west. On July 25 Guilfoyle managed to surprise their camp in the San Andres, capturing all their camp goods and more than a dozen head of stock, mostly mules; the lieutenant also believed his men had killed two of the enemy.

In making his escape from Guilfoyle, Nana continued westward; the raiding Tci-he-nde and Mescaleros crossed the Rio Grande about six miles below San Jose, where they killed a Mexican and two miners. The Apaches reached the foothills of the San Mateo Mountains on July 30, where they came upon and slaughtered four more Mexicans and continued west into the mountains.

The pace that Nana and his men were keeping was spectacular—on some days the stove-up old man led his warriors seventy hard-riding miles. Nana himself credited his awesome stamina in the saddle to his knowledge of the geese. He knew their songs and had their power, which came from heaven, he said, and not from earth. In the Chiricahua power-associations Goose represented speed and endurance; the fact that Nana could draw on the power of the geese undoubtedly helped him, at his age and physical condition, to recruit a party to follow him. "Old Nana used to tell a story about the geese" one informant said later. "He said that some old men used to tell him when he was young about how some geese started from the north. Each of them had twelve pieces of bread. They were going far to the south. A large group went. They kept going for twelve days without stopping and then they got there."[7]

The geese must have favored the raid, for the panic Nana's renegades caused among the citizens spread like shock waves from their horses' hooves. As Nana swept the countryside for ammunition, stock, and plunder, civilian "ranger" forces—mounted posses of local citizens—took the field to protect their homes. Indian hunting had never ceased to be a popular pastime, and it was a hobby given added importance by Nana's presence in the territory, but few of the "ranger" excursions seriously thought to encounter the wizened old Indian. One such posse Nana caught literally napping, taking a siesta on a blistering afternoon about the first of August. Of three dozen white settlers, the Apaches killed only one, but wounded seven more. Their principal object was fresh horses, and they got every one—thirty-eight head. Another Mexican was cut down as the renegades pounded out of the area.

Lieutenant Guilfoyle retook eleven head of stock a couple of days later, still in the San Mateos, and also some more hastily made camp goods. But again Nana melted away; for nearly a week the Apaches lay dormant, their presence unknown until two more bodies were found, near La Savoya.

By the second week in August the continuing Nana raid was an even greater sensation, and General Hatch had blanketed his district with eighteen companies of troops and scouts. Guilfoyle had run his own men to a frazzle and pulled out of the chase, but on August 12 Nana was overtaken twenty-five miles west of Sabinal by another unit of regulars.

The troops believed, without conclusive evidence, that they killed four of the renegades, while themselves losing three wounded, one missing, and one killed. On the sixteenth troops again got too close and Nana ambushed them fiercely, killing two and wounding three. When the Indians disengaged from this fight they began moving to complete their circuit, heading west for the familiar Black Range, but before they could get a good start they were struck by yet another army patrol, which snatched some of their horses and goods before they could get away.

The Black Range also proved too hotly patrolled for safety, as while there they fought another party of troops. Here Nana claimed the greatest single victory of his raid; of twenty soldiers, his warriors killed six and wounded three, the eleven survivors withdrawing. Soon after this Nana faded back across the border into the Sierra Madre, his New Mexico blitz complete.

No historical accounts of the Nana raid begrudge its audacity and flash[8] —covering over a thousand miles in six weeks, the Apaches had garnered a great deal of stolen property while inflicting much heavier casualties than they sustained, all the while living off the land. In all the later frontier Indian wars, including those against the Apaches, the warriors' greatest liability was the exposure of their families to death or capture. The American army was composed of nothing but fighting men; in Indian terms it was a gigantic warrior society, the elite strike force of the white civilization. If the Apaches had ever been able to mount for any period of time such a force, unencumbered by their women and children, Nana's raid, and one or two subsequent ones under other leaders, offer a frightening suggestion of what they might have accomplished.

Victorio:
NOTES

1. See Opler, "Myths and Tales of the Chiricahua Apache Indians," p. 15.

2. Gatewood, "Campaigning Against Victorio in 1879," pp. 101-2, quoted in Thrapp, Conquest of Apacheria, p. 185.

3. Ibid.

4. Utley, "Fort Davis Guidebook."

5. Diary at Fort Davis National Historic Monument.

6. Eve Ball asserted that three hundred Apaches were killed, but that is almost certainly much too high. Letter to Sylvia Dunn, Mar. 25, 1957, Southwest Collection, Texas Tech. University.

7. The Mescaleros, Nana's wife's people, had a belief similar to this one, which was Chiricahua. Opler, "Myths and Tales of the Chiricahua Apache Indians," p. 72.

8. Record of Engagements, pp. 99-100.

Chatto, the Chiricahua leader, was an effective raider until his change of heart led him to join the scouts. He gained the trust of the officers he served under; many Chiricahuas more hostile than he came to loathe him. *National Archives*.

Charlie McComas, white captive held and later killed by Apaches. *National Archives*.

This group of Britton Davis' Apache scouts refused to have their picture taken until they were bought new suits of clothes. Front center is First Sergeant Chatto. Mickey Free is at lower left. Photo taken in El Paso, Texas, at the conclusion of a fruitless chase after Gerónimo. *National Archives*.

Sierra Madre of old Mexico; arrow marks the peak near which Crawford was killed. *National Archives.*

Captain Emmet Crawford. *National Archives.*

The Gray Fox returns for another go: General Crook poses on his favorite riding mule, Apache, in Apache Pass. *Arizona Historical Society.*

Portrait of four: Scout Dutchy, Apache the mule, General Crook, and Alchise. *National Archives.*

One of the series of photographs by Camillus S. Fly. No peace had been concluded when Fly posed the heavily

Ka-ya-ten-nae, once the nemesis of Britton Davis, underwent a change of heart during his incarceration in Alcatraz and returned to help Crook negotiate the surrender of March 1886, according to the traditional history. Better accounts, thanks in some measure to his stepson Kaywaykla, shown here with his mother, Guyan, indicate that Ka-ya-ten-nae's paramount interest was to guard his people against treachery by Crook and his interpreters. *Museum of New Mexico, photo by Ben Wittick.*

Chihuahua, Chiricahua chief. *National Archives*.

Gerónimo surrenders to General Crook; detail of the conference photograph. General Crook is at right, in helmet, with Captain Bourke sitting on his right. Beyond Bourke, three interpreters, and beyond them in rumpled hat and mustache, Lieutenant Maus. Gerónimo sits at extreme left, with silver conchos on shoulders of his coat. Man sitting between Gerónimo and Lieutenant Maus is the old chief Nana. *Arizona Historical Society.*

Cibicue

By the time the New Mexico excitement over the Nana raid ended it had already begun to be overshadowed by a new round of trouble from San Carlos. During the summer a White Mountain di-yin named Nakai-doklini had gained a large and devoted following to a doctrine that better times were ahead and their dead would return to life. He was a tiny wisp of a man, one of the first scouts that Crook had recruited in 1871, being characterized then as a "kindly White Mountain herb doctor." That same year or the year following, according to some, he was part of an Apache delegation to Washington, although there is little evidence to support that assertion,[1] and he later attended a school in Santa Fe. One result of his white contact was an inquiry into the religion of the pindahs, the rudiments of which he managed to learn and assimilate into his own movement. The blend suited his mystic nature, and he spent a good deal of time wandering alone in the wilderness as he had heard Christ had done, fasting and praying.

The agent at San Carlos now was J. C. Tiffany, not the most satisfactory within memory, and he had not made much attempt to understand the culture of his charges, his greater interest in Apaches allegedly stemming from the potential profit of their administering. When Tiffany learned of the new movement, and that Nakai-doklini was teaching a new religious dance to his followers to bring about his millennium (part of which, Tiffany heard, was the disappearance of the pindahs from the country), he summoned a few of the chiefs and warned them from any action against the government.

The military learned about the first of August that a performance of the mysterious new dance was in progress on Carrizo Creek, about twenty miles west of Fort Apache, and a chief of scouts, a Choctaw-Negro named Sam Bowman, was sent to investigate it. When he returned he appeared deeply troubled and upset; he sought out his company commander and tried to resign. "That kind of dance always meant trouble," the company packmaster quoted Bowman, "and he didn't want to get mixed up in it."[2]

Nakai-doklini's ceremony was a variation of the Wheel Dance, in which all the performers face a central focus, aligned outward like the spokes of a wheel, and dance a forward-backward time step, irregularly, so that the wheel slowly revolves. The religious significance of the new rite was attested by the extensive sprinkling of the sacred ha-dintin pollen. For a time Nakai-doklini moved his ceremony closer to Fort Apache, and a cavalry lieutenant rode out to witness it himself. He too found it ominous to see "the swaying, engrossed figures, moving like automatons to the thump of the drums."[3] What the lieutenant found even more frightening was that Nakai-doklini had established through his movement a degree of unity among Apaches of bands who had theretofore felt a great aversion to one another.

Shortly after this Nakai-doklini relocated farther away, on Cibicue Creek, nearly fifty miles from the agency. By means of his Wheel Dance Nakai-doklini announced he would restore two dead chiefs—one of them the revered Diablo—to life.

Diablo's declining years are something of a mystery. John Clum had studiously courted his good will, no doubt being coached in the wisdom of this policy by his friend—and Diablo's relative by marriage—Eskiminzin. Diablo's influence began to wane in the late 1870s because of his age. However, his counsel was apparently still sought by his people until he was snubbed by the Indian Bureau: when the authorities passed him over and failed to recognize him as a tag band chief his influence was destroyed at a blow. Other, lesser men rose to influence, and Diablo sank into the benign neglect that was the lot of every old Apache. "I remember him when he was a very old man living at Dewey Flat," an informant told Grenville Goodwin. "One time a big cloudburst came, and with it a wall of water descending the river. This old man was camped close to the river with other people. They left the bottom, seeking higher ground, forgetting about the old man. I saw him coming along by himself, dragging his blanket, crying and saying, 'Nothing is afraid of me anymore. Long ago it was not that way. Then [even the water] was afraid of me.' "[4] Diablo was killed during the winter of 1880–81, during one of the feuds that continually beset his Nadotsusn clan. Historical treatments of the Nakai-doklini trouble and subsequent difficulty with the White Mountain Apaches have not given sufficient thought to the possible incendiary effect the Indian Bureau's abandonment of Diablo might have had. When the time came for the civilian authorities to name what leaders would be recognized as tag band chiefs, it is impossible that a man of Diablo's stature was simply overlooked; the real motivations of the agent—or the Tucson Ring—can only be conjectured. Moreover, Diablo had spent a large portion of his time during his last active years in quelling just the kind of clan and band fighting that finally claimed his life. He was a firm but beloved peacemaker; the men most likely to take advantage of his downfall were his enemies, factious and divisive. It is not beyond possibility that much of the violence among the White Mountain Apaches during the early eight-ies could have been avoided if Diablo had been kept in power by the white agency instead of undercut. Indeed, it seems likely that the rank and file of the White Mountain Indians soon grew sick of the power struggle that came after Diablo's killing. It is certain that when Nakai-doklini said he would bring Diablo back to life, his own influence spread even further. What alarmed both civil and military authorities enough to spur them to action was, first, that many of the army's Apache scouts and the agency's Apache Police became caught up in the movement, became unco-operative and sometimes belligerent, openly grumbling against white mastery of their homeland. Second, Nakai-doklini failed in his attempt to resurrect the two chiefs, and blamed the failure of his medicine on the presence of pindahs, allegedly asserting that better times for the Apaches would never come as long as there were whites in their country. And he said he had dreamed that the white-eyes would be gone "when the corn was ripe." The Apaches later asserted that Nakai-doklini's dreams had charged him to keep peace with the whites, and indeed it seems difficult to believe that a genuinely violent message would have gained much fol-lowing among the White Mountain Indians, who had always been the most hospitable of the Arizona Apaches. But in his religion the army saw a threat of insurrection that had to be dealt with. On August 6 the com-mandant of Fort Apache, General Eugene A. Carr, wired out that trouble appeared to be brewing, an impression that was not changed when Nakai-doklini, or the Prophet, as he was now called, ignored a joint invitation from Carr and Agent Tiffany to come in for an interview. By the middle of the month the excitement had reached such a level that Tiffany, at San Carlos, wired Carr bluntly that the White Mountain di-yin was to be "arrested or killed or both." Carr responded to the telegram with greater reason, issuing a second invitation to the medicine man to come in to the fort for a talk. But when this, too, was ignored, Carr laid plans to go out with a strong escort and arrest him. He marched out on Monday, August 29, with a force of 117, including eighty-four regulars and twenty-three Apache scouts, the latter being a source of great concern to him.

Many of the scouts had very obviously been slipping away at night to participate in Nakai-doklini's dance, and had become increasingly less trustworthy; ammunition had not been issued them for more than two weeks, and they had not been given access to their firearms. General Carr strongly sensed the possibility of mutiny, but as he wrote later, "I had to take chances. They were enlisted soldiers of my command for duty; and I could not have found the medicine man without them." The night of their first camp, Carr had a meeting with the scouts in front of his tent, where he issued them their guns and ammunition. He waited until then, he reported, because "I deemed it better also that if they should prove unfaithful it should not occur at the Post."[5]

In a long and earnest remonstration Carr tried to calm his scouts, insisting that he was not going to kill or hurt Nakai-doklini, but was only going out "to show him that he must come when sent for." One of the Apache scouts, a sergeant called Mose, was a personal acquaintance of the di-yin's, and protested with some vigor that Nakai-doklini had done nothing wrong. Carr explained that he heard of the prediction that the whites would be gone when the corn ripened, but that the whites had no intention of leaving. Sergeant Mose appeared satisfied with Carr's argument that "When there is a misunderstanding between friends they should talk it over." Mose did ask permission, though, to ride ahead of the command and warn Nakai-doklini's group that the troops were coming; Carr, reasoning that this would help prevent a panic, assented, and Mose went on ahead.

As Carr led his command into the Cibicue Valley he handled his mission with an admirable blend of caution and restraint. The trail forked as it approached the rancheria and Carr, suspecting that some of Nakai-doklini's more radical followers had prepared an ambush along the more direct route and not wishing to provoke a fight, took the roundabout trail. When one of the White Mountain chiefs, named Sanchez, rode out to meet the column, Carr registered no distrust as the Indian rode down the line, very obviously sizing up their strength and makeup. When they reached the crossing of the Cibicue some of the Apache scouts tried to persuade Carr to camp there for the night, but the general, either fearing treachery or just prudently wanting to get the arrest over with quickly, said they would take Nakai-doklini before camping.

When Carr's force drew up in a line before the Prophet's wickiup the general saw a number of the medicine man's followers standing about. To ease their tension he explained through his interpreter what he had come for and why, that Nakai-doklini had failed to come when summoned. The di-yin replied that he was caring for a patient when sent for, but now he was well and he could go with the troops. Tensions suddenly increased when Nakai-doklini was warned that if he tried to escape he would be killed. "I could actually *feel* the stiffening in that crowd," wrote one of the officers later. "I thought that the clash was coming then." Quickly Sergeant Mose and several of the other scouts approached Nakai-doklini and reassured him and his followers that if he just did as he was told no harm would be done him. The di-yin himself smiled and told his believers they could be easy on his account. He had done nothing wrong, he said, and would do nothing to get himself killed.

When Nakai-doklini agreed to come peacefully, Carr turned back down the trail toward Fort Apache, leaving almost half his force to follow along behind with the Prophet. After Carr was well out of sight, however, Nakai-doklini sat down to his evening meal, delaying their start until Carr was several miles away. Violence nearly flared again when the medicine man was finally taken into custody and led away. More of his believers had shown up, heavily armed and very belligerent, and the officers charged with the di-yin's removal expressed their great relief at having escaped from the rancheria without a fight.

General Carr went into camp for the night after he had regained Cibicue Creek, and only then learned how far he had been separated from the rest of his column. When the second group did catch up, Carr was surprised to learn what a close scrape they had had and demanded an explanation of how the force could have let themselves in for such danger. Lieutenant Thomas Cruse explained that "The Indians kept pouring into the trail out of every little side canyon. They were all stripped and painted for fighting. It looked to Stanton and me like an attack at any minute." This conference was interrupted when Cruse spied several Indians from the Nakai-doklini rancheria slipping across the creek ford toward the camp, and Carr ordered his second-in-command, Captain Edmund C. Hentig, to order them away. Hentig walked toward the approaching Indians, motioning them off, calling "*Uca-shay* [Leave]!" At the same time, the lieutenant in charge of scouts was instructing his men to make camp, but they found the spot unsuitable. One of them, a sergeant called Dead Shot, protested, "Too much anthills." The officer agreed that they could move beyond the anthills, when suddenly a number of the scouts knelt and loaded their rifles, and as war whoops rang out, crashing volleys erupted both from them and from hostiles who had been stealthily making their way toward the camp. Captain Hentig was dropped in his tracks, and his orderly blown off his feet by eight simultaneous hits. Another private was killed as other Indians stampeded the horses and pack animals, succeeding in getting about half of them.

After the first explosive moment the hostiles and mutineers took cover in the brush surrounding the camp and kept up a steady fire, killing two additional troopers immediately and mortally wounding two more. At the height of the firing the di-yin Nakai-doklini was reportedly seen crawling off into the bushes to escape, but was shot and killed by the wounded sergeant of his guard, John MacDonald, and a bugler named Benites. As the firing continued, Carr's men hurriedly constructed barricades of rocks and baggage, including even a carton of tinned rations that began leaking its contents after being struck numerous times.

By evening additional Indians had come on the scene from nearby rancherias, until there were possibly over a thousand of them. Six of the Apache scouts who mutinied had been killed, and an estimated dozen of the attacking White Mountains. After nightfall General Carr had the bodies of his dead tagged for future identification and buried in a mass grave beneath his tent. Carr and his men dug in for a night of siege, as one friendly Apache and a former Mexican captive galloped away from the scene and into Fort Apache, where they gave the "news" that Carr and his column had been annihilated to the last man. That was the story that went out on the telegraph, and it made banner headlines.

But the White Mountain Apaches abandoned the attack during the night, many of the bands slipping out to hide themselves in the wilderness. And still, the question has to be asked, why did they attack Carr, and when they had such an overwhelming advantage, why did they not press the attack? When General Crook made his own inquiry into the matter he wrote, "I have no doubt . . . that if the Indians had been in earnest not one of our soldiers would have gotten away from there alive."[6] Crook was probably overstating his case, but the attack by White Mountain Apaches was in dramatic contradiction to their previous attitude toward the pindahs, which from their earliest contact had been, if not cordial, at least practical. Seemingly, a rumor must have spread through Nakai-doklini's rancheria that he either had been or would shortly be put to death. His followers went out to rescue him, and vented their anger and frustration on the pinned soldiers before deciding upon flight. That is speculative, but Nakai-doklini's death was held in such bitter memory by the White Mountains, who vehemently expressed the view that the army had planned his end, that it seems unlikely that they intended a full-blown war. Had they intended a serious conflict, Nakai-doklini's killing would have been a foregone conclusion.

In fact, the version of the di-yin's death that became traditional among the Indians bears little resemblance to that asserted by the army. According to Mike Burns, an Apache boy about seventeen years old at the time, who had been orphaned by the annihilation of Nanni-chaddi's band at Skull Cave on the Salt River in 1872, Nakai-doklini never moved from the rock where he had been seated under guard, but in the confusion his wife and child reached his side. "When his wife tried to get him to go away over the hills to where the rest had gone," related Burns, "he told her to go alone; that there was no use for him to go anywhere after there had been so much killing on his account, as they would kill him no matter where he went, and it was just as well for him to meet his fate where he was. Just then one of the soldiers who had hidden among some saddles came out, pulled out his pistol and shot the medicine man through the head while his wife had her arm around him."[7] The woman and child were not harmed.

But whether or not the White Mountains were earnest in their brief venture into war, they had certainly handed Carr a bruising defeat. He limped into Fort Apache the next afternoon, grateful to be alive but somewhat surprised to find himself reported the victim of a Custer-vintage massacre. In addition to his dead and wounded he had lost some supplies, including three thousand rounds of ammunition, to his assailants. Three of the Apache scouts who mutinied, Dead Shot, who evidently touched off the affair, Jim Dandy, who had shot Captain Hentig, and Private Skippy, were tried and convicted of mutiny and hanged on March 3 of the following year. Later it was charged that the traitorous scouts had flashed intelligence by mirror to the ambushers, revealing how many soldiers were coming and where they would make camp. That accusation rings hollow, though, if, as Carr reported, scout Sergeant Mose went ahead to the rancheria to warn Nakai-doklini that they were coming, and the more so because of Chief Sanchez's close inspection of Carr's troops and disposition.

For one element of the White Mountain group, though, the di-yin's death was not the end of the affair. The tribe had long had a radical war element, but they had always been small and under control. Now, however, a few of them, particularly a band of men under a minor war leader named Na-tio-tish, committed a string of depredations around Fort Apache. At first they were joined by the more peaceable Indians, no doubt venting their grief over relatives killed in the Carr fight, though these latter soon gave up. But for a time the blood flowed. Soon after Carr arrived back at Fort Apache three soldiers were killed a few miles away, and four civilians were killed and mutilated perhaps a mile from the fort. And briefly, the enraged Indians even laid siege to Fort Apache itself, which was an extremely rare occurrence in frontier history. Fort Apache, like most "forts" in the West, was not a stockade but an open collection of barracks, stables, and warehouses. The Indians kept it under fire for several hours, sniping in among the unprotected buildings, even setting fire to some, until they slipped away during the night. At least one depredation occurred as far as thirty miles from the fort, where a party of Apaches attacked a ranch and killed two whites, numerous others making dramatic escapes.

Though reports of Carr's death were decidedly premature, the uncertainty over his fate, and the high and rare drama that attended a fort being attacked, electrified the country and put the army in motion with unaccustomed speed. Department Commander Orlando Willcox staged such a show of force on and around the White Mountain Reservation that nearly all those who had forgotten themselves in the Nakai-doklini religion surrendered quickly. The small radical element of the tribe disappeared into the mountains, where eventually they would have to be hunted down.

Nakai-doklini's religious movement broke apart soon after his death, never to be resurrected. In 1887 a Yavapai living at the San Carlos Reservation attempted to make medicine similar to the di-yin's but gained no followers.[8] However, the form of Wheel Dance that Nakai-doklini had instituted and taught to other White Mountain medicine men became the single most prominent form of ceremonial dance to the White Mountains division of the Western tribe.[9]

Cibicue:
NOTES

1. Nakai-doklini is sometimes credited as having been part of General Howard's delegation in the summer of 1872. Howard, however, had four chiefs with him: Santo, who was Eskiminzin's father-in-law, Miguel, Pedro, and the great Diablo. Crook's Tonto War did not end until spring of 1873; Nakai-doklini could not have gone to Washington before that time. Commissioner of Indian Affairs, *Annual Report* for 1872, pp. 156, 174; Lori Davisson to James L. Haley, Aug. 3, 1976.
2. Thrapp, *Conquest of Apacheria*, p. 220.
3. Ibid.
4. Goodwin, *Social Organization of the Western Apache*, p. 690.
5. Ibid., p. 221.
6. Thrapp, *Conquest of Apacheria*, pp. 225–26.
7. Farish, *History of Arizona*, Vol. III, pp. 335–39.
8. Gifford, "The Southeastern Yavapai," pp. 238–39.
9. Reagan, "Notes on Indians of the Fort Apache Region," p. 328.

The San Carlos Raid

In many respects the White Mountain trouble of August was the percussion cap that detonated the Chiricahua explosion in October.

Throughout the Nakai-doklini conflict the Chiricahuas had stayed in relative quiet at the San Carlos sub-agency of Camp Goodwin, about seven miles downstream on the Gila from Fort Thomas. By this time practically all the Chiricahuas were living on the reservation, including the Nde-nda-i leader Juh. Evidently the last of the Nde-nda-i holdouts, he had surrendered in January of 1880. Nana and the survivors of Victorio's Tci-he-nde Mimbres were raiding and hiding in Old Mexico, but apart from them virtually all the Chiricahuas had been keeping out of trouble.

However, the military response to the Nakai-doklini uprising, if it can be properly called an uprising, was so swift and overwhelming that, although it did have the desired effect of cowing the White Mountains without bloodletting, it also demoralized and terrified the Tsoka-ne-nde and Nde-nda-i at the Goodwin sub-agency. General Willcox himself took the field and planted his ensign at Fort Thomas. There on September 25 he received the surrender of two White Mountain bands involved in the Nakai-doklini fight, and "paroled" them to Camp Goodwin. But five days later, September 30, Willcox changed his mind and dispatched Major James Biddle with a force of cavalry to Goodwin to put them back under guard. It was an exceptionally stupid move. Five days after they had been "forgiven" the White Mountains found themselves suddenly staring at clattering battle lines of three cavalry companies, and they understandably bolted in terror for the camp of the Chiricahuas. The latter had gone into San Carlos numerous times, the most recent only a week or so before, nervously asking reassurance that the troops would not molest them. Biddle's stark materialization destroyed their already battered sense of security, and during the night seventy-four of the Chiricahua warriors with many of their families fled to Mexico. The Tsoka-ne-nde were led by Cochise's son Naiche, and the Nde-nda-i by Juh, his kinsman and partner

Gerónimo, and a lesser leader, but one who still controlled his own band, named Chatto.

These Chiricahuas, though restive and unhappy, had been at peace, and while at several times in their history they had staged raids deserving of punishment, it was in this instance nothing but their fear and the army's vacillating self-contradiction that sparked the outbreak. Admittedly the Goodwin sub-agency was rife with dissension and bad blood, and the situation there was dangerously unstable, but it was rashness and imprudence on the army's part that, for one of several times in its frontier record, brought an Indian war upon itself. And, as might sadly be expected, the army refused to acknowledge any error, General Willcox righteously claiming that the Chiricahuas had broken out because the agent had refused to authorize an irrigation ditch.

For the time being the new renegades made for the safety of the Sierra Madre of Old Mexico, pausing long enough near the west slope of the Pinaleno Mountains to overwhelm and plunder a wagon train. This action slowed them up enough to permit Willcox to overtake them with more than a battalion of regulars and scouts, but the Chiricahuas, most of whom were not sorry to be back to a life of excitement, scampered up into the mountains and hooted insults to the soldiers to come and get them. In response Willcox ordered an advance, losing three dead and three wounded while hitting none of his enemy. Far from just having a high time, though, the Chiricahuas must have felt closely pressed, for about dusk the warriors staged a ferocious attack on Willcox's position to keep the soldiers tied down while their women and children got higher in the mountains. Up there during the night they quietly killed any animals that could give them away—their dogs, who might bark, and the horses light enough in color to be seen clearly in the night—and melted away. There was no mention, however, that any babies were sacrificed in this instance. Before reaching the border the Chiricahuas managed to steal some $20,000 in prize horses from a Tucson breeder, then slipped down to lair in the Sierra Madre, while the army set about defending the country once more.

Things stayed relatively quiet all through the fall and midway through the winter, but the feeling was universal that it was the calm before a storm. In January 1882, the fear proved correct, as a warning came into San Carlos that the escaped Chiricahuas hiding in Mexico planned to raid the agency and capture Loco and his large band of Tci-he-nde Mimbres. Once the army learned of it, Willcox sent out the alarm in Arizona, and Ranald Mackenzie, the new commander of the District of New Mexico, strung six troops of his 4th Cavalry along the Southern Pacific Railroad line, these units commanded by Lieutenant Colonel George A. Forsyth. Smaller patrols were also kept on the lookout, but by the time they found traces of invading Chiricahuas, in the Peloncillo Mountains around the first of April, it was too late.

The scar-faced old Loco commanded probably the largest single following of any of the remaining Chiricahua chiefs, about seven hundred people. Though he was regarded as being as courageous as he was wise, he had spurned the October breakout. This was a sore spot with the renegade leaders, who finally determined that he must be captured and shamed back onto the warpath. Loco, in his rancheria near Camp Goodwin, received messengers from Juh and Naiche, who told him they would be coming for him soon. On reflection, Loco had little cause to feel any obligation to join the renegades; not only did he himself see no future in war against the pindahs, he also was tied by no blood duty to help the other Indians. Although the time spent on the reservation had already begun to break down the divisions between the groups, Juh was still a Nde-nda-i and Naiche a Tsoka-ne-nde. Loco was a Tci-he-nde, and they were not his people. Still, word of the impending raid got out, and for weeks, then months, speculation was rife when and how the capture would be attempted.

After dark on April 18 the telegraph operator at Camp Goodwin discovered that his instrument had gone dead, an almost sure sign that the renegades were close at hand and ready to attempt the raid. With considerable courage he rode out to find and repair the vandalism, then returned to tick out an alarm to San Carlos. When the telegraph operator there was finally awakened it was not long before the chief of the Apache Police, Albert D. Sterling, and a single policeman raced off toward Camp Goodwin. The renegades were not concentrating on Loco for the moment, however, and had pounded off to work some mischief at San Carlos. On their way up the road they suddenly encountered and quickly killed the two officers. Sterling, although well liked by the friendly Tci-he-nde of Loco's camp, had made himself particularly unpopular with the renegade element, who were said to have kicked his head around "like a football" for a time before they abandoned the scheme of attacking San Carlos, and returned to fetch old Loco.

The sudden invasion caught the reservation Apaches by surprise. One of them heard the commotion and, he recalled, "Running out of our tepee we saw a line of Apache warriors spread out along the west side of camp and coming our way with guns in their hands. Others were swimming horses across the river or pushing floating logs ahead of themselves. One of their leaders was shouting, 'Take them all! No one is to be left in the camp. Shoot anyone who refuses to go with us! Some of you men lead them out.' . . . We did everything they told us to. We were given no time to look for our horses and round them up but were driven from our village on foot. We weren't allowed to snatch up anything but a handful of clothing and other belongings."[1] One of the warriors was showing off Albert Sterling's boots.

(There was at least one instance in this period when a peaceable Chiricahua saved himself from being kidnapped by the hostiles by obeying a muscular tremor-sign. According to one of Opler's Chiricahua informants, "Once a bunch of Geronimo's band saw C. and his wife working in the distance. They planned to catch C. and force him to go with them. All of a sudden they saw C. and the woman drop everything, jump on a horse, and head back to the reservation. Many years later someone reminded C. of this. They asked him what warned him. He said, 'Oh, yes! I remember the time. I was working and all of a sudden I got a muscular tremor sign which I knew from experience meant, 'Something bad is going to happen. Drop everything.' So I did.' "[2])

Loco offered no resistance to his captors. Some of his people, however, did refuse to go and ran away to seek refuge, it was said, with the Navajos, but the army intercepted them and interned them at Fort Union, New Mexico. Along with Loco's Tci-he-nde families the hostiles also took a small number of White Mountains caught in the trap.

On their way back to Mexico the combined party raided incessantly, killing during their spree between thirty and fifty white men, women, and children, mostly the work of Juh, not Loco. Whites taken alive were tortured with an inhumanity not justified by any amount of hatred for the pindahs. People were cut or roasted to death; in one instance a small child was heaved into a dense cactus bed and left to flounder about. It was Juh's nature, and there was no one now to stop him.

A few days into the flight to Mexico the daughter of one of the White Mountain families entered her first menstrual period. Even in the haste of this situation, time was taken to give her an abbreviated Puberty Ceremony. As a skirmish with soldiers erupted on the other side of the hill from where it was held, they observed all the rites—the massage, the running to the feather, blessing the people—although the four-day ceremony was condensed to less than one day and there were few gifts to distribute.

The civilian population was panic-stricken, though the military was doing its best to corral the bloodthirsty renegades. Scout units crisscrossed the deserts in attempts to find the hostiles. So great was the general fear of the hideous torture death that once, when a unit of Yuma Indian scouts attached to Forsyth's troops in the Peloncillos followed a trail and overtook two prospectors, the bewhiskered mountain men were temporarily insane with fright. When the lieutenant in charge rode up he discovered "These two men ran in circles, with their hands, jaws and apparently the very skin of their bodies shaking and quivering, the guns in their hands oscillating like the hands of a palsied person. Perspiration in huge drops ran down their faces, hair and beard, and they were utterly incapable of making the slightest defense. Although I stood before them in my uniform and spoke to them, telling them who we were, it was several moments before they seemed to realize they were not to be massacred."³ The Indian scouts, especially a famously skilled one named Yuma Bill, thought it was hysterically funny.

Almost immediately thereafter, however, on April 23, some of these very scouts, including Yuma Bill, lost their lives in a hostile ambush that was so expertly laid that not even Yuma Bill detected it before it was too late. As recorded later by the lieutenant, David McDonald, the party had been following a suspicious trail at the foot of a mountain ledge, when the scouts saw two hostile warriors, afoot, about a half mile away. Suddenly Yuma Bill realized he had been concentrating so hard on the distant warriors that he had neglected to check the rocky ledge itself, and, according to Lieutenant McDonald, he "jerked his face so quickly to the front that he came near striking it against mine as I was leaning looking to the right. I believe the portion of a second that I gained in suddenly jerking my face out of the way saved my life, for in a flash I saw poked over the rock a thick array of gun barrels, with twelve or fifteen Indian heads and faces showing behind them." Yuma Bill screamed a warning to the officer, who threw himself "forward on my horse's neck, grasp[ing] the reins close to the bit on each side to turn him away, and then came the volley, and with the smoke in my face and eyes, I threw my horse's head to the left-about, over the bodies of the three dead Yumas, that had been riding on my left . . . I knew from an exclamation, that Bill had been struck, and somehow was conscious that he had not fallen from his saddle. I heard the corporal, who, being a little behind and lower down the slope, had not been exposed to the volley, wheel to the rear and call, 'Come on, Lieutenant,' and I galloped after him."⁴

As Lieutenant McDonald fled the scene the horses that the dead scouts had been riding whirled and kept pace with him, as they had been trained. When out of immediate danger the officer turned and looked back, in time to see Yuma Bill blasted from his saddle by a second quick volley. When the two soldiers had regrouped with their scouts the full force of Indians, about 150, evidently of Loco's following, beset them determinedly. McDonald managed to get off couriers to Colonel Forsyth while desperately holding the hostiles at gun range, until the colonel came thundering up at the head of six companies of cavalry. "Splendid," wrote McDonald, "beautiful order." He might well have thought so.

The combatants found themselves in Horseshoe Canyon, an extremely rough and vertical defile. Loco's men balked momentarily at the sudden appearance of three hundred regulars, and they ignited an extensive brush fire to conceal themselves as they improved their positions. Leaving one troop of cavalry to guard the horses, Forsyth deployed his small army effectively in three units, one company to assault the center and two to attack the flanks. All day the blue force ground up the canyon like an amoeba, assaulting the center to expose the flanks, then wearing down the flanks to attack the front again. The process was consumptive of time and ammunition, and it was wretchedly hot and thirsty work. Repeatedly Loco gave ground only to regroup on a higher ridge. By the end of the day Forsyth held the canyon, and had lost three dead and four wounded. The hostile Apaches melted away, less thirteen horses but otherwise none the worse for the encounter. Forsyth's prize, the canyon, was useless, and he pulled back to rest his command as the hostiles filtered down to the Tsoka-ne-nde home range, the Chiricahua Mountains, where they mauled a tent city of prospectors before swarming down into Mexico.

Their escape from San Carlos had taken a week. They had fought like ghosts, disappearing here and materializing there. They had demoralized the army and cut down dozens of pindahs while raking in a fortune in food, supplies, and ammunition. And now they would have been safe in the Sierra Madres, except for the determination of two tough-skinned veteran horse captains, Tullius C. Tupper, 6th Cavalry, and William A. Rafferty, 4th Cavalry.

At the time of the Chiricahua raid on the mining camp these two officers' units were nearest the scene of the action, and on hearing of the attack they took their columns on a chase southward with strike-force speed and iron determination. All that night and the next day they maintained a punishing pace, pausing to rest only once, when Al Sieber and his scouts lost the trail briefly. They were back in the saddle before dawn April 27, and when it became apparent they could not overtake the renegades before they crossed the border, they elected to plunge illegally into Mexico after them. The scouts finally found them camped about twenty miles deep into that country, just east of the Sonora–Chihuahua line near a low ridge of hills. Tupper's simple but effective strategy was to attack the rancheria frontally with his two companies of cavalry, driving the hostiles back into the low hills where he knew they would take refuge, and where he would leave his two scout companies waiting for them. The trap was prematurely tripped, however; as the scouts were sneaking into position in the wee hours of April 28 they were discovered by four mescal gatherers, who were quickly shot dead before they could spread the alarm. Among the dead was a son of Chief Loco. Once they started shooting, the scouts blasted an estimated eight hundred rounds into the rancheria in less than five minutes, as the cavalry hastened up somewhat before they were ready.

In spite of this blunder, the White Mountain scouts acquitted themselves commendably in most of their clashes. One of them later said his father-in-law called him by his given name during a fight. To call any Apache warrior by his name in battle had a profound effect on him, but this was increased when done by his wife's father. "While we were shooting at the Chiricahuas," he said, "my father-in-law called me by my real name, even though I was married to his daughter. This was in battle. 'You are enlisted as a scout, so go to these Chiricahua now and fight them.' When he said that, I got up and started running for the bluff where the enemy were, as fast as I could. There were little winds around my legs as I ran.[5] Three of us started up then, my father-in-law, myself, and another man."

A half dozen of Loco's people were killed in the first firing and the chief himself was wounded, but the positions of the scouts and soldiers were very hastily chosen, and according to Chief of Scouts Sieber, if the renegades had not panicked, they could have defeated the Tupper command handily. But in their frightened reaction they shot too high for the range and failed to do much damage. However, the hostiles had selected the site of their camp with sufficient care that they had no need to seek the protection of the hills to defend themselves, and once Tupper understood he could not overrun them, he withdrew, being sent off by an explosive barrage from the rancheria that cost him one dead and one wounded. His men were also desperately low on ammunition, and as he had managed to secure several dozen of Loco's horses and mules, he called off the fight.

Shortly after Tupper took his bone-weary men into camp he was joined by Colonel Forsyth and his force, who had followed their trail south. During the last few days Forsyth had been prowling southern New Mexico, absorbing smaller, more mobile commands into his own until he rumbled along with not less than ten companies of scouts and regulars under his personal command. Because of this ego-building practice Forsyth soon found himself plodding ineffectively along cold trails, to the undisguised disgust of Chief of Scouts Sieber and other more experienced Apache fighters. But notwithstanding the growing criticism of him, Forsyth also assumed control of the Tupper-Rafferty force and energetically directed an immediate advance after the hostiles, but agreed to wait when Tupper pointed out that his men had not rested in a day and a half.

Once Tupper's men had rested, the combined army plunged deeper into Mexico, but on April 30 they met Colonel Lorenzo García and a force of 250 Mexican infantry. García informed the Americans that the Apaches, preoccupied with the trailing soldiers, had walked into an ambush he had prepared. Against the still considerable loss to himself of twenty-two dead and sixteen wounded, García claimed seventy-eight Apache dead—mostly women and children, and thirty-three captives, all women and children. The surviving Apaches had melted into their Sierra Madre lair, and García ordered Tupper and Forsyth out of the country. The border crossing had been completely illegal, but because of their fight against a common enemy the exchange with García was not unfriendly. Nevertheless, because of diplomatic repercussions no report of the affair reached Washington. It was said that Forsyth made out a report and gave it to his District commander General Mackenzie, whose experience in such matters prompted him to return it unendorsed, with the advisory to keep quiet.

García was enabled to ambush the Apaches because the scouts that Gerónimo had sent ahead, fifteen of them, had failed to report back, and after the bloodbath was ended they were discovered in the shade of a tree, smoking and talking. They were in disgrace. García had laid his ambush with sufficient skill that the Indians were not aware of it until they were completely within the cross fire. A young Apache boy who was farther back in the line of march later said, "The first thing I saw was Mexicans firing at the Apache women who were about a quarter of a mile ahead of where my mother, sister, and I were. Almost immediately Mexicans were right among us all, shooting down women and children right and left. Here and there a few Indian warriors were trying to protect us while the rest of the band were running in all directions."[6]

The majority of García's casualties came after Gerónimo fiercely rallied about thirty of his men to dig in, with some women and children who were with them, to cover the getaway of the families. The men started to shoot with a good store of ammunition, covering the women as they threw up makeshift breastworks. The Mexicans became overconfident and tried to take the position but were driven back. At one point Gerónimo's men began running low on ammunition, and an old woman volunteered to run out into the open to fetch a sack containing five hundred rounds. If she were killed it would be no great loss to the rest, an example of the elderly striving to demonstrate their usefulness to the community. The old woman dashed out into the heavy fire and returned safely with the cartridges.

When García understood he could not storm the position he ordered his men to withdraw, and forced one of his prisoners up into an exposed tree to call to Gerónimo and his men that the Mexicans had gone. It didn't work, and soon García resumed the attack, lighting a ring of fire around the small ditch where the Apaches were entrenched. Night had fallen, and with the fire burning closer the Apaches knew they had to make their move to escape. Their predicament was extreme, and some of the women in the hole with Gerónimo had with them two or three infants, and everyone knew what had to be done. After asking the permission of the women, some of the warriors choked the babies to ensure that the escape would not be foiled by sudden crying.

The battered Apaches spent a miserable night, not daring once they found a hiding place to build campfires. From there they saw the meeting between García's men and the Americans, and saw the latter turn back north. Though García had surprised them, he lacked the strength to follow them into the mountains; thus the Indians moved into higher country to regroup.

The San Carlos Raid:
NOTES

1. Betzinez, *I Fought with Geronimo*, p. 56.
2. Opler, *An Apache Life-way*, p. 189.
3. Quoted in Thrapp, *Conquest of Apacheria*, p. 242.
4. Ibid., p. 243.
5. Goodwin, *Social Organization of the Western Apache*, p. 257.
6. Betzinez, *I Fought with Geronimo*, p. 72.

Na-tio-tish

The hostile Chiricahuas with their captive Loco had been hiding in the Sierra Madre just over two months when the situation at San Carlos again boiled over. After Nakai-doklini's medicine movement was smashed the preceding September, the small group of White Mountain Apache warriors who constituted the war element soon came out of their wilderness hiding and began committing depredations. By summer they had mostly coalesced under the man Na-tio-tish, whose leadership gained considerable influence among his followers, who numbered at most sixty renegade warriors.

On July 6, 1882, some of Na-tio-tish's warriors cut down from ambush four San Carlos policemen, among them the late Albert Sterling's successor as police chief, J. L. "Cibicue Charley" Colvig, which gave that position a rather alarming mortality rate. Other whites approaching the scene, who would have fallen victim, were turned away by a friendly White Mountain Indian; they raced into the town of Globe, whose telegraph clicked out the monstrous news of more trouble on the Fort Apache Reservation. All during the Chiricahua break-in and capture of Loco's people, the army—indeed the whole country—had kept a wary and suspicious eye on the White Mountain Apaches. The Nakai-doklini trouble was still fresh in memory, and instead of the allegedly peaceful intentions of the religious movement, the country preferred instead to remember the "massacre" of General Carr and the dramatic attack upon Fort Apache. Central Arizona residents followed in disbelief the horrible torture deaths devised by Juh and his Chiricahuas, and news that Fort Apache was again aflame resulted in an unprecedented cry for protection.

During the second week in July Na-tio-tish led his sixty disaffected rowdies generally northwest through the Tonto Basin, raiding as they went. In no way did they have the sanction of the legitimate White Mountain leadership. Indeed, several of the chiefs said publicly the band was evil and could not be allowed to remain out, a refuge for "every Indian who had done a bad thing."[1] If the white people would provide troops, they pledged, they would provide scouts. The army's reaction to the Na-tio-tish band and the citizen uproar was swift and overwhelming. To engage five dozen Apaches, fourteen companies of cavalry poured from forts Apache and McDowell on the Salt, Fort Thomas southeast of San Carlos, and forts Verde and Whipple to the north up the Verde River. What was envisioned was a swift and crushing re-enactment of Crook's 1872–73 Tonto War.

By the middle of the month the Na-tio-tish group was trekking upstream on Cherry Creek to the Mogollon Rim, intending to reach General Springs, the much-used water hole on "Crook's Trail" between Fort Verde and Fort Apache. As they scrambled up the mighty cliff the Apaches saw in the distance that they were being trailed by a single troop of cavalry (it was Captain Adna R. Chaffee's company of the 6th), and laid an ambush. Continuing on seven miles north of General Springs to where a fork of East Clear Creek cut a narrow and precipitous gorge into the rim, Na-tio-tish's men hid themselves on the far side and waited.

What Na-tio-tish did not suspect was that Chaffee was guided by the superbly experienced Al Sieber, fresh from Tupper's Mexican adventure. Himself undetected, Sieber discovered the trap and warned the troops. Neither did Na-tio-tish learn that during the night of the sixteenth Chaffee's lone company was reinforced by four more from Fort Apache, two of the 6th and two of the 3rd, under Major A. W. Evans. The troops attacked early on the seventeenth. Evans, though superior to Chaffee in rank, let the latter conduct the operation; Chaffee had found the Indians, of course, but it was still a gentlemanly act to occur in an army where promotions rested primarily on skill and experience at killing Indians. Chaffee's tactics were uncomplicated, but they worked to perfection. With one company of cavalry he opened fire from the rim facing the Apaches, and while keeping the hostiles busy there, he split the remaining four cavalry troops, dividing the Indian scouts between them, sending them two companies upstream and two downstream, to sneak across the canyon and smash the Apaches from both sides. It was believed that every last warrior was wounded; from sixteen to twenty-seven were killed, including Na-tio-tish. The survivors drifted back to the reservation, never to rebel again.

The engagement became known as the Battle of Big Dry Wash, even though the canyon did contain water in the branch of East Clear Creek. Except for fights against the Mimbres and other Chiricahuas concealed in the Sierra Madre, it was the last battle ever fought between army regulars and Apache Indians.

Big Dry Wash also marked one of the few times that white soldiers fought and bested Apaches in actual battle, but this was mainly because "it was one of the few instances in which Apaches allowed themselves to be drawn into conventional battle."[2] But more than that, Na-tio-tish seems to have been a war leader of inferior capabilities. In the first place, after committing to the warpath, instead of fleeing to Mexico and comparative safety, he led his warriors into the Tonto Basin, a region ringed with forts and camps in which there was no possibility of escape or concealment. Tribal factionalism probably played a part in this; for Na-tio-tish's White Mountain rebels to have sought refuge in the Sierra Madre with the Chiricahuas might easily have rekindled the inter-band strife that was a large part of the San Carlos trouble to begin with. But Crook had demonstrated ten years earlier that Indians raiding in the Tonto Basin could be trapped and crushed.

In preparing to ambush Chaffee, Na-tio-tish was not hard pressed, and if he was outnumbered it was only barely so. He should have kept Chaffee's camp under surveillance during the night to ensure that he was not reinforced, and if he were, that the Indians could slip away without being drawn into a fight. During the battle at Big Dry Wash Na-tio-tish allowed four companies of cavalry, an aggregate of two hundred men, plus scouts, to cross the canyon undetected. In both cases, by Apache standards, Na-tio-tish had men to spare as lookouts, but did not use them. Thus, while a large part of the criticism of Na-tio-tish is from the benefit of hindsight, and while the White Mountains generally did not have the same expertise in war as the three Chiricahua groups, Na-tio-tish himself simply did not have that almost demonic instinct for war that characterized the really capable leaders like Victorio and Nana, and increasingly, Gerónimo.

Na-tio-tish:
NOTES

1. Quoted in Thrapp, Conquest of Apacheria, p. 254.
2. Utley, Frontier Regulars, p. 387.

The Gray Fox

On July 14, 1882, three days before the decisive action at Big Dry Wash, orders were issued relieving Orlando Willcox as commanding general of the Arizona Department. The feeling against him had been on the upswing for some time, both in and out of the army. Citizen discontent with his management led to an ever increasing rash of local "ranger" forces that fared no better against marauding Apaches than he did. General Sherman had castigated him for mishandling the Nakai-doklini trouble, for which Willcox laid the blame on, and court-martialed, General Carr; Willcox was continuing to discredit himself with self-righteous grabbing at straws of vindication. The few successes in the field during his tenure were mostly the result of quick thinking by those under fire; Willcox himself in the field against Apaches was almost a joke, and his confused and ambiguous orders kept his columns moving for the most part in ineffectual stabs and chases. Sherman, while on an inspection tour of Arizona, was almost caught in the middle of the Camp Goodwin raid that lost Loco and his people to the hostiles, and that seemed to seal Willcox's fate. His replacement was no stranger to the territory: George Crook, Department commander from 1871 to 1875, was returning to have another go.

Crook arrived at Whipple Barracks and assumed command on September 4, defining his mission in his *Résumé* as of three objectives: to bring the reservation Indians under control, protect the lives and property of the citizenry, and defeat the remaining hostiles in the Sierra Madre.

Easier said than done, he knew, but he set to work with his customary methodology, his first attention going to the Apaches still at San Carlos. Assisted by his protégé and aide since the beginning of his first Arizona duty, Lieutenant John G. Bourke, Crook within a week of his return held exhaustive meetings with the Western Apaches at Fort Apache, even going into their rancherias to hear their version of how the agencies had been run. The Indians told him a horror story that put him in uncontainable anger, but deepened his understanding of how suffering and discontent could give rise to an outbreak. "Bad as Indians often are," he wrote hotly, "I have never yet seen one so demoralized that he was not an example . . . to the wretches who enrich themselves by plundering him of the little our Government appropriates for him."[1]

By shocking coercion the San Carlos agents—and Crook included their current one, Tiffany, among the worst—had forced the Apaches to buckle under to rations that sometimes amounted to one cup of flour per adult per week, and about as much meat, while their crops of corn and melons were destroyed to increase their dependence upon the agent. Blankets and other supplies shipped for issuance to the Indians were undisguisedly sold in nearby towns as the agent's private property, and the reservation boundaries had been adjusted five times, each time to remove Indian claim to a particularly good piece of land. Affairs had declined a long way since John Clum ran San Carlos, and the wonder was not that a man like Na-tio-tish gained followers, but that the White Mountain chiefs still refused open resistance. Lieutenant Bourke, who participated in meetings with more than a hundred of the Apaches, agreed that, seemingly, "the Great Father would send in ten regiments to carry out the schemes of the [Indian] ring, but he would never send one honest, truthful man to inquire whether the Apaches had a story or not."[2] Now, fortunately, the scandal caught the attention, and wrath, of a remarkable Secretary of the Interior, German-born Civil War general and pioneering conservationist Carl Schurz. In a rage he swept the Indian Office clean, reportedly giving the commissioner himself one hour to gather his personal effects, and restaffed it top to bottom.

The new agent at San Carlos was P. P. Wilcox, and General Crook lost no time in calling on him, ready to bluff and bully him into submission, but to his surprise Wilcox proved amenable from the start to Crook's design of stationing troops on the reservations and assuming partial control of the Indians. In fact, P. P. Wilcox proved such a just agent to the Apaches that the Indian Ring soon started moving against him, and Crook, to his honor, helped fight them off. Normally the Apaches would have opposed the scheme to quarter troops in their midst, but so great was Crook's show of indignation at their past treatment that they trusted him to work for their benefit, and Crook proved his good faith by winning for the White Mountains the right to return to their home territory in the lofty ranges above Fort Apache. Thus, for Crook, the government was breaking down even its detested concentration policy, and the Western Apaches sensed perhaps a broad change in their fortunes. Then, too, they undoubtedly remembered what the Gray Fox could do to them if he were angry, but still Crook was not wrong to report late in the month that the agency Indians were pacified.

To represent him at the agencies Crook resumed his policy of stationing officers answerable only to him personally, and after interviewing all his officers, just as he had in 1871, he selected efficient and capable men, each of whom had either commendable experience with handling Apaches or an exceptional aptitude for it. In selecting officers to command the Apache scouts Crook kept in mind that the Indians placed paramount importance on the physical condition of their leaders. They themselves would not follow weak or infirm men into war. An Apache "cares very little about our idea of rank," he wrote. "Efficiency, and efficiency only, is what he looks for in the man who is to lead him on the war-path. Their leaders necessarily have to be of the best physique, in robust health, capable of enduring great fatigue, of undisputed courage, of great patience, good judgment and discretion. The commanders of Indian scouts have therefore, as a rule, been selected from the younger officers, whose health is still unimpaired and whose ambition is a guiding motive, rather than from officers of more experience, upon whose vigor and energy the effects of long service have began [sic] to tell."[3] To control the Indians at Fort Apache Crook dispatched Charles B. Gatewood; he was something of an exception to the requirement for robust health, but he had commanded Apache scouts since the Victorio campaign and was a good man with his Indians; at Apache he was to be assisted by Lieutenant Hamilton Roach. To manage the San Carlos agglomeration of bands he sent Lieutenant Britton Davis, who had just entered the service with his West Point commission. In one sense Davis' memory of Indians went back further than most other officers', however. His father, E. J. Davis, was the Reconstruction governor of Texas who had paroled the marauding Kiowa chiefs Santana and Big Tree in 1873. From his childhood Britton Davis had evinced an intense curiosity about and respect for Indians, and Crook was willing to let him get his fill as a scout commander. To oversee the entire operation, stationed in San Carlos, Crook detailed Emmet Crawford, a captain in the 3rd Cavalry.

To govern the Apaches Crook issued a series of orders that were exemplary of his philosophy of Indian management. Against hostiles he was a relentless and terrible foe, but to the Indians who tried to make a genuine go of it on the reservation he was a staunch and tireless friend. "Officers and soldiers serving in this department," he admonished, "are reminded that one of the fundamental principles of the military character is justice to all—Indians as well as white men—and that a disregard of this principle is likely to bring about hostilities, and cause the death of the very persons they are sent here to protect. In all their dealings with the Indians, officers must be careful not only to observe the strictest fidelity, but to make no promises not in their power to carry out. . . . Each officer will be held to a strict accountability . . . that Indians evincing a desire to enter upon a career of peace shall have no cause for complaint through hasty or injudicious acts of the military."[4]

The four officers renewed Crook's previously tried methods of Indian management: census records and metal identification tags, planted spies ("Confidential Indians" Crook called them; Britton Davis called them his Secret Service), the recruitment of Indian scouts who lived with their people when not on duty, and most importantly, a "judicious exercise of firmness tempered by honesty, justice, tact, and patience."[5] Aside from the inherent "rightness" of a good-faith-oriented Indian policy, its most important advantage lay in cracking tribal solidarity of opposition to white control and engendering factions within the Apache rancherias favorable to Crook. Probably the most objectionable portion of the scheme was the hanging on the Indians of the metal tag-bands to identify them. The dehumanizing census method was not done away with officially until 1913, and continued in some cases for forty years past that date.

Still mindful that one requirement of winning the Apaches' confidence was to trust them first with responsibility, Crook continued his field meetings with huge gatherings of them, through October and into November. He told them he knew the San Carlos area was too small to subsist them all, and chiefs who wished to take their bands to more productive areas of the reservation would be permitted to do so, and would be responsible for their conduct. He told them he was removing the bulk of the soldiers from their reservation and that the Apache Police would be reformed (it had fallen into disrepair after the Nakai-doklini trouble), and they should keep order among themselves. The Apaches responded favorably, but expressed distrust of their agent Wilcox, or any other agent they should be sent, until Crook gave Wilcox his personal endorsement.

But the Apaches would not be entirely on their own; the hundreds of Indians listened soberly as the Gray Fox told them he would be keeping his eye on them, and if any of them wanted to go to war they had better leave while the going was good, and he would settle accounts with them later. Crook also reinforced the previous bans on the manufacture of tizwin and tula-pah, and renewed the stricture against beating wives or slitting the noses of wives caught in or suspected of adultery. This second provision, especially, seems now to have been of obvious propriety, but in reality it was still a serious interference with the Apache Life-way. John Clum was nearly killed when he tried to tell Des-a-lin how to treat his wives, and Crook's similar directions would cause a great deal of trouble later on.

Nevertheless, by the advent of the 1882–83 winter Crook had the San Carlos and Fort Apache reservations fairly well in hand, and he turned his attention to the Chiricahuas laired south of the border. By this time the renegades in the Sierra Madre had repaired far to the south, to the headwaters of the Yaquí River, a country of rugged clefts and gorges. After the hostiles had taken Loco and his people back south with them the Apache population in Mexico was greater than it had been in a long time, and the

Indians resumed the ages-old cycle of trading massacres with the Mexicans.

During the summer of 1882 the renegades attempted on one occasion to make a peace accord with the citizens of the town of Casas Grandes, in Chihuahua. "I think that Geronimo was responsible for this," one of the Apaches related, "his motive being to get whiskey."[6] A woman who spoke Spanish was sent into the town to bring back the leading men for a council, at which the Mexicans professed their willingness to forget the past and live at peace. Juh and Gerónimo and several other men went into town for a monstrous drunk, and for two days there was no sign of treachery. Then the women and children came in. On the third night the Indians were bedded down outside the town walls, near a stream, many of them passed out. In the pre-dawn gloom an organized band of Mexicans crept into their midst and started killing. Before the hung-over Apaches could awaken and flee, between twelve and fifteen men were killed and thirty or forty women and children captured. There was some evidence later that the prisoners were killed in a public free-for-all of an execution in the town plaza, but these might also have been prisoners taken in the earlier García fight. But whether they were killed or sold, the surviving Apaches never saw most of the prisoners again, and among the lost were a wife of Gerónimo, and Chatto's family.

The Nde-nda-i and other Chiricahuas, in turn, made things very hot for the isolated ranches and villages of Chihuahua and Sonora, the Arizona newspapers reporting regularly on the fierce depredations and speculating on how long it would take the renegades to return to the United States. While the winter was actually fairly quiet in the American Southwest, Chihuahua state suffered heavily from raids along the eastern slope of the Sierra Madre. Around the first of December a sizable war party under Juh and Gerónimo stole horses from the village of Galeana, not far from Casas Grandes, for the purpose of drawing the small soldier garrison out into an ambush. The Mexicans predictably fell into the trap. One of the warriors, at this time a novice carrying the drinking tube and scratching stick, later recalled that "As the Mexicans swept past the ravine our detachments hidden there came out and began attacking the enemy from the rear. Then when the Mexicans were within range of our main body they were heavily fired upon from the front. Their commander saw that they . . . had been decoyed too far, maybe eight miles from the safety of Galeana. . . . Meantime the Indians rode behind another knoll. Here they dismounted and turned their horses over to a few apprentices. I was one of the latter. We horseholders were able to peer over the hill and watch the whole attack from short range."[7]

At the first blinding fusillade the Mexican troops dug in on a low hill to make a fight of it, but the Apaches approached nearer and nearer, employing the unique strategy of crawling along the ground, each man rolling a head-sized rock before him to protect him from the Mexicans' fire. Finally they got so close that they staged a rush, and twenty-one of the soldiers were killed. One fled afoot back toward town. He could easily have been dropped, but Gerónimo prevailed upon the others to let him go, for the purpose of bringing out another group of soldiers to ambush. Incredibly, this scheme, too, worked, and soon another squadron of troops came storming out of Galeana. By the time they arrived at the scene of the massacre the Apaches had mounted their stolen stock, and when the Mexicans caught sight of them they dismounted and began feverishly digging rifle pits. Instead of attacking, the Apache warriors seated themselves on the hillside, in plain sight of the soldiers, and chuckled quietly among themselves at the scared fools below. It was nearly sunset, and they did not like night fighting. After dark they filtered back into the mountains, having lost only two dead and partially avenged the Casas Grandes slaughter. But as they had suffered losses, they held no victory dance. Later they learned that the major in command of the Mexican troops had been a leader at the Victorio fight under General Terrazas, which gave the Indians added satisfaction with the victory.

The prospect of renewed Chiricahua violence worried General Crook mightily, and though he traveled to southern Arizona and sent his Indian scouts in small groups sneaking through the Sierra Madre to try to contact them and induce their return to the reservation, he felt deep within himself that he would have to lead a campaign south of the border to whip them into submission. His projected operations in Mexico would be legal, because of a limited "hot-pursuit" treaty with Mexico signed on July 29, 1882, after a long delay.

Going into the new year, 1883, reports of hostile activity increased, some of the stories being true, most of them either entirely false or blown far out of proportion. From the emotional and continuous coverage given the Apaches in Mexico, the question of Indian Ring influence again arises, but in Chihuahua the situation was indeed serious enough to prompt Governor General Terrazas to sign an authorization to enlist civilian militia to engage the Chiricahuas wherever they could be struck. The policy yielded a result in late January, when the militia of the mountain village of Temósachic attacked a rancheria that proved to be Juh's camp. A dozen or so of the renegades were killed, including Juh's wife; his only daughter was desperately wounded. More than thirty Apaches were taken prisoner and nearly ninety head of stock captured. Juh counterattacked and killed six Mexicans, but failed to regain his captive people. It was learned later that the defeat caused a split among Juh's surviving followers, which suggests that perhaps the fat old chief was becoming more skilled at downing his beloved aguardiente than at choosing defensible campsites. At any rate, Juh left the main band and lived by himself, leaving his kinsman and personal partner Gerónimo in charge of the rancheria.

By well into the spring of 1883 Crook had laid in enough rations, forage, and war matériel to mount a major offensive as soon as he acquired two things he considered imperative: a sudden reappearance of the Chiricahuas in Arizona to give him the needed "hot pursuit" excuse, and a guide from the hostile rancherias who knew the Sierra Madre, a mountain range that was, if anything, more rugged and vertical than the worst Arizona had to offer. He was not long in waiting for the first, as in March of 1883 the Sierra Madre bands initiated two raids of uncommon size. One, led by Gerónimo, rode southwest into Sonora to steal stock. Chatto, Benito, and a chief named Chihuahua led the other, an ammunition-gathering foray into the United States. It was fortunate that Crook's principal objective was an excuse to cross the border, because he never came close to touching Chatto while he was in the country, and that leader took his men on a hard-riding blitz that threw the citizens into near hysteria and humiliated the army.

Chatto crossed the line southwest of Tombstone, attacking four white men at a charcoal camp near Charleston, killing three. Immediately thereafter his band set upon another camp, killing one more. There was a tent in this camp, and Chatto's men positioned themselves behind a close-by corral and shouted in both English and Spanish for anyone inside to surrender. There was no sign of movement from the tent, however, and two of the raiders, partners, one named Tzo-e (or alternatively, Bariotish), and the other a former scout named Beneactiney, approached it warily. When they got too close a rifle cracked, dropping Beneactiney; Tzo-e dove for cover and made his way back to the others, and the party moved off without further fighting. The man in the tent, a local resident named Childs, was glad to see them go.

Within a couple of days at least eight more whites had fallen victim, including three workers at a mine called, with appropriate local color, the Total Wreck, and several dozen head of stock had been stolen. The people around Tombstone were almost lathered in terror and the newspapers shrieked for protection from the army. Crook agreed willingly that this was "the worst band of Indians in the country," but gently reminded those within hearing that he had wanted to corral the Chiricahuas in 1872, but they had been given instead to General Howard and Tom Jeffords.

For a time it was feared that Chatto's warriors would raid San Carlos for ammunition and possibly recruits, but that never developed, and the army officers in charge of the reservation expressed no little surprise when the rancherias of the "disarmed" Western Apaches disgorged impressive caches of weaponry to fight off the Chiricahuas if they did show. As Chatto's band swept past San Carlos, one of their number announced he was quitting and returning to the reservation. It was Tzo-e. He and Beneactiney had been companions in a degree that was remarkable even for Apache partners. Tzo-e was unable to shake off the grief; he had no more heart for raiding and was going in. Doubtless the others in the band tried to talk him out of it, but if Tzo-e's medicine had told him to do it, then it was not their place to accuse him of cowardice or treason. He left, alone, with no hard feelings; some of Chatto's men even gave him some things he might need when he settled down. (It might also be noted that Tzo-e was himself of White Mountain extraction. He had married into Chatto's group but was not, reportedly, overly fond of his wife's people. Neither had he been too keen on raiding, but he had performed well, and had been wounded in the García fight.)

Instead of continuing north to the reservations, the rampaging hostiles swung eastward when they reached the Gila, crossed into New Mexico, then turned back south through the soaring country of the Tci-he-nde. Between Lordsburg and Silver City they committed a depredation that genuinely stunned the country. Their victims in this case were federal judge and noted legal authority H. C. McComas, and his socially prominent wife. The couple was attacked while traveling by wagon on the main road; their six-year-old son, Charlie, was taken captive. An extensive and somewhat sensational manhunt failed to find any trace of him, and a massive dragnet of both army troops and civilian volunteers failed to intercept the renegades before they had stormed back south into Mexico. In less than a week the couple of dozen Chiricahuas had killed an equal number of whites, garnered a handy supply of stock and ammunition, and were never touched, though their wake of destruction trailed over four hundred miles. Truly it was a raider's raid.

Three days after Tzo-e left his band he was picked up by the San Carlos Apache Police while camped about twelve miles from the agency. As Britton Davis related the story, Davis had gone to bed on the night of March 30, but was awakened about midnight by the squeak of his door hinges. As he made out the form of an armed Indian slipping into his bedroom he fingered his pistol and demanded an identification. It was one of his "Secret Service" Indians, who said tersely, "Chiricahua come."[8] Thinking that it was the long expected invasion, Davis leaped from his bed, rousted out his chief of scouts, Sam Bowman, and was on the trail to the located camp with nearly forty of the San Carlos policemen and Tonto auxiliaries. Before dawn they rushed the camp and, somewhat to their relief, found only the one man, Tzo-e, who just smiled. Davis took him back to San Carlos and shackled him for interrogation. Tzo-e freely told all he knew, and Davis telegraphed it on to Crook, who was in the southern part of the territory readying his expedition. Part of the information Tzo-e gave was that most of the Apaches who were out wanted to surrender but the main leaders wouldn't let them; Crook was aware of the circumstances of the Loco breakout, and was not surprised to learn that Loco, too, wanted to come back in, and was living with his people some distance removed from the real fire-eaters, not joining in the depredations and tortures. At once Crook saw his opportunity, and telegraphed Davis to ask Tzo-e if he would guide the soldiers to his people and get them to surrender, too. To Crook's joy, Tzo-e said yes, and soon found himself on the way, still in chains, to the general's bivouac in the southeastern corner of the territory. When Crook and his men saw him they were struck by his open, sensitive, handsome face and his light—extraordinarily fair for an Indian—complexion. The soldiers gave him an appropriate nickname that stayed with him for good: Peaches.[9] It was said that when Crook ordered Tzo-e's chains removed, the warrior-turned-guide offered to wear them until he had proven himself trustworthy. Crook freed him nonetheless, appreciative of the good attributes of this remarkable young Indian.

The Gray Fox:
NOTES

1. Quoted in Bourke, On the Border, p. 445.
2. Ibid., p. 438. For an excellent precis of Tiffany's career, see Worcester, The Apaches, pp. 359–61.
3. Crook, "The Apache Problem," pp. 263–64.
4. General Orders No. 43, Department of Arizona, Oct. 5, 1882, quoted in Thrapp, Conquest of Apacheria, p. 260.
5. Utley, Frontier Regulars, p. 388.
6. Betzinez, I Fought with Geronimo, p. 77.
7. Ibid., p. 94.
8. Davis, The Truth About Geronimo, p. 57.
9. The name Peaches could, however, stem from a corruption of another rendition of his Apache name, Pe-nal-tishu. Lummis, General Crook and the Apache Wars, p. vi.

The Mexican Invasion, 1883

Before Crook could get away to Mexico he had several lesser business items to deal with at home, not the least of which was a threatened citizen invasion of San Carlos. The awesome swiftness and voracity of Chatto's and Chihuahua's free-wheeling raid across the Southwest had put the settlers in unparalled frenzy. The people of Tombstone had taken a particular battering, and in heavily attended public rallies they organized a force of rangers to deal with the problem. Unready to go trailing off into the Sierra Madre lair, however, they determined to vent their wrath upon the Apaches at San Carlos, who, the territorial newspapers kept insisting, were just as bad anyway. Crook sympathized with their frustration but knew he had to stop them. A Camp Grant-style massacre of San Carlos Apaches would have ignited an Indian war that no number of troops could have quelled, so when word was received that the Tombstone rangers were out, Crook alerted all his forces and ordered their arrest on sight. There is no mention of it, but one hopes that his thoughts turned at least briefly to Royal Whitman.

According to both lieutenants Bourke and Davis, the Tombstone ranger expedition fizzled on a par with the other territorial ranger forces. Davis compared them to a celebrated posse of rangers from the town of Globe, noting that they were "under the same or a better brand of stimulant."[1] Just as the rangers entered the reservation, the massacre exploded when "they met with an old Indian who was gathering mescal for a mescal bake. They fired at him, but fortunately missed. He fled north and they fled south." Davis was being perhaps a bit unfair toward their bravery; to their confused way of thinking the old Indian might have been trying to lure them into an ambuscade, from which, in their minds, they were wise enough to escape. Bourke agreed with Davis that the force broke up when they exhausted their supply of liquor—or as he put it, the scheme "expired of thirst."[2]

Under the terms of the July convention, Crook had to warn the Mexican authorities that he contemplated a border crossing in pursuit of hostiles, and to that effect he telegraphed all the Mexican line generals on their northern frontier, but received no replies. He had to take time out to clamber aboard a train and personally call on Governors Torres of Sonora and Terrazas of Chihuahua, and important garrison commanders, and win their promise that if he did cross they would not harass his movements. He believed he succeeded in this, and hoped that it would satisfy General Sherman, who had been repeatedly cautioning him not to cause an international incident while operating south of or even along the border. But, trusting the good faith of the Mexican army as well as generous loopholes in the treaty, Crook was ready to start out by the last week in April 1883. He spent the last few days moving men and supplies from Willcox station to his border bivouac, and his force finally struck out on May 1, as large a command as he could expect to be manageable in the rugged Sierra Madre. He had with him only one cavalry troop, I Company of the 6th, mounting forty-two regulars. His main reliance was on the 193 Indian scouts, an agglomeration of White Mountain, Tonto, and Chiricahua Apaches augmented by Mojaves and Yumas, under the direction of Emmet Crawford, Charles Gatewood, Al Sieber, and Archie MacIntosh. And, of course, there was his ace in the hole, Peaches.

Although the scouts worked in co-operation with the pindahs, they retained much of their tribal way; they made medicine before going out on service, and in this instance the Chiricahua scouts held a war dance that was notable for its emphasis on the individuals who were going out. The singer, it was reported, "called to a certain man by name. He said, 'C., you are a man. You are known to be a great warrior. You have fought your enemies in close battle. We are calling on you to dance.' As soon as he said this, C. had his gun ready. He sprang out there, shooting into the air. Then they kept singing and called another name and another until four or five were out there dancing.

"The women were at the war dance. But they didn't dance or mix with the men. They stayed about six or eight yards away in a circle around the fire. They made that noise they make in the big tepee at the girl's puberty ceremony. At this war dance the women are all called White Painted Woman. . . . And the men are all called Child of the Water."[3]

Crook's five pack trains carried over two months' rations; each man carried forty rounds of ammunition and had 160 more rounds in the trains. Once under way they were gone six silent weeks, disappeared into the womb of what are among the toughest mountains anywhere, and as the silence lengthened, terrible speculation went on as to their fate. Rumors filtered back, all of them seemingly making headlines in the Arizona papers, of terrible massacres that had Crook the victim of, alternately, hostile attacks and mutinies by his nearly two hundred scouts. But the army high command discounted them hopefully and awaited real news.

In early May a genuine fight was reported by the governor of Sonora, General Luis Torres. The official version had Torres, in conjunction with Lorenzo García and three hundred Mexican regulars, attacking and over-running the great, secreted stronghold of Juh and Gerónimo, and carrying the field after delivering a blistering defeat to the renegades. Not long after, one of Crook's detachments inspected the battlefield and reported it certain that "the Indians had enticed the Mexicans into an ambuscade, killed a number with bullets and rocks, and put the rest to . . . flight." One of the men in Gerónimo's camp later said that after the ambush the fight was very difficult, and the Mexicans fought with courage but lost. According to Lieutenant Bourke, Peaches, when told the Mexican side of the affair, "smiled quietly, but said nothing."[4]

For two days after entering Mexico the Crook force made good time, covering thirty miles in two days, when they struck the Bavispe River, just at the point where the stream makes a broad, north-facing bend, with one fork leading southwest, downstream, to its confluence with the Yaquí, the other southeast, upstream, into the heart of the Sierra Madre. Crook took the latter route, reaching the town of Bavispe two days later. Even as soon as this the scouts began to uncover hostile sign in the form of old trails. At the next town south of Bavispe, Bacerac, Sieber and some of the others took advantage of the opportunity to make a last fling, and went on a rolling Saturday night mescal drunk in town, but Crook soon had them rounded up and back on their way. Since the third day the country had become progressively more rugged, the trails steeper and the air thinner and hotter as they gained steadily in altitude. Signs of the renegade presence began to grow fresher, the scouts locating butchered carcasses of animals slaughtered for food along broad trails made as the stolen herds were driven along. After a week they were deep into Mexico, skirting the Continental Divide; frequently the men had to dismount and climb afoot, leading their horses. Mules lost their footing and fell struggling down the mountainsides. (One of the pack animals carried over with him plates and chemicals belonging to A. Frank Randall. The famous photographer had won permission to accompany the expedition, but never got the chance to take pictures. A few days into Mexico, Randall proudly captured an owl and tied him to his saddle. The scouts were mortified, and refused to go another step until Crook made Randall free the terrible being. One wonders what the scouts' thoughts might have been to see then his mule plummet squealing from a precipice.) A few days more and ten miles became a successful day's march. About a week and a half into the march Crook sent his scouts to cast about in the mountains to contact the hostiles. His instructions to Crawford were simple: if they found a rancheria and held the advantage, attack and kill as many of the men as they could. If they were at a disadvantage, attack and hold while sending for the main body. In no event were the scouts to kill women or children deliberately, and captives were to be treated with scrupulous care.

On May 15 a courier brought Crook a message that Crawford's scouts had crossed a very fresh renegade trail; he was cutting loose from his pack trains to take after them, and Crook should lie low until Crawford communicated again. And he added a postscript to the note: "I don't think the Indians know we are in the country." Crook co-operated, and soon a second messenger arrived with the advisory that they had struck the Indians, but one of the scouts had sprung the trap prematurely, the hostiles had bolted, and they were in hot pursuit. Crook was to follow along with all possible haste, guided by Crawford's courier.

Crook followed, and by early afternoon he and his command could hear rifle fire in the distance, but before they could reach the scene it had stopped. Before sunset a weary Crawford came into Crook's camp. Seven renegades were dead, he said, and he had in tow four children, one the daughter of Naiche, and a young woman, the daughter of Chief Benito. Also in the rancheria, although Crawford was unaware of it, had been six-year-old Charlie McComas, son of the judge killed in the Chatto raid. Since his capture he had learned to speak some Apache and, according to one of the renegades, was well on his way to becoming assimilated into the tribe. During Crawford's attack, however, one of the Apaches killed was a certain old woman, whose son then in a rage stoned the little boy. Chihuahua's daughter witnessed the incident, but never divulged the secret, answering questions about Charlie's fate by speculating idly that he must have run away.[5]

To Crook, Benito's daughter confessed that most of the hostiles genuinely wanted to come in, and there had been a council that considered sending two people in to San Carlos to try to arrange terms. To the young woman Crook retained the image of the Gray Fox, who would as soon kill Indians as talk, but inwardly his heart leaped. He gave some food to Benito's daughter and the eldest boy of the children, and told them they could go back out and find their people. If they truly wanted peace they could come in to him and not be harmed; he would wait for three days before coming after them again.

At noon the next day two Chiricahua women came timidly into Crook's camp; three hours later came two more, and other women could be seen peering over the cliffs to observe their fate. Among those who ventured in was the sister of Chihuahua, who told the general that the chief would come in the next morning. True to her word, Chihuahua entered camp on the morning of the eighteenth; he had a long interview with Crook, and was satisfied to the extent that he went back out and returned before dark with his entire following. By noon of May 19 Crook held in custody one hundred Chiricahuas.

By a combination of guts, determination, and bluff Crook was winning an impressive victory, but he had also received help from another factor, about which he was soon to learn: Chihuahua and the marginally hostile had been able to surrender because Gerónimo and the hard-core fighters were not there to stop them. They had left on a raid in the direction of Chihuahua City, their purpose being to take captives with which to bargain for the return of Chiricahuas taken in the treacherous Casas Grandes massacre. A remarkable event occurred as the hostiles, with Mexican prisoners in tow, were returning to their people. A few apprentice warriors were with the Gerónimo group, and one of them, named Batsinas, had, according to his regimen, cooked the evening meal for the others. As Gerónimo was eating he dropped his knife and in a stunned voice announced that their women and children had been taken captive. It was one example of the di-yin chief's clairvoyance that kept his following in no little awe of him. They rode hard back northward, and at one point Gerónimo said, "Tomorrow afternoon as we march along the north side of the mountains we will see a man standing on a hill to our left. He will howl to us and tell us that the troops have captured our base camp." The event occurred just as he predicted. There was no way Gerónimo could have been receiving information not readily visible to the other Apaches. Batsinas, who lived to be a very old man and became a devout Christian, never retreated from his belief that Gerónimo had harnessed a great power.[6]

At a quarter of nine in the morning of May 20, General Crook's scouts suddenly began shrieking and howling as they grabbed their arms and took cover in the trees; when Crook and the other officers demanded to know the cause, the scouts pointed upward. There, on the cliff edge more than a thousand feet above, stood the war di-yin Gerónimo and his fighters.

The renegades called down into the camp, asking if Chihuahua's people were all right, and inquiring whether they would be permitted to come in for a council with Crook. Once permission was given, the warriors came stealthily into the camp from all directions, ready to flee at the first sign of treachery. When Gerónimo finally appeared he had a very short interview with Crook, who deliberately maintained a cold and hateful attitude toward him. In a second talk Gerónimo told his version of the wicked agents who had misruled his people, confessed he wanted to surrender, and would do so if Crook could guarantee that no more wrongs would be done them by the whites. Crook replied sharply that Gerónimo had the choice of war or peace and that was all. Crook had already proven himself sympathetic to the problem of wicked men running the agencies, but he also knew the value of truculent bluff when dealing with hostiles. Gerónimo said with candor that he could fight indefinitely against the Mexicans, even saving ammunition and killing them with rocks (meaning presumably by luring them into landslide ambushes), but once the Gray Fox came, guided by his own people, he knew he must either make terms or die fighting. Crook said little else, and Gerónimo promised to return the next day for further talk.

General Crook knew that he was playing boldly for high stakes; what he did not know was, he nearly overplayed his hand. Gerónimo wanted very much to surrender, but was shocked by Crook's intransigence. At a council that night, the frustrated di-yin put forward an alternative plan, to invite Crook's White Mountain Apache scouts to a big social dance, there to ambush and kill as many of them as they could and flee. What probably saved Crook's scouts was the fact that Gerónimo's father-in-law had ties with the White Mountains, and refused to back him. Gerónimo insisted, and was dressed down in a manner that was perhaps the exclusive privilege of an Apache father-in-law: "You chiefs don't mean anything to me. I have been with you many times and helped you kill lots of Mexicans and whites, and that's the way you got the clothes you are wearing now. I am the one who has killed these people for you, and you have just followed behind me. I don't want to hear you talking this way again."[7] One cannot imagine anyone other than a father-in-law talking like that to Gerónimo, and the invulnerability of his position is attested by the fact he was not himself even an Indian; he was a white captive raised by White Mountains, highly respected by Chiricahuas and other Western groups alike.[8]

After this altercation, Gerónimo's father-in-law stalked out of the council and Gerónimo went ahead with his plan, but it failed, either because of a warning slipped to the scouts, or because the untimely death of one of the scouts made their participation in a dance improper.[9] Crook of course knew nothing of this. He only knew that if Gerónimo stampeded back to the mountains the whole expedition would have been useless; Crook would have come in for the severest censure from all quarters and what was worse, the Apache wars would have been extended indefinitely. He knew he had to end the expedition quickly or face being out of rations and overstaying the duration allowed by the July treaty. Crook spent a restless night, but in the morning Gerónimo returned with his decision: surrender.

For a few days more Crook held a sort of court high in the Sierra Madre. Old Nana came in with his small band, and Loco, whom Crook already knew had never wanted a war. Then, too, came a mysterious young Chiricahua leader who had never been at the agency, named Ka-ya-ten-nae. He had been among Gerónimo's scouts disgraced by failing to report the García ambush, but still he was not unimportant and he commanded his own following. By the end of the month Crook had marshaled nearly 375 hostile Indians, including virtually all the renegade chiefs. Gerónimo asked for more time to locate and bring in the rest of his people, but Crook could wait no longer. He was averse to leaving Gerónimo behind, but to attempt to force his return was too risky, and Crook had to settle for his promise to follow along behind as soon as he could. Crook started his homeward journey on May 30 with 325 Indians, including fifty-two warriors under Benito, Loco, and Nana. They crossed into Arizona three weeks later and made their dusty way back to San Carlos, a long, tired line of Indians, mostly afoot, to arrive there on June 23.

Nothing seriously detracts from the size of Crook's accomplishment, but the unanimous willingness among the renegades to surrender had been facilitated by one additional significant happening: the monster Juh was dead. According to tradition (and some of the Indians), he was killed in a drunken fall from his mount into a stream, where he drowned. Juh's son Asa Daklugie always stoutly maintained that his father fell into the river after suffering a heart attack. The truth probably lies somewhere in between.

The Mexican Invasion:
NOTES

1. Davis, The Truth About Geronimo, pp. 55–56.
2. Bourke, Apache Campaign, p. 30.
3. Opler, An Apache Life-way, p. 339.
4. Bourke, Apache Campaign, p. 67.
5. Betzinez, I Fought with Geronimo, pp. 118–20. Betzinez believed that the boy was killed, but apparently he was not, at least not at once. He was found badly wounded by the mother and aunt of Sam Houzous. The two women wanted to take him in to Crook, but left him for dead out of fear of being blamed for what had happened. Debo, Geronimo, p. 190, n. 39.
6. Betzinez, I Fought with Geronimo, p. 115.
7. Rope, "Experiences of an Indian Scout," p. 69.
8. Goodwin, Western Apache Raiding and Warfare, pp. 110, 165–67, 318.
9. Debo, Geronimo, pp. 187–88.

Be Patient, and Fear Not

Unfortunately, no sooner were the surrendered bands back at San Carlos than inter-band squabbling broke out again. The Western Apaches wanted nothing to do with the late hostiles, and Britton Davis wisely had the Chiricahuas make their camp adjacent to the agency compound so he could manage them closely. There they appeared to be satisfied for the time being, except for the mysterious one named Ka-ya-ten-nae, who went into a sulk, grumbling that they should never have come in but settled things in the hills. That attitude seems understandable, since this was the leader's first experience with reservation confinement. The others were more used to it, but Ka-ya-ten-nae held a following of more than thirty warriors, and Britton Davis knew if he wanted to make trouble he could do a good job of it.

Crook meanwhile found himself a hero. His presence disproved the numerous reports of his massacre, and his long lines of captive Apaches demonstrated his success. He was lionized at banquets and in the press, and on July 7 the government had him assume police control of the San Carlos Reservation, a consolidation of authority he had long sought. But Crook's own thoughts were on Gerónimo and the others he had trusted to follow him home. There was as yet no word of their coming, and the silence was becoming embarrassing. After a few weeks Crook's adoring press and public turned on him, as he no doubt expected, with speculation and then the expressed certainty that the crafty Gerónimo had tricked him. Crook, too, began to have his doubts, but officially the army said nothing.

On September 1 Crook was, after traveling to Washington for conferences with the War and Interior secretaries and the Indian Commissioner, finally awarded sole control of the San Carlos Apaches, and he undertook an administration of greater fairness to the Indians than any since John Clum's. In establishing the cornerstones of his government, Crook noted that "The Apaches had such a deep-seated distrust of all Americans that four points of policy at once obtruded themselves. First, to make them no promises that could not be fulfilled. Second, to tell them the exact truth at all times. Third, to keep them at labor and to find remuneration for that labor. Fourth, to be patient, to be just, and to fear not."[1]

But the Gerónimo question nagged. The months of silence turned into whole seasons, and increasingly the hero became the fool. It even began to be charged that Crook had not captured the Indians at all, but had been himself collared by Gerónimo and forced to make terms. The rumor was wildly observed but it was so sensational that it was widely printed and accepted, to Crook's private but intense fury. But all the business of building him up and tearing him down was in the press; Crook himself never changed, and quietly he set about discovering what had gone wrong. The general sent Britton Davis to the border to wait on Gerónimo, and scouts were sent—not legally this time—into Mexico to try to find him. They failed, and as autumn turned into winter the Tucson Indian Ring began looking hopefully for a continuation of the Apache wars. But for the time being they were disappointed. Five days before Christmas thirteen of the Sierra Madre renegades crossed into Arizona, followed by more after the new year. On February 7 Chatto and nineteen from his band showed up, and then, climactically, the elusive Gerónimo himself. As each group reached the border a military escort raced them north to San Carlos before the sundry forces of civilian rangers, volunteers, and deputized legal authorities could nab them for trial and certain execution. Gerónimo's following presented a larger problem, as they were driving along with them a dusty, lowing herd of three hundred fifty cattle newly stolen in Mexico. When Britton Davis stared agape at the massive dust cloud Gerónimo reportedly pointed and said, "*Ganado*." One presumes that· Lieutenant Davis already knew they were cattle.

Far from embarrassed at crossing the border with so much booty, Gerónimo truculently required to know what Davis meant by having scouts (whom Gerónimo knew had little affection for himself) escort them north. Davis pacified the angry di-yin by explaining that people in the towns might get drunk and try to seize the cattle, and the scouts were now like soldiers, sworn to protect the surrendering Apaches from trouble. Satisfied on that point, Gerónimo next complained that he had been required to drive the cattle too hard to escape Mexican pursuit, and he demanded a layover of three days to rest the animals. Davis tactfully agreed to rest the remainder of that day but insisted that they begin moving north in the morning. This was done, and the large group managed to make some twenty miles per day, over Gerónimo's incessant growling. When the party reached the ranch and comparative oasis at Sulphur Springs, Gerónimo refused absolutely to proceed farther without a rest for the cattle, and Davis gave in.

That evening two characters from Tucson arrived, announcing themselves as a customs inspector and federal marshal. (Davis accepted their credentials as legitimate, which indeed they possibly were. They were still characters.) They told Davis they were to arrest the Indians and take them to Tucson for trial, and they commanded his assistance. Davis replied that he was under General Crook's authority, at which the marshal subpoenaed him to aid in the arrest. If Davis refused, he said, he would subpeona the ranch hands and, if necessary, raise a posse in Willcox. Davis' position was grim. If he held to his orders and defied the marshal, there could be a fight; the Indians would bolt for Mexico, and if he lost the fight, a federal court would be waiting in Tucson. If he obeyed the subpoena, the Indians would bolt for Mexico, the marshal would release him with thanks and leave him to face General Crook. The answer seemed to lie in which fate he feared more; this was quickly resolved in Crook's favor, but the nearest reinforcements he could count on were at Fort Bowie, thirty miles away. Davis was still scheming how to get Gerónimo to agree to flee north without spooking him into blasting his way back to Mexico, when there arrived in camp Davis' West Point buddy Lieutenant J. Y. F. "Bo" Blake.

Davis had previously sent a message to Blake, who was stationed at Bowie, advising when he would arrive at Sulphur Springs and inviting him out for a reunion. Together they concocted a plan, the first part of which was to get the two citizens drunk. That proved easy, as the marshal and inspector sauntered over after supper to socialize. Blake had brought a bottle of whiskey for his get-together with Davis, and the two officers made certain that it was the civvies who consumed the bulk of it. The two characters soon bedded down on the porch of the ranch house, some ten feet from the nearest of the Apaches. As soon as it was safe, Davis had his scouts awakened and sent his Apache sergeant to roust Gerónimo from his bedding. In a tense conference with Mickey Free interpreting, Davis told Gerónimo that the customs men had come, and if a thousand-dollar tax were not paid on the cattle, he and his men would take them. Davis wisely omitted any reference to Tucson, trials, or hanging, but insisted that it was imperative that they start out at once, in absolute silence, for the reservation to avoid trouble. Gerónimo was simply livid; if those pindahs wanted his cattle, he was ready for a good fight, he would be pleased to fight them in the morning, and good night. Just then Davis' scout sergeant hissed something at Gerónimo that demoralized him. There were too many whispers shooting about for Mickey Free to interpret them all, and Davis never learned what it was that broke Gerónimo. With the diyin acquiescent, however, Davis played up to him what a good joke it would be to slip away unheard and leave the citizens to awaken alone. When Gerónimo saw that he had no support among his own people, his face, too, creased into a leering kind of smile.

As the Apache informant Kanseah told Eve Ball, "If any people knows how to be quiet it is the Apache. . . . We shook with laughter as we got everything ready to move. It did not take ten minutes. Not a dog barked. Not a baby cried. We tied children's feet together under the bellies of the horses. We tied small children to adults. And we started. At first we moved slowly, very slowly. We had to, because of the cattle. But after we got out of hearing we put boys with lances to keep the cattle moving, and we made time."[2] When the inspector and the marshal awakened in the morning, only Davis remained behind, sitting on a crate holding his mule by the bridle, to tell them that Blake, his superior by a year's seniority, had assumed his command and started out with the Indians, but that he (Davis) was remaining behind in obedience to the subpoena. When the citizens demanded to know in what direction they had gone, Davis pleaded ignorance: perhaps north to Fort Grant, maybe east to Fort Bowie; the Apaches might have struck out for Mexico with Blake in pursuit. The marshal and the inspector didn't believe a word of it, but had no choice but to go back where they came from. Davis overtook Blake and Gerónimo just south of the reservation a couple of days later.

The whole incident at Sulphur Springs is repeated here in such detail because it presents a microcosm of what Crook called "The Apache Problem." It illustrates the tact and resourcefulness constantly required of Crook's subordinates in the field, the degree to which loyal Apache scouts were indispensable for keeping hostiles in line, the seriousness of trouble that meddlesome citizens could cause, and the Apaches' ever present need of luck, that not a dog would bark nor a baby cry. The wonder of it is that Crook and his officers accomplished as much as they did.

Once Gerónimo's people safely reached San Carlos, the stolen cattle were sold at auction and the proceeds returned to Mexican authorities for payment to the rightful owners. Gerónimo was furious; he claimed then and ever afterward that he intended the cattle to give his people a start at ranching. Once stripped of them, however, he did not break out again, for the time being.

After the conclusion of his Mexican campaign General Crook reassigned Gatewood to handle the Indians at Fort Apache, and Britton Davis the more dangerous ones at San Carlos, regretting even as he did so the risk to the officers' lives. He knew the situation with at least some of the former hostiles was very precarious, and in event of another breakout their lives would be the first on the line. But Crook did take comfort in trusting his men to the Apache scouts. They had proved their loyalty magnificently in the late effort, certainly enough in Crook's mind to wipe the slate clean for the Cibicue mutiny. In fact, none of the white regulars except Crawford had fired a shot in the Sierra Madre. The Indian scouts had done it all, and no further proof could be asked of the value of using Apaches to fight Apaches.

As affairs at San Carlos settled into a routine Lieutenant Davis noticed that the late hostiles, the last stragglers of whom had come in by mid-

May, began to form into two groups. One became quite friendly and trac-
table. Chiefs of this group, old Loco and Benito, the younger Chatto, and
another chief called Zele, came to visit Davis often. The lieutenant
formed a particularly close relationship with the chief Chatto, whom he
regarded as a man of superior character and intellect; Davis made him a
sergeant of scouts and came to depend on him heavily. Davis also considered Nana to be in this group, speculating that the infirmities of his age
kept him from coming in more often, but he was probably giving the irritable old man too much credit.

On the other hand a "bad element" also began to coalesce under the
wilder and more suspicious chiefs, Mangus of the Tci-he-nde, Naiche of
the Tsoka-ne-nde and Gerónimo of the Nde-nda-i were among them, but
the immediate problem was Ka-ya-ten-nae. That leader turned from silent
and sullen to belligerent; he beat his women viciously and forced them to
make tizwin in large quantities, until Captain Crawford hit on the idea of
recruiting him among the scouts and giving him some responsibility to
carry out. That scheme seemed to work for a time, but soon Ka-ya-ten-nae
grew more restless than ever, and Davis heard from his Secret Service Indians that not only was the mysterious young chief's own conduct unsatis-
factory, but he had begun inciting the other wilder chiefs to break back
out with him. Davis relied increasingly on Chatto and another of his most
reliable scouts, a Christian convert called Dutchy, to keep him in line.

Ka-ya-ten-nae finally committed a crime that could not be ignored when
he attempted to assassinate Davis, who escaped only because of a timely
diversion from the path he was treading. When tried before the Apache
Court, by a jury genuinely of his peers, Ka-ya-ten-nae was sentenced to
three years, and was taken away to the military prison on Alcatraz Island
in San Francisco Bay. As far as Crook was concerned, however, the incarceration was intended more to reconstruct the turbulent young leader
than to inflict punishment. If Ka-ya-ten-nae could be won over, he could
wield immense influence for good among his people. Though Crook consented that he be sent away, Ka-ya-ten-nae stayed very much in his
thoughts.

The difficulty with Ka-ya-ten-nae and the other troubled spirits was not
typical of the rest of the Apaches at San Carlos and Fort Apache.
Through 1884 Crook's control of the Indians was virtually unfettered and
the Apaches began to respond to his combination of firmness and fairness,
just as they had to John Clum. Crops were heavily planted in the spring,
and it can be taken as some measure of Crook's success that in the fall the
Apaches harvested more than 4,000 tons of fruit, vegetables, and grain.[3]
Even the grumblers took up some farming, although Lieutenant Davis'
view of them was not untouched by a little jaundice. "Geronimo's efforts
at self-support were typical of the efforts of many," he recalled. "He came
to me one day with the request that I visit his 'farm.' I could not go at the

moment but went the following morning. He had shown me a small blister on the palm of one of his hands, of which he was very proud. When I arrived at the section of river bottom that had been allotted to him and his band he was sitting on a rail in the shade of a tree with one of his wives fanning him. The other two were hoeing a quarter-acre patch of partially cleared ground, in which a few sickly looking sprouts of corn were struggling for life." Davis readily admitted, however, that the inattention to farming on the part of some leaders was not all their fault, for their plots were as infertile and unarable as desert gravel could be. "The most suitable sections . . . had been assigned to the White Mountain, Cibicue, and Coyotero several years before. The newcomers had to take what was left."[4] One Gerónimo scholar went so far as to make the excuse that Gerónimo might have been ill at the time Davis saw him,[5] but it was doubtless true among the Chiricahua, as it was among the Westerns, that "the dignity of subchiefs and wealthy men put them above certain types of more menial work. They did not work on their farms but hired poorer people to help their own family in planting, cultivating, and harvesting. They sometimes supported poor relatives who, in turn, did work for them."[6]

Crook, for his part, continued to try to earn the Chiricahuas' trust. Late in 1883 local legal authorities tried and succeeded in indicting Davis' scout Dutchy on a murder charge, and began to apply pressure on the military to turn him over. Crook knew that the charges, which stemmed from the Cibicue affair, were very possibly true, but he also knew that Dutchy had since proven himself, and he knew what the reaction of the Chiricahuas would be if one of their number long since held up as exemplary were suddenly taken from them and put to trial. That he would be hanged was a foregone conclusion. The Justice Department finally gave a decision favorable to Crook, but for months before that and after, the general had to play a light-fingered shell game to keep Dutchy from falling into the clutches of the territorial authorities. The Apaches knew what was going on and were grateful.

Long time ago they say.

Coyote killed a bear and made an arrow quiver from its hide. Some other people saw him and told him he had better stop, because bears have dangerous power and it is forbidden to touch them, but he went ahead anyway.

Pretty soon Coyote set the quiver down so he could gather some nuts, and when he wasn't looking that quiver turned into a big bear and started to chase him. Coyote ran hard, and soon he met his friend, Gopher. "Help me, old man," said Coyote. "A bear is after me."

"All right," said Gopher. "Get in my mouth." So Coyote crawled into Gopher's mouth.

Just then Bear ran up and said, "Where did that Coyote go?"
"I haven't seen any Coyote."
"What's that in your mouth?" said Bear.
"Teeth," said Gopher.
Bear got angry and kicked Gopher. Coyote fell out and started running
again. Bear chased him some more, but he got away.
I am talking about fruit.[7]

Throughout this same period Crook labored to achieve the release of the Chiricahua families held in Casas Grandes, some of whom had been in bondage since the massacre of summer 1882. After being taken into the city the prisoners were "reconstructed" by housing them among several prominent families, where the attempt to better them was almost universally minimal. With a few possible exceptions they were nothing but slaves kept at labor in the stables and sculleries; some of the women were, in all probability, prostituted. Over a long period Crook tried to foster negotiations between Washington and Mexico City, and at one point himself contacted the appropriate Mexican generals in an attempt to make them weigh the benefits of keeping them as slaves in Casas Grandes against ensuring future peace. It was finally agreed to return a very limited number of the captives, but by then—May of 1885—it was too late. The San Carlos kettle had bubbled over again.

Be Patient, and Fear Not:
NOTES

1. Crook, "The Apache Problem," p. 267.
2. Kaywaykla, *In the Days of Victorio*, pp. 152–53; Debo, *Geronimo*, p. 201, n. 12.
3. Hodge, "Handbook of Indians North of Mexico," p. 65.
4. Davis, *The Truth About Geronimo*, pp. 136–37.
5. Debo, *Geronimo*, p. 233.
6. Goodwin, *Social Organization of the Western Apache*, p. 166.
7. This illustrative motif is found in two of the Opler treatises on mythology: "Myths and Tales of the Chiricahua Apache Indians," pp. 69–70; and "Myths and Tales of the Jicarilla Apache Indians," pp. 326–27. See also Goodwin, "Myths and Tales of the White Mountain Apache," pp. 172–73.

Canyon of the Tricksters

Regardless of how admirably Crook labored for his Indians, his gains were always offset in some measure by their resentment of the restrictions he placed on their Life-way, most particularly his ban on wife beating and the making of tizwin. He also had under his roof some genuinely ugly and uncontrollable spirits. Chihuahua, Mangus, and Naiche were always prone to be violent and troublesome but Britton Davis, for all his respect and fascination for Indians, thought the worst of the lot was Gerónimo, whom he characterized as "a thoroughly vicious, intractable and treacherous man. His only redeeming traits were courage and determination. His word, no matter how earnestly pledged, was worthless."[1] The dissatisfaction with the tizwin rule was widespread, to be sure, but it was primarily premeditation on the part of Gerónimo that led to the outbreak of May 1885.

On the morning of May 12, when Britton Davis awoke and opened his tent, he found himself staring at an impressive array of chiefs, heavily armed and obviously drunk. Gerónimo was at the head, with Naiche, Mangus, and Chihuahua, but there, too, were the once friendlier Loco and Zele. When they demanded a talk, Davis had little choice but to invite them in. They were sick of rules, they said. They insisted on their right to brew tizwin and beat their wives; moreover, they boasted that they had been on a rousing tizwin drunk all night and demanded to know what Davis was going to do about it. There was little Davis *could* do, except stall the bleary-eyed Indians, saying he could see the situation was too serious to act himself, and he would send word to the general for instructions.

Instead of sending the wire directly to General Crook, Davis properly directed it to Captain Francis Pierce, who had freshly replaced Emmet Crawford as Crook's number two man over the whole Apache matter. Pierce, at Crawford's old station at San Carlos, showed the telegram to an extremely sleepy and hung over Al Sieber. Pierce was still new enough at his job to want Sieber's advice, and the chief of scouts mumbled thickly that it was just a tizwin drunk and Davis could handle it by himself. Pierce, too, failed to perceive the telegram's importance and laid it aside, unwilling to trouble the general with it. Crook did not see it for months. If Sieber had been coherent, he undoubtedly would have handled it properly; Crook, recognizing Sieber's past service and unique abilities, never disciplined him for the lapse.

Three days passed, the Indians growing increasingly fearful of the ominous silence from the Gray Fox. Perhaps he was so angry at their effrontery that he was coming with troops to really punish them. They knew he would not ignore the message and Gerónimo knew that whatever Crook's response, it was time for him to leave. He also knew he must take enough warriors with him to make a show of it. The question was, how?

Gerónimo selected three of his most trusted men and dispatched them to the agency to assassinate Lieutenant Davis and his touted Chatto. The men approached the agency as bidden, but on finding Davis not in his quarters—he was umpiring an agency baseball game—they lost heart and fled. Gerónimo meanwhile, almost certainly in league with Mangus, engaged in some disreputable trickery, seeking out Naiche and Chihuahua, telling them Davis and Chatto were dead and they four were to be arrested for the murders. The ruse worked, and the four leaders collected their bands and bolted the reservation.

When the Choctaw-Negro chief of scouts at San Carlos, Sam Bowman, was told of the impending outbreak by one of the Secret Service Indians he rushed word to Davis, who was returning from the baseball game, but it was too late. Loco and Zele, who had been involved in the tizwin drunk, refused to leave, but the unreconstructed old fire-eater Nana left with Gerónimo. Apparently, at least part of Nana's incentive to leave came only a short time before, when Britton Davis made the perennial mistake of enthusiastic young whites at San Carlos: he tried to tell him how to treat his women. Nana was aghast and vituperative at the affront, huffing to Davis that he had been killing men before Davis was ever born. The total number of the new bustout was 134, including forty-two warriors and apprentices.

The Chiricahuas under Davis' charge had established their rancherias some distance from San Carlos, in between that place and Fort Apache. When Davis tried to telegraph news of the trouble to Pierce, who was at San Carlos station, he found the wire had been cut. Unlike the time the line was severed during the Loco capture, this time the cut in the wire was not found at first. The hostiles had become canny enough to cut the wire where it was hidden in a tree fork, and then splice it back together with a thin strand of hide. The vandalism was found only after a close search, Davis meanwhile sending out messengers to spread the alarm. He waited for Charles B. Gatewood to come down from Fort Apache with a detachment of his White Mountain scouts, and joined him with a force of his own Chiricahuas, including Benito and Chatto, both of whom Davis reported were bitterly angry at the trouble. Davis and Gatewood knew they couldn't possibly catch the fleeing Indians; they only wanted to get a bearing on where they might be headed. After a chase of sixty-five miles, during which they sometimes saw the renegades' dust cloud in the haze across a desert valley, they concluded they were making generally southeast, toward the Black Range of New Mexico.

When Crook learned of the developments he rifled a dual message to San Carlos, one to the reservation Apaches that the outbreak was placing the long-negotiated return of their Casas Grandes captives in jeopardy, and one to Davis that any Indians who volunteered to join the renegades for the purpose of spreading dissension among them, should be encouraged to go.

The outlaws were not long on the trail before Naiche and Chihuahua learned that Gerónimo had duped them, and they were furious with him and disgusted with themselves. Chihuahua, in fact, left his camp with his brother and another Indian to kill Gerónimo, but one of the old di-yin's men got the warning to him in time for him and Mangus to pack up their goods and people and strike out south. Mangus had, apparently, resigned himself to becoming something of a protégé of Gerónimo's. Although himself a son of the mighty Mangas Coloradas, he had managed to keep only an embarrassingly small following, and so attached himself to a star he believed was on the rise. Naiche was still with Gerónimo at this time, but he had left his family with Chihuahua; after the bands split both Naiche and Chihuahua wanted to go back in and take their chances with a surrender, and they would have, but for unfortunate happenstances that prevented either from doing so. Naiche sent word back to his wife and child to return to San Carlos, where he would rejoin them shortly. They obeyed willingly enough, but before they regained the reservation they were spotted by Davis' scouts and panicked into returning to Chihuahua. The latter chief, after Gerónimo had split off for the south, determined to swing back around to the north, re-establish himself on the reservation and surrender. Chihuahua had the largest single following of all the Indians out, about eighty individuals, and if he had done so Gerónimo's break would have been crippled from the first days.

However, when the San Carlos scouts attained the spot where Gerónimo's trail separated from Chihuahua's, they elected to concentrate on the northern one, relying on other army units to intercept the southbound Indians before they reached Mexico. Chihuahua, unnerved that all the scouts should stick to his trail and none to Gerónimo's, elected to finally throw in his lot with the crafty di-yin he had just tried to kill, and he steered his people back south. When he did commit himself to hostility, though, he did it with a vengeance. Where Gerónimo sneaked his way through the posts and troop columns to reach the Sierra Madre, Chihuahua shot his way through, in a series of raids and killings that were reminiscent of the work of fat, sadistic old Juh. Because of his indecisive milling and mulling over whether to surrender, Chihuahua had a longer and more hazardous journey ahead of him than Gerónimo. Gatewood and his scouts kept up the chase but wore their horses down badly in the process. About two weeks after the escape there was a report of a family massacred near Silver City; one girl was taken alive and hanged from a meat hook jammed under the base of her skull. She was still alive when found but died shortly after. Up to this time the army made only one hostile contact, when a detachment was ambushed from a position that was conceded to be unassailable, and three regulars were wounded.

General Crook knew that once Gerónimo took the trouble to break out it would be a long and arduous task to bring him back in, and he wearily began to lay plans for another extended effort, moving his headquarters from Whipple to Fort Bayard, New Mexico, to be nearer the action. Meticulously he positioned his troops to cut the hostiles off from reaching Mexico if they went by any of the most frequented trails, and he sent to Texas for the return of Emmet Crawford to command the scouts. Readying for the worst, he also requested that he be assigned extra surgeons. Crook's force amounted to not less than a crushing twenty companies of cavalry and an indeterminable number of Indian scouts, including many Mescaleros newly rousted from their reservation for service. But the maddened Chiricahuas eluded them all. With their women and children hidden deep in the mountains of southwest New Mexico, the warriors splintered into small groups to raid wherever they could for supplies, horses, and ammunition. By the end of the first week in June perhaps twenty whites had been killed in that vicinity.

Evidence was mounting that Chihuahua was readying for his break to Old Mexico, as he moved from the mountains of New Mexico into the Tsoka-ne-nde stronghold of the Chiricahua Mountains. To deal with him there Crook had only one unit of regulars, Captain Henry Lawton's squadron of 4th Cavalry, whom Crook ordered out of their post at Camp Huachuca in southeast Arizona to try to block Chihuahua as best they could. The general then resignedly ordered Britton Davis and Emmet Crawford to unite their scout commands at the mouth of Guadalupe Canyon and prepare to trail into the Sierra Madre after him. Crawford, Davis, and Al Sieber had with them one cavalry company and just over ninety Indian scouts, including Chatto, when they crossed into Mexico on June 11, 1885. A month later they were reinforced by a second, independent force under Captain Wirt Davis, 4th Cavalry, and about a hundred scouts under Lieutenant Matthias Day. Behind them Crook established a defensive net of cavalry lines along the border, hoping they would never be tested, as he knew the angry Chiricahuas could make them all look like fools.

Crawford's unit was not long in striking pay dirt. On June 23 a group of scouts under Chatto—there were no white men present—were trudging along a mountainside in a drenching downpour. They almost walked into a small rancheria before they saw it. The renegades saw them about the same time and fled, losing only one killed, but Chatto managed to collar fifteen of them, and sent them north under guard. The victory was incomplete but not small. The camp was that of Chihuahua, and two of the prisoners were his children.

The two scout groups soon found themselves working their way deeper into Mexico than any other penetration. "In the little town of Nacori," wrote Britton Davis, "I met a curious state of affairs. The population was 313 souls; but of these only fifteen were adult males. Every family had lost one or more male members at the hands of the Apaches."[2] They were combing in and out of the mountains southeast of Nácori, when suddenly attention was focused back on Arizona as Crook was rudely awakened to the fact that not all the renegades had yet gone south of the border. It was nearly July when a few Chiricahuas, less than a dozen, swooped down out of the Tci-he-nde stronghold toward Mexico, driving before them at least forty head of stolen horses. They burst through Crook's cavalry net and drew pursuit after them sixty miles deep into Mexico before they were lost. The hostiles were forced, however, to abandon their booty.

Crawford himself had turned back north as far as Bavispe to replenish supplies and rations, while Britton Davis and his scouts continued to wind through the mountain ridges of the central Sierra Madre. Eventually they too swung back north, believing there would be no hostiles farther south than Nácori. But there were, and the mistake spared Mangus and his small following additional pursuit. When Crawford arrived with freshly laden pack trains he and Davis struck eastward back into the highest part of the range, where they soon encountered Lieutenant Day, the scout commander from Wirt Davis' force. Day gave the information that on July 28 he had attacked a rancheria believed to be Gerónimo's, killing a boy and a woman, and just over a week after that, on August 7, they hit it again, causing the death of five and taking fifteen prisoners. As the second attack had taken place only three days since, Crawford assigned the job to Britton Davis of getting on the trail of the survivors and staying on it until the issue was decided. Davis took about forty men, including Chatto, Mickey Free, and Al Sieber, and set off on a bewildering chase. The renegades led them down off the eastern slope of the Sierra Madre into the heart of Chihuahua state, where they raced northward, constantly stealing fresh horses as they were needed, and disappearing in the direction of the American border. Davis' group, without the advantage of fresh horses, floundered along behind, making their way almost due north to El Paso, Texas. There Lieutenant Davis bought his scouts fresh clothes, had their picture taken, and took them back to Arizona on a train. He had

Frank Randall's photograph of Fort Bowie in Apache Pass was taken in 1886, the year Miles assumed command from Crook. *Arizona Historical Society.*

Marvelously handsome as a young man, General Nelson A. Miles still cut a fine profile in his later years. *Courtesy the Kansas State Historical Society, Topeka.*

One of the camouflaged heliograph stations that General Miles had constructed on strategic mountaintops across Chiricahua country. *National Archives.*

Scene of Gatewood's Mission, near the head of the Bavispe River. *National Archives.*

General Miles and his staff officers pose for a victory portrait soon after the final surrender of Gerónimo. Miles is directly in the center, fifth from left. *National Archives.*

Wagons laden with Apache prisoners of war rumble out of Fort Bowie. Eventual destination: Fort Marion prison, Florida. *National Archives.*

Chiricahua prison train pauses in San Antonio, Texas. Front row at left are two relatives of Gerónimo, Fun and Perico. Naiche is in tall boots front center, and Gerónimo sitting on his left. Third woman from the right, second row, was identified by Kayway-kla as Lozen, a woman di-yin who was a sister of Victorio and fought alongside the men. Her name does not appear on the roll, however. *National Archives.*

Chiricahua chiefs imprisoned at Mount Vernon Barracks, Alabama. Left to right: Chihuahua, Naiche, Loco, Nana, Gerónimo. *National Archives.*

Gerónimo as a prisoner of war at Fort Sill, c. early 1900s, shown here with his sixth wife, Zi-yeh, and children. *Courtesy U. S. Army Field Artillery Museum.*

Medicine Bluffs, Fort Sill, Oklahoma, scene of Apache farming and ranching. Those of Ka-ya-ten-nae, Mangas, and Loco were atop the north bank (right); those of Chatto and Naiche were on the south bank between the bluffs and the blockhouse in the distance. *Photo by the author.*

finally had enough of Indians and Indian fighting, and resigned his commission soon after his return.

Long time ago they say.

Coyote came up on Frog Old Woman. She was sitting there in her squash, I guess. Coyote said, "Grandmother, let's have a race and see which of us is faster."

Frog Old Woman looked at him and said, "Don't make fun of me. I may just be an old woman, but I could still whip you in a race."

Coyote said, "Let us race, then, and we'll see about it."

"All right," said Frog Old Woman. "I have to go over here in the bushes first."

Coyote thought she was going to urinate or something and let her go. Once she was out of sight, she got to her village of Frog People. She said, "You people come here and listen. Coyote wants to race me. I want you all to space yourselves along the path. While he runs, each of you jump a couple of times and then the next take over. We all look alike and he won't know about it. Whoever is at the finish can make fun of him."

Frog Old Woman went back to Coyote and they started racing. Coyote ran hard, but every time he looked a frog was in front of him jumping. When they got to the finish, another Frog Old Woman said, "My grandson, what's the matter? You're not so fast as you thought. You're no man, just a boy. Go away and leave me alone."

Coyote went off and sat down. "How did she do that?" he said.

I am talking about fruit.[3]

Crawford and Captain Wirt Davis stayed on in the Sierra Madre well into the autumn. They lost one man dead to the enemy on September 22, while claiming one renegade killed and two wounded. At one in the morning of that same day, at the Chiricahua rancheria near Fort Apache in the White Mountains, Gerónimo suddenly burst onto the scene, took his wife, child, and a second woman, and vanished. In doing so Gerónimo frustrated the army's exhaustive effort to prevent its happening, which had reportedly included everything short of locking the family in the guardhouse.

Hostile activity began in general to take a more northerly course about this time, with twenty renegades regaining American territory around September 28 at Guadalupe Canyon, with Crawford and Wirt Davis close on their heels. Crook sent out the alarm to the southern Arizona and New Mexico towns, readying himself for the inevitable storm of citizen abuse, but Crawford and Davis were after them with determination. The Apaches hid in the Chiricahua Mountains for some days, killing two pindahs while they were there, until a heavy concentration of cavalry troops flushed them out. Sometime before the first of October they stole fresh horses, but once they were out in the open, Crawford's tough scouts chased them in a high-speed zigzag like a coyote after a jackrabbit. Just as their new horses were about played out the hostiles had an incredible stroke of luck.

When General Crook warned the settlements to be wary of a new Indian invasion, he told them explicitly that the renegades would be short of stock and would steal horses at every opportunity, and settlers should keep their animals closely corralled. The fall roundup of cattle was under way in the San Simon Valley, and after a day's roping and branding a large number of the cowboys were spending the night at a ranch house. Their horses were tied up outside, unguarded. Sometime before sunrise Gerónimo made off with thirty of the strongest, fastest, best-trained, and most intelligent horses in the territory. The embarrassingly easy triumph sent Gerónimo and his people storming back into Mexico. Crawford, his scouts' enlistments nearly up, marched disgustedly back to the reservation to recruit new ones.

No sooner had Gerónimo regained the still relative safety of the Sierra Madre than New Mexico and Arizona suffered another high-speed blitz by a small group of warriors, reminiscent of the flashing raids of Nana and Chatto. This one was led by a hitherto little-known younger brother of Chihuahua, called Ulzanna. They crossed into New Mexico below the Florida Mountains about the first of November, shooting their way through to the Tci-he-nde homeland. Ulzanna had with him fewer than a dozen men, and in the couple of days it took them to reach a hideout they had killed a scout, two citizens, a White Mountain Apache, and two Navajos. Their only loss was one man who suffered a broken leg and, in the exigency of the situation, was abandoned. In the New Mexico mountains the Ulzanna group united briefly with another less spectacular raiding party of sixteen, but the latter soon returned to Mexico and Ulzanna continued on with his handful. For three weeks they lay low before storming off to punish the reservation Indians at Fort Apache who had refused to join the outbreak. On November 23 Crook's telegraph began ticking out a message from the officer temporarily in charge of Fort Apache that renegades were sighted less than four miles from the fort and he was preparing to go after them. Even as Crook was receiving the message the wire was cut and the key fell dead. Four days later Crook learned that the fiends had killed twenty of their own people including, shockingly, fifteen women and children. They had also stolen Chief Benito's horse herd, while themselves losing only one dead, a sentry who was ambushed and decapitated by a reservation Apache.

The military had been offering bounties to the scouts for the heads of Chiricahua renegades, and when victims were taken the hate that the Chiricahuas felt for the peaceful Indians was akin to that of the Tontos toward the White Mountains in the early seventies. In this instance a

Chiricahua account provides some interesting details: "Some Chiricahua had been away from the reservation. The U.S. army men had been after them and offered twenty-five dollars for every hostile Chiricahua's head brought in. This bunch of Chiricahua decided to come in. They came close to the agency and were eating there. They put one on a ridge to watch and stand guard. Finally J. was relieved by another boy, a good-looking young Chiricahua. A few minutes later, as he was sitting on the ridge with his gun across his knees, looking in the opposite direction, a San Carlos Indian crept up behind him and shot him. As soon as he shot, he was on this boy with his knife and cut his head off.

"The rest of the Chiricahua camp came up and saw what had been done. They were angry as could be. They found out who had done this and went down to his camp to get him. But he had been warned and got away. His wife and several children were there, though, and they killed them and left them lying right there. They went out and began shooting into other near-by San Carlos camps. They were so angry they didn't care what they did. Then they made for the hills."⁴ Although the informant never mentioned Ulzanna by name the events and circumstances match precisely; the assertion that they came to the reservation to surrender is not without historical import, but possibly stems from the informant's being a Chiricahua himself.

On Benito's horses Ulzanna's men stormed back south through Arivaipa Canyon, raiding as they went, then swung back around to the north. Not far from Solomonville they stole more horses, and a group of locals, believing from the small size of the party they were just thieves, galloped out after them. They learned differently when two of their posse were killed in a flashing ambush. George Crook was applying every scrap of his skill, experience, and intuition to trapping the rampaging hostiles. Chatto was after them, Crawford was after them, and a huge army of cavalry units was either after them or lying in wait for them. But still the terror went on.

On December 8 two more whites were killed near the small town of Alma, but for once Ulzanna showed himself at a time and place he could be struck. The next night, after a breathless stalk and approach, Lieutenant Sam Fountain, 8th Cavalry, ambushed the Chiricahuas' camp. He killed none of them but captured all their camp goods, blankets, and horses. The day after that Ulzanna killed two ranchers nearby; Fountain led his troops in pursuit for several days but found no trace. Fountain's own scouts were Navajo Indians, who were continuing their dismal record of stalling and ineptitude at finding and engaging their more ferocious cousins, and on the nineteenth the lieutenant left his own compay to return to his rear and hurry them up. While he was gone his troop walked straight into a trap Ulzanna had prepared, and in a deafening ambuscade five soldiers were killed and two wounded. The renegades melted away to work over the town of Alma once more.

On December 25 the renegades stole enough horses to start working their way back south, and under cover of a heavy snowfall nobody could stop them. Ulzanna was believed to have recrossed into Mexico about December 28, having killed perhaps forty people in two months, against a loss to himself of one dead and one abandoned. Quietly Emmet Crawford and Wirt Davis went back into the Sierra Madre after them. The success of the Ulzanna raid had Crook almost crazed with frustration. "Every conceivable effort was made and artifice employed which an experience of a generation of Indian wars could suggest," he wrote. "But, although the party was so closely followed that twice they were compelled to abandon their horses and plunder and take to the rocks on foot . . . in their next flight [they] left no more trail than so many birds, [and] finally crossed back into Mexico with no loss that can be positively stated beyond one of their number killed by the friendly Apaches near Fort Apache."5 Old Nana must have been proud.

Crawford and Davis, in pursuit, followed a new policy of penetrating deeper than ever into Mexico. Marching parallel to the downstream course of the Bavispe they passed Oputo and Nácori, and on January 9, 1886, made hostile contact in the western edge of the Sierra Madre, just west of the headwaters of the Haros River. They were at least two hundred miles deep into Mexico, about one hundred fifty miles west of Chihuahua City. The rancheria they struck was a major one, and the scouts used the greatest care in surrounding it after a silent eighteen-hour march through fiercely rugged country. Though most of the renegades escaped the attack, the rancheria was seized with all its equipment and horses. Bleakly the renegades realized they had been surprised and whipped in the most secure place they had ever known, and it was time to give up. They sent a woman into the American camp, where she arranged for a talk to be held the following day.

On the morning of January 10 the valley of Crawford's camp was covered by a heavy mist, and when the scouts made out the approach of a large body of troops they assumed it was Captain Davis joining up. They were wrong. It was a force of Mexican irregulars guided by Tarahumara Indians, on the trail of the same Apaches Crawford had just struck. Their identity was not discovered until Crawford found his camp under heavy fire from the advancing Mexicans. At first it might perhaps have been a case of the Mexicans thinking Crawford's camp was the hostile rancheria. That seems doubtful, but even if it was true, after the Mexicans learned the camp was of Americans and Apache scouts it didn't make any difference. Unknown to Crawford, tensions between Mexico and the United States had been building for some time, as the Mexicans began to accuse, without much justification, that the Apache scouts had been committing offenses against Mexican citizens. Dispatches from Crook were on their way to Crawford at that instant ordering him to examine his scouts as to their conduct.

Ignorant of the situation, Crawford, wearing his captain's tunic, in the company of his number two, Lieutenant Marion Maus, and Chief of Scouts Tom Horn, ran out from their camp toward the Mexicans, shouting that they were Americans and to hold their fire. After a quarter hour the Mexicans stopped shooting, and Crawford and Maus ventured out for a talk. Maus explained in Spanish that they were Americans, what they were doing there, and called attention to their uniforms. Crawford told Maus to return to their own camp and make sure no more fire erupted from there. Then, according to Maus, "I started back, when again a volley was fired. . . . When I turned again I saw the Captain lying on the rocks with a wound in his head, and some of his brains upon the rocks."[6] Chief of Scouts Horn was wounded slightly. Crawford did not die immediately. With his shattered head gently bandaged he was taken and left in Nácori, where he lingered for a week. He died without regaining consciousness. It was said, with some evidence, that the fatal shot was fired by the Tarahumara scout Mauricio, using the nickel-plated rifle awarded him for the slaying of Victorio in 1881.

(C. F. Lummis reported back to the Los Angeles Times that one of the scouts was wounded as well, shot through both hips, "doing him the utmost damage that can be done a man. The poor devil had six holes in him, all made by one bullet. When I went to the hospital to see him he was feeling pretty blue, apparently, and was singing a doleful ululation to the earth-mother, the sun, the winds, and various spare entities, calling on them to give him a new lease on life. He wouldn't pay any attention to visitors until he had finished."[7])

The next day Lieutenant Maus negotiated with the Mexicans, whom he found very truculent and belligerent. They demanded and got some of Maus's mules to carry their wounded away, and Maus then moved his camp a few miles to the north to have his meeting with the renegades. The Indians were all ready to surrender, they said, and would begin moving back north, if they could be assured that they could bargain with the Gray Fox before coming back into the United States. As evidence of their good faith they gave hostages in the persons of Old Nana, another warrior, and the families of Naiche and Gerónimo. Satisfied, Maus headed north with relief and sent messages to Crook, who began soliciting assurances from the territorial authorities not to attempt seizing Nana as he came back into the country. About a month later, on February 10, Maus sent word that he was back at the border, and the hostiles were coming in behind him. There was some delay in their movement, however, as they stopped to uncache matériel hidden at various places in the mountains.

To get ready for his conference with Gerónimo, Crook had the

Chiricahua leader Ka-ya-ten-nae released from Alcatraz and sent back to use his influence in arguing for the renegades' surrender. Crook believed the turbulent young chief had been sufficiently chastened by his time in prison to be released, but he remained sulky and prone to violence. He did promise to be helpful, however. An enterprising photographer from Tombstone, Camillus S. Fly, asked and received permission to record the historic meeting. It was the middle of March before Crook received word that the renegade Chiricahuas were waiting for him, in the Cañón de los Embudos, or the Canyon of the Tricksters, just across the border in Sonora, on the San Bernardino River. The meeting would not take place entirely without terms; the Apaches stipulated that Crook must bring no force of soldiers with him, and the general, knowing what the result would be of obstinance or bad faith on his part, consented.

Toward the end of the month Crook struck out from Fort Bowie, arriving at Maus's camp just south of the border in time for lunch on March 26, 1886. After the meal he had his first meeting with the renegades. "So suspicious were they," he wrote in his *Résumé*, "that never more than from five to eight of the men came into our camp at one time."[8] The Chiricahuas had established their own rancheria on an eminently defensible lava hill about a quarter mile from Maus's camp.

The negotiations continued over three days, the Indians insisting that if they were to be imprisoned in the East, and they were, it must not be for more than two years, thence to be returned home. Crook bluffed tersely that they had to make up their minds at once for peace or war. If it were peace, he would do what he could for them. If it were war, he would kill them all "if it took fifty years." Crook knew very well that if they fled again their defeat might very well take just that long, and he dispatched two of his best Indians to the hostile rancheria to speed a favorable decision. The first was the White Mountain scout, Alchise, and the other was Lieutenant Davis' erstwhile nemesis, Ka-ya-ten-nae. In his report to General Sheridan, Crook gave credit that "Ka-e-te-na, the young chief, who less than two years ago was the worst Chiricahua of the whole lot, is now perfectly subdued. He is thoroughly reconstructed, has rendered me valuable assistance, and will be of great service in helping me to control these Indians in the future. His stay at Alcatraz has worked a complete transformation on his character."[9] Although Crook was pleased with Ka-ya-ten-nae's progress, the latter was not entirely broken to Crook's scheme. He knew that to be present was the best way to protect his family and band against treachery by Crook or the White Mountains and Chiricahuas who were genuinely receptive to his thinking. Real animosity had been growing between the wilder Chiricahuas and those of Chatto's mold, and it was almost certainly to keep the latter honest that Ka-ya-ten-nae was playing up to Crook.

Early on the twenty-seventh Chihuahua sent a message that he was sure the decision would be for surrender, but whatever the others decided he would bring his own following in that noon, and he proved as good as his word. He was accompanied by Naiche and Gerónimo, and also Nana, whose importance the officers erroneously discounted because of his age and limp, and the chiefs asked Crook for a conference.

It seems to have been Chihuahua who took some measure of charge, and he was the first to speak. "I am very glad to see you and have this talk with you," he began. "It is as you say, we are always in danger out here. I hope from this time on we may live better with our families and not do any harm to anybody. I am anxious to behave. I think the sun is looking down upon me and the earth is listening. I am thinking better." Chihuahua then turned his thoughts to Crook himself, and showered him with effusive flattery: "There are many men in the world who are big chiefs and command many people, but you, I think, are the greatest of them all, or you wouldn't come out here to see us. . . . You must be our God. You must be the one who makes the green pastures, who sends the rain, who commands the winds. You must be the one who sends the fresh fruits that appear on the trees every year." After these blandishments Chihuahua got to the point. "I want you to have pity on me. . . . I am now in your hands. I place myself at your disposition. I surrender myself to you. Do with me as you please. I shake your hand."

General Crook took his hand and he continued, "I want to come right into your camp with my family and stay with you. I don't want to stay away at a distance. I want to be right where you are. . . . Whenever a man raises anything, even a dog, he thinks well of it and tries to raise it right and treat it well. So I want you to feel toward me and be good to me and don't let people say bad things about me. Now I surrender to you and go with you. When we are travelling together on the road or anywhere else, I hope you'll talk to me once in a while."

Mindful of the waiting prison cell in the East, Chihuahua recalled the loss of his camp to Chatto on June 23, telling Crook, "If you don't let me go back to the reservation, I would like you to send my family with me wherever you send me. I have a daughter at Camp Apache, and some others. . . ." Crook questioned whether his family would want to accompany him, and Chihuahua concluded that he would be satisfied for them to make up their own minds. The conference record indicates that Chihuahua shook hands with Crook—the good four times—before letting Naiche speak his mind.

"What Chihuahua says I say. I surrender just the same as he did. What he has said I say. I give you my word, I give you my body. I surrender; I have nothing more to say than that. When I was free I gave orders, but now I surrender to you. I throw myself at your feet. You now order and I obey. What you tell me to do I do." The two men shook hands and it was done, but soon Naiche began to speak again to Crook, "[I] hope you will be kind to us, as you have always been a good friend to the Indians and tried to do what was right for them . . . You don't lie to me. I hope from this day on you will see that I am in earnest, and will believe what I say." The heir of Cochise was not known ever to have spoken so to any other army officer.

After stalling as long as he could, the old di-yin told Crook, "Two or three words are enough. I have little to say. I surrender myself to you. We are all comrades, all one family, all one band. What the others say I say also. I give myself up to you. Do with me what you please. I surrender. Once I moved about like the wind. Now I surrender to you and that is all. I don't want any one to say any wrong thing about me in any way. I surrender to you and want it to be just as if I were in your pocket. My heart is yours, and I hope yours will be mine. . . . I have no lies in my heart. Whatever you tell me is true. We are all satisfied of that. I hope the day may come when my word shall be as strong with you as yours is with me." During the course of the short speech Gerónimo also shook hands with Crook, four times.

The general informed the Apaches that he was returning to Arizona the following day because he was nearly out of rations, but that they might follow him at their own speed. Chihuahua registered surprise at the unexpected kindness. "Our stock is very poor," he said. "I was afraid that I'd have to travel too fast."

"Not at all," said Crook. "You will come along in good time." Chihuahua promised to send word each day and shook his hand again emphatically.

Gerónimo asked that his wife and daughter be sent to him, and Crook agreed that they could meet him on the road, although he could not yet say where. The general's business seemed very well concluded indeed. Back at Bowie, Crook wired the good news to Sheridan, including the information that he had granted the Apaches' condition that their confinement East would be limited to two years. When Sheridan saw the agreement he quickly had it submitted to Grover Cleveland and replied bleakly, "The President cannot assent to the surrender of the hostiles on the [stated] terms. . . . He instructs you to enter again into negotiations on the terms of their unconditional surrender, only sparing their lives." Crook was then ordered to back up his new conference with enough troops to annihilate the renegades, and was cautioned, inevitably, that "the escape of the hostiles . . . must not be allowed under any circumstances." The sweet political fruits of humiliating Gerónimo were to take precedence over finding a workable peace.

Before Crook could compose a response to his latest lack of support from higher authority, he received news that must have put him in shock: Naiche and his band, with Gerónimo, were gone.

Crook's talks with the Chiricahuas had taken place on the sprawling

San Bernardino Ranch, which straddled the international boundary. A well-known fence, bootlegger and profiteer, a Swiss-American named Tribolett, had established his residence—no doubt for legal reasons—some yards south of the Arizona line on this ranch. Unknown to Crook and his troops, Tribolett set up shop near the Chiricahua rancheria and sold the leaders enough whiskey to get them royally drunk. And once he got them pliable, allegedly, he "warned" them that Crook intended to massacre them as soon as he had them under guard. Either in response or just because they were drunk, some of the Indians fled back into the mountains, led by Gerónimo and Naiche. One of the chiefs of scouts, "Buckskin" Frank Leslie, later told Captain Bourke that he had once seen Tribolett sell "thirty dollars' worth of mescall in less than one hour—all to Chiricahuas—and upon being remonstrated with, the wretch boasted that he could have sold one hundred dollars' worth. . . ."[10] Regarding the unsavory character, Crook fumed to Charles Lummis, "That man is the cause of this whole trouble now. . . . Oh no, there's no way of dealing with Tribolet. He has been tried before, but bought his way out. If we had shot him down like a coyote, as he deserved, it would have raised a terrible row. Why, that man has a beef contract for our army!"[11] (The cultural historian only wishes that Crook had realized the full truth, in his peculiar circumstance, of calling Tribolett a Coyote.) Crook later wrote on the same topic that "the greed and rapacity of the vultures who fatten on Indian wars have been a greater obstruction in the path of civilization than the ferocity of the wildest savages who have fought them."[12]

Although Crook blamed the new trouble with Gerónimo and Naiche entirely on Tribolett, when the Chiricahuas who made good on their surrender followed Chihuahua to Fort Bowie on April 3, Crook held another conference with them at which another aspect of it surfaced. It seemed that during the party they held with Tribolett's whiskey, Naiche caught his wife and another man flirting. Drunk and enraged, Naiche shot the woman through the knee—his impromptu equivalent, one supposes, of slitting her nose. Other men criticized this extreme behavior, and the band had split over the issue. Chihuahua registered the opinion to Crook that he thought Naiche would come back in once he had calmed down, although he couldn't say for sure, but he thought Gerónimo was now out for good.[13] (A second version of the shooting incident gained preeminence in the Apache oral tradition, that the wife, E-clah-heh, the mother of Dorothy Naiche, overheard Naiche's and Gerónimo's scheming to break back for the mountains in response to Tribolett's "warning." Fed up with life as a fugitive, E-clah-heh made a dash for the American's camp, and Naiche shot her in the leg to prevent the warning from being delivered.[14])

Chihuahua and the other leaders who came in, Nana, Ulzanna, and Cut-le, set up camp a short distance from Fort Bowie, and Crook paroled to them the Chiricahua prisoners previously taken here and there and kept at the post. One woman, however, tearfully refused to budge from the guardhouse. Her husband had been killed during the fighting the previous year, and she had no more relatives in his local group. "She foresaw," reported Lummis, "that if she rejoined the band . . . she would be kicked from pillar to post, and have to work like a slave to be tolerated at all."[15] Crook let her stay where she wished.

At the new rancheria near Bowie the Chiricahuas were issued firewood and rations, but their stay was brief. The Apaches had surrendered to Crook in good faith on the terms he had agreed to, and Crook kept the news of the repudiation from them as he tried feverishly to bargain with Sheridan. But, there was nothing doing. The exchange of telegrams with Sheridan resulted in Crook being ordered, angrily and directly, to take all Chiricahua prisoners in his custody up to Bowie Station and entrain them for Florida, at once. Crook had no choice but to obey, and shipped all seventy-seven prisoners—including the families of Gerónimo and Naiche —to prison at Fort Marion in St. Augustine.

On reading Crook's wire that Gerónimo had escaped, Sheridan lost his temper again, and blamed the misfortune on treachery by Crook's Apache auxiliaries, with the observation, "It seems strange that Geronimo could have escaped without knowledge of the scouts."

It was not the first time that Sheridan had spoken sharply without full knowledge of the facts, by any means,[16] but that was little comfort to Crook. He returned the message, hotly defending his scouts, telling Sheridan as diplomatically as he could that he didn't know what he was talking about. "To enable you to understand situation," he wired, "it should be remembered that the hostiles had an agreement with Lieut. Maus that they were to be met by me twenty-five miles below the line, that no regular troops were to be present. While I was very averse to such an agreement, I had to abide by it. . . . They were armed to the teeth, having the most improved guns and all the ammunition they could carry. The clothing and other supplies lost in the fight with Crawford had been replaced by new blankets and shirts obtained in Mexico. Lieutenant Maus with Apache scouts was camped at the nearest point the hostiles would agree to his approaching. Even had I been disposed to betray the confidence they placed in me, it would have been simply an impossibility to get white troops to that point either by day or by night without their knowledge, and had I attempted to do this the whole band would have stampeded back to the mountains. . . . My only hope was to get their confidence on the march through Ka-ya-ten-nae and other confidential Indians, and finally put them on the cars; and until this was done it was impossible even to disarm them."[17]

Sheridan interpreted Crook's message not as a vindication of a good strategy foiled, but as a recital of folly. At the most charitable, Crook had depended entirely on scouts who should not have been trusted to tell their own ages truthfully, and then himself took a foolish personal risk and had been fortunate to get out alive. Then, most insufferably of all, Sheridan talked down to Crook. "I do not see what you can do now except to concentrate your troops at the best points and give protection to the people. . . . As the offensive campaign . . . with scouts has failed, would it not be best to take up defensive and give protection to the people and business interests. . . . Please send me a statement of what you contemplate for the future."[18]

This latest communiqué was just too much for the overburdened Crook. In his reply he insisted that maintenance of an offensive was imperative, as given the rugged terrain and the Apaches' singular understanding of it, "Troops cannot protect property beyond a radius of one-half mile from their camps." Adding that he had done all along the best he could to protect white lives and property, he concluded that his plan of operations, including reliance on Indian scouts, "is the one most likely to prove successful in the end. It may be, however, that I am too wedded to my own views in this matter, and as I have spent nearly eight years of the hardest work of my life in this Department, I respectfully request that I may now be relieved from its command."

Sheridan complied with relief, quickly transferring Crook to the North Plains to command the Department of the Platte, moving in to Arizona one of his special favorites, Brigadier General Nelson A. Miles. Of all the generals who had commanded troops against the Apaches, none had ever equaled Crook in understanding and respect for his adversary. In governing the Indians he went farther than any other military man to root his policy in honesty, prudence, and good faith toward the Apaches. Crook's great mistake lay in committing his government to ethics equal to his own.

From the Indian point of view, probably the best tribute came from the Chiricahua warrior Batsinas, later much better known as Jason Betzinez. "He was a hard fighter," he wrote, "a strong enemy when we were hostile. But he played fair with us afterwards and did what he could to protect the Indians. We actually loved General Crook, and even today think of him, and talk about him, with genuine affection. He probably never knew that."[19]

By another reckoning, however, George Crook only got as bad as he gave. At this stage of his career, most historians are so sympathetic to the besieged general that they forget his shameful treatment of Lieutenant Whitman after the Camp Grant massacre. Whitman's great mistake, too, lay in committing others beyond his control to an Indian policy of humanity and non-recrimination. Inasmuch as Crook had hounded and humiliated Whitman through three courts-martial on trumped-up charges, his own downfall over the disposition of the surrendered Chiricahuas strikes one as irony that is painful but not unjust.

Canyon of the Tricksters:
NOTES

1. Davis, *The Truth About Geronimo*, p. 206.
2. Ibid., p. 170.
3. I have adapted this from the version contained in Goodwin, "Myths and Tales of the White Mountain Apache," pp. 171–72.
4. Opler, *An Apache Life-way*, p. 343.
5. Crook, "The Apache Problem," p. 266.
6. Thrapp, *Conquest of Apacheria*, p. 341.
7. Lummis, *General Crook and the Apache Wars*, p. 64.
8. The many published accounts of the following transactions stem mostly from U. S. Senate, Exec. Doc. No. 88, 51st Cong., 1st sess.
9. Quoted in Davis, *The Truth About Geronimo*, p. 284.
10. Bourke, *On the Border*, pp. 480–81. C. F. Lummis did not regard Leslie as a consistently truthful individual. The two men stood on opposite sides of the question of Apache scouts—Lummis siding with Crook—and in one of his dispatches back to the Los Angeles *Times*, Lummis wrote that he "may add that the howl against Apache scouts comes largely from alleged white scouts of the Frank Leslie stamp, who want the positions for themselves. The real white scouts, men like Al Seeber [*sic*] . . . cheerfully admit that Apache scouts are indispensible." Lummis, *General Crook and the Apache Wars*, p. 21. Leslie was, wrote Lummis elsewhere, "for a few weeks connected with Captain Crawford's command, hunting Geronimo, but was directly discharged for his inability to tell an Indian trail from a box of flea-powder." Ibid., p. 60. Lummis did credit Leslie's bravery and stamina, however, and they were in agreement in their estimation of Tribolett, if nothing else.
11. Lummis, *General Crook and the Apache Wars*, p. 16.
12. Crook, "The Apache Problem," p. 268.
13. Lummis, *General Crook and the Apache Wars*, p. 32.
14. See Debo, *Geronimo*, pp. 265–66.
15. Lummis, *General Crook and the Apache Wars*, p. 39. There may have been more afoot here than met Crook's eye. If the woman had been a respected one, of good family, she probably would not have married a man with no family. Then, if what few relatives the man had did not like her, they might have tried to bind her by the levirate to stay with them for a year or so, to benefit from her labor, but with no realistic prospect for remarriage.
16. One other notable example of this penchant of Sheridan's was his attack on General John Pope during the Red River War of 1874. See Haley, *The Buffalo War*, pp. 102–3.
17. Crook, *Résumé of Operations*, pp. 13–14.
18. Ibid., p. 15.
19. Betzinez, *I Fought with Geronimo*, pp. 120–21.

Canyon of the Skeletons

Sheridan's white ethnocentrism and outright distrust of Indian scouts found a kindred spirit in Nelson Miles. General Crook's view that regular troops could not perform well against Apaches was now in very official disfavor, and Miles was to conquer the enemy while giving particular emphasis to the role of the fighting white soldier.[1] The execution of this policy, though, wound up being rather less puristic than its jargon.

Miles was one of the most controversial officers in the army, and had been since the close of the Civil War. He was a good soldier, with brains, nerves, and ability. In his younger days his personal bravery was near legendary, but as he grew older his less fortunate qualities gained in prominence: he was a propagandist and a consumptively ambitious schemer who, many of his colleagues believed, would stop at nothing to reach the pinnacle of power. He was talented enough to win advancement or at least glory on the battlefield (with perhaps a little help from the news reporters who were sometimes to be found in his entourage),[2] but as battlefields became scarcer Miles seemed almost equally adept at plotting promotions from his writing desk. He developed an uncanny ability to be in the right place at the right time. In the Nez Perce war, Oliver Howard had fought and hounded those Indians to exhaustion, only to lose his command to Miles in time for the latter to receive the surrender of Chief Joseph; now it was Crook's turn. Miles was one of the line colonels galled by Crook's irregular promotion after the Tonto War; Miles did not make brigadier until (it was alleged) he engineered the forced retirement of E. O. C. Ord in 1880, an affair that scandalized the officer corps. General Sherman, Miles's uncle by marriage, saw through him and gave him no favors, but when Sherman retired in 1883 and Sheridan became General of the Army, Miles's prospects brightened. Two major generalcies opened in 1886 and Sheridan backed Miles for one, but the animosity in other quarters was too great, and the two-starred billets went to Howard and Terry.[3]

Miles arrived at Bowie Station on April 11, accompanied by his clerk-stenographer, Frank Brown, whose fare Miles had paid from Leavenworth, Kansas. "I think this is the most barren region I have ever seen," Miles wrote his wife, Mary. "From what I can see and hear of the troops, they are very much discouraged by being kept in the field so long and by the prospect that the campaign must be continued for some time to come. General Crook leaves tomorrow. He appears to feel very much disappointed but does not say much. He tells me that only two of the Apache warriors have been killed since they broke out."[4]

Crook had every reason to be downcast. It was barely two weeks since Gerónimo surrendered to him at Cañón de los Embudos, and the Apache wars had seemed at an end. Eight years of his life had been wrecked by a profiteering bootlegger named Tribolett and three demijohns of whiskey, and Sheridan could only blame the failure on Crook and the scouts who had proven themselves loyal time after time. Faced with the prospect that his career was going to end unrewarded and jeered, Crook finally broke his disciplined silence and wrote an article defending himself and his scouts, and paying tribute to the enemy he had fought for so long. It was the sunset of Apache resistance, and Crook's eulogy for them was the kindest words they would hear for a long time, that an Apache warrior "is perfectly at home, anywhere in the immense country over which he roams and which affords him all the sustenance he requires. Even in his rapid flights he gets a rabbit here or a rat there, and this, with the wild roots and the mescal, gives him all the food he needs. It is, therefore, unnecessary for him to carry provisions. They have no property which they cannot carry on their backs in their most rapid marches; nor have they, when on the war-path, any settled habitations of any kind, and their temporary resting places are chosen with the instinct resulting from the experience of generations.

"The Apache can endure fatigue and fasting and can live without water for periods that would kill the hardiest mountaineer. Every thing he has ever received from the white man is a luxury which he can do without as he has done from time immemorial . . . In fighting them we must of necessity be the pursuers, and unless we can surprise them by sudden and unexpected attack, the advantage is all in their favor. In Indian combats it must be remembered that you rarely see an Indian; you see the puff of smoke and hear the whiz of his bullets, but the Indian is thoroughly hidden in the rocks and even his exact hiding-place can only be conjectured. The soldier on the contrary must expose himself, and exposure is fatal. A dozen Indians in the rocks can withstand the onset of a battalion of soldiers, and though they can be driven from their position at the cost of many lives in the attacking party, it only results in their attaining another position equally as strong as the first, or in their scattering like quail in the rocks, to appear at some point miles away, in front, on either flank, or in rear, as may seem to them desirable. The Apaches only fight with regular soldiers when they choose and when the advantages are all on their side. If pursued to their rocky strongholds, they send their families to some other point beyond immediate reach of danger, while the bucks absolutely without impedimenta swarm your column, avoid, or attack, as their interests dictate, dispute every foot of your advance, harass your rear and surround you on all sides. Under such conditions regular troops are as helpless as a whale attacked by a school of sword-fish. The tendency of military drill and discipline is to make the individual soldier a machine, dependent upon the officer in command for its movement and action, and upon cohesion with its fellow machines for its efficiency. His individuality is completely lost in his organization and he therefore cannot compete on equal terms with an enemy whose individuality under all circumstances is perfect. In operating against them the only hope of success lies in using their own methods, and with the above facts in view, it must be evident that to successfully operate against them a partial tribal disintegration must take place, and that a portion of the tribe must be arrayed against the other."

Crook went on to mention bitterly "the prejudices of army officers" against his Apache scouts and against his belief that they could do what white men could not. "For months the statement has been industriously disseminated by interested parties that the Apache scouts were untrustworthy, that they had mutinied, and every thing of that kind. But in none of these reports is there a spark of truth. The Apache scouts, for this class of warfare, are as worthy of trust as any soldiers in the world, and in all the experience I have had with them they have proved themselves energetic, reliable, truthful, and honest."[5]

"I am . . . annoyed by the statements thrown out by Crook," wrote Miles. "He made a dead failure of this, as he has every other campaign."[6] Crook did find he had one group of friends left, strange allies that they made; William Sanders Oury and the other Tucson veterans of the Camp Grant massacre stuck by him robustly.[7] Sheridan, however, wanted results that were measured in Apache heads, and Nelson Miles was the man of the day.

The new commanding general soon journeyed down to Fort Huachuca near the Mexican border. To acquaint himself with the terrain there Miles, in the company of James Parker (later a brigadier general himself), hiked to the top of nearby El Moro Mountain. In discussing the problem of coaxing Gerónimo and his band to surrender, Parker later asserted that he told Miles, "I have recently come from Fort Apache, where the Chiricahuas not with Geronimo are located . . . Whenever there is news of a raid, the Chiricahuas, in order not to become involved in the fighting, go into the post and are quartered in the quartermaster corral."

Parker then suggested that "a false report of a raid be spread and when the Indians are in the corral, they can be surrounded by the troops, disarmed, taken to the railroad and shipped east as prisoners of war. Geronimo's band in the field will then be isolated . . . and will surrender."[8]

Miles dismissed the idea as treacherous and something he could never bring himself to do, and the subject was dropped. At the time Miles took command, the total number of hostile Apaches was thirty-six, including twenty warriors—three with Mangus and seventeen with Gerónimo. At first Miles divided his troops conventionally, garrisoning supply bases and key water holes with infantry, reserving his cavalry for rapid sorties and scouts. But Miles was not without innovation. As one of his first orders of business he tended to the construction of some thirty heliographic signal stations atop important mountain peaks across Apachería. Operating by the mirrored reflection of sunlight, the heliographs were perfectly suited to the great visibility and the almost never failing sun of the southwestern desert. Their signals could be read over tremendous distances, giving Miles unprecedented effectiveness in communication.

On April 17 General Miles wrote his wife that the "latest news of Geronimo was that his band had gone four hundred miles down into Old Mexico, and I shall not object if they keep going. We can spare them and others as well. But Indians are very unreliable, and when we think them the fartherest away some times they come back. I will endeavor to arrange the command so that it may be as effective as possible in case they do come back."[9]

The remark was prophetic: on April 27 Gerónimo and Naiche led a raid across the border into the Santa Cruz Valley, after which they split into smaller groups and committed depredations as far north as San Carlos and even Fort Apache without being touched. But, reported Miles heartily, they were in the country only three weeks, and killed only fourteen people, before he "drove them" back into Mexico!

When the time came for Miles to carry his campaign to the renegade hideouts in Old Mexico he selected two officers who shared in the "confident belief that Apaches could be outmanuevered, worn down, and subjugated by white soldiers."[10] One was Captain Henry W. Lawton of the 4th Cavalry, a physical giant of a man with a wrestler's physique and furry handlebarred mustache. Lawton had made a reputation for himself as a brilliant and resourceful quartermaster to Ranald Mackenzie during the 1874 Comanche war. The other was Captain Leonard Wood, once a surgeon's assistant and also a big, tough athletic man. As finally outfitted, their expedition was comprised of thirty-five hand-picked cavalry, a company of infantry and twenty Indian scouts under the direction of Tom Horn. To supply them they had thirty packers and a team of a hundred mules. Although Miles did deploy cavalry here, he was not so critical of Crook's methodology as not to use pack trains and Indian scouts.

Not until May 5 was any serious contact made, this in the Pinito Mountains of Sonora by a unit under Captain T. C. Lebo. In the fray he lost one dead and one wounded. Lebo claimed to have killed two hostiles and wounded a third, but Britton Davis, soon back West as a ranch foreman, claimed to know better.[11] (Meanwhile, word from Lawton and Wood indicated that the great experiment in white mastery of Indian warfare was not going well. Five days in the desert mountains of Sonora had ruined the horses, forcing the cavalry to march alongside the infantry.)

Also operating in Old Mexico, Captain Charles A. P. Hatfield, another tough veteran of the 4th Cavalry, struck another group of renegades believed to be Gerónimo's in some low mountains between the San Pedro and Santa Cruz rivers. He succeeded in seizing their camp goods and twenty head of horses, but his report of the affair gave Miles little room to celebrate. As Hatfield was threading his way through a deep canyon leading out of the mountains the hostiles ambushed him. With ferocious suddenness two sergeants were wounded, the cook and blacksmith killed, and the captured stock lost again. And as if that weren't enough, Hatfield's own horse herd was stampeded, though he recovered all but two of the animals. "His skirmishers were too far in advance," clucked Miles, "which was a mistake. I presume he was too confident and too elated with his success."[12] That was an unlikely charge to level at an officer who learned to fight Indians under Ranald Mackenzie. "The Indians have enough ammunition to last them five years," Miles continued, "upwards of one hundred thousand rounds."

Two days after the Hatfield fight, Indians thought to be the same ones swept close enough to the Fort Apache Reservation for one of their number, a warrior named Ki-e-ta, to defect to the peaceful agency Indians in the White Mountains. "I am anxiously waiting to hear from different officers in charge of the troops [there]," wrote Miles to his wife. "There is a band of Indians near the Apache agency, and I am anxious to know whether they can be made to surrender or whether they will turn back south again and continue hostilities. If they do, the campaign may last much longer."[13] After less than six weeks in command, Miles was evidently backing off from the objective of total victory, and casting about for a settlement. And, like the defections of Peaches and Ka-ya-ten-nae before him, that of Ki-e-ta was filed away for later use.

Although Miles was incrementally adopting Crook's method of warfare, his letters of June 7 and 8 show that he was still working under serious misapprehensions about Apache character and tactics. He wrote his wife that "the reports of Indians escaping or avoiding the troops and occasionally killing some one have annoyed me very much. Last night I was tossing about restlessly and could not sleep. Finally about one o'clock I heard the sound of horses' feet, and was very glad to hear from the couriers who arrived that they were from Lt. Walsh. He had been quite successful in intercepting the Indians and capturing their horses, saddles, supplies, etc., putting them on foot in the mountains. This occurred just before dark and Walsh will continue the pursuit at daybreak. . . . They are heading now straight for Old Mexico and may go far down into that country. I am glad they have been driven out of our country and hope to keep them out."[14] Miles's experience with the Plains Indians was that dismounted warriors were as good as caught, but if he still thought having hostile Apaches "on foot in the mountains" was to his advantage, it probably did not change his mind any to learn that during the night, Walsh's Chiricahua quarry slipped away, part going to Mexico and the remainder continuing to raid in the area. And, although Miles conceded grudgingly that the Apaches seemed to recoup readily after losing stock and supplies, Britton Davis expounded that the hostiles had been dismounted "seven times in fifteen months . . . and seven times within a week or ten days they re-equipped themselves through raids on Mexican settlements or American ranches."[15]

The whole of June 8 Miles spent in the telegraph office tending to dispatches. He was increasingly disgusted over the failure of his troops to defeat or capture the hostiles, but his respect for the Apaches was beginning to grow. "When we think we have the best of them," he wrote to Mary that night, "they seem to make some move to slip out. But we will get them in time, in spite of their cunning and activity. Yesterday I felt sure they would be driven into Old Mexico today, as a part of them was; but a part slipped out and have been committing some depredations today."[16] Miles's continuing emphasis on driving the Apaches out of American territory also was misplaced. First of all, he probably was not "driving" them anywhere; the Chiricahuas seem to have been crossing the border with only slightly greater difficulty than they ever had. To those fugitives in the Sierra Madre, moreover, the Arizonans offered better harvest than the impoverished peons of Sonora and Chihuahua and, in the second place, the Sierra Madre remained a safer haven than anyplace in Arizona, for troop movements south of the border still risked an international incident. It was only about six months since Captain Crawford had been killed in the most sinister of circumstances. The feeling against the *yanquis* was still high south of the border, and the hate was reciprocated by most of the troops. In one of Miles's own letters of the time he wrote that "nearly every American expects war [with Mexico] and most desire it, strange as it may seem. Although it is only about twenty years since the Civil War . . . our people are again anxious for war. . . . The result undoubtedly would be that Mexico would be absorbed. . . . I am not sure our country would be any better off, and it might not be as well off."[17] On some points, at least, Miles's vision was clear.

During the third week in June a rumor drifted in, and was printed in local newspapers, that Gerónimo's renegades were willing to talk surrender. "There is no truth in the report," huffed Miles, "and in fact nearly everything you see in these Arizona [newspapers] are made up out of nothing. The correspondents send anything for a sensation, and seem not to care whether it be true or false."[18] Yet the rumor was not unwelcome. By the middle of summer Miles had all but abandoned finally his scheme of using fast-pursuit cavalry units. Their futility was driven home when on July 13 a young Lieutenant Brown from West Point (who had been making quite a name for himself with constant Apache skirmishes) led a force of Indian scouts to surprise a hostile encampment and seize their camp goods and horses. After things quieted down again, Captain Lawton arrived, leading not a mounted strike force, but a ragtag mixed bag of infantry and horseless, footsore cavalry troops.

Also on July 13 a peace mission left Fort Apache for the Mexican hinterland. Miles had received information again that the renegades were discussing possible surrender with Mexicans at Fronteras, and so dispatched Lieutenant Gatewood with two Chiricahuas, one named Martine and the other, the defector from Gerónimo's band, Ki-e-ta, to try to obtain their surrender. Gatewood's orders authorized him to request assistance from any officer except those already in Mexico, but constrained him not to approach the hostiles with a smaller escort than twenty-five regulars. Although he was sick and weak, Gatewood went to Bowie to put together an expedition. The commanding officer there had too few soldiers to detail twenty-five to Gatewood, which probably did not bother him too much, as he knew he could never get within hailing distance of Gerónimo with twenty-five troops. Gatewood pushed on to the border station at Cloverdale, where again he could not obtain an escort, so he struck into Mexico accompanied only by an interpreter, a packer, a courier, and the two Indians.

They met Lieutenant James Parker, 4th Cavalry, soon after crossing. Parker, too, was unable to provide an escort, so Gatewood continued on to Carretas, about fifty miles south, pausing there to rest, as his infirmities were giving him much pain. Parker overtook him there and finally agreed to act as temporary escort; together the two units continued south, contacting Captain Lawton on the Haros River on August 3. Lawton had seen or heard nothing of the hostiles in two weeks, and when he took on Gatewood's mission, Parker turned back north. Captain Wood at this time was farther south with twenty-five men, accomplishing little. Both units were too far north to strike the quietly hiding Mangus, and far to the southwest of Gerónimo. But on receiving Gatewood's news that Gerónimo had sent a peace feeler into Fronteras they turned north and made good time.

On August 15 several of the scouts apparently rode into the village of Bacadéhuachi, east of Bavispe, for a mescal drunk, and caused a disturbance. The trouble was minor enough to be handled by other, sober scouts, and the white soldiers were not called in. Nevertheless, it was possibly this kind of activity that led the Mexican authorities to resent the scouts, and which may have helped create the ill feeling that resulted in Crawford's death. Lawton and Gatewood made such good time on their northward journey that they overtook Lieutenant Parker, even though a rash of storms put some of the mountain rivers in flood and time was lost waiting for them to fall enough to ford them. On the nineteenth the soldiers received intelligence that two of Gerónimo's women had ventured into Fronteras to investigate peace terms. Urgently Gatewood was sent ahead with twenty-two scouts, marching the eighty miles to Fronteras without a single lengthy stop. In the town he learned that the Mexican authorities had held the Apache women prisoners until an American army detachment under Lieutenant Wilber E. Wilder convinced the prefect to release them to return to their people with a surrender message made more palatable by three pony loads of mescal liquor and food. Then, however, in typically Mexican fashion, the prefect sent for his own army, secreting about two hundred irregulars in the buildings around the plaza to annihilate Gerónimo's band when they came in to talk.

When Gatewood arrived in town the prefect informed him of his plan and instructed him not to trail the women and foil his scheme, with the genius of which he seemed thoroughly carried. Wilder offered Gatewood a half dozen of his men, which Gatewood accepted, and then outwardly agreeing with the prefect he turned back in the direction he had come, in the company of Tom Horn, José Maria, and his scouts. "Beak" Gatewood intended to go the prefect one better at his own game, however. About six miles out of town Gatewood and his men "darted up a convenient arroyo," doubled back northward, and began tracking Gerónimo's women at what they hoped was a safe distance. Doggedly they kept to the trail, protected, they hoped, by their white flag, a stick with a rag made from a flour sack. After three days the squaws' trail joined that of Gerónimo's main band and descended into a yawning chasm that fell away to the Bavispe River. At the edge of the canyon Gatewood found a faded pair of trousers strung from a bush. Hoping it was a sign for them to continue but not at all sure that was the case, they descended the steep, narrow trail without incident and camped near the river. Gatewood attached his white flag high on an agave and sent Ki-e-ta and Martine out to discover what they could, and waited. They were about twenty-five miles southeast of Fronteras.

After dark Martine returned to camp and announced they had found and spoken with the elusive Gerónimo, in the Torres Mountains about four miles distant. They had delivered General Miles's surrender ultimatum; Gerónimo said he would talk, but only with the Beak, kept Ki-e-ta hostage, and sent Martine back to fetch him. In fact, Martine said, Gerónimo was angry that Gatewood himself had not first come. "I had my opinion of that," wrote the Beak,[19] not knowing how close to the mark his savvy genuinely was: the scouts' approach had been seen by Gerónimo's lookout, an apprentice named Kanseah, who recognized them. Upon hearing of their presence Gerónimo snapped that he didn't care who they were; if they came any closer, shoot them. A widely respected warrior in Gerónimo's camp, Yanozha, took strong exception to killing men who were so well known to them and brave enough to risk bringing a message. When Gerónimo insisted that they be killed, Yanozha threatened that if there was any shooting to be done, Gerónimo would be the first to die. Yanozha was supported by Fun, a young relative of Gerónimo, who promised to help kill the old di-yin if necessary. Gerónimo backed down and muttered his assent, again faced down by men of superior reputation, and Ki-e-ta and Martine were allowed to approach. If Gatewood had delivered the message himself he probably would not have been so lucky.

Gatewood was still hesitant to venture out, but in a separate message to Martine, Naiche had guaranteed the Beak's safety, so he agreed. That same night Lawton's thirty scouts arrived in the camp with the information that Lawton was following behind, he hoped close enough to help if needed but far enough not to stampede the renegades.

The next morning, August 24, Gatewood left his camp with Lawton's scouts in the direction of Gerónimo's rancheria. About a mile from it some of the renegade warriors materialized from trailside cover and ordered the scouts back to Gatewood's camp, with the instruction that any soldiers coming up must also approach no nearer than there. Gatewood must go on alone.

At the same time this was going on, Lawton and Wood reached Fronteras, as did Captain Forsyth, who had made a hard ride down from Huachuca with a support column. Gatewood had regularly sent word back to Lawton of his situation, but only after Lawton reached Fronteras did he learn of Gatewood's hair-raising mission. "I have just arrived . . . and rec'd your notes," he wrote the Beak. "My Pack Train got off the trail yesterday, and will not be in until the night. I have sent Lt. Smith back on fresh horse to bring up your tobacco and some rations and will send them over to you as soon as they arrive. I have ordered them to come forward if it kills the mules. It will be too late for me to go over tonight, and besides I do not wish to interfere with you, but will come over if you wish me. Send a man back to conduct the pack mules over, and write me what you want. I *hope* and *trust* your efforts will meet with success."[20]

With Lawton's scouts left behind, Gatewood was alone amid desperately hostile Indians and completely at their mercy, which was, he well knew, not reputable. He went with the renegades to the place they selected, where several groups arrived, unsaddling and freeing their horses to graze. By the time Gerónimo rode in, Gatewood's heart was pounding, but the chief put him a little more at ease. "He laid his rifle down twenty feet away," wrote the lieutenant, "and came and shook hands, said he was

glad to see me again, and . . . the tobacco having been passed around . . .
he took a seat alongside as close as he could get, the revolver bulge under
his coat touching my right thigh."

When they asked what terms Gatewood had to offer, he related the
message succinctly: "Surrender, and you will be sent with your families to
Florida, there to await the decision of the President as to your final disposition. Accept these terms or fight it out to the bitter end." There was a
long silence; the Indians "sat there with never a movement, regarding me
intently. I felt the strain. Finally, Gerónimo passed a hand across his eyes,
then held both hands before him making them tremble and asked me for
a drink." Gatewood knew then he was not to be killed, at least not right
then, and explained that he had none. Gerónimo said he and his men had
been on a three-day drunk with the mescal brought from Fronteras, were
badly hung over and needed a drink to think straight, but Gatewood let
it pass. When he began trying to haggle for terms Gatewood quickly said
that he had no authority to negotiate, only to convey the message from
General Miles. Numerous times Gerónimo shuttled between Gatewood
and his people, finally stating that if they could not go back to the reservation they would go on fighting. Gatewood figured his own life hung in
the balance. "I couldn't take him to the reservation; I couldn't fight, neither could I run, nor yet feel comfortable."[21]

Then Gatewood played his only ace. If they returned to the reservation
they would only be among their enemies the White Mountains and Gilas,
he said. Their own people had already been sent to Florida. The sudden
revelation hit them broadside and with noticeable effect, Gerónimo leaving to caucus with his group once more. When he returned he answered
they had decided to continue the war; Gatewood must have come near to
fainting. But, said Gerónimo, if they could round up a beef to kill, they
would continue the talk after eating. None was located.

Gerónimo elected to continue the conference, however, even without
the beef, and suddenly turned the conversation to the General Miles
whom he had never met. With a quiet intensity he asked Gatewood a bat-
tery of questions about the new commander: "What is his age, his size,
the color of his hair and eyes; is his voice harsh or agreeable; does he talk
much or little, say less or more than he means? Does he look you in the
eyes or not? Has he many friends? Do people believe what he says? Do
officers and soldiers like him? Has he had experience with other Indians?
Is he cruel or kind-hearted?" To each query Gatewood answered as
honestly as he knew, and finally Gerónimo concluded, "He must be a
good man, since the Great Father sent him from Washington, and he
has sent you to us."[22]

Then Gerónimo put a new question to Gatewood, telling him to put
himself in their situation, as he knew it to be, and advise them what to
do. Earnestly and solemnly Gatewood said they should trust Miles and

surrender. When the Chiricahuas still made no commitment Gatewood pled with them to discuss it further among themselves. He then returned to Lawton's camp, briefed the captain on what had occurred, and crept into his blanket.

After dawn the renegades began calling for him, using his nickname, Baychendaysen, or Long Nose. Gatewood found Gerónimo several hundred yards from Lawton's camp. "I went out to meet him," Gatewood recalled. "He said to me, 'You can come to my camp anywhere. You are no more responsible for this war than I. I know you . . . I will go with you now alone to Capt. L[awton]'s camp if you desire it. That's the way I feel towards you.'"[23] A second time the old di-yin repeated his scrutinizing interrogation about General Miles. After repeating his answers, Gatewood heard Gerónimo say that his band would go north with him and meet and surrender to General Miles.

The renegades seemed in a much better frame of mind than on the previous day, trusting—or at least putting up the hopeful front—that Miles must have been sincere to have sent Gatewood among them. "They cracked lots of jokes and smoked lots of tobacco," Gatewood noted, "& were in a jolly good humor generally, except Natchez. He seemed very blue. All he had to say was that he wanted to meet his children. I really felt sorry for him . . . It makes me homesicker than usual to look at him." Gerónimo disarmed himself and accompanied Gatewood into Lawton's camp, where the two "had a hugging match before the whole command. [The renegades] really want to surrender," Gatewood wrote his wife the following day, "but they want their families with [them]. Can any one blame a man for wanting to see his wife and children. Wouldn't I prance around lively if they moved you off to Florida?"

As conditions of the surrender, Gatewood had to agreed to travel with Gerónimo's band as a hostage, the Apaches were to be allowed to keep their arms until they actually surrendered, and Lawton was to escort them and protect them from the Mexicans. Gatewood and then Lawton agreed, and messages were sent to Miles to meet them in Skeleton Canyon near the international boundary.

Gerónimo's band now numbered thirty-eight, fourteen of them women and children. They set off for the American boundary shortly after the talk with Gatewood, and on the third day of their march, August 28, the wisdom of Gerónimo's insistence that Lawton stay nearby, and that his people keep their arms, became apparent. Visible a great distance across the desert floor, headed toward them, was a strike force of nearly two hundred Mexicans. Lawton's scouts, whose hatred for Mexicans was only slightly less than Gerónimo's, began buckling on belts of additional ammunition. To prevent a genuine battle Lawton sent Captain Wood and a lieutenant down to stall them. "Gerónimo," wrote Wood, "kindly sent me word that he was on our side in case of a row."[24]

The Mexicans dismounted in a cane thicket and were preparing a battle advance when Wood and the lieutenant reached them. They were cold and hateful to the American officers, ignoring their outstretched hands. Wood therefore bluffed them about the great size of the American force, cautioning them that an advance would be ill advised. Most of the Mexicans stayed put, but a dozen or so, some of them former Apache captives, went with their commander, the prefect of Arispe, to Lawton's camp. While they were there Gerónimo, too, came in. Although the men of low rank on both sides caught up on family news, among the brass the meeting was fraught with terrible potential. As Gerónimo and the prefect were introduced they started to draw their guns on each other, but slowly relaxed. Gatewood noted that when the prefect asked why Gerónimo had not surrendered at Fronteras the chief answered, "Because I did not want to get murdered." Sending the women in had only been a ploy to get supplies. He did not know an ambush had been prepared, but he did not need his celebrated clairvoyance to suspect it.

After this crisis had passed, Lawton continued northward with his group, but difficulty was not through with him yet. As they passed Guadalupe Canyon, the scene of a successful Apache ambush of a cavalry unit in 1885, some of the white troops began grumbling against the Indians, mentioning the propriety of taking revenge as they passed the spot. Word of this got back to Gerónimo, and suddenly Gatewood discovered some of the Apaches silently sneaking away, the women and children before them. In a flash the Beak was on a mule after them. When he caught up with them Gerónimo asked him what Gatewood would do if the soldiers turned on them; the lieutenant answered he would try to stop them, but if he failed he would run away with the Indians. Naiche, on hearing this, suggested Gatewood stay very close to the chiefs, where they could protect him from angry men of their band.

Still dissatisfied, Gerónimo asked that he and Gatewood ride on ahead and meet with Miles at Fort Bowie; Gatewood, sensibly, demurred. They would still be subject to ambush by avenging soldiers, and besides, he did not think Miles was really at Bowie.

When Lawton and his group reached the Canyon of the Skeletons they found it bare. General Miles had not come. Couriers were dispatched to find out what was going on, and the surrendering renegades grew exceedingly nervous. It was later charged that Miles delayed the meeting in order not to miss a Tucson banquet.[25] Miles's character was such that it is easy for historians to be unfair with him, but it has also been charged more seriously that Miles was stalling, hoping that Lawton would arrange to have Gerónimo and Naiche killed and simply bring in the survivors.[26] It is true that on August 31 Miles instructed Lawton to "secure the person of Gerónimo and Natchez . . . by any means, and don't fail to hold them beyond the possibility of escape." The same day he repeated that Lawton could capture them by "saying you have a message from me and from the President . . . [and then] you can do whatever you think best." Still a third communique emphasized that "you will be justified in using *any* measures." Twenty years earlier an officer for General West would have known what that meant, but Lawton was either unwilling or slow to take the hint, if it was a hint. It is possible that all Miles wanted was to avoid what happened to General Crook. "Gerónimo and Natchez pretend they want to surrender," he wrote to Mary, "but they are very unreliable. . . . I do not know whether I will go or not."[27] If Nelson Miles possessed one instinct, it was shielding his career from any association with a failure, but by September 2 Lawton had prevailed upon him to come down.

By this time Gerónimo had sat in an exposed canyon surrounded by troops for five days, and not bolted. He had not fled in the face of the prefect of Arispe and his two hundred soldiers, and had been convinced to stay in spite of the threat of massacre by his own escort. If Gerónimo was going to run, he would have run by now, and Miles could not have helped but know it, and also that a new outbreak would have fallen on Lawton's head, not his own. (However, if Miles was playing a game with Lawton's stakes, it was a game that two could play. By courier from the Mexican interior Lawton had written his wife, who had come in to Bowie, "Be nice to Miles for I am working for a reputation and I want his good favor and all the credit I can get from him." It was amid this kind of maneuvering that the Apaches surrendered the final time.)

Miles arrived in Skeleton Canyon on September 3. At the first meeting of the two principals, the interpreter introduced Miles as Gerónimo's friend.

Gerónimo sized him up quickly. "I never saw him," he cracked, "but I have been in need of friends. Why has he not been with me?" The soldiers laughed appreciatively to have the ice broken. Miles found himself impressed and bemused by his adversary, and Sheridan's command to spare only the hostiles' lives was lost in the new respect. He put the best possible face on the inevitable exile in Florida, saying it was the President's desire to reunite them with their families in a new country. Their misdeeds were not to be held against them; with the back of his hand he swept clean a patch of dust: surrender to him, he said, and the past would be wiped clean. Here and later he said something, the words have been lost, that led the Chiricahuas to insist that Miles promised them a reservation of their own.

Gerónimo surrendered, to outward appearances, with relief, but Naiche had not yet come in. The explanation was given to Miles that he was in the mountains mourning for a brother he believed had been killed a short time before. Naiche's only brother, of course, was Taza, who died in 1876, but in Apache kinship terms it could apply to about any close relative. Or, Naiche could have been about other business—rounding up cached wealth, or perhaps he had gone over to see his sister-in-law and her people, who had been quietly hiding out near Cananea ever since Tom Jeffords erased them from the rolls. At any rate, Gatewood, Gerónimo, two scouts and two interpreters went out to fetch him. When Naiche finally came down, Miles reported him "wild and suspicious, and evidently fear[ing] treachery,"[28] which the general attributed to Naiche's memory of Mangas Coloradas' fate, and his own position as the last hereditary chief of the Chiricahuas. Conferences finally took place that resulted in the capitulation of both chiefs, and the next day Miles, Naiche, Gerónimo, and some others made a fast ride to Fort Bowie in Miles's wagon, leaving Lawton to bring in the rest.

As the ambulance approached Bowie, Gerónimo gazed out at the Chiricahua Mountains, and said to Miles, "This is the fourth time I have surrendered." The general replied unmoved that he thought it would be the last. Lawton arrived at Bowie three days later, with six fewer Apaches —three men and three women—than he started with. The runaways headed south again, probably to take refuge with the tiny colony that had been in hiding since the Taza removal in the mid-seventies.

His enthusiasm undimmed by the escape, Miles that night wrote a jubilant letter to his wife:

"We have at last been most successful.

"I am making a clean sweep of the hostile Apaches out of this country and it has given a feeling of relief and security to thousands of homes that they have never felt before." Miles confided to Mary that his own performance had been "brilliant."

"If you had been here, you would have seen me riding in over the mountains with Gerónimo and Natchez as you saw me ride . . . down to the Yellowstone with Chief Joseph."[29]

The truth was that Miles had had about as significant a role in causing the surrender of Chief Joseph as he did in bringing about that of Gerónimo. During that same day, September 7, Miles's method of making a clean sweep became stunningly apparent to the 382 Chiricahuas left at Fort Apache in the White Mountains. The post commander called them in for what was said to be a routine count; the men were suddenly disarmed and confined, and the women sent to pack their belongings. They were loaded onto wagons and taken to the train station at Holbrook, where they were forced with some panic and terror onto a train for Florida. Included among the prisoners of war were many of General Crook's most faithful scouts. Gerónimo and Naiche were entrained the next day.

It has been very hard for historians to resist the conclusion that Miles finally usurped James Parker's idea for corralling the Chiricahuas (including former scouts) who were beginning a new life at Fort Apache, and even speculate that he was motivated by the knowledge that the more "prisoners" he had to show, the bigger splash he would make. That, however, almost certainly goes too far, and at this juncture Miles must be given his due. He had, as one writer observed, "his own way of keeping faith."[30] All summer Miles had been arguing—vigorously—against the barbarity of sending Indians acclimated to the desert mountains to a sea-coast climate where they could only sicken and die. Even into early September he suggested to Sheridan reservations in the Indian Territory or even Kansas, but without effect. There was no hope for the Fort Apache Chiricahuas in any case; the commanding officer rounded them up on September 5. Incontrovertible orders for their removal arrived on the seventh, and they reached the rail station at Holbrook on the twelfth.

On September 7 orders were also sent down to Miles *not* to remove Gerónimo, Naiche, and the other men who surrendered to him, but only their women and children. He was to hold the men in "close confine-ment" at Bowie pending their trial and execution (one hopes it would have been in that order) by civil authorities in Arizona. Miles was aghast. The Apaches under Gerónimo "had surrendered like brave men to brave men," he wrote Mary. "We were in honor bound not to give them up to a mob."[31] On September 8 he piled all his Chiricahuas onto a train for Florida. Sheridan and the other Washington authorities were outraged, halted the train in San Antonio, Texas, on the tenth, and demanded an explanation. Miles answered inanely that they were already en route when he received the order to hold them for civil trial. (Of course, if Miles was at all savvy in the workings of the Indian Ring, he must have known that Gerónimo in a civilian jail likely would have "escaped" and continued to fight.)

As the telegraphic fallout began to settle it became clear to Sheridan that Miles, contrary to his expectation of an unconditional surrender, had given the Apaches terms. What terms, exactly? Miles hedged, unwilling to admit straight out that he had induced Gerónimo to surrender with a deal even more generous than Crook's. Sheridan must have been disgusted with his protégé, but Miles had presented him with a *fait accompli*. To return Gerónimo and his men to Arizona for hanging, when they had not only surrendered but were halfway across the continent, would have raised a scandal such as not even Sheridan could face. Reluctantly he let them proceed to Florida.

Then the celebrations began; banquets were held, and tribute poured in for Miles, Lawton, Wood, and, as Miles summarized to the Secretary of War, "the gallant officers and soldiers, who, despite every hardship and adverse circumstance, have achieved the success their endurance and fortitude so richly deserved."[32] The role of the scouts was pooh-poohed, and Miles saw to it that Gatewood was excluded from the festivity. It seemed to be the hour of triumph for Sheridan and the white Olympian ideal.

The process of lionizing Wood and Lawton had its detractors, and not all of them from the Crook element, and the argument raged for decades.

On hearing the frequent assertion that Wood and Lawton were the only two soldiers to last the entire campaign, one of the junior officers on their sweep hotly pointed out to the *Army and Navy Journal* in 1909 that "this is not true . . . I was present during the entire time, and as a matter of fact was on the expedition longer than either Captain Lawton or Doctor Wood." He did not dispute that the campaign was a tough one on everybody, but he debunked the amount of romanticized glory heaped on the two Miles protégés. "While it is never necessary to tell a lie," he wrote, "it is not always wise to tell *all* the truth, consequently many facts connected with this campaign will probably never be known; but this much is certain: First, that Lawton and Wood were not the only men who endured the whole campaign; second, water was not scarce nor did the command ever travel where there was no shade nor grass visible; third, that the command was never without supplies; fourth, that no company of soldiers ever became exhausted and were ordered back to barracks for this reason; fifth, that no portion of Lawton's command, except Troop B of the 4th Cavalry, ever had a fight with the Indians during the entire campaign, and at this fight Doctor Wood was not present; sixth, that Doctor Wood never saw a hostile Indian from the time he started until Gerónimo came into Captain Lawton's camp to talk surrender, and that he never heard a shot fired at hostile Indians."[33] The same officer also took up the cudgels for poor Gatewood, but after the lapse of twenty-three years called him by the wrong name.

Old Nana said, when the world is about to end, there will be no water and no rain. That's how we will know. There will be maybe two or three springs left on all the earth. To these people will come and fight over the water and kill each other. That's how people will end.

After that the world will be made over. Those who had been white will be Indian, and we who were Indians will be white.

I don't know how he knew that. He had a power, I guess.[34]

Canyon of the Skeletons:

NOTES

1. Thrapp, *Conquest of Apacheria*, p. 350. Some writers have construed this to be volitional racism on the part of the Miles-Sheridan faction of the argument, but it seems to be an easy matter to overstate when writing in our own age of what we suppose to be racial enlightenment. I can't help but think that it was Sheridan's genuine distrust of the Apache scouts' loyalty, which may in fact have been rooted in racist background, that precipitated the new turn in Apache fighting tactics.

2. During Miles's 1874 campaign against the Southern Cheyennes one of his scouts, J. T. Marshall, was a traveling correspondent for the Kansas *Daily Commonwealth* who shared Miles's disdain for his superior officer, John Pope, who had refused to give Miles supreme command of all the columns in the field. See Lonnie J. White, ed., *The Miles Expedition of 1874–1875*.

3. Miles left two rather self-righteous autobiographies, *Personal Recollections and Observations*, published in 1896, and *Serving the Republic*, in 1911; and two competent if uncritical biographies have appeared, Virginia Johnson's *The Unregimented General* and Newton Tolman's *The Search for General Miles*. Miles died in 1925, at the age of eighty-five; in one of those moments of exquisite symbolism that history allows only rarely, Miles had taken his grandchildren to the circus, and dropped dead while saluting the flag under the big top.

4. Miles to Mary, Apr. 11, 1886, quoted in Johnson, *The Unregimented General*, p. 230, and Tolman, *The Search for General Miles*, pp. 136–37.

5. Crook, "The Apache Problem," pp. 261–63.

6. Johnson, *The Unregimented General*, p. 240.

7. Thrapp, *Conquest of Apacheria*, p. 96 n. 3.

8. Quoted in Davis, *The Truth About Geronimo*, pp. 334–35. General Parker's account has always been a subject of controversy.

9. Johnson, *The Unregimented General*, p. 231.

10. Lockwood, *Apache Indians*, p. 296.

11. Davis, *The Truth About Geronimo*, p. 219.

12. Miles to Mary, May 16, 1886, quoted in Johnson, *The Unregimented General*, p. 234, and in Tolman, *The Search for General Miles*, p. 137.

13. Miles to Mary, May 25, 1886, quoted in Johnson, *The Unregimented General*, pp. 236–37, and in Tolman, *The Search for General Miles*, p. 138.

14. Miles to Mary, June 7, 1886, quoted in Johnson, *The Unregimented General*, pp. 237–38.

15. Davis, *The Truth About Geronimo*, p. 221.

16. Miles to Mary, June 8, 1886, quoted in Tolman, *The Search for General Miles*, p. 140.

17. Ibid.

18. Miles to Mary, June 23, 1886, quoted in Johnson, *The Unregimented General*, p. 245.

19. Quoted in Thrapp, *Conquest of Apacheria*, p. 357.

20. Davis, *The Truth About Geronimo*, p. 228.

21. Quoted in Thrapp, *Conquest of Apacheria*, p. 359.

22. Ibid.

23. This and following from Gatewood, "Gatewood Reports to His Wife from Geronimo's Camp," pp. 78–80.

24. Thrapp, *Conquest of Apacheria*, p. 360.

25. Ibid., p. 362.

26. Parker, *Old Army*, p. 183ff.; Debo, *Geronimo*, p. 290.

27. Miles to Mary, Aug. 29, 1886, quoted in Johnson, *The Unregimented General*, p. 247.

28. Gerónimo, *Geronimo's Story of His Life*, p. 190, rev. ed.

29. Miles to Mary, Sept. 7, 1886, quoted in Johnson, *Unregimented General*, p. 250.

30. Debo, *Geronimo*, p. 298.

31. Faulk, *The Geronimo Campaign*, p. 170.

32. Secretary of War, *Annual Report* for 1886, p. 176.

33. Benson, "Geronimo Campaign."

34. Opler, "Myths and Tales of the Chiricahua Apache Indians," p. 100. Except for the Jicarillas, other Apache tribes seemed less concerned in their mythology with the end of the world, certainly less so than the Navajo. See Opler, "Interpretation of Ambivalence," pp. 111–13.

Epilogue

The Apache wars were over, but some of the local citizens had trouble accepting that as fact. Two days before Christmas 1886—with the Chiricahuas safely in Florida—the newspaper in Silver City reported that "Yesterday afternoon a citizen's meeting was called to devise means for immediate relief from the present Indian troubles. . . . A motion was put and carried that the board of county commissioners be requested to offer a reward of $250 for the scalps of marauding Indians. To this amount Lyons and Campbell offered an additional reward of $500 for Geronimo's scalp."[1]

When the decision was made to send the Chiricahua prisoners of war to Florida, they began an odyssey of dislocation and suffering as terrible as any ever inflicted on American Indians. In Florida the warriors pulled time at Fort Pickens, their families at Fort Marion. The subtropical humidity ravaged the Indians, who were accustomed to the air of desert mountains; perhaps a third of them died there. Some of the children—those regarded as most amenable to elevation—were sent to the famous Indian school at Carlisle, Pennsylvania. There some, like Batsinas, became white men inside red skins; they adjusted and prospered. Others died of cold. The rest turned upon themselves inwardly in despair and self-disgust. In a few years the families were reunited, at Mount Vernon Barracks, Alabama; and in 1894—eight years after the surrender—they were removed to Fort Sill, Oklahoma, and settled on land that had belonged to the Comanche and Kiowa Indians, who gave it to them with little grudging.

At Fort Sill many of the older generation passed away. Tall, crippled old Nana died in 1896, a fire-eater to the last. Chihuahua, whom the soldiers had taken to calling "Chesterfield" for his impeccable manners, and also Mangus, followed in 1901. Loco, sad, bitter, and confused, survived until 1905. Here, too, some adjusted and prospered; Medicine Bluff Creek northwest of the post hospital became the center of the Apache ranching and farming operation, and one who profited well during the time of captivity was Gerónimo.

Just as his personal role in unifying Apache resistance had been overrated by the frontier press, Gerónimo now found himself the most famous of the Apache prisoners, widely sought for interviews or just a souvenir, and the old di-yin had no difficulty accumulating a small fortune. His first big commercial venture was in the autumn of 1898, as an attraction of the Trans-Mississippi Exhibition in Omaha. Naiche and his family, as well as several other Apaches, also went, but it quickly became clear that Gerónimo was the real draw. At each train station sightseers pressed forward to see him, and in a short time he had sold them all the buttons on his coat for a quarter each, and his hat for five dollars. When the train would start up again, Gerónimo would select another hat from his store of them, and settle in his seat to sew more buttons on his coat. It was a killing rather different from those he made in the old days, but he was adaptable.

Many members of Gerónimo's family fell ill and died during the bondage, however, which led to a final surfacing of the fear and suspicion that many other Apaches felt toward the man who had manipulated them in the old days and now had, it was rumored, perhaps ten thousand dollars in the bank in Lawton. Since the final surrender Gerónimo had lost two wives, his sons Chappo (in Alabama) and Fenton (at Sill), and his daughter Lulu and her husband and daughter. Their son Thomas died in 1908, and then Gerónimo began to notice his cherished daughter Eva beginning to weaken. He suspected that he was the victim of witchcraft, and held a dance to determine who was hexing his family. The ceremony ended abruptly when the divining di-yin he had hired pointed the accusation at Gerónimo himself, claiming that he had witched his children to prolong his own life.[2] Many Apaches frowned and nodded.

In one of the last interviews he gave, Gerónimo said plaintively, "I want to go back to my old home before I die. Tired of fight and want to rest. Want to go back to the mountains again. I asked the Great White Father to allow me to go back, but he said no."[3] In February of 1909 he rode into Lawton to sell the bows and arrows that he crafted as souvenirs, and while there he asked a son of Chihuahua, Eugene, to obtain some liquor for him. It was procured (illicitly, of course, though getting it was not difficult), and that evening Gerónimo became drunk while riding home and fell off his horse into Cache Creek, where he lay all night before being found. He died six days later of pneumonia, aged probably about eighty-five years.

Not until 1913, the year before World War I began, did the government allow the Chiricahuas to settle any further west. Many had set roots so deep around the Fort Sill area that they chose to remain. The rest were allowed to travel only as far west as the Mescalero Reservation in eastern New Mexico; the feeling against them in Arizona was still too volatile to allow them to return. Not even then could the government have guaranteed their safety there.

Epilogue:
NOTES

1. Lummis, *General Crook and the Apache Wars*, p. x.
2. Debo, *Geronimo*, p. 437.
3. Quoted in Adams, *Geronimo*, pp. 313–14.

Bibliography

GOVERNMENT DOCUMENTS

Secretary of War, *Annual Reports*, 1849–1887.
Commissioner of Indian Affairs, *Annual Reports*, 1854–1887.
National Archives and Records Service, Army Record Groups 75, 98.

BOOKS

Adams, Alexander B. *Geronimo: A Biography*. New York: G. P. Putnam's Sons, 1971.

Adams, Evelyn C. *American Indian Education, Government Schools and Economic Progress*. New York: King's Crown Press, 1946.

Alsberg, Henry G., and Hansen, Harry, eds. *Arizona: A Guide to the Grand Canyon State*. Rev. ed. New York: Hastings House, 1966.

Baldwin, Gordon C. *The Warrior Apaches*. Tucson, Arizona: Dale Stuart King, 1965.

Bancroft, Hubert Howe. *History of Arizona and New Mexico, 1530–1888*. Vol. XVII of collected *Works*. San Francisco: The History Co., 1889.

————. *History of the North Mexican States and Texas*. 2 vols. San Francisco: The History Co., 1884, 1889.

Bandelier, Adolph F. *The Southwestern Journals, 1883–1884*. Albuquerque New Mexico: University of New Mexico Press, 1970.

————, and Bandelier, Fanny R. *Historical Documents Relating to New Mexico, Neuva Vizcaya, and Approaches Thereto to 1773*. Edited by Charles Wilson Hackett. 3 vols. Washington, D.C.: Carnegie Institution, 1923, 1926, 1937.

Banta, Alfred Franklin. *Albert Franklin Banta: Arizona Pioneer*. Edited by Frank D. Reeve. Albuquerque, New Mexico: Historical Society of New Mexico, 1953.

Barnes, Will Croft. *Arizona Place Names*. Tucson, Arizona: University of Arizona, 1935.

Barney, James M. *Tales of Apache Warfare: True Stories of Massacres, Fights, and Raids in Arizona and New Mexico.* Phoenix, Arizona: priv. pub., 1933.

Bartlett, John R. *Personal Narrative of Explorations and Incidents in Texas, New Mexico, California, Sonora, and Chihuahua, Connected with the United States and Mexican Boundary during the Years, 1850, '51, '52, '53 . . .* 2 vols. New York: D. Appleton & Co., 1854.

Basso, Keith H. *The Cibicue Apache.* New York: Holt, Rinehart & Winston, 1970.

Baylor, George Wythe. *John Robert Baylor, Confederate Governor of Arizona.* Tucson: Arizona Pioneers' Historical Society, 1966.

Bell, William A. *New Tracks in North America: A Journal of Travel and Adventure Whilst Engaged in the Survey for a Southern Railroad to the Pacific Ocean during 1867–1868.* 2 vols. New York: Scribner, Welford & Co., 1869.

Bellah, Robert N. *Apache Kinship Systems.* Cambridge, Massachusetts: Harvard University Press, 1942.

Benavides, Fray Alonso de. *The Memorial of Fray Alonso de Benavides.* Edited by Frederick Webb Hodge and C. F. Lummis. Translated by Mrs. Edward E. Ayer. Chicago: priv. pub., 1916.

———. *Benavides Memorial of 1630.* Edited by Cyprian J. Lynch. Translated by Peter P. Forrestal. Washington, D.C.: Academy of American Franciscan History, 1954.

Bender, Averam Burton. *A Study of the Mescalero Apache Indians, 1846–1880.* New York: Garland Publishing Co., 1960.

Bennett, James A. *Forts and Forays: A Dragoon in New Mexico, 1850–56.* Albuquerque, New Mexico: University of New Mexico Press, 1948.

Betzinez, Jason. *I Fought with Geronimo.* Edited by Wilbur Sturtevant Nye. Harrisburg, Pennsylvania: Stackpole Co., 1959.

Bieber, Ralph P., ed. *Exploring Southwestern Trails.* Glendale, California: Arthur H. Clarke Co., 1938.

———. *Marching with the Army of the West, 1846–48.* Glendale, California: Arthur H. Clarke Co., 1936.

Bigelow, John, Jr. *On the Bloody Trail of Geronimo.* Edited by Arthur Woodward. Los Angeles: Westernlore Press, 1958.

Bleeker, Sonia. *The Apache Indians.* New York: William Morrow & Co., 1951.

Bolton, Herbert E. *Athanase de Mezieres and the Louisiana-Texas Frontier, 1768–1780.* Cleveland, Ohio: Arthur H. Clarke Co., 1914.

———. *The Rim of Christendom: A Biography of Eusebio Francisco Kino, Pacific Coast Pioneer.* New York: Macmillan Co., 1936.

———. *The Spanish Borderlands: A Chronicle of Old Florida and the Southwest.* New Haven: Yale University Press, 1921.

Bourke, John G. *An Apache Campaign in the Sierra Madre: An Account of the Expedition in Pursuit of the Hostile Chiricahua Apaches in the Spring of 1883.* New York: Charles Scribner's Sons, 1886. Rev. eds. 1953, 1958.

———. *On the Border with Crook.* New York: Charles Scribner's Sons, 1891.

Box, Michael James. *Captain James Box's Adventures and Explorations in New and Old Mexico.* New York: J. Miller, 1869.

Brandes, Ray. *Frontier Military Posts of Arizona.* Globe, Arizona: Dale Stuart King, 1960.

————, ed. *Troopers West: Military & Indian Affairs on the American Frontier.* San Diego, California: Frontier Heritage Press, 1970.

Browne, J. Ross. *A Tour Through Arizona.* Tucson, Arizona: Arizona Silhouettes, 1951.

Burlison, Irene. *Yesterday and Today in the Life of the Apache.* Philadelphia: Dorrance & Co., 1973.

Calhoun, James S. *The Official Correspondence of James S. Calhoun, while Indian Agent at Santa Fe and Superintendent of Indian Affairs in New Mexico.* Edited by Anne Heloise Abel. Washington, D.C.: U. S. Government Printing Office, 1915.

Callahan, James Morton. *American Foreign Policy in Mexican Relations.* New York: Macmillan Co., 1932.

Carpenter, John H. *Sword and Olive Branch: Oliver Otis Howard.* Pittsburgh: University of Pittsburgh Press, 1964.

Carter, W. H. *From Yorktown to Santiago with the Sixth Cavalry.* Baltimore: Lord Baltimore Press, 1900.

————. *The Life of Lieutenant General Chaffee.* Chicago: University of Chicago Press, 1917.

Catlin, George. *The Indians of North America.* London: Chatto & Windus, 1876.

————. *Last Rambles Amongst the Indians of the Rocky Mountains and the Andes.* London: Sampson Low, Son, and Marston, 1868.

Cattermole, E. G. *Famous Frontiersmen, Pioneers and Scouts.* Chicago: W. H. Harrison, Jr., 1886.

Clarke, Dwight L. *Stephen Watts Kearny: Soldier of the West.* Norman, Oklahoma: University of Oklahoma Press, 1961.

Cleland, Robert Glass. *This Reckless Breed of Men.* New York: Alfred A. Knopf, 1950.

Clendenen, Clarence C. *Blood on the Border: The United States Army and the Mexican Irregulars.* New York: Macmillan Co., 1969.

Clum, John P. *The Truth about the Apaches Told in the Annual Reports.* Los Angeles: n. p., 1931.

Clum, Woodworth. *Apache Agent: The Story of John P. Clum.* Boston: Houghton Mifflin Co., 1936.

Cochise, Niño. *The First Hundred Years of Niño Cochise.* Edited by A. Kinney Griffith. New York: Abelard-Schuman, 1971.

Collier, John. *The Indians of the Americas.* New York: W. W. Norton & Co., 1947.

————. *Patterns and Ceremonials of the Indians of the Southwest.* New York: E. P. Dutton & Co., 1949.

Colyer, Vincent. *Peace with the Apaches of New Mexico and Arizona.* Washington, D.C.: U. S. Government Printing Office, 1872.

Comfort, Will Levington. *Apache.* New York: E. P. Dutton & Co., 1931.

Condition of the Indian Tribes: Report of the Joint Special Committee Appointed under Joint Resolution of March 3, 1865. Washington, D.C.: U. S. Government Printing Office, 1867.

Conner, Daniel Ellis. *Joseph Reddeford Walker and the Arizona Adventure.* Norman, Oklahoma: University of Oklahoma Press, 1956.

Cook, James H. *Fifty Years on the Old Frontier.* New Haven: Yale University Press, 1923.

Coues, Elliott. *The Expeditions of Zebulon Montgomery Pike.* New York: F. P. Harper, 1895.

Cozzens, Samuel W. *The Marvellous Country: or, Three Years in Arizona and New Mexico, the Apaches' Home.* Boston: Lee & Shepard, 1874.

Cremony, John C. *Life Among the Apaches.* San Francisco: A. Roman & Co., 1868. Reprint. Tucson, Arizona: Arizona Silhouettes, 1954.

Crook, George. *General George Crook: His Autobiography.* Edited by Martin F. Schmitt. Norman, Oklahoma: University of Oklahoma Press, 1946.

———. *Crook's Résumé of Operations against Apache Indians, 1882–1886.* London: Johnson-Taunton Military Press, 1971.

Cruse, Thomas. *Apache Days and After.* Caldwell, Idaho: Caxton Press, 1941.

Cullum, George W. *Biographical Register of the Officers and Graduates of the U. S. Military Academy at West Point, New York.* 8 vols. Boston: Houghton Mifflin Co., 1891–1910.

Curtis, Edward S. *The North American Indian.* 20 vols. Cambridge, Massachusetts: The University Press, 1907–30. Reprint, edited by Frederick Webb Hodge. New York: Johnson Reprint Corp., 1970.

Dale, Edward Everett. *The Indians of the Southwest.* Norman, Oklahoma: University of Oklahoma Press, 1949.

Davis, Britton. *The Truth About Geronimo.* Edited by M. M. Quaif. New Haven: Yale University Press, 1929.

Day, James M., and Winfrey, Dorman, eds. *Texas Indian Papers, 1860–1916.* Austin, Texas: Texas State Library, 1961.

Debo, Angie. *Geronimo: The Man, His Time, His Place.* Norman, Oklahoma: University of Oklahoma Press, 1976.

Deibert, Ralph Conrad. *A History of the Third United States Cavalry.* Harrisburg, Pennsylvania: Telegraph Press, 1953.

Dellenbaugh, F. S. *The North Americans of Yesterday.* New York: G. P. Putnam's Sons, 1901.

DeLong, S. R. *The History of Arizona from the Earliest Times.* San Francisco: Whitaker & Ray Co., 1905.

Diccionario Porrua: Historia, Biografía y Geografía de México. 2nd ed. Mexico City: Libreria Porrua, 1965.

Dorsey, George. *Indians of the Southwest.* Chicago: Passenger Department, Atchison, Topeka and Santa Fe Railway System, 1903.

Dunn, J. P., Jr. *Massacres of the Mountains: A History of the Indian Wars of the Far West.* New York: Harper & Bros., 1886.

Dutton, Bertha P. *Indians of the Southwest.* Santa Fe, New Mexico: Southwestern Association on Indian Affairs, 1965.

Eggan, Fred. *Social Anthropology of North American Tribes.* Chicago: University of Chicago Press, 1937.

Emerson, Dorothy. *Among the Mescalero Apaches: The Story of Father Albert Braun, O. F. M.* Tucson, Arizona: University of Arizona Press, 1973.

Erwin, Allen A. *The Southwest of John Horton Slaughter: Cattleman, Sheriff.* Glendale, California: Arthur H. Clarke Co., 1965.

Falconer, Thomas. *Letters and Notes of the Texan Santa Fe Expedition.* Edited by Frederick Webb Hodge. New York: Dauber & Pine Bookshops, 1930.

Farish, Thomas Edwin. *History of Arizona.* 8 vols. San Francisco: Filmer Brothers Electrotype Co., 1915–18.

Faulk, Odie B. *The Geronimo Campaign.* New York: Oxford University Press, 1969.

———. *Too Far North, Too Far South.* Los Angeles: Westernlore Press, 1967.

Feder, Norman. *American Indian Art.* New York: Harry N. Abrams, 1969.

Fehrenbach, T. R. *Comanches: The Destruction of a People.* New York: Alfred A. Knopf, 1974.

Ferguson, Erna. *Dancing Gods.* Albuquerque, New Mexico: University of New Mexico Press, 1966.

Fireman, Bert. *Historical Markers of Arizona.* Phoenix, Arizona: Arizona Development Board, n.d.

Forbes, Jack D. *Apache, Navajo, and Spaniard.* Norman, Oklahoma: University of Oklahoma Press, 1960.

———. *The Indian in America's Past.* Englewood Cliffs, New Jersey: Prentice-Hall, 1964.

Forsyth, George A. *Thrilling Days in Army Life.* New York: Harper & Bros., 1900.

Frazer, Robert. *The Apaches of White Mountain Reservation.* Philadelphia, Pennsylvania: Indian Rights Association, 1885.

Froebel, Julius. *Seven Years' Travel in Central America, Northern Mexico, and the Far West of the United States.* London: R. Bentley, 1859.

Fuchs, Estelle, and Havighurst, Robert J. *To Live on this Earth: American Indian Education.* Garden City: Doubleday & Co., 1972.

Gálvez, Bernardo de. *Instruction for Governing the Interior Provinces of New Spain, 1786.* Translated and edited by Donald E. Worcester. Berkeley, California: Quivira Society, 1951.

Garces, Francisco. *On the Trail of a Spanish Pioneer: the Diary and Itinerary of Francisco Garces in his Travels through Sonora, Arizona and California, 1775–1776.* Edited by Elliott Coues. 2 vols. New York: Macmillan Co., 1900.

Gerónimo. *Geronimo's Story of His Life.* Edited by S. M. Barrett. New York: Duffield & Co., 1906. Rev. ed. New York: Ballantine Books, 1971.

Gillett, James B. *Six Years with the Texas Rangers.* New Haven: Yale University Press, 1925. Reprint. 1963.

Glass, E. L. N., comp. and ed. *The History of the Tenth Cavalry, 1866–1921.* Tucson, Arizona: Acme Printing Co., 1921.

Goddard, Pliny Earle. *Indians of the Southwest.* New York: American Museum of Natural History, 1921.

Goodman, David Michael. *A Western Panorama, 1849–1875: The Travels, Writings and Influence of J. Ross Browne on the Pacific Coast, and in Texas, Nevada, Arizona and Baja California, as the First Mining Commissioner, and Minister to China.* Glendale, California: Arthur H. Clarke Co., 1966.

Goodwin, Grenville. *The Social Organization of the Western Apache.* Chicago: University of Chicago Press, 1942.

————. *Western Apache Raiding and Warfare.* Edited by Keith H. Basso. Tucson: University of Arizona Press, 1971.

Greene, A. C. *The Last Captive.* Austin, Texas: Encino Press, 1972.

Gregg, Josiah. *Commerce of the Prairies: The Journal of a Santa Fe Trader during Eight Expeditions across the Great Western Prairies.* 2 vols. New York: Langley, 1845.

Gregg, Robert D. *The Influence of Border Troubles on Relations Between the United States and Mexico, 1876–1910.* Baltimore: Johns Hopkins Press, 1937.

Gunnerson, Dolores. *The Jicarilla Apaches: A Study in Survival.* DeKalb, Illinois: Northern Illinois University Press, 1973.

Hafen, Leroy R. *The Indians of Colorado.* Denver: State Historical Society of Colorado State Museum, 1952.

Hagedorn, Herman. *Leonard Wood: A Biography.* 2 vols. New York: Harper & Bros., 1931.

Haight, Theron Wilbur. *Three Wisconsin Cushings.* Madison, Wisconsin: Wisconsin History Commission, 1910.

Haley, James L. *The Buffalo War: The History of the Red River Indian Uprising of 1874.* Garden City: Doubleday & Co., 1976.

Hamilton, Patrick. *The Resources of Arizona.* 3rd ed. San Francisco: A. L. Bancroft & Co., 1884.

Hein, O. L. *Memories of Long Ago, by an Old Army Officer.* New York: G. P. Putnam's Sons, 1925.

Henson, Pauline. *Founding a Wilderness Capital: Prescott, A. T., 1864.* Flagstaff, Arizona: Northland Press, 1965.

Hinton, Richard G. *The Handbook to Arizona.* San Francisco: Payot Upham Co., 1878. Reprint. Tucson, Arizona: Arizona Silhouettes, 1954.

History of Arizona Territory Showing Its Resources and Advantages; With Illustrations. San Francisco: W. W. Elliott & Co., 1884. Reprint. Flagstaff, Arizona: Northland Press, 1964.

Hodge, Frederick Webb, ed. *The Indian Tribes of North America; with Biographical Sketches and Anecdotes of the Principal Chiefs.* 3 vols. Edinburgh: J. Grant, 1933–34.

Hoijer, Harry. *Chiricahua and Mescalero Apache Texts.* Chicago: University of Chicago Press, 1938.

Hoopes, Alban W. *Indian Affairs and Their Administration, with Special Reference to the Far West, 1849–60.* Philadelphia: University of Pennsylvania Press, 1932.

Horgan, Paul. *Lamy of Santa Fe: His Life and Times.* New York: Farrar, Straus & Giroux, 1975.

Horn, Tom. *Life of Tom Horn: A Vindication.* Denver: Louthan Co., 1904.

Horr, David Agee, comp. and ed. *American Indian Ethnohistory: The Indians of the Southwest: The Apache Indians.* 12 vols. New York: Garland Publishing, 1974.

Howard, Oliver O. *My Life and Experiences Among Our Hostile Indians.* Hartford, Connecticut: A. D. Worthington & Co., 1907.

Hrdlička, Aleš. *Stature of Indians of the Southwest and of Northern Mexico.* New York: Putnam Anniversary Volume, 1909.

Hughes, Annie E. *The Beginnings of Spanish Settlement in the El Paso District.* Berkeley, California: University of California Press, 1914.

Hughes, John T. *Reprint of Doniphan's Expedition.* Topeka, Kansas: William E. Connelly, 1907.

Hunt, Aurora. *The Army of the Pacific.* Glendale, California: Arthur H. Clarke Co., 1951.

————. *Major James Henry Carleton, 1814–1873: Western Frontier Dragoon.* Glendale, California: Arthur H. Clarke Co., 1958.

Jackson, Orick. *The White Conquest of Arizona.* Los Angeles: Grafton Co., 1908.

Johnson, Virginia W. *The Unregimented General: A Biography of Nelson A. Miles.* Boston: Houghton Mifflin Co., 1962.

Jones, Jonathan H. *A Condensed History of the Apache and Comanche Indian Tribes.* San Antonio, Texas: Johnson Bros. Printing, 1899.

Josephy, Alvin M., Jr. *The Patriot Chiefs: A Chronicle of American Indian Resistance.* New York: Viking Press, 1958.

Kappler, Charles J., comp. *Indian Affairs: Laws and Treaties.* 3 vols. Washington, D.C.: U. S. Government Printing Office, 1904.

Kaywaykla, James. *In the Days of Victorio: Recollections of a Warm Springs Apache.* Recorded by Eve Ball. Tucson, Arizona: University of Arizona Press, 1970.

Keleher, William A. *Turmoil in New Mexico.* Santa Fe, New Mexico: Rydal Press, 1952.

Kerby, Robert Lee. *The Confederate Invasion of New Mexico and Arizona, 1861–62.* Los Angeles: Westernlore Press, 1958.

King, James T. *War Eagle: A Life of General Eugene A. Carr.* Lincoln, Nebraska: University of Nebraska Press, 1963.

Leckie, William H. *The Buffalo Soldiers: A Narrative of the Negro Cavalry in the West.* Norman, Oklahoma: University of Oklahoma Press, 1967.

Lockwood, Frank C. *The Apache Indians.* New York: Macmillan Co., 1938.

————. *Arizona Characters.* Los Angeles: Times-Mirror Press, 1928.

————. *More Arizona Characters.* Tucson, Arizona: University of Arizona Press, 1943.

————. *Pioneer Days in Arizona: from the Spanish Occupation to Statehood.* New York: Macmillan Co., 1932.

Lummis, Charles F. *The Land of Poco Tiempo.* New York: Charles Scribner's Sons, 1933. Original. London: Sampson, Low, Marston & Co., 1893.

————. *General Crook and the Apache Wars.* Flagstaff, Arizona: Northland Press, 1966.

Lutrell, Estelle. *Newspapers and Periodicals of Arizona, 1859–1911.* Tucson, Arizona: University of Arizona Press, 1950.

McClintock, James H. *Arizona: Prehistoric, Aboriginal, Pioneer, Modern.* 3 vols. Chicago: S. J. Clarke Publishing Co., 1916.

Mails, Thomas E. *Dog Soldiers, Bear Men and Buffalo Women.* Englewood Cliffs, New Jersey: Prentice-Hall, 1973.

————. *The Mystic Warriors of the Plains.* Garden City: Doubleday & Co., 1972.

————. *The People Called Apache.* Englewood Cliffs, New Jersey: Prentice-Hall, 1974.

Marion, John H. *Notes of Travel through the Territory of Arizona, Being an Account of the Trip Made by General George Stoneman and Others in the Autumn of 1870.* Edited by Donald M. Powell. Tucson, Arizona: University of Arizona Press, 1965.

Marshall, James. *Santa Fe: The Railroad That Built an Empire.* New York: Random House, 1945.

Mason, Otis Tufton. *North American Bows, Arrows and Quivers.* Washington, D.C.: Smithsonian Institution, 1891. Reprint. New York: Carl J. Pugliese, 1972.

Material Culture Notes. Denver: American Indian Art Department, Denver Art Museum, 1967.

Mazzanovitch, Anton. *Trailing Geronimo.* Los Angeles: Gem Publishing Co., 1926.

Memorial and Affidavits Showing Outrages Perpetrated by Apache Indians in the Territory of Arizona for the Years 1869–1870. San Francisco: Francis & Valentine, Printers, 1871.

Miles, Nelson A. *Personal Recollections and Observations.* Chicago: Werner Co., 1897.

————. *Serving the Republic.* New York: Harper & Bros., 1911.

Miller, Joseph. *The Arizona Story.* New York: Hastings House, 1952.

Moorhead, Max L. *The Apache Frontier: Jacobo Ugarte and Spanish–Indian Relations in Northern New Spain, 1769–1791.* Norman, Oklahoma: University of Oklahoma Press, 1968.

Morfi, Fray Juan Augustin. *History of Texas, 1673–1779.* Albuquerque, New Mexico: Quivira Society, 1935.

Mullane, William H. *Indian Raids, as Reported in the Silver City Enterprise, Silver City, New Mexico: 1882–1886.* Silver City, New Mexico: Enterprise, 1968.

————. *This is Silver City, New Mexico: 1882–1883–1884.* Silver City, New Mexico: Enterprise, 1963.

National Cyclopedia of American Biography. 20 vols. New York: James T. White & Co., 1898–1926.

Newcomb, W. W. *The Indians of Texas, from Prehistoric to Modern Times.* Austin, Texas: University of Texas Press, 1961.

Nye, Wilbur S. *Plains Indian Raiders.* Norman, Oklahoma: University of Oklahoma Press, 1968.

Ogle, Ralph H. *Federal Control of the Western Apaches, 1848–1886.* Albuquerque, New Mexico: University of New Mexico Press, 1940.

Opler, Morris E. *An Apache Life-way: The Economic, Social and Religious Institutions of the Chiricahua Indians.* Chicago: University of Chicago Press, 1941.

————. *Apache Odyssey: A Journey Between Two Worlds.* New York: Holt, Rinehart & Winston, 1969.

———. *Childhood and Youth in Jicarilla Apache Society*. Los Angeles: Southwest Museum, 1946.

———. *Grenville Goodwin Among the Western Apaches: Letters from the Field*. Tucson, Arizona: University of Arizona Press, 1973.

Parker, James. *The Old Army: Memories 1872–1918*. Philadelphia: Dorrance & Co., 1929.

Parsons, John E. *Smith & Wesson Revolvers*. New York: William Morrow & Co., 1957.

Pattie, James O. *Personal Narrative of James O. Pattie*. Cincinnati, Ohio: Timothy Flint, 1831. Reprint (edited by William H. Goetzman). New York: J. B. Lippincott, 1962.

Paxson, Frederic L. *The Last American Frontier*. New York: Macmillan Co., 1910.

Pearce, T. M., ed. *New Mexico Place Names: A Geographical Dictionary*. Albuquerque, New Mexico: University of New Mexico Press, 1965.

Peplow, Edward Hadduck. *History of Arizona*. 3 vols. New York: Lewis Historical Publishing Co., 1958.

Pettis, George H. *The California Column*. Santa Fe, New Mexico: New Mexican Printing Co., 1908.

Pope, Captain John. *Report of Exploration of a Route for the Pacific Railroad near the Thirty-second Parallel of Latitude, from the Red River to the Rio Grande*. 33rd Cong., 2nd sess., H. R. Exec. Doc. No. 129 (1885).

Price, George F. *Across the Continent with the Fifth Cavalry*. New York: D. Van Nostrand, 1883. Reprint. New York: Antiquarian Press, 1959.

Prominent Men of Mexico. Mexico City: La Patria, 1888.

Prucha, Francis Paul. *Guide to the Military Posts of the United States*. Madison, Wisconsin: State Historical Society of Wisconsin, 1964.

Pumpelly, Raphael. *Across America and Asia: Notes of a Five Years' Journey Around the World and of Residence in Arizona, Japan, and China*. 4th ed. New York: Leypoldt & Holt, 1870.

Raht, Carlysle Graham. *The Romance of Davis Mountains and Big Bend Country*. El Paso, Texas: Rahtbooks Co., 1919.

Record of Engagements with Hostile Indians within the Military Division of the Missouri, from 1868 to 1882. Washington, D.C.: U. S. Government Printing Office, 1882.

Remington, Frederic. *Crooked Trails*. New York: Harper & Bros., 1899.

Rice, William B. *The Los Angeles Star, 1851–1864*. Berkeley, California: University of California Press, 1947.

Rickey, Don. *Forty Miles a Day on Beans and Hay: The Enlisted Soldier Fighting the Indian Wars*. Norman, Oklahoma: University of Oklahoma Press, 1963.

Risch, Erna. *Quartermaster Support of the Army: A History of the Corps, 1775–1939*. Washington, D.C.: Office of the Quartermaster General, 1962.

Rister, Carl Coke. *The Southwestern Frontier, 1865–1881*. Glendale, California: Arthur H. Clarke Co., 1928.

Robinson, Bert. *The Basket Weavers of Arizona*. Albuquerque, New Mexico: University of New Mexico Press, 1954.

Roca, Paul M. *Paths of the Padres Through Sonora*. Tucson, Arizona: Arizona Pioneers' Historical Society, 1967.

Rodenburgh, Theophilus F. *From Everglade to Canon with the Second Dragoons*. New York: D. Van Nostrand, 1875.

Rushmore, Elsie Mitchell. *The Indian Policy During Grant's Administration*. Jamaica, New York: Marion Press, 1914.

Russell, Don. *One Hundred and Three Fights and Scrimmages*. Washington, D.C.: U. S. Cavalry Association, 1936.

Sabin, Edwin L. *Kit Carson Days (1809–1868)*. Chicago: A. C. McClurg & Co., 1914.

Santee, Ross. *Apache Land*. New York: C. Scribner's Sons, 1947.

Schellie, Don. *Vast Domain of Blood*. Los Angeles: Westernlore, 1968.

Schmeckebier, Laurence F. *The Office of Indian Affairs: Its History, Activities, and Organization*. Baltimore: Johns Hopkins Press, 1927.

Schneider, David M., and Gough, Kathleen, eds. *Matrilineal Kinship*. Berkeley, California: University of California Press, 1961.

Schoolcraft, Henry R. *Information Respecting the History, Condition and Prospects of the Indian Tribes of the United States*. 6 vols. Philadelphia: Lippincott, Grambo & Co., 1852–57.

Schroeder, Albert H. *A Study of the Apache Indians*. 5 vols. New York: Garland Publishing, 1974.

Sheridan, Philip H. *Personal Memoirs*. New York: Charles L. Webster & Co., 1888.

Sherman, William T. *Memoirs of General W. T. Sherman*. New York: Charles L. Webster & Co., 1891.

Simpson, Lesley Byrd. *The San Saba Papers: A Documentary Account of the Founding and Destruction of San Saba Mission*. San Francisco: John Howell Books, 1959.

Sloan, Richard E. *Memories of an Arizona Judge*. Stanford, California: Stanford University Press, 1932.

Smith, Anne N. *New Mexico Indians: Economic, Educational and Social Problems*. Santa Fe, New Mexico: University of New Mexico Press, 1966.

Smith, Cornelius C. *William Sanders Oury: History Maker of the Southwest*. Tucson, Arizona: University of Arizona Press, 1967.

Smith, Dama Margaret (Mrs. White Mountain). *Indian Tribes of the Southwest*. Stanford, California: Stanford University Press, 1933.

Sonnichsen, C. L. *The Mescalero Apaches*. Norman, Oklahoma: University of Oklahoma Press, 1958.

Spicer, Edward H. *Cycles of Conquest: The Impact of Spain, Mexico, and the United States on the Indians of the Southwest: 1533–1960*. Tucson, Arizona: University of Arizona Press, 1962.

————, ed. *Perspectives in American Indian Cultural Change*. Chicago: University of Chicago Press, 1961.

Spier, Leslie, et al., eds. *Language, Culture, and Personality*. Menasha, Wisconsin: Banta, 1941.

Stanley, F. *The Apaches of New Mexico 1540–1940*. Pampa, Texas: Pampa Print Shop, 1962.

————. *The Jicarilla Apaches of New Mexico*. Pampa, Texas: Pampa Print Shop, 1967.

Summerhayes, Martha. *Vanished Arizona*. Chicago: Lakeside Press, 1939.

Tanner, Clara Lee. *Southwest Indian Craft Arts*. Tucson, Arizona: University of Arizona Press, 1968.

Terrell, John Upton. *Apache Chronicle*. New York: World Publishing Co., 1972.

———. *The Plains Apache*. New York: Thomas Y. Crowell, 1976.

Tevis, James H. *Arizona in the '50's*. Albuquerque, New Mexico: University of New Mexico Press, 1954.

Thomas, Alfred Barnaby. *After Coronado*. Norman, Oklahoma: University of Oklahoma Press, 1935.

———. *Forgotten Frontiers: A Study of the Spanish Indian Policy of Don Juan Bautista de Anza, Governor of New Mexico, 1777–87*. Norman, Oklahoma: University of Oklahoma Press, 1932.

———. *The Plains Indian and New Mexico, 1751–78. A Collection of Documents Illustrative of the Eastern Frontier of New Mexico*. Albuquerque, New Mexico: University of New Mexico Press, 1935.

———. *Teodoro de Croix and the Northern Frontier of New Spain, 1776–83*. Norman, Oklahoma: University of Oklahoma Press, 1941.

Thrapp, Dan L. *Al Sieber: Chief of Scouts*. Norman, Oklahoma: University of Oklahoma Press, 1964.

———. *The Conquest of Apacheria*. Norman, Oklahoma: University of Oklahoma Press, 1967.

———. *General Crook and the Sierra Madre Adventure*. Norman, Oklahoma: University of Oklahoma Press, 1972.

———. *Victorio*. Norman, Oklahoma: University of Oklahoma Press, 1974.

Tolman, Newton F. *The Search for General Miles*. New York: G. P. Putnam's Sons, 1968.

Twitchell, Ralph Emerson. *The Leading Facts of New Mexican History*. 2 vols. Albuquerque, New Mexico: Horn & Wallace, Publishers, 1963.

Utley, Robert M. *Frontier Regulars: The United States Army and the Indians, 1866–1891*. New York: Macmillan Co., 1973.

———. *Frontiersmen in Blue: The United States Army and the Indians, 1848–1865*. New York: Macmillan Co., 1967.

Vanderwerth, W. C., comp. *Indian Oratory*. Norman, Oklahoma: University of Oklahoma Press, 1971.

Van Roekel, Gertrude B. *Jicarilla Apaches*. San Antonio, Texas: Naylor Company, 1971.

Van Tramp, John C. *Prairie and Rocky Mountain Adventures, or, Life in the Far West*. Columbus, Ohio: Segner & Condit, 1868.

Villagra, Gaspar Perez de. *History of New Mexico*. Edited by Frederick Webb Hodge and George P. Hammond. Los Angeles: Quivira Society, 1933.

Villasenor, David V. *Tapestries in the Sand: The Spirit of Indian Sandpainting*. Heraldsburg, California: Naturegraph Co., 1963.

Wallace, Andrew, ed. *Pumpelly's Arizona*. Tucson, Arizona: Palo Verde Press, 1965.

Wallace, Ernest. *Ranald S. Mackenzie on the Texas Frontier*. Lubbock, Texas: West Texas Museum Association, 1964.

The War of the Rebellion: A Compilation of the Official Records of the

Union and Confederate Armies. Series I. 53 vols. Washington, D.C.: U. S. Government Printing Office, 1880–1901.

Webb, George W. *Chronological List of Engagements Between Regular Army of the United States and Various Tribes of Hostile Indians Which Occurred During the Years 1790–1898, Inclusive.* St. Joseph, Missouri: Wing Printing and Publishing Co., 1939.

Weight, Harold, and Weight, Lucile. *William B. Rood: Death Valley 49er, Arizona Pioneer, Apache Fighter, River Ranchero.* Twentynine Palms, California: Calico Press, 1959.

Wellman, Paul I. *Bronco Apache.* Garden City: Doubleday & Co., 1936.

———. *Death in the Desert.* New York: Macmillan Co., 1935.

———. *Indian Wars of the West.* Garden City: Doubleday & Co., 1947.

Welsh, Herbert. *The Apache Prisoners in Fort Marion, St. Augustine, Florida.* Philadelphia: Indian Rights Association, 1887.

Wharfield, Colonel H. B. *Alchesay.* El Cajon, California: priv. pub., 1969.

———. *Apache Indian Scouts.* El Cajon, California, priv. pub., 1964.

———. *Cooley: Army Scout, Arizona Pioneer, Wayside Host, Apache Friend.* El Cajon, California: priv. pub., 1966.

White, Lonnie J., ed. *The Miles Expedition of 1874–75: An Eyewitness Account of the Red River War.* Austin, Texas: Encino Press, 1971.

Whitman, S. E. *The Troopers: An Informal History of the Plains Cavalry, 1865–1890.* New York: Hastings House, 1962.

Willson, Roscoe. *Pioneers and Well Known Cattlemen of Arizona.* 2 vols. Phoenix, Arizona: Valley National Bank, 1951, 1956.

Wilson, Neill C., and Taylor, Frank J. *Southern Pacific: The Roaring Story of a Fighting Railroad.* New York: McGraw-Hill Book Co., 1952.

Winship, George Parker. *The Journey of Coronado, 1540–42.* New York: Barnes, 1904.

Worcester, Donald E. *The Apaches: Eagles of the Southwest.* Norman, Oklahoma: University of Oklahoma Press, 1979.

Wyllys, Rufus Kay. *Arizona: The History of a Frontier State.* Phoenix, Arizona: Hobson & Herr, 1950.

———. *Pioneer Padre: The Life and Times of Eusebio Francisco Kino.* Dallas, Texas: Southwest Press, 1935.

PERIODICALS

Abarr, James W. "Fort Ojo Caliente." *Desert Magazine,* Vol. XXII (Apr. 1959).

Abel, Annie Heloise. "Indian Affairs in New Mexico Under the Administration of William Carr Lane," *New Mexico Historical Review,* Vol. XVI (Apr. 1941).

Andrews, E. "Military Surgery Among the Apache Indians." *Chicago Medical Examiner,* Vol. XVI (1869).

Ball, Eve. "The Apache Scouts: A Chiricahua Appraisal." *Arizona and the West,* Vol. VII (Winter 1965).

Bandelier, Adolph F. A. "Final Report of Investigation Among the Indians of the Southwestern United States, Carried on Mainly in the Years from 1880 to 1885." *Papers of the Archaeological Institute of America*, No. 3. 2 vols. Cambridge, Massachusetts: John Wilson & Sons, 1890.

Barnes, Will C. "The Apaches' Last Stand in Arizona." *Arizona Historical Review*, Vol. III (Jan. 1931).

Barney, James M. "The Townsend Expedition." *Arizona Highways*, Vol. XIII (Mar. 1937).

Barrett, Arrie. "Western Frontier Forts of Texas, 1845–61." *West Texas Historical Association Yearbook*, Vol. VII (1931).

Barrett, Lenora. "Transportation, Supplies, and Quarters for the West Texas Frontier Under the Federal Military System." *West Texas Historical Association Yearbook*, Vol. V (1929).

Basso, Keith H. "The Gift of Changing Woman." *Bulletin of the Bureau of American Ethnology*, No. 196 (1966).

———. "In Pursuit of the Apaches." *Arizona Highways*, Vol. LIII (July 1977).

———. "Western Apache Witchcraft." *Anthropological Papers of the University of Arizona*, No. 15 (1969).

Becknell, P. C., and Matthews, Washington. "Why the Apaches Eat No Fish." *Journal of the American Folklore Society*, Vol. XI (1898).

Bender, A. B. "Frontier Defense in the Territory of New Mexico." *New Mexico Historical Review*, Vol. IX (July, Oct. 1934).

Benson, H. C. "The Geronimo Campaign." *Army and Navy Journal*, July 3, 1909.

Bieber, Ralph P. "Some Aspects of the Santa Fe Trail, 1848–1880." *Chronicles of Oklahoma*, Vol. II (Mar. 1924).

Bishop, W. H. "Across America." *Harper's New Monthly*, Vol. LVI (1883).

Blazer, A. N. "Beginnings of an Indian War." *New Mexico*, Vol. VI (Feb. 1938).

———. "Blazer's Mill." *New Mexico*, Vol. VI (Jan. 1938).

Bolton, Herbert E. "The Jumanos Indians in Texas." *Texas State Historical Association Quarterly*, Vol. XV (July 1911).

Borden, W. C. "The Vital Statistics of an Apache Indian Community." *Boston Medical & Surgical Journal*, July 6, 1893.

Bourke, John G. "The Folk Foods of the Rio Grande and Northern Mexico." *Journal of American Folklore*, Vol. VIII (1895).

———. "General Crook in the Indian Country." *Century*, Vol. XLI (Mar. 1891).

———. "Medicine-Men of the Apache." *Annual Report of the Bureau of American Ethnology*, No. 9 (1892).

———. "Notes and News." *American Anthropologist*, Vol. VIII (1895).

———. "Notes on Apache Mythology." *Journal of the American Folklore Society*, Vol. III (1890).

———. "Notes upon the Gentile Organization of the Apaches of Arizona." *Journal of the American Folklore Society*, Vol. III (1890).

Brandes, Ray. "Don Santiago Kirker, King of the Scalp Hunters." *The Smoke Signal*, No. 6 (Fall 1962).

————. "A Guide to the History of the U. S. Army Installations in Arizona, 1849–1886." *Arizona and the West*, Vol. I (Spring 1959).

Brosius, S. M. "The Apache Prisoners of War." *Annual Report of the Indian Rights Association*, No. 30, in *Publications*, Series II, No. 68 (1912).

Burton, Estelle Bennett. "Volunteer Soldiers of New Mexico and Their Conflicts with the Indians in 1862 and 1863." *Old Santa Fe*, Vol. I (Apr. 1914).

Cabannis, A. A. "Troop and Company Pack Trains." *Journal of the U. S. Cavalry Association*, Vol. III (1890).

Carter, R. G. "Lawton's Capture of Geronimo." *Collier's Weekly*, Vol. XXIV (Jan. 27, 1900).

Charles, Tom. "Old Scouts of the Mescaleros." *New Mexico*, Vol. IX (Aug. 1931).

Clay, Thomas J. "Some Unwritten Incidents of the Geronimo Campaign." *Proceedings of the Annual Meeting and Dinner of the Order of Indian Wars of the United States*, 1929.

Clendenen, Clarence C. "General James Henry Carleton." *New Mexico Historical Review*, Vol. XXX (Jan. 1955).

Clum, John P. "The Apaches." *New Mexico Historical Review*, Vol. IV (Oct. 1929).

————. "Apache Misrule." *New Mexico Historical Review*, Vol. V (Apr., July 1930).

————. "Es-kim-in-zin." *New Mexico Historical Review*, Vol. III (Oct. 1928); Vol. IV (Jan. 1929).

————. "Geronimo." *New Mexico Historical Review*, Vol. III (Jan., Apr., July 1928).

————. "It All Happened in Tombstone." *Arizona Historical Review*, Vol. II (Oct. 1929).

————. "The San Carlos Apache Police." *New Mexico Historical Review*, Vol. IV, (July 1929); Vol. V (Jan. 1930).

Cooper, Thomas C. "Arizona History in *Arizona Highways*: An Annotated Bibliography," *Arizona and the West*, Vol. XVI (Spring, Summer 1974).

Corbusier, Dr. William F. "The Apache-Yumas and Apache-Mojaves." *American Antiquarian*, Vol. VIII (Sept. 1886).

Crane, R. C. "Settlement of Indian Troubles in West Texas, 1874–75." *West Texas Historical Association Yearbook*, Vol. I (1925).

Creelman, Henry. "Leonard Wood—The Doctor Who Became a General." *Pearson's Magazine*, Vol. XXI (Apr. 1909).

Cremony, John C. "The Apache Race." *Overland Monthly*, Vol. I (1868).

Crimmins, Martin L., ed. "Colonel Buell's Expedition into Mexico in 1880." *New Mexico Historical Review*, Vol. X (Apr. 1935).

————. "The Mescalero Apaches." *Frontier Times*, Vol. VIII (Sept. 1931).

Crook, George. "The Apache Problem." *Journal of the Military Service Institution of the United States*, Vol. XXVII (1886).

Culin, Stewart. "Games of the North American Indians." *Annual Report of the Bureau of American Ethnology*, No. 24 (1907).

Curtis, Edward S. "Vanishing Indian Types: The Tribes of the Southwest." *Scribner's Magazine*, May 1906.

Daklugie, Asa. "Coyote and the Flies." Recorded by Eve Ball. *New Mexico Folklore Record*, Vol. X (1955–56).

Daly, Henry W. "The Geronimo Campaign." *Journal of the U. S. Cavalry Association*, Vol. XIX (1908).

———. "Scouts Good and Bad." *American Legion Monthly*, Vol. V (Aug. 1928).

Davis, Ann Pence. "Apache Debs." *New Mexico*, Vol. XV (Apr. 1937).

Davis, Britton. "The Difficulties of Indian Warfare." *Army-Navy Journal*, Oct. 24, 1885.

Davis, O. K. "Our Prisoners of War." *North American Review*, Vol. XCV (Mar. 1912).

Dockstader, Frederick J., ed. "The American Indian in Graduate Studies: A Bibliography of Theses and Dissertations." *Contributions from the Museum of the American Indian Heye Foundation*, Vol. XV (1957).

Dunlap, H. E. "Clay Beauford—Wilford C. Bridwell." *Arizona Historical Review*, Vol. III (Oct. 1930).

Dunn, William Edward. "The Apache Mission on the San Saba River: Its Founding and Failure." *Southwestern Historical Quarterly*, Vol. XVII (Apr. 1914).

———. "Apache Relations in Texas, 1718–90." *Texas State Historical Association Quarterly*, Vol. XIV (Jan. 1911).

———. "Missionary Activities Among the Eastern Apaches Previous to the Founding of the San Saba Mission." *Southwestern Historical Quarterly*, Vol. XV (Jan. 1912).

Eaton, George O. "Stopping an Apache Battle." Edited by Don Russell. *Journal of the U. S. Cavalry Association*, Vol. XLII (July–Aug. 1933).

Essin, Emmett M. III. "Mules, Packs, and Packtrains." *Southwestern Historical Quarterly*, Vol. LXXIV (July 1970).

Fatty, Eustace. "Chiricahua Legends." Recorded by Eve Ball. *Western Folklore*, Vol. XV (Apr. 1956).

French, David. "Comparative Notes on Chiricahua Apache Mythology." *Memoirs of the American Folklore Society*, Vol. XXXVII (1942).

Froman, Robert. "The Red Ghost." *American Heritage*, Vol. XII (Apr. 1961).

Fuente, Pedro José de la. "Diary of Pedro José de la Fuente, Captain of the Presidio of El Paso del Norte, January to July, 1765." Translated and edited by James M. Daniel. *Southwestern Historical Quarterly*, Vol. LX (Oct. 1956).

Gatewood, Charles B. "Campaigning Against Victorio in 1879." *The Great Divide*, no vol., no no. (April 1894).

———. "The Surrender of Geronimo." *Proceedings of the Annual Meeting and Dinner of the Order of Indian Wars of the United States*, 1929.

———. "Gatewood Reports to His Wife From Geronimo's Camp." Edited by Charles Byars. *Journal of Arizona History*, Vol. VII (Summer 1966).

"General Crook's Apache Campaign." *Frank Leslie's Illustrated Newspaper*, June 2, 1883.

———. "The San Carlos Indian Cattle Industry." *Anthropological Papers of the University of Arizona*, No. 7 (1963).

Gifford, E. W. "The Southeastern Yavapai." *University of California Publications in American Archaeology and Ethnology,* Vol. XXIX (1930–32).

Goddard, Pliny E. "Apache Tribes of the Southwest." *Southern Workman,* Vol. XXXIX (1910).

———. "Jicarilla Apache Texts." *Anthropological Papers of the American Museum of Natural History,* Vol. VIII (1911).

———. "Myths and Tales from the San Carlos Apache." *Anthropological Publications of the American Museum of Natural History,* No. 24, part 1 (1918).

———. "Myths and Tales from the White Mountain Apache." *Anthropological Publications of the American Museum of Natural History,* No. 24, part 2 (1919).

———. "San Carlos Apache Texts." *Anthropological Publications of the American Museum of Natural History,* No. 24, part 3 (1919).

———. "White Mountain Apache Texts." *Anthropological Publications of the American Museum of Natural History,* No. 24, part 4 (1920).

Goodwin, Grenville. "The Characteristics and Function of Clan in Southern Athapascan Culture." *American Anthropologist,* Vol. XXXIX (1937).

———. "Clans of the Western Apaches." *New Mexico Historical Review,* Vol. VIII (July 1933).

———. "Myths and Tales of the White Mountain Apache." *Memoirs of the American Folklore Society,* No. 33 (1939).

———. "The Social Divisions and Economic Life of the Western Apache." *American Anthropologist,* Vol. XXXVII (1935).

———. "White Mountain Apache Religion." *American Anthropologist,* Vol. XL (1938).

———, and Kaut, Charles R. "A Native Religious Movement Among the White Mountain and Cibicue Apaches." *Southwestern Journal of Anthropology,* Vol. X (1954).

———, and Kluckhohn, Clyde. "A Comparison of Navaho and White Mountain Ceremonial Forms and Categories." *Southwestern Journal of Anthropology,* Vol. I (1945).

Gould, M. K. "Mohave-Apache Legends." *Journal of the American Folklore Society,* Vol. XXXIV (1921).

Gregg, Robert Danforth. "The Influence of Border Troubles on Relations Between the United States and Mexico, 1876–1910." *Johns Hopkins University Studies in History and Political Science,* Vol. LV (1937).

Greiner, John. "The Journal of John Greiner." Edited by Annie Heloise Abel. *Old Santa Fe,* Vol. III (July 1916).

Guenther, Rev. Arthur. "50 Years in Apache Land." *White Mountains of Arizona,* Vol. XVII (Fall 1971–Summer 1972).

Gunnerson, Dolores A. "The Southwestern Athapascans: Their Arrival in the Southwest." *El Palacio,* Vol. LXIII (Nov.–Dec. 1956).

———, and Gunnerson, James H. "Apachean Culture History and Ethnology." *Anthropological Papers of the University of Arizona,* No. 21 (1971).

Gwyther, George M. D. "An Indian Reservation." *Overland Monthly,* Vol. X (Feb. 1873).

Hall, Edward J., Jr. "Recent Clues to Athapaskan Prehistory in the Southwest." *American Anthropologist*, Vol. XLVI (1944).

Hanna, Robert. "With Crawford in Mexico." *Arizona Historical Review*, Vol. VI (Apr. 1935).

Harmon, George D. "The United States Indian Policy in Texas, 1845–1860." *Mississippi Historical Review*, Vol. XVII (Dec. 1930).

Harrington, M. R. "The Devil Dance of the Apaches." *Museum Journal of the University of Pennsylvania*, Vol. III (1929).

Harris, Francis. "Where Did the Plains Indians Get Their Horses?" *American Anthropologist*, Vol. XL (Jan.–Mar. 1937).

Harte, John Bret. "Conflict at San Carlos: The Military–Civilian Struggle for Control, 1882–1885." *Arizona and the West*, Vol. XV (Spring 1973).

Hastings, James K. "A Boy's-Eye View of the Old Southwest." *New Mexico Historical Review*, Vol. XXVI (Oct. 1951).

Hastings, James R. "The Tragedy of Camp Grant in 1871." *Arizona and the West*, Vol. I (Summer 1959).

Hill, Joseph J. "New Light on Pattie and the Southwestern Fur Trade." *Southwestern Historical Quarterly*, Vol. XXVI (Apr. 1923).

Hodge, Frederick Webb. "The Early Navajo and Apache." *American Anthropologist*, Vol. VIII (July 1895).

———. "Early Western History." *Land of Sunshine*, Vol. XII (Dec. 1900).

———. "Handbook of Indians North of Mexico." *Bulletin of the Bureau of American Ethnology*, No. 30 (1907).

———. "In Memoriam: John Gregory Bourke." *Journal of American Folklore*, Vol. IX (Apr.–June 1896).

Hoijer, Harry. "The Southern Athapaskan Languages." *American Anthropologist*, Vol. XL (1938).

Hollon, W. Eugene. "Great Days of the Overland Stage." *American Heritage*, Vol. VIII (June 1957).

Hough, Walter. "Environmental Interrelations in Arizona." *American Anthropologist*, Vol. XI (1898).

Hrdlička, Aleš. "Method of Preparing Tesvino Among the White River Apaches." *American Anthropologist*, Vol. VI (1904).

———. "Notes on the San Carlos Apache." *American Anthropologist*, Vol. VIII (1905).

Irwin, General B. J. D. "The Apache Pass Fight." *Infantry Journal*, Vol. XXXII (Apr. 1928).

Johnson, Carl P. "A War Chief of the Tontos." *Overland Monthly*, Vol. XXVIII (Nov. 1896).

Kaut, Charles R. "The Western Apache Clan System: Its Origins and Development." *University of New Mexico Publications in Anthropology*, No. 9 (1957).

Kroeber, A. L. "Cultural and Natural Areas of Native North America." *University of California Publications in American Archaeology and Ethnology*, Vol. XXXVIII (1939).

La Farge, Oliver. "Assimilation—The Indian View." *New Mexico Quarterly*, Vol. XXVI (Spring 1956).

Lane, William Carr. "The Letters of William Carr Lane, 1852–1854." Edited by Ralph P. Bieber. *New Mexico Historical Review*, Vol. III (Apr. 1928).

"List of Actions, etc., with Indians and Other Marauders, Participated in by the Tenth United States Cavalry, Chronologically Arranged—1867 to 1897." *Cavalry Journal*, Vol. X (1897).

Lyon, Juana Fraser. "An Apache Branch of Clan MacIntosh." *Clan Chattan*, Vol. IV (Jan. 1961).

———. "Archie MacIntosh, the Scottish Indian Scout." *Journal of Arizona History*, Vol. VII (Autumn 1966).

McClintock, James H. "Fighting Apaches—A Narrative of the Fifth Cavalry's Deadly Conflict in the Superstition Mountains of Arizona." *Sunset*, no vol., no no. (Feb. 1907).

McNeil, Irving. "Indian Justice." *New Mexico Historical Review*, Vol. XIX (Oct. 1944).

Matthews, Washington. "Ichthyophobia." *Journal of American Folklore*, Vol. XI (Apr.–June 1898).

Merritt, General Wesley. "Three Indian Campaigns." *Harper's Magazine*, Vol. LXXX (Apr. 1890).

Middleton, Hattie (Mrs. G. M. Allison). No title—account of the Indian fight in Pleasant Valley. *Frontier Times*, June 1928. Reprinted in *True West*, Vol. XI (Mar.–Apr. 1964).

———. "The Jicarilla Genesis." *American Anthropologist*, Vol. XI (1898).

———. "The Kiowa Indians." *Annual Report of the Bureau of American Ethnology*, No. 17, part 1 (1897).

Moorhead, Max L. "Spanish Deportation of Hostile Apaches: the Policy and the Practice," *Arizona and the West*, Vol. XVII (Autumn 1975).

Morice, A. G. "Unity of Speech Among the Northern and Southern Dine." *American Anthropologist*, Vol. IX (1896).

Mulligan, R. A. "Apache Pass and Old Fort Bowie." *The Smoke Signal* (Spring 1965).

———. "Down the Butterfield Trail." *Arizona and the West*, Vol. I (Winter 1959).

———. "Sixteen Days in Apache Pass." *The Kiva*, Vol. XXIV (1958).

Murdock, John R. "Arizona Characters in Silhouette." *Arizona State Teacher's College Bulletin*, No. 9 (1933).

Murphy, Nellie. "Recollections of the Walapai." *The Native American*, Vol. VIII (Dec. 21, 1907).

Myers, Lee. "The Enigma of Mangas Coloradas' Death." *New Mexico Historical Review*, Vol. XLI (Oct. 1966).

———. "Fort Webster on the Mimbres River," *New Mexico Historical Review*, Vol. XLI (Jan. 1966).

———. "Military Establishments in Southwestern New Mexico: Stepping Stones to Settlement." *New Mexico Historical Review*, Vol. XLIII (Jan. 1968).

Nalty, Bernard C., and Strobridge, Truman R. "Captain Emmet Crawford: Commander of Apache Scouts: 1882–1886." *Arizona and the West*, Vol. VI (Spring 1964).

Nelson, Al B. "Campaigning in the Big Bend of the Rio Grande in 1787." *Southwestern Historical Quarterly*, Vol. XXXIX (Jan. 1936).
———. "Juan de Ugalde and Picax-Ande Ins-Tinsle." *Southwestern Historical Quarterly*, Vol. XLIII (Apr. 1940).
Nicholas, Dan. "Mescalero Puberty Ceremony." *El Palacio*, Vol. XLVI (Sept. 1939).
Nickerson, A. H. "An Apache Indian Raid, and a Long-Distance Ride." *Harper's Magazine*, Vol. XLI (July 10, 1897).
Officer, James E. "A Note on the Elias Family of Tucson." *Arizona and the West*, Vol. I (Winter 1959).
———. "Chiricahua Apache Material Relating to Sorcery." *Primitive Man*, Vol. XIX (1946).
———. "A Chiricahua Apache's Account of the Geronimo Campaign of 1886." *New Mexico Historical Review*, Vol. VIII (Oct. 1938).
———. "The Concept of Supernatural Power Among the Chiricahua and Mescalero Apaches." *American Anthropologist*, Vol. XXXVII (Jan.–Mar. 1937).
———. "Dirty Boy: A Jicarilla Tale of Raid and War." *Memoirs of the American Anthropological Association*, No. 52 (1938).
———. "Further Comparative Data Bearing on the Solution of a Psychological Problem." *Journal of Social Psychology*, Vol. IX (1938).
———. "Humor and Wisdom of Some American Indian Tribes." *New Mexico Anthropologist*, Vol. III (1938).
———. "An Interpretation of the Ambivalence of Two American Indian Tribes." *Journal of Social Psychology*, Vol. VII (1936).
———. "The Kinship Systems of the Southern Athapaskan-Speaking Tribes: A Comparative Study." *American Anthropologist*, Vol. XXXVIII (1936).
———. "Mythology and Folk Belief in the Maintenance of Jicarilla Tribal Endogamy." *Journal of American Folklore*, Vol. LX (Apr.–June 1947).
———. "Myths and Legends of the Lipan Apache Indians." *Memoirs of the American Folklore Society*, No. 36 (1940).
———. "Myths and Tales of the Chiricahua Apache Indians." *Memoirs of the American Folklore Society*, No. 37 (1942).
———. "Myths and Tales of the Jicarilla Apache Indians." *Memoirs of the American Folklore Society*, No. 31 (1938).
———. "Notes on Chiricahua and Apache Culture: Supernatural Power and the Shaman." *Primitive Man*, Vol. XX (Jan.–Apr. 1947).
———. "Reaction to Death Among the Mescalero Apache." *Southwestern Journal of Anthropology*, Vol. II (Winter 1946).
———. "The Role of Creative Shamanism in Mescalero Apache Mythology." *Journal of American Folklore Society*, Vol. LIX (July–Sept. 1946).
———. "The Sacred Clowns of the Chiricahua and Mescalero Apache Indians." *El Palacio*, XLIV (Mar. 1938).
———. "The Slaying of the Monsters." *El Palacio*, Vol. LIII (Aug.–Sept. 1946).
———. "Some Points of Comparison and Contrast Between the Treatment of Functional Disorders by Apache Shamans and Modern Psychiatric Practice." *American Journal of Psychiatry*, Vol. XCII, (1936).

————. "A Summary of Jicarilla Apache Culture." *American Anthropologist*, Vol. XXXVIII (1936).

————, and Basso, Keith H., eds. "Apachean Culture, History and Ethnology." *Anthropological Papers of the University of Arizona*, No. 21 (1971).

————, and Castetter, Edward F. "The Ethnobotany of the Chiricahua and Mescalero Apaches." *Ethnobiological Studies in the American Southwest*, Vol. VII (1936).

————, and Hoijer, Harry. "The Raid and Warpath Language of the Chiricahua Apache." *American Anthropologist*, Vol. XLII (Oct.–Dec. 1942).

————, and Opler, Catherine H. "Mescalero Apache History in the Southwest." *New Mexico Historical Review*, Vol. XXV (Jan. 1950).

Oskison, John M. "An Apache Problem." *Quarterly Journal of the Society of American Indians*, Vol. I (Apr. 1913).

Parker, James. "The Geronimo Campaign." *Proceedings of the Annual Meeting and Dinner of the Order of Indian Wars of the United States*, 1929.

Pettit, James S. "Apache Campaign Notes." *Journal of the Military Service Institution of the United States*, Vol. VIII (1896).

Poston, Charles. "Building a State in Apache Land." *Overland Monthly*, Vol. XXIV (Sept. 1894).

Rafferty, Ken. "Mission at Mescalero." *New Mexico*, Vol. XVII (Oct. 1940).

Reagan, Albert. "Notes on the Indians of the Fort Apache Region." *Anthropological Publications of the American Museum of Natural History*, No. 31, part 5 (1929).

Reeve, Frank D. "The Federal Indian Policy in New Mexico, 1858–1880." *New Mexico Historical Review*, Vol. XII (July 1937), Vol. XIII (Jan., Apr., July 1938).

Rippy, Fred J. "The Indians of the Southwest in the Diplomacy of the United States and Mexico, 1848–1853." *Hispanic American Review*, Vol. II (Aug. 1919).

Rister, Carl Coke. "Harmful Practices of Indian Traders of the Southwest, 1865–1876." *New Mexico Historical Review*, Vol. VI (July 1931).

Roberts, Helen. "Basketry of the San Carlos Apache Indians." *Anthropological Papers of the American Museum of Natural History*, No. 31, part 2 (1929).

Rope, John. "Experiences of an Indian Scout." Recorded by Grenville Goodwin. *Arizona Historical Review*, Vol. III (Jan., Apr. 1936).

Royce, Charles C. "Indian Land Cessions in the United States." *Annual Report of the Bureau of American Ethnology*, No. 18 (1899).

Rush, Rita. "El Chivero—Merejildo Grijalva." *Arizoniana*, Vol. I (Fall 1960).

Russell, Frank. "Myths of the Jicarilla Apache." *Journal of American Folklore*, Vol. XI (1898).

Sacks, Benjamin H. "New Evidence on the Bascom Affair." *Arizona and the West*, Vol. IV (Autumn 1962).

Salzman, M., Jr. "Geronimo: The Napoleon of the Indians." *Journal of Arizona History*, Vol. VIII (Winter 1967).

Scholes, France V. "Troublous Times in New Mexico." *New Mexico Historical Review*, Vol. XII (Apr., Oct. 1937).

Schwatka, Frederick. "Among the Apaches." *Century Magazine*, Vol. XXXIV (May 1887).

"Select Picture List: The American West, 1848–1912." *National Archives General Information Leaflet*, No. 23 (1971).

Shipp, Lieutenant W. E. "Captain Crawford's Last Expedition." *Journal of the U. S. Cavalry Association*, Vol. XIX (Oct. 1905).

Sjoberg, Andree F. "Lipan Apache Culture in Historical Perspective." *Southwestern Journal of Anthropology*, Vol. IX (1953).

Smith, Cornelius. "The Fight at Cibicu." *Arizona Highways*, Vol. XXXII (May 1956).

Smith, Ralph A. "John Joel Glanton, Lord of the Scalp Range." *The Smoke Signal*, No. 6 (Fall 1962).

———. "Apache Plunder Trails Southward, 1831–1840." *New Mexico Historical Review*, Vol. XXXVII (Jan. 1962).

———. "Apache 'Ranching' Below the Gila, 1841–1845." *Arizoniana*, Vol. III (Winter 1962).

———. "The Scalp Hunter in the Borderlands." *Arizona and the West*, Vol. VI (Spring 1964).

———. "The Scalp Hunt in Chihuahua—1849." *New Mexico Historical Review*, Vol. XL (Apr. 1965).

Sniffen, M. K. "The Record of Thirty Years." *Publications of the Indian Rights Association*, Series II, No. 90 (Apr. 1913), rev. ed.

Spicer, Edward H. "European Expansion and the Enclavement of Southwestern Indians." *Arizona and the West*, Vol. I (Summer 1959).

———. "Spanish-Indian Acculturation in the Southwest." *American Anthropologist*, Vol. LVI (1954).

Stevens, Robert C. "The Apache Menace in Sonora, 1831–49." *Arizona and the West*, Vol. VI (Autumn 1964).

Stottler, V. E. "Pressure as a Civilizer of Wild Indians." *The Outlook*, Vol. LVI (Jan. 12, 1897).

Swanton, John R. "The Indian Tribes of North America." *Bulletin of the Bureau of American Ethnology*, No. 145 (1953).

Tassin, A. G. "Reminiscences of Indian Scouting." *Overland Monthly*, Series II, Vol. XIV (Aug. 1889).

Teal, John W. "Soldier in the California Column: The Diary of John W. Teal." Edited by Henry P. Walker. *Arizona and the West*, Vol. XIII (Spring 1971).

Thomas, Alfred Barnaby. "Antonio de Bonilla and Spanish Plans for the Defense of New Mexico, 1772–78." *New Spain and the Anglo-American West*, Vol. I (1932).

Thompson, Gerald, comp. "New Mexico History in New Mexico Magazine: An Annotated Bibliography." *Arizona and the West*, Vol. XVII (Autumn, Winter 1975).

———. " 'To the People of New Mexico': General Carleton Defends the Bosque Redondo." *Arizona and the West*, Vol. XIV (Winter 1972).

Thrapp, Dan L. "Dan O'Leary: Apache Scout." *Arizona and the West*, Vol. VII (Winter 1965).

Torrans, Mary Powell. "Tubac's Rightful Place in the Sun." *Arizona and the West*, Vol. I (Winter 1959).

Turner, W. "The Fearless Apaches." *National Republic*, Vol. XVI (Jan. 1929).

Tyler, Barbara A. "Cochise, Apache War Leader." *Journal of Arizona History*, Vol. VI (Spring 1965).

Utley, Robert M. "The Bascom Affair: A Reconstruction." *Arizona and the West*, Vol. III (Spring 1961).

———. "Fort Davis." Guidebook to Fort Davis National Historic Monument, 1972.

———. "The Surrender of Geronimo." *Arizoniana*, Vol. IV (Spring 1963).

Van de Mark, Dorothy. "The Raid on the Reservations." *Harper's*, Vol. CCXII (Mar. 1956).

Wallace, Edward S., and Anderson, Adrian S. "R. S. Mackenzie and the Kickapoos: The Raid into Mexico in 1873." *Arizona and the West*, Vol. VII (Summer 1965).

Waller, John L. "Colonel George Wythe Baylor." *Southwestern Social Science Quarterly*, Vol. XXIV (June 1943).

Ward, John (Abel, Annie Heloise, ed.). "Indian Affairs in New Mexico Under the Administration of William Carr Lane, from the Journal of John Ward." Edited by Annie Heloise Abel. *New Mexico Historical Review*, Vol. XVI (Apr. 1941).

Wayland, Virginia. "Apache Playing Cards." *Southwest Museum Leaflet*, No. 28 (1961).

Wheat, Carl I. "Trailing the Forty-Niners Through Death Valley." *Sierra Club Bulletin*, Vol. XXIV (June 1939).

Whitaker, Kathleen. "Na Ih Es: An Apache Puberty Ceremony." *The Masterkey*, Vol. XLV (Jan.–Mar. 1971).

Williamson, Dan R. "Al Sieber: Famous Scout of the Southwest." *Arizona Historical Review*, Vol. III (Jan. 1931).

———. "The Story of Oskay De No Tah, 'The Flying Fighter,'" *Arizona Historical Review*, Vol. III (Oct. 1930).

Wilson, Benjamin David. "Benjamin David Wilson's Observations on Early Days in California and New Mexico." *Historical Society of Southern California Quarterly*, no vol., no no. (1934).

Wissler, Clark. "The Apache Indian." *Target*, Vol. LXXXIII (1923).

Woodward, Arthur. "Side Lights on Fifty Years of Apache Warfare, 1836–1886." *Arizoniana*, Vol. II (Fall 1961).

Woody, Clara T. "The Woolsey Expeditions of 1864." *Arizona and the West*, Vol. IV (Summer 1962).

Worcester, Donald E. "The Beginning of the Apache Menace in the Southwest." *New Mexico Historical Review*, Vol. XVI (Jan. 1941).

Wyman, Walker D. "The Military Phase of Santa Fe Freighting, 1846–1865." *Kansas Historical Quarterly*, Vol. I (Nov. 1932).

Index